mochi
mochi
mochi
mochi

尾田栄一郎

Every once in a while, there's a craze for that sticky, chewy, "mochi-mochi" texture in foods. Well, I've discovered the perfect mochi-mochi food—it's mochi.

Here comes mochi-mochi volume 74!!!

-Eiichiro Oda, 2014

Eiichiro Oda began his manga career at the age of 17, when his one-shot cowboy manga **Wanted!** won second place in the coveted Tezuka manga awards. Oda went on to work as an assistant to some of the biggest manga artists in the industry, including Nobuhiro Watsuki, before winning the Hop Step Award for new artists. His pirate adventure **One Piece**, which debuted in **Weekly Shonen Jump** in 1997, quickly became one of the most popular manga in Japan.

ONE PIECE VOL. 74
NEW WORLD PART 14

SHONEN JUMP Manga Edition

STORY AND ART BY EIICHIRO ODA

Translation/Stephen Paul
Touch-up Art & Lettering/Vanessa Satone
Design/Fawn Lau
Editor/Alexis Kirsch

ONE PIECE © 1997 by Eiichiro Oda. All rights reserved.
First published in Japan in 1997 by SHUEISHA Inc., Tokyo.
English translation rights arranged by SHUEISHA Inc.

The stories, characters and incidents mentioned
in this publication are entirely fictional.

Printed in the U.S.A.

Published by VIZ Media, LLC
P.O. Box 77010
San Francisco, CA 94107

10 9 8 7 6 5 4 3 2 1
First printing, April 2015

SHONEN JUMP MANGA

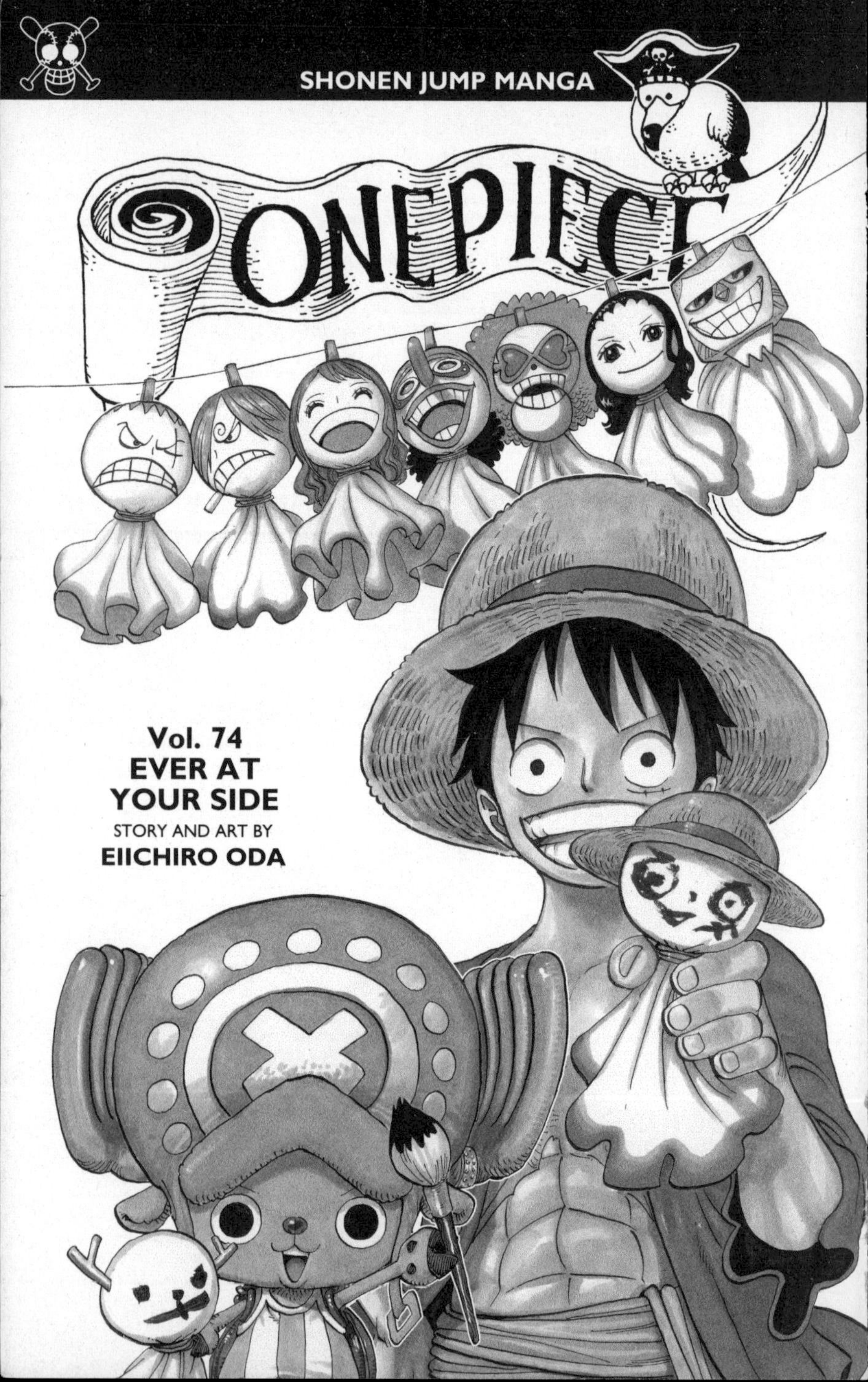
ONE PIECE

Vol. 74
EVER AT YOUR SIDE

STORY AND ART BY
EIICHIRO ODA

The Straw Hat Crew

Monkey D. Luffy

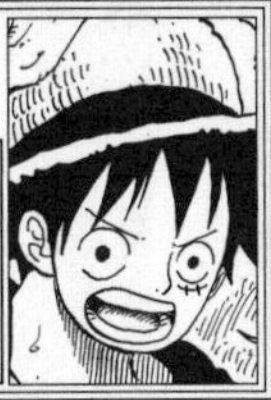

A young man who dreams of becoming the Pirate King. After training with Rayleigh, he and his crew head for the New World!

Captain, Bounty: 400 million berries

Roronoa Zolo

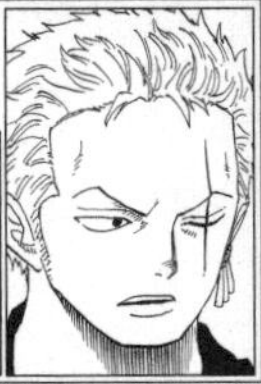

He swallowed his pride and asked to be trained by Mihawk on Gloom Island before reuniting with the rest of the crew.

Fighter, Bounty: 120 million berries

Tony Tony Chopper

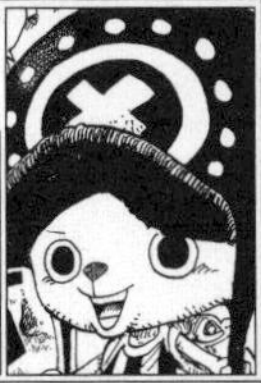

After researching powerful medicine in Birdie Kingdom, he reunites with the rest of the crew.

Ship's Doctor, Bounty: 50 berries

Nami

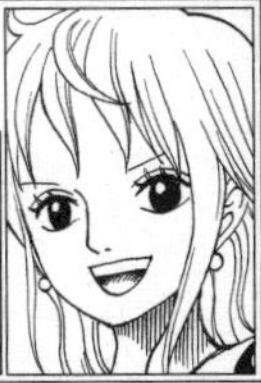

She studied the weather of the New World on the small Sky Island Weatheria, a place where weather is studied as a science.

Navigator, Bounty: 16 million berries

Nico Robin

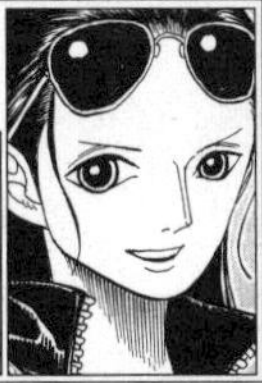

She spent her time in Baltigo with the leader of the Revolutionary Army: Luffy's father, Dragon.

Archeologist, Bounty: 80 million berries

Usopp

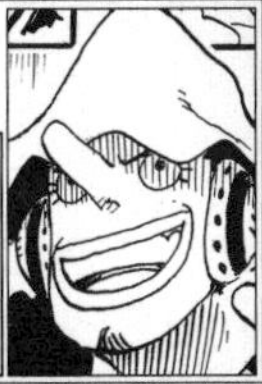

He trained under Heracles at the Bowin Islands to become the King of Snipers.

Sniper, Bounty: 30 million berries

Franky

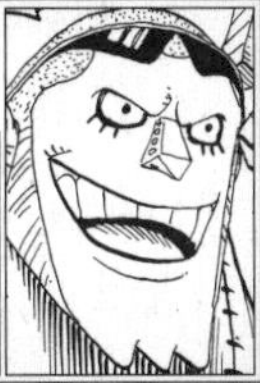

He modified himself in Future Land Baldimore and turned himself into Armored Franky before reuniting with the rest of the crew.

Shipwright, Bounty: 44 million berries

Sanji

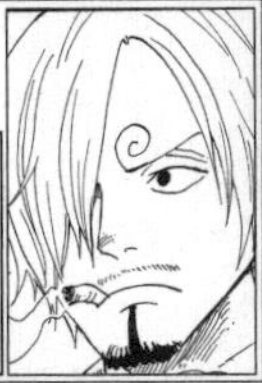

After fighting the New Kama Karate masters in the Kamabakka Kingdom, he returned to the crew.

Cook, Bounty: 77 million berries

Brook

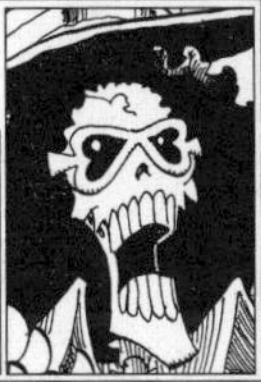

After being captured and used as a freak show by the Longarm Tribe, he became a famous rock star called "Soul King" Brook.

Musician, Bounty: 33 million berries

Doflamingo. Things start off according to plan, but Law is abducted after falling into a trap set by Doflamingo. The rest of the crew meets a toy soldier who informs them of the nation's hidden darkness. Furious at Doflamingo's evil machinations, they decide to help the little Tontattas in their fight for freedom. Luffy prepares to leave the coliseum to help rescue Law when he comes across a very unexpected face...

The story of ONE PIECE 1»74

Shanks

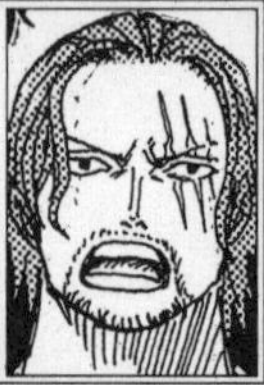

One of the Four Emperors. He continues to wait for Luffy in the second half of the Grand Line, called the New World.

Captain of the Red-Haired Pirates

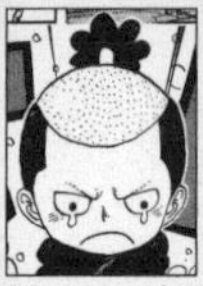

Momonosuke

Kin'emon's Son

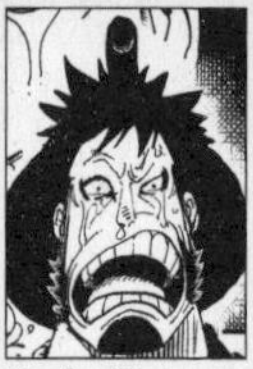

Foxfire Kin'emon

Samurai of Wan

Don Quixote Pirates

Don Quixote Doflamingo (Joker)

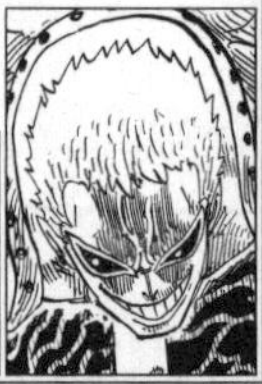

One of the Seven Warlords of the sea and a weapons broker. He works under the alias of "Joker."

Pirate, Warlord (former)

Trafalgar Law

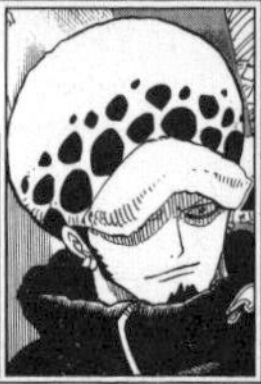

The Surgeon of Death, wielder of the Op-Op Fruit's powers. Currently allied with Luffy.

Pirate, Warlord

Master Caesar Clown

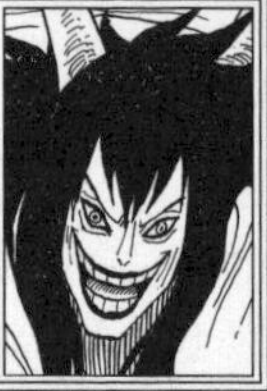

An authority on weapons of mass murder. Kidnapped by Law in an attempt to goad Doflamingo out of hiding.

Former government scientist

Don Quixote Family

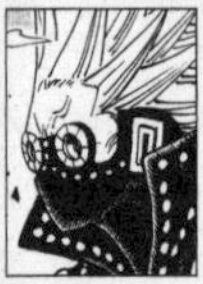

Gladius

♠ Pica Army

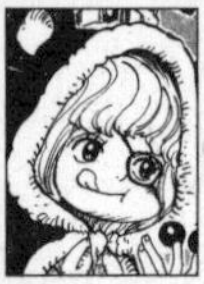

Sugar

♣ Trebol Army

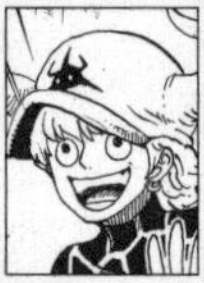

Dellinger

♦ Diamante Army

Fujitora (Issho)

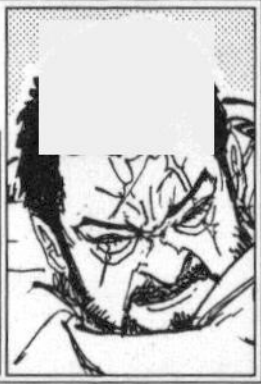

A blind swordsman. One of the Three Admirals after Aokiji's departure.

Naval HQ Admiral

Tontatta Kingdom

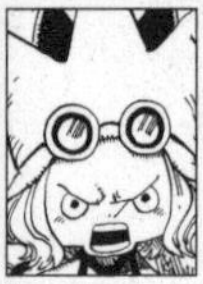

Leo

Warrior

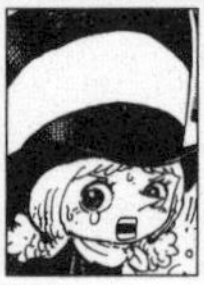

Wicka

Reconnaissance

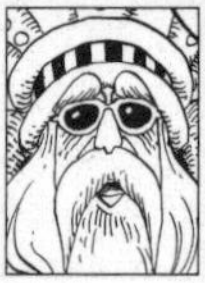

Gancho

King of the Tontattas

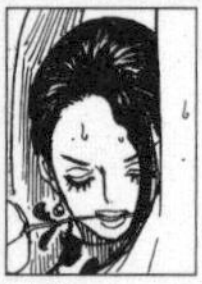

Violet

Dancer

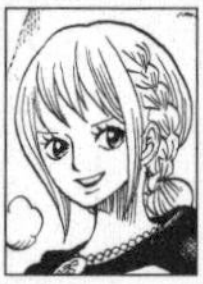

Rebecca

Gladiator

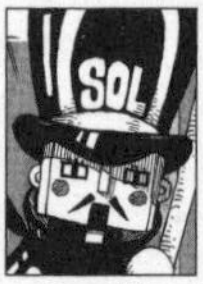
SOL

One-Legged Soldier

Toy

Story

After two years of hard training, the Straw Hat pirates are back together, first at the Sabaody Archipelago and then through Fish-Man Island to their next stage: the New World!!

The crew happens across Trafalgar Law on the island of Punk Hazard, run by Caesar Clown. At his suggestion, they form a new pirate alliance that seeks to take down one of the Four Emperors. In order to draw Doflamingo's attention, they first capture Caesar and infiltrate Dressrosa, which is governed by

NEW WORLD ONE PIECE

Vol. 74
Ever at Your Side

CONTENTS

Chapter 732:
AN UNDER-GROUND WORLD

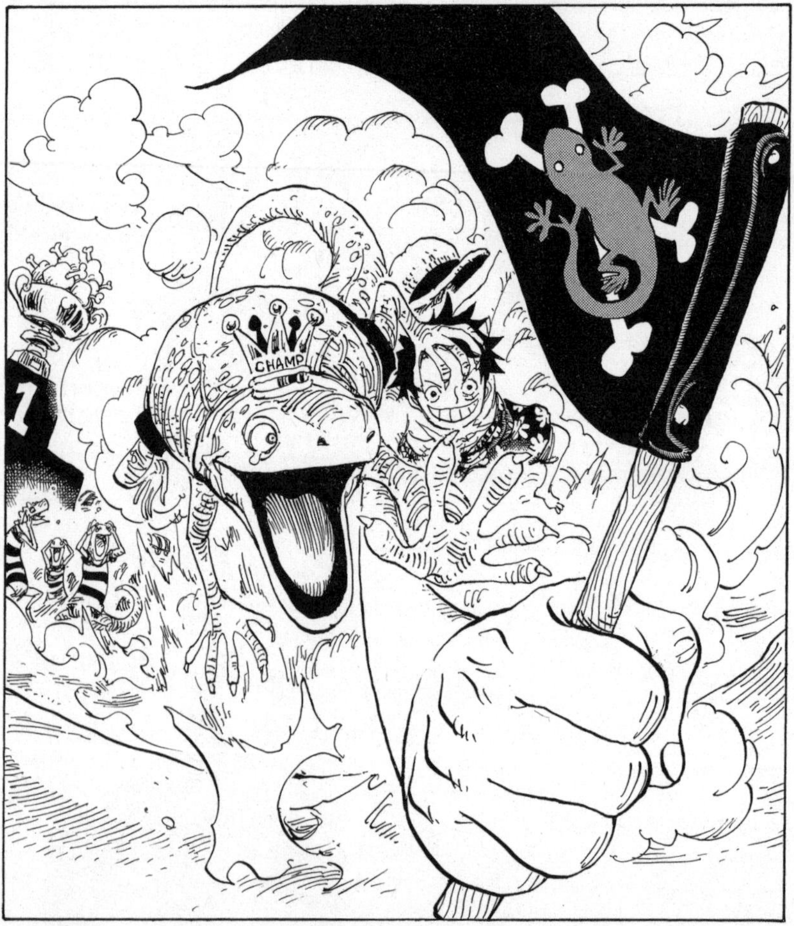
CHAMP
1

REQUEST: "LUFFY AND A LIZARD IN A BEACH FLAG RACE"
BY TAZ FROM KYOTO

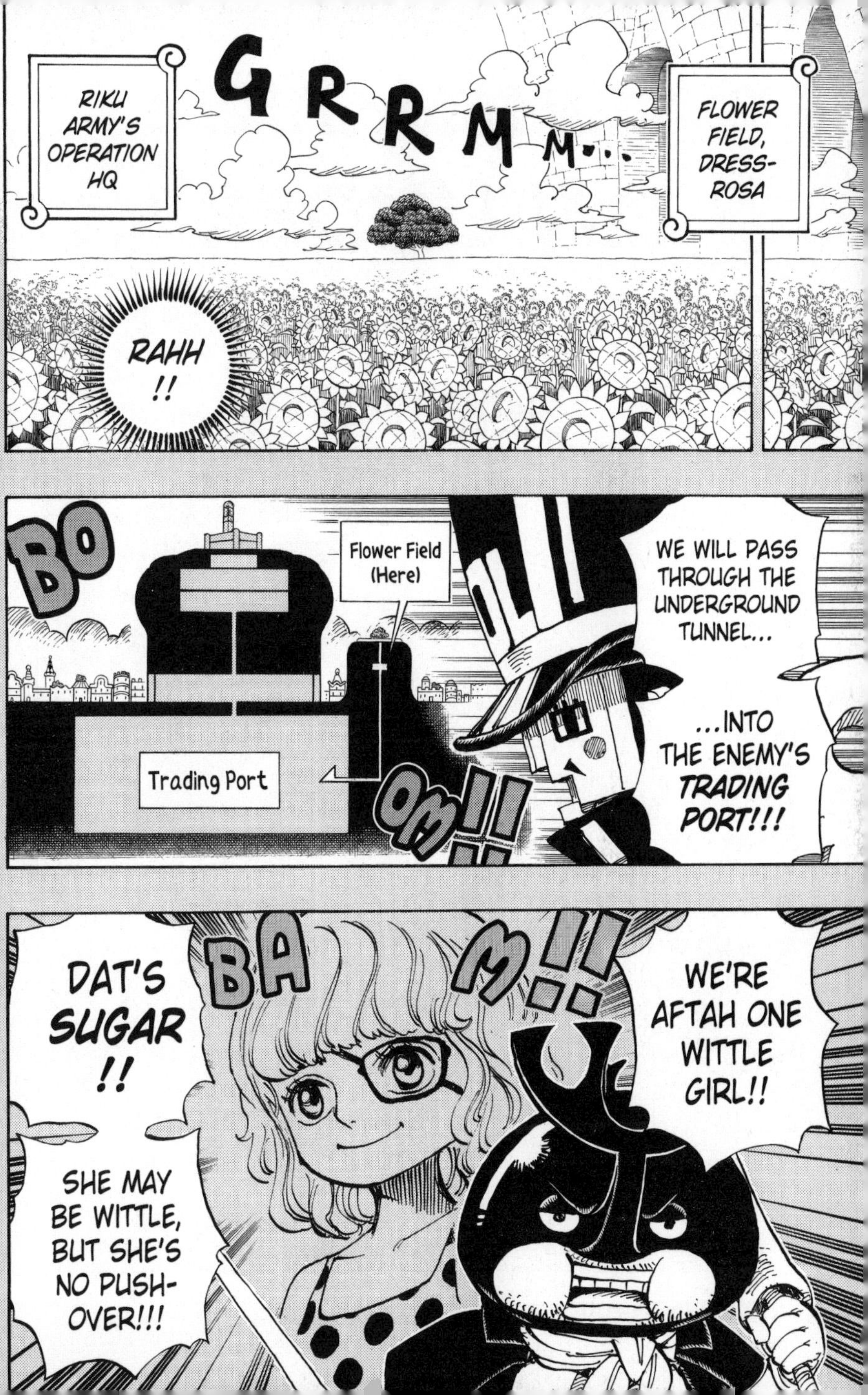
FLOWER FIELD, DRESS-ROSA
GRRRMM...
RIKU ARMY'S OPERATION HQ
RAHH!!
WE WILL PASS THROUGH THE UNDERGROUND TUNNEL...
...INTO THE ENEMY'S TRADING PORT!!!
Flower Field (Here)
BOOM!!
Trading Port
WE'RE AFTAH ONE WITTLE GIRL!!
BAM!!
DAT'S SUGAR!!
SHE MAY BE WITTLE, BUT SHE'S NO PUSH-OVER!!!

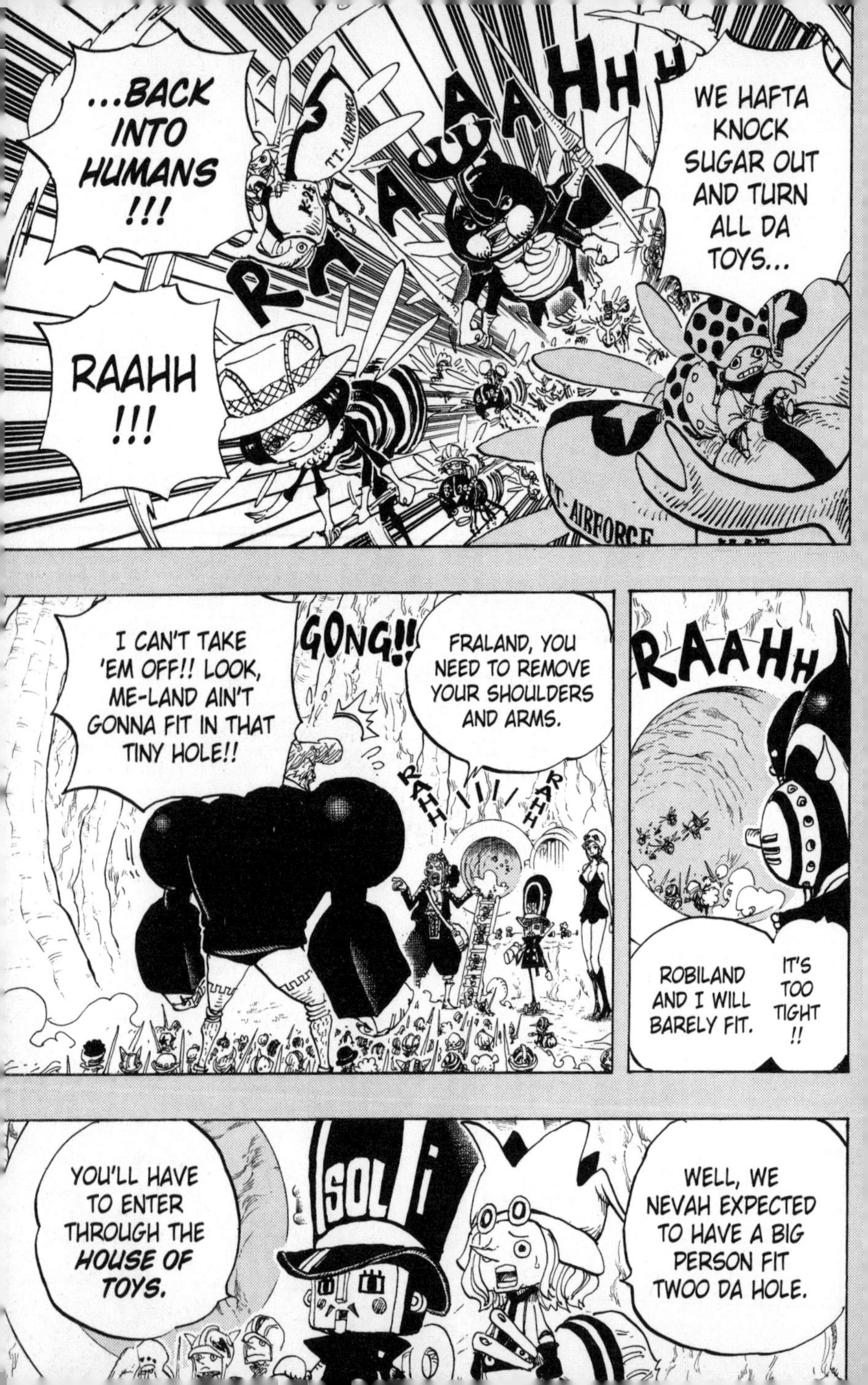
WE HAFTA KNOCK SUGAR OUT AND TURN ALL DA TOYS...
RAAAAAHHH
...BACK INTO HUMANS!!!
RAAHH!!!
TT-AIRFORCE
TT-AIRFORCE
RAAHH
IT'S TOO TIGHT!!
ROBILAND AND I WILL BARELY FIT.
FRALAND, YOU NEED TO REMOVE YOUR SHOULDERS AND ARMS.
GONG!!
I CAN'T TAKE 'EM OFF!! LOOK, ME-LAND AIN'T GONNA FIT IN THAT TINY HOLE!!
RAHH
RAHH
WELL, WE NEVAH EXPECTED TO HAVE A BIG PERSON FIT TWOO DA HOLE.
YOU'LL HAVE TO ENTER THROUGH THE *HOUSE OF TOYS.*
SOL

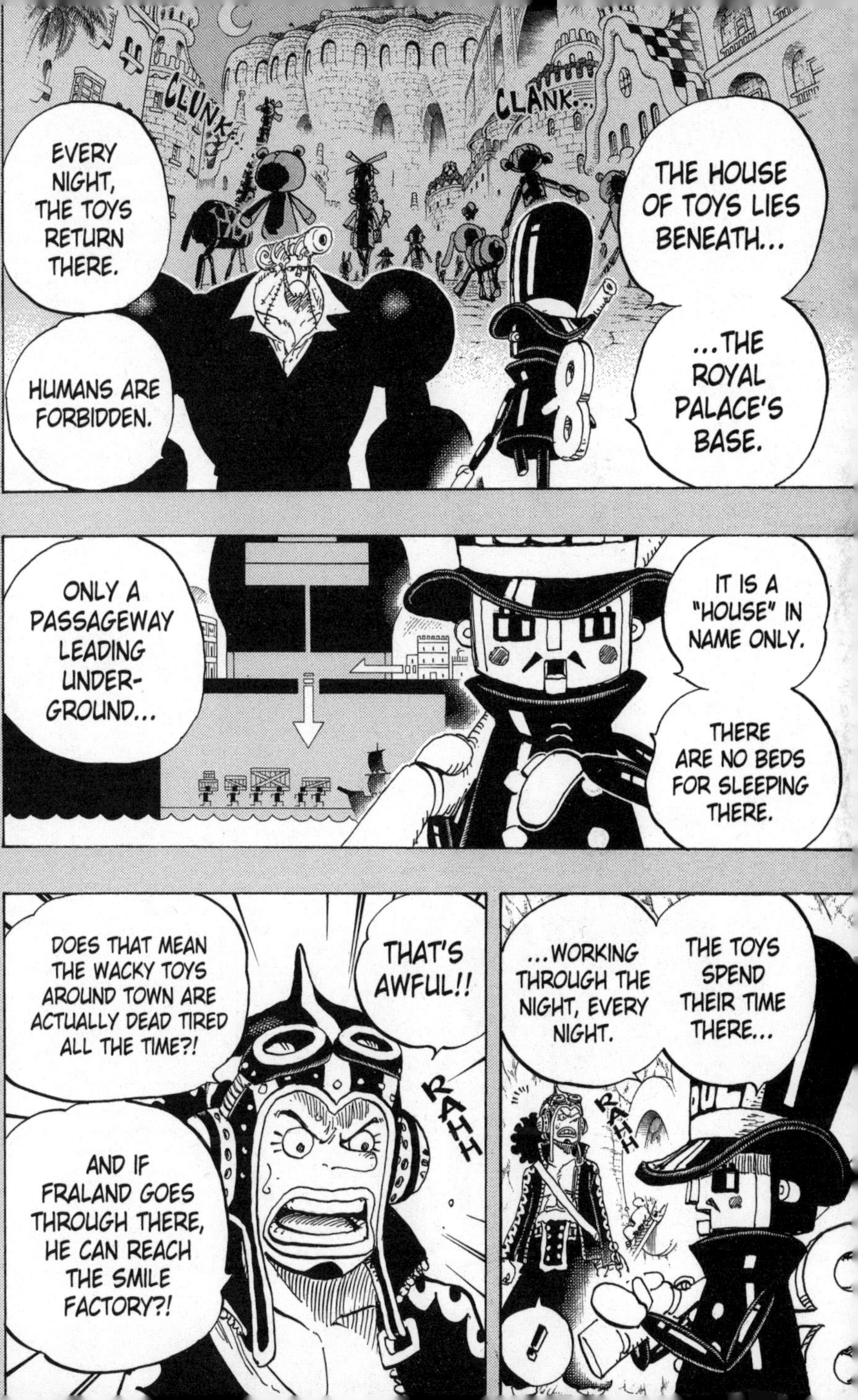

CLANK...
CLUNK
THE HOUSE OF TOYS LIES BENEATH...
...THE ROYAL PALACE'S BASE.
EVERY NIGHT, THE TOYS RETURN THERE.
HUMANS ARE FORBIDDEN.
IT IS A "HOUSE" IN NAME ONLY.
THERE ARE NO BEDS FOR SLEEPING THERE.
ONLY A PASSAGEWAY LEADING UNDER-GROUND...
THE TOYS SPEND THEIR TIME THERE...
...WORKING THROUGH THE NIGHT, EVERY NIGHT.
RAHH
THAT'S AWFUL!!
DOES THAT MEAN THE WACKY TOYS AROUND TOWN ARE ACTUALLY DEAD TIRED ALL THE TIME?!
RAHH
AND IF FRALAND GOES THROUGH THERE, HE CAN REACH THE SMILE FACTORY?!

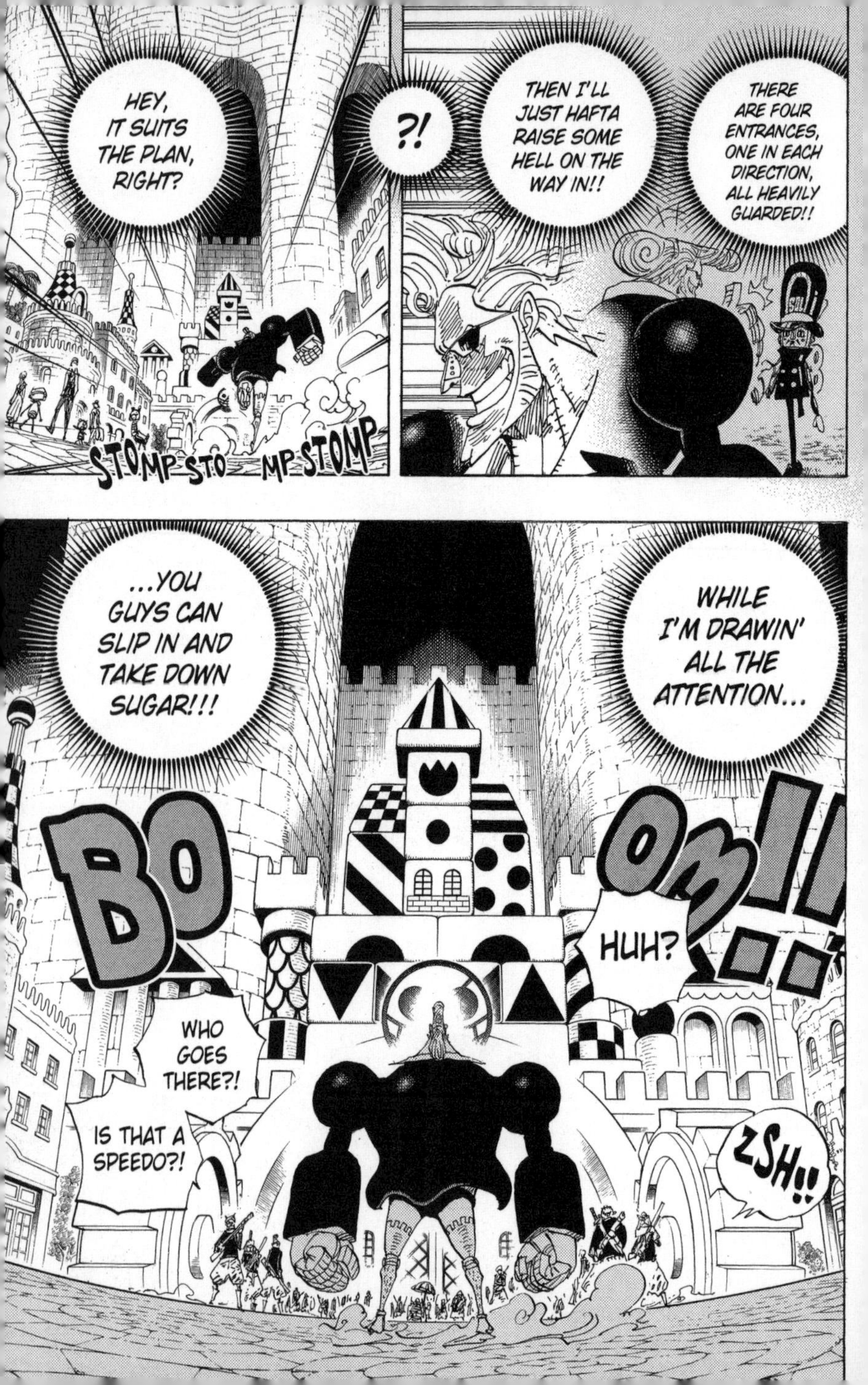
THERE ARE FOUR ENTRANCES, ONE IN EACH DIRECTION, ALL HEAVILY GUARDED!!
THEN I'LL JUST HAFTA RAISE SOME HELL ON THE WAY IN!!
?!
HEY, IT SUITS THE PLAN, RIGHT?
STOMP STO MP STOMP
WHILE I'M DRAWIN' ALL THE ATTENTION...
...YOU GUYS CAN SLIP IN AND TAKE DOWN SUGAR!!!
BOOM!!
HUH?
ZSH!!
WHO GOES THERE?!
IS THAT A SPEEDO?!

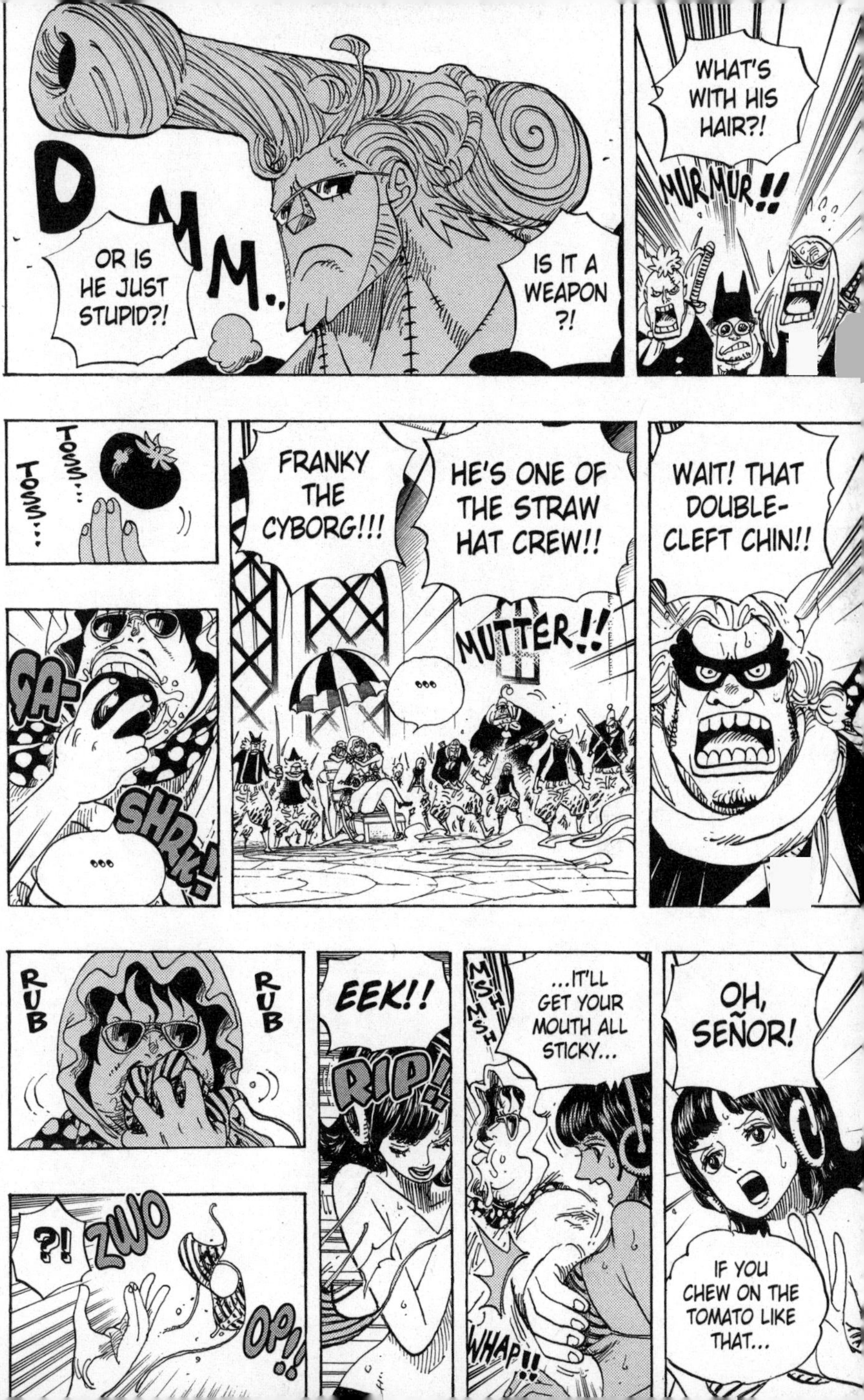

WHAT'S WITH HIS HAIR?!
MURMUR!!
IS IT A WEAPON ?!
OR IS HE JUST STUPID?!
DMM..
WAIT! THAT DOUBLE-CLEFT CHIN!!
HE'S ONE OF THE STRAW HAT CREW!!
FRANKY THE CYBORG!!!
MUTTER!!
...
TOSS... TOSS...
GA-
SHRK!
...
OH, SEÑOR!
IF YOU CHEW ON THE TOMATO LIKE THAT...
...IT'LL GET YOUR MOUTH ALL STICKY...
MSH MSH
WHAP!!
EEK!!
RIP!!
RUB RUB
?!
ZWOOP!!

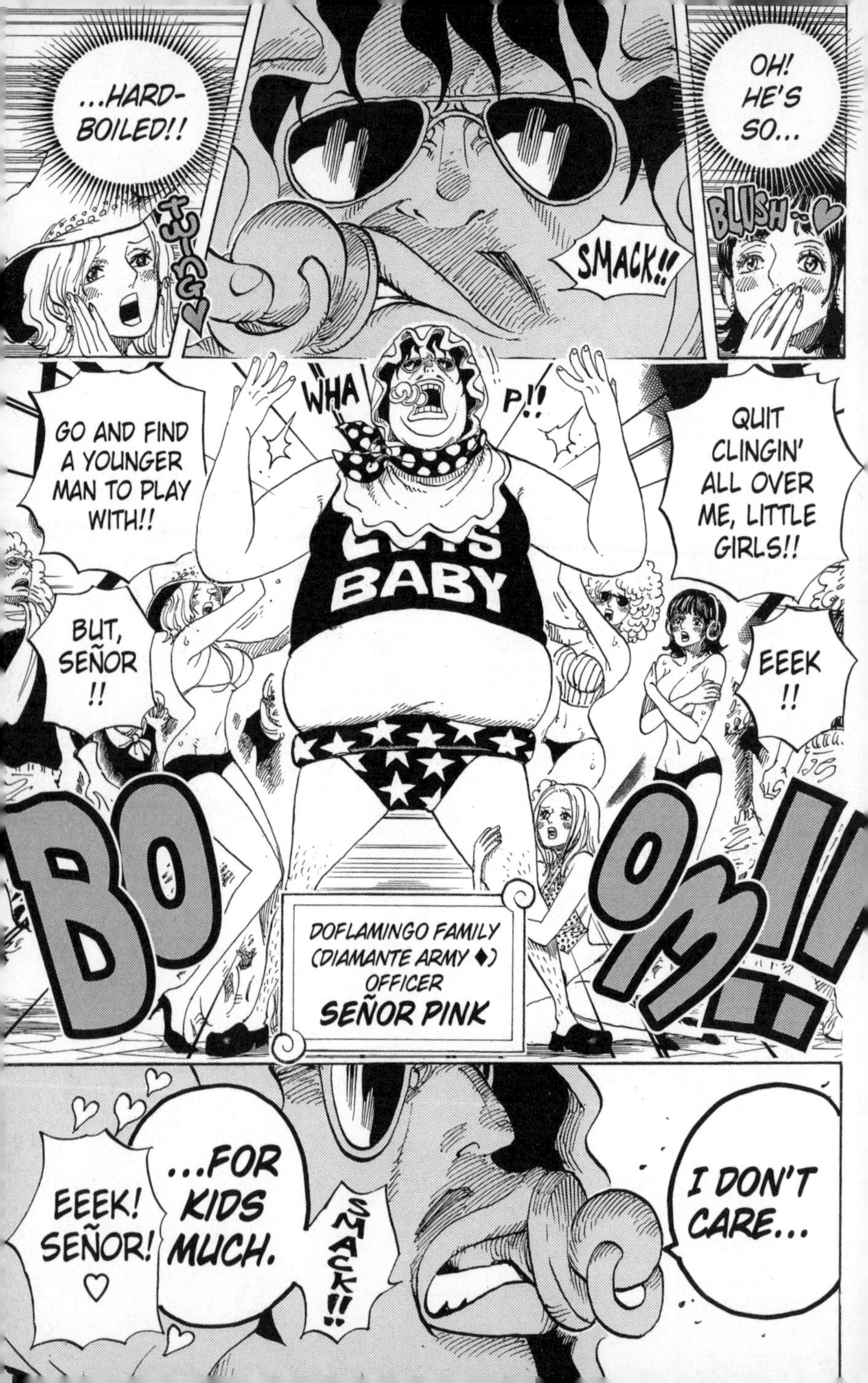
OH! HE'S SO...
BLUSH
SMACK!!
...HARD-BOILED!!
TUG
WHAP!!
QUIT CLINGIN' ALL OVER ME, LITTLE GIRLS!!
GO AND FIND A YOUNGER MAN TO PLAY WITH!!
BABY
EEEK !!
BUT, SEÑOR !!
BOOM!!
DOFLAMINGO FAMILY (DIAMANTE ARMY ♦) OFFICER SEÑOR PINK
I DON'T CARE...
SMACK!!
...FOR KIDS MUCH.
EEEK! SEÑOR! ♡

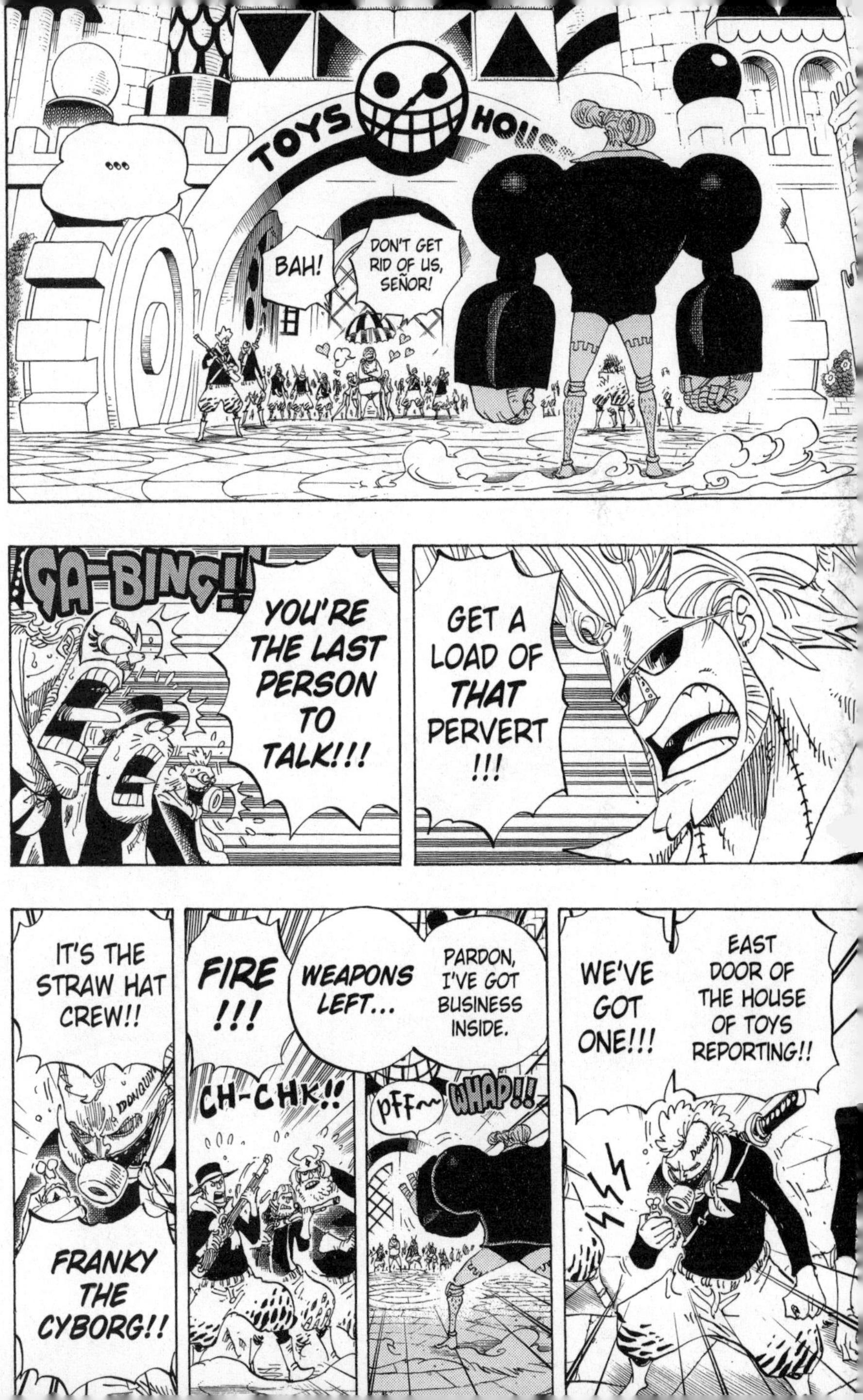
TOYS
...
DON'T GET RID OF US, SEÑOR!
BAH!
GET A LOAD OF THAT PERVERT!!!
GA-BING!!
YOU'RE THE LAST PERSON TO TALK!!!
EAST DOOR OF THE HOUSE OF TOYS REPORTING!!
WE'VE GOT ONE!!!
PARDON, I'VE GOT BUSINESS INSIDE.
WHAP!!
pFF~
WEAPONS LEFT...
FIRE!!!
CH-CHK!!
IT'S THE STRAW HAT CREW!!
FRANKY THE CYBORG!!

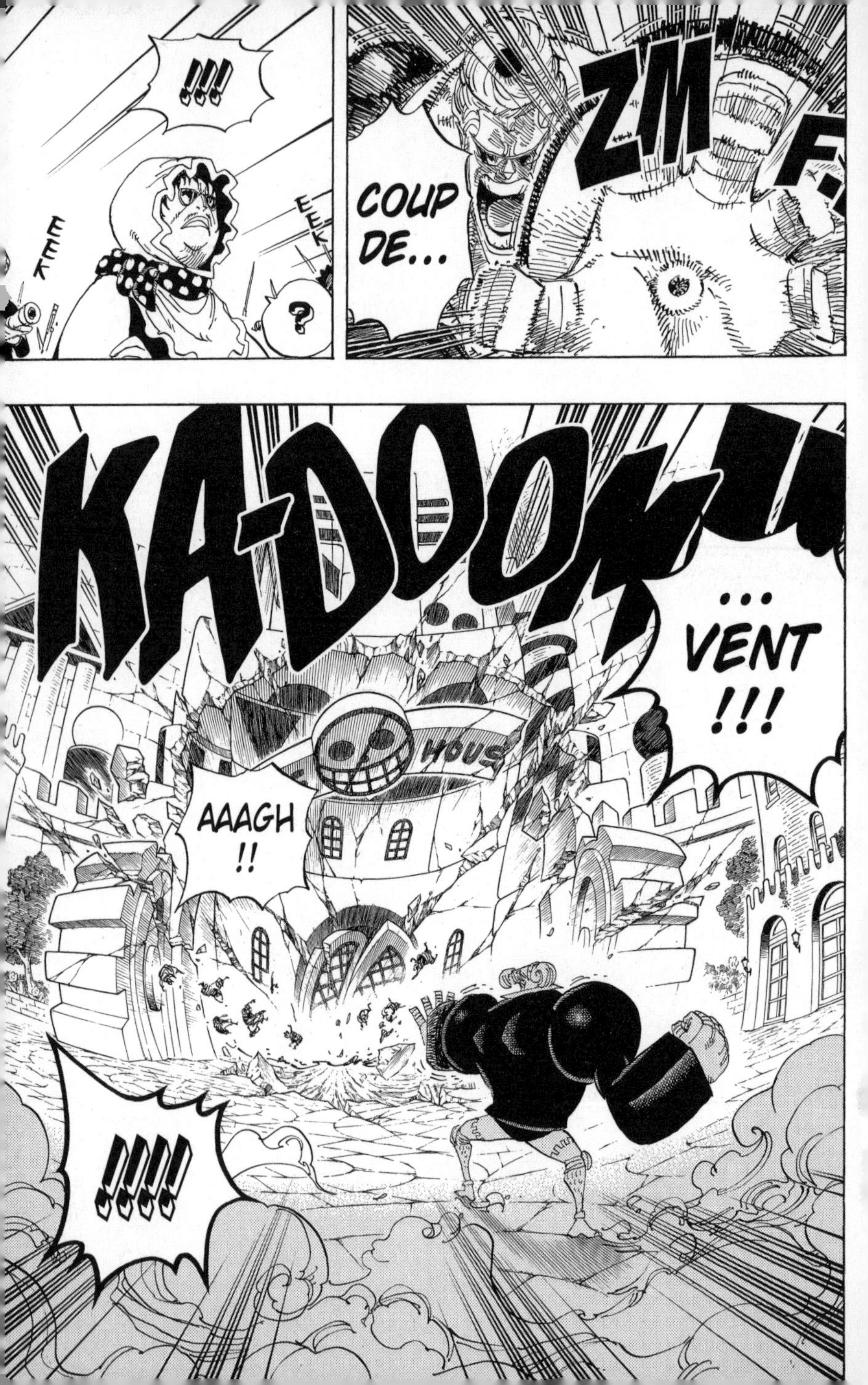
ZM
COUP DE...
!!!
EEK
EEK
?
KA-DOO
... VENT !!!
VOUS
AAAGH !!
!!!!

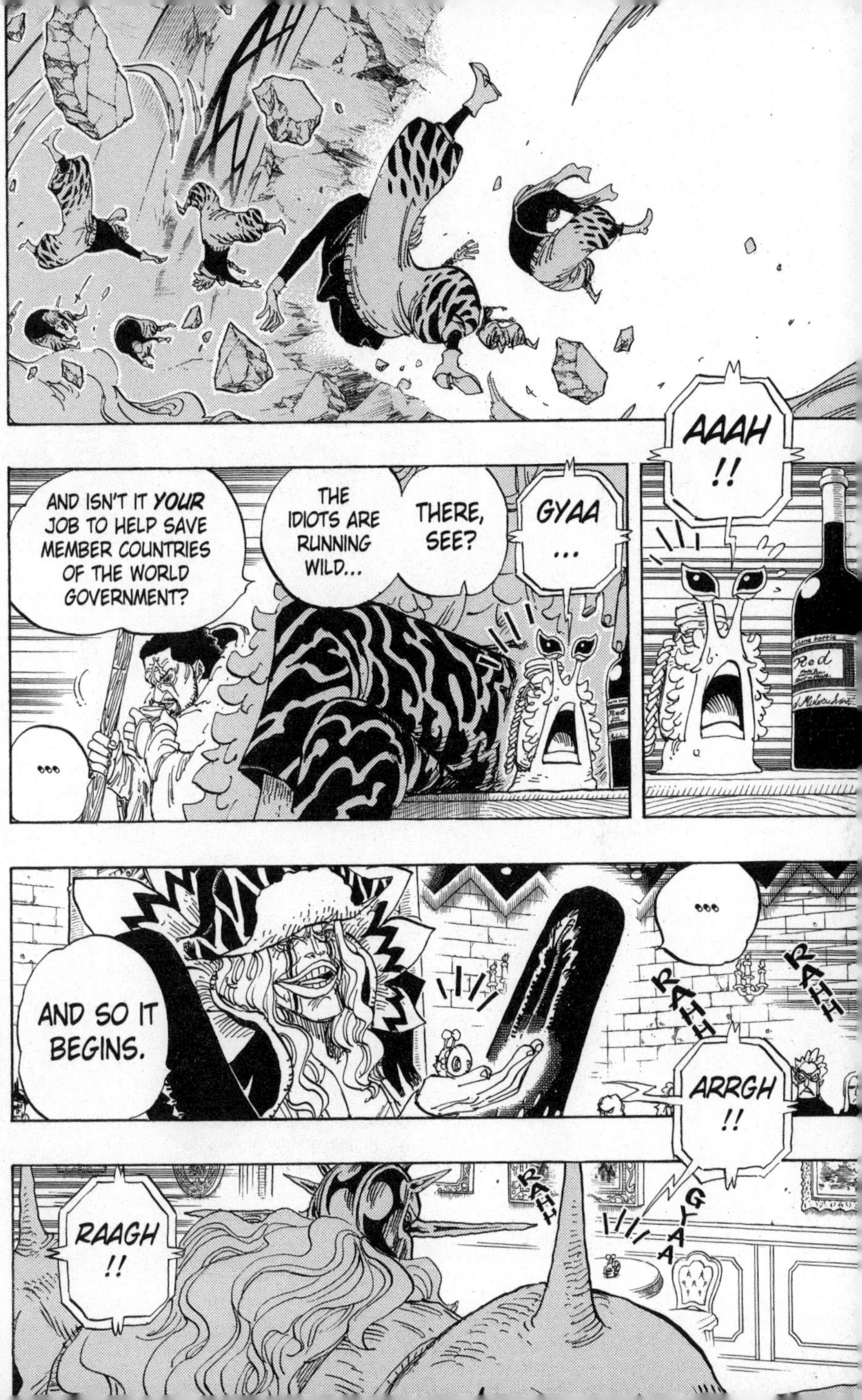
AAAH!!
GYAA...
THERE, SEE?
THE IDIOTS ARE RUNNING WILD...
AND ISN'T IT *YOUR* JOB TO HELP SAVE MEMBER COUNTRIES OF THE WORLD GOVERNMENT?
...
...
RAHH
RAHH
ARRGH!!
AND SO IT BEGINS.
RAHH
GYAAA
RAAGH!!

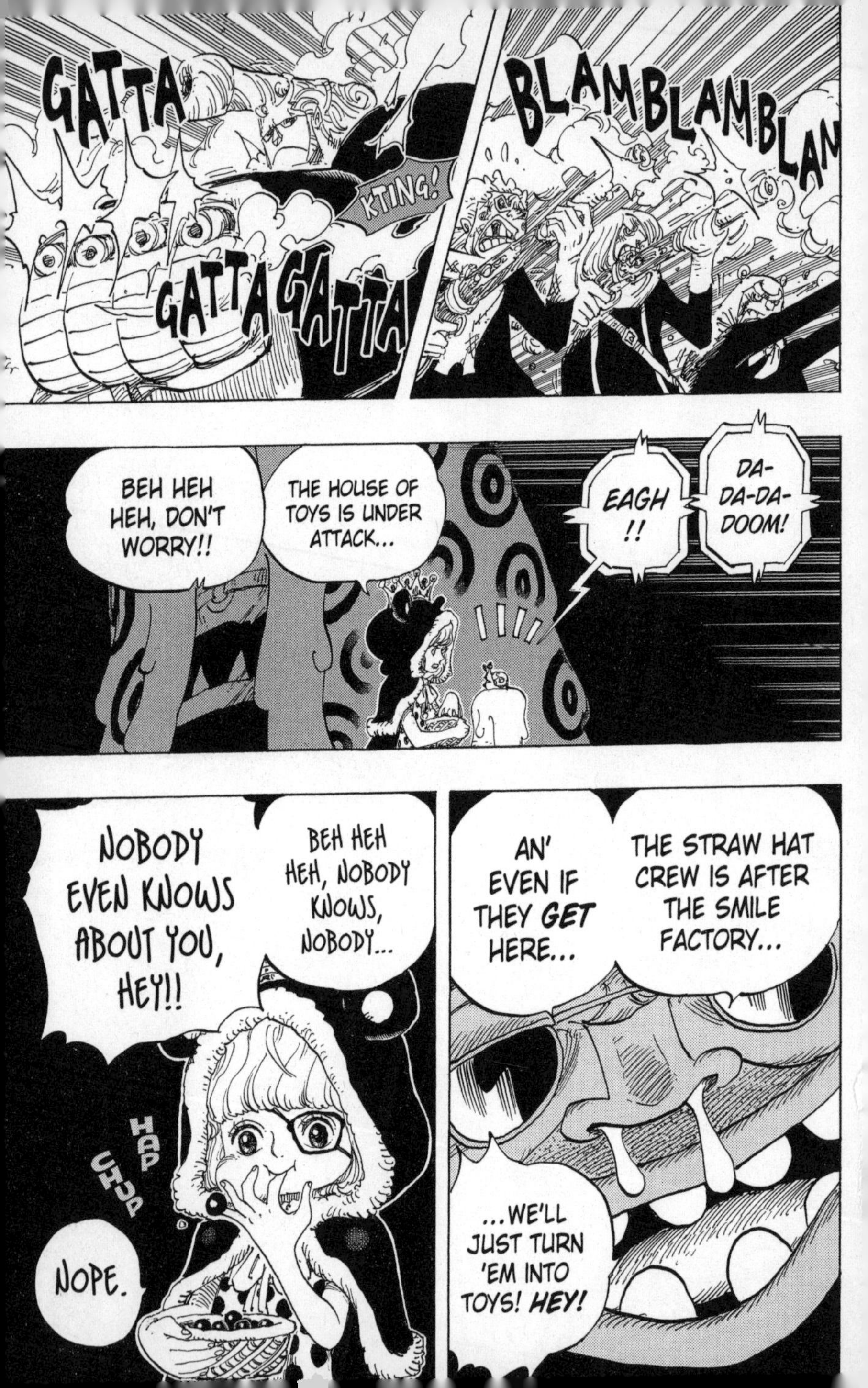
BLAMBLAMBLAM
GATTA
KTING!
GATTA GATTA
DA-DA-DA-DOOM!
EAGH!!
THE HOUSE OF TOYS IS UNDER ATTACK...
BEH HEH HEH, DON'T WORRY!!
THE STRAW HAT CREW IS AFTER THE SMILE FACTORY...
AN' EVEN IF THEY GET HERE...
...WE'LL JUST TURN 'EM INTO TOYS! HEY!
BEH HEH HEH, NOBODY KNOWS, NOBODY...
NOBODY EVEN KNOWS ABOUT YOU, HEY!!
NOPE.

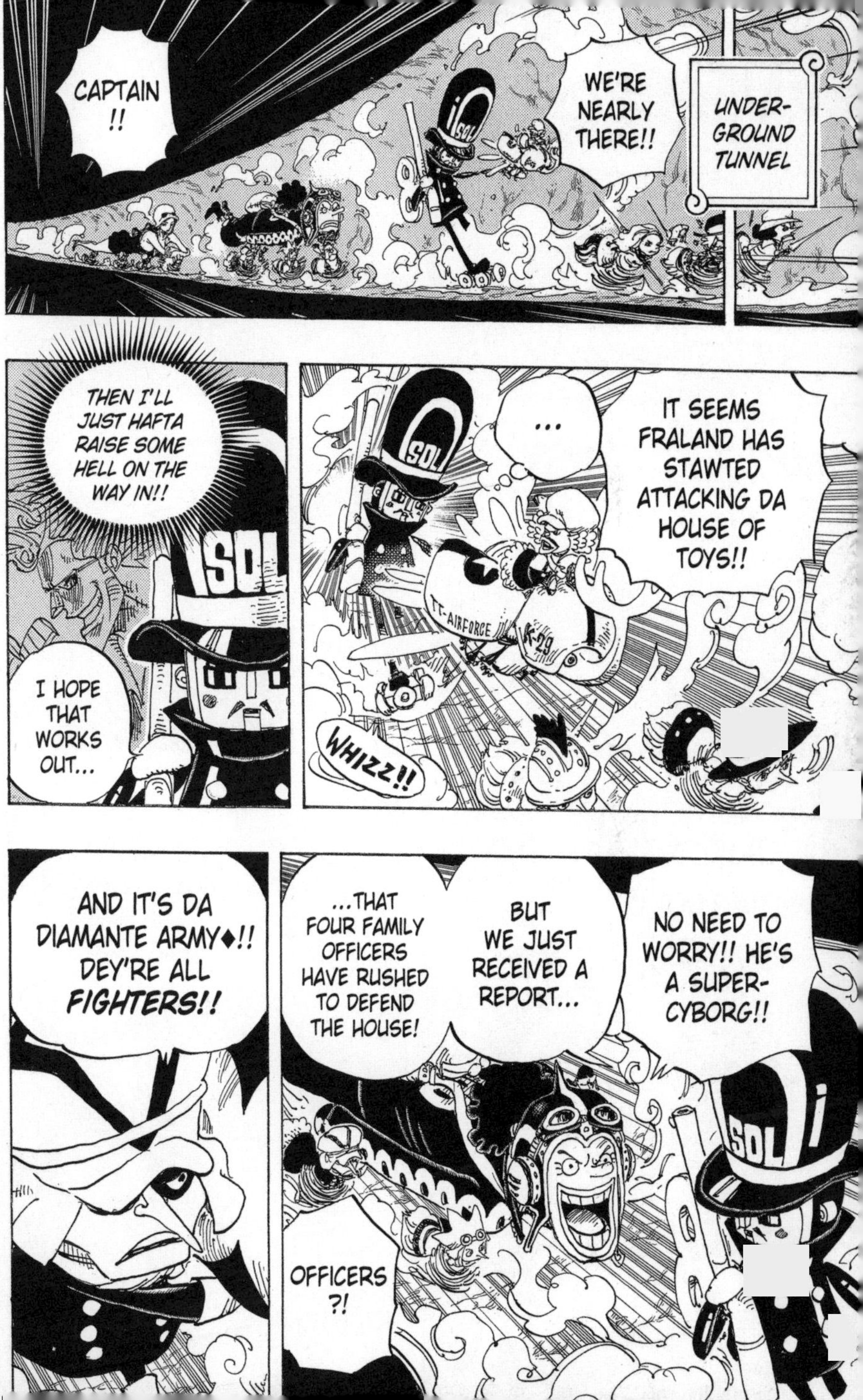
UNDERGROUND TUNNEL
WE'RE NEARLY THERE!!
CAPTAIN!!
IT SEEMS FRALAND HAS STAWTED ATTACKING DA HOUSE OF TOYS!!
...
TT-AIRFORCE
K-29
WHIZZ!!
THEN I'LL JUST HAFTA RAISE SOME HELL ON THE WAY IN!!
I HOPE THAT WORKS OUT...
NO NEED TO WORRY!! HE'S A SUPER-CYBORG!!
BUT WE JUST RECEIVED A REPORT...
...THAT FOUR FAMILY OFFICERS HAVE RUSHED TO DEFEND THE HOUSE!
OFFICERS?!
AND IT'S DA DIAMANTE ARMY♦!! DEY'RE ALL *FIGHTERS!!*

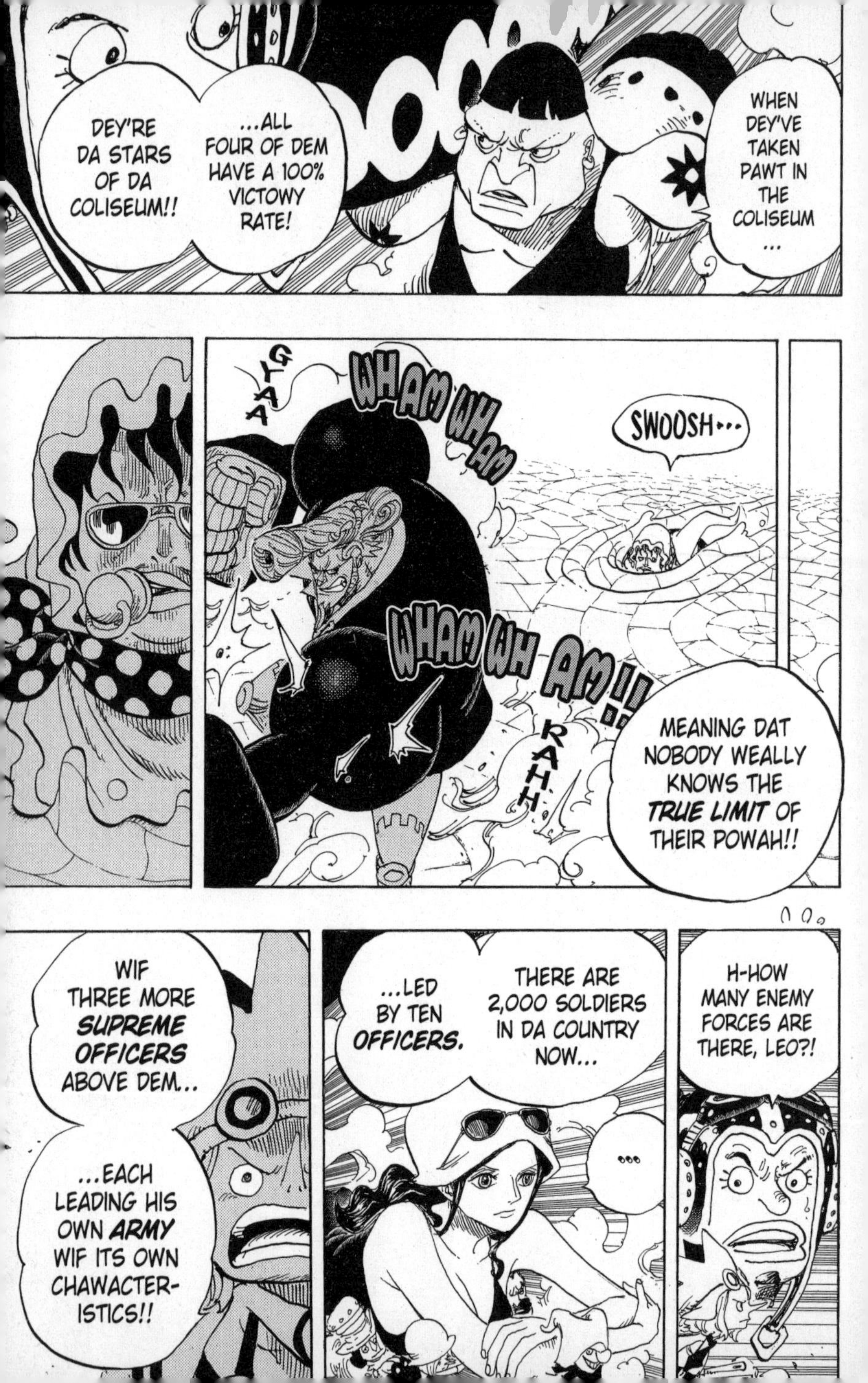
WHEN DEY'VE TAKEN PAWT IN THE COLISEUM...
...ALL FOUR OF DEM HAVE A 100% VICTOWY RATE!
DEY'RE DA STARS OF DA COLISEUM!!
SWOOSH...
WHAM WHAM
GYAA
WHAM WHAM!!
RAHH
MEANING DAT NOBODY WEALLY KNOWS THE TRUE LIMIT OF THEIR POWAH!!
H-HOW MANY ENEMY FORCES ARE THERE, LEO?!
THERE ARE 2,000 SOLDIERS IN DA COUNTRY NOW...
...LED BY TEN OFFICERS.
...
WIF THREE MORE SUPREME OFFICERS ABOVE DEM...
...EACH LEADING HIS OWN ARMY WIF ITS OWN CHAWACTER-ISTICS!!

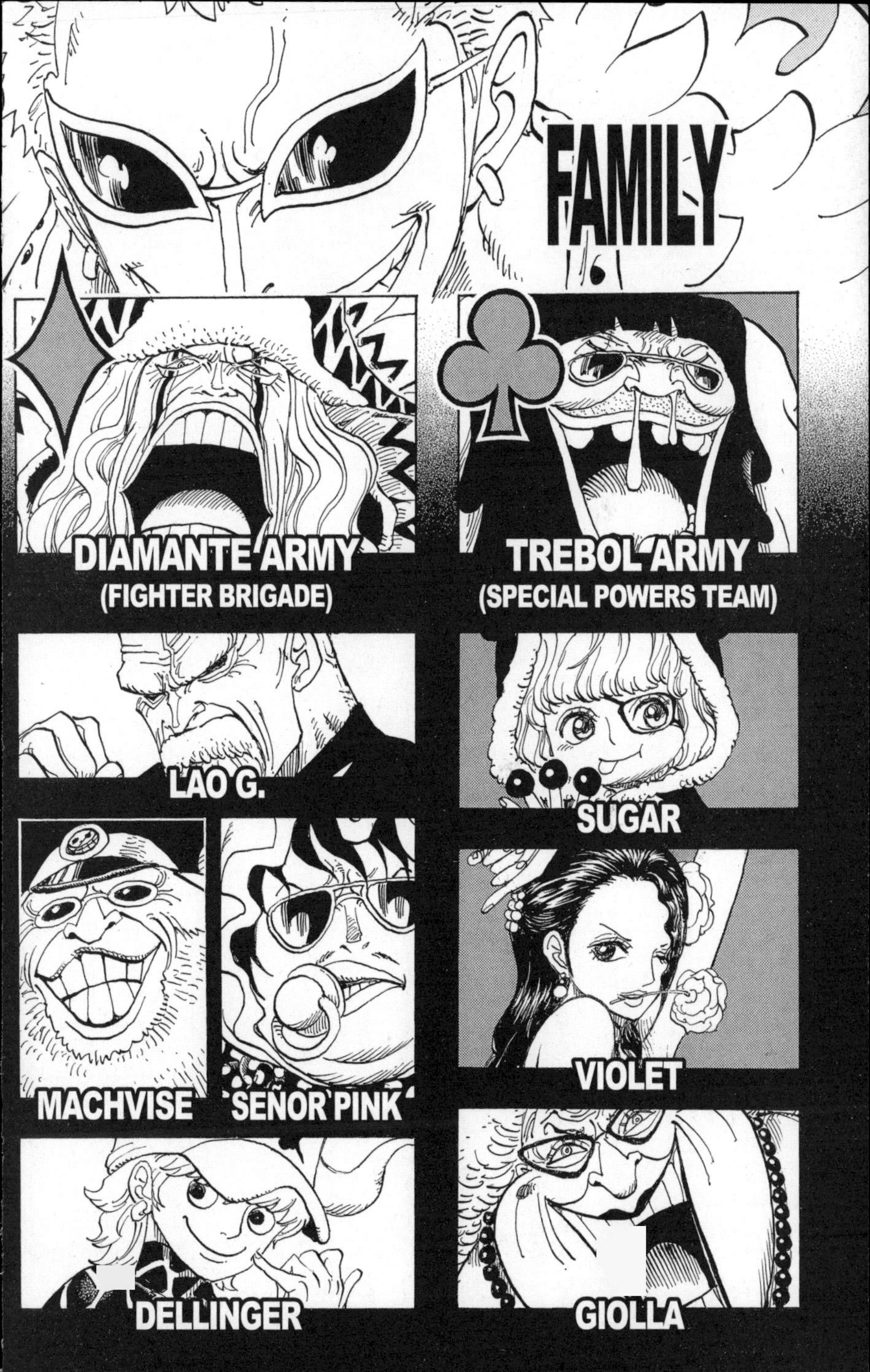
FAMILY
TREBOL ARMY
(SPECIAL POWERS TEAM)
DIAMANTE ARMY
(FIGHTER BRIGADE)
SUGAR
LAO G.
VIOLET
SEÑOR PINK
MACHVISE
GIOLLA
DELLINGER

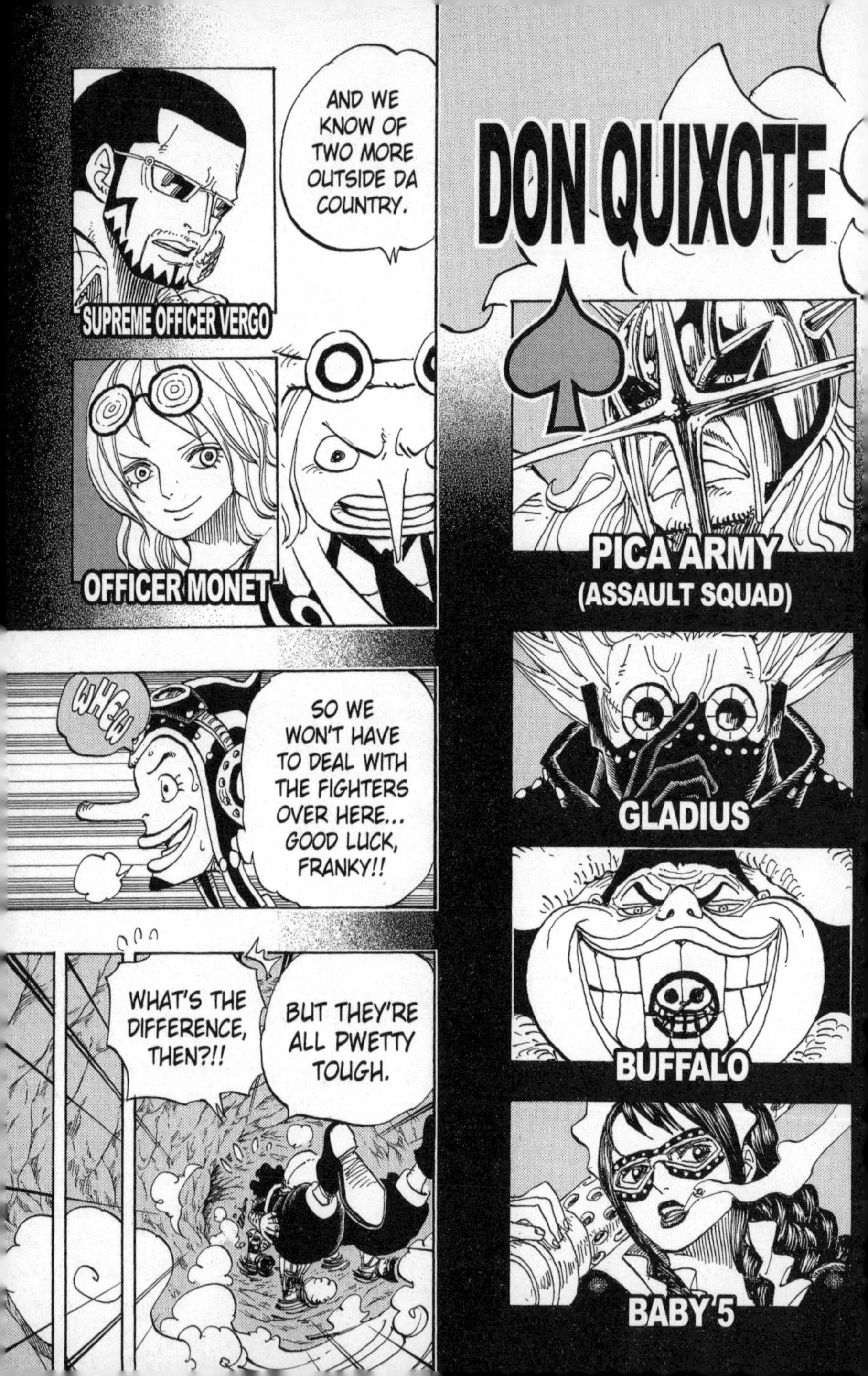
DON QUIXOTE
PICA ARMY
(ASSAULT SQUAD)
GLADIUS
BUFFALO
BABY 5
AND WE KNOW OF TWO MORE OUTSIDE DA COUNTRY.
SUPREME OFFICER VERGO
OFFICER MONET
SO WE WON'T HAVE TO DEAL WITH THE FIGHTERS OVER HERE... GOOD LUCK, FRANKY!!
WHEW
BUT THEY'RE ALL PWETTY TOUGH.
WHAT'S THE DIFFERENCE, THEN?!!

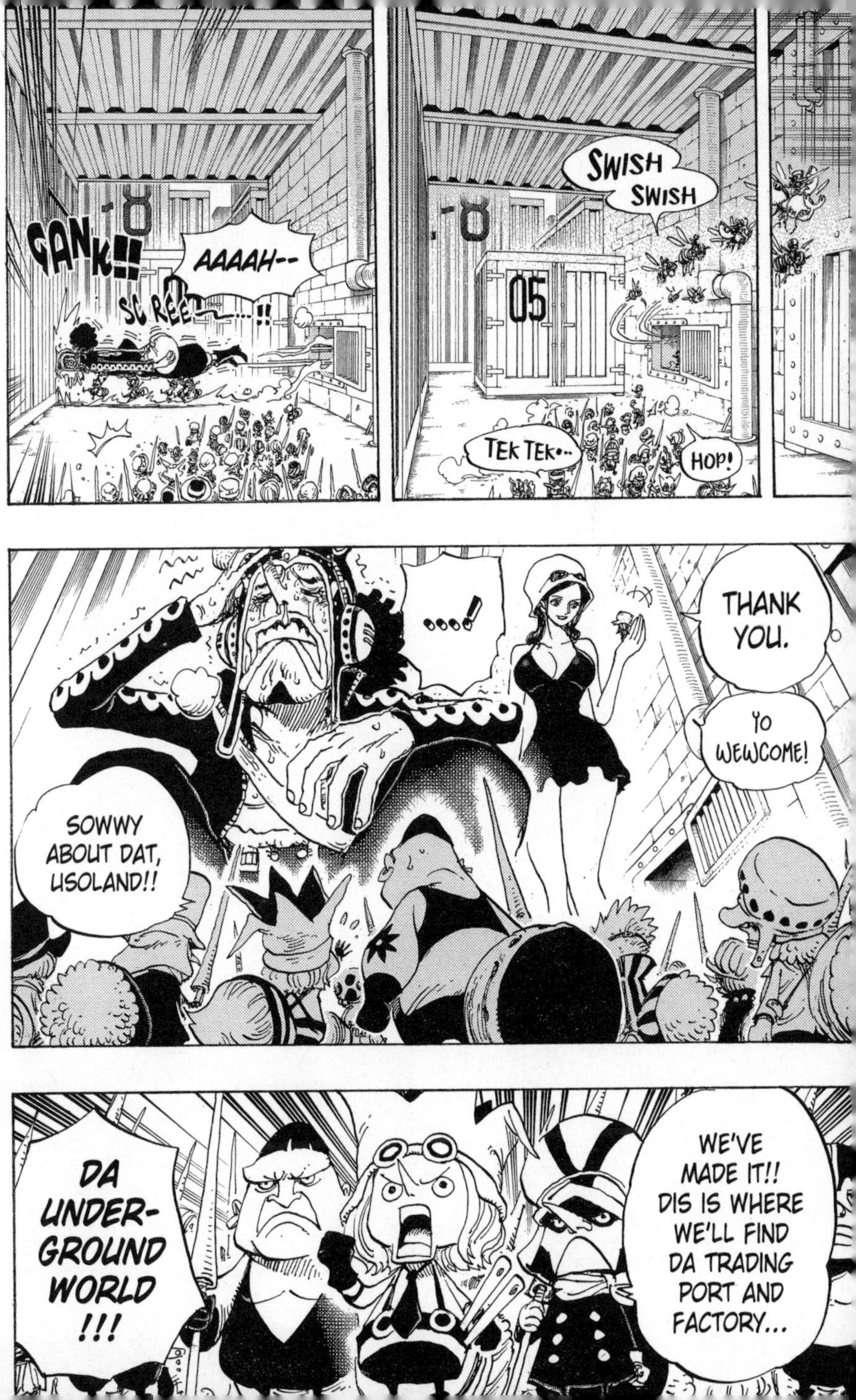
SWISH SWISH
HOP!
TEK TEK..
AAAAH--
GANK!!
SCREE...!!
THANK YOU.
YO WEWCOME!
...!
SOWWY ABOUT DAT, USOLAND!!
WE'VE MADE IT!! DIS IS WHERE WE'LL FIND DA TRADING PORT AND FACTORY...
DA UNDER-GROUND WORLD!!!

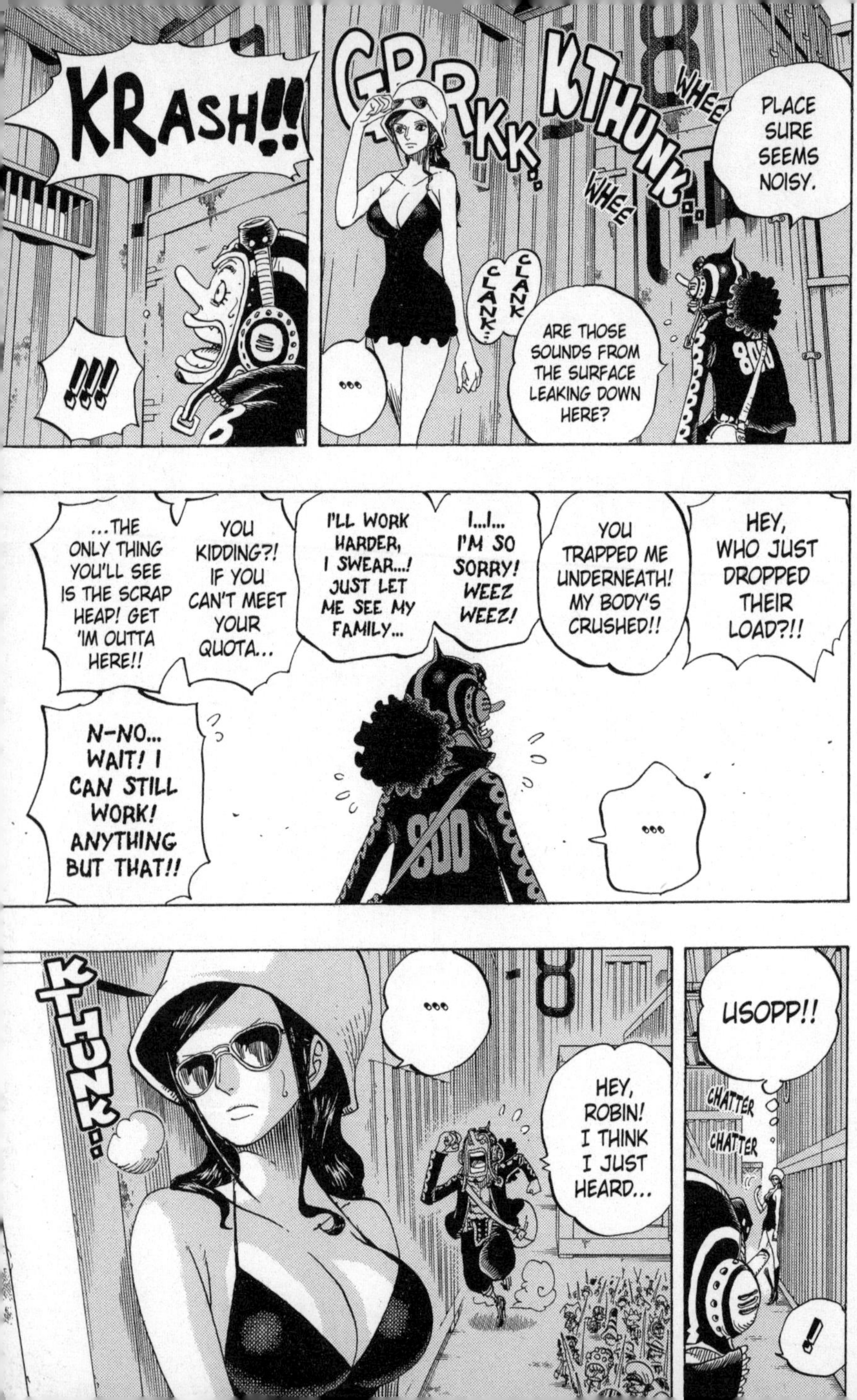

GRRKK..
KTHUNK..
WHEE
WHEE
PLACE SURE SEEMS NOISY.
ARE THOSE SOUNDS FROM THE SURFACE LEAKING DOWN HERE?
CLANK CLANK..
...
KRASH!!!
!!!
HEY, WHO JUST DROPPED THEIR LOAD?!!
YOU TRAPPED ME UNDERNEATH! MY BODY'S CRUSHED!!
I...I... I'M SO SORRY! WEEZ WEEZ!
I'LL WORK HARDER, I SWEAR...! JUST LET ME SEE MY FAMILY...
YOU KIDDING?! IF YOU CAN'T MEET YOUR QUOTA...
...THE ONLY THING YOU'LL SEE IS THE SCRAP HEAP! GET 'IM OUTTA HERE!!
...
N-NO... WAIT! I CAN STILL WORK! ANYTHING BUT THAT!!
USOPP!!
CHATTER
CHATTER
!
HEY, ROBIN! I THINK I JUST HEARD...
...
KTHUNK..

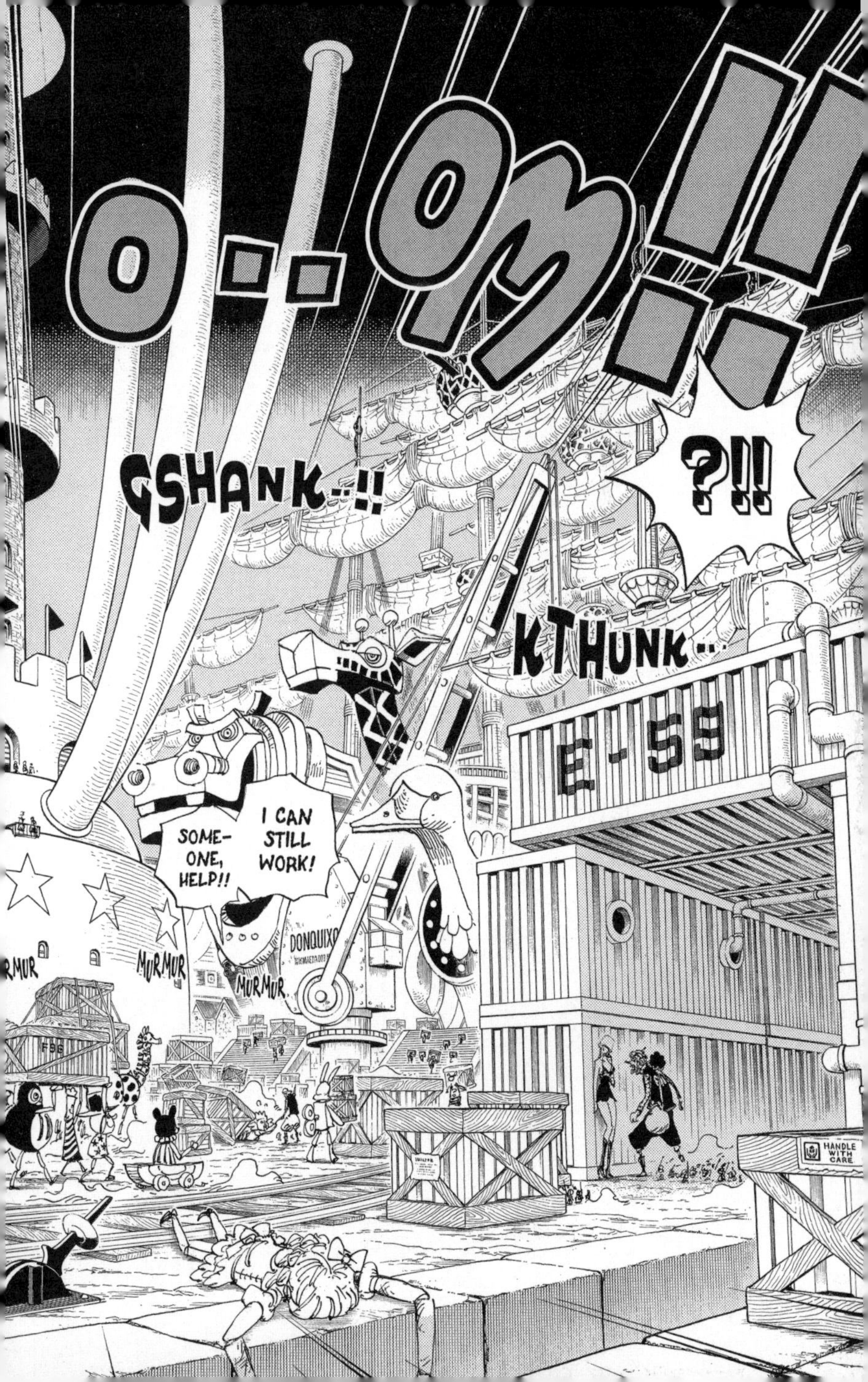
?!!
GSHANK..!!
KTHUNK..
E-59
I CAN STILL WORK!
SOME-ONE, HELP!!
MURMUR
MURMUR
MURMUR
MURMUR
HANDLE WITH CARE

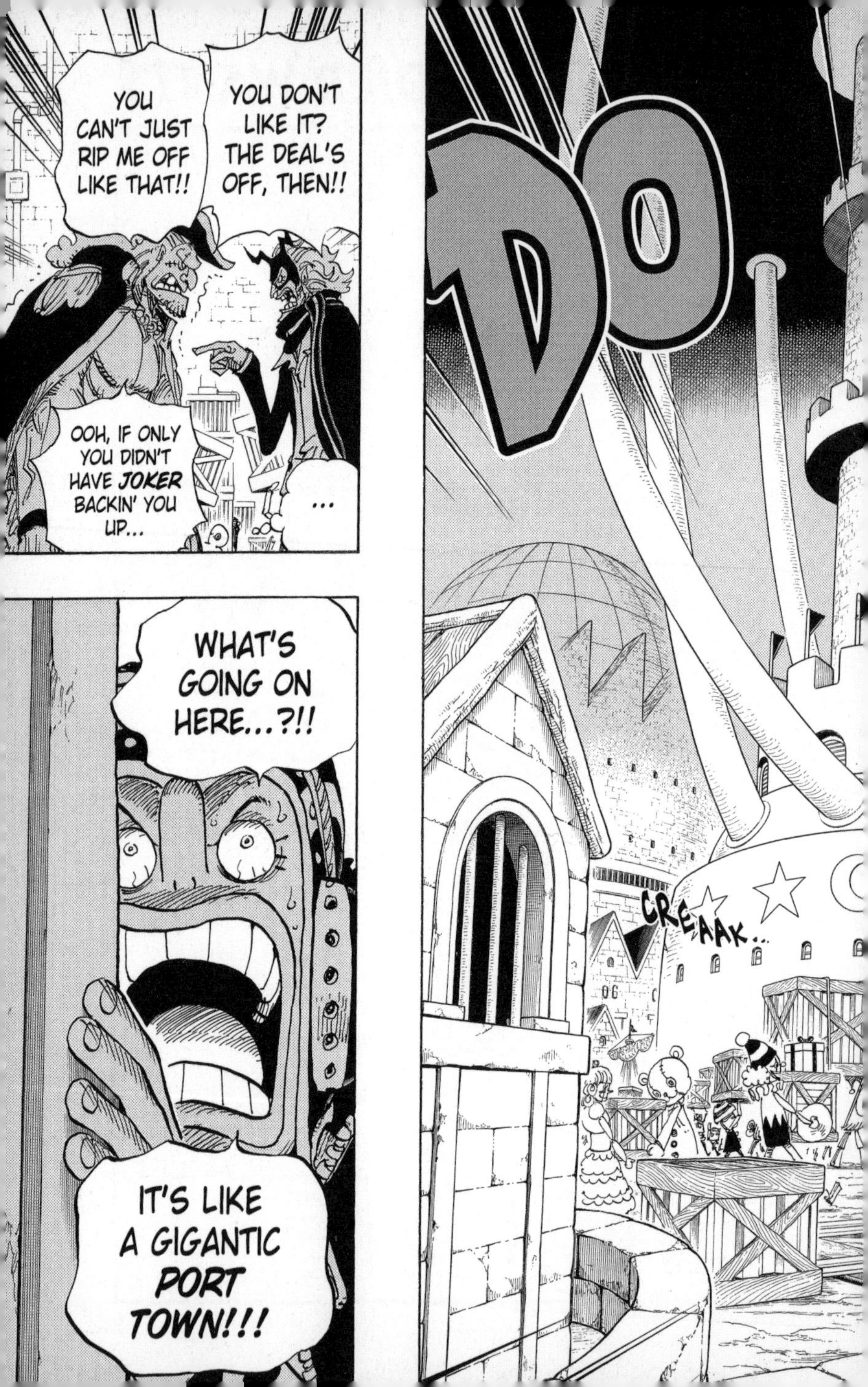
DO
CREAAK...
YOU DON'T LIKE IT? THE DEAL'S OFF, THEN!!
YOU CAN'T JUST RIP ME OFF LIKE THAT!!
...
OOH, IF ONLY YOU DIDN'T HAVE JOKER BACKIN' YOU UP...
WHAT'S GOING ON HERE...?!!
IT'S LIKE A GIGANTIC PORT TOWN!!!

WHAT THE SOLDIER WANTS

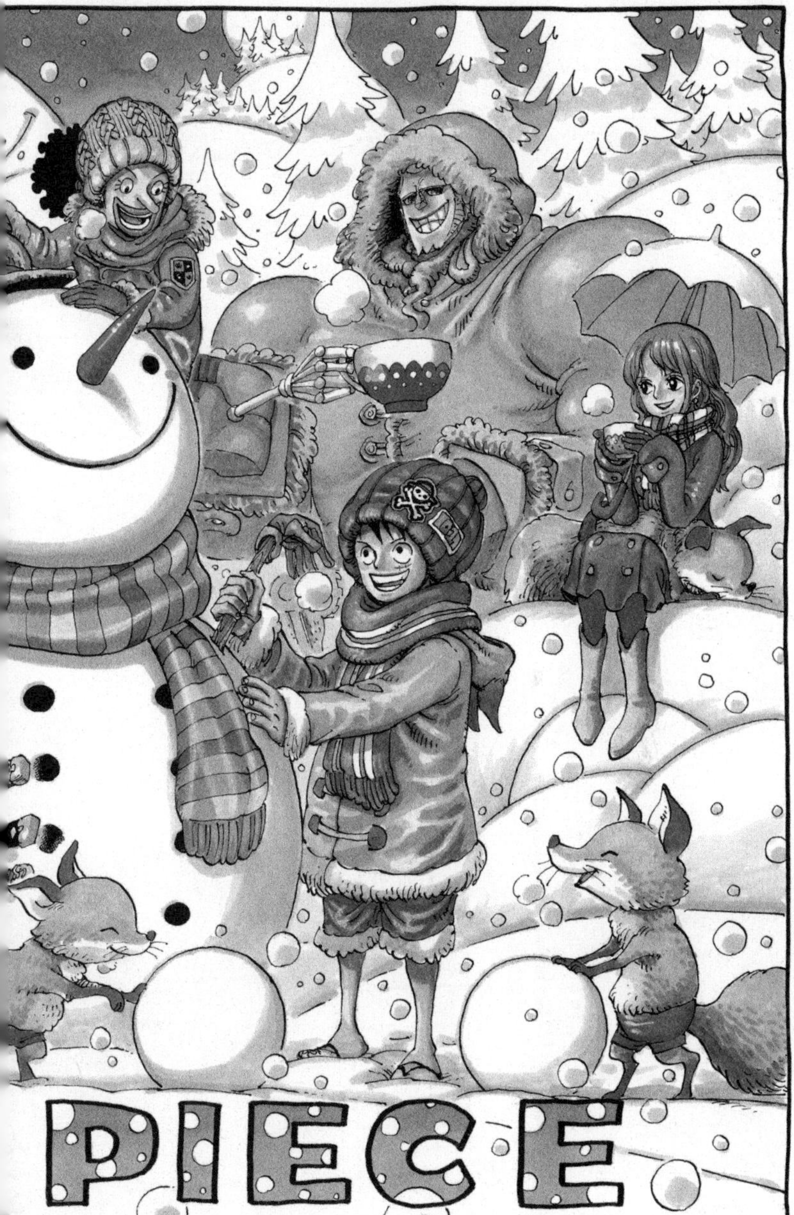
PIECE

Chapter 733:

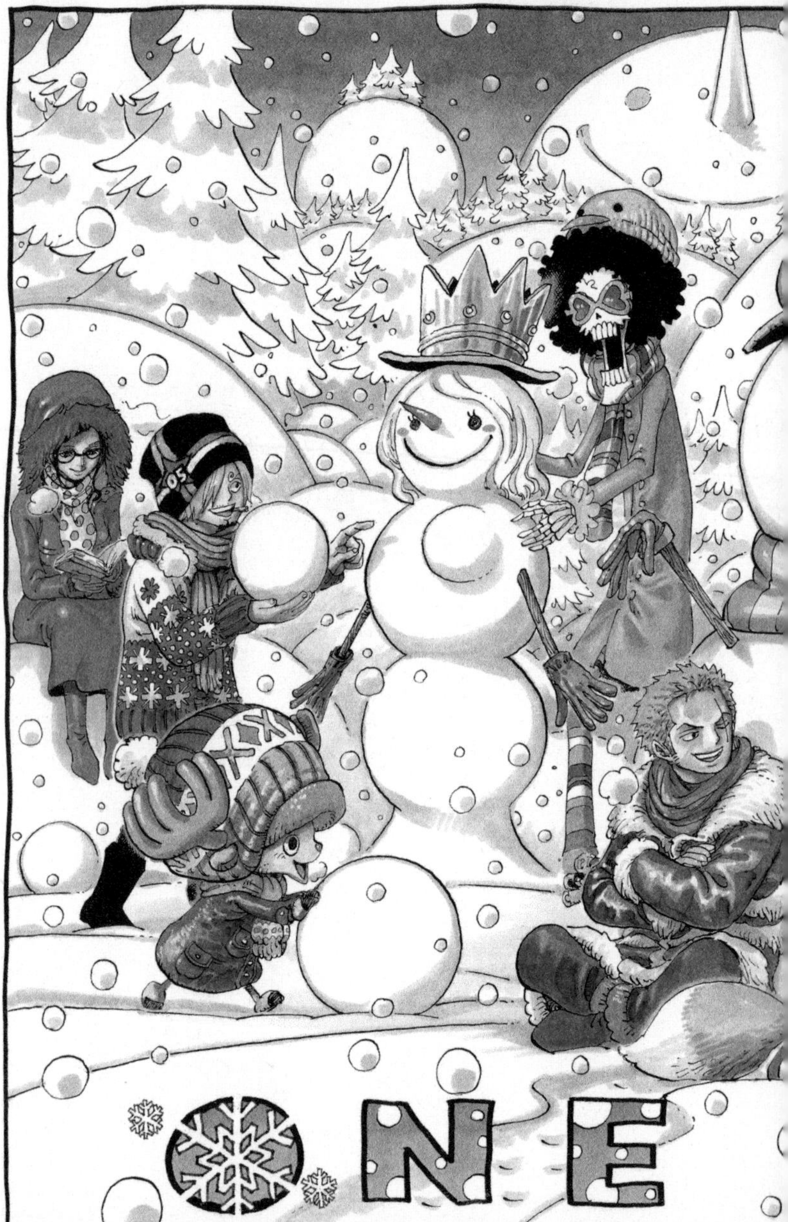
05
ONE

vol.74
ONE PIECE

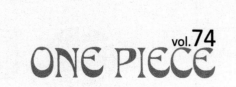

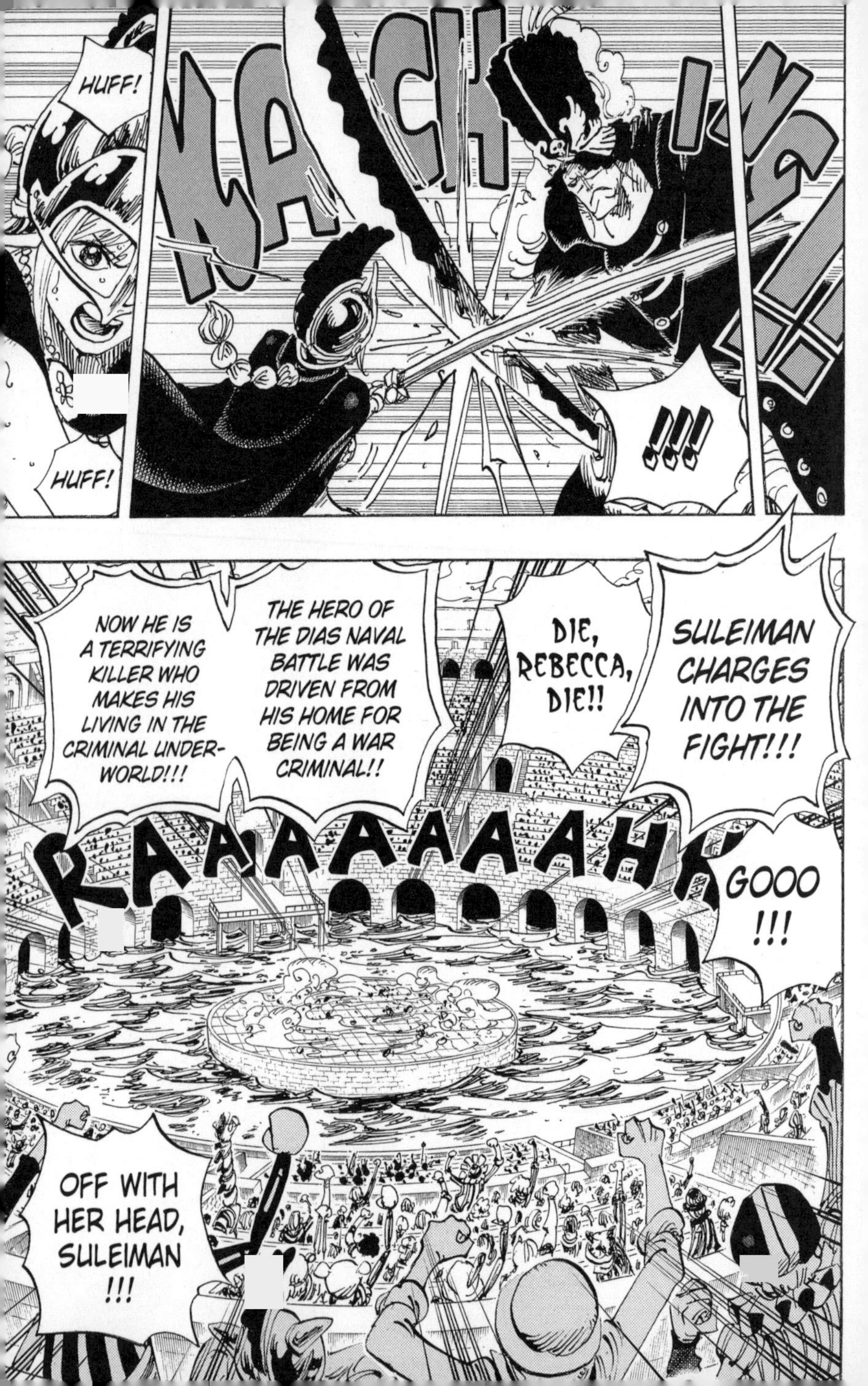

WACHING!!
!!!
HUFF!
HUFF!
SULEIMAN CHARGES INTO THE FIGHT!!!
DIE, REBECCA, DIE!!
THE HERO OF THE DIAS NAVAL BATTLE WAS DRIVEN FROM HIS HOME FOR BEING A WAR CRIMINAL!!
NOW HE IS A TERRIFYING KILLER WHO MAKES HIS LIVING IN THE CRIMINAL UNDER-WORLD!!!
RAAAAAAAHH
GOOO!!!
OFF WITH HER HEAD, SULEIMAN!!!

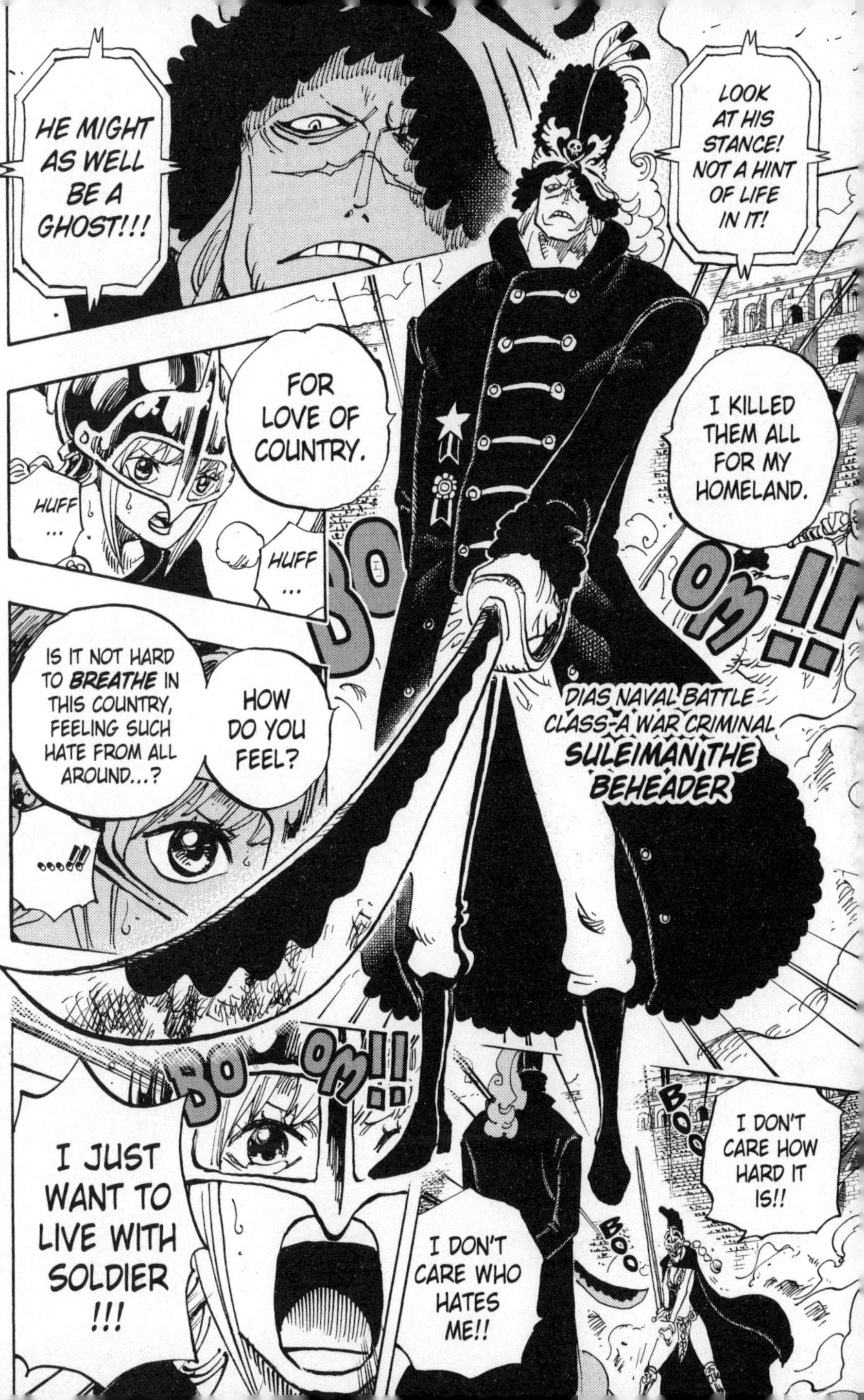
LOOK AT HIS STANCE! NOT A HINT OF LIFE IN IT!
HE MIGHT AS WELL BE A GHOST!!!
I KILLED THEM ALL FOR MY HOMELAND.
BOOM!!
DIAS NAVAL BATTLE CLASS-A WAR CRIMINAL
SULEIMAN THE BEHEADER
FOR LOVE OF COUNTRY.
HUFF...
HUFF...
HOW DO YOU FEEL?
IS IT NOT HARD TO BREATHE IN THIS COUNTRY, FEELING SUCH HATE FROM ALL AROUND...?
...!!
BOOM!!
BOO
I DON'T CARE HOW HARD IT IS!!
BOO
I DON'T CARE WHO HATES ME!!
I JUST WANT TO LIVE WITH SOLDIER!!!

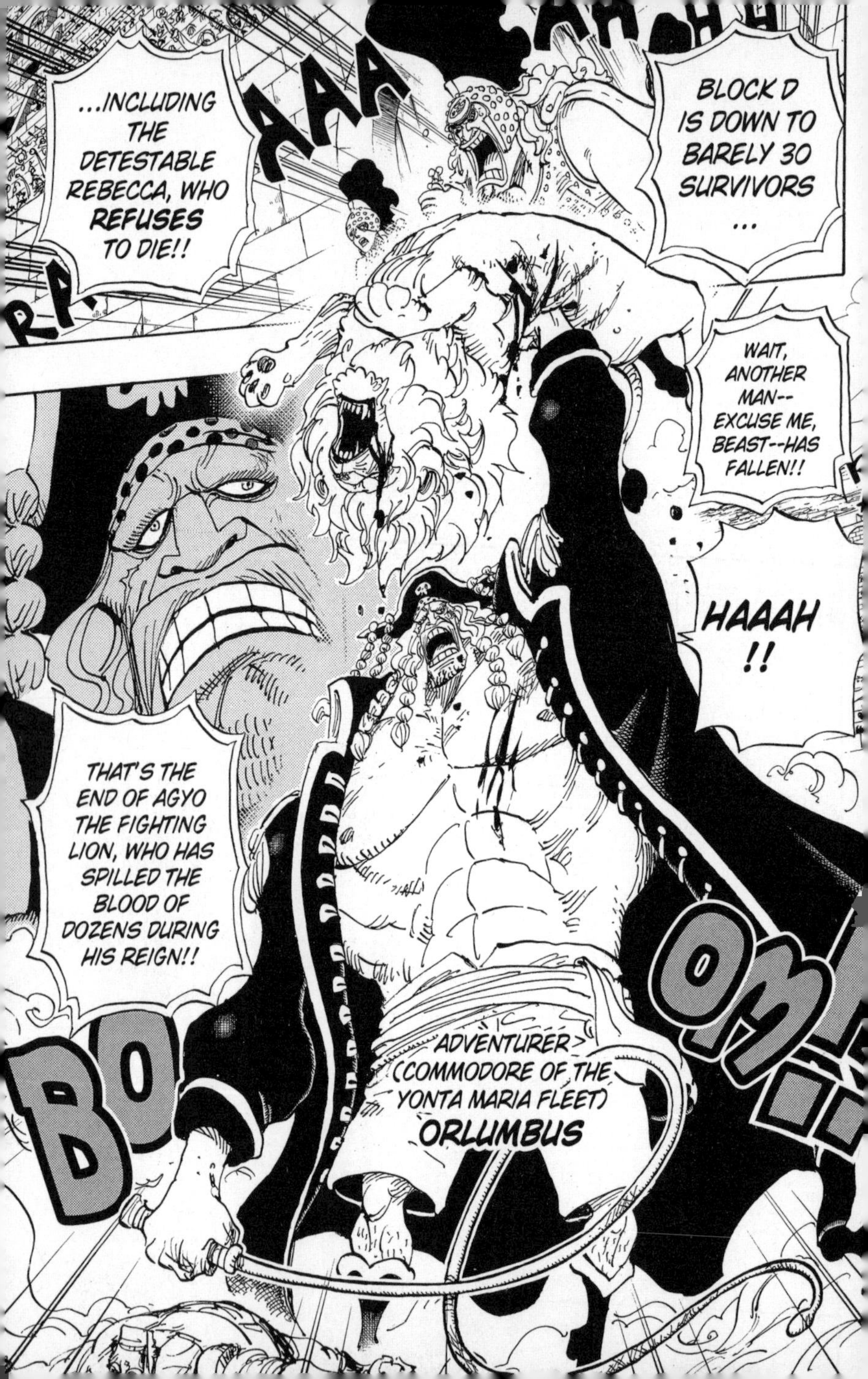
BLOCK D IS DOWN TO BARELY 30 SURVIVORS ...
...INCLUDING THE DETESTABLE REBECCA, WHO REFUSES TO DIE!!
AAA
WAIT, ANOTHER MAN-- EXCUSE ME, BEAST--HAS FALLEN!!
HAAAH !!
THAT'S THE END OF AGYO THE FIGHTING LION, WHO HAS SPILLED THE BLOOD OF DOZENS DURING HIS REIGN!!
OM!!
BO
ADVENTURER (COMMODORE OF THE YONTA MARIA FLEET) ORLUMBUS

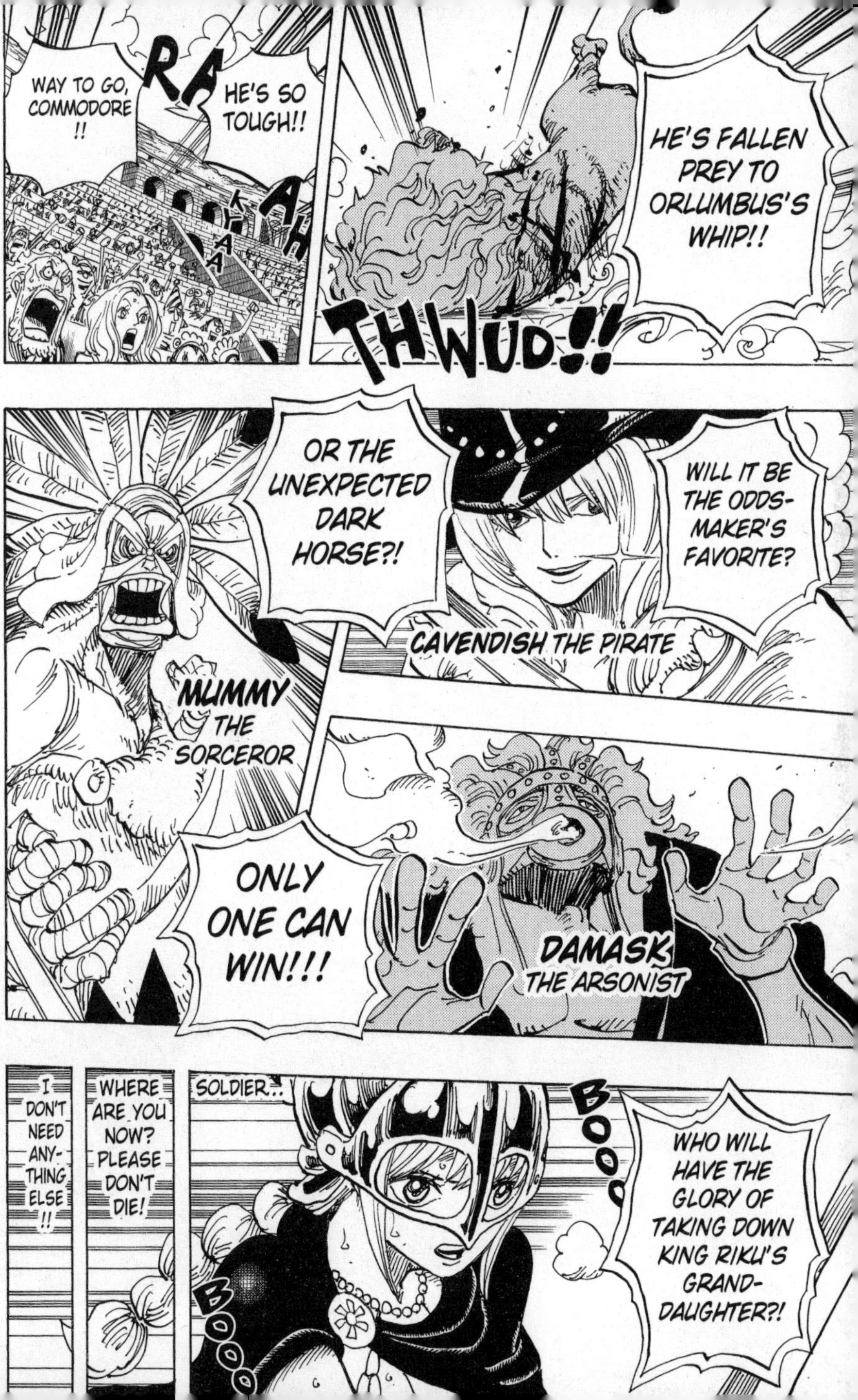
HE'S FALLEN PREY TO ORLUMBUS'S WHIP!!
THWUD!!
HE'S SO TOUGH!!
RAAH
WAY TO GO, COMMODORE !!
KYAAA
WILL IT BE THE ODDS-MAKER'S FAVORITE?
CAVENDISH THE PIRATE
OR THE UNEXPECTED DARK HORSE?!
MUMMY THE SORCEROR
DAMASK THE ARSONIST
ONLY ONE CAN WIN!!!
WHO WILL HAVE THE GLORY OF TAKING DOWN KING RIKU'S GRAND-DAUGHTER?!
BOOO
BOOO
SOLDIER...
WHERE ARE YOU NOW? PLEASE DON'T DIE!
I DON'T NEED ANYTHING ELSE !!

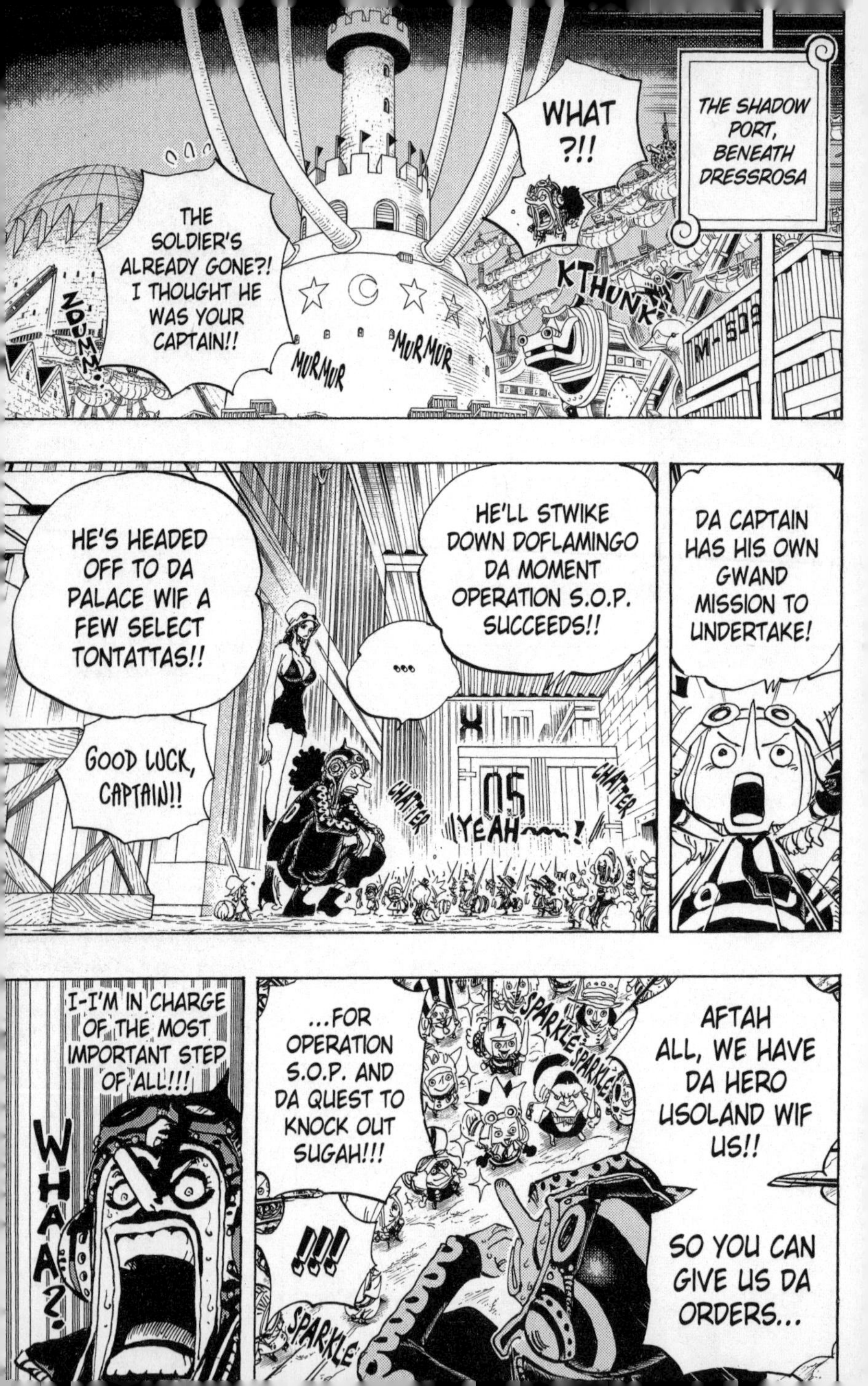
THE SHADOW PORT, BENEATH DRESSROSA
WHAT ?!!
KTHUNK
M-509
MURMUR
MURMUR
THE SOLDIER'S ALREADY GONE?! I THOUGHT HE WAS YOUR CAPTAIN!!
ZDUMM
DA CAPTAIN HAS HIS OWN GWAND MISSION TO UNDERTAKE!
HE'S HEADED OFF TO DA PALACE WIF A FEW SELECT TONTATTAS!!
HE'LL STWIKE DOWN DOFLAMINGO DA MOMENT OPERATION S.O.P. SUCCEEDS!!
...
CHATTER
CHATTER
GOOD LUCK, CAPTAIN!!
YEAH~~!
AFTAH ALL, WE HAVE DA HERO USOLAND WIF US!!
SO YOU CAN GIVE US DA ORDERS...
SPARKLE
SPARKLE
...FOR OPERATION S.O.P. AND DA QUEST TO KNOCK OUT SUGAH!!!
!!!
SPARKLE
I-I'M IN CHARGE OF THE MOST IMPORTANT STEP OF ALL!!!
WHAA?!

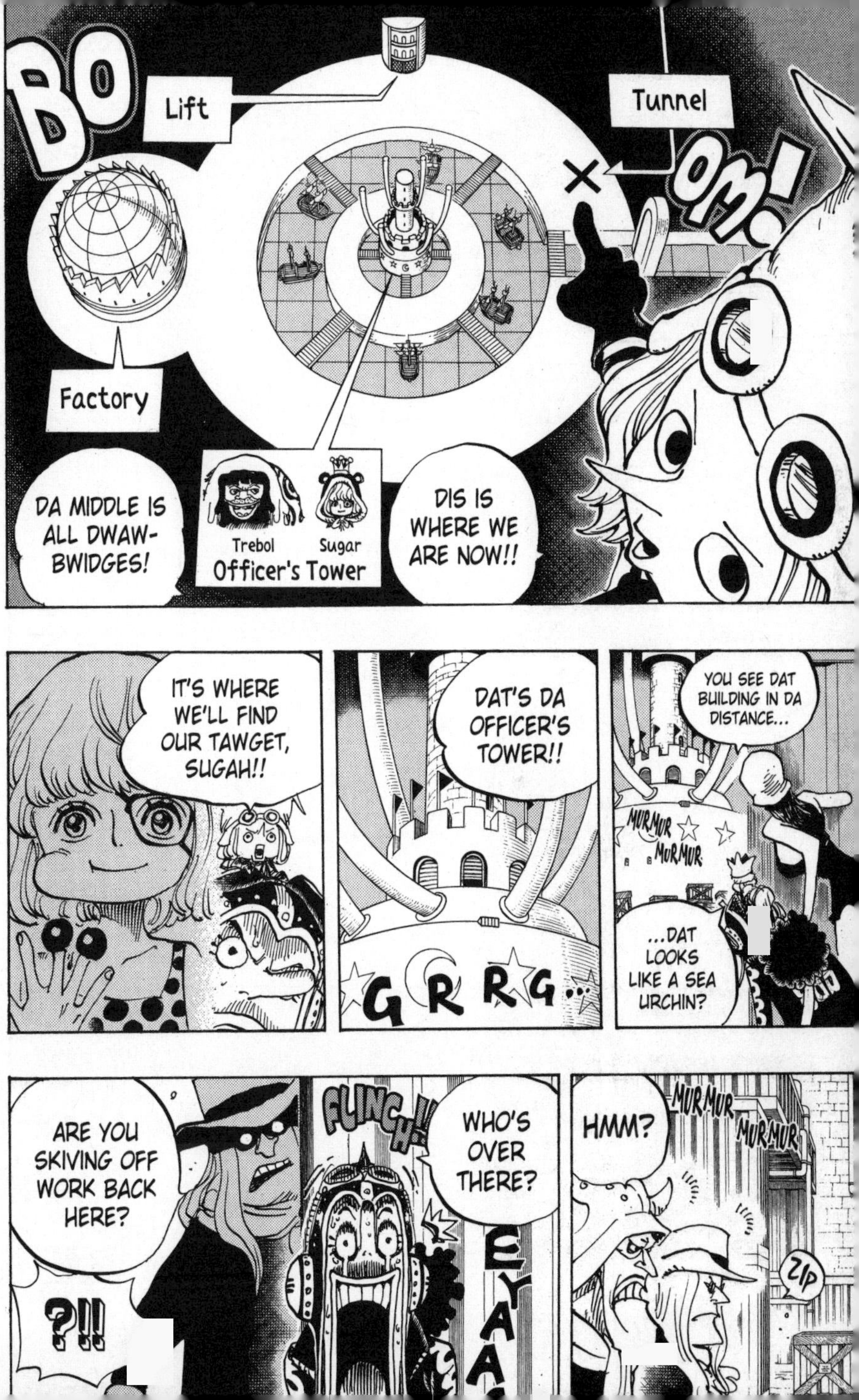
BOOM!
Tunnel
Lift
Factory
Trebol
Sugar
Officer's Tower
DIS IS WHERE WE ARE NOW!!
DA MIDDLE IS ALL DWAW-BWIDGES!
YOU SEE DAT BUILDING IN DA DISTANCE...
MURMUR
MURMUR
...DAT LOOKS LIKE A SEA URCHIN?
DAT'S DA OFFICER'S TOWER!!
GRRG...
IT'S WHERE WE'LL FIND OUR TAWGET, SUGAH!!
MURMUR
MURMUR
HMM?
ZIP
WHO'S OVER THERE?
FLINCH!!
EYAA
ARE YOU SKIVING OFF WORK BACK HERE?
?!!

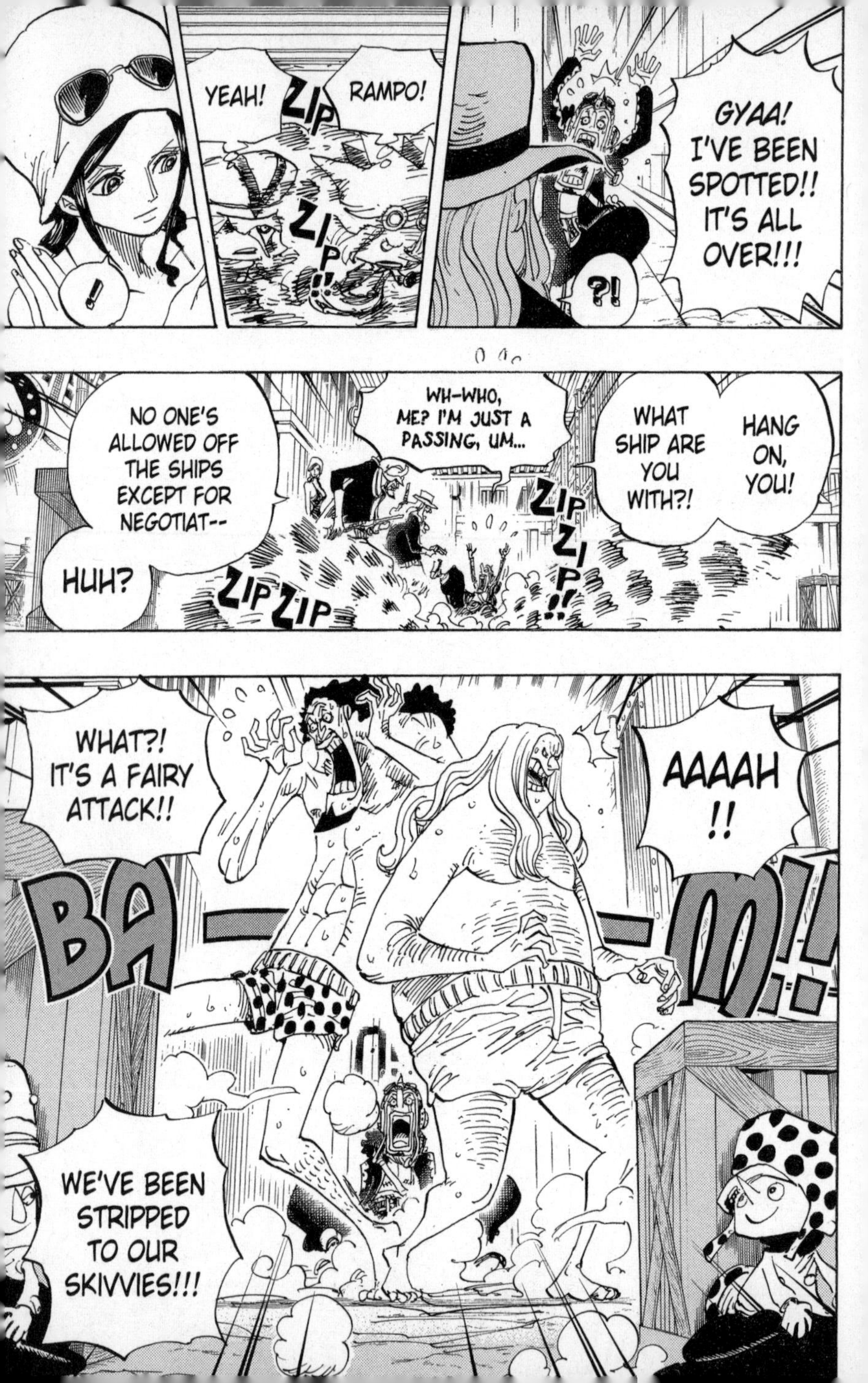
GYAA! I'VE BEEN SPOTTED!! IT'S ALL OVER!!!
?!
RAMPO!
ZIP
YEAH!
ZIP!!
!
HANG ON, YOU!
WHAT SHIP ARE YOU WITH?!
ZIP
ZIP!!
WH-WHO, ME? I'M JUST A PASSING, UM...
NO ONE'S ALLOWED OFF THE SHIPS EXCEPT FOR NEGOTIAT--
ZIP ZIP
HUH?
AAAAH!!
WHAT?! IT'S A FAIRY ATTACK!!
BA--M!!
WE'VE BEEN STRIPPED TO OUR SKIVVIES!!!

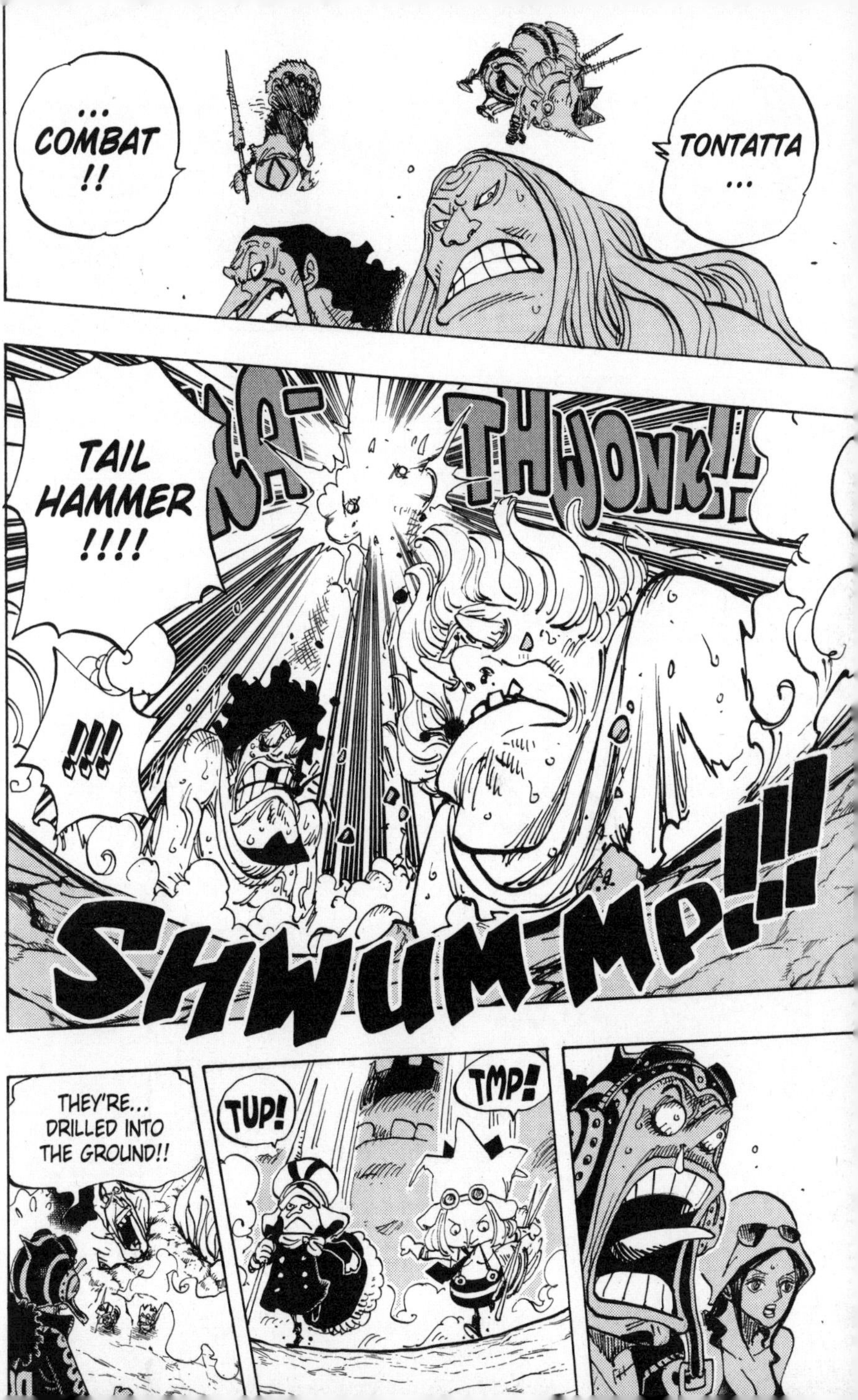
TONTATTA ...
... COMBAT !!
THWONK!!
TAIL HAMMER !!!!
!!!
SHWUM-MP!!!
TMP!
TUP!
THEY'RE... DRILLED INTO THE GROUND!!

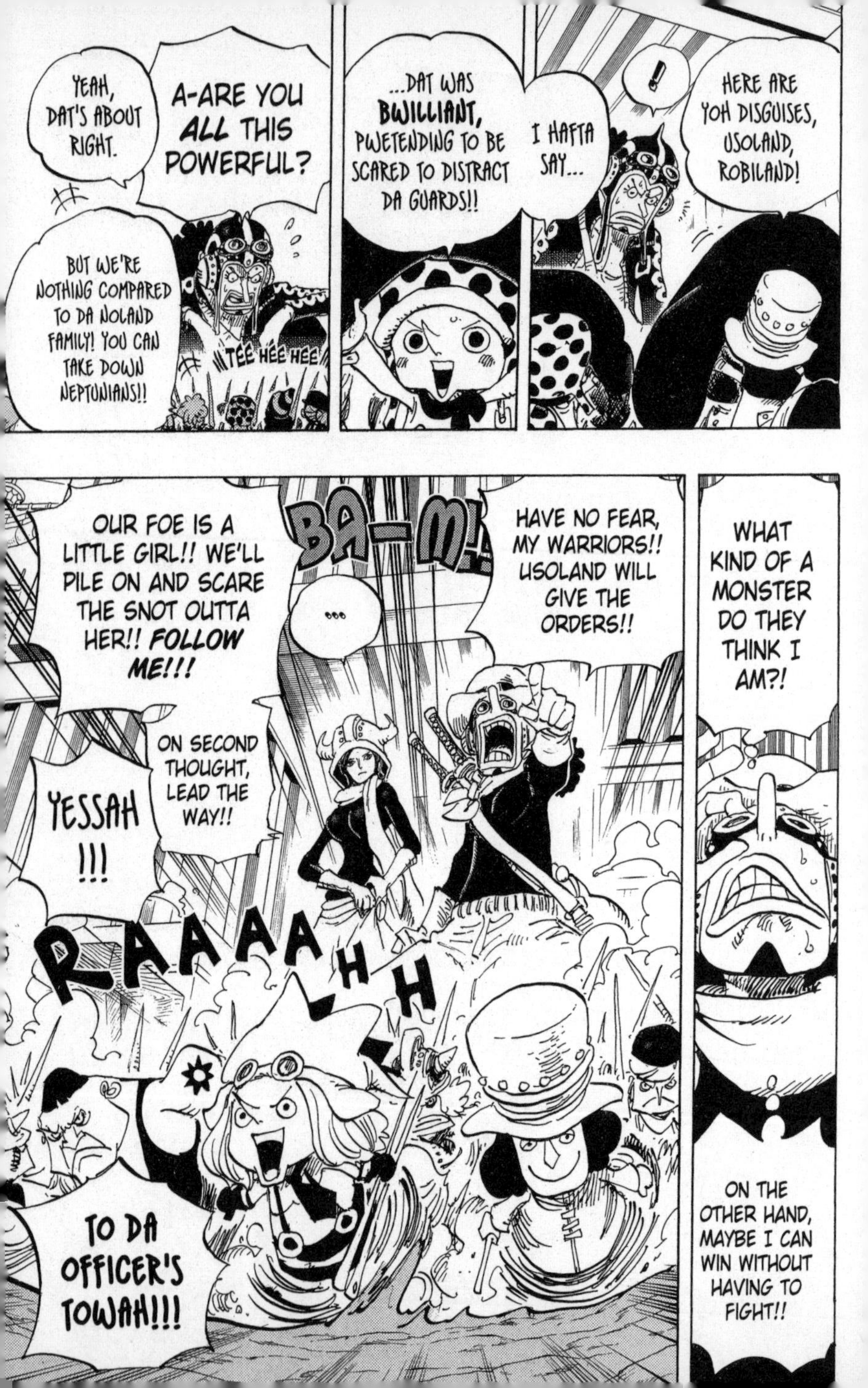
!
HERE ARE YOH DISGUISES, USOLAND, ROBILAND!
I HAFTA SAY...
...DAT WAS BWILLIANT, PWETENDING TO BE SCARED TO DISTRACT DA GUARDS!!
A-ARE YOU ALL THIS POWERFUL?
YEAH, DAT'S ABOUT RIGHT.
BUT WE'RE NOTHING COMPARED TO DA NOLAND FAMILY! YOU CAN TAKE DOWN NEPTUNIANS!!
TEE HEE HEE
WHAT KIND OF A MONSTER DO THEY THINK I AM?!
ON THE OTHER HAND, MAYBE I CAN WIN WITHOUT HAVING TO FIGHT!!
HAVE NO FEAR, MY WARRIORS!! USOLAND WILL GIVE THE ORDERS!!
BA-M!!
...
OUR FOE IS A LITTLE GIRL!! WE'LL PILE ON AND SCARE THE SNOT OUTTA HER!! FOLLOW ME!!!
ON SECOND THOUGHT, LEAD THE WAY!!
YESSAH!!!
RAAAAHH
TO DA OFFICER'S TOWAH!!!

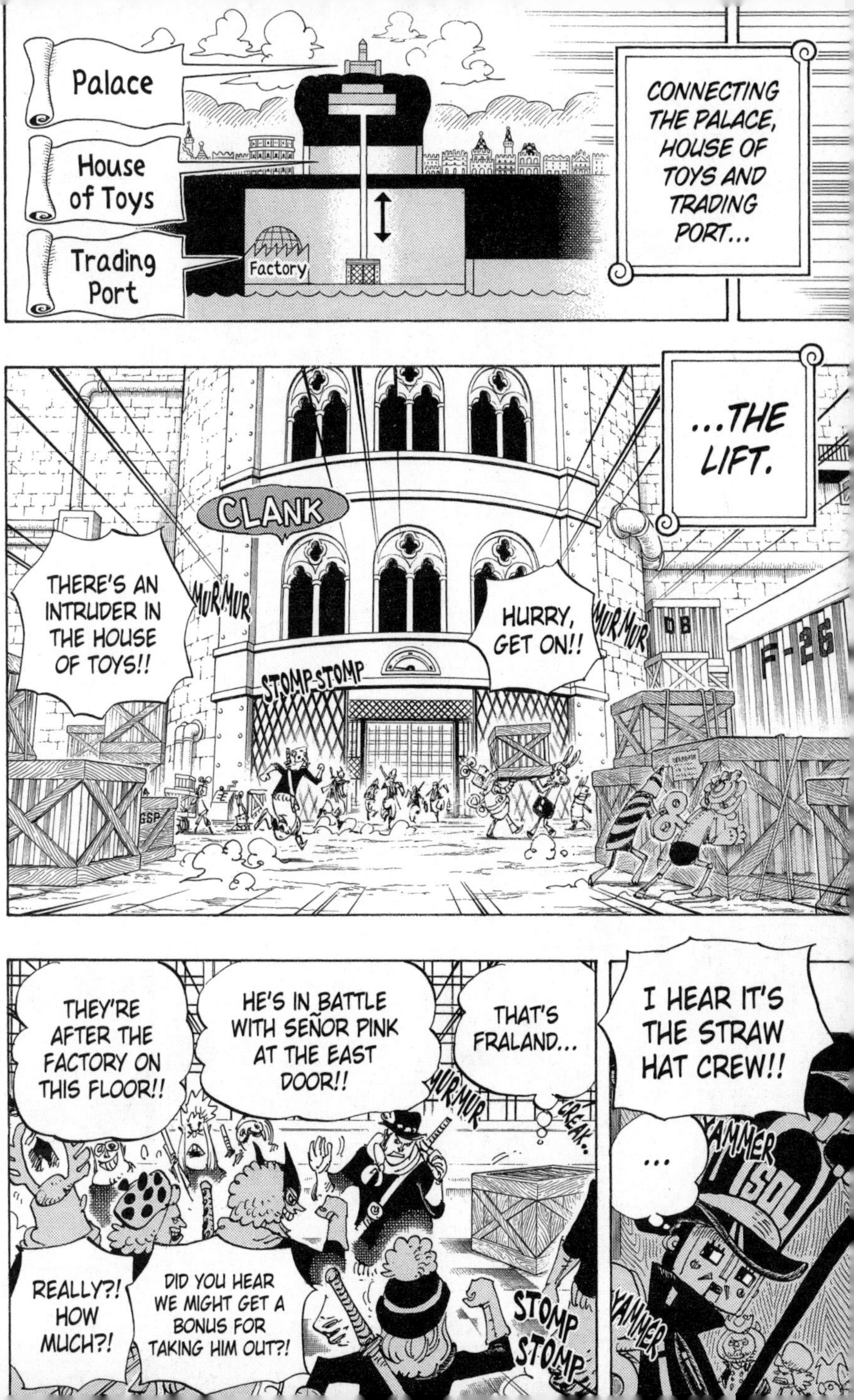
CONNECTING THE PALACE, HOUSE OF TOYS AND TRADING PORT...
Palace
House of Toys
Trading Port
Factory
...THE LIFT.
HURRY, GET ON!!
MUR MUR
CLANK
THERE'S AN INTRUDER IN THE HOUSE OF TOYS!!
MUR MUR
STOMP-STOMP
DB
F-26
I HEAR IT'S THE STRAW HAT CREW!!
...
YAMMER
YAMMER
THAT'S FRALAND...
CREAK...
HE'S IN BATTLE WITH SEÑOR PINK AT THE EAST DOOR!!
MUR MUR
THEY'RE AFTER THE FACTORY ON THIS FLOOR!!
STOMP STOMP
DID YOU HEAR WE MIGHT GET A BONUS FOR TAKING HIM OUT?!
REALLY?! HOW MUCH?!

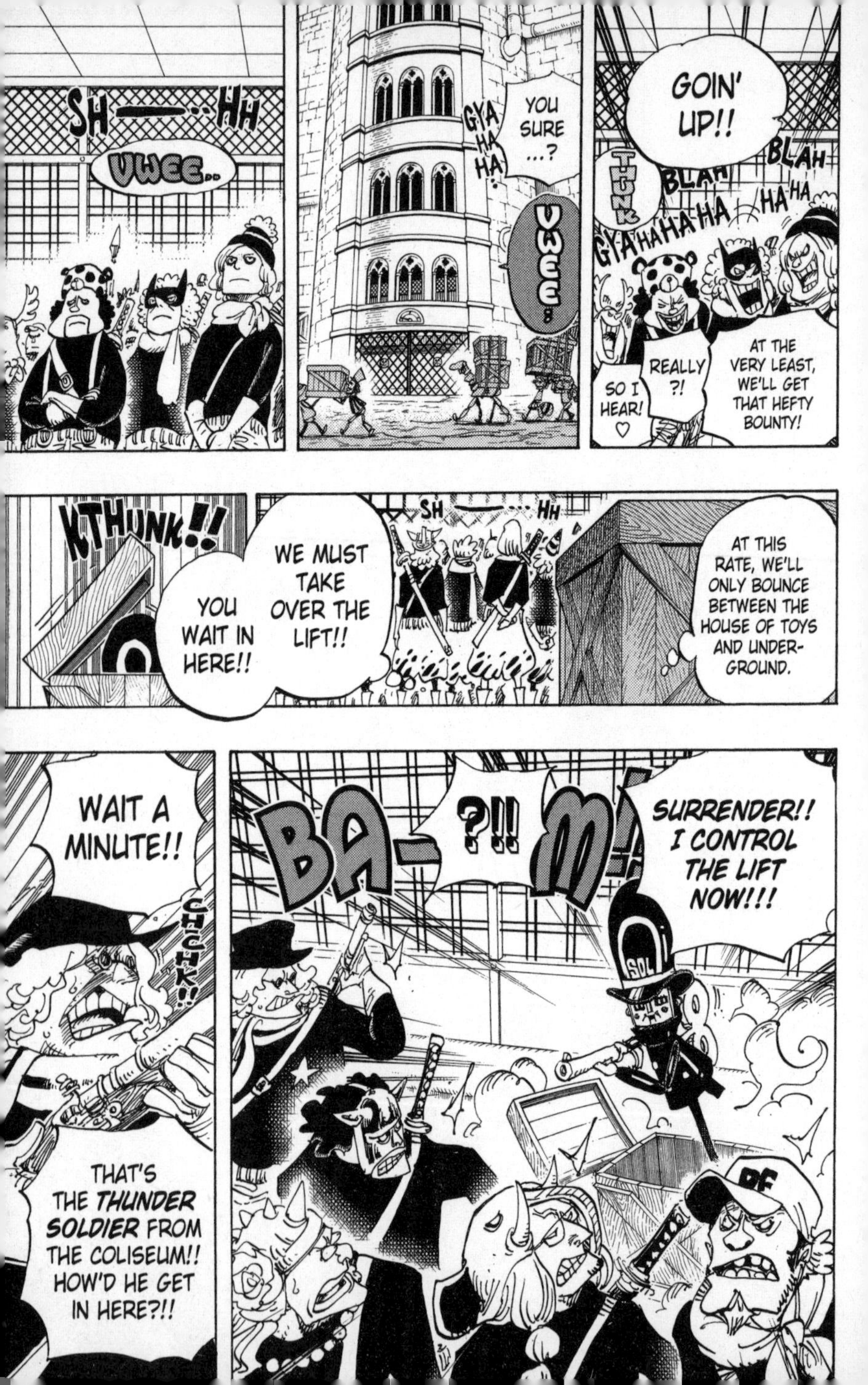
GOIN' UP!!
THUNK
BLAH BLAH
GYAHAHAHAHA HAHA
AT THE VERY LEAST, WE'LL GET THAT HEFTY BOUNTY!
REALLY?!
SO I HEAR! ♡
YOU SURE ...?
GYAHAHA
UWEE...
SH——...HH
UWEE...
SH——...HH
AT THIS RATE, WE'LL ONLY BOUNCE BETWEEN THE HOUSE OF TOYS AND UNDER-GROUND.
WE MUST TAKE OVER THE LIFT!!
YOU WAIT IN HERE!!
KTHUNK!!
SURRENDER!! I CONTROL THE LIFT NOW!!!
BA-M!
?!!
WAIT A MINUTE!!
CHCHK!!
THAT'S THE THUNDER SOLDIER FROM THE COLISEUM!! HOW'D HE GET IN HERE?!!

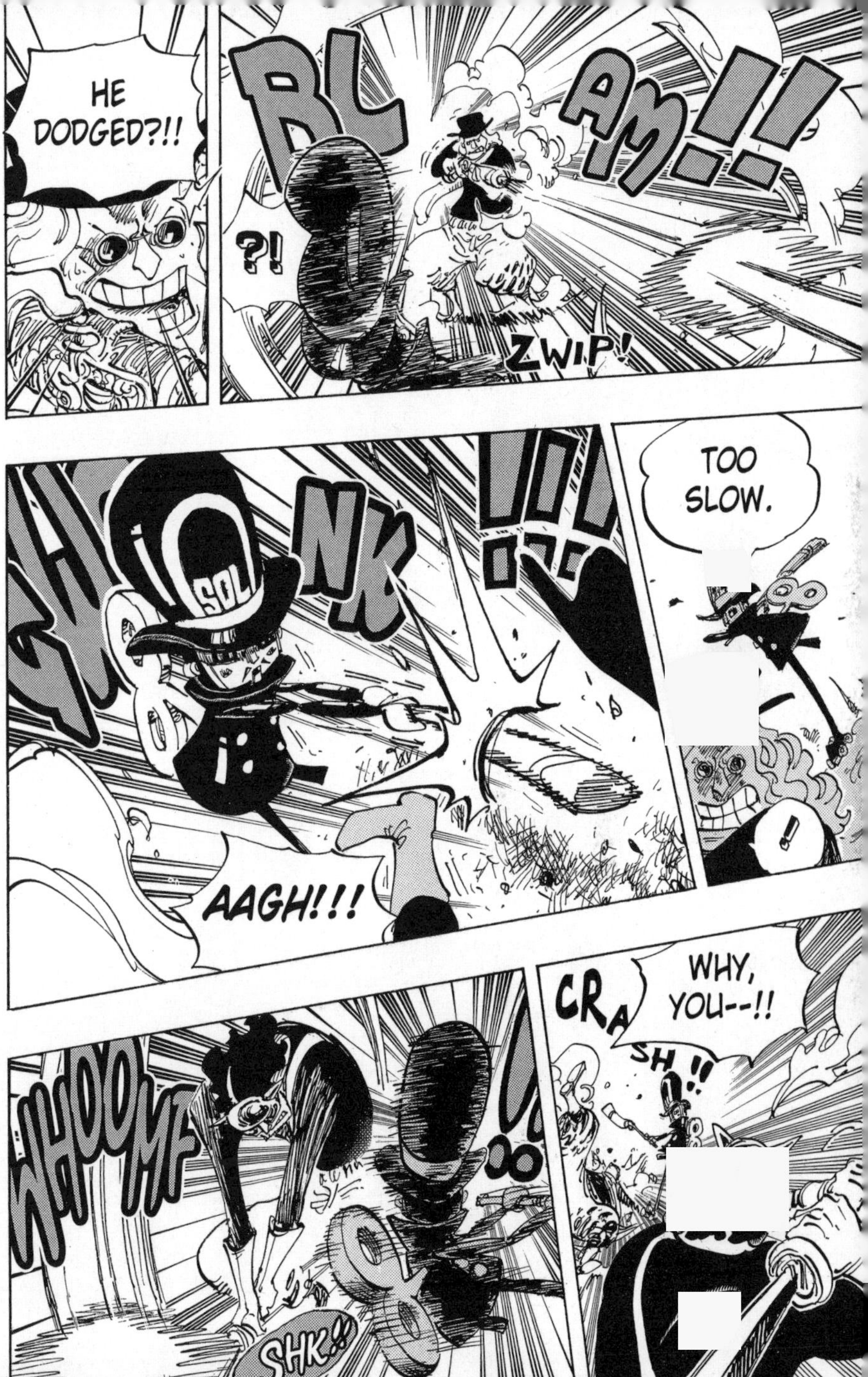
BLAM!!
?!
ZWIP!
HE DODGED?!!
TOO SLOW.
!
SOL
AAGH!!!
WHY, YOU--!!
CRASH!!
WHOOMF
SHK!!

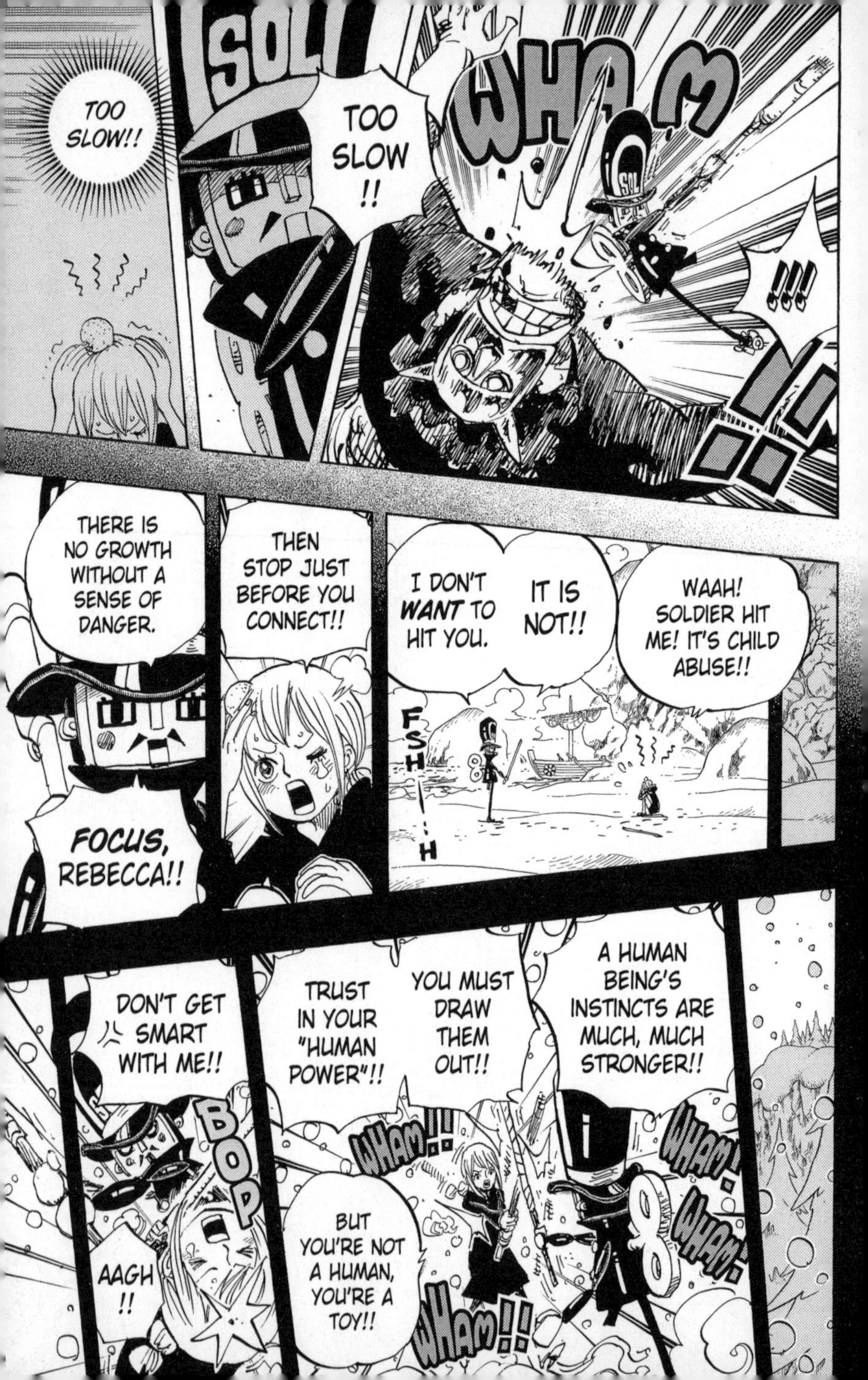
WHAM
!!!
TOO SLOW !!
SOL!
TOO SLOW!!
WAAH! SOLDIER HIT ME! IT'S CHILD ABUSE!!
IT IS NOT!!
I DON'T WANT TO HIT YOU.
FSH...H
THEN STOP JUST BEFORE YOU CONNECT!!
THERE IS NO GROWTH WITHOUT A SENSE OF DANGER.
FOCUS, REBECCA!!
A HUMAN BEING'S INSTINCTS ARE MUCH, MUCH STRONGER!!
YOU MUST DRAW THEM OUT!!
WHAM!
WHAM!
TRUST IN YOUR "HUMAN POWER"!!
WHAM!!
BUT YOU'RE NOT A HUMAN, YOU'RE A TOY!!
WHAM!!
DON'T GET SMART WITH ME!!
BOP
AAGH !!

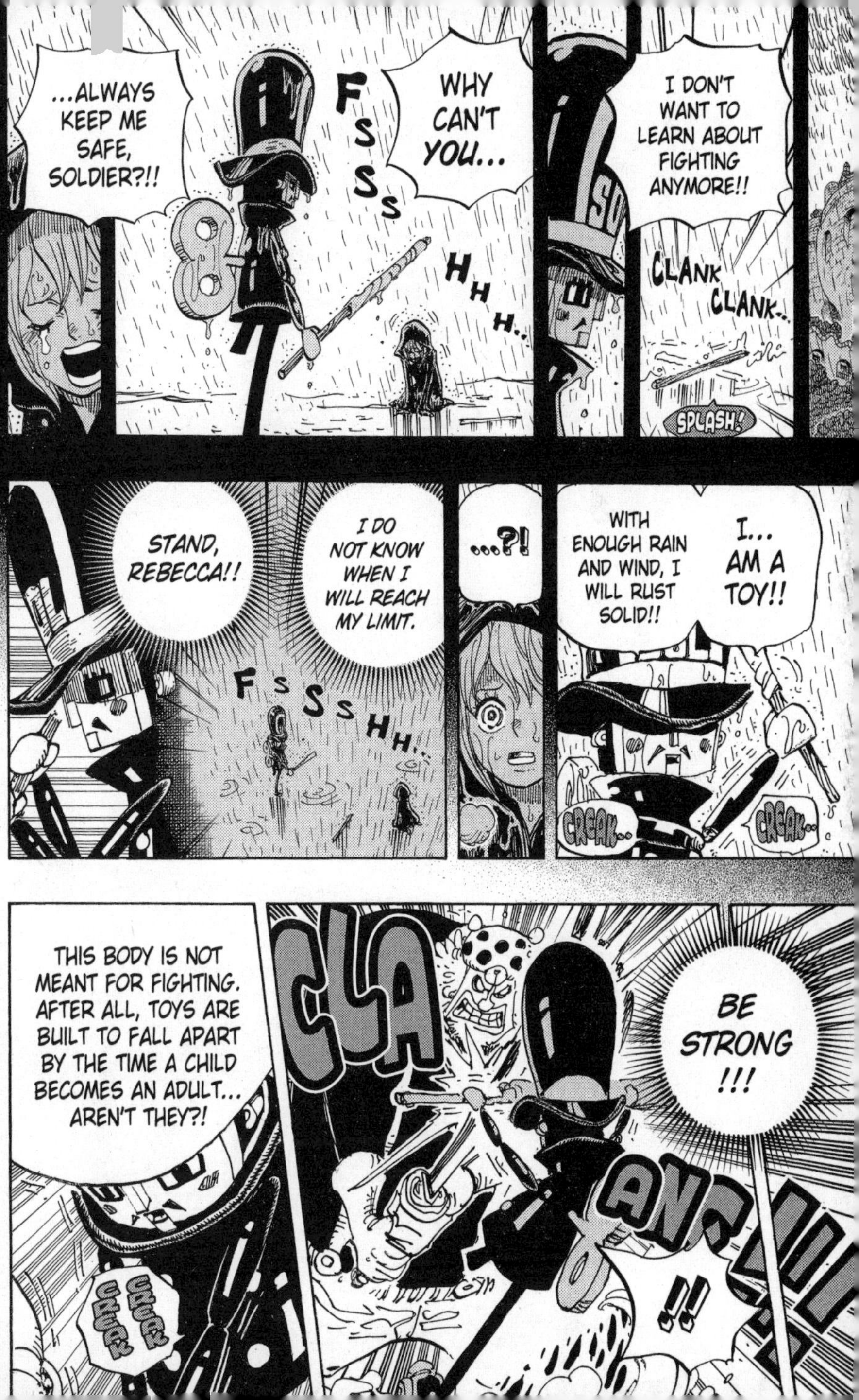

I DON'T WANT TO LEARN ABOUT FIGHTING ANYMORE!!
CLANK
CLANK...
SPLASH!
WHY CAN'T YOU...
FSSSHHH...
...ALWAYS KEEP ME SAFE, SOLDIER?!!
I... AM A TOY!!
WITH ENOUGH RAIN AND WIND, I WILL RUST SOLID!!
CREAK...
CREAK...
...?!
I DO NOT KNOW WHEN I WILL REACH MY LIMIT.
FSSSHHH...
STAND, REBECCA!!
BE STRONG!!!
CLA
ANG!!
THIS BODY IS NOT MEANT FOR FIGHTING. AFTER ALL, TOYS ARE BUILT TO FALL APART BY THE TIME A CHILD BECOMES AN ADULT... AREN'T THEY?!
CREAK
CREAK

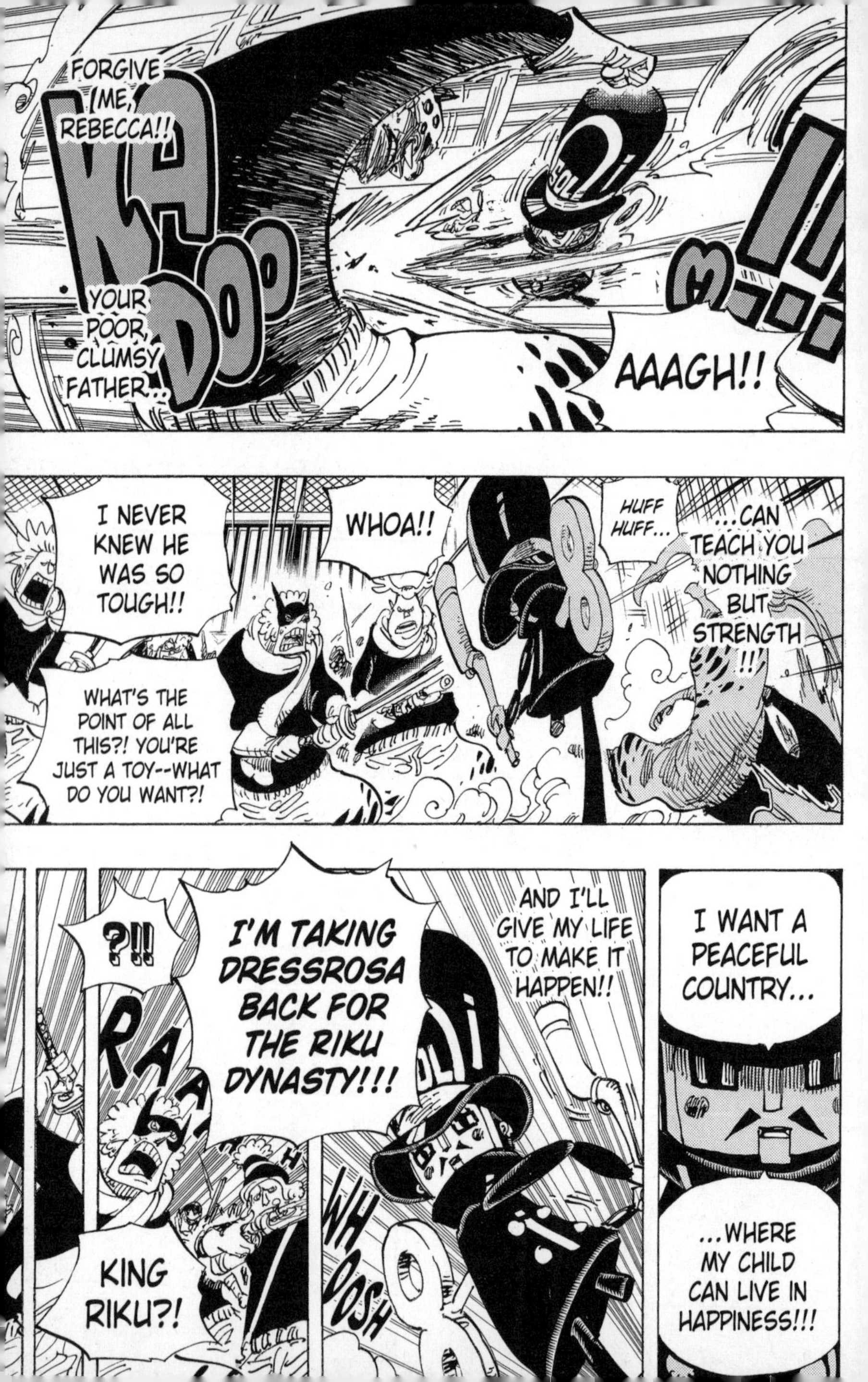
M..!!
FORGIVE ME, REBECCA!!
KADOOO
AAAGH!!
YOUR POOR, CLUMSY FATHER..
...CAN TEACH YOU NOTHING BUT STRENGTH!!!
HUFF HUFF...
WHOA!!
I NEVER KNEW HE WAS SO TOUGH!!
WHAT'S THE POINT OF ALL THIS?! YOU'RE JUST A TOY--WHAT DO YOU WANT?!
I WANT A PEACEFUL COUNTRY...
...WHERE MY CHILD CAN LIVE IN HAPPINESS!!!
AND I'LL GIVE MY LIFE TO MAKE IT HAPPEN!!
I'M TAKING DRESSROSA BACK FOR THE RIKU DYNASTY!!!
WHOOSH
?!!
KING RIKU?!

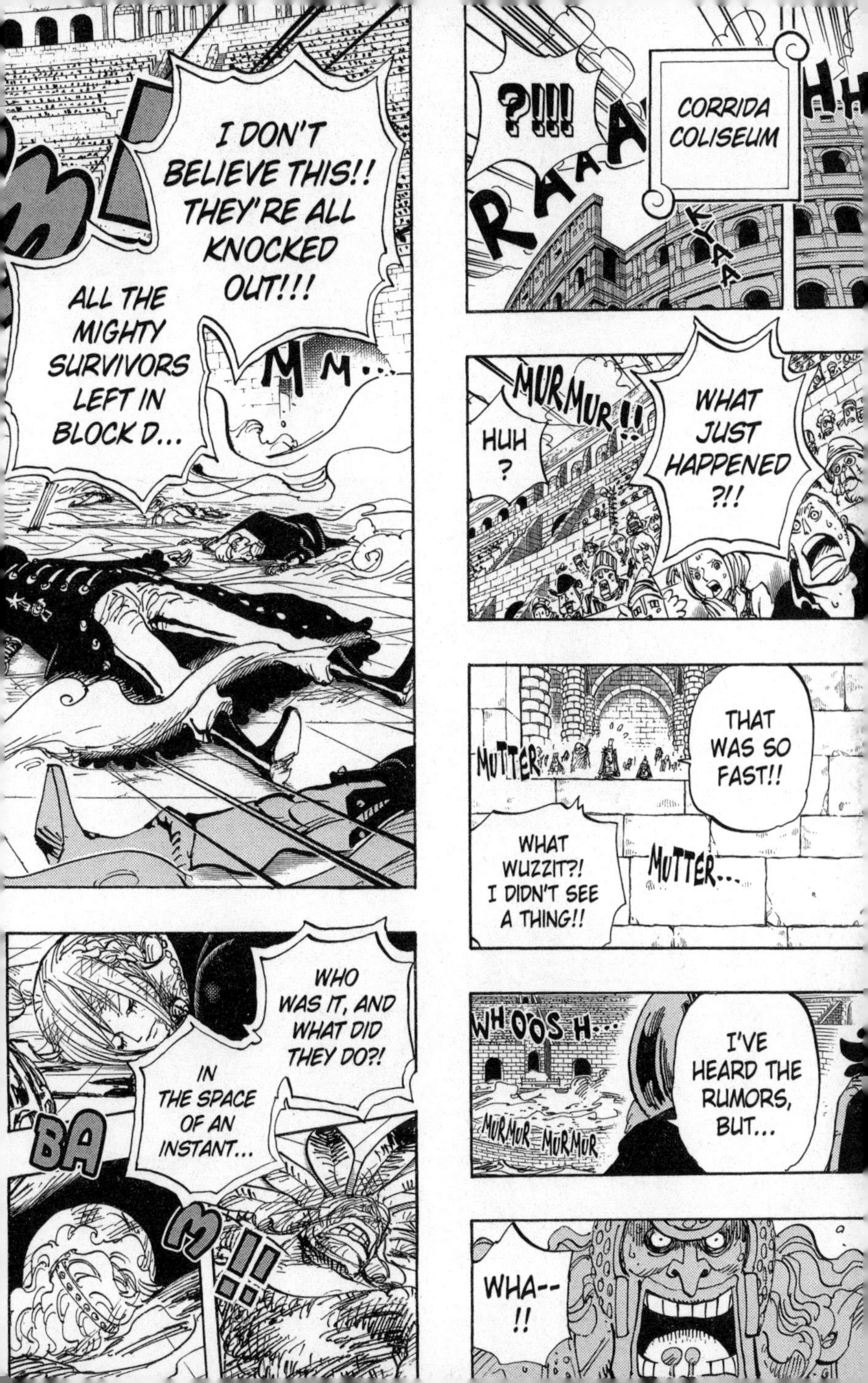

CORRIDA COLISEUM
?!!!
RAAAAHH
KYAAA
WHAT JUST HAPPENED ?!!
MURMUR!!
HUH ?
THAT WAS SO FAST!!
MUTTER
WHAT WUZZIT?! I DIDN'T SEE A THING!!
MUTTER...
I'VE HEARD THE RUMORS, BUT...
WHOOSH...
MURMUR MURMUR
WHA-- !!
I DON'T BELIEVE THIS!! THEY'RE ALL KNOCKED OUT!!!
ALL THE MIGHTY SURVIVORS LEFT IN BLOCK D...
MM...
WHO WAS IT, AND WHAT DID THEY DO?!
IN THE SPACE OF AN INSTANT...
BAM!!

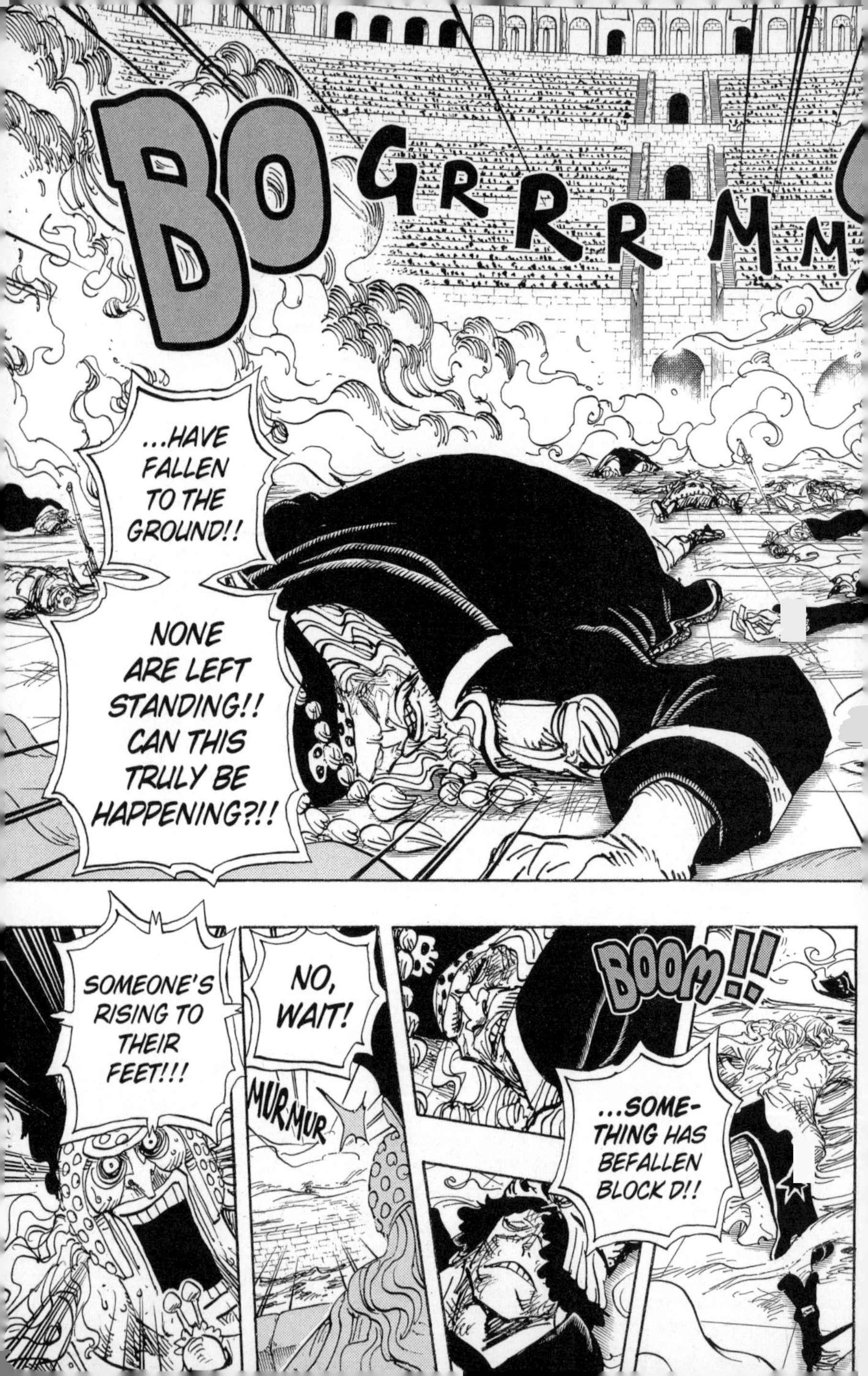
BOGRRRMM
...HAVE FALLEN TO THE GROUND!!
NONE ARE LEFT STANDING!! CAN THIS TRULY BE HAPPENING?!!
BOOM!!
...SOME-THING HAS BEFALLEN BLOCK D!!
NO, WAIT!
MUR MUR
SOMEONE'S RISING TO THEIR FEET!!!

SBS Question Corner

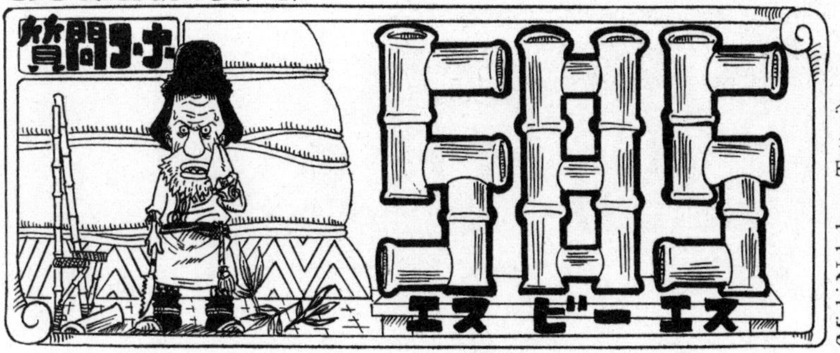
エス ビー エス

(Michi Nakahara, Tottori)

Q: Heeey!! I'll get things started without Odacchi. So let's get things going with a bang! Here goes! Ready, set…

"S.O.S.!!!"

--Klutzy Candy Apple

A: Help!! Someone, help!! Klutzy Candy Apple is drowning! S.O.S., S.O.S.!! It's S.B.S.!!!

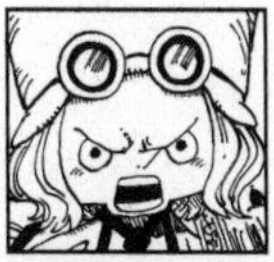

Q: Odacchi, I fowgive you.

--Kozuetty

A: Excuse me?! Are you implying that my joke fell flat?!

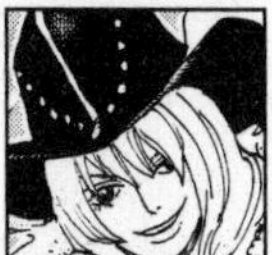

Q: Hello. I fell in love with Cavendish at first sight. So Odacchi, I'd love to know his birthday… How about this? Caven sounds like Cabbage, which is a vegetable, which is yasai in Japanese, and that becomes 8/31 when you turn it into numbers. Sound good?

--Prince with Shining Teeth

A: Hmmm... (pretending to mull it over) Hmmm... (pretending to mull it over) Okay. (doesn't really care)

Q: In Chapter 731, when the toy soldier is explaining Operation S.O.P., I noticed that there are little Tontatta versions of Luffy, Zolo, Sanji, Chopper, Nami, Brook and even Pandaman! What does this mean?! I'm sure my **beloved** Mr. Oda has a **very, very deep** reason behind it! If you don't tell me,

--I'll Start the S.B.S.

A: Whoa, you started the S.B.S.! But... it's already going? Anyway, well spotted. Reason? None whatsoever. I just challenged my readers to see if I could slip it past them. Well, I lost.

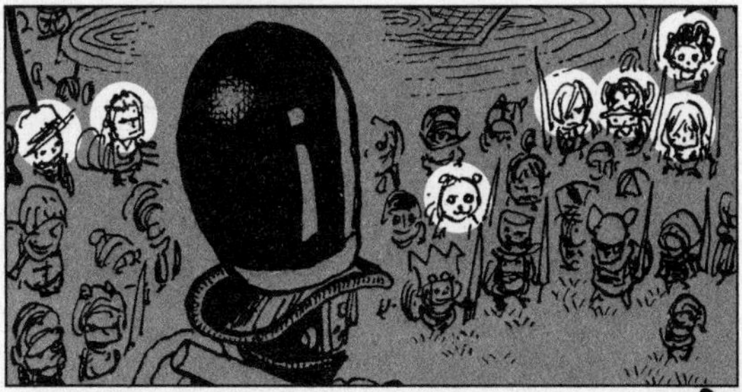

Chapter 734:
THE SLICING WINDS OF ROMMEL

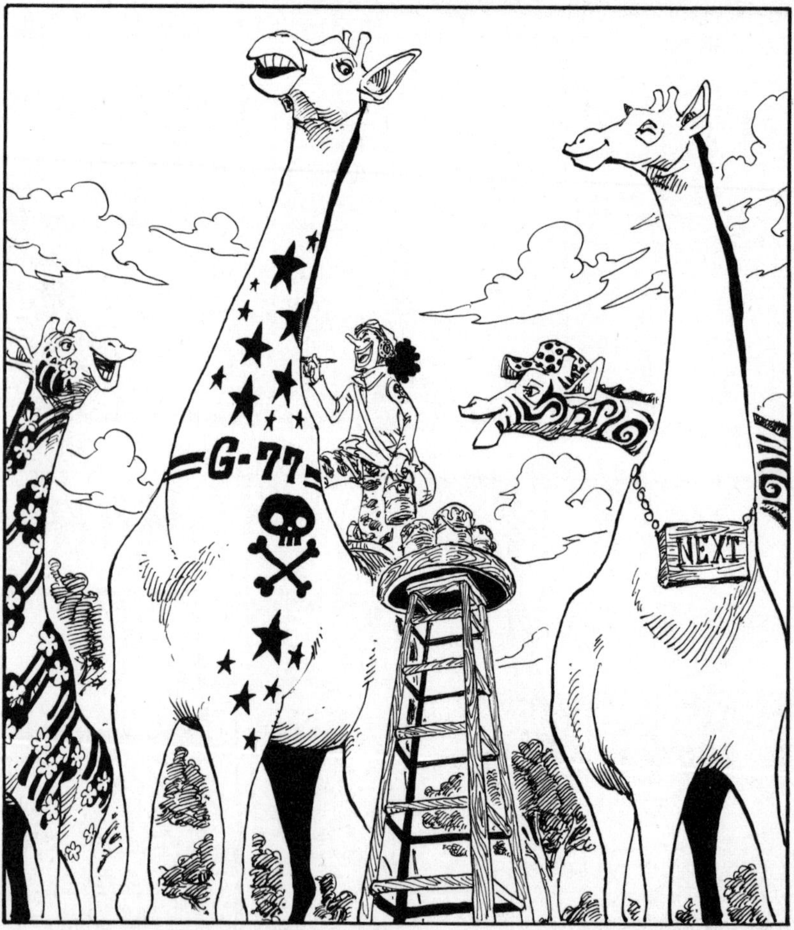
G-77
NEXT

REQUEST: "USOPP RIDING A PLAIN GIRAFFE AND DRAWING IT SOME NEW SPOTS" BY CROQUETTE FROM AICHI

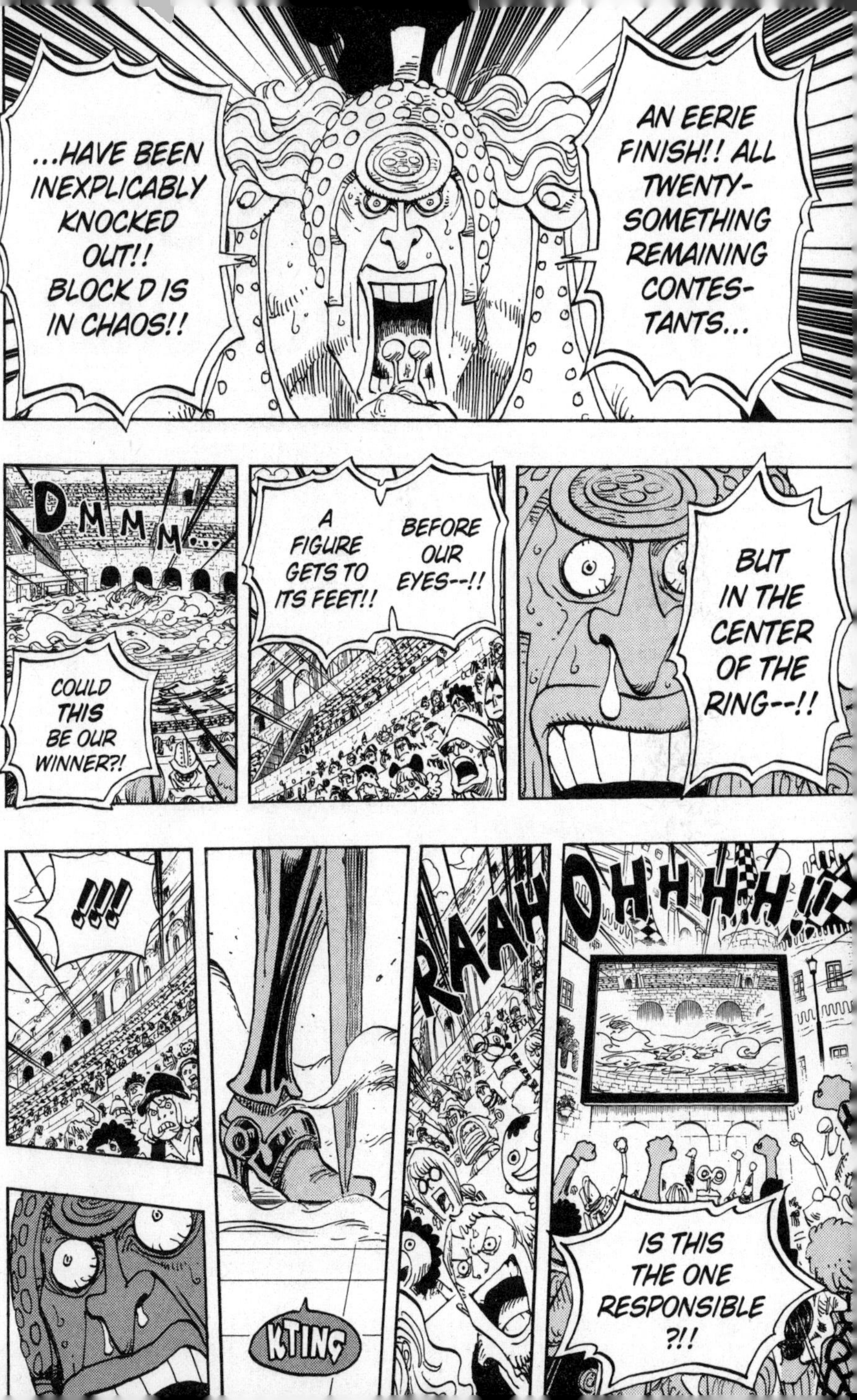
AN EERIE FINISH!! ALL TWENTY-SOMETHING REMAINING CONTES-TANTS...
...HAVE BEEN INEXPLICABLY KNOCKED OUT!! BLOCK D IS IN CHAOS!!
BUT IN THE CENTER OF THE RING--!!
BEFORE OUR EYES--!!
A FIGURE GETS TO ITS FEET!!
DMMM...
COULD THIS BE OUR WINNER?!
RAAHOHHHHH!!!
IS THIS THE ONE RESPONSIBLE?!!
KTING
!!!

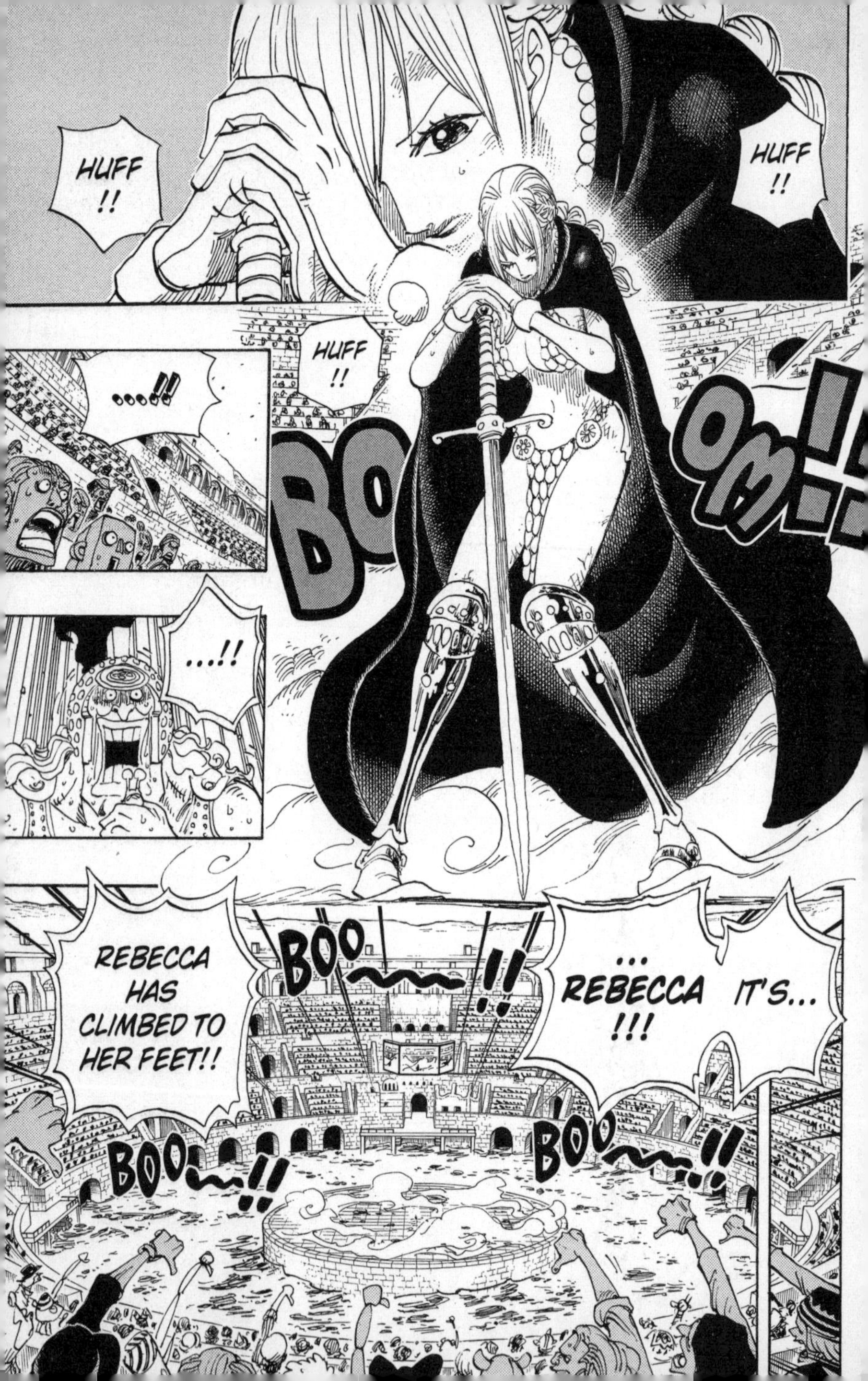
HUFF!!
HUFF!!
HUFF!!
BOOM!!
...!!
...!!
IT'S... ...REBECCA!!!
BOO~~!!
REBECCA HAS CLIMBED TO HER FEET!!
BOO~~!!
BOO~~!!

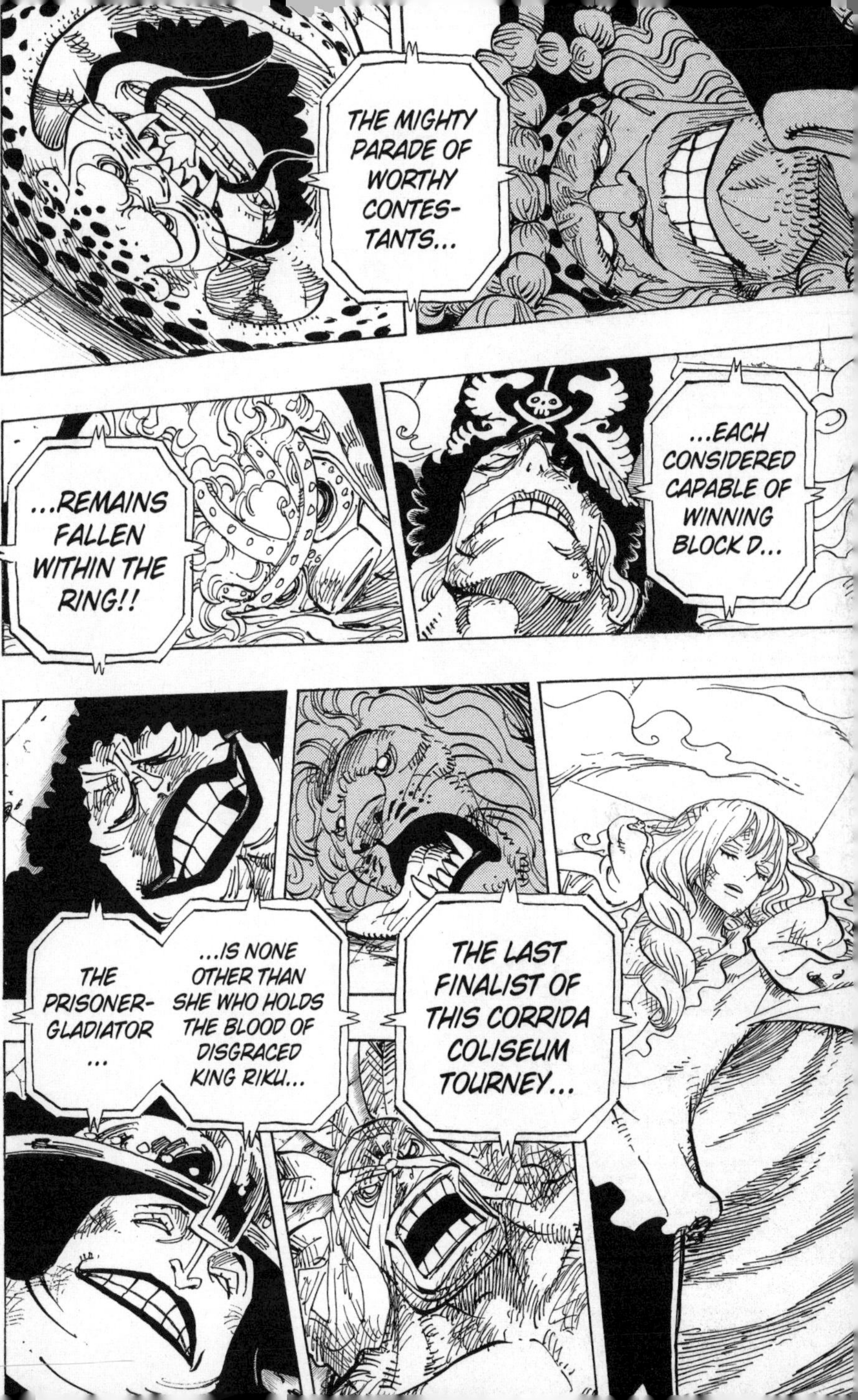
THE MIGHTY PARADE OF WORTHY CONTES-TANTS...
...EACH CONSIDERED CAPABLE OF WINNING BLOCK D...
...REMAINS FALLEN WITHIN THE RING!!
THE LAST FINALIST OF THIS CORRIDA COLISEUM TOURNEY...
...IS NONE OTHER THAN SHE WHO HOLDS THE BLOOD OF DISGRACED KING RIKU...
THE PRISONER-GLADIATOR ...

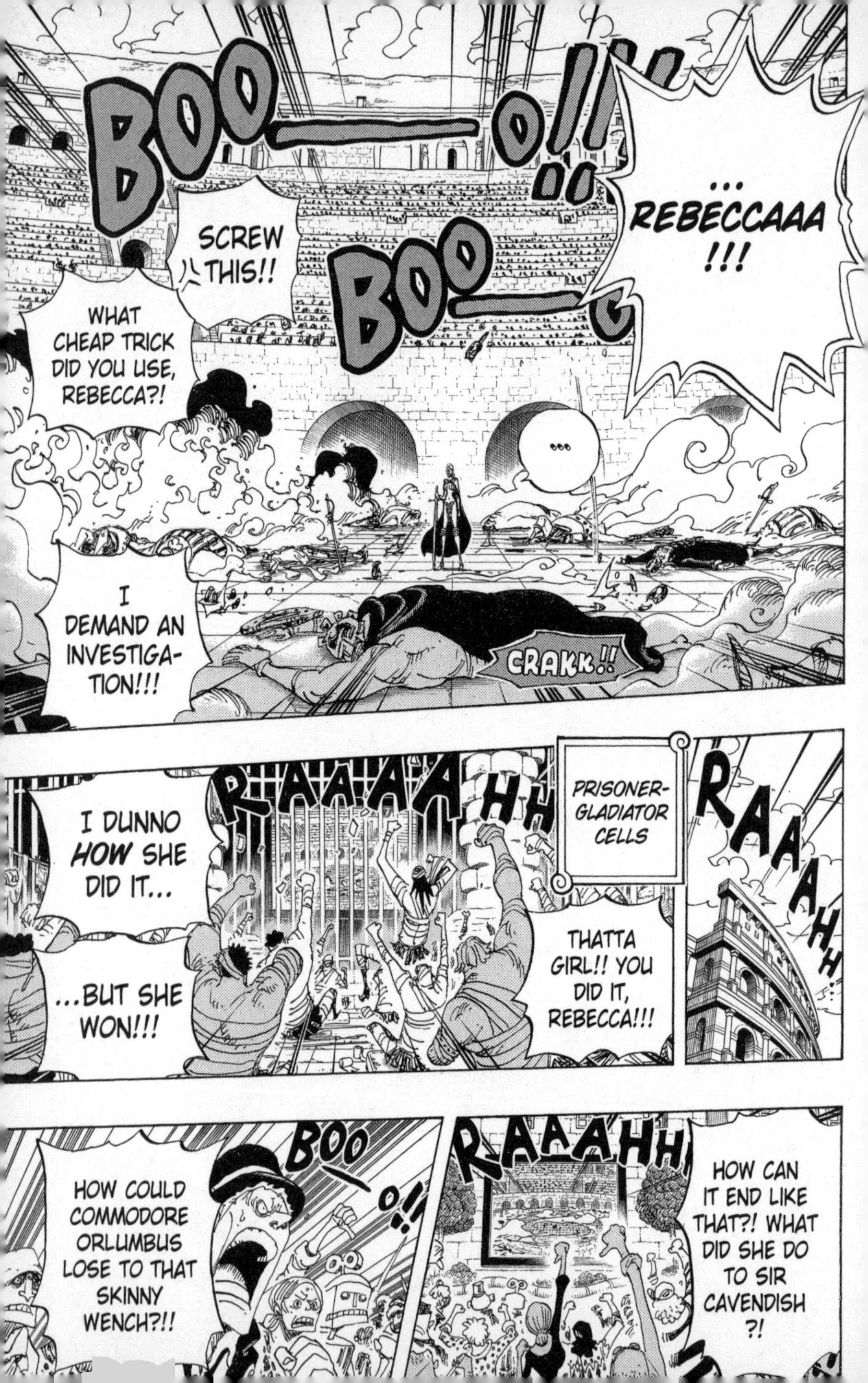
...REBECCAAA!!!
BOO—O!!
BOO—O
...
SCREW THIS!!
WHAT CHEAP TRICK DID YOU USE, REBECCA?!
CRAKK!!
I DEMAND AN INVESTIGATION!!!
RAAAHH
PRISONER-GLADIATOR CELLS
RAAAAHH
THATTA GIRL!! YOU DID IT, REBECCA!!!
I DUNNO *HOW* SHE DID IT...
...BUT SHE WON!!!
RAAAHH
HOW CAN IT END LIKE THAT?! WHAT DID SHE DO TO SIR CAVENDISH ?!
BOO—O!!
HOW COULD COMMODORE ORLUMBUS LOSE TO THAT SKINNY WENCH?!!

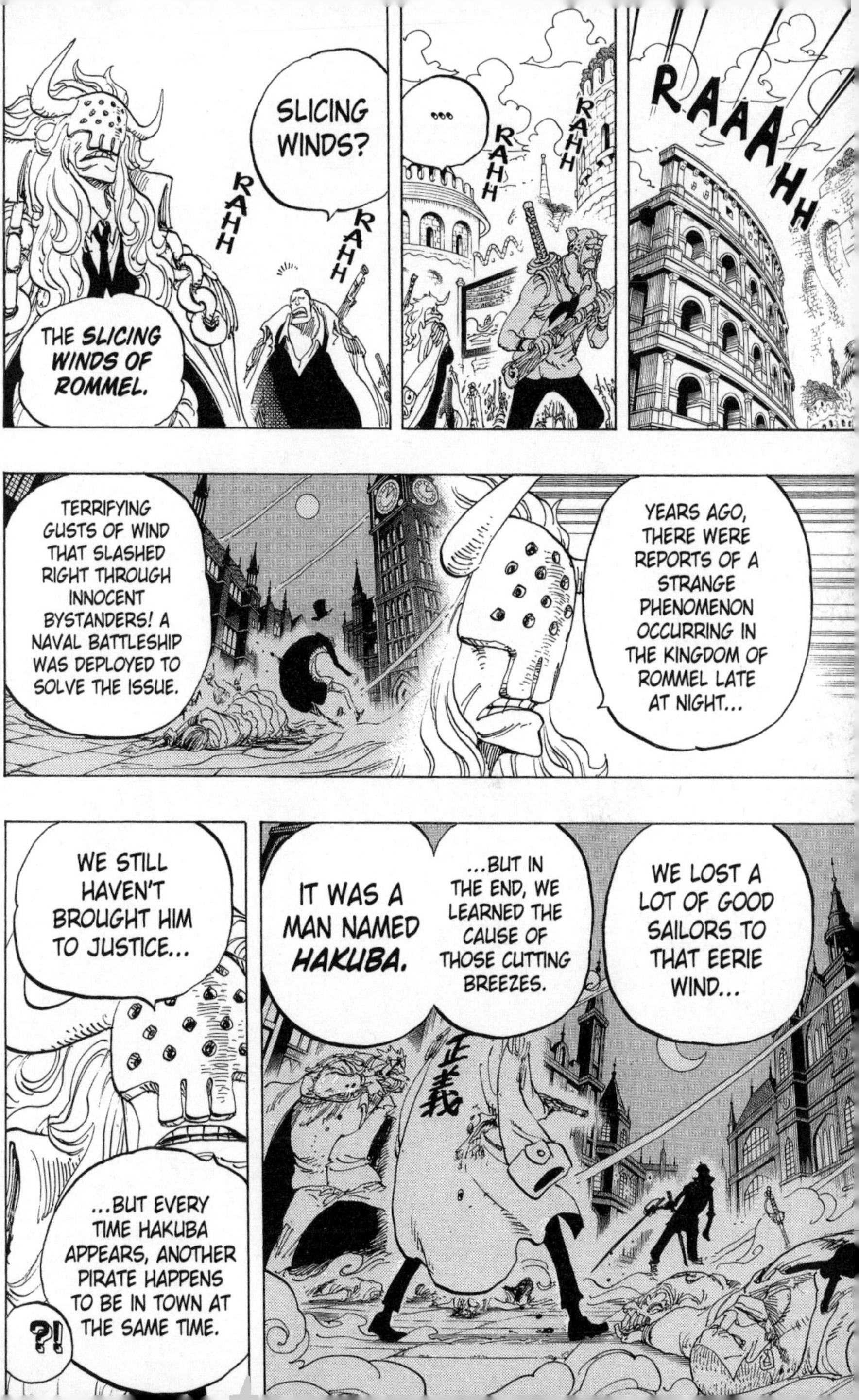
RAAAAHH
RAHH
...
RAHH
SLICING WINDS?
RAHH
RAHH
THE *SLICING WINDS OF ROMMEL.*
YEARS AGO, THERE WERE REPORTS OF A STRANGE PHENOMENON OCCURRING IN THE KINGDOM OF ROMMEL LATE AT NIGHT...
TERRIFYING GUSTS OF WIND THAT SLASHED RIGHT THROUGH INNOCENT BYSTANDERS! A NAVAL BATTLESHIP WAS DEPLOYED TO SOLVE THE ISSUE.
WE LOST A LOT OF GOOD SAILORS TO THAT EERIE WIND...
...BUT IN THE END, WE LEARNED THE CAUSE OF THOSE CUTTING BREEZES.
IT WAS A MAN NAMED ***HAKUBA.***
正義
WE STILL HAVEN'T BROUGHT HIM TO JUSTICE...
...BUT EVERY TIME HAKUBA APPEARS, ANOTHER PIRATE HAPPENS TO BE IN TOWN AT THE SAME TIME.
?!

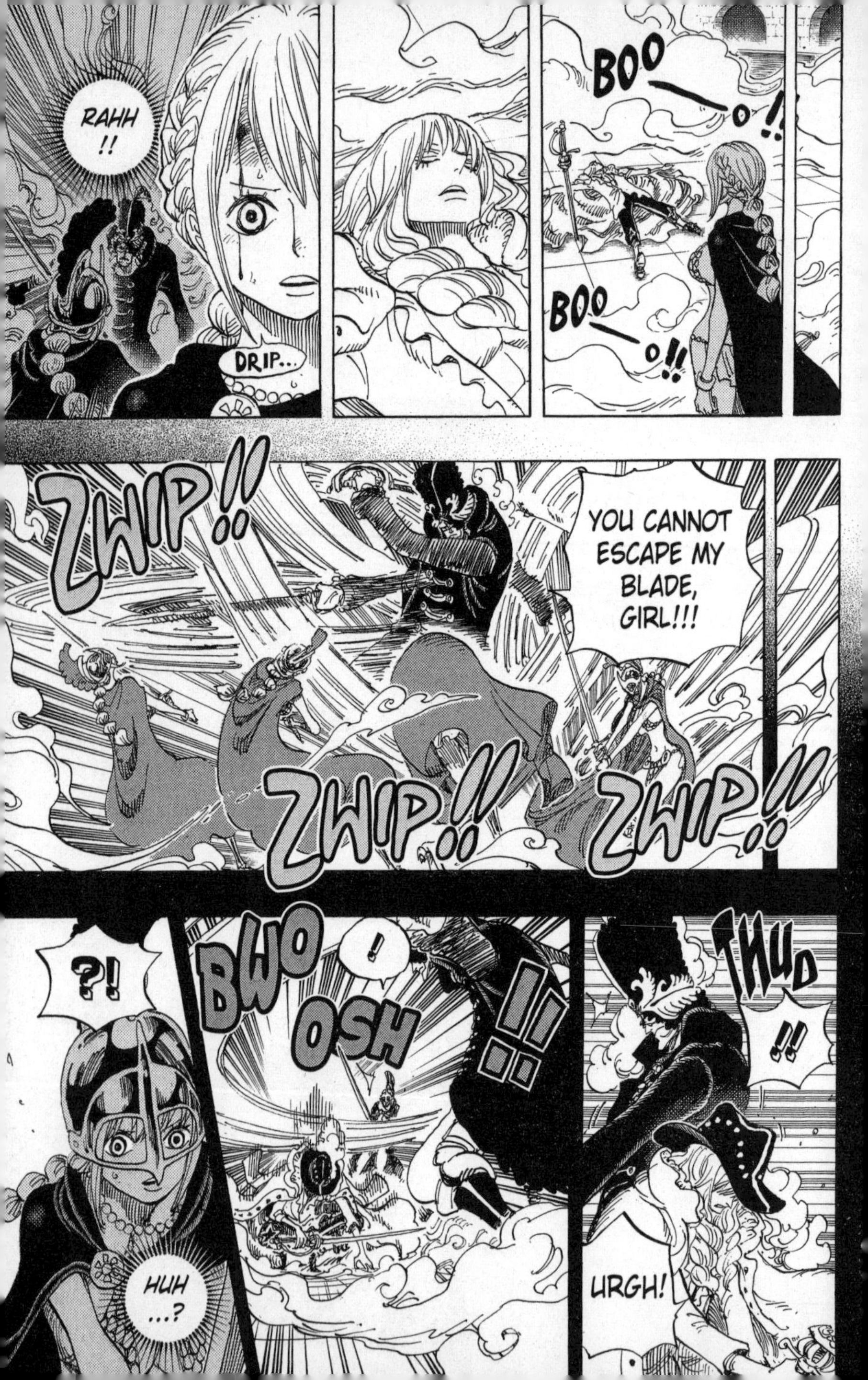
BOO—O!!
BOO—O!!
RAHH!!
DRIP...
YOU CANNOT ESCAPE MY BLADE, GIRL!!!
ZWIP!!
ZWIP!!
ZWIP!!
THUD!!
URGH!
!
BWOOSH!!
?!
HUH...?

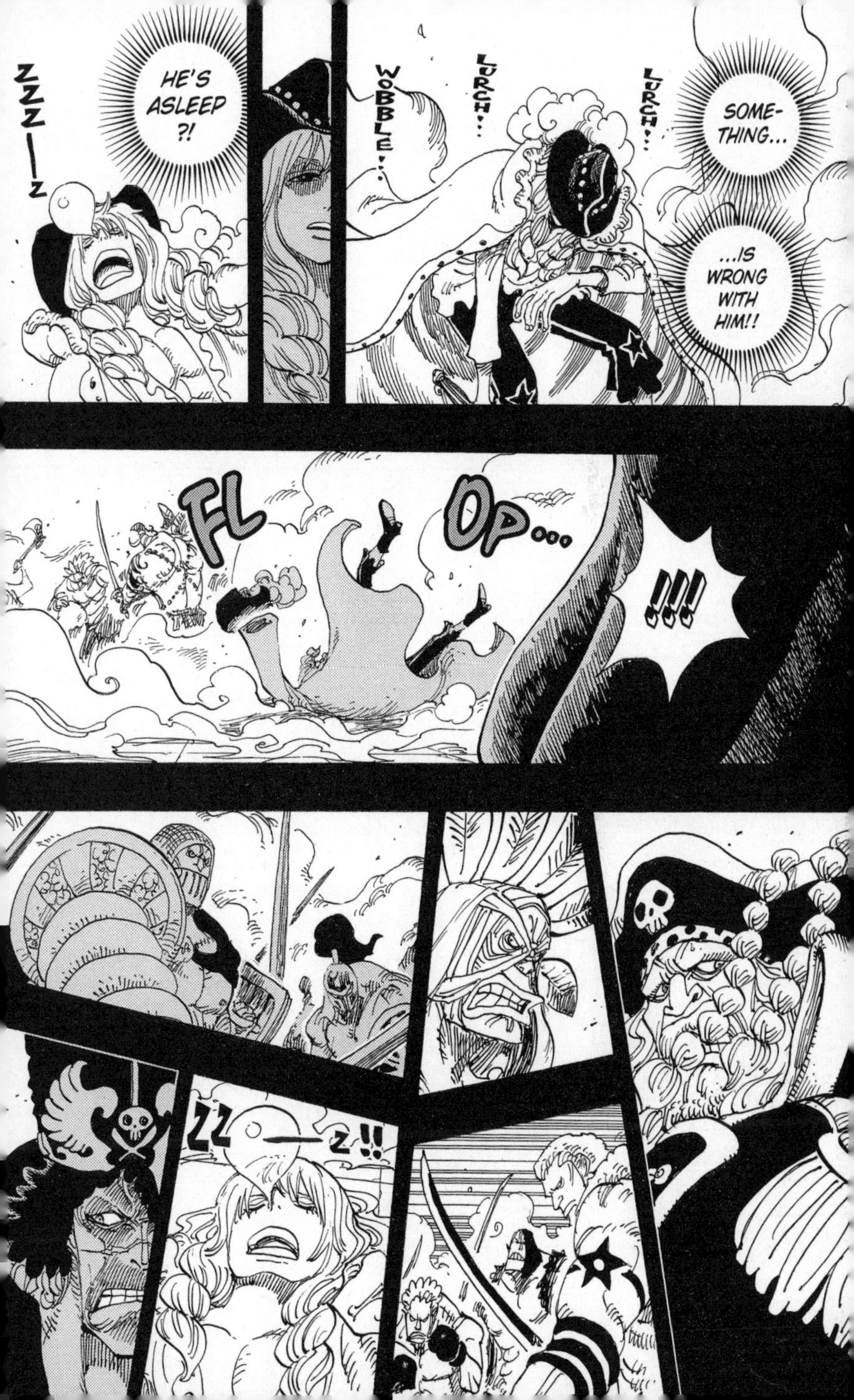
SOME-THING...
...IS WRONG WITH HIM!!
LURCH..
LURCH..
WOBBLE..
HE'S ASLEEP?!
ZZZ—Z
!!!
FLOP...
ZZ—Z!!

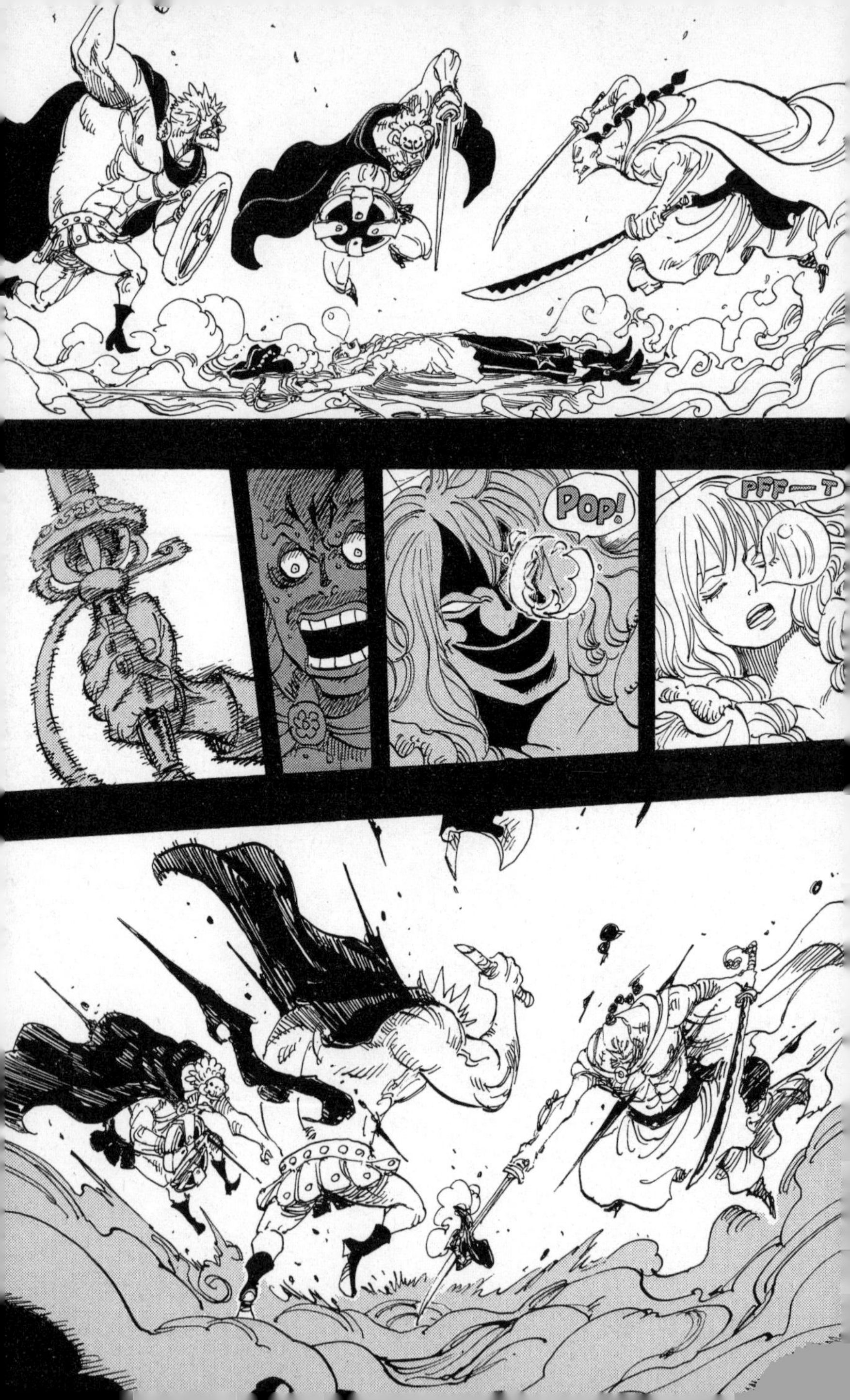
PFF— T
POP!

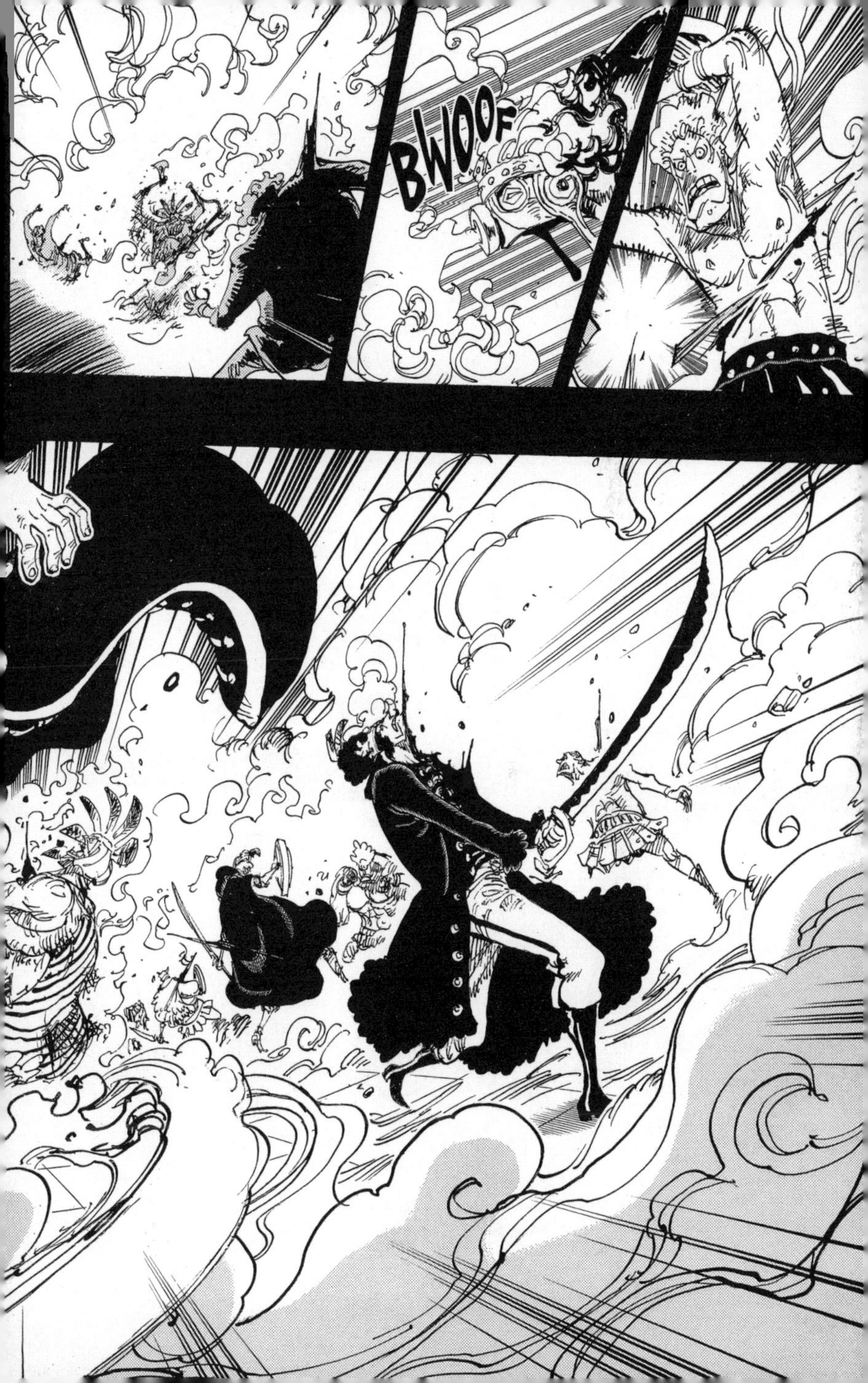
BWOOF

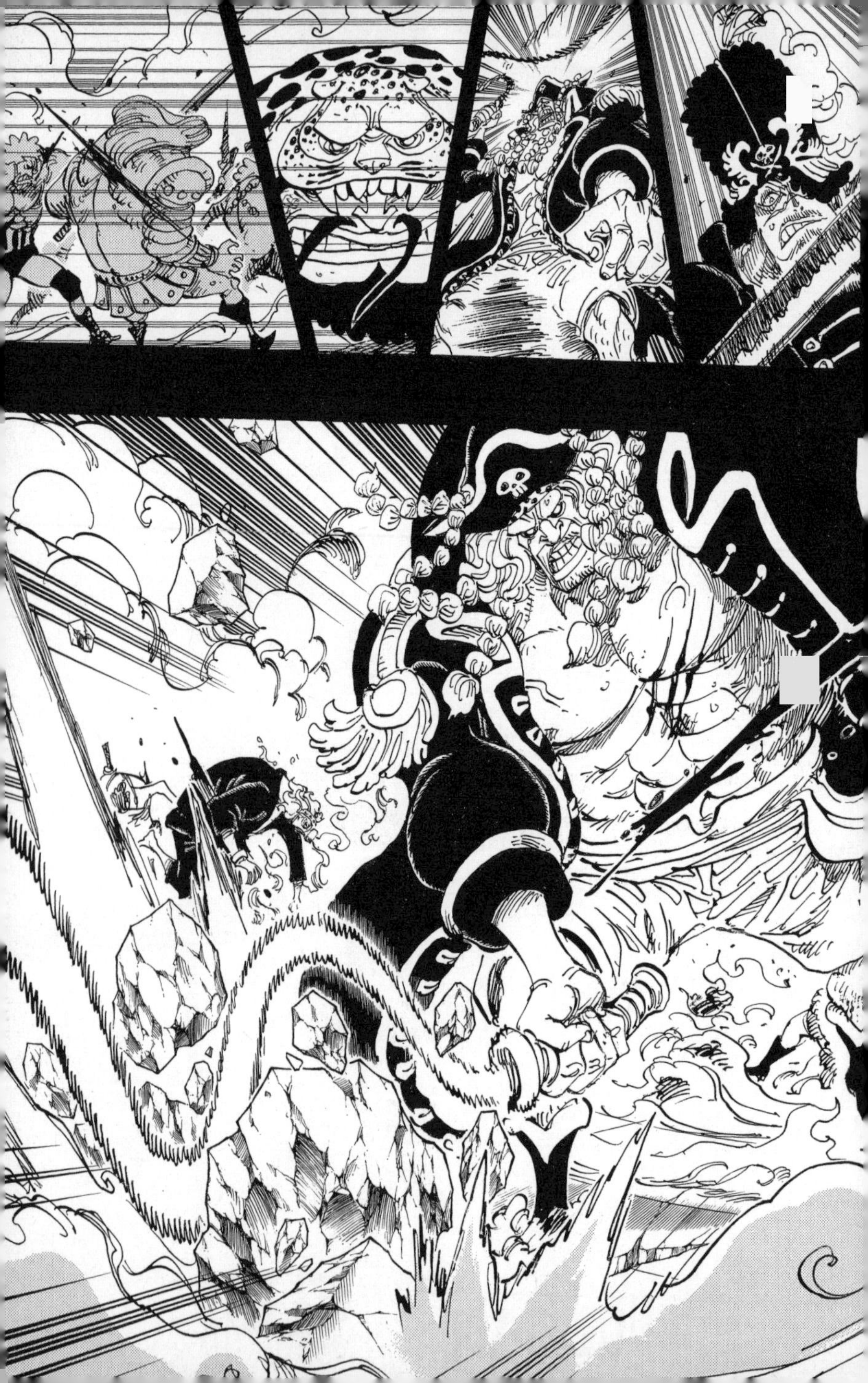

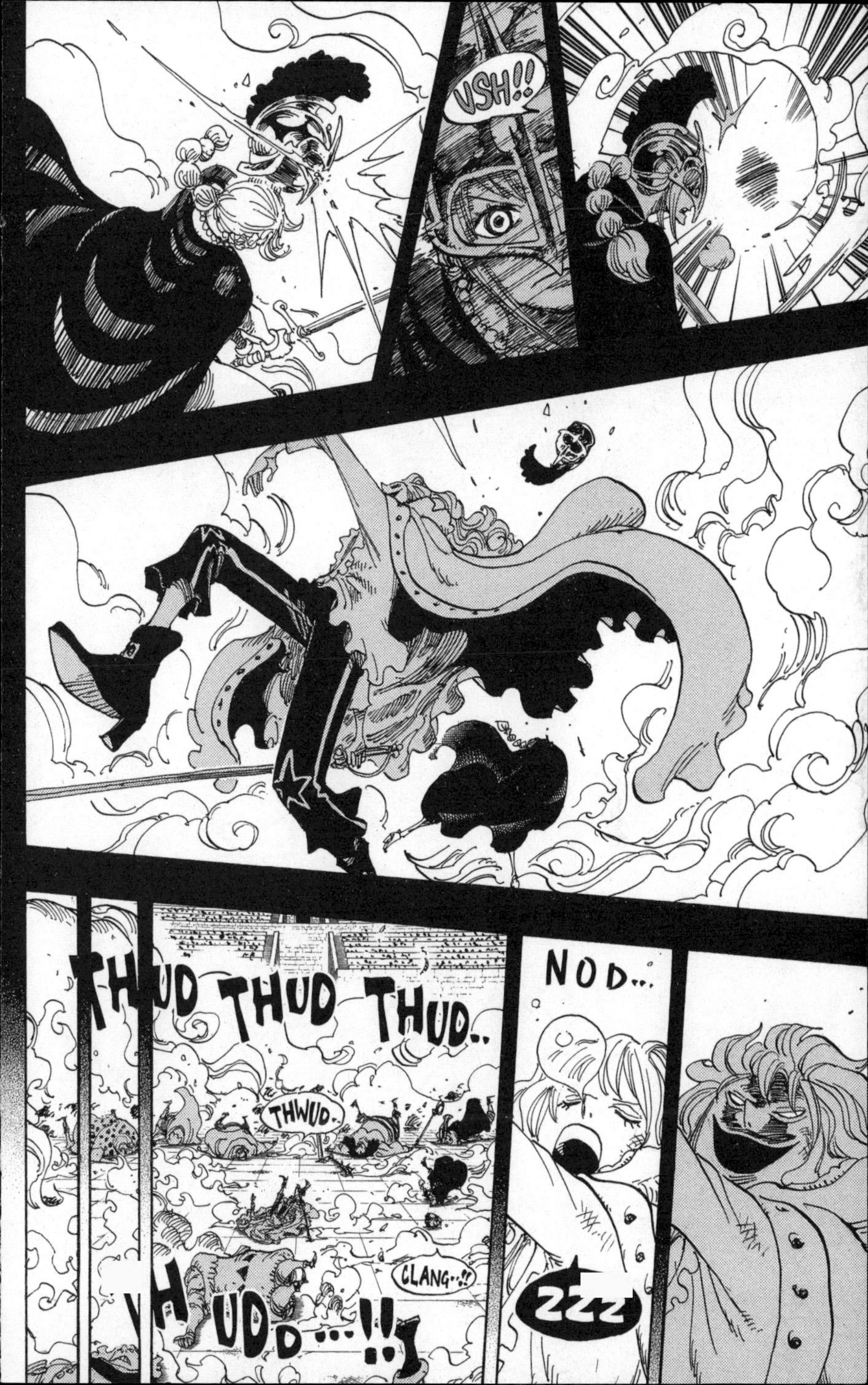
VSH!!
NOD...
ZZZ
THUD THUD THUD..
THWUD..
CLANG..!?
HUDD...!!

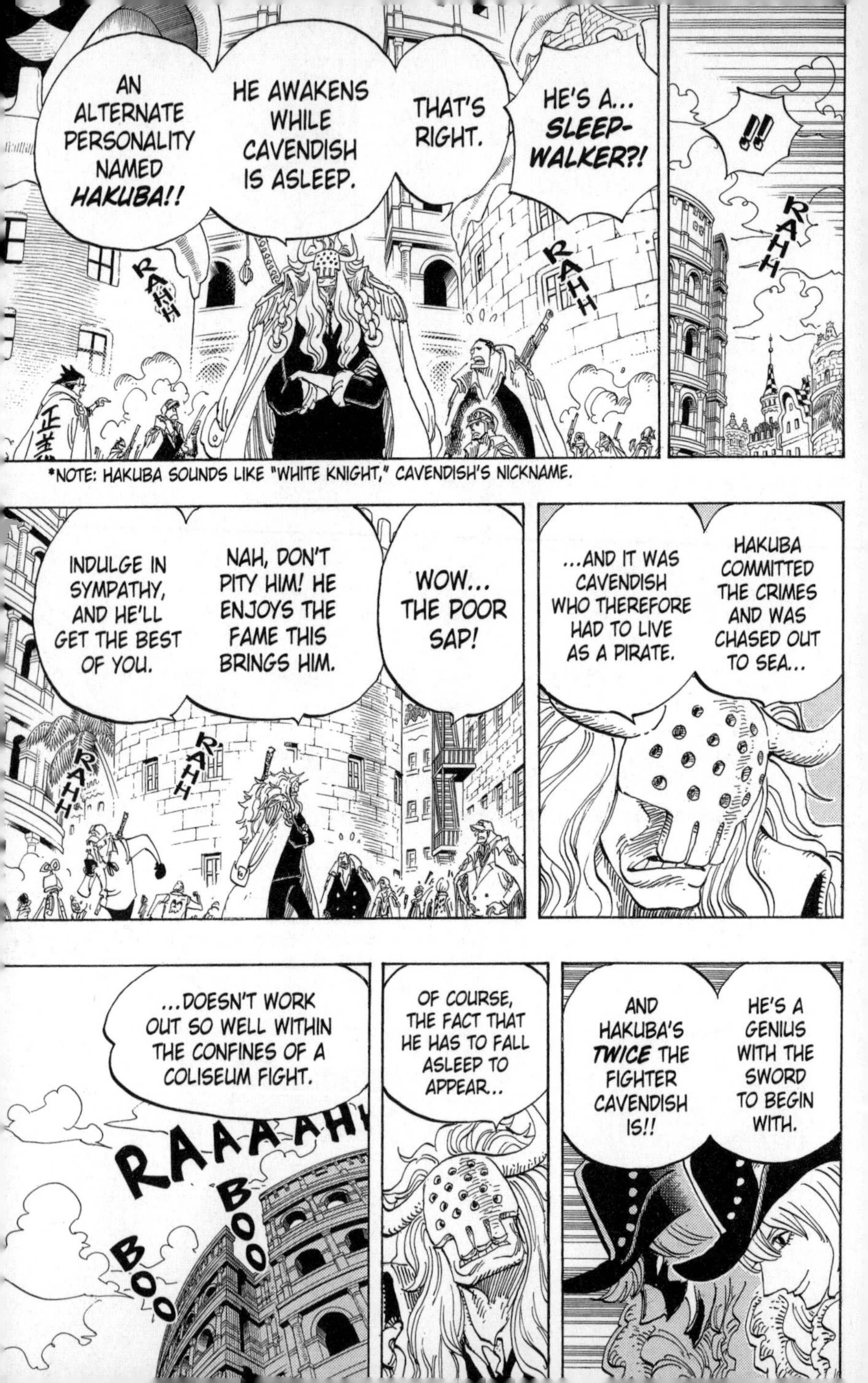
!!
RAHH
HE'S A... SLEEP-WALKER?!
THAT'S RIGHT.
HE AWAKENS WHILE CAVENDISH IS ASLEEP.
AN ALTERNATE PERSONALITY NAMED HAKUBA!!
RAHH
RAHH
*NOTE: HAKUBA SOUNDS LIKE "WHITE KNIGHT," CAVENDISH'S NICKNAME.
HAKUBA COMMITTED THE CRIMES AND WAS CHASED OUT TO SEA...
...AND IT WAS CAVENDISH WHO THEREFORE HAD TO LIVE AS A PIRATE.
WOW... THE POOR SAP!
NAH, DON'T PITY HIM! HE ENJOYS THE FAME THIS BRINGS HIM.
INDULGE IN SYMPATHY, AND HE'LL GET THE BEST OF YOU.
RAHH
RAHH
HE'S A GENIUS WITH THE SWORD TO BEGIN WITH.
AND HAKUBA'S TWICE THE FIGHTER CAVENDISH IS!!
OF COURSE, THE FACT THAT HE HAS TO FALL ASLEEP TO APPEAR...
...DOESN'T WORK OUT SO WELL WITHIN THE CONFINES OF A COLISEUM FIGHT.
RAAAAHH
BOO
BOO

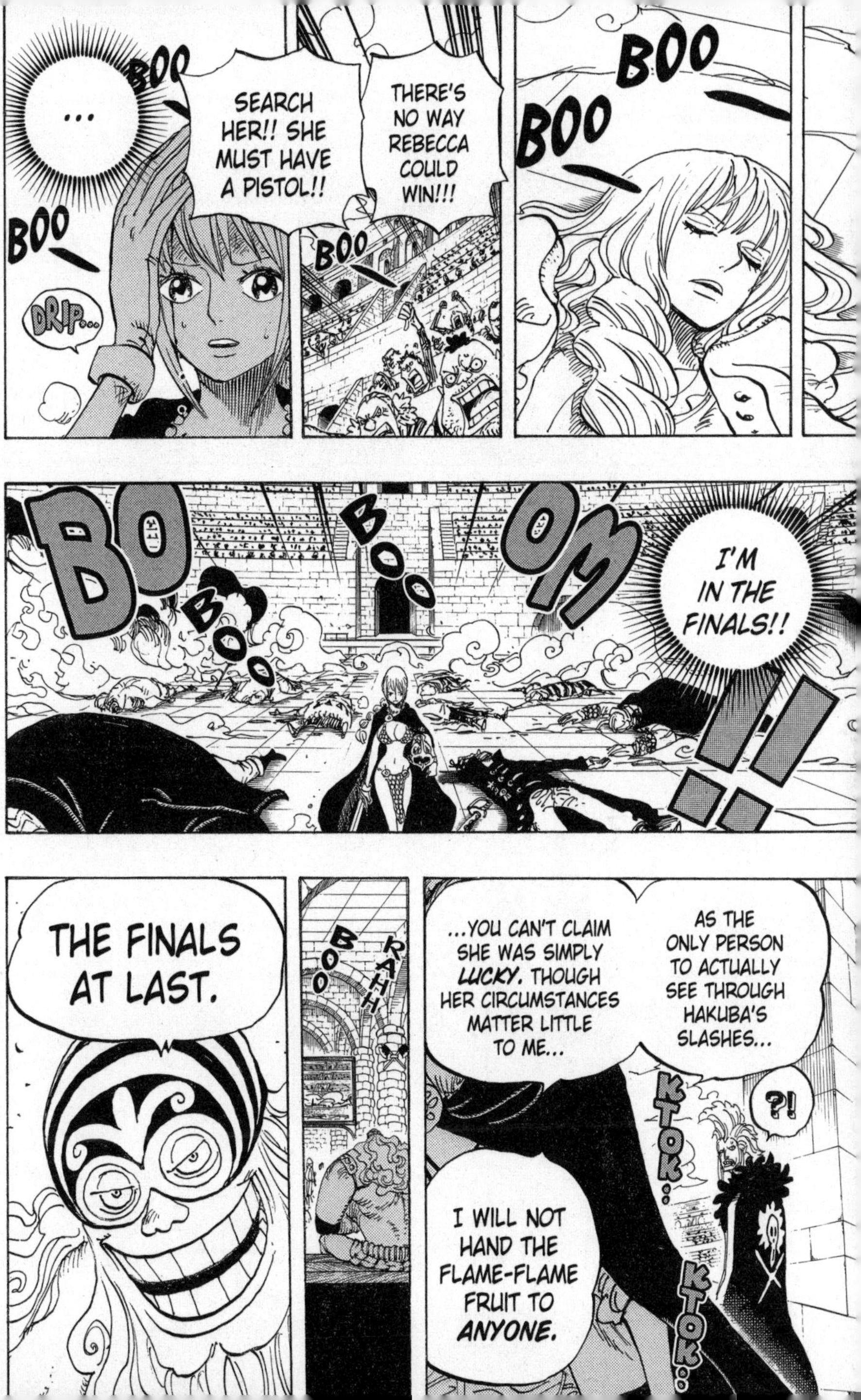
BOO
BOO
THERE'S NO WAY REBECCA COULD WIN!!!
SEARCH HER!! SHE MUST HAVE A PISTOL!!
BOO
...
BOO
BOO
DRIP...
I'M IN THE FINALS!!
!!
!!
BOOM
BOO
BOO
AS THE ONLY PERSON TO ACTUALLY SEE THROUGH HAKUBA'S SLASHES...
...YOU CAN'T CLAIM SHE WAS SIMPLY *LUCKY*. THOUGH HER CIRCUMSTANCES MATTER LITTLE TO ME...
?!
KTOK..
I WILL NOT HAND THE FLAME-FLAME FRUIT TO ***ANYONE***.
KTOK..
RAHH
BOO
THE FINALS AT LAST.

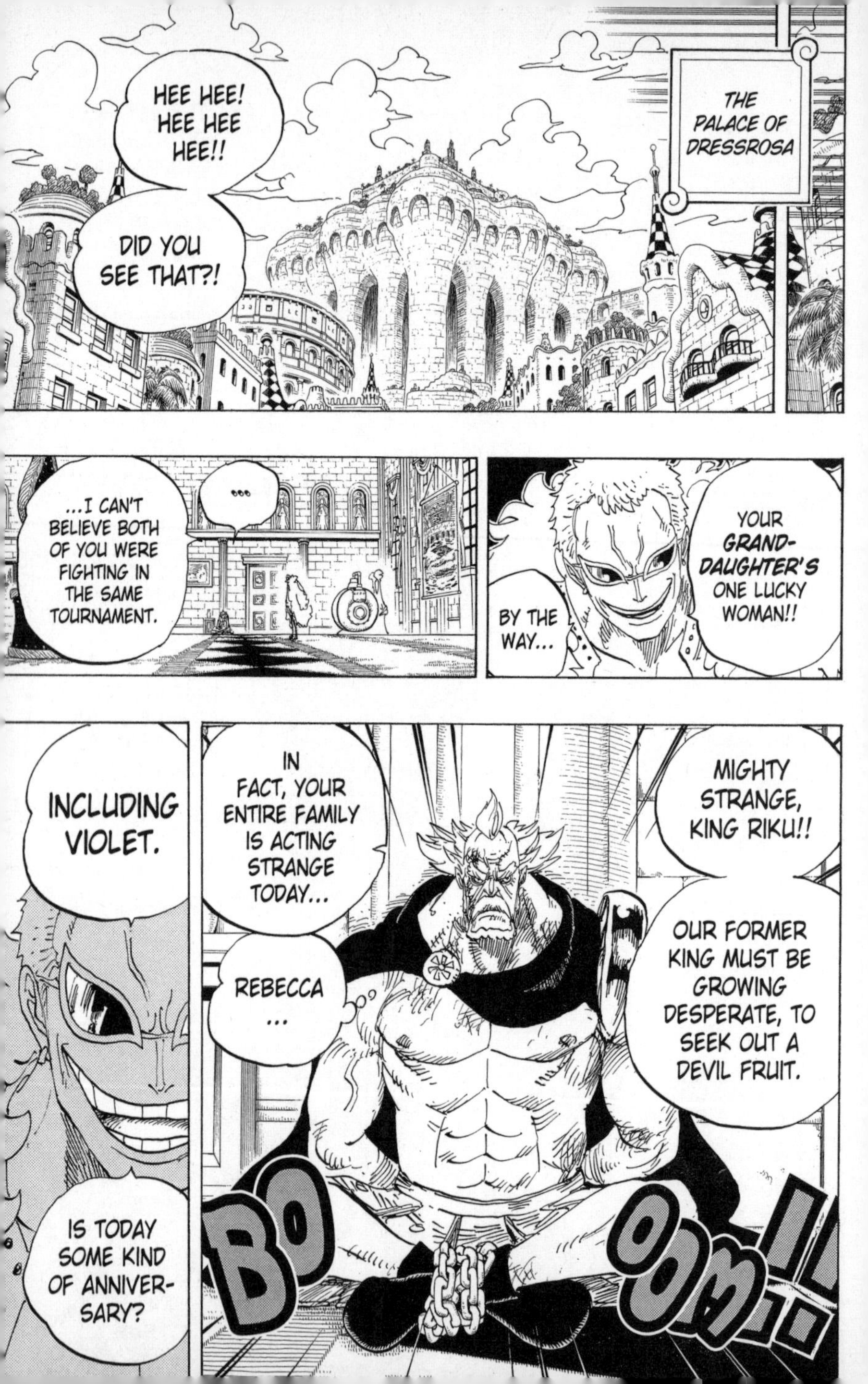
THE PALACE OF DRESSROSA
HEE HEE! HEE HEE HEE!!
DID YOU SEE THAT?!
YOUR GRAND-DAUGHTER'S ONE LUCKY WOMAN!!
BY THE WAY...
...
...I CAN'T BELIEVE BOTH OF YOU WERE FIGHTING IN THE SAME TOURNAMENT.
MIGHTY STRANGE, KING RIKU!!
IN FACT, YOUR ENTIRE FAMILY IS ACTING STRANGE TODAY...
OUR FORMER KING MUST BE GROWING DESPERATE, TO SEEK OUT A DEVIL FRUIT.
REBECCA ...
BOOOM!!
INCLUDING VIOLET.
IS TODAY SOME KIND OF ANNIVER-SARY?

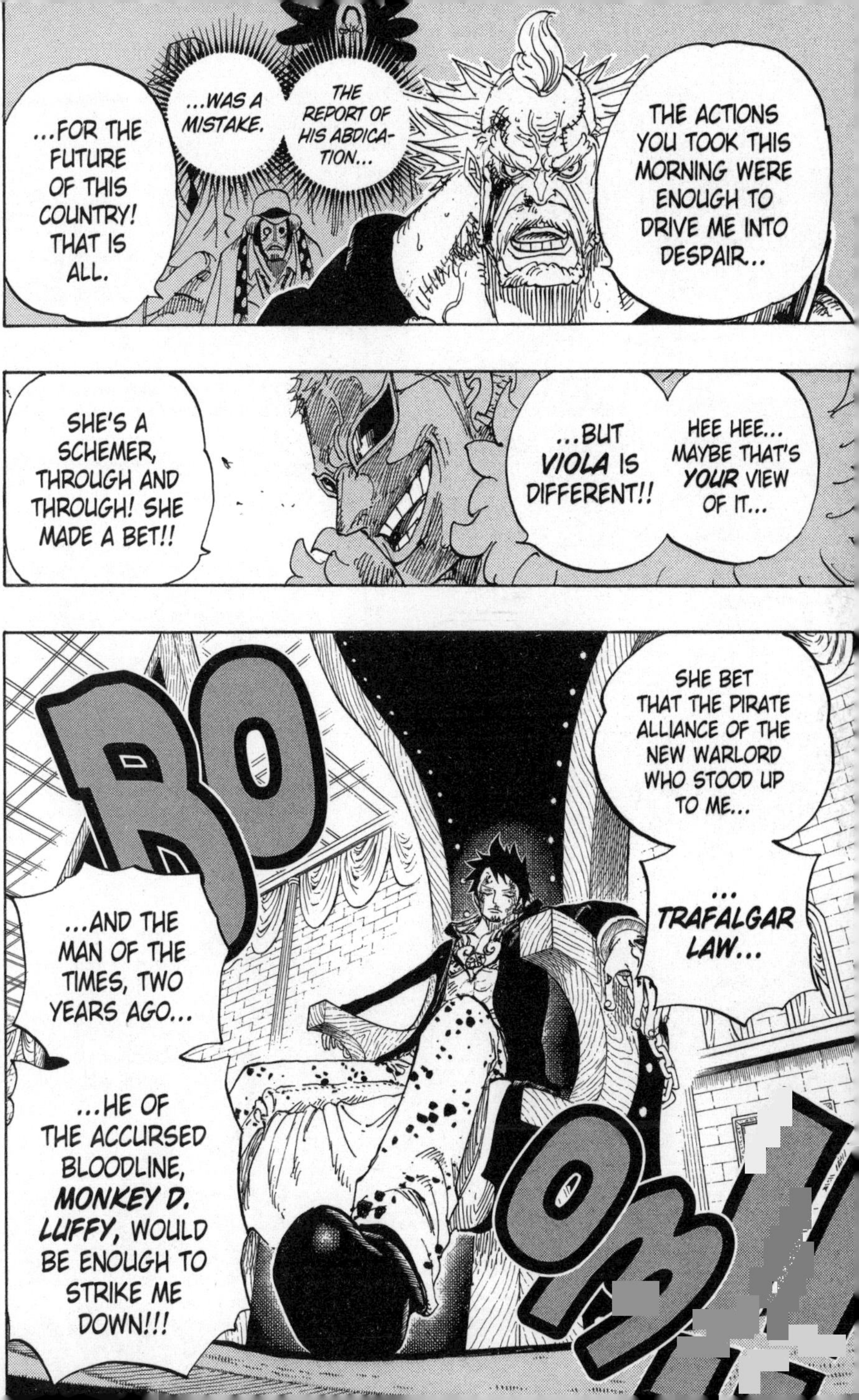
THE ACTIONS YOU TOOK THIS MORNING WERE ENOUGH TO DRIVE ME INTO DESPAIR...
THE REPORT OF HIS ABDICA-TION...
...WAS A MISTAKE.
...FOR THE FUTURE OF THIS COUNTRY! THAT IS ALL.
HEE HEE... MAYBE THAT'S *YOUR* VIEW OF IT...
...BUT *VIOLA* IS DIFFERENT!!
SHE'S A SCHEMER, THROUGH AND THROUGH! SHE MADE A BET!!
SHE BET THAT THE PIRATE ALLIANCE OF THE NEW WARLORD WHO STOOD UP TO ME...
... *TRAFALGAR LAW*...
...AND THE MAN OF THE TIMES, TWO YEARS AGO...
...HE OF THE ACCURSED BLOODLINE, *MONKEY D. LUFFY*, WOULD BE ENOUGH TO STRIKE ME DOWN!!!
BOOM!!

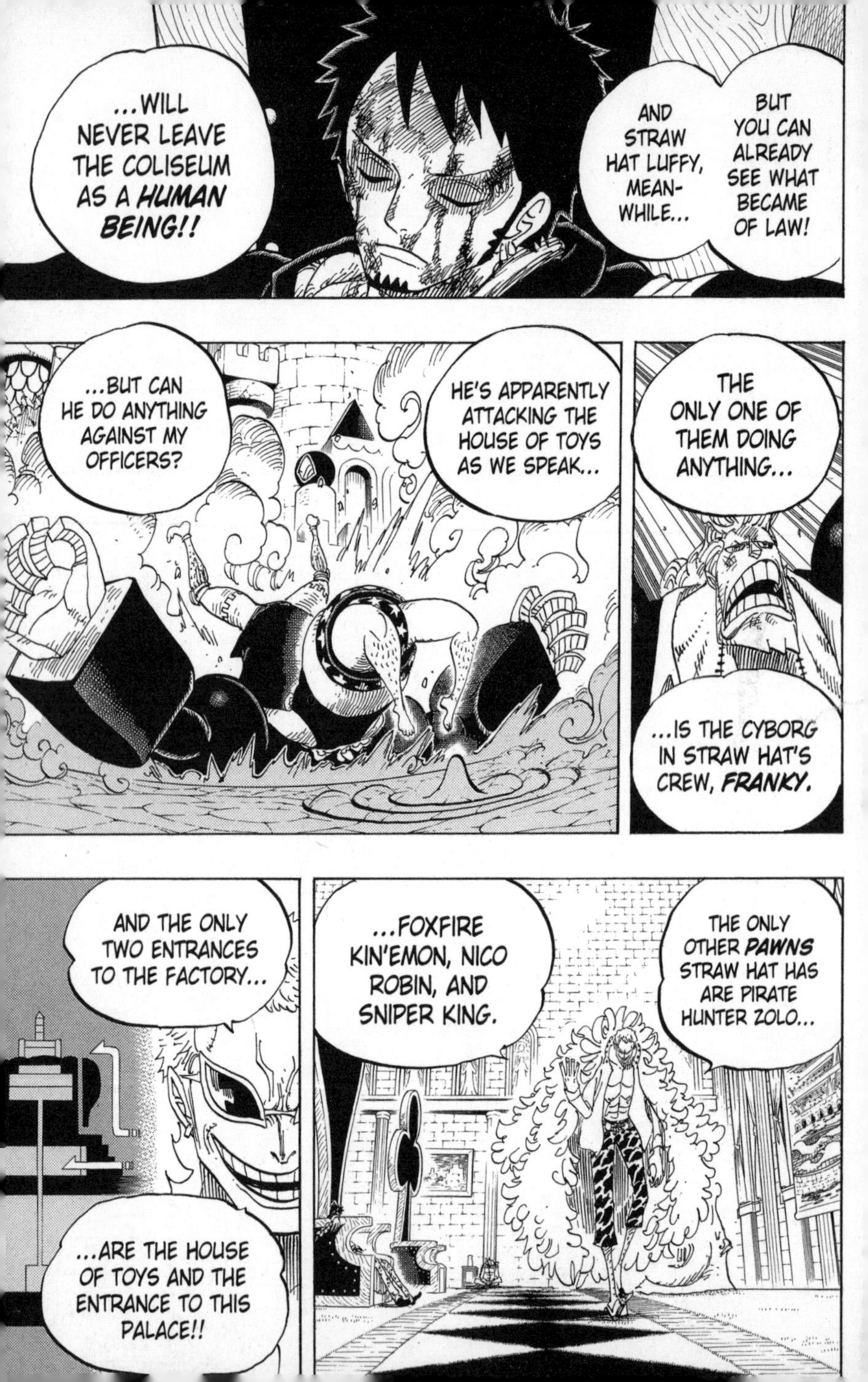
BUT YOU CAN ALREADY SEE WHAT BECAME OF LAW!
AND STRAW HAT LUFFY, MEAN-WHILE...
...WILL NEVER LEAVE THE COLISEUM AS A ***HUMAN BEING!!***
THE ONLY ONE OF THEM DOING ANYTHING...
...IS THE CYBORG IN STRAW HAT'S CREW, ***FRANKY.***
HE'S APPARENTLY ATTACKING THE HOUSE OF TOYS AS WE SPEAK...
...BUT CAN HE DO ANYTHING AGAINST MY OFFICERS?
THE ONLY OTHER ***PAWNS*** STRAW HAT HAS ARE PIRATE HUNTER ZOLO...
...FOXFIRE KIN'EMON, NICO ROBIN, AND SNIPER KING.
AND THE ONLY TWO ENTRANCES TO THE FACTORY...
...ARE THE HOUSE OF TOYS AND THE ENTRANCE TO THIS PALACE!!

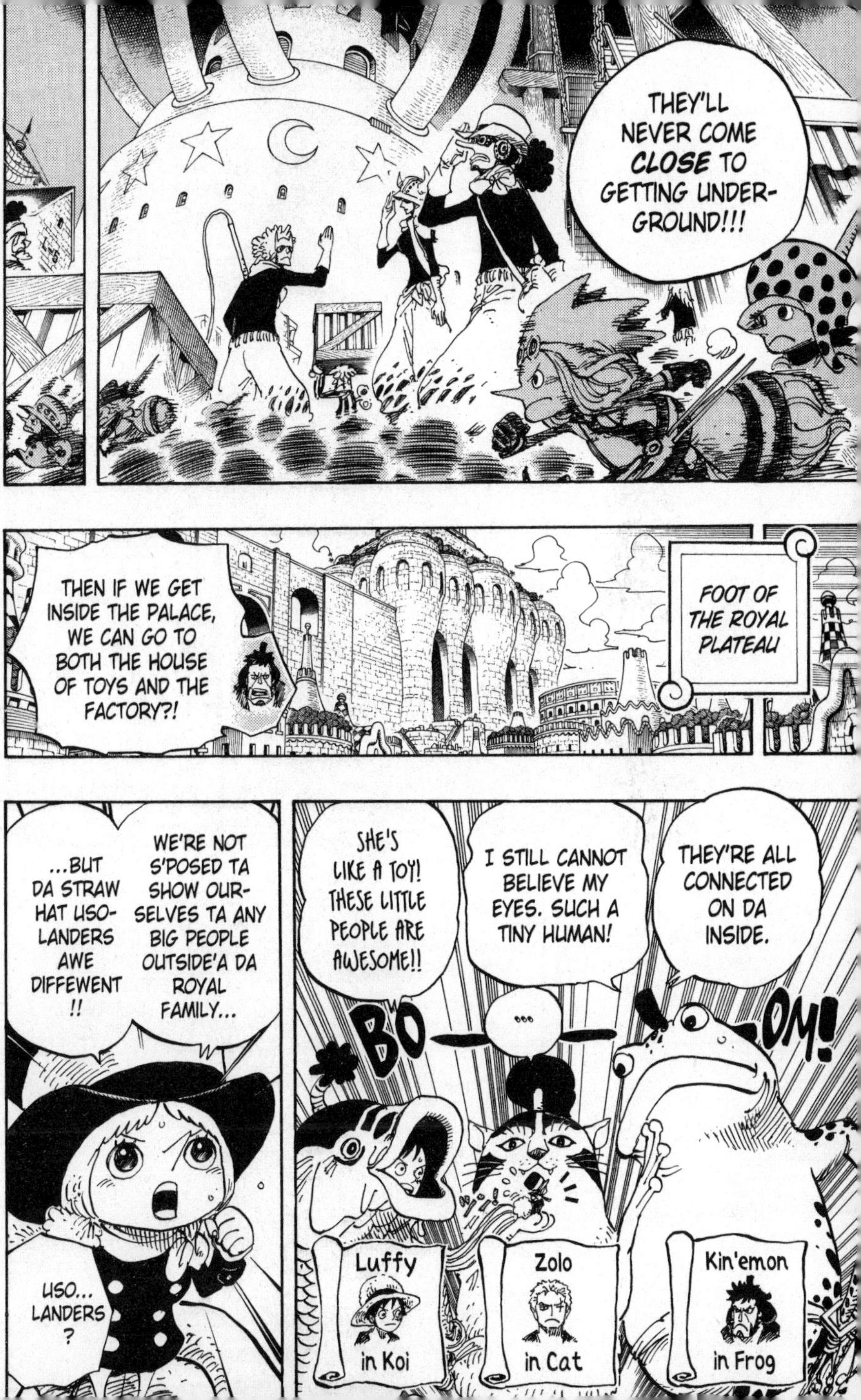

THEY'LL NEVER COME CLOSE TO GETTING UNDER-GROUND!!!
FOOT OF THE ROYAL PLATEAU
THEN IF WE GET INSIDE THE PALACE, WE CAN GO TO BOTH THE HOUSE OF TOYS AND THE FACTORY?!
THEY'RE ALL CONNECTED ON DA INSIDE.
I STILL CANNOT BELIEVE MY EYES. SUCH A TINY HUMAN!
SHE'S LIKE A TOY! THESE LITTLE PEOPLE ARE AWESOME!!
BO—OM!
...
Kin'emon in Frog
Zolo in Cat
Luffy in Koi
WE'RE NOT S'POSED TA SHOW OUR-SELVES TA ANY BIG PEOPLE OUTSIDE'A DA ROYAL FAMILY...
...BUT DA STRAW HAT USO-LANDERS AWE DIFFEWENT!!
USO... LANDERS?

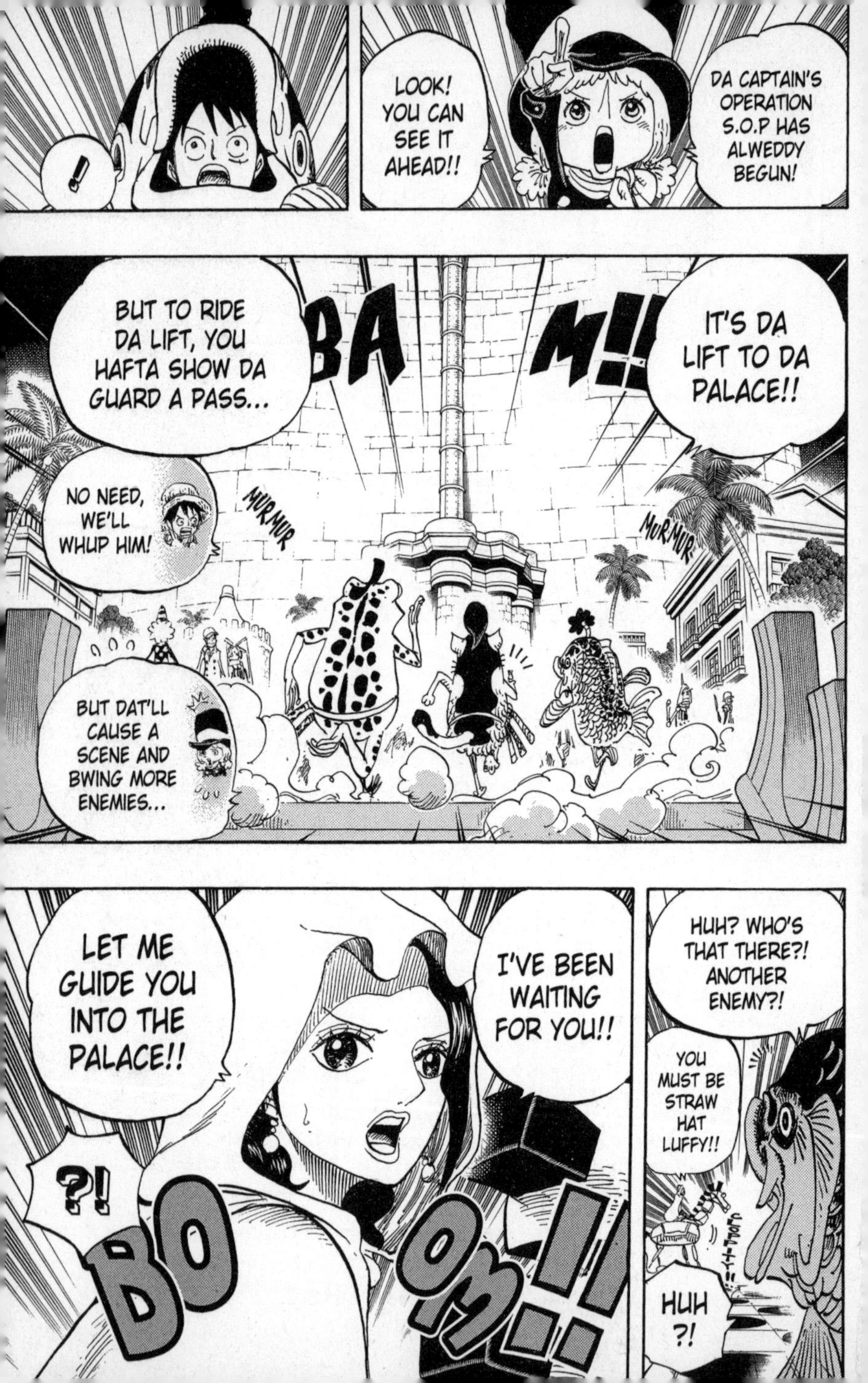
DA CAPTAIN'S OPERATION S.O.P HAS ALWEDDY BEGUN!
LOOK! YOU CAN SEE IT AHEAD!!
!
IT'S DA LIFT TO DA PALACE!!
BAM!!
MURMUR
BUT TO RIDE DA LIFT, YOU HAFTA SHOW DA GUARD A PASS...
MURMUR
NO NEED, WE'LL WHUP HIM!
BUT DAT'LL CAUSE A SCENE AND BWING MORE ENEMIES...
HUH? WHO'S THAT THERE?! ANOTHER ENEMY?!
YOU MUST BE STRAW HAT LUFFY!!
HUH ?!
I'VE BEEN WAITING FOR YOU!!
LET ME GUIDE YOU INTO THE PALACE!!
BOOM!!
?!

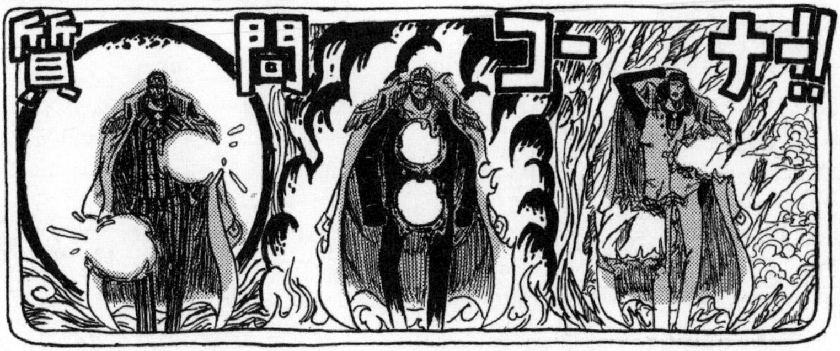
質問コーナー!!

(Bokuo Okubo, Kagoshima)

Q: Oda! I was playing Underwear Man with my little sister yesterday, putting underwear on my head. Want to play? It's simple, just put the underwear on and run around saying, "You'll pay if you don't put underwear on your head!" That's it! Try it out! It's fun!

--Maebara

A: Wow, that does sound fun! Wheee!! Knock it off!! That's disgusting!!

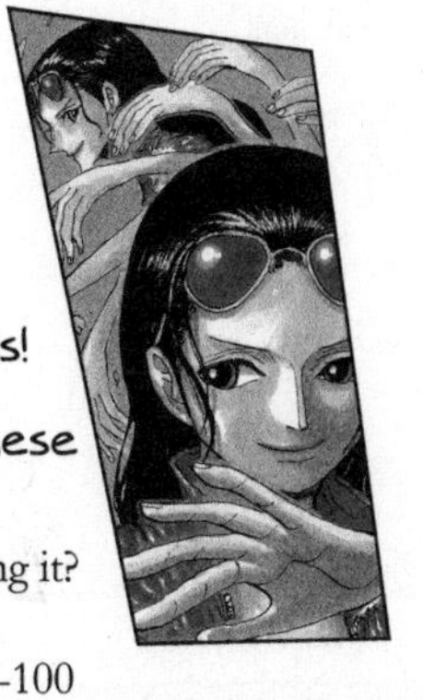

Q: Robin's hands are truly **gorgeous.** Please let me rub them.

--Yoshikage 0130

A: Pervert!!! Please, you have to stop this! I'm getting constant complaints from the PTA about this section. Stop sending in these undignified comments and questions!

Q: Which scene made you cry the most as you were drawing it? Please tell me.

--ca-100

A: Ahh, now this... This is the kind of serious question I want. There are plenty of scenes that got me teary as I drew them. In fact, it's often so difficult to draw that I have to get up out of my chair. The one that made me cry the most, or at least was the most painful, was probably the scene where Vivi says, "Stop all the fighting!!" in volume 23. That was so hard I couldn't finish it for a while. There are plenty of scenes I can think of, but that might be the one.

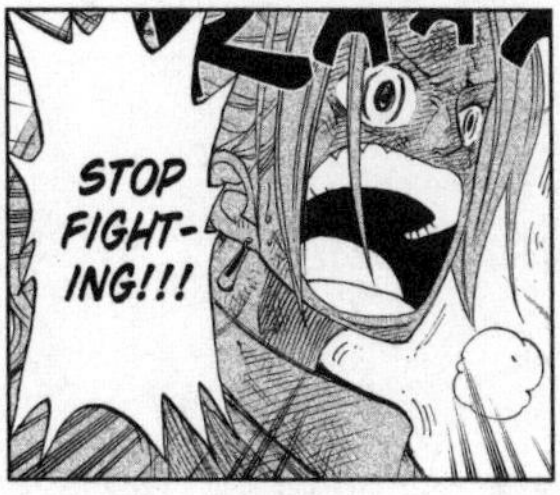
STOP FIGHT-ING!!!

Q: Here's a question. If Marco's wiener gets cut off, will it grow back?

--Seigan

A: Yes, even his marcus can grow back. Hey!!!

Chapter 735:
FUJITORA'S PLAN

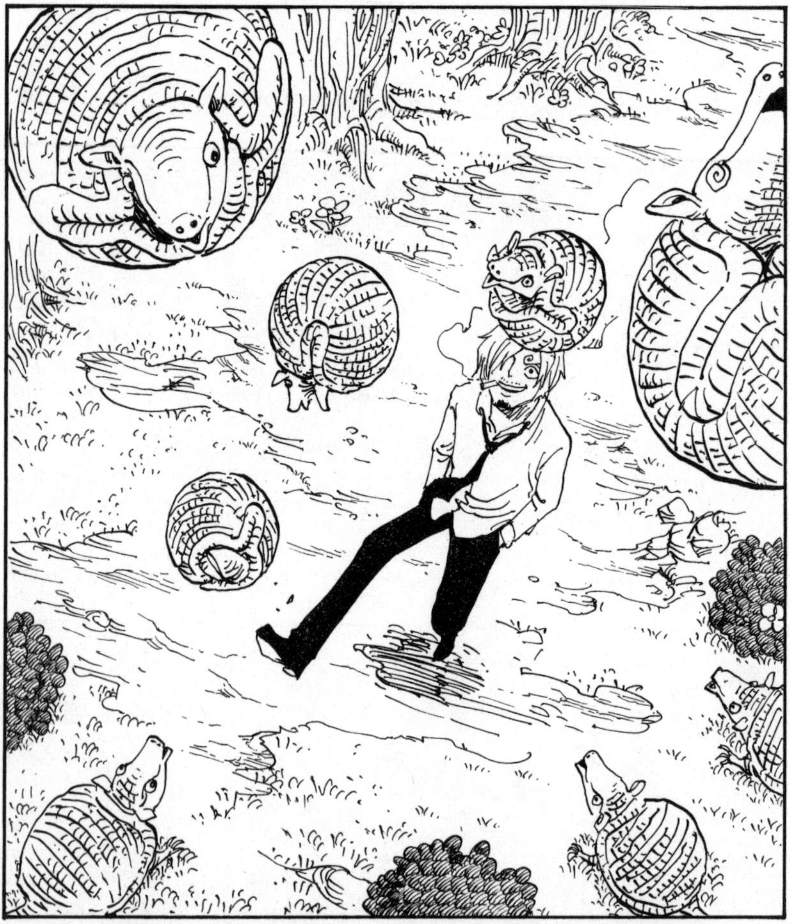

REQUEST: "SANJI PRACTICES HIS JUGGLING WITH ARMADILLOS" BY KOGE-BUTA FROM KYOTO

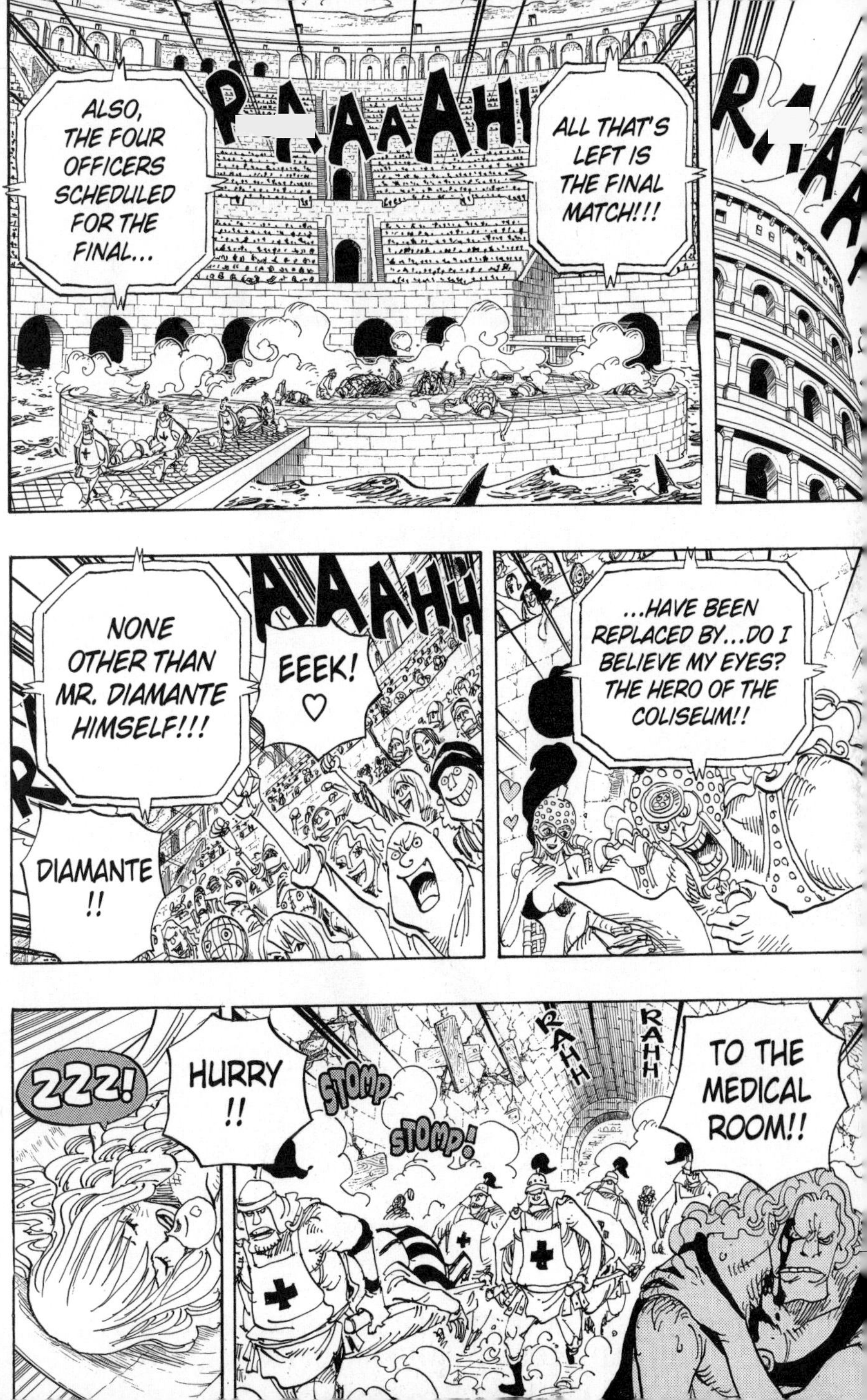
ALL THAT'S LEFT IS THE FINAL MATCH!!!
ALSO, THE FOUR OFFICERS SCHEDULED FOR THE FINAL...
...HAVE BEEN REPLACED BY...DO I BELIEVE MY EYES? THE HERO OF THE COLISEUM!!
AAAHH
EEEK! ♡
NONE OTHER THAN MR. DIAMANTE HIMSELF!!!
DIAMANTE !!
TO THE MEDICAL ROOM!!
RAHH
RAHH
STOMP!
STOMP
HURRY !!
ZZZ!

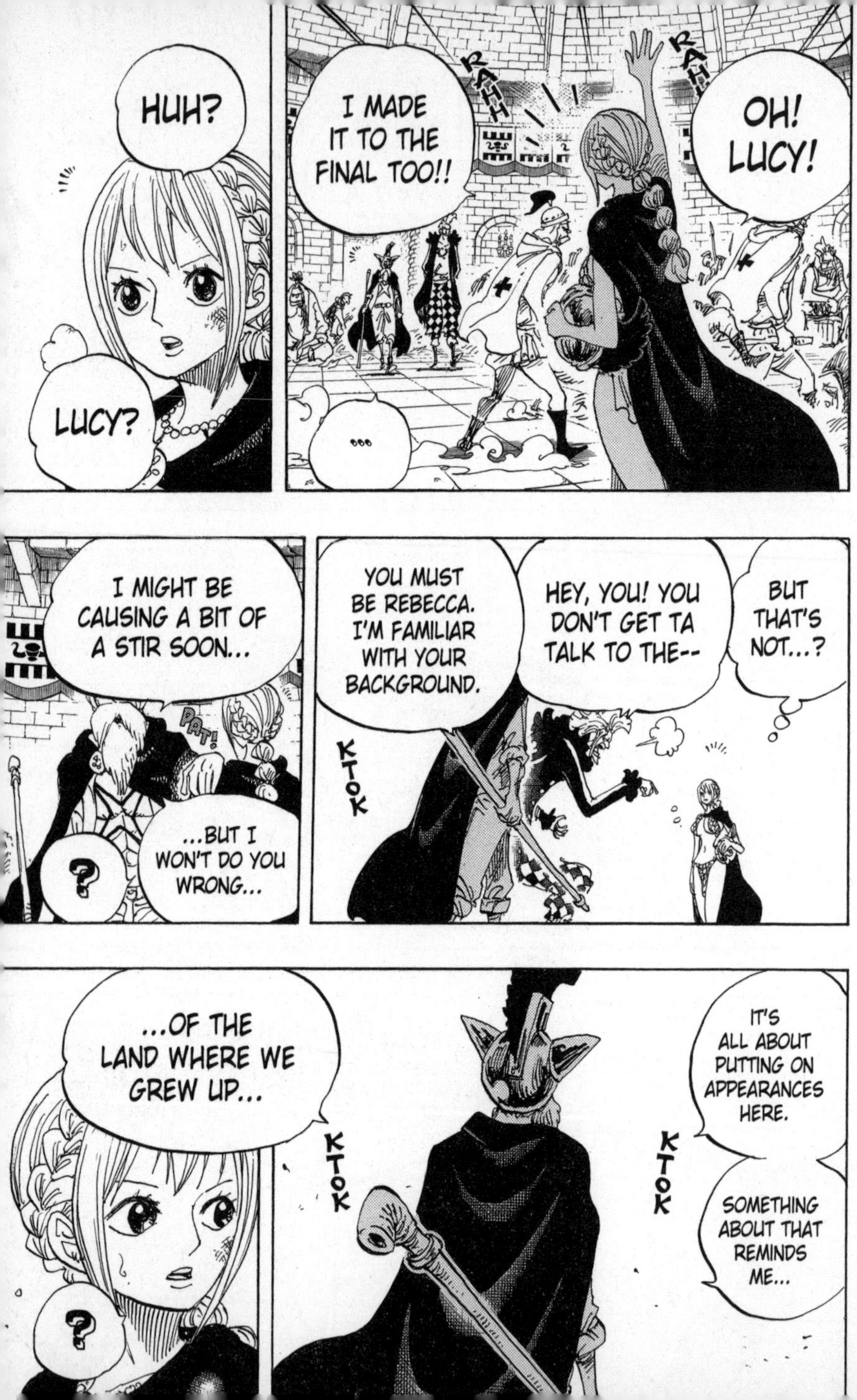
OH! LUCY!
RAHH
RAHH
I MADE IT TO THE FINAL TOO!!
...
HUH?
LUCY?
BUT THAT'S NOT...?
HEY, YOU! YOU DON'T GET TA TALK TO THE--
YOU MUST BE REBECCA. I'M FAMILIAR WITH YOUR BACKGROUND.
KTOK
I MIGHT BE CAUSING A BIT OF A STIR SOON...
PAT!
...BUT I WON'T DO YOU WRONG...
?
IT'S ALL ABOUT PUTTING ON APPEARANCES HERE.
SOMETHING ABOUT THAT REMINDS ME...
KTOK
KTOK
...OF THE LAND WHERE WE GREW UP...
?

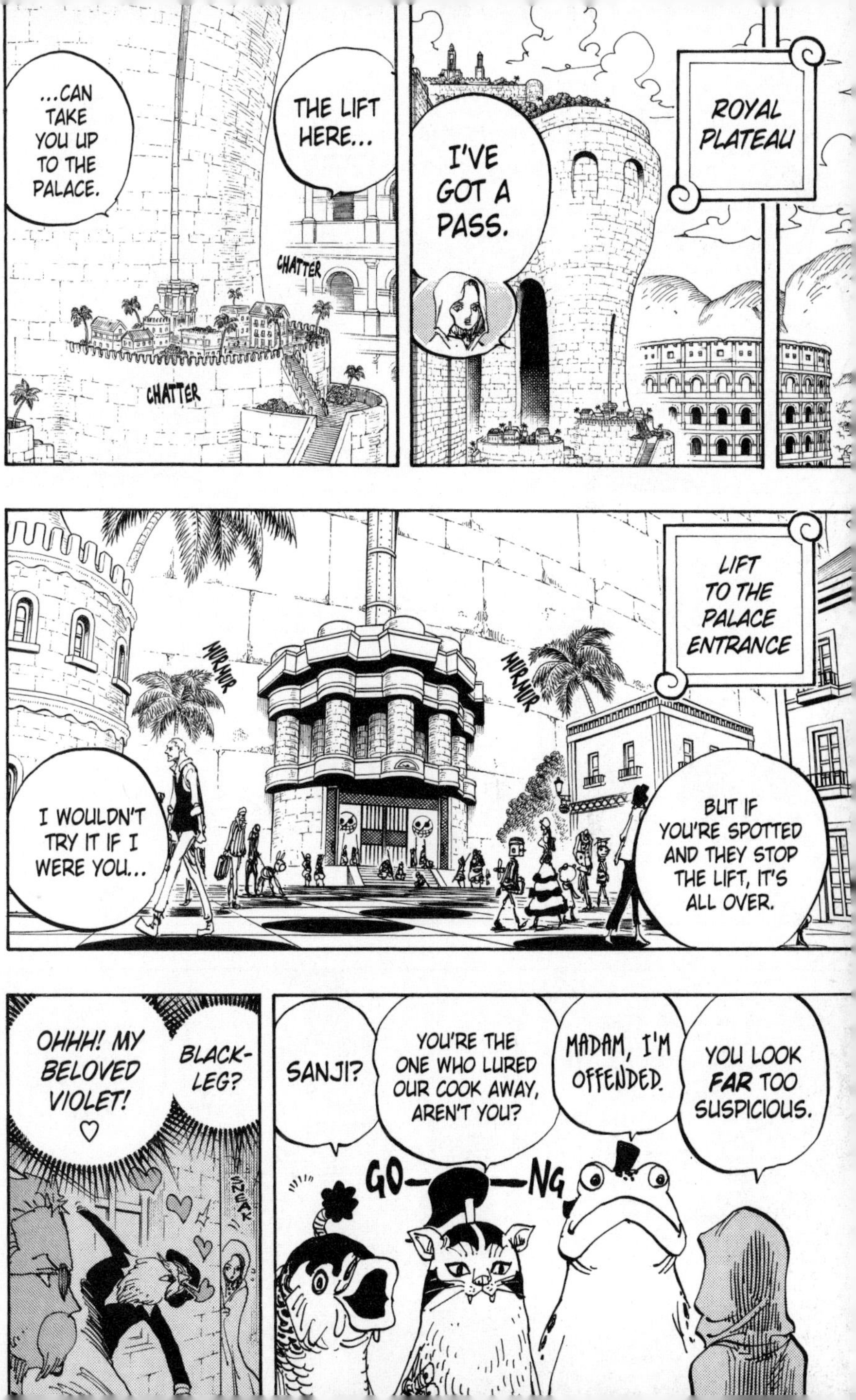
ROYAL PLATEAU
I'VE GOT A PASS.
THE LIFT HERE...
...CAN TAKE YOU UP TO THE PALACE.
CHATTER
CHATTER
LIFT TO THE PALACE ENTRANCE
MURMUR
MURMUR
BUT IF YOU'RE SPOTTED AND THEY STOP THE LIFT, IT'S ALL OVER.
I WOULDN'T TRY IT IF I WERE YOU...
YOU LOOK **FAR** TOO SUSPICIOUS.
MADAM, I'M OFFENDED.
YOU'RE THE ONE WHO LURED OUR COOK AWAY, AREN'T YOU?
SANJI?
GO—NG
BLACK-LEG?
OHHH! MY BELOVED VIOLET! ♡
SNEAK

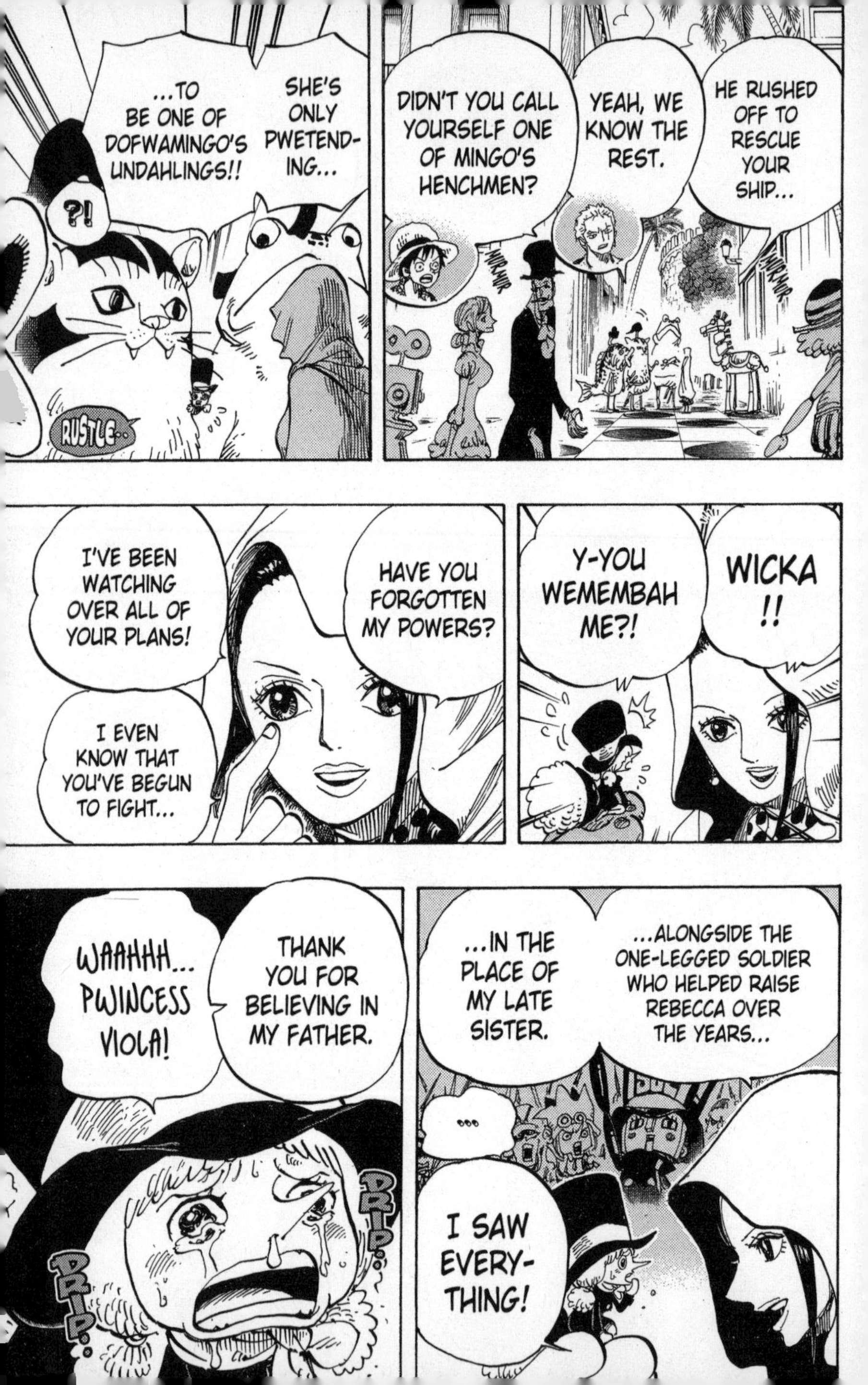
HE RUSHED OFF TO RESCUE YOUR SHIP...
YEAH, WE KNOW THE REST.
DIDN'T YOU CALL YOURSELF ONE OF MINGO'S HENCHMEN?
SHE'S ONLY PWETEND-ING...
...TO BE ONE OF DOFWAMINGO'S UNDAHLINGS!!
?!
RUSTLE..
WICKA !!
Y-YOU WEMEMBAH ME?!
HAVE YOU FORGOTTEN MY POWERS?
I'VE BEEN WATCHING OVER ALL OF YOUR PLANS!
I EVEN KNOW THAT YOU'VE BEGUN TO FIGHT...
...ALONGSIDE THE ONE-LEGGED SOLDIER WHO HELPED RAISE REBECCA OVER THE YEARS...
...IN THE PLACE OF MY LATE SISTER.
...
I SAW EVERY-THING!
THANK YOU FOR BELIEVING IN MY FATHER.
WAAHHH... PWINCESS VIOLA!
DRIP.
DRIP.

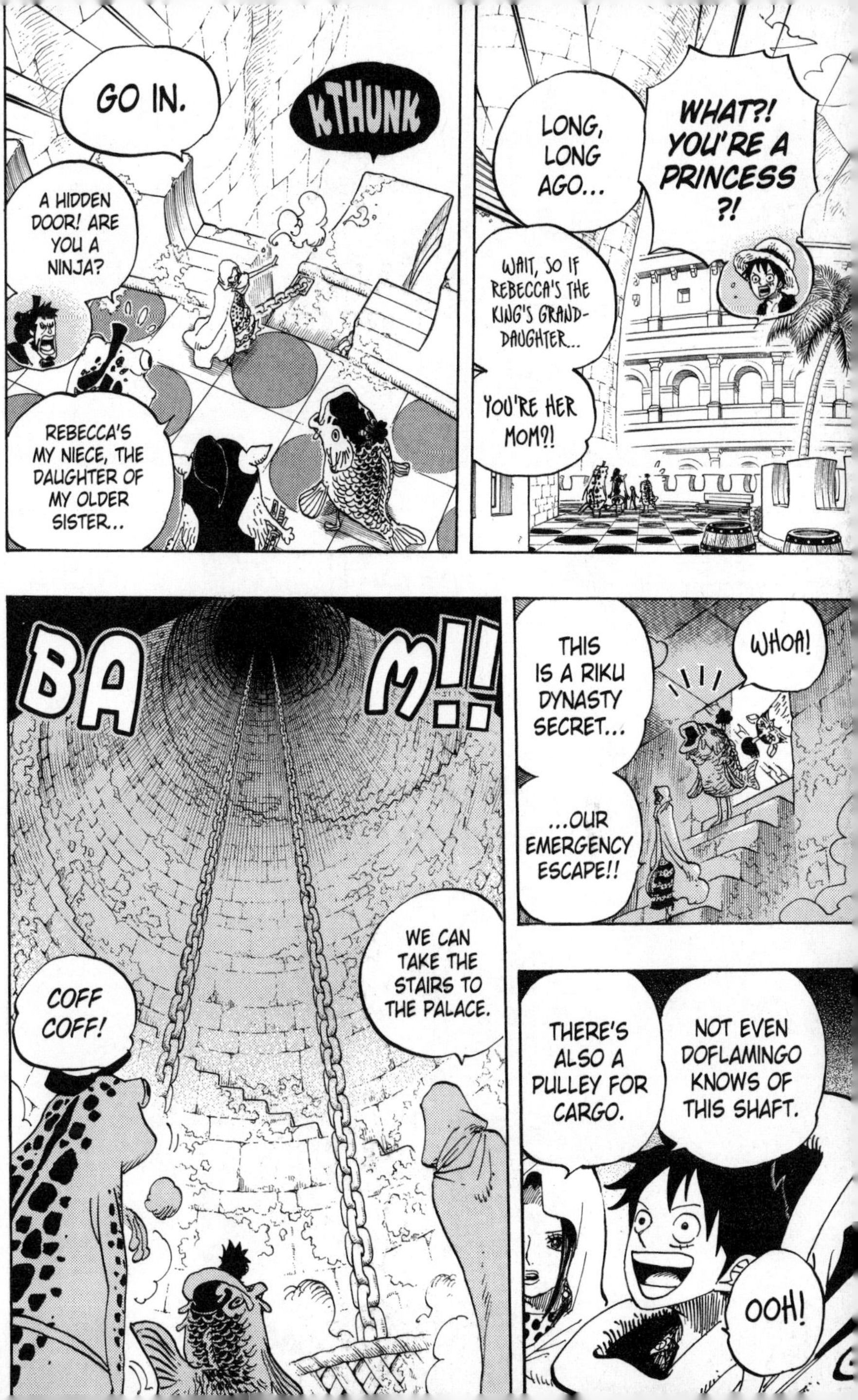
WHAT?! YOU'RE A PRINCESS?!
LONG, LONG AGO...
WAIT, SO IF REBECCA'S THE KING'S GRAND-DAUGHTER...
YOU'RE HER MOM?!
GO IN.
KTHUNK
A HIDDEN DOOR! ARE YOU A NINJA?
REBECCA'S MY NIECE, THE DAUGHTER OF MY OLDER SISTER...
WHOA!
THIS IS A RIKU DYNASTY SECRET...
...OUR EMERGENCY ESCAPE!!
NOT EVEN DOFLAMINGO KNOWS OF THIS SHAFT.
THERE'S ALSO A PULLEY FOR CARGO.
OOH!
BAM!!
WE CAN TAKE THE STAIRS TO THE PALACE.
COFF COFF!

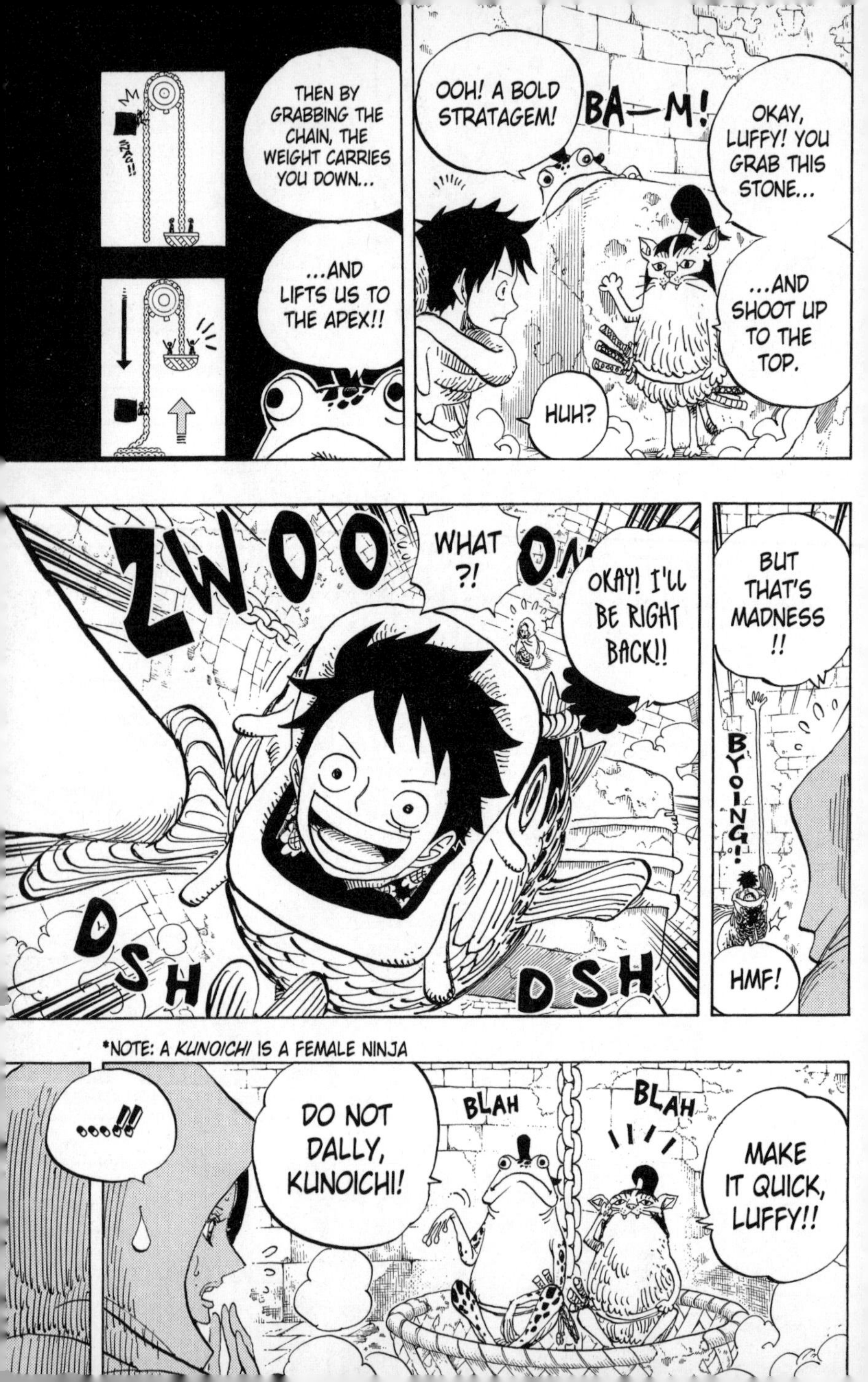
OKAY, LUFFY! YOU GRAB THIS STONE...
...AND SHOOT UP TO THE TOP.
BA-M!
OOH! A BOLD STRATAGEM!
HUH?
THEN BY GRABBING THE CHAIN, THE WEIGHT CARRIES YOU DOWN...
SNAG!!
...AND LIFTS US TO THE APEX!!
BUT THAT'S MADNESS!!
BYOING!
HMF!
OKAY! I'LL BE RIGHT BACK!!
WHAT?!
ZWOOOM
DSH
DSH
MAKE IT QUICK, LUFFY!!
BLAH
BLAH
DO NOT DALLY, KUNOICHI!
...!!

*NOTE: A *KUNOICHI* IS A FEMALE NINJA

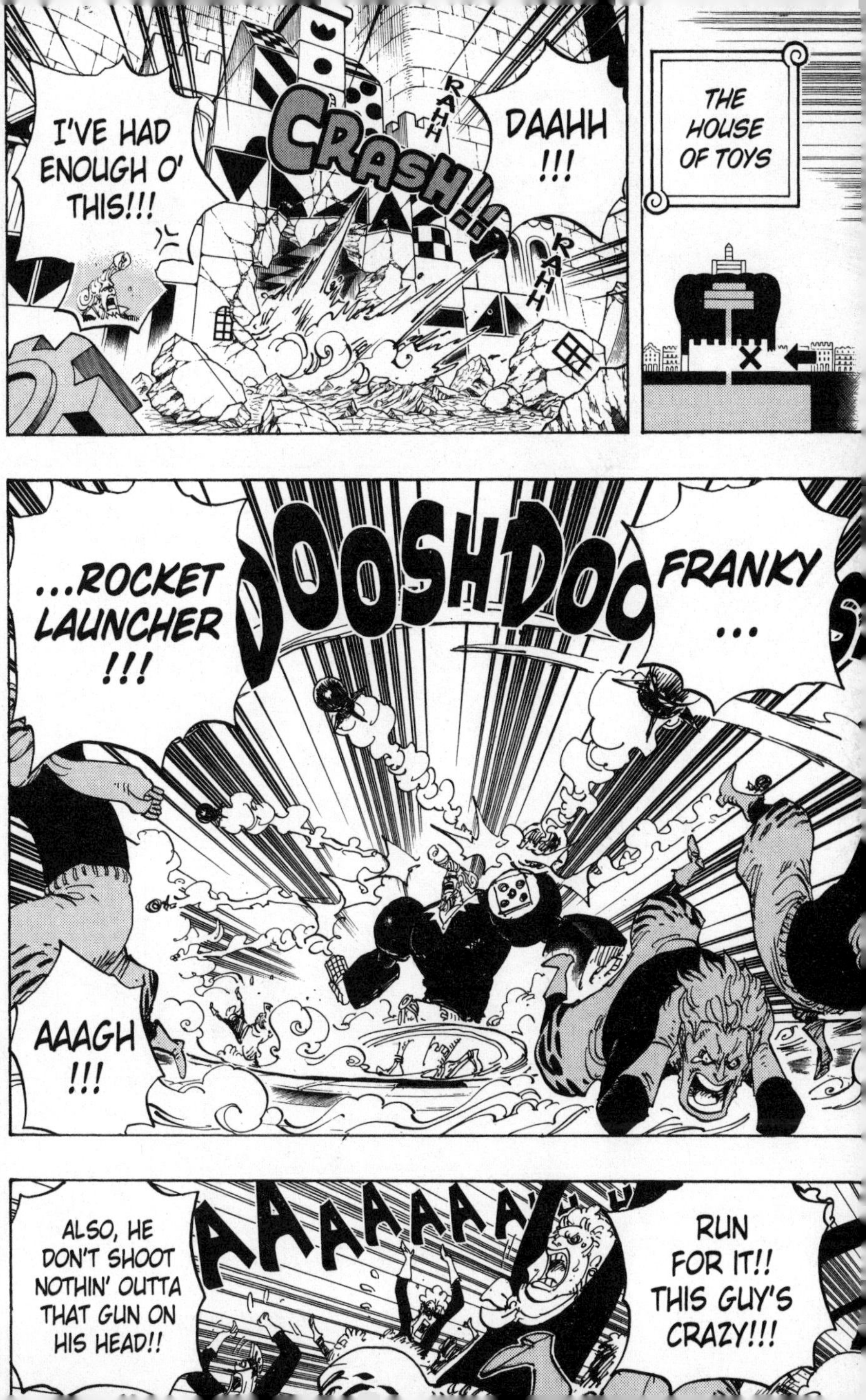
THE HOUSE OF TOYS
DAAHH!!!
RAHH
CRASH!!
RAHH
I'VE HAD ENOUGH O' THIS!!!
FRANKY...
DOOSHDOO
...ROCKET LAUNCHER!!!
AAAGH!!!
RUN FOR IT!! THIS GUY'S CRAZY!!!
AAAAAAA
ALSO, HE DON'T SHOOT NOTHIN' OUTTA THAT GUN ON HIS HEAD!!

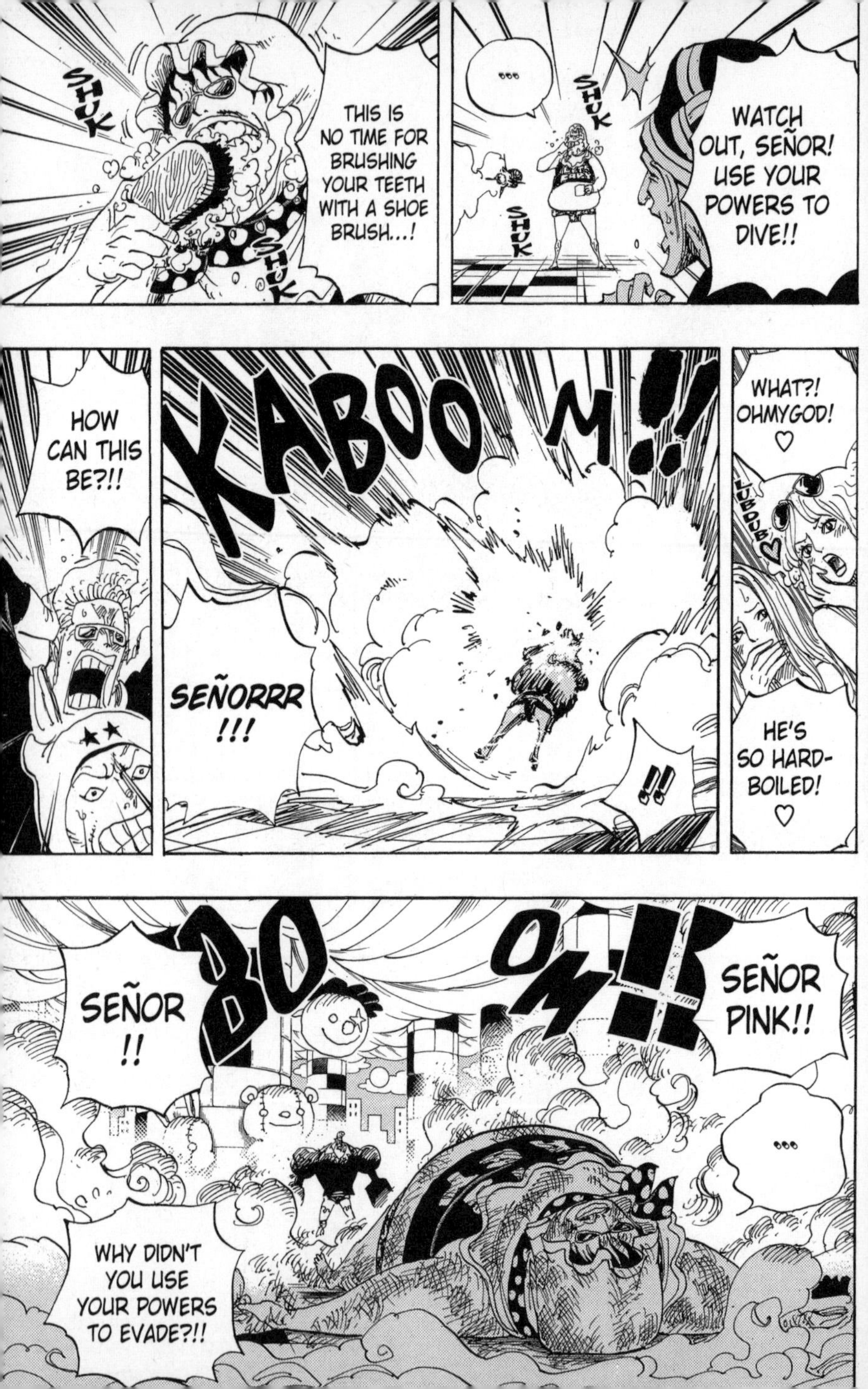
WATCH OUT, SEÑOR! USE YOUR POWERS TO DIVE!!
...
SHUK
SHUK
THIS IS NO TIME FOR BRUSHING YOUR TEETH WITH A SHOE BRUSH...!
SHUK
SHUK
WHAT?! OHMYGOD! ♡
LUBDUB ♡
HE'S SO HARD-BOILED! ♡
KABOOM!!
!!
SEÑORRR!!!
HOW CAN THIS BE?!!
SEÑOR PINK!!
BOOM!!
...
SEÑOR!!
WHY DIDN'T YOU USE YOUR POWERS TO EVADE?!!

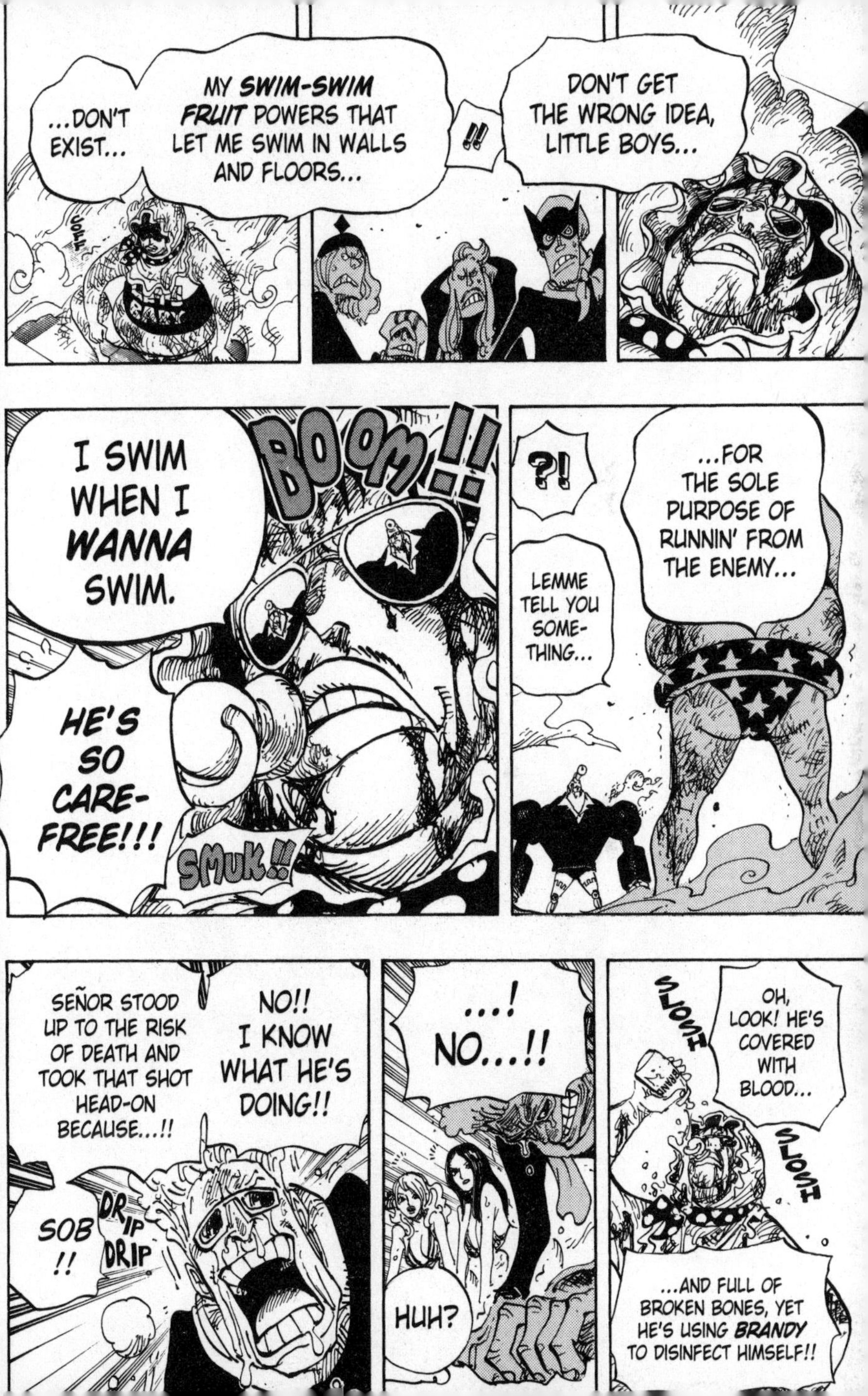
DON'T GET THE WRONG IDEA, LITTLE BOYS...
!!
MY SWIM-SWIM FRUIT POWERS THAT LET ME SWIM IN WALLS AND FLOORS...
...DON'T EXIST...
...FOR THE SOLE PURPOSE OF RUNNIN' FROM THE ENEMY...
?!
LEMME TELL YOU SOME-THING...
BOOM!!
I SWIM WHEN I WANNA SWIM.
HE'S SO CARE-FREE!!!
SMUK!!
SLOSH
OH, LOOK! HE'S COVERED WITH BLOOD...
SLOSH
...AND FULL OF BROKEN BONES, YET HE'S USING BRANDY TO DISINFECT HIMSELF!!
...! NO...!!
HUH?
NO!! I KNOW WHAT HE'S DOING!!
SEÑOR STOOD UP TO THE RISK OF DEATH AND TOOK THAT SHOT HEAD-ON BECAUSE...!!
DRIP DRIP
SOB!!

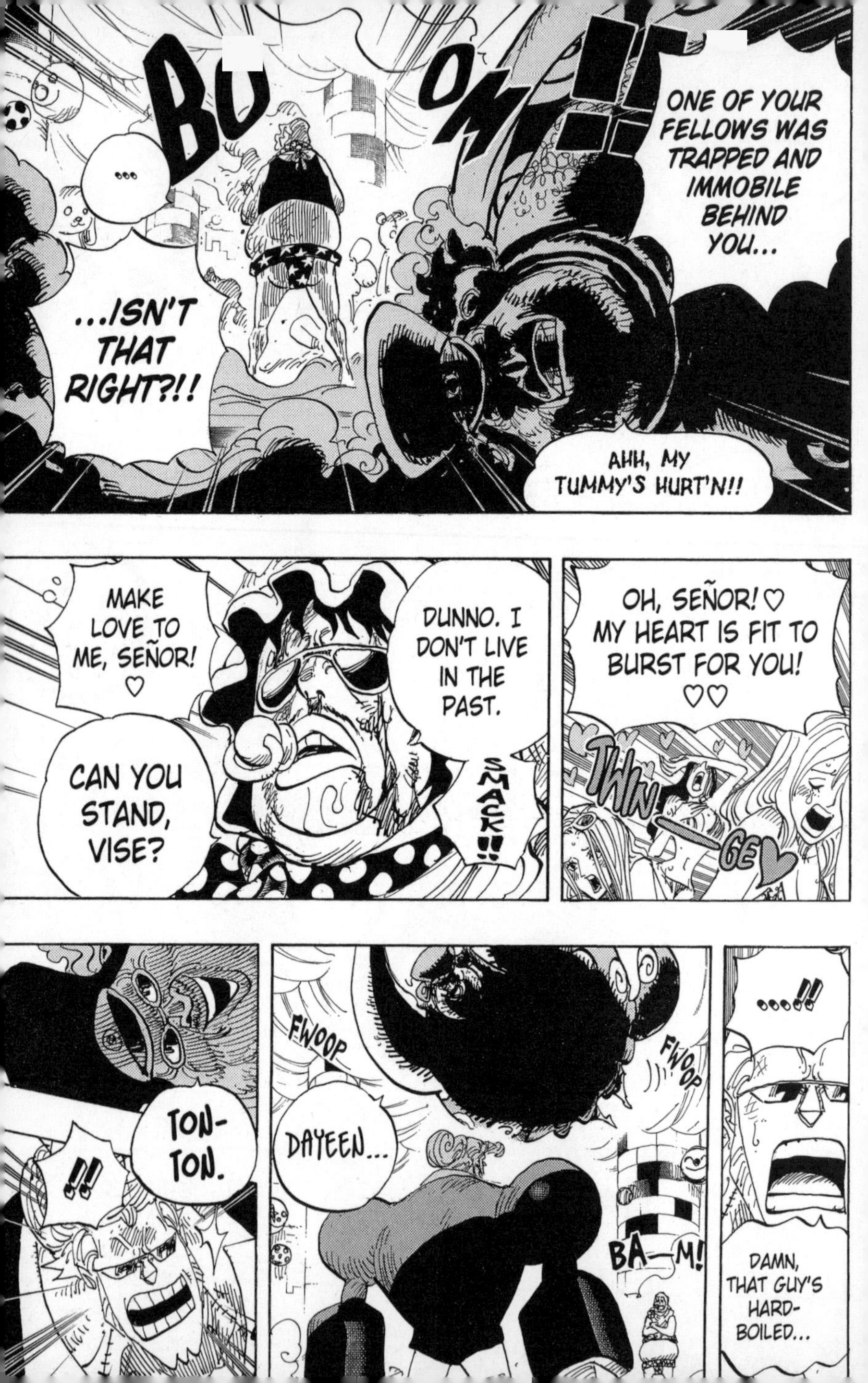
BOOM!!
ONE OF YOUR FELLOWS WAS TRAPPED AND IMMOBILE BEHIND YOU...
...
...ISN'T THAT RIGHT?!!
AHH, MY TUMMY'S HURT'N!!
OH, SEÑOR! ♡ MY HEART IS FIT TO BURST FOR YOU! ♡♡
THWINGE♡
DUNNO. I DON'T LIVE IN THE PAST.
SMACK!!
MAKE LOVE TO ME, SEÑOR! ♡
CAN YOU STAND, VISE?
...!!
DAMN, THAT GUY'S HARD-BOILED...
FWOOP
FWOOP
DAYEEN...
BA—M!
TON-TON.
!!

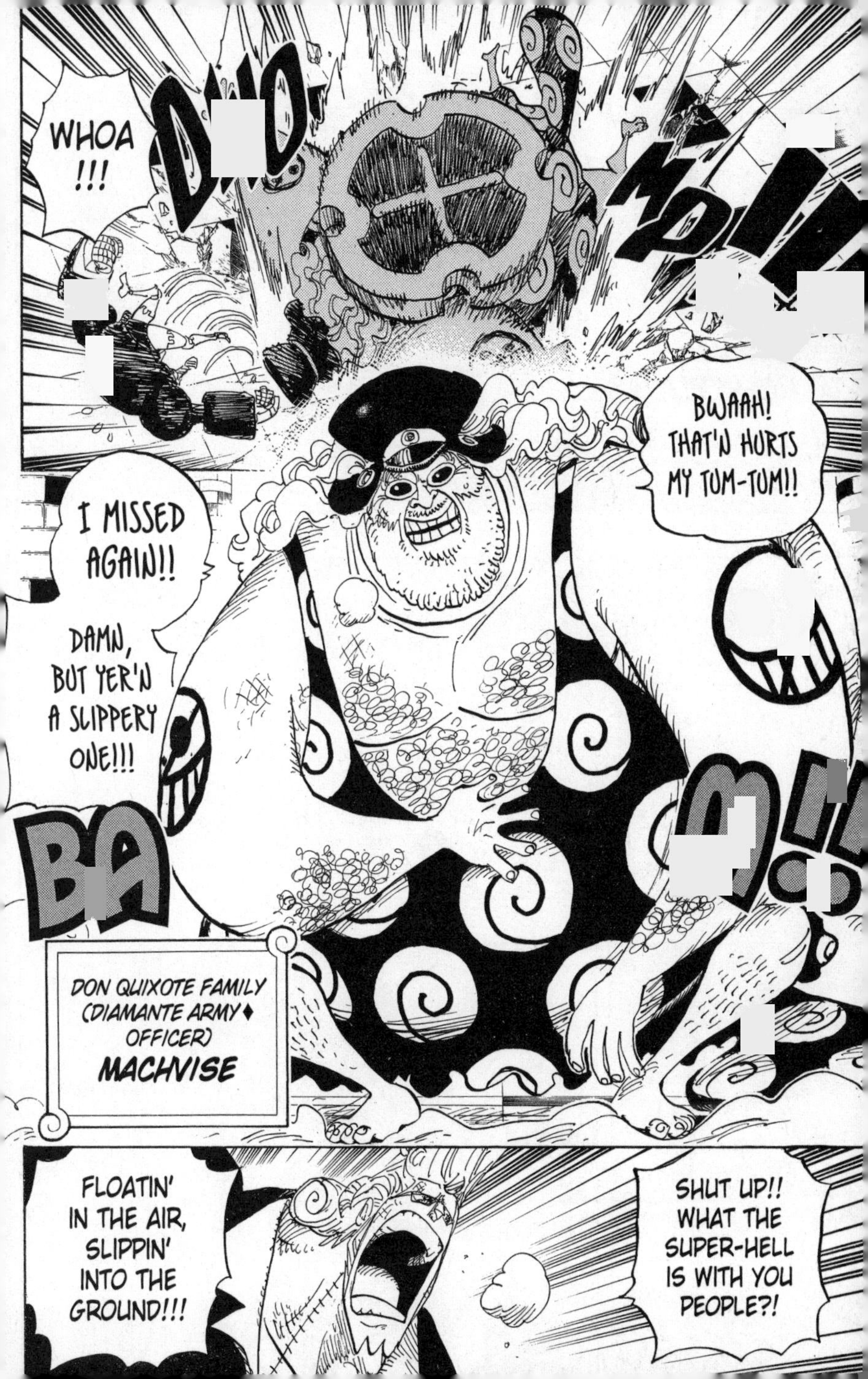
WHOA!!!
BWAAH! THAT'N HURTS MY TUM-TUM!!
I MISSED AGAIN!!
DAMN, BUT YER'N A SLIPPERY ONE!!!
DON QUIXOTE FAMILY (DIAMANTE ARMY ♦ OFFICER) MACHVISE
SHUT UP!! WHAT THE SUPER-HELL IS WITH YOU PEOPLE?!
FLOATIN' IN THE AIR, SLIPPIN' INTO THE GROUND!!!

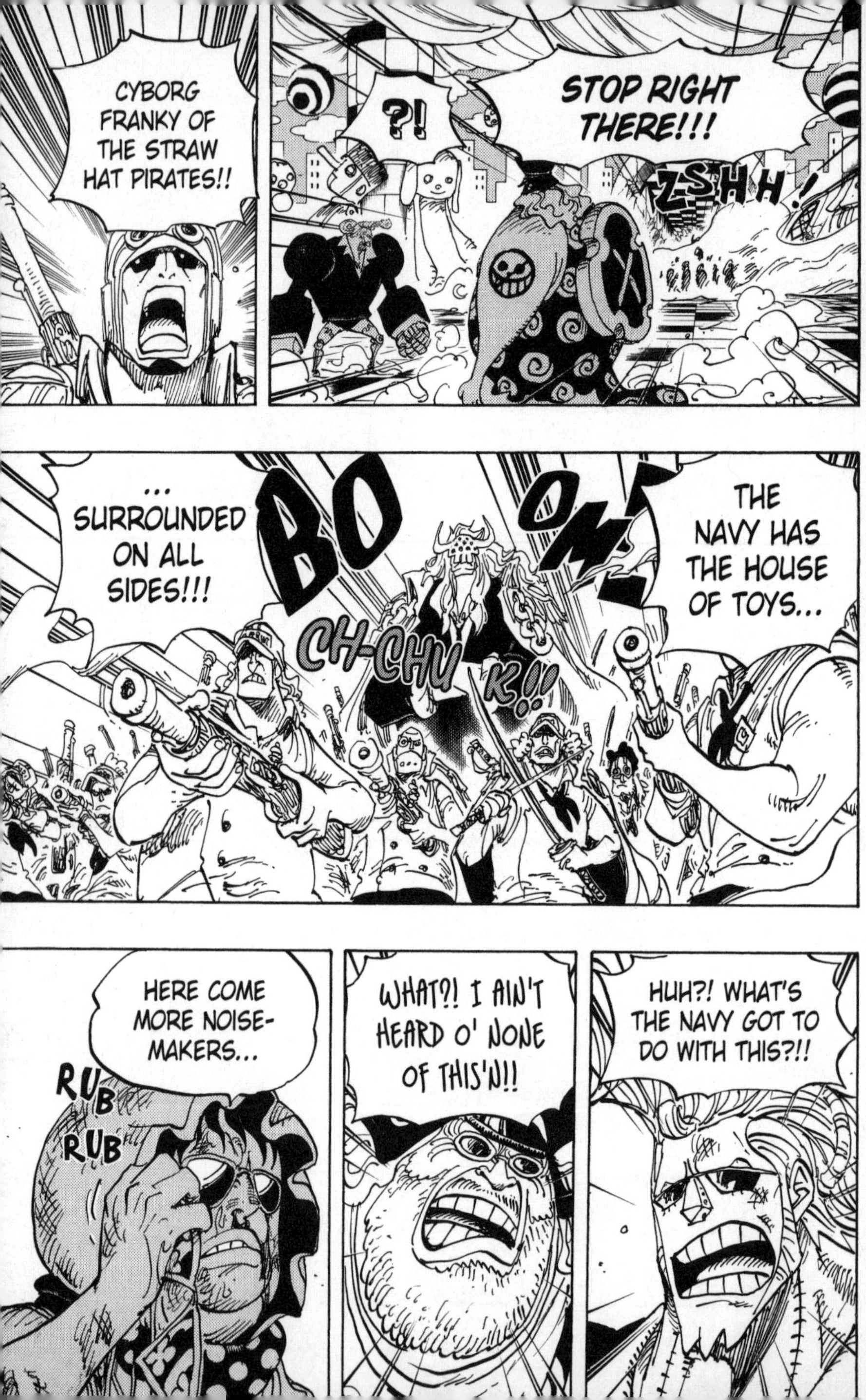
STOP RIGHT THERE!!!
?!
ZSHH!
CYBORG FRANKY OF THE STRAW HAT PIRATES!!
THE NAVY HAS THE HOUSE OF TOYS...
BOOM
... SURROUNDED ON ALL SIDES!!!
CH-CHUK!!
HUH?! WHAT'S THE NAVY GOT TO DO WITH THIS?!!
WHAT?! I AIN'T HEARD O' NONE OF THIS'N!!
HERE COME MORE NOISE-MAKERS...
RUB RUB

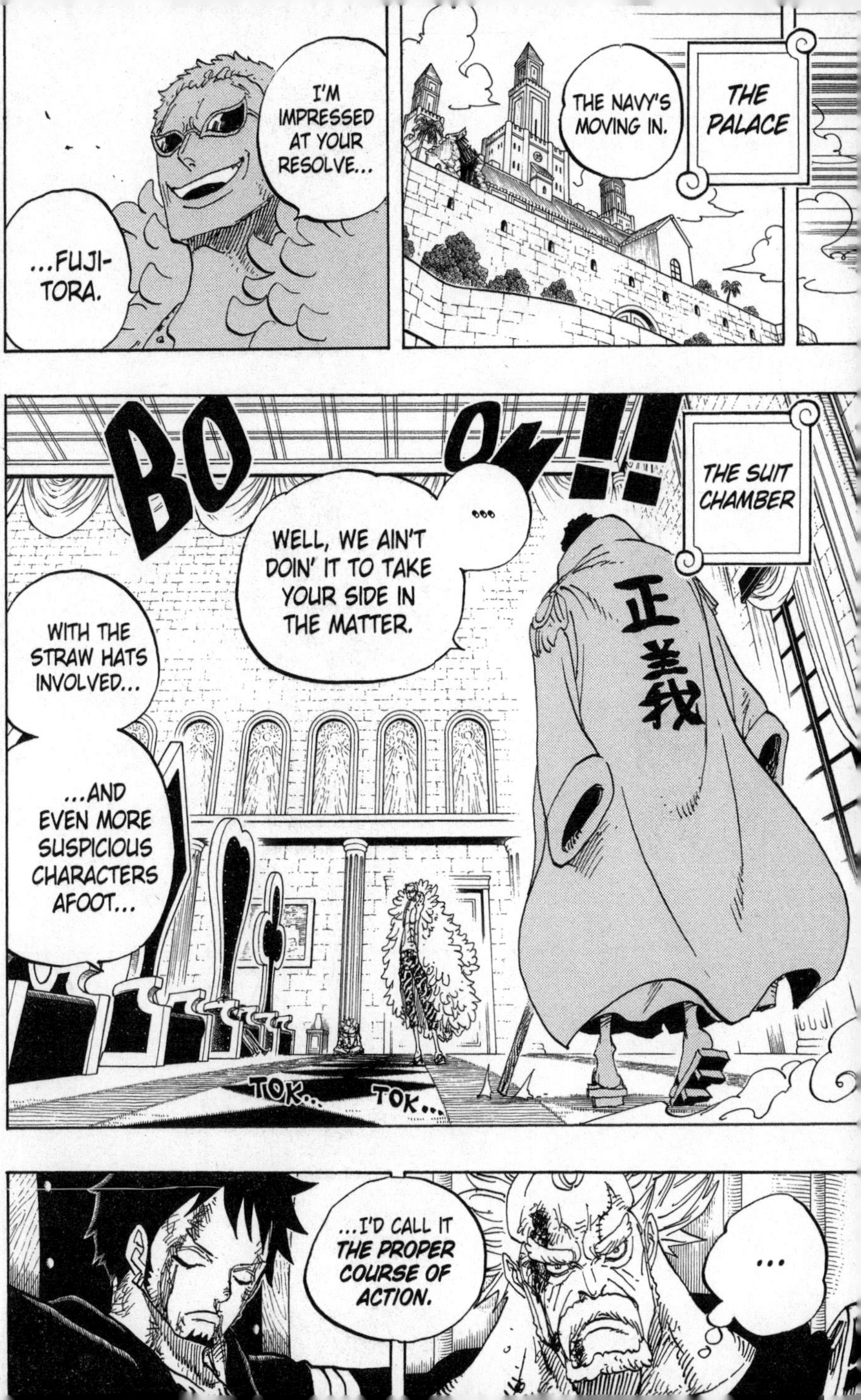
THE PALACE
THE NAVY'S MOVING IN.
I'M IMPRESSED AT YOUR RESOLVE...
...FUJI-TORA.
BOOM!!
THE SUIT CHAMBER
正義
...
WELL, WE AIN'T DOIN' IT TO TAKE YOUR SIDE IN THE MATTER.
WITH THE STRAW HATS INVOLVED...
...AND EVEN MORE SUSPICIOUS CHARACTERS AFOOT...
TOK... TOK...
...
...I'D CALL IT THE PROPER COURSE OF ACTION.

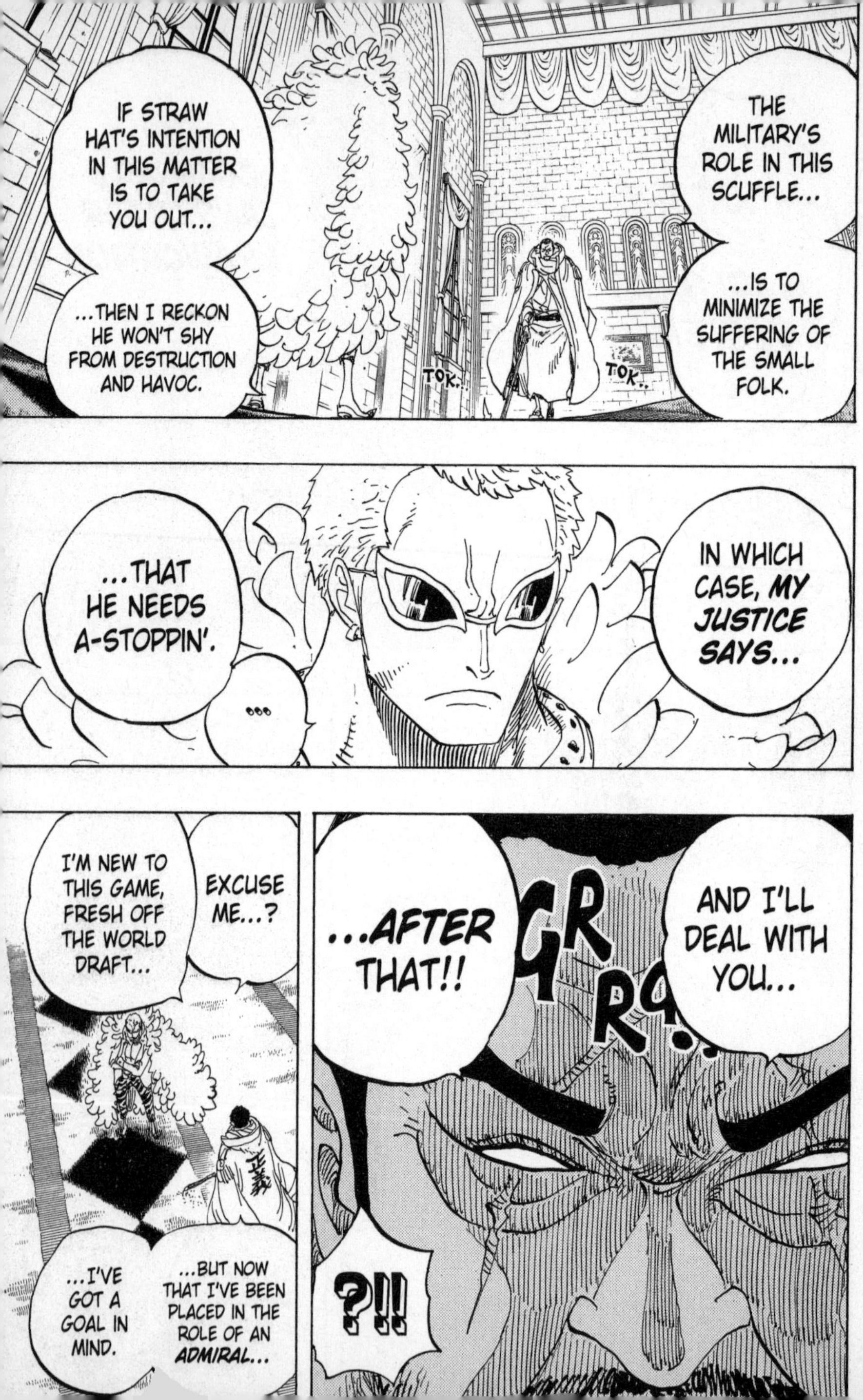

THE MILITARY'S ROLE IN THIS SCUFFLE...
...IS TO MINIMIZE THE SUFFERING OF THE SMALL FOLK.
TOK..
TOK..
IF STRAW HAT'S INTENTION IN THIS MATTER IS TO TAKE YOU OUT...
...THEN I RECKON HE WON'T SHY FROM DESTRUCTION AND HAVOC.
IN WHICH CASE, ***MY JUSTICE SAYS...***
...THAT HE NEEDS A-STOPPIN'.
...
AND I'LL DEAL WITH YOU...
...***AFTER*** THAT!!
?!!
EXCUSE ME...?
I'M NEW TO THIS GAME, FRESH OFF THE WORLD DRAFT...
...BUT NOW THAT I'VE BEEN PLACED IN THE ROLE OF AN ***ADMIRAL...***
...I'VE GOT A GOAL IN MIND.

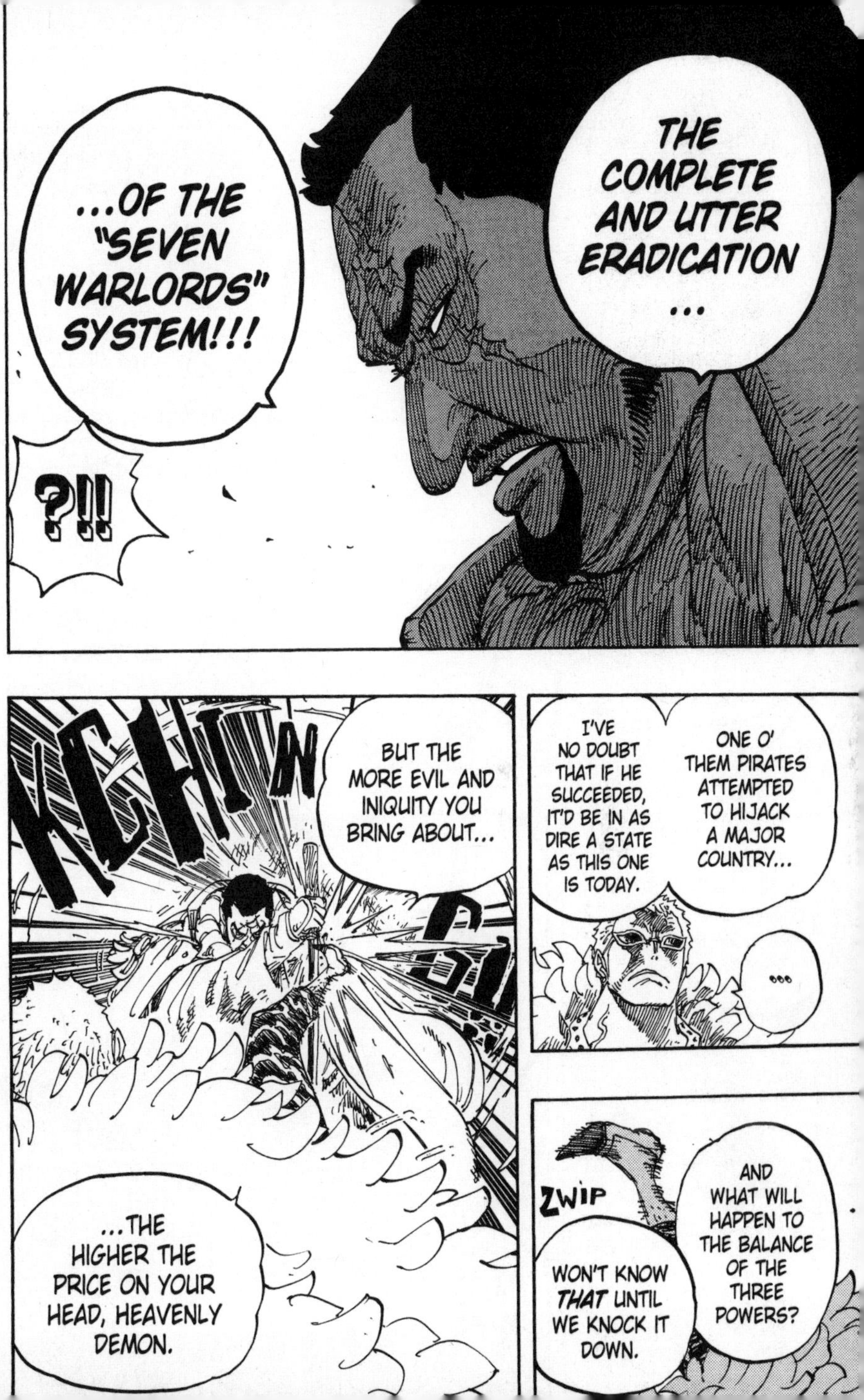
THE COMPLETE AND UTTER ERADICATION ...
...OF THE "SEVEN WARLORDS" SYSTEM!!!
?!!
ONE O' THEM PIRATES ATTEMPTED TO HIJACK A MAJOR COUNTRY...
I'VE NO DOUBT THAT IF HE SUCCEEDED, IT'D BE IN AS DIRE A STATE AS THIS ONE IS TODAY.
...
AND WHAT WILL HAPPEN TO THE BALANCE OF THE THREE POWERS?
ZWIP
WON'T KNOW *THAT* UNTIL WE KNOCK IT DOWN.
BUT THE MORE EVIL AND INIQUITY YOU BRING ABOUT...
...THE HIGHER THE PRICE ON YOUR HEAD, HEAVENLY DEMON.

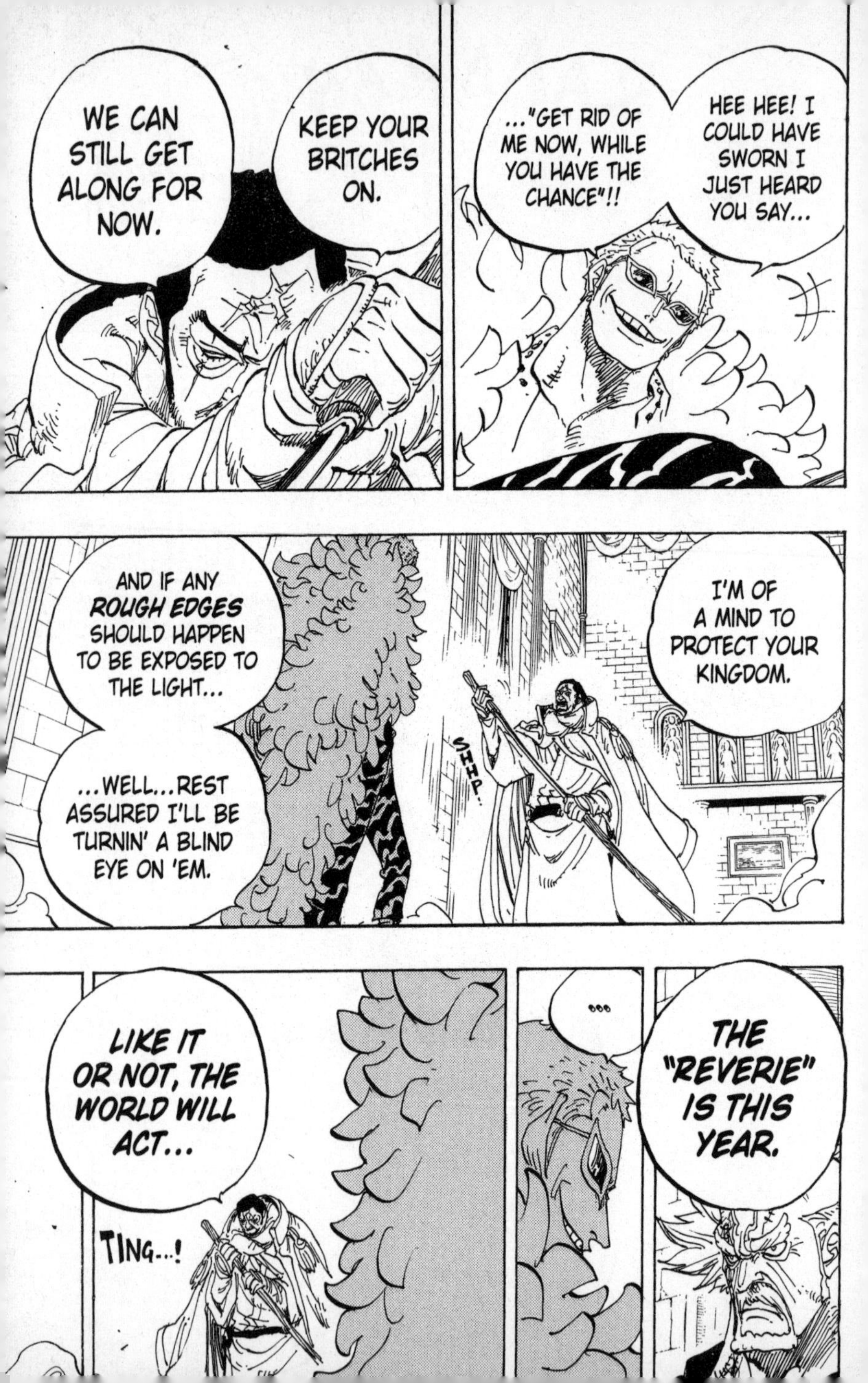
HEE HEE! I COULD HAVE SWORN I JUST HEARD YOU SAY...
..."GET RID OF ME NOW, WHILE YOU HAVE THE CHANCE"!!
KEEP YOUR BRITCHES ON.
WE CAN STILL GET ALONG FOR NOW.
I'M OF A MIND TO PROTECT YOUR KINGDOM.
SHHP.
AND IF ANY ROUGH EDGES SHOULD HAPPEN TO BE EXPOSED TO THE LIGHT...
...WELL...REST ASSURED I'LL BE TURNIN' A BLIND EYE ON 'EM.
THE "REVERIE" IS THIS YEAR.
...
LIKE IT OR NOT, THE WORLD WILL ACT...
TING...!

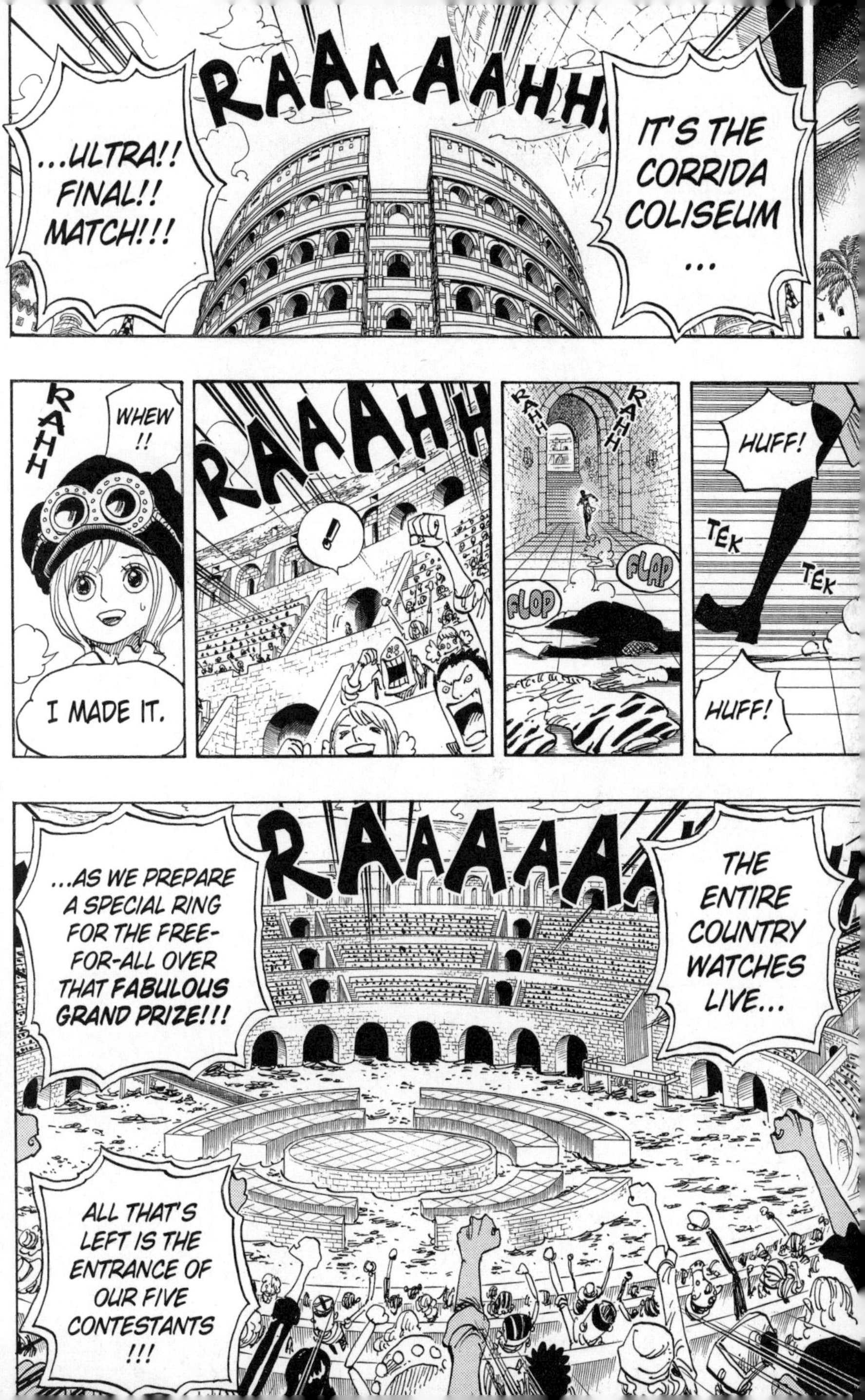
IT'S THE CORRIDA COLISEUM ...
RAAAAAHHH
...ULTRA!! FINAL!! MATCH!!!
HUFF!
TEK
TEK
HUFF!
RAHH
RAHH
FLAP
FLOP
RAAHH
!
RAHH
WHEW !!
I MADE IT.
THE ENTIRE COUNTRY WATCHES LIVE...
RAAAAA
...AS WE PREPARE A SPECIAL RING FOR THE FREE-FOR-ALL OVER THAT FABULOUS GRAND PRIZE!!!
ALL THAT'S LEFT IS THE ENTRANCE OF OUR FIVE CONTESTANTS !!!

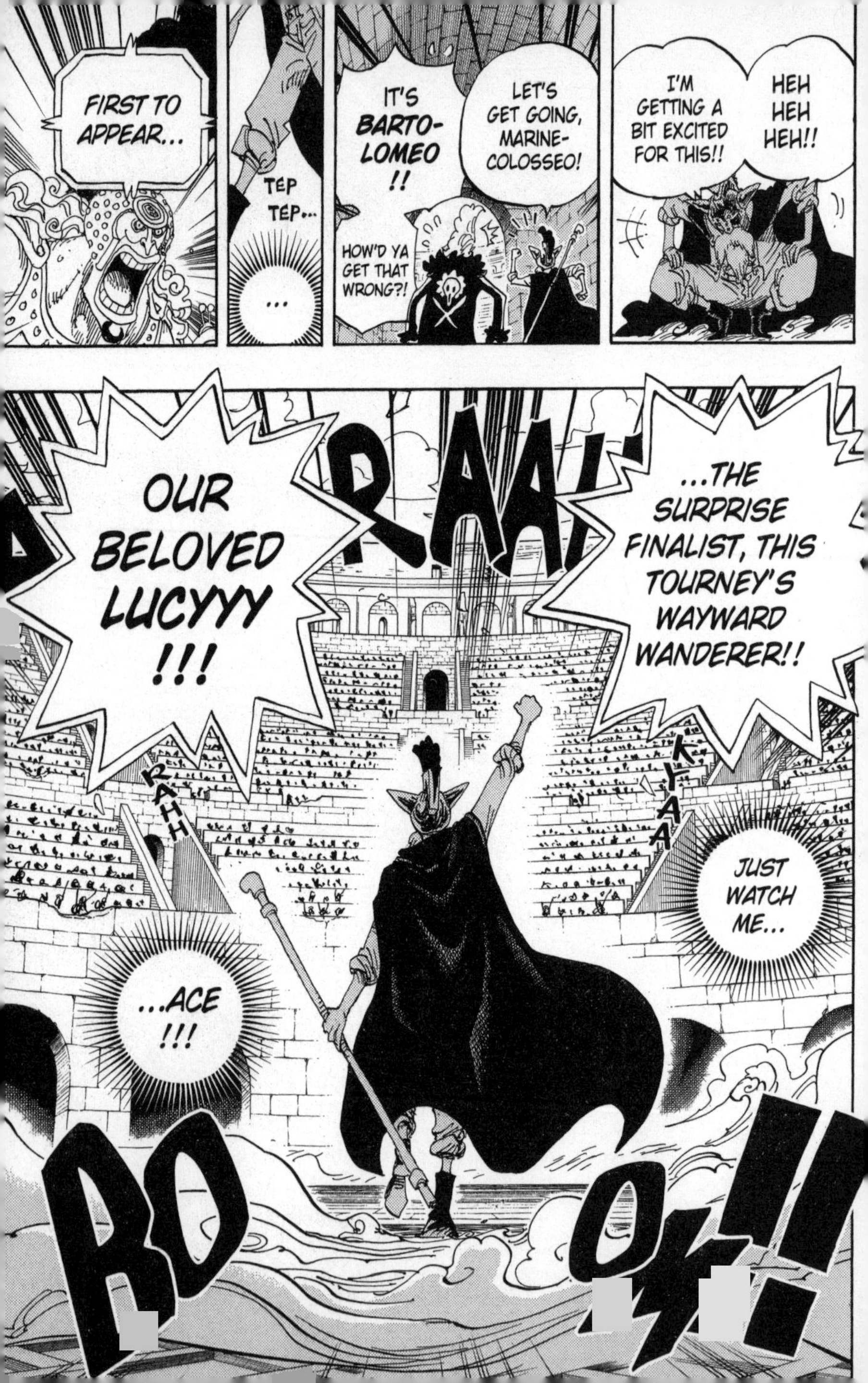
HEH HEH HEH!!
I'M GETTING A BIT EXCITED FOR THIS!!
LET'S GET GOING, MARINE-COLOSSEO!
IT'S BARTO-LOMEO!!
HOW'D YA GET THAT WRONG?!
TEP TEP...
...
FIRST TO APPEAR...
...THE SURPRISE FINALIST, THIS TOURNEY'S WAYWARD WANDERER!!
RAA
OUR BELOVED LUCYYY!!!
KYAA
JUST WATCH ME...
RAHH
...ACE!!!
RO
O!!

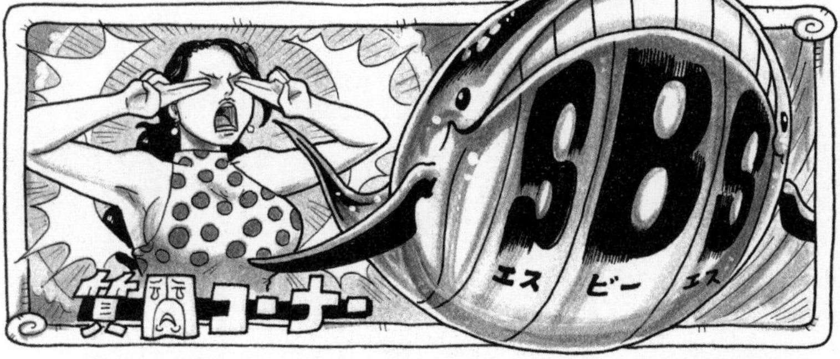
SBS
エス ビー エス

(Hippo Iron, Saitama)

Q: Can Fujitora's birthday be August 10? "Fu" can refer to 8, and "to" can be 10.

--Torohitamanu

A: Hmm... (pretending to mull it over) Hmm... (pretending to mull it over) Zzz... (fell asleep) Ah!! (Woke up) Okay. (doesn't really care)

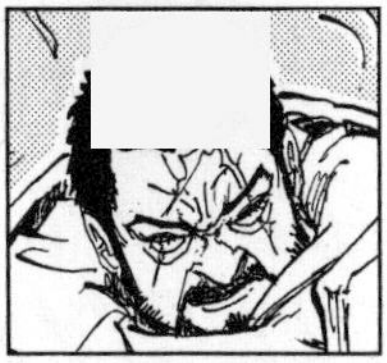

Q: Heya, Odacchi! Is Fujitora based on the role of Zatoichi, the blind swordsman played by Shintaro Katsu? I don't know who that is, but Mommy and Daddy said so.

--Mitarashi Dango

A: Yes, that's right. My generation would never mistake good old "Katsu-Shin," but I suppose the younger folks wouldn't know him. There are plenty of newer movies with the Zatoichi title, but he was originally a sub-character from a totally different story played by an actor named Shintaro Katsu. Between TV productions and movies, there are over a hundred pieces of film based on this famous character. Let me guess, you're not interested? I know that! So anyway, Katsu-Shin really hated reading scripts, so when it came to the TV shows...

Q: Mr. Oda, when will we get to see Naval Admiral Momousagi (Pink Rabbit)? Sexy dynamite Momousagi, with her lethal knockout beauty! I can barely sleep at night from all the anticipation.

--Sanji's Brother, Yonji 2

A: Hmm? Momousagi...?
Umm, the current admirals are Kizaru...Fujitora...Ryokugyu...
Momousagi? Oh! I know who you mean.
Y-yeah, of course! The vice admiral! She was one of the candidates for admiral, right? Yeah, totally! I can show you right now. This is Vice Admiral Momousagi. ➡
Some say she might be modeled after a young Michiyo Kogure.

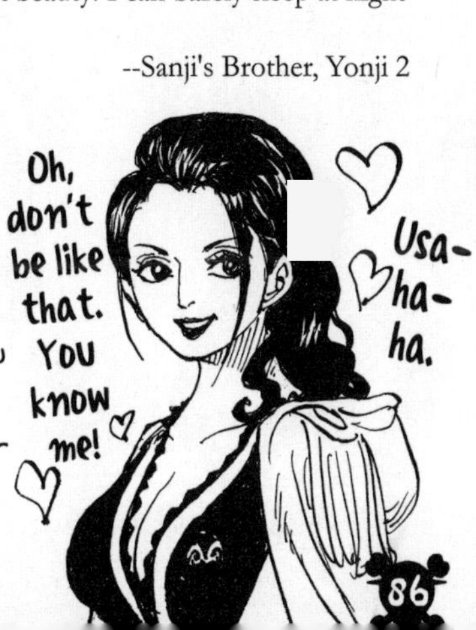
Oh, don't be like that. You know me!
Usa-ha-ha.

Chapter 736:
SUPREME OFFICER DIAMANTE

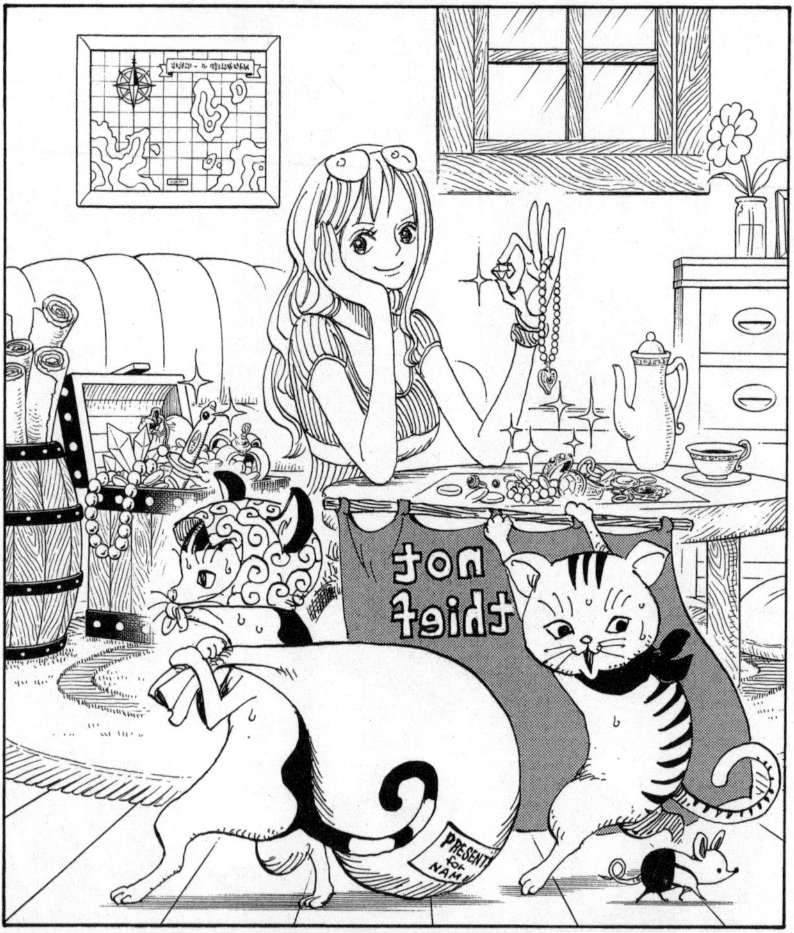
PRESENT
for
NAM

REQUEST: "NAMI THE CAT BURGLAR GETS BURGLARIZED BY SOME CATS" BY JUN SANPEI (FEMALE)

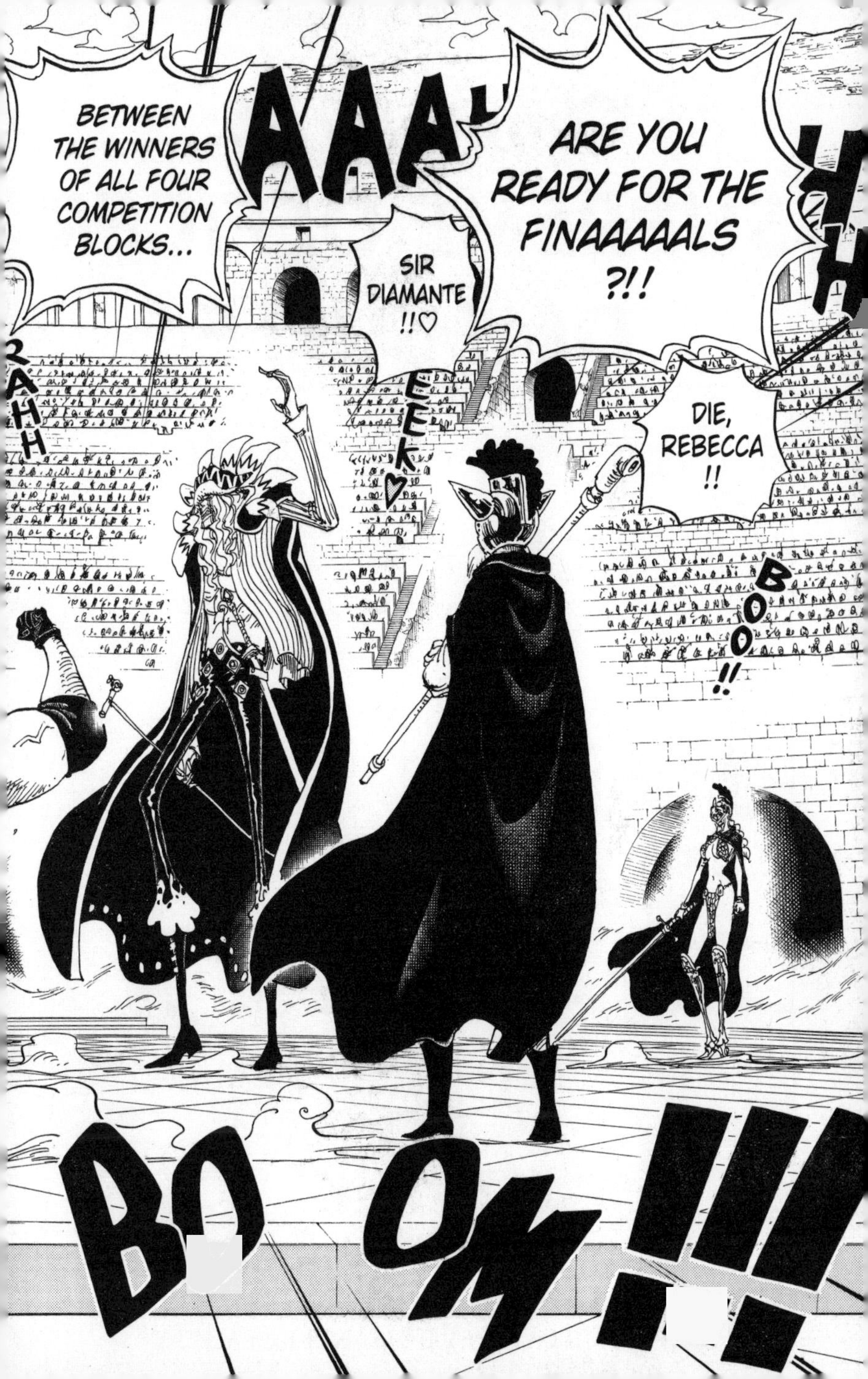

BETWEEN THE WINNERS OF ALL FOUR COMPETITION BLOCKS...
ARE YOU READY FOR THE FINAAAAALS ?!!
AAAAH
SIR DIAMANTE !!♡
DIE, REBECCA !!
RAHH
EEEK♥
BOO!!
BOOM!!!!

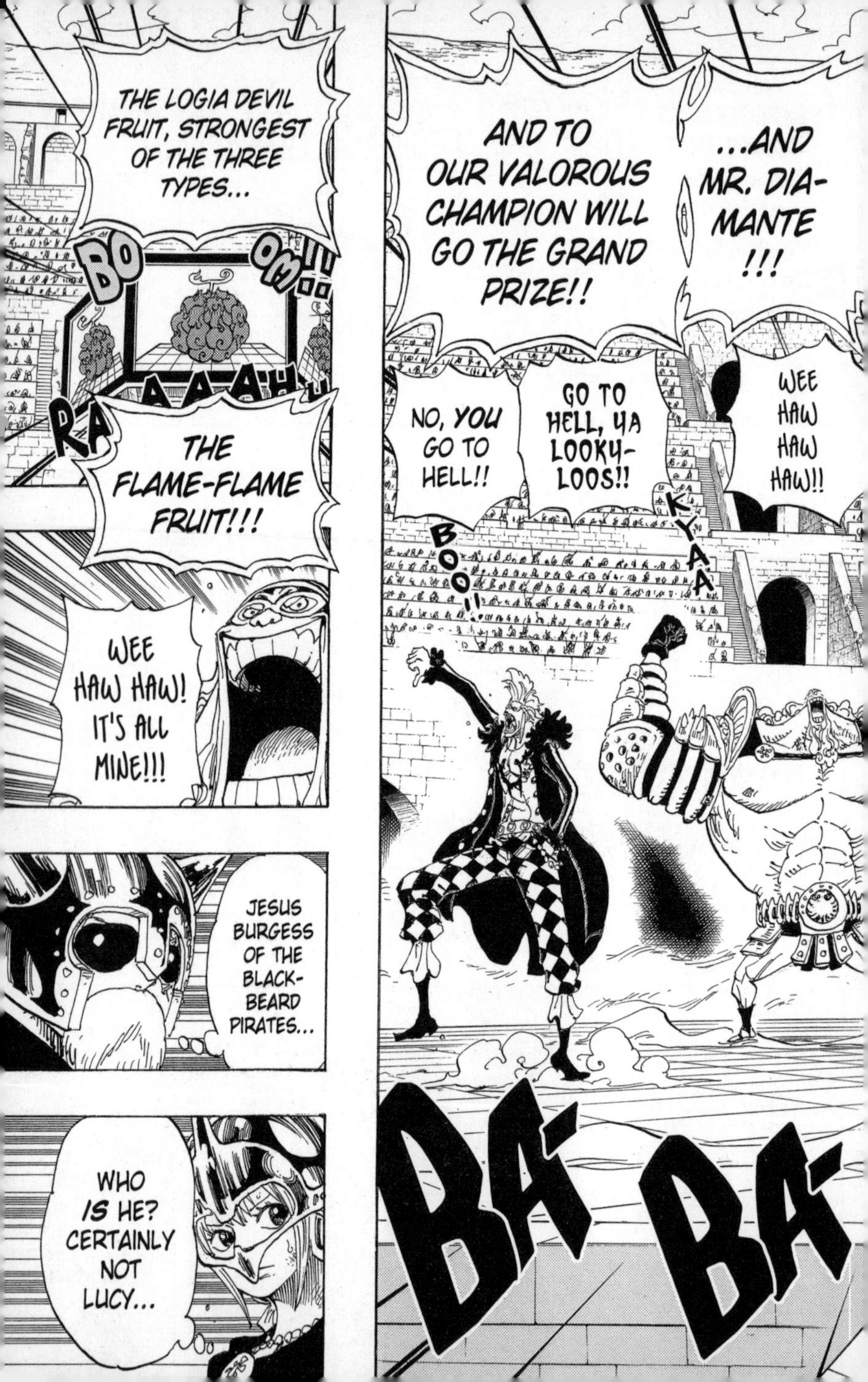
THE LOGIA DEVIL FRUIT, STRONGEST OF THE THREE TYPES...
BOOM!!
RAAAAH!!
THE FLAME-FLAME FRUIT!!!
WEE HAW HAW! IT'S ALL MINE!!!
JESUS BURGESS OF THE BLACKBEARD PIRATES...
WHO IS HE? CERTAINLY NOT LUCY...
AND TO OUR VALOROUS CHAMPION WILL GO THE GRAND PRIZE!!
...AND MR. DIAMANTE!!!
NO, YOU GO TO HELL!!
GO TO HELL, YA LOOKY-LOOS!!
WEE HAW HAW HAW!!
BOO!!
KYAA
BA BA

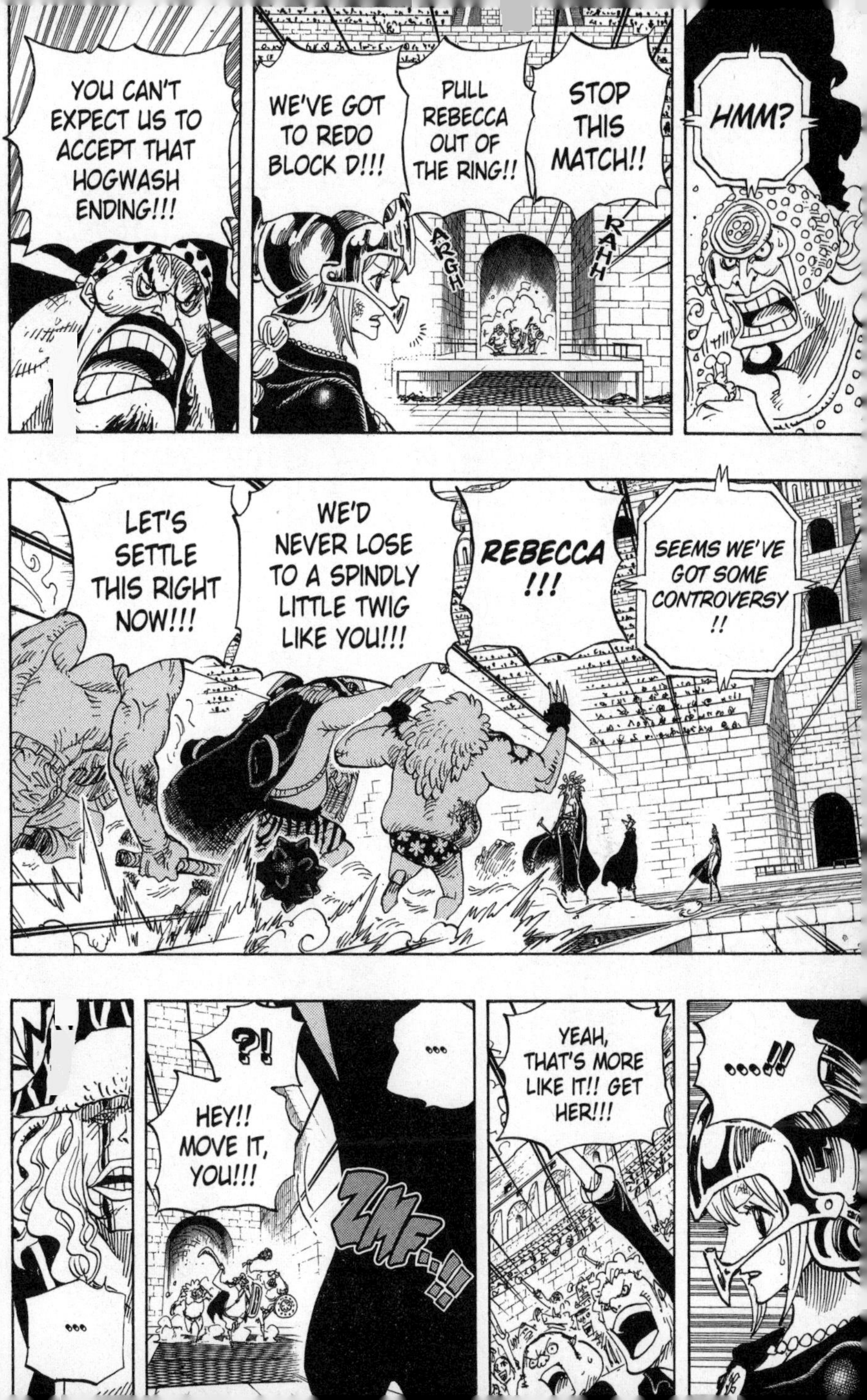
HMM?
STOP THIS MATCH!!
RAHH
PULL REBECCA OUT OF THE RING!!
ARGH
WE'VE GOT TO REDO BLOCK D!!!
YOU CAN'T EXPECT US TO ACCEPT THAT HOGWASH ENDING!!!
SEEMS WE'VE GOT SOME CONTROVERSY !!
REBECCA !!!
WE'D NEVER LOSE TO A SPINDLY LITTLE TWIG LIKE YOU!!!
LET'S SETTLE THIS RIGHT NOW!!!
...!!
YEAH, THAT'S MORE LIKE IT!! GET HER!!!
...
?!
HEY!! MOVE IT, YOU!!!
ZMF...!!
...

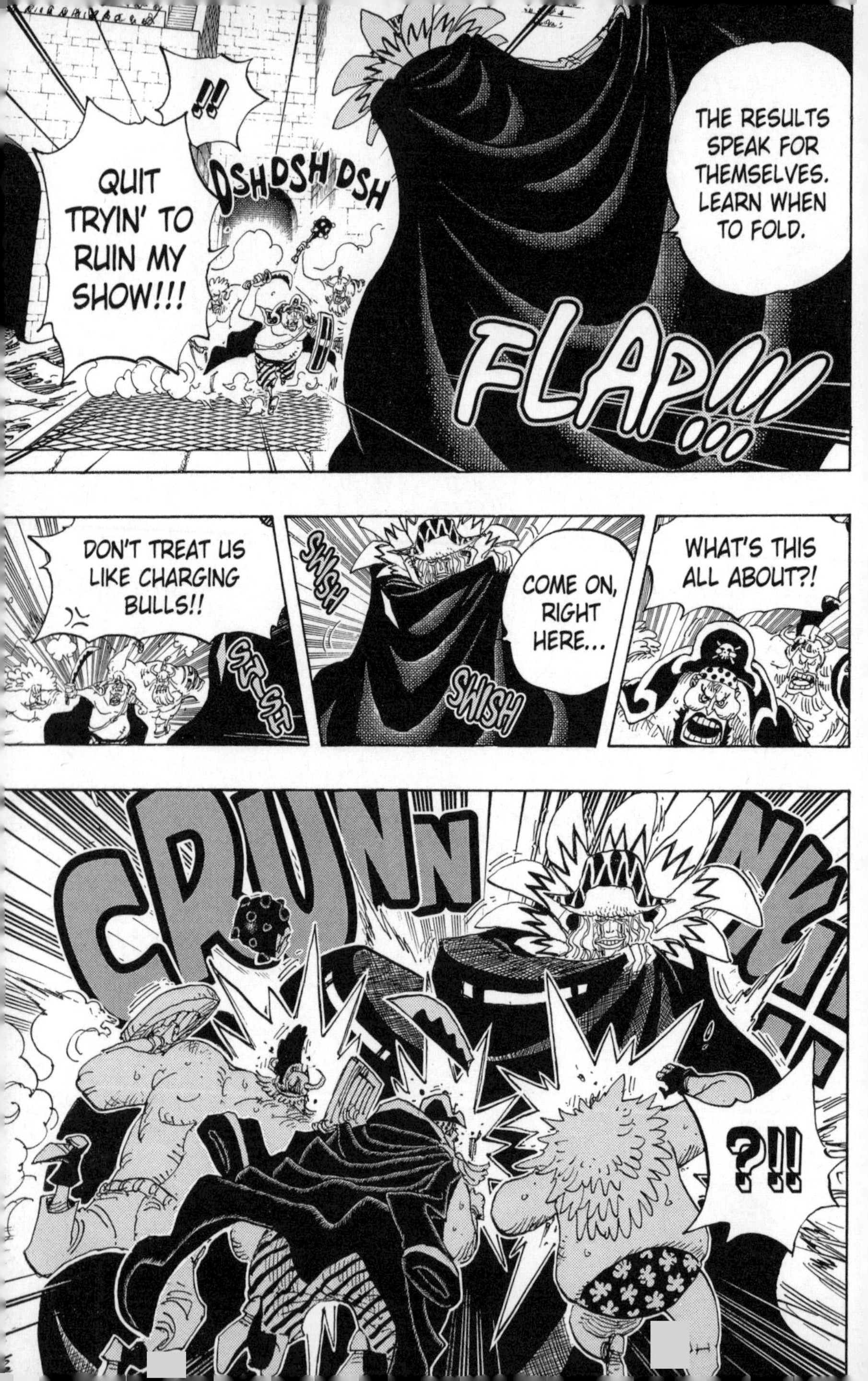
THE RESULTS SPEAK FOR THEMSELVES. LEARN WHEN TO FOLD.
FLAP!!!
!!
DSHDSHDSH
QUIT TRYIN' TO RUIN MY SHOW!!!
WHAT'S THIS ALL ABOUT?!
COME ON, RIGHT HERE...
SHISH
SHISH
DON'T TREAT US LIKE CHARGING BULLS!!
SHISH
CRUNN
?!!

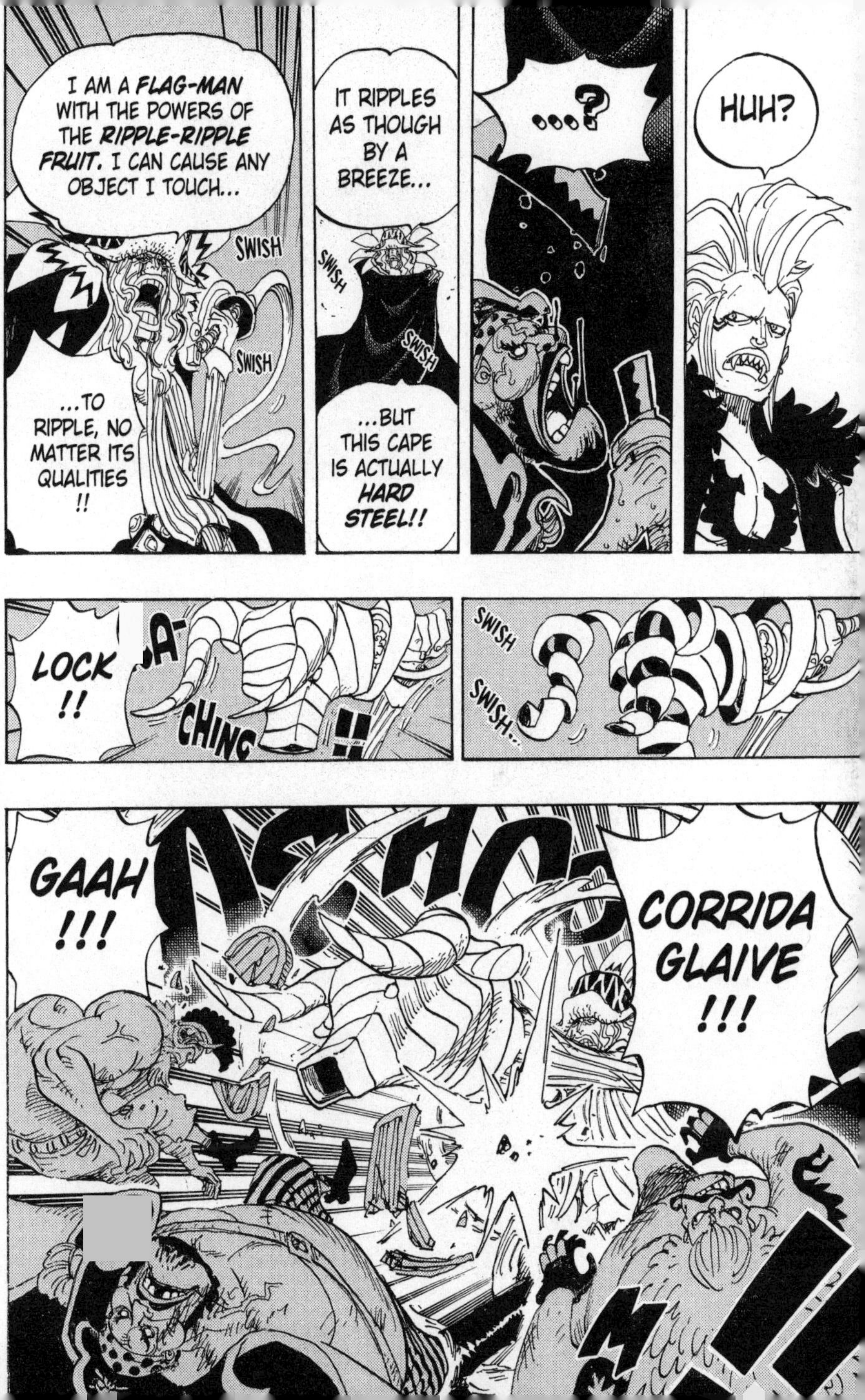
HUH?
...?
IT RIPPLES AS THOUGH BY A BREEZE...
SWISH
SWISH
...BUT THIS CAPE IS ACTUALLY HARD STEEL!!
I AM A FLAG-MAN WITH THE POWERS OF THE RIPPLE-RIPPLE FRUIT. I CAN CAUSE ANY OBJECT I TOUCH...
SWISH
SWISH
...TO RIPPLE, NO MATTER ITS QUALITIES!!
SWISH
SWISH...
LOCK!!
CHING
CORRIDA GLAIVE!!!
GAAH!!!

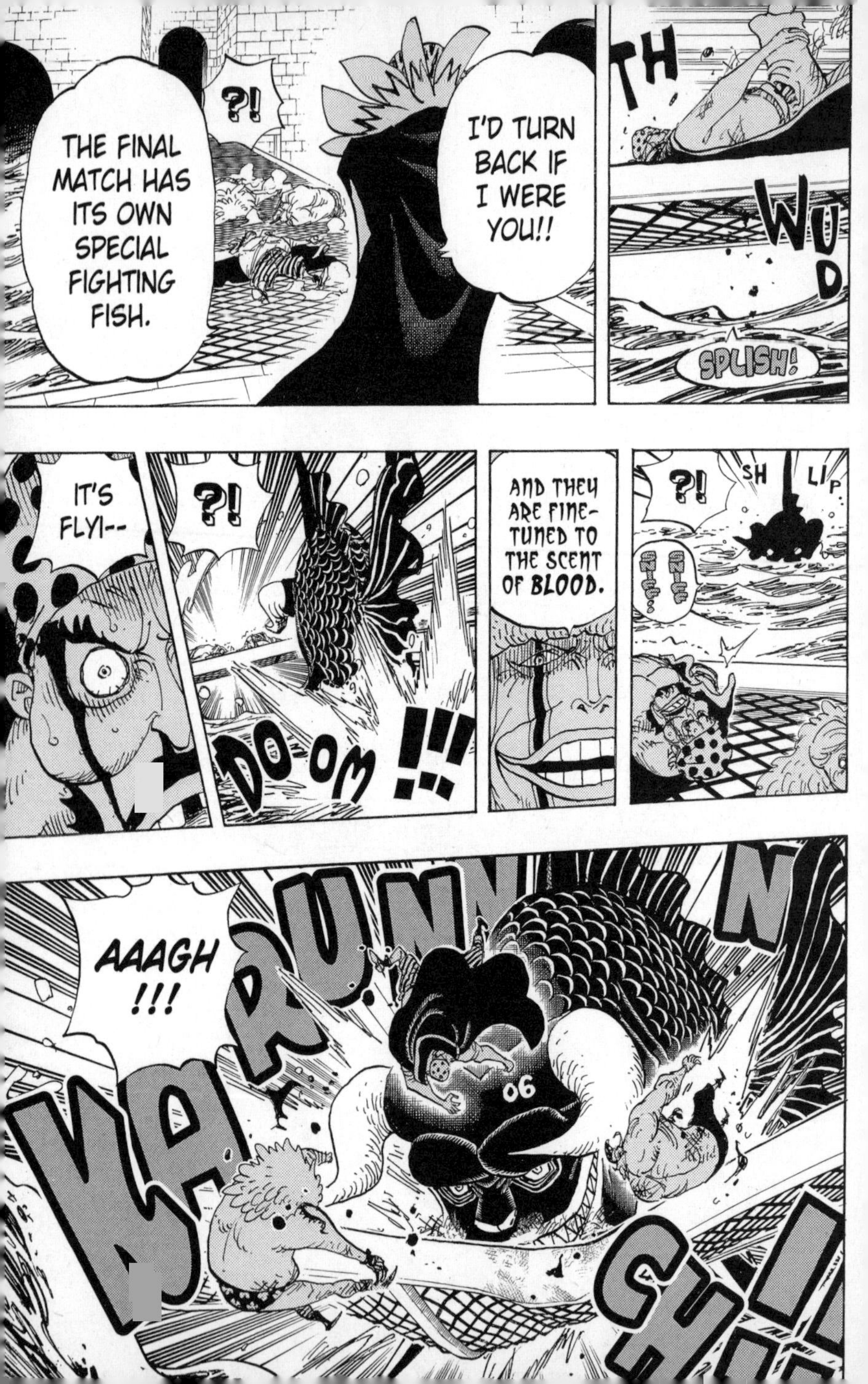
TH
WUD
SPLISH!
I'D TURN BACK IF I WERE YOU!!
?!
THE FINAL MATCH HAS ITS OWN SPECIAL FIGHTING FISH.
?!
SHLIP
SNIFF SNIFF
AND THEY ARE FINE-TUNED TO THE SCENT OF BLOOD.
?!
DOOM!!!
IT'S FLYI--
AAAGH!!!
KARUNNN

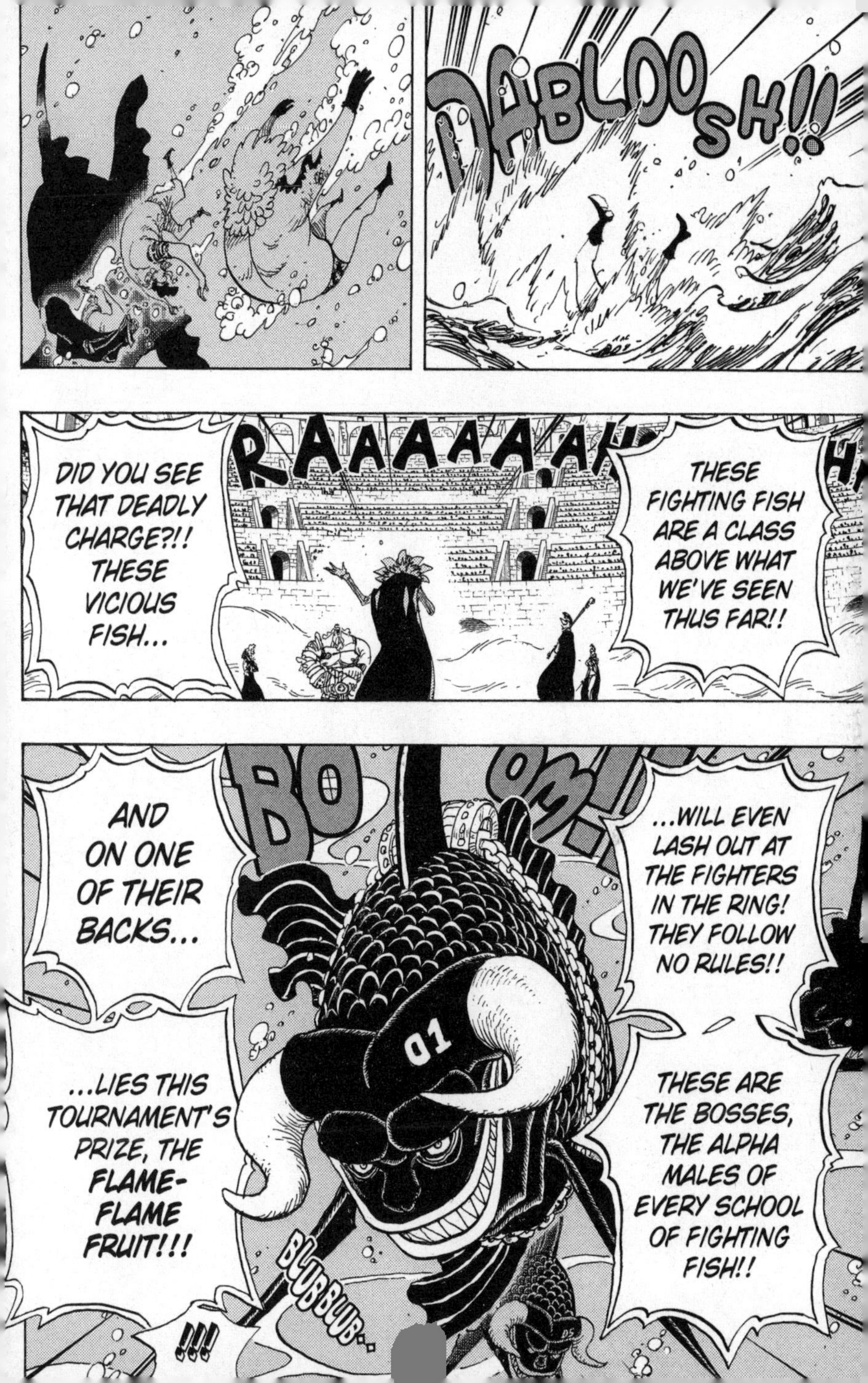
DABLOOSH!!
RAAAAAA
THESE FIGHTING FISH ARE A CLASS ABOVE WHAT WE'VE SEEN THUS FAR!!
DID YOU SEE THAT DEADLY CHARGE?!! THESE VICIOUS FISH...
BOOM!!
...WILL EVEN LASH OUT AT THE FIGHTERS IN THE RING! THEY FOLLOW NO RULES!!
AND ON ONE OF THEIR BACKS...
THESE ARE THE BOSSES, THE ALPHA MALES OF EVERY SCHOOL OF FIGHTING FISH!!
...LIES THIS TOURNAMENT'S PRIZE, THE FLAME-FLAME FRUIT!!!
01
BLUBBLUB
!!!

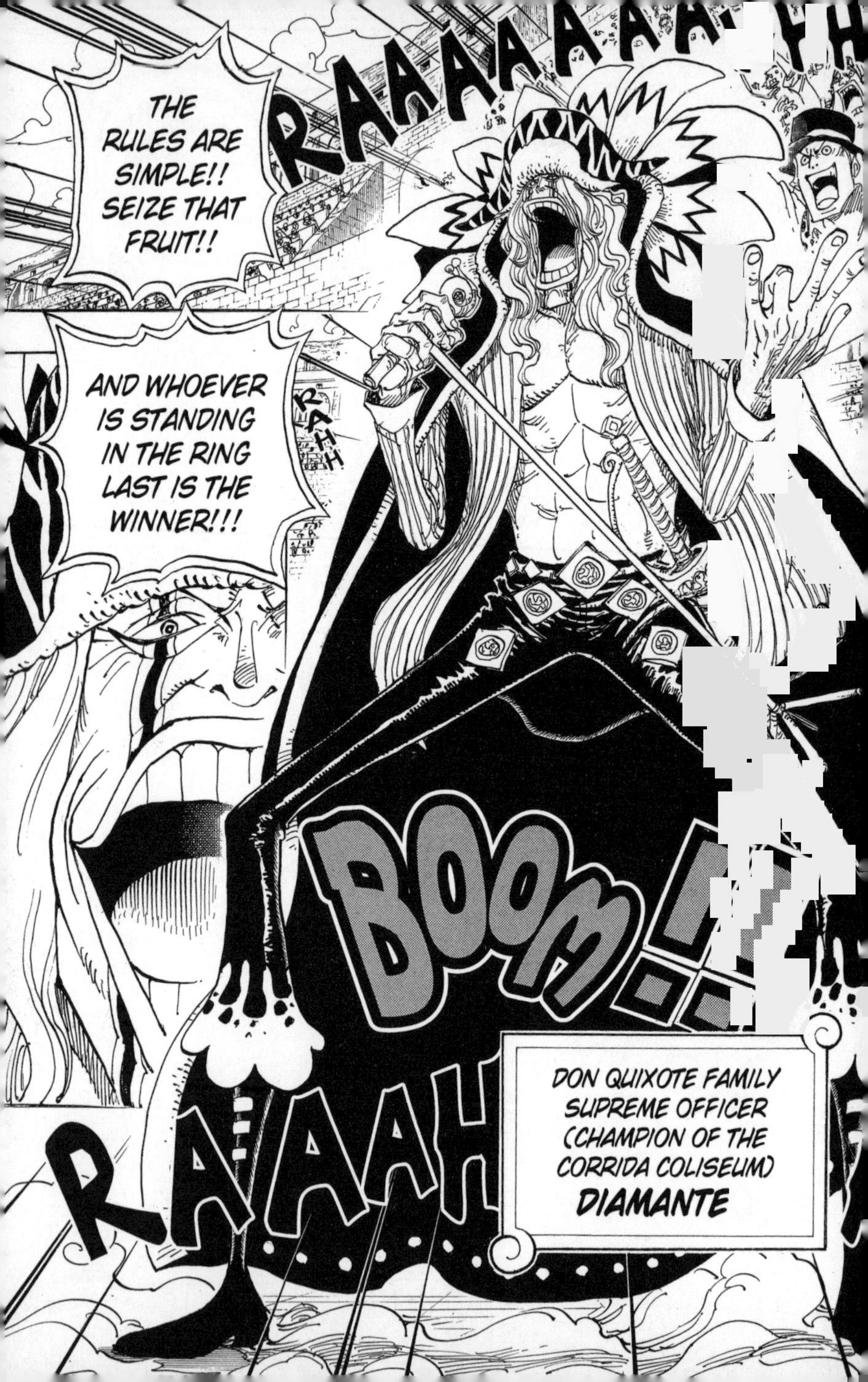
THE RULES ARE SIMPLE!! SEIZE THAT FRUIT!!
AND WHOEVER IS STANDING IN THE RING LAST IS THE WINNER!!!
RAHH
BOOM!!
RAAAH
DON QUIXOTE FAMILY SUPREME OFFICER (CHAMPION OF THE CORRIDA COLISEUM) DIAMANTE

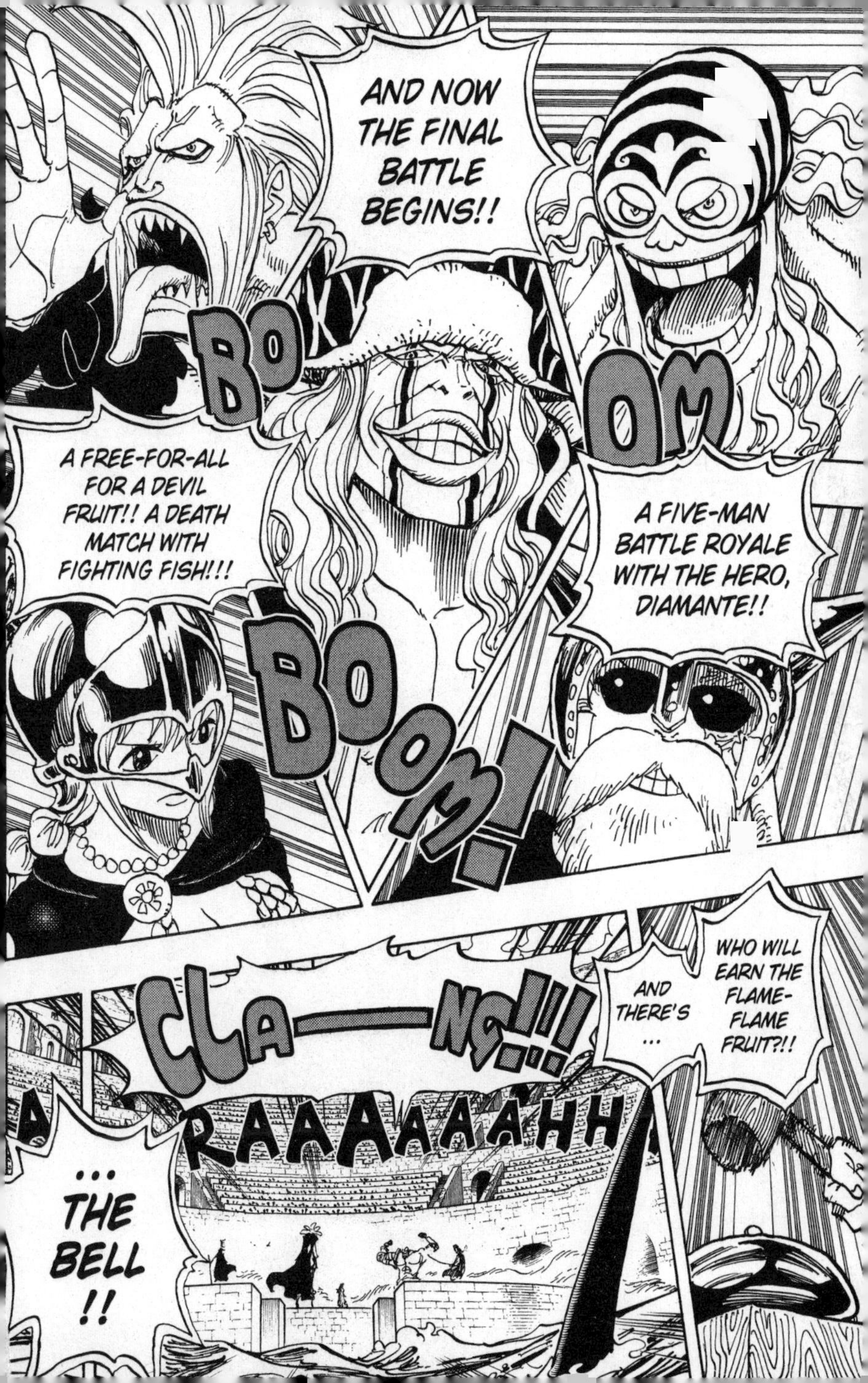
AND NOW THE FINAL BATTLE BEGINS!!
BO OM
A FIVE-MAN BATTLE ROYALE WITH THE HERO, DIAMANTE!!
A FREE-FOR-ALL FOR A DEVIL FRUIT!! A DEATH MATCH WITH FIGHTING FISH!!!
BOOOM!!
WHO WILL EARN THE FLAME-FLAME FRUIT?!!
AND THERE'S ...
CLA——NG!!!
RAAAAAAHH
... THE BELL !!

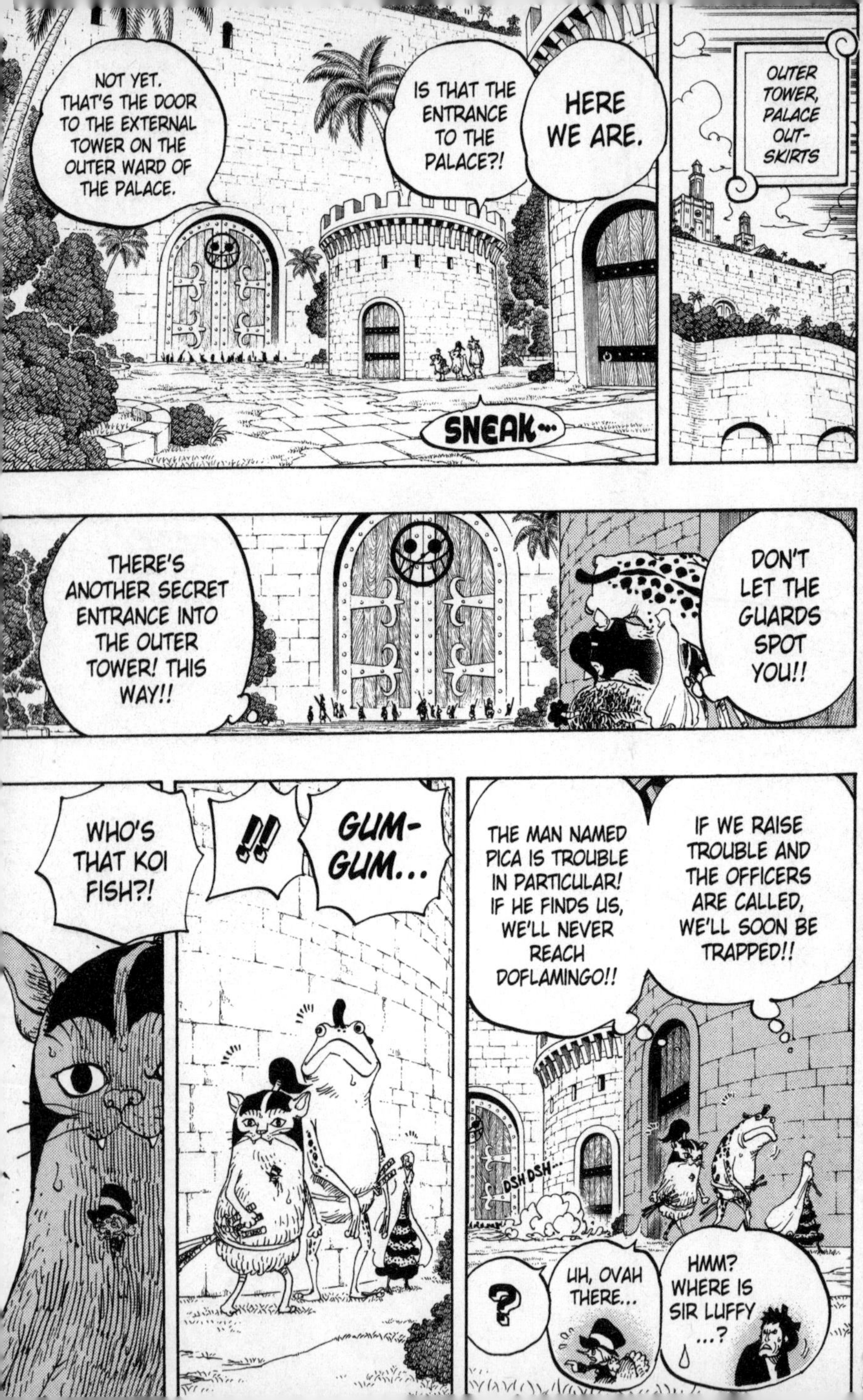

OUTER TOWER, PALACE OUT-SKIRTS
HERE WE ARE.
IS THAT THE ENTRANCE TO THE PALACE?!
NOT YET. THAT'S THE DOOR TO THE EXTERNAL TOWER ON THE OUTER WARD OF THE PALACE.
SNEAK...
DON'T LET THE GUARDS SPOT YOU!!
THERE'S ANOTHER SECRET ENTRANCE INTO THE OUTER TOWER! THIS WAY!!
IF WE RAISE TROUBLE AND THE OFFICERS ARE CALLED, WE'LL SOON BE TRAPPED!!
THE MAN NAMED PICA IS TROUBLE IN PARTICULAR! IF HE FINDS US, WE'LL NEVER REACH DOFLAMINGO!!
DSH DSH...
HMM? WHERE IS SIR LUFFY ...?
UH, OVAH THERE...
?
GUM-GUM...
!!
WHO'S THAT KOI FISH?!

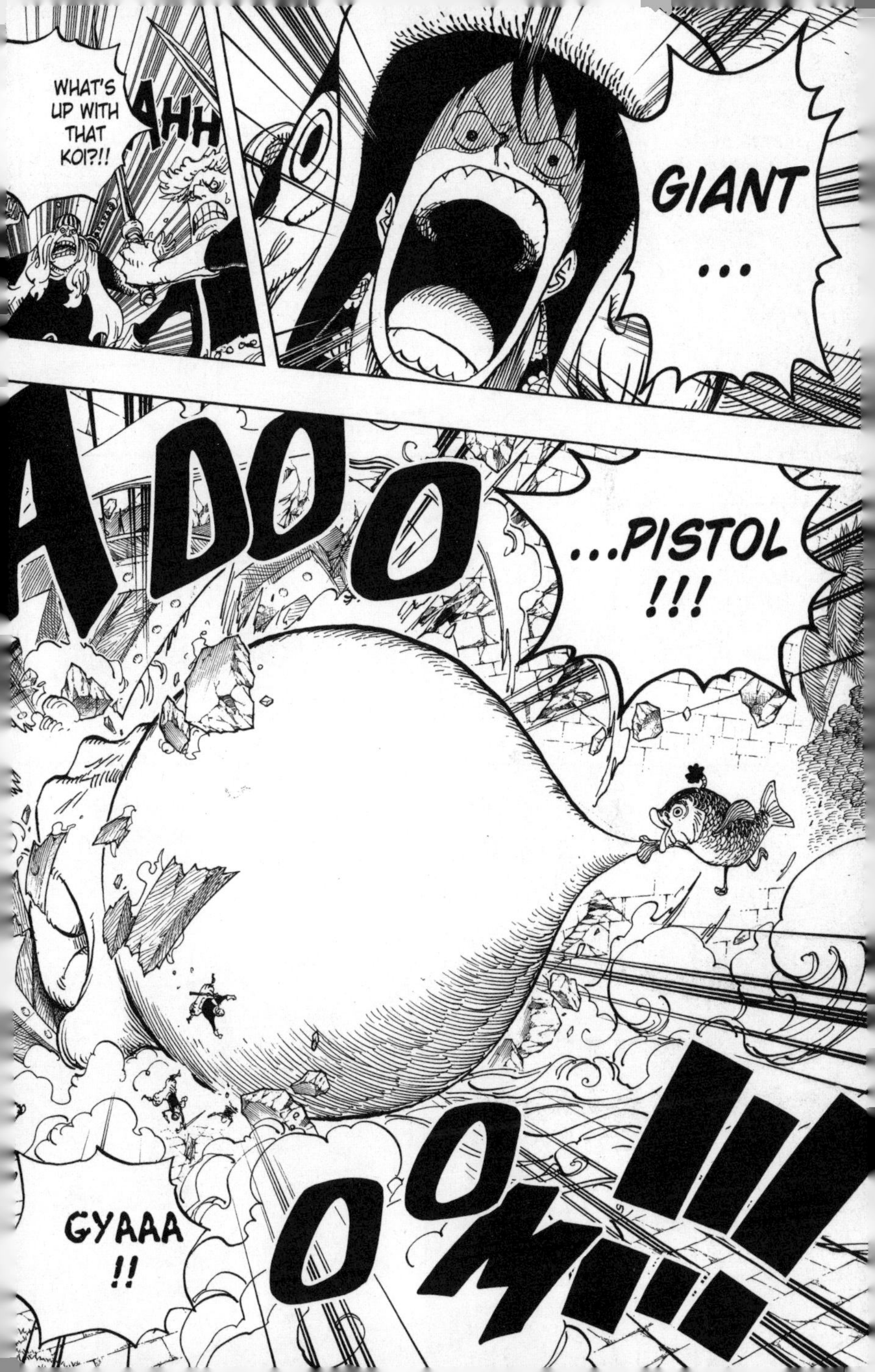
GIANT ...
AHH
WHAT'S UP WITH THAT KOI?!!
...PISTOL !!!
ADOOO
OOOM!!!
GYAAA !!

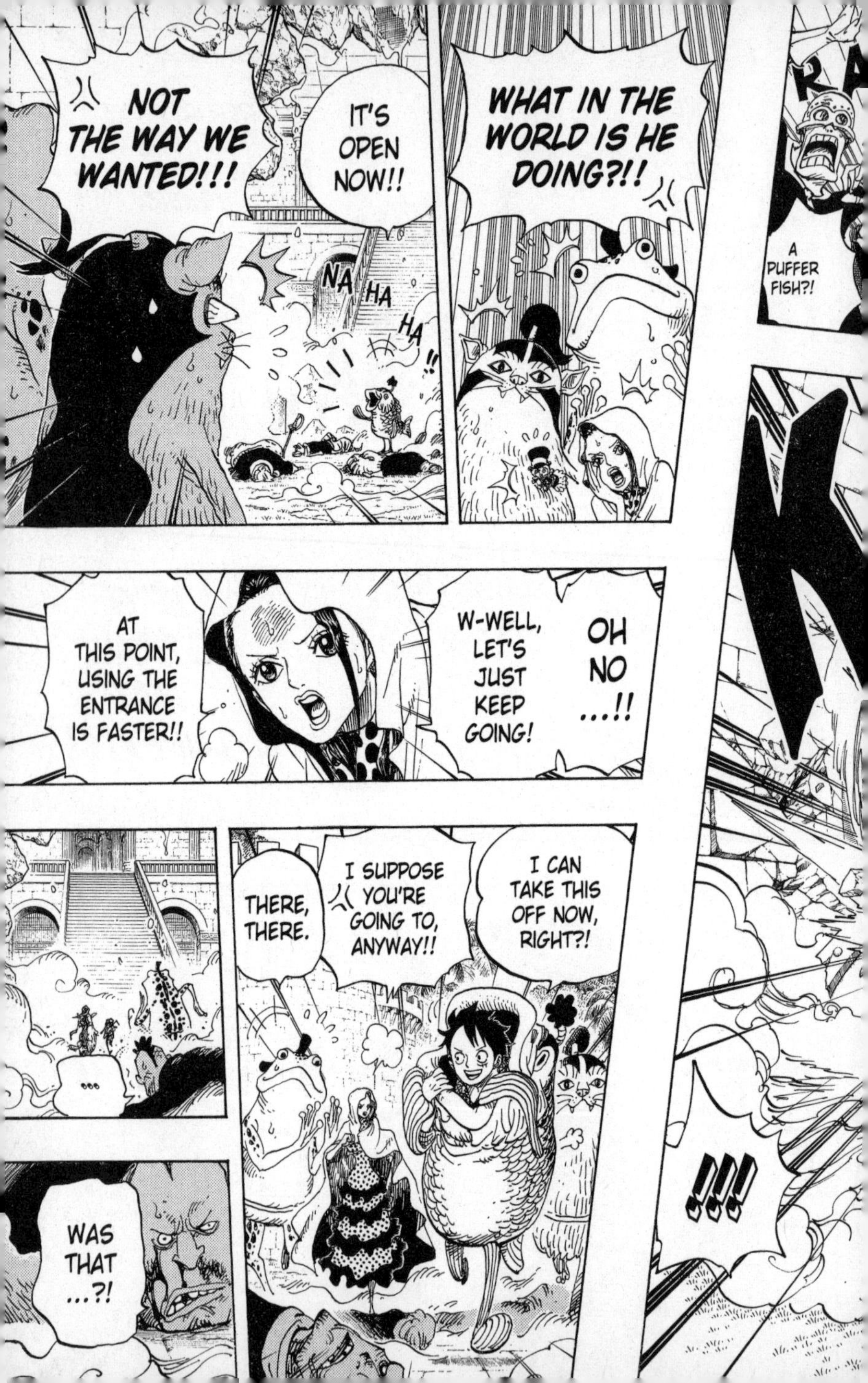

RA
A PUFFER FISH?!
!!!
WHAT IN THE WORLD IS HE DOING?!!
IT'S OPEN NOW!!
NOT THE WAY WE WANTED!!!
NA HA HA
OH NO ...!!
W-WELL, LET'S JUST KEEP GOING!
AT THIS POINT, USING THE ENTRANCE IS FASTER!!
I CAN TAKE THIS OFF NOW, RIGHT?!
I SUPPOSE YOU'RE GOING TO, ANYWAY!!
THERE, THERE.
...
WAS THAT ...?!

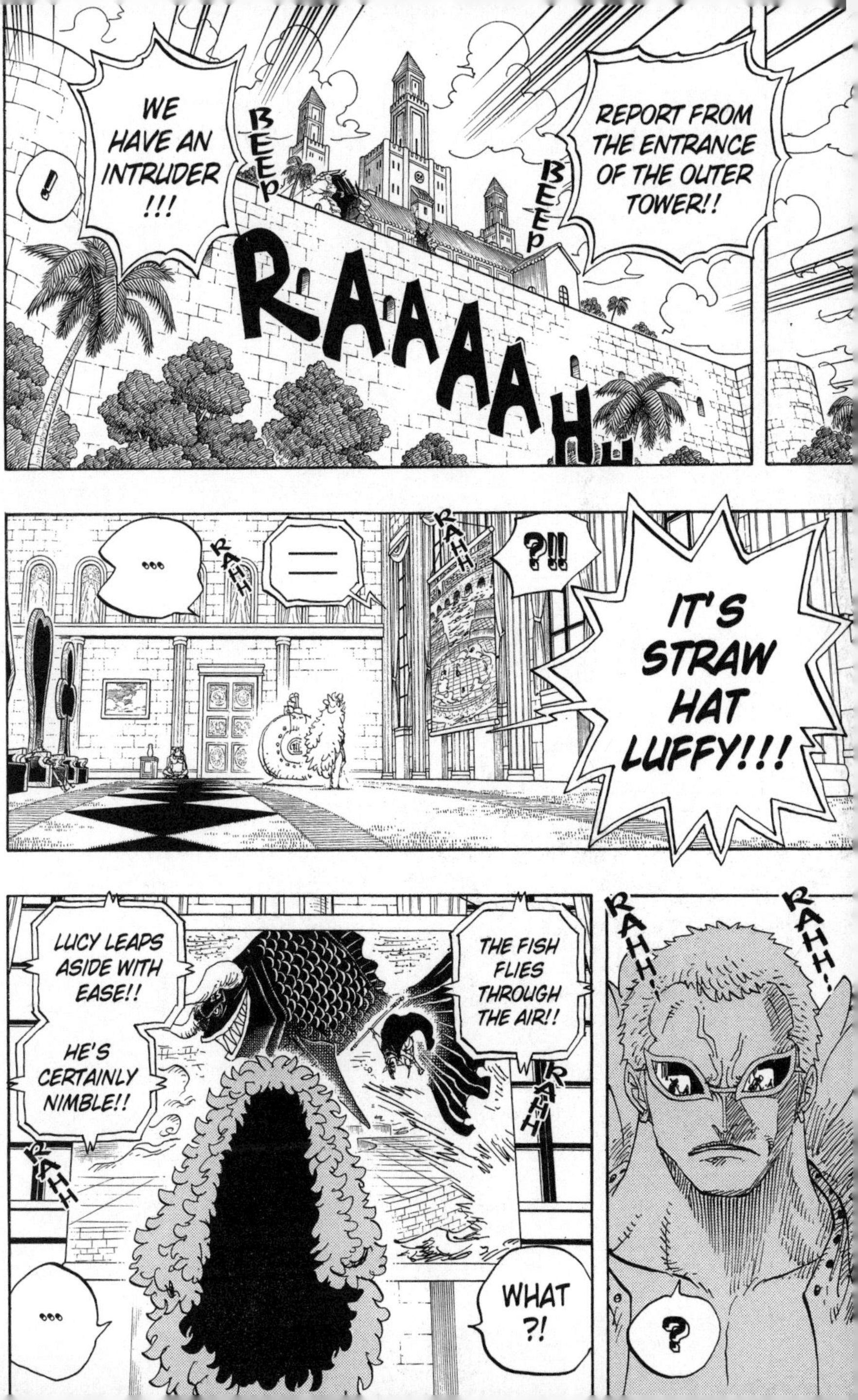
REPORT FROM THE ENTRANCE OF THE OUTER TOWER!!
BEEP
BEEP
WE HAVE AN INTRUDER!!!
!
RAAAAAH
IT'S STRAW HAT LUFFY!!!
?!!
RAHH
—
RAHH
...
RAHH
RAHH
?
THE FISH FLIES THROUGH THE AIR!!
RAHH
LUCY LEAPS ASIDE WITH EASE!!
HE'S CERTAINLY NIMBLE!!
RAHH
WHAT?!
...

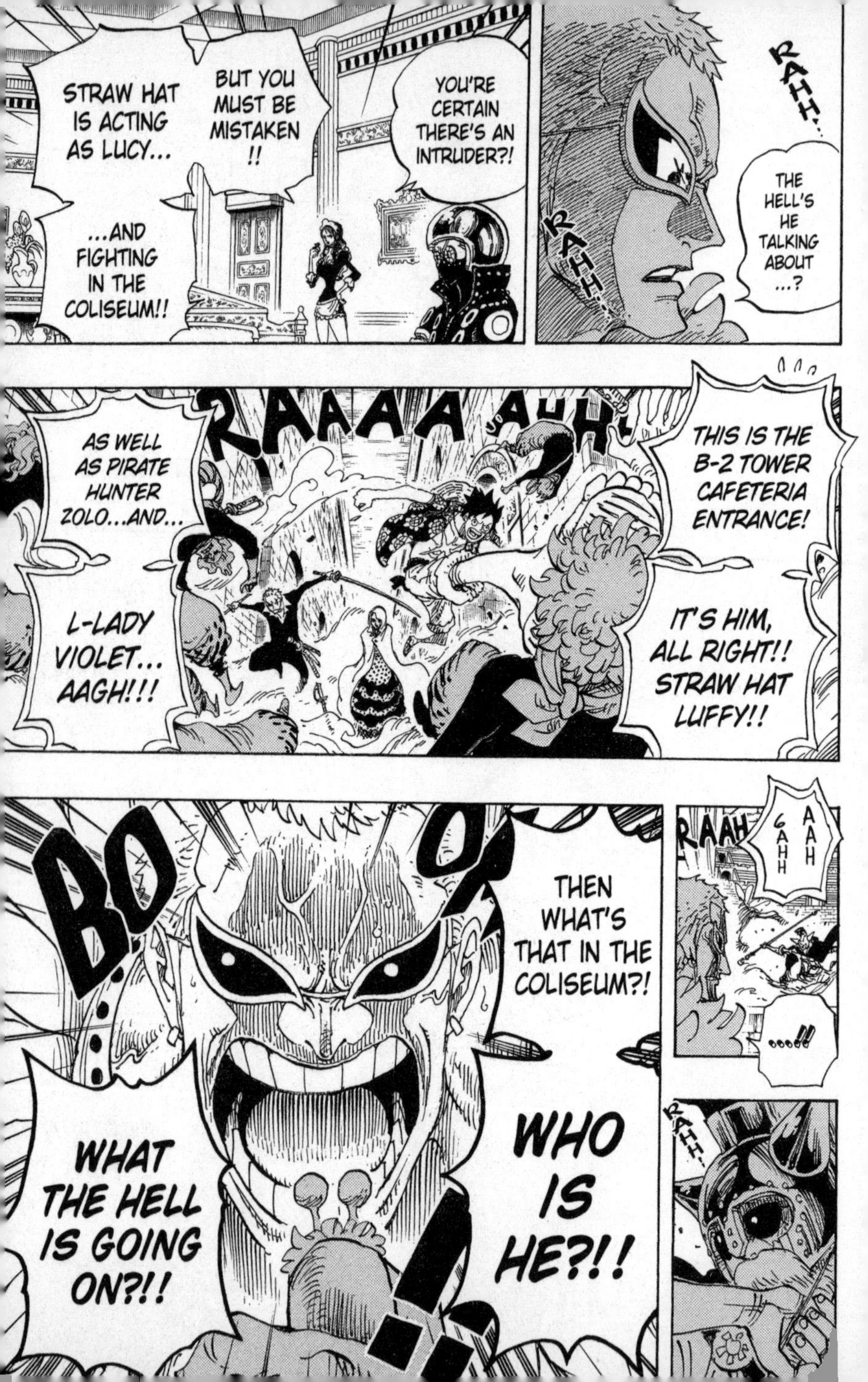
RAHH...
THE HELL'S HE TALKING ABOUT ...?
RAHH...
YOU'RE CERTAIN THERE'S AN INTRUDER?!
BUT YOU MUST BE MISTAKEN !!
STRAW HAT IS ACTING AS LUCY...
...AND FIGHTING IN THE COLISEUM!!
THIS IS THE B-2 TOWER CAFETERIA ENTRANCE!
IT'S HIM, ALL RIGHT!! STRAW HAT LUFFY!!
RAAAAAAHH
AS WELL AS PIRATE HUNTER ZOLO...AND...
L-LADY VIOLET... AAGH!!!
RAAH
AAH GAHH
....!!
RAHH..
BO
THEN WHAT'S THAT IN THE COLISEUM?!
WHO IS HE?!!
WHAT THE HELL IS GOING ON?!!

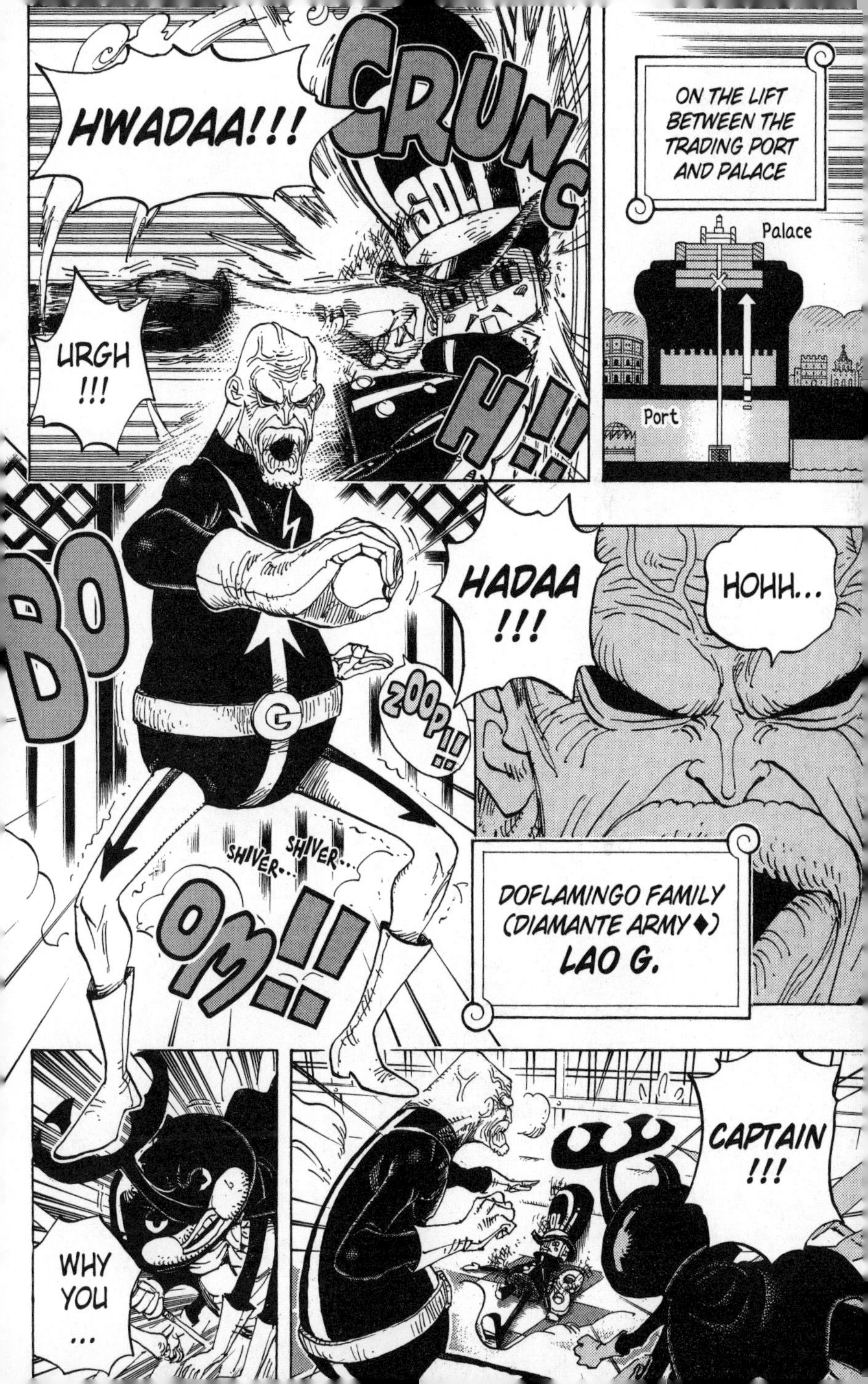
ON THE LIFT BETWEEN THE TRADING PORT AND PALACE
Palace
Port
HWADAA!!!
CRUNCH!!
URGH!!!
HOHH...
HADAA!!!
DOFLAMINGO FAMILY (DIAMANTE ARMY ♦) LAO G.
BOOM!!
ZOOP!!
SHIVER...
SHIVER...
CAPTAIN!!!
WHY YOU...

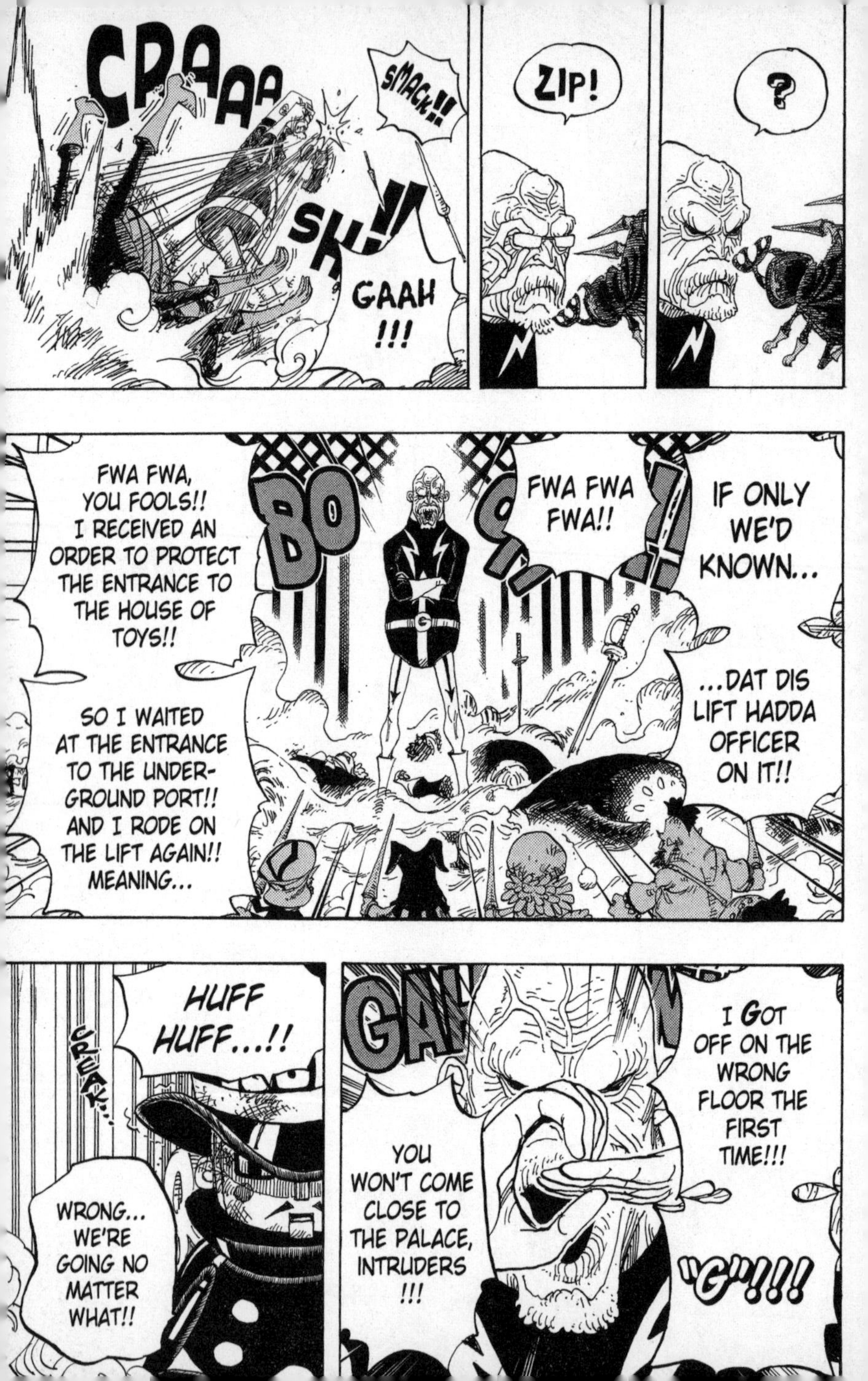
?
ZIP!
SMACK!!
CRAAAA
GAAH!!!
IF ONLY WE'D KNOWN...
...DAT DIS LIFT HADDA OFFICER ON IT!!
FWA FWA FWA!!
FWA FWA, YOU FOOLS!! I RECEIVED AN ORDER TO PROTECT THE ENTRANCE TO THE HOUSE OF TOYS!!
SO I WAITED AT THE ENTRANCE TO THE UNDER-GROUND PORT!! AND I RODE ON THE LIFT AGAIN!! MEANING...
I GOT OFF ON THE WRONG FLOOR THE FIRST TIME!!!
YOU WON'T COME CLOSE TO THE PALACE, INTRUDERS!!!
"G"!!!
HUFF HUFF...!!
CREAK...
WRONG... WE'RE GOING NO MATTER WHAT!!

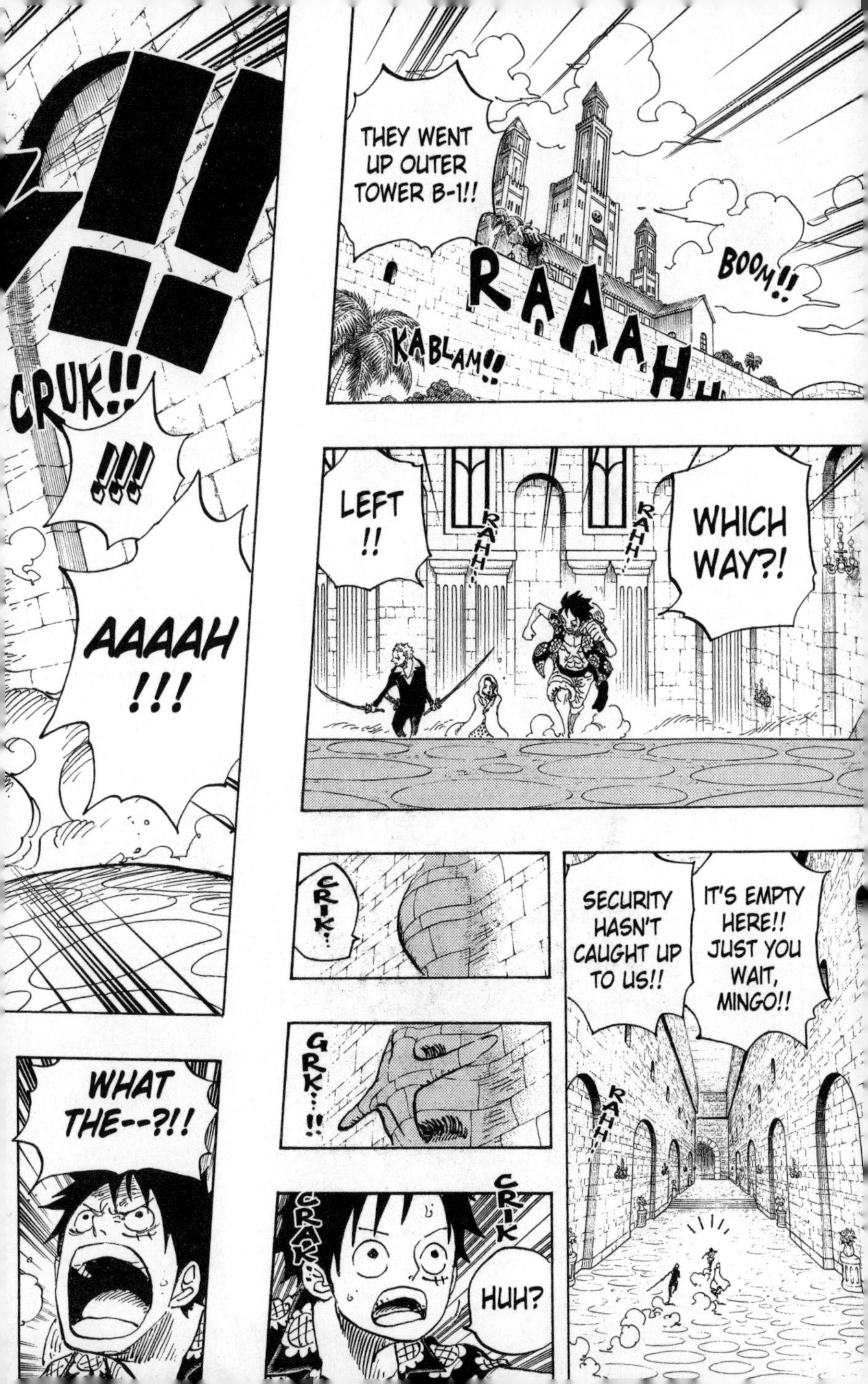
THEY WENT UP OUTER TOWER B-1!!
RAAAAHH
BOOM!!
KABLAM!!
WHICH WAY?!
RAHH...
RAHH...
LEFT!!
IT'S EMPTY HERE!! JUST YOU WAIT, MINGO!!
SECURITY HASN'T CAUGHT UP TO US!!
RAHH...
CRIK...
GRK...!!
CRIK
CRAK
HUH?
WHAT THE--?!!
CRUK!!
!!!
AAAAH!!!

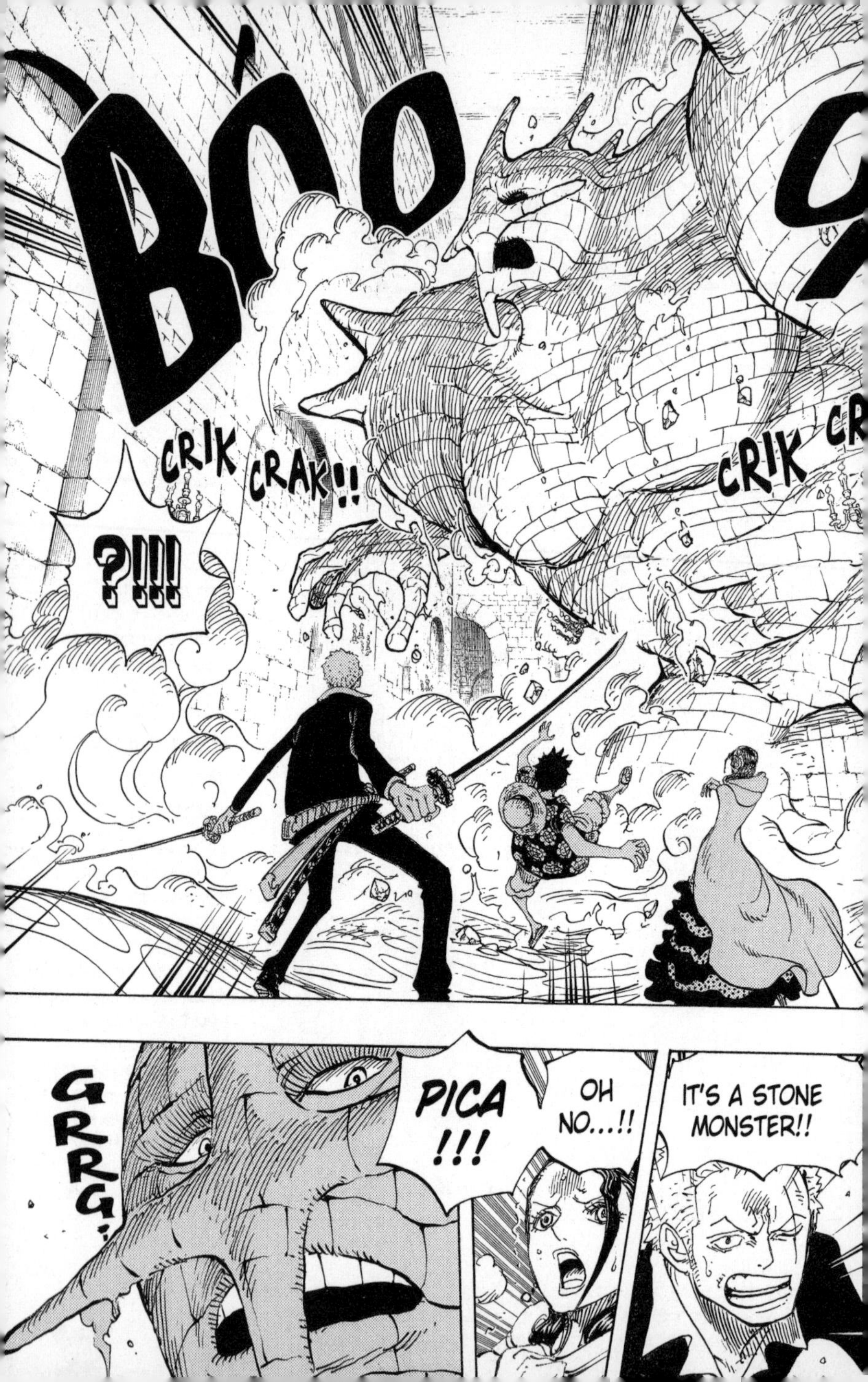
BOO
CRIK CR
CRIK CRAK!!
?!!!
IT'S A STONE MONSTER!!
OH NO...!!
PICA!!!
GRRG

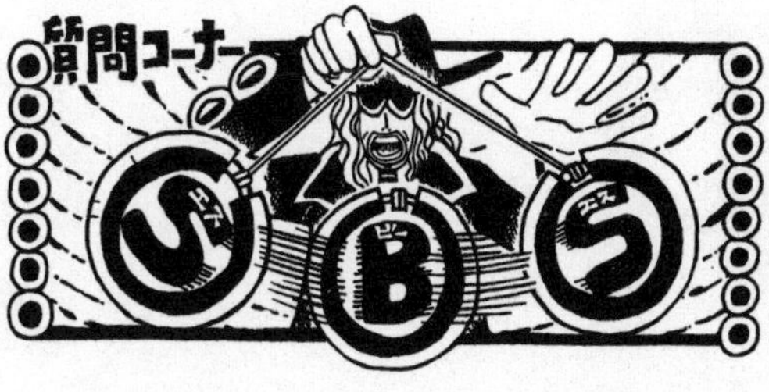
質問コーナー
S
B
S

(Fujima, Fukuoka)

Q: We're a husband and wife who love *One Piece* with all of our hearts. We made an eraser stamp of Trebol's face and came up with a quiz question for you!

--Ryo and Kyoko Yamamoto

Question: Select the correctly dressed Trebol from the four choices below.

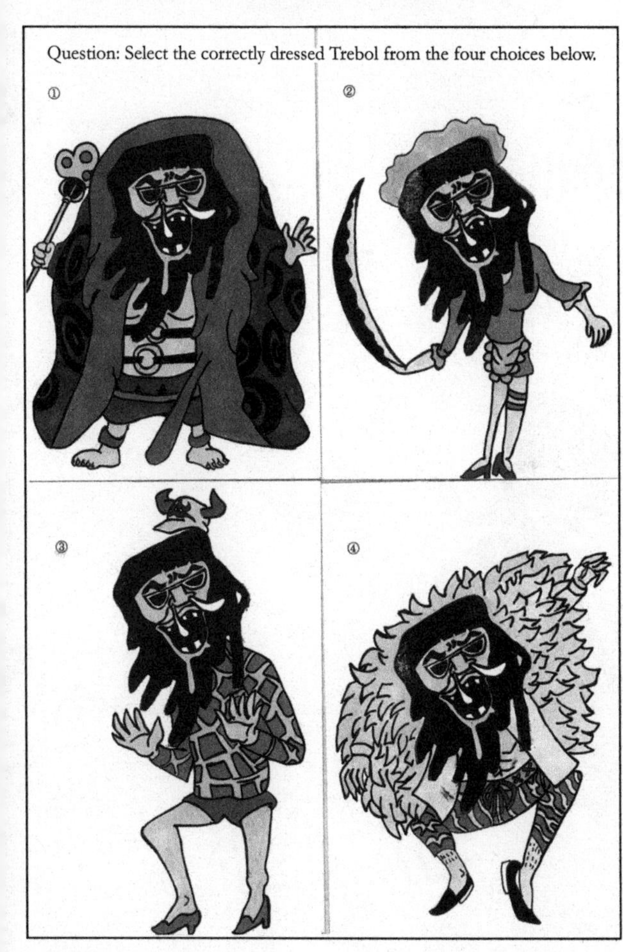
①
②
③
④

A: Thank you very much. Nice work, you lovebirds! Let's try this quiz together!!

A: Did you all figure it out? To find out if you answered correctly, turn to page-- **why would you need to look up the answer?!!** Come on, you lovebirds! That's obvious! Oops, sorry, flew off the handle a bit there. Anyways, I put this one in the book not because of the quiz, but because I liked the drawings. (Guess what? The answer is (1).)

*By the way, in volume 72, I said the coliseum was based on ancient Greece, but that was wrong. I was thinking of ancient Rome. Sorry about the mistake.

Chapter 737:
OFFICER'S TOWER

REQUEST: "ZOLO HAVING A DRINKING CONTEST WITH
A MONKEY BOSS" BY NODA SKYWALKER FROM OSAKA

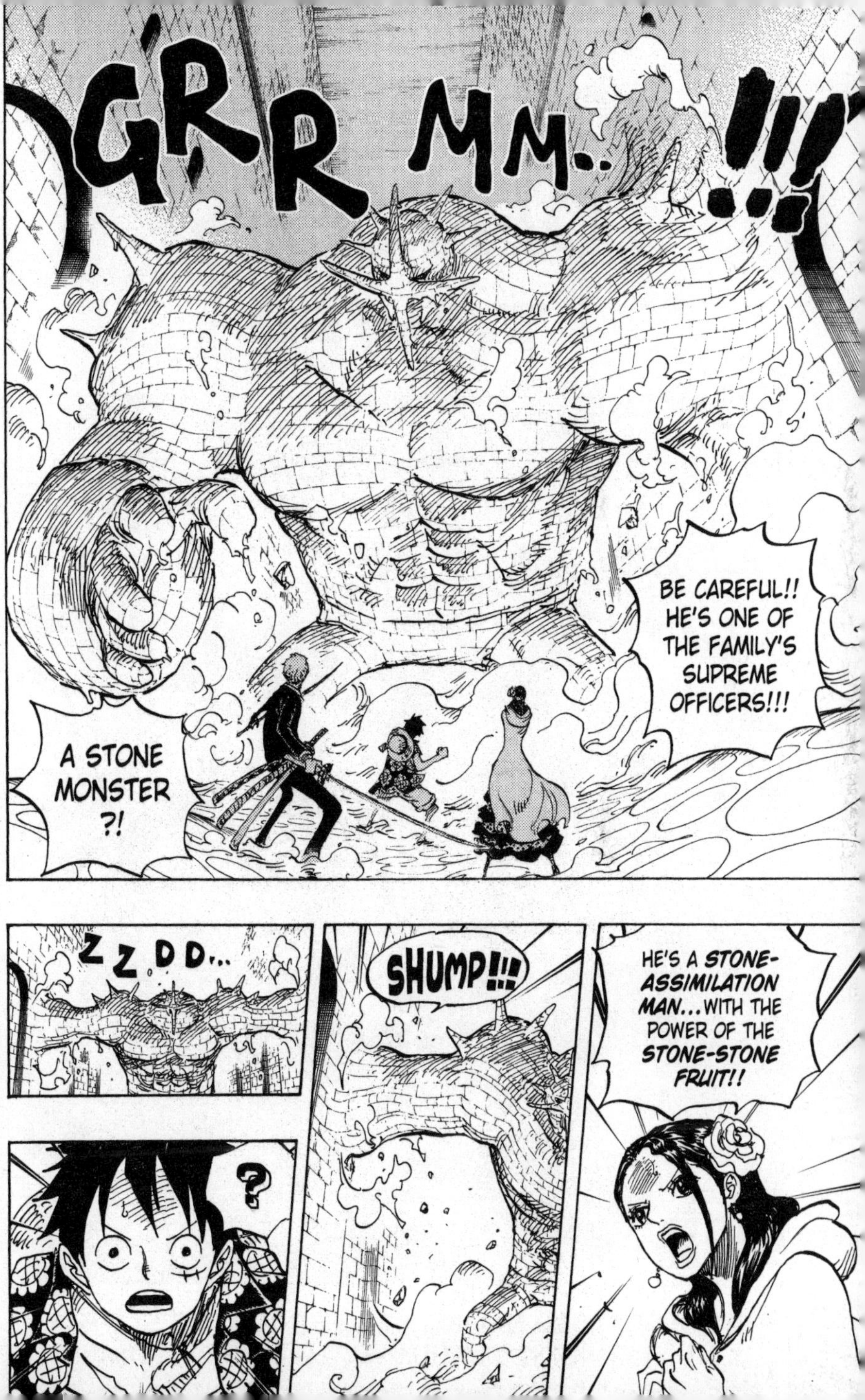
GRRMM...!!!
BE CAREFUL!! HE'S ONE OF THE FAMILY'S SUPREME OFFICERS!!!
A STONE MONSTER ?!
HE'S A *STONE-ASSIMILATION MAN*...WITH THE POWER OF THE *STONE-STONE FRUIT!!*
SHUMP!!!
ZZDD...
?

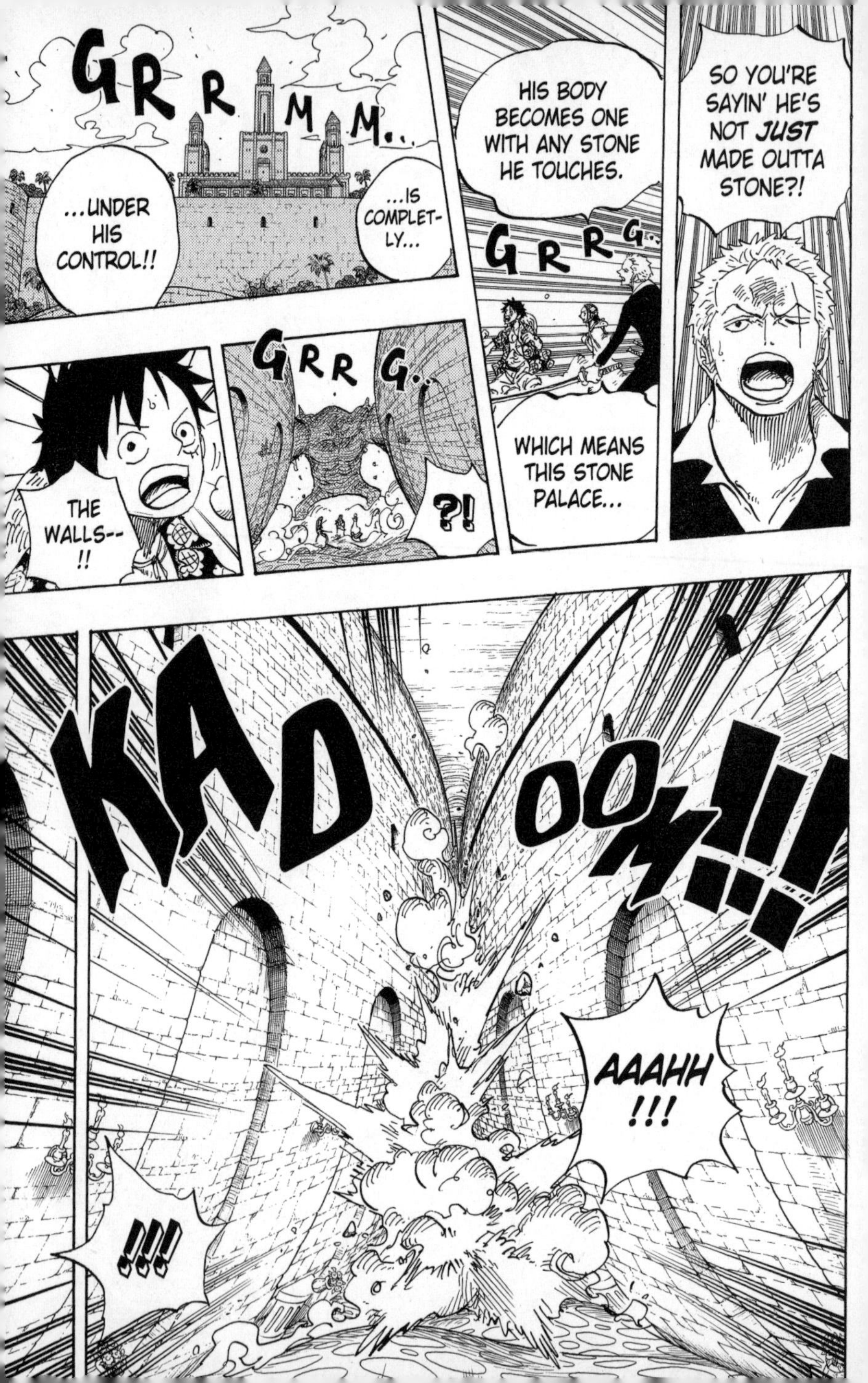
SO YOU'RE SAYIN' HE'S NOT *JUST* MADE OUTTA STONE?!
HIS BODY BECOMES ONE WITH ANY STONE HE TOUCHES.
GRRRG..
WHICH MEANS THIS STONE PALACE...
GRRRMM..
...IS COMPLET-LY...
...UNDER HIS CONTROL!!
GRRRG..
?!
THE WALLS--!!
KADOOM!!!
AAAHH!!!
!!!

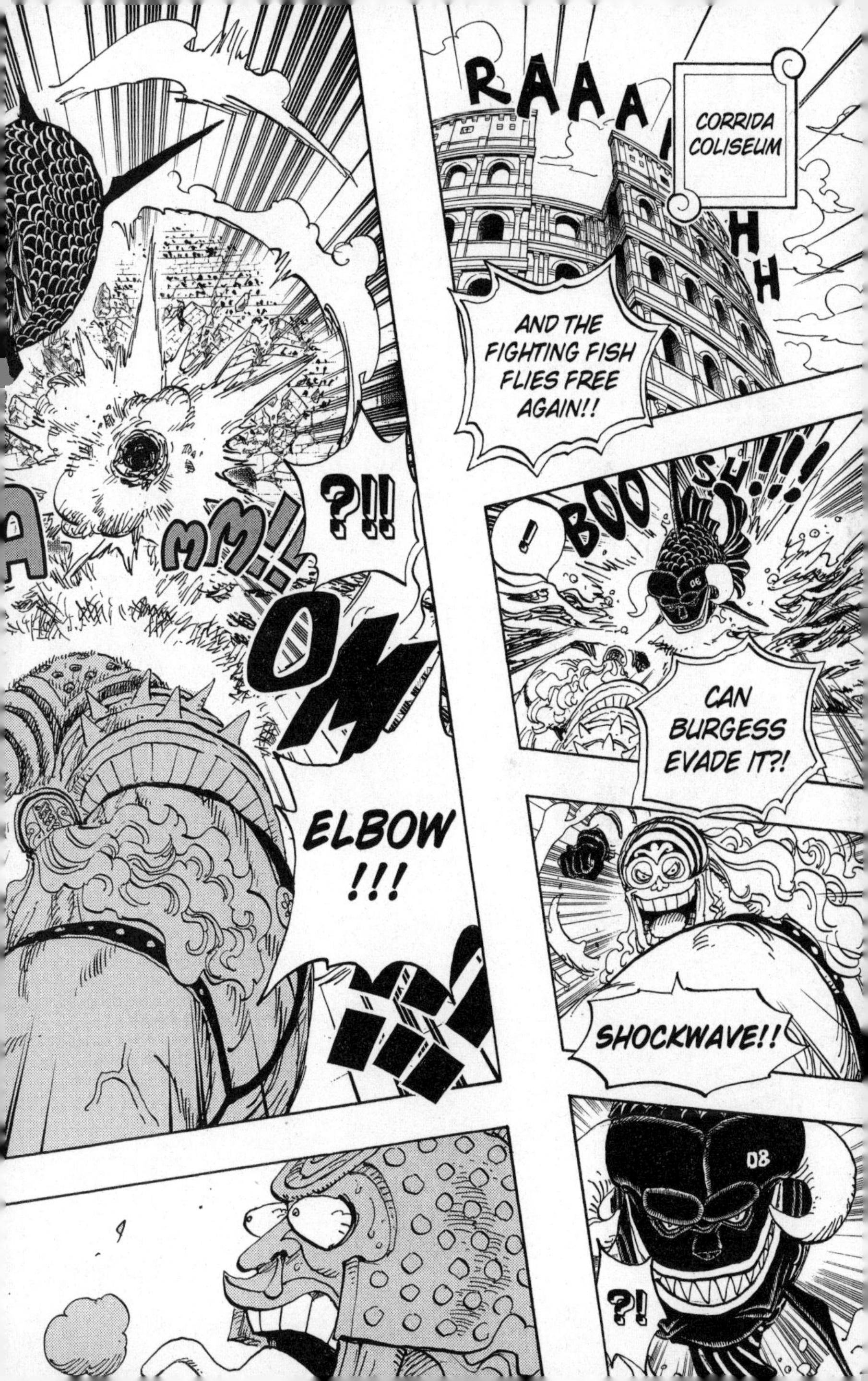
CORRIDA COLISEUM
RAAAAHH
AND THE FIGHTING FISH FLIES FREE AGAIN!!
!
BOOSH!!!
CAN BURGESS EVADE IT?!
SHOCKWAVE!!
?!
?!!
ELBOW !!!

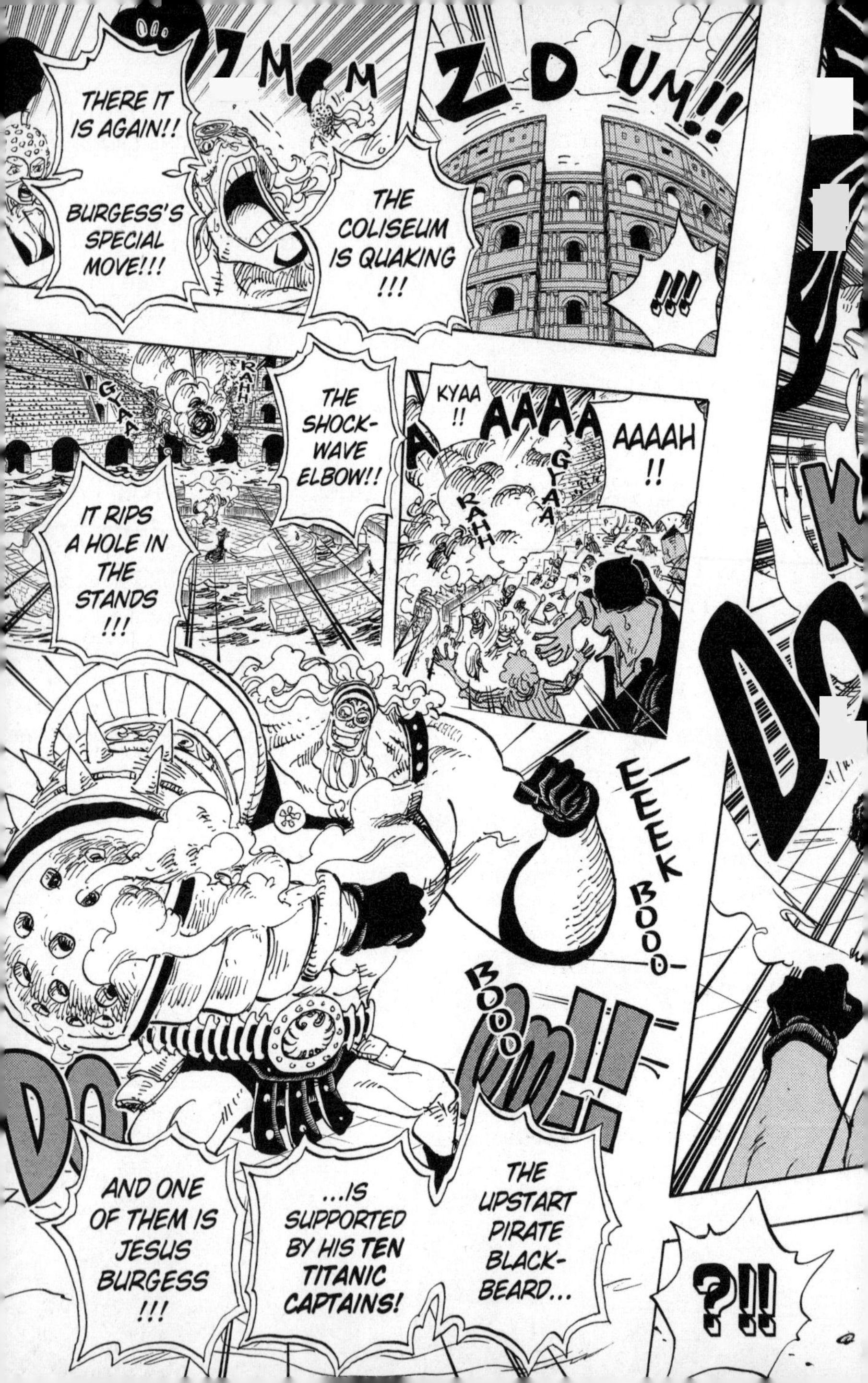
?!!
MMM ZDUM!!
THE COLISEUM IS QUAKING!!!
!!!
THERE IT IS AGAIN!!
BURGESS'S SPECIAL MOVE!!!
KYAA!!
AAAA
AAAAH!!
GYAA
RAHH
THE SHOCK-WAVE ELBOW!!
GYAA
RAHH
IT RIPS A HOLE IN THE STANDS!!!
EEEEK
BOOO
BOOOM!!
THE UPSTART PIRATE BLACKBEARD...
...IS SUPPORTED BY HIS TEN TITANIC CAPTAINS!
AND ONE OF THEM IS JESUS BURGESS!!!

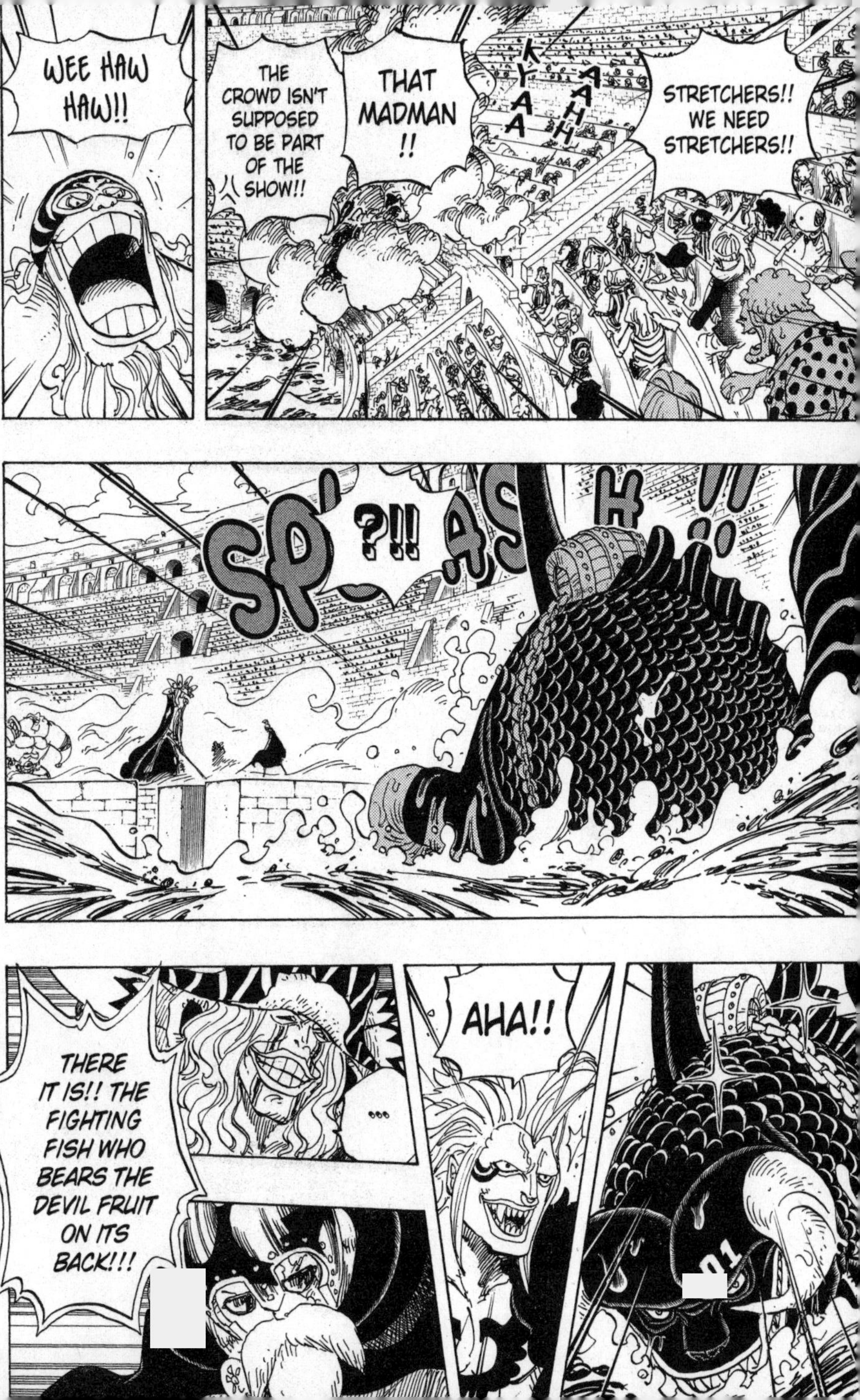
STRETCHERS!! WE NEED STRETCHERS!!
KYAAA
AAAHH
THAT MADMAN!!
THE CROWD ISN'T SUPPOSED TO BE PART OF THE SHOW!!
WEE HAW HAW!!
?!!
AHA!!
THERE IT IS!! THE FIGHTING FISH WHO BEARS THE DEVIL FRUIT ON ITS BACK!!!
...

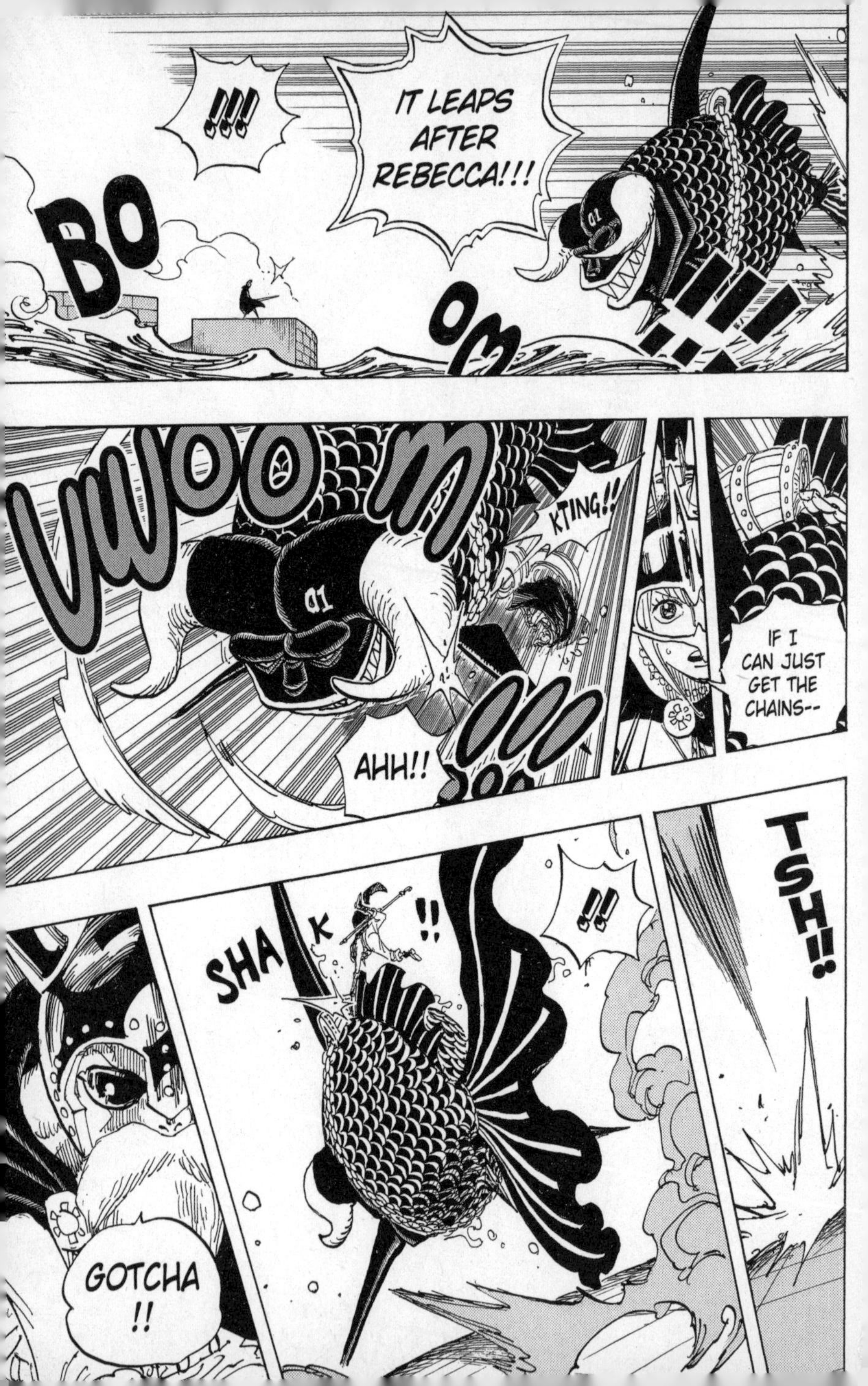
IT LEAPS AFTER REBECCA!!!
!!!
BOOM
IF I CAN JUST GET THE CHAINS--
KTING!!
WOOM
AHH!!
TSH!!
!!
SHAK!!
GOTCHA !!

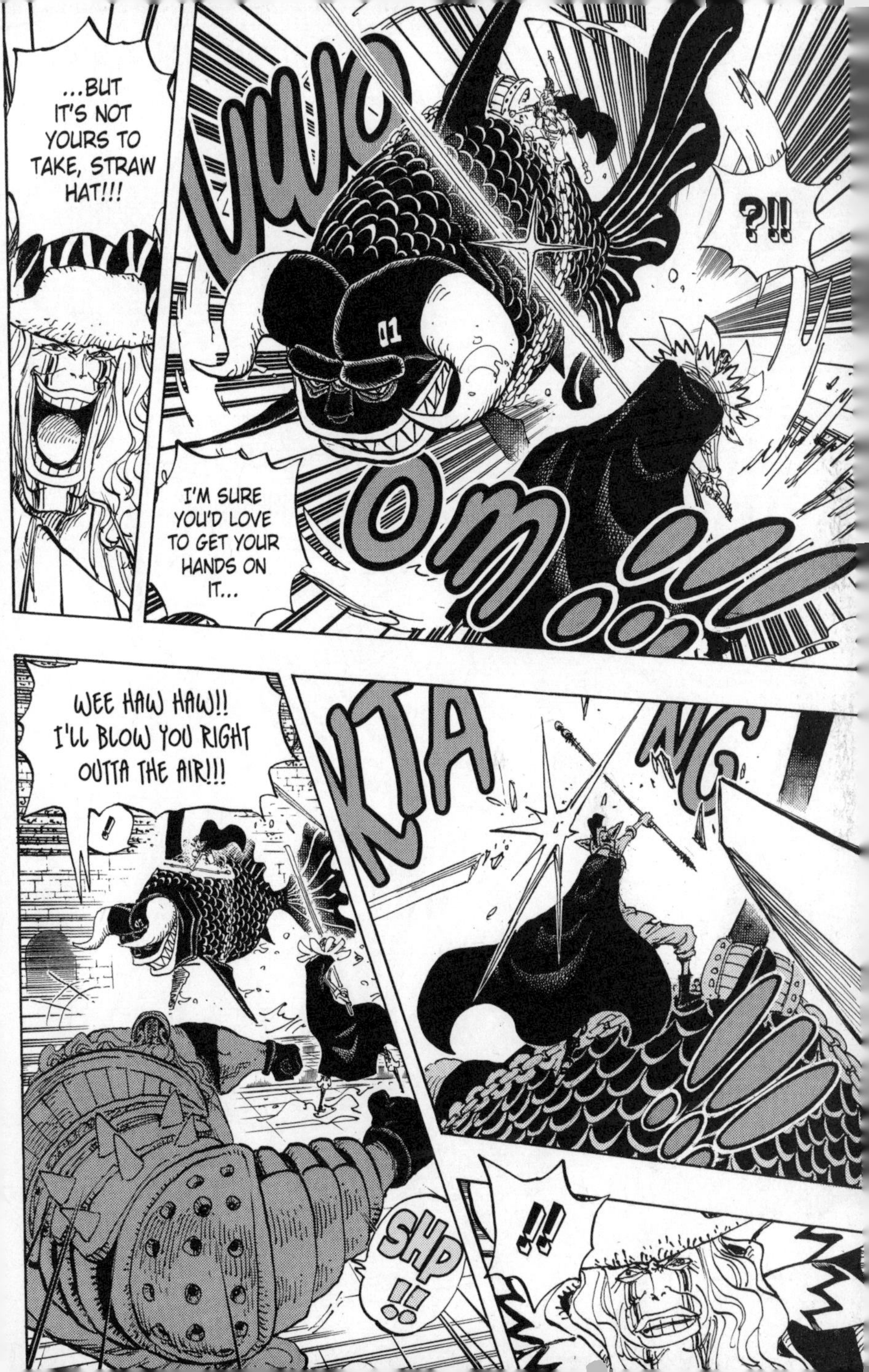
?!!
UWO
OM
I'M SURE YOU'D LOVE TO GET YOUR HANDS ON IT...
...BUT IT'S NOT YOURS TO TAKE, STRAW HAT!!!
KTA
NG
!!
WEE HAW HAW!! I'LL BLOW YOU RIGHT OUTTA THE AIR!!!
!
SHP!!

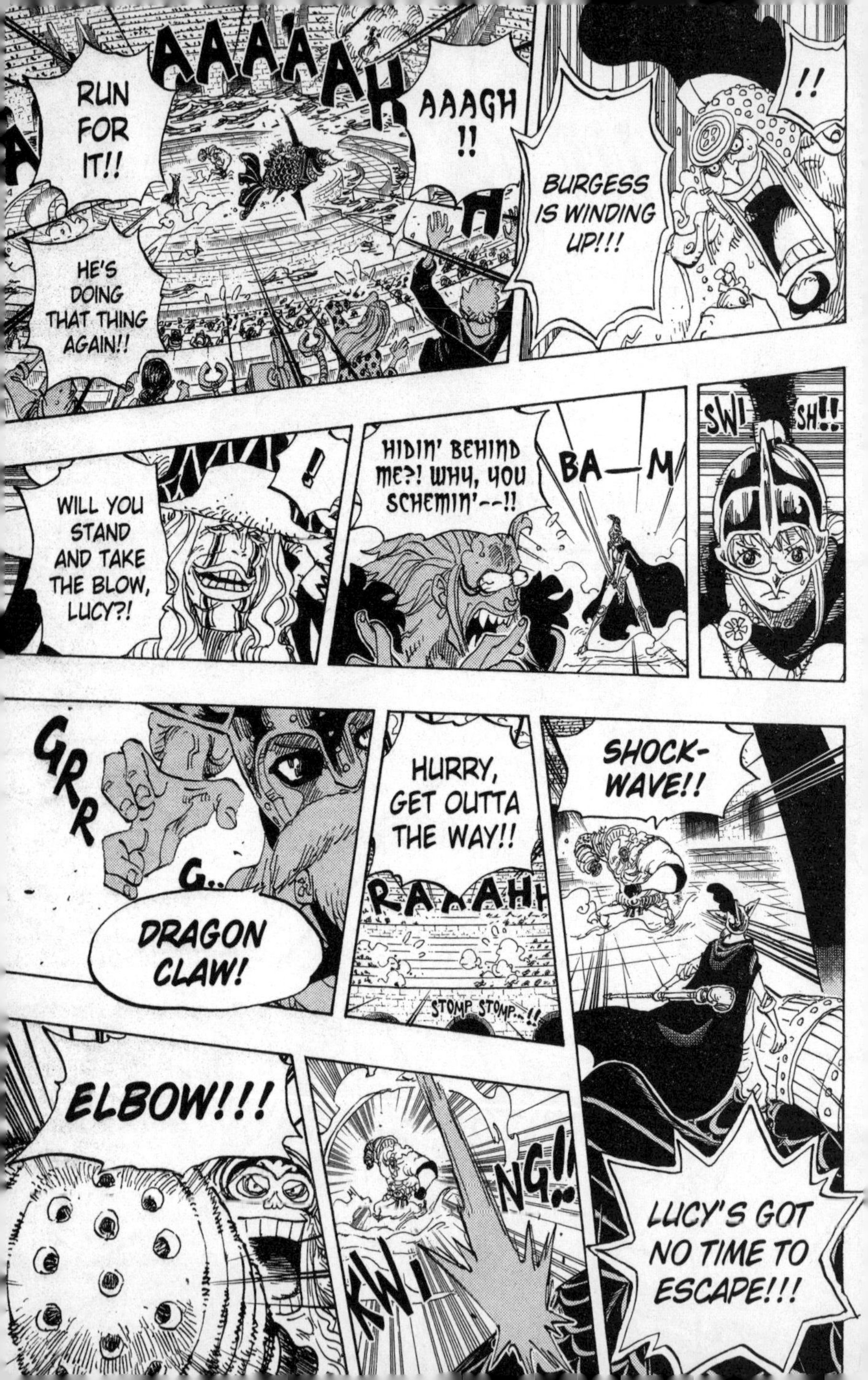
!!
BURGESS IS WINDING UP!!!
AAAGH !!
AAAAAK
RUN FOR IT!!
HE'S DOING THAT THING AGAIN!!
SWISH!!
BA—M
HIDIN' BEHIND ME?! WHY, YOU SCHEMIN'--!!
!
WILL YOU STAND AND TAKE THE BLOW, LUCY?!
SHOCK-WAVE!!
LUCY'S GOT NO TIME TO ESCAPE!!!
HURRY, GET OUTTA THE WAY!!
RAAAHH
STOMP STOMP..!!
GRR
G..
DRAGON CLAW!
KWING!!
ELBOW!!!

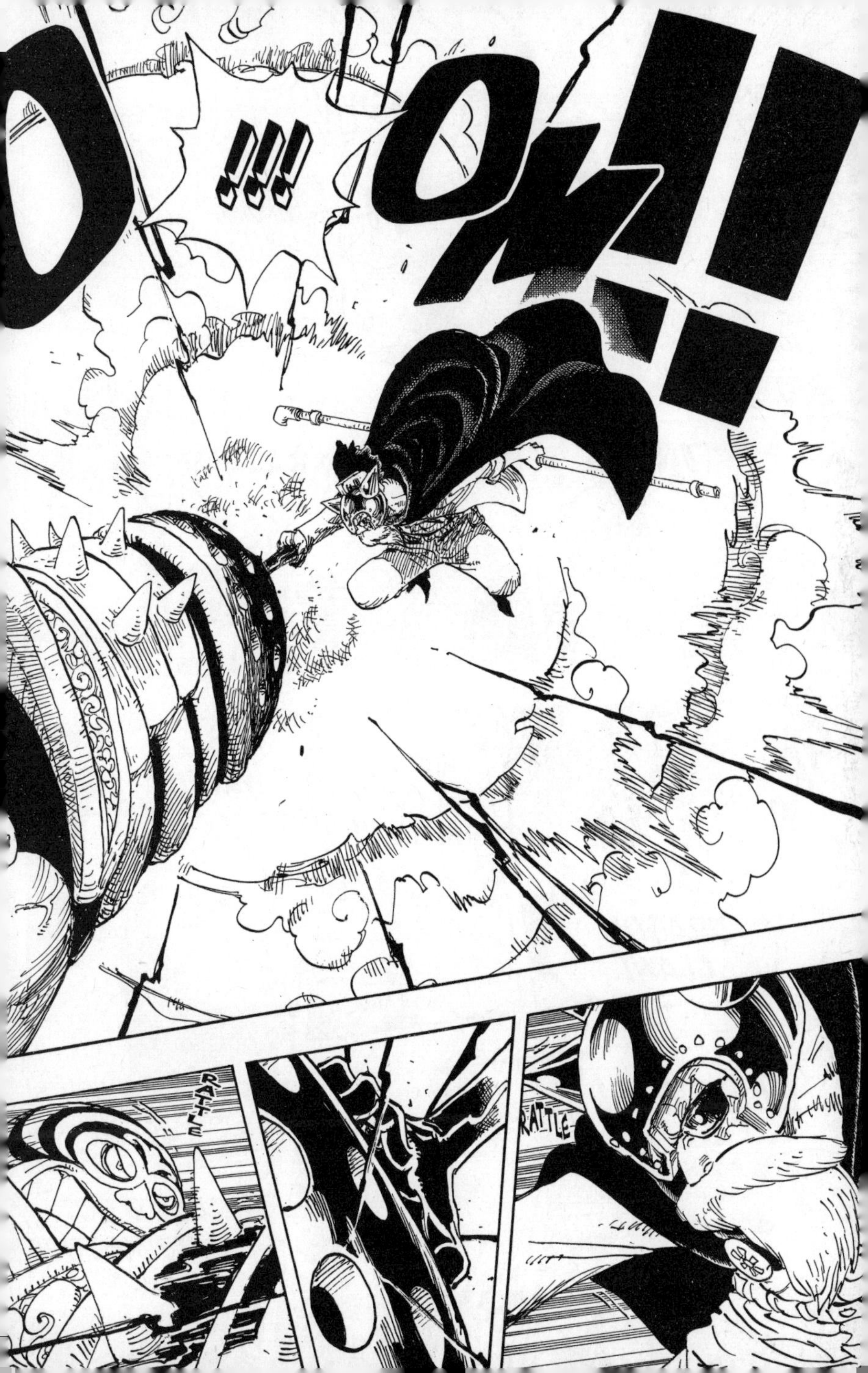
O
OH!!
!!!
RATTLE
RATTLE

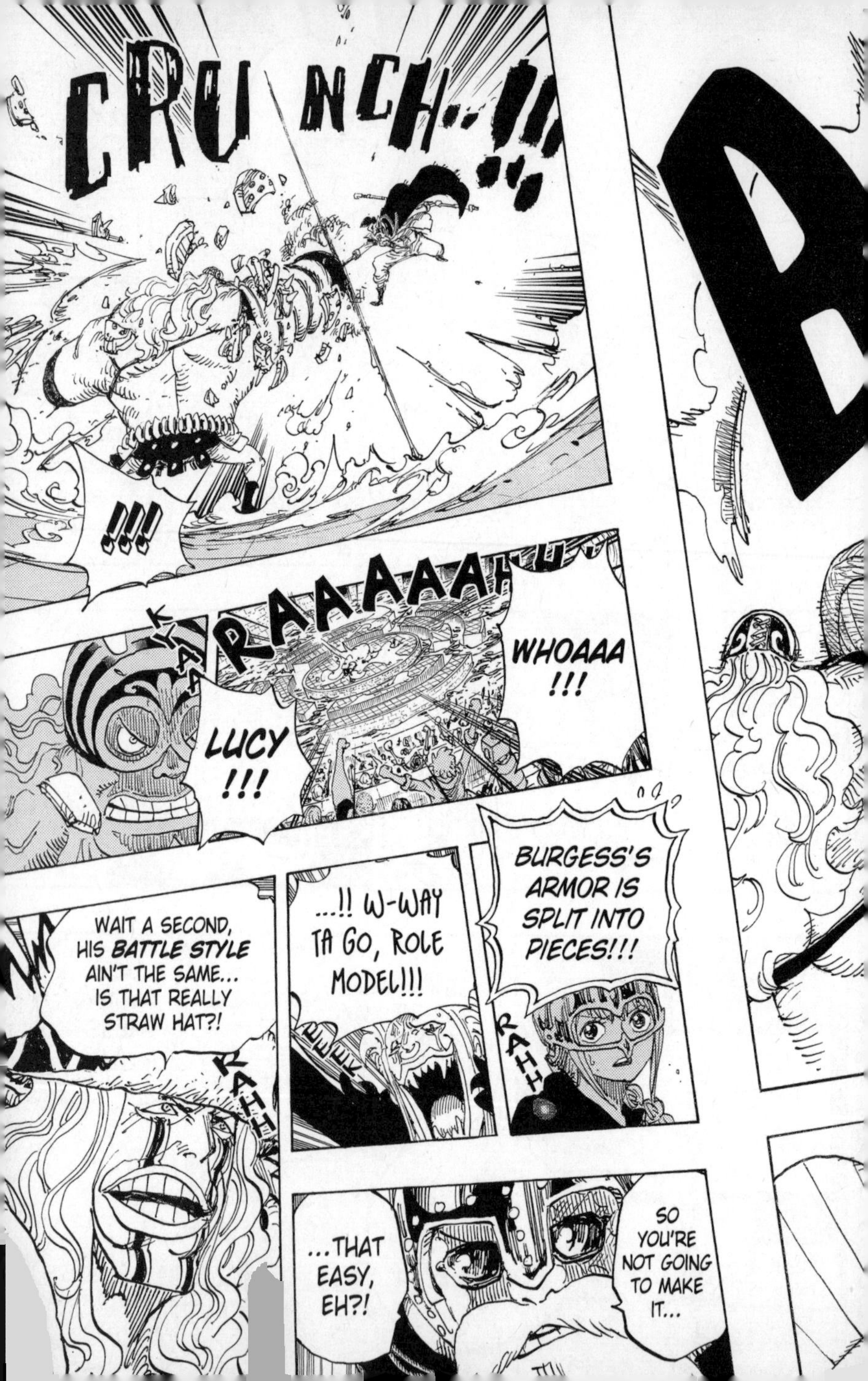

B
CRUNCH..!!!
!!!
RAAAAAAH
KYAA
WHOAAA !!!
LUCY !!!
BURGESS'S ARMOR IS SPLIT INTO PIECES!!!
RAHH
...!! W-WAY TA GO, ROLE MODEL!!!
WAIT A SECOND, HIS BATTLE STYLE AIN'T THE SAME... IS THAT REALLY STRAW HAT?!
RAHH
SO YOU'RE NOT GOING TO MAKE IT...
...THAT EASY, EH?!

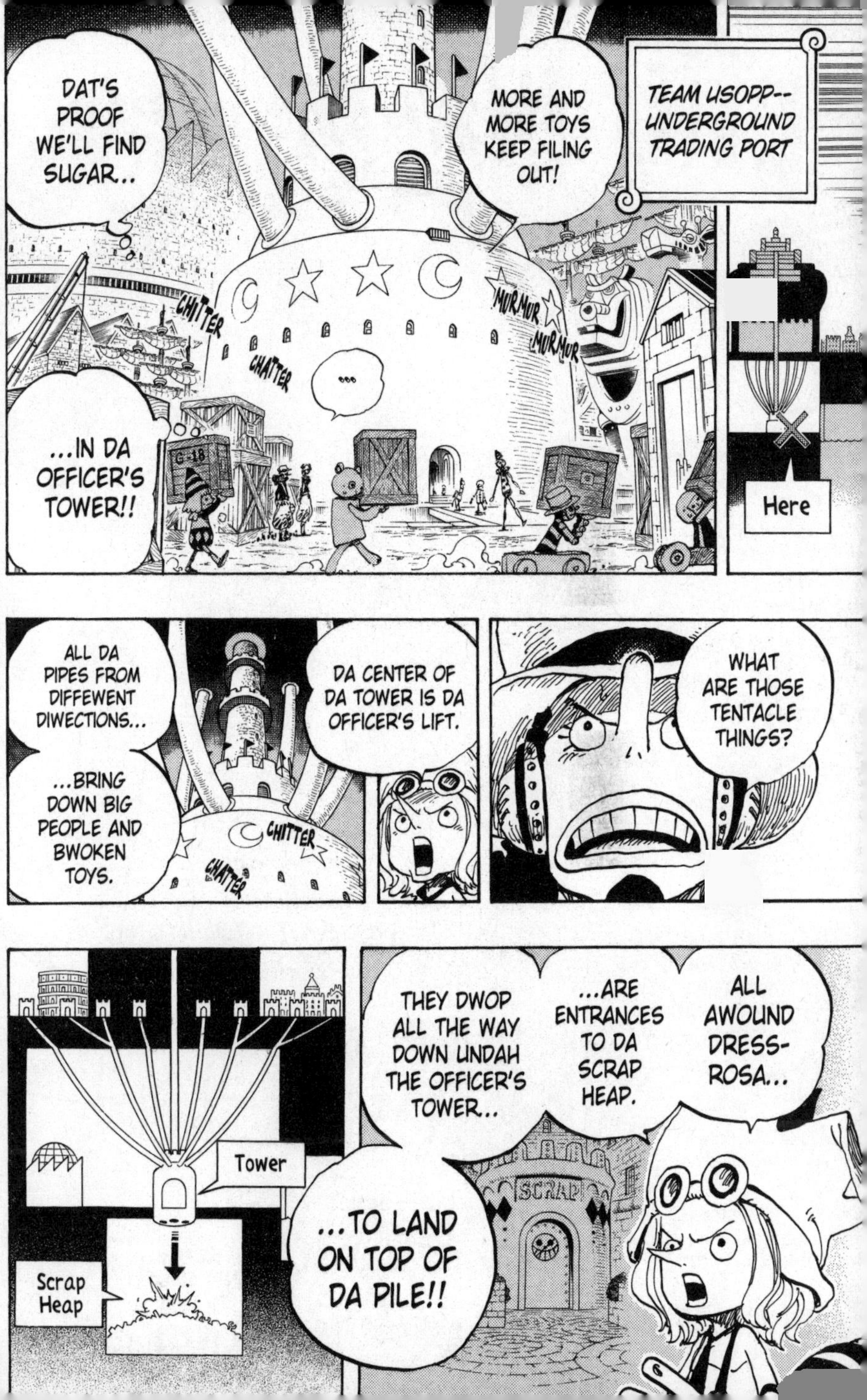
Here
TEAM USOPP-- UNDERGROUND TRADING PORT
MORE AND MORE TOYS KEEP FILING OUT!
MURMUR
MURMUR
DAT'S PROOF WE'LL FIND SUGAR...
CHITTER
CHATTER
...
...IN DA OFFICER'S TOWER!!
G-18
WHAT ARE THOSE TENTACLE THINGS?
DA CENTER OF DA TOWER IS DA OFFICER'S LIFT.
ALL DA PIPES FROM DIFFEWENT DIWECTIONS...
...BRING DOWN BIG PEOPLE AND BWOKEN TOYS.
CHITTER
CHATTER
ALL AWOUND DRESS-ROSA...
...ARE ENTRANCES TO DA SCRAP HEAP.
THEY DWOP ALL THE WAY DOWN UNDAH THE OFFICER'S TOWER...
SCRAP
...TO LAND ON TOP OF DA PILE!!
Tower
Scrap Heap

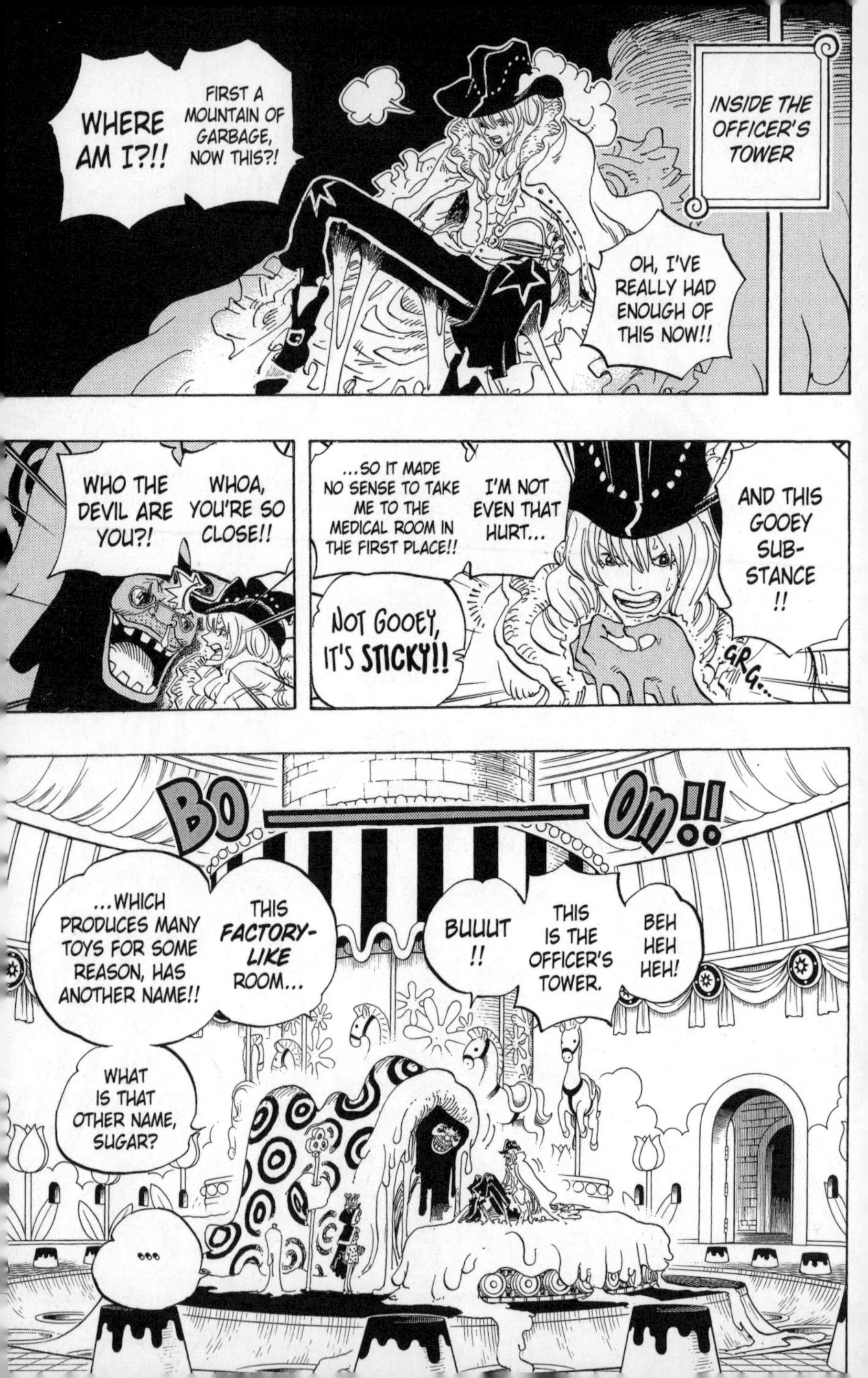
INSIDE THE OFFICER'S TOWER
FIRST A MOUNTAIN OF GARBAGE, NOW THIS?!
WHERE AM I?!!
OH, I'VE REALLY HAD ENOUGH OF THIS NOW!!
AND THIS GOOEY SUBSTANCE!!
I'M NOT EVEN THAT HURT...
...SO IT MADE NO SENSE TO TAKE ME TO THE MEDICAL ROOM IN THE FIRST PLACE!!
NOT GOOEY, IT'S STICKY!!
GRG...
WHOA, YOU'RE SO CLOSE!!
WHO THE DEVIL ARE YOU?!
BO—OM!!
BEH HEH HEH!
THIS IS THE OFFICER'S TOWER.
BUUUT!!
THIS FACTORY-LIKE ROOM...
...WHICH PRODUCES MANY TOYS FOR SOME REASON, HAS ANOTHER NAME!!
WHAT IS THAT OTHER NAME, SUGAR?
...

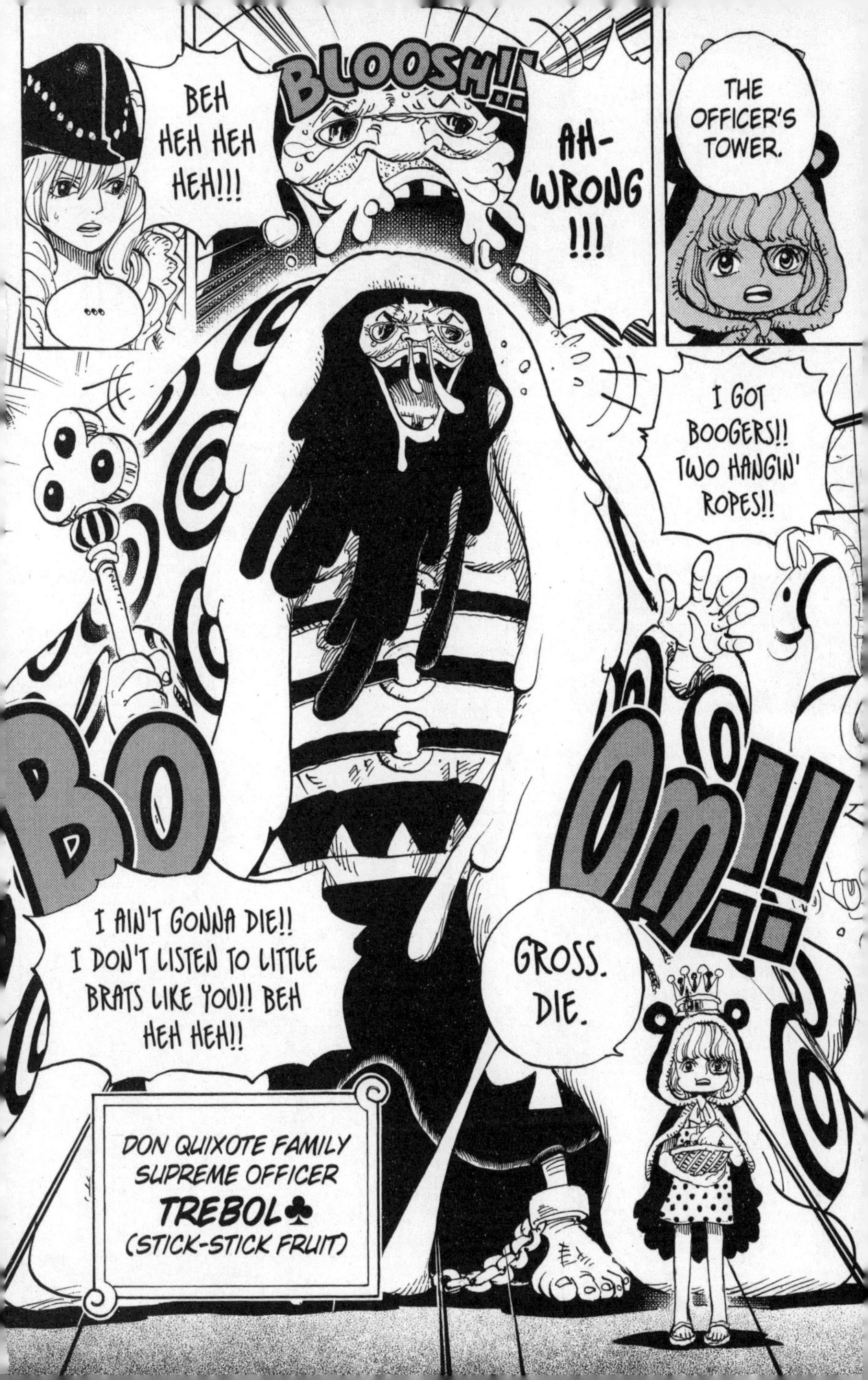
THE OFFICER'S TOWER.
BLOOSH!!
AH-WRONG!!!
BEH HEH HEH HEH!!!
...
I GOT BOOGERS!! TWO HANGIN' ROPES!!
BOOM!!
GROSS. DIE.
I AIN'T GONNA DIE!! I DON'T LISTEN TO LITTLE BRATS LIKE YOU!! BEH HEH HEH!!
DON QUIXOTE FAMILY SUPREME OFFICER
TREBOL♣
(STICK-STICK FRUIT)

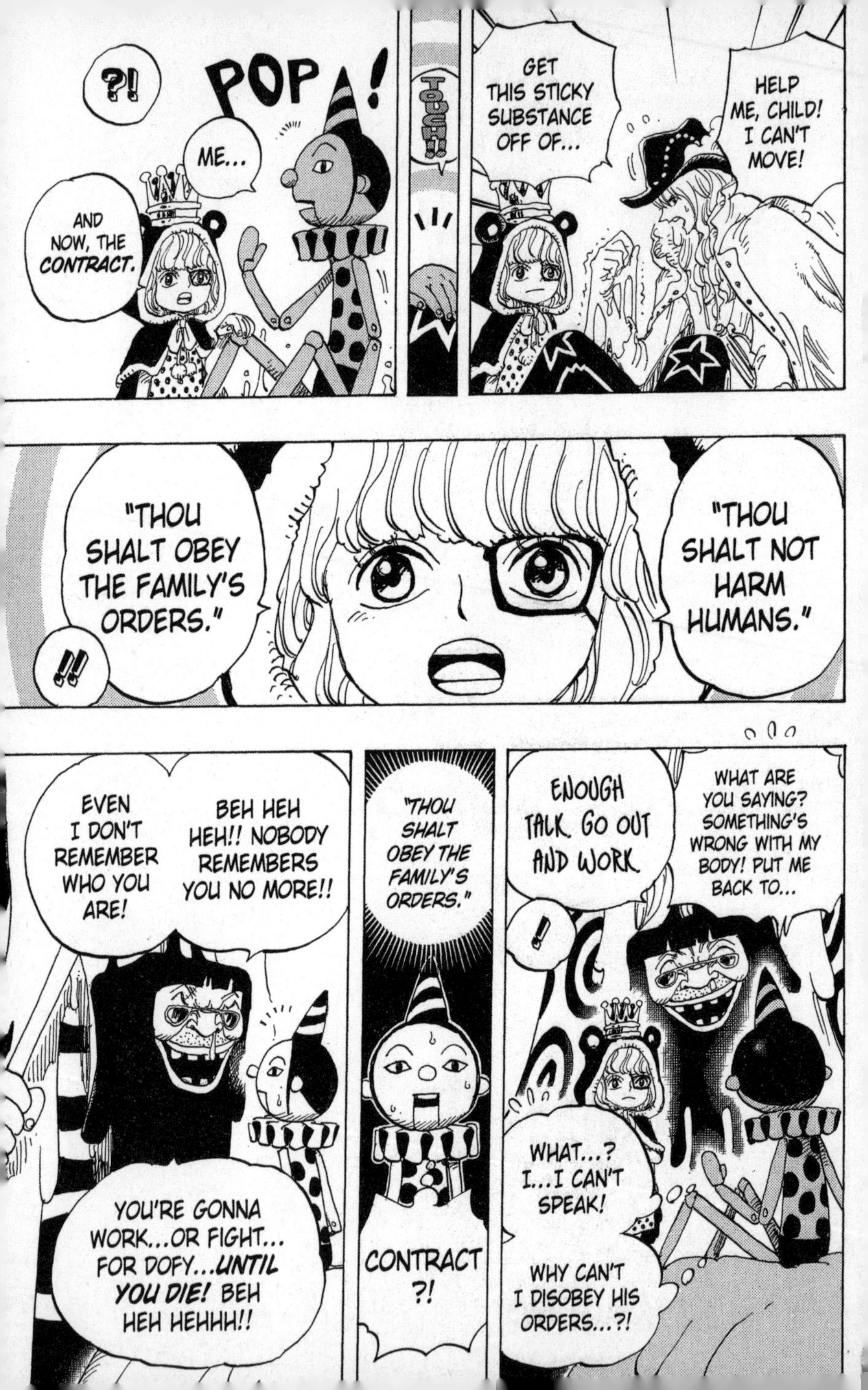
HELP ME, CHILD! I CAN'T MOVE!
GET THIS STICKY SUBSTANCE OFF OF...
TOUCH!!
!
POP
ME...
?!
AND NOW, THE *CONTRACT.*
"THOU SHALT NOT HARM HUMANS."
"THOU SHALT OBEY THE FAMILY'S ORDERS."
!!
WHAT ARE YOU SAYING? SOMETHING'S WRONG WITH MY BODY! PUT ME BACK TO...
ENOUGH TALK. GO OUT AND WORK.
!
WHAT...? I...I CAN'T SPEAK!
WHY CAN'T I DISOBEY HIS ORDERS...?!
"THOU SHALT OBEY THE FAMILY'S ORDERS."
CONTRACT ?!
BEH HEH HEH!! NOBODY REMEMBERS YOU NO MORE!!
EVEN I DON'T REMEMBER WHO YOU ARE!
YOU'RE GONNA WORK...OR FIGHT... FOR DOFY...*UNTIL YOU DIE!* BEH HEH HEHHH!!

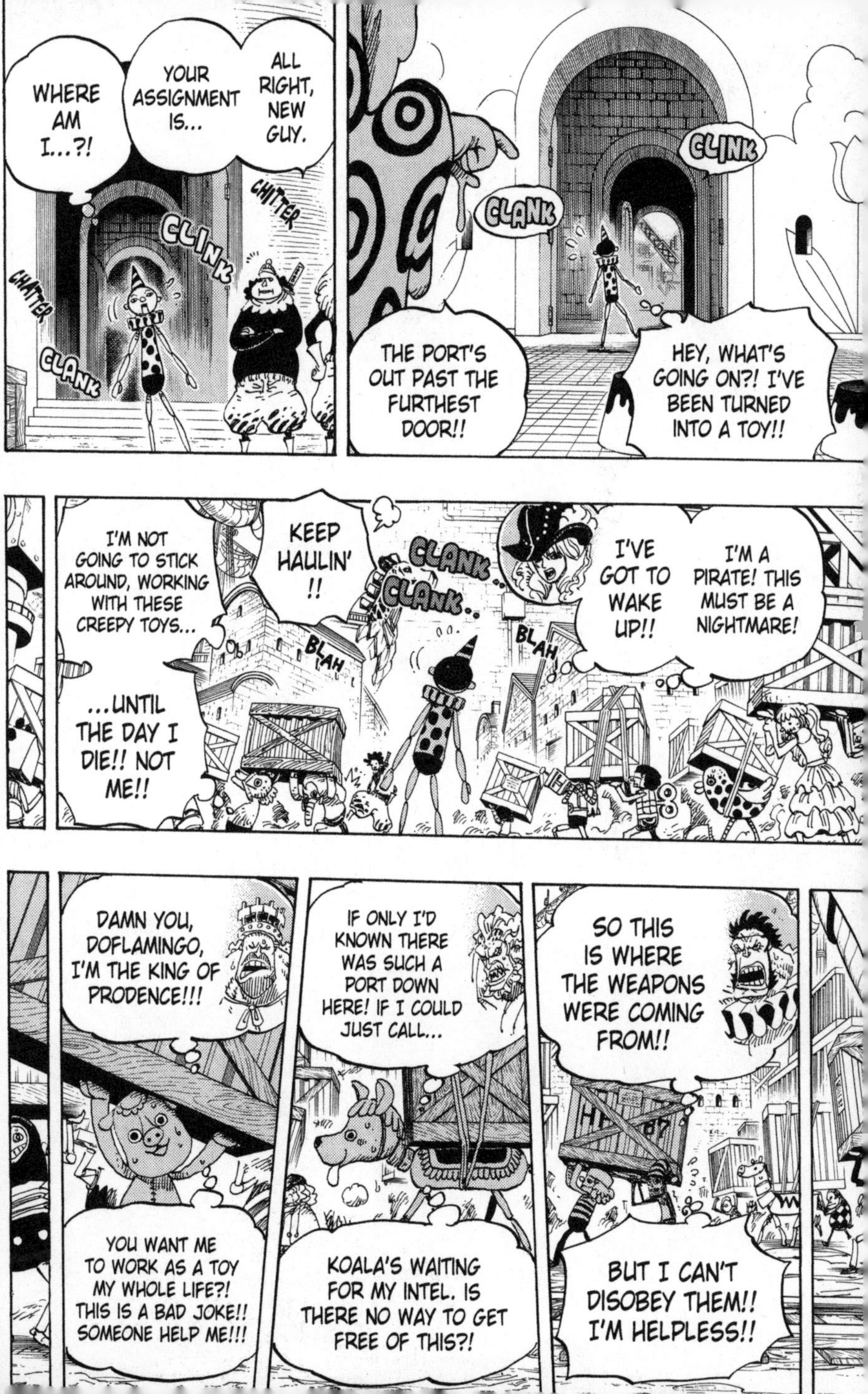
CLINK
CLANK
HEY, WHAT'S GOING ON?! I'VE BEEN TURNED INTO A TOY!!
THE PORT'S OUT PAST THE FURTHEST DOOR!!
ALL RIGHT, NEW GUY.
YOUR ASSIGNMENT IS...
WHERE AM I...?!
CHITTER
CLINK
CHATTER
CLANK
I'M A PIRATE! THIS MUST BE A NIGHTMARE!
I'VE GOT TO WAKE UP!!
CLANK
CLANK
KEEP HAULIN'!!
BLAH
BLAH
I'M NOT GOING TO STICK AROUND, WORKING WITH THESE CREEPY TOYS...
...UNTIL THE DAY I DIE!! NOT ME!!
SO THIS IS WHERE THE WEAPONS WERE COMING FROM!!
BUT I CAN'T DISOBEY THEM!! I'M HELPLESS!!
IF ONLY I'D KNOWN THERE WAS SUCH A PORT DOWN HERE! IF I COULD JUST CALL...
KOALA'S WAITING FOR MY INTEL. IS THERE NO WAY TO GET FREE OF THIS?!
DAMN YOU, DOFLAMINGO, I'M THE KING OF PRODENCE!!!
YOU WANT ME TO WORK AS A TOY MY WHOLE LIFE?! THIS IS A BAD JOKE!! SOMEONE HELP ME!!!

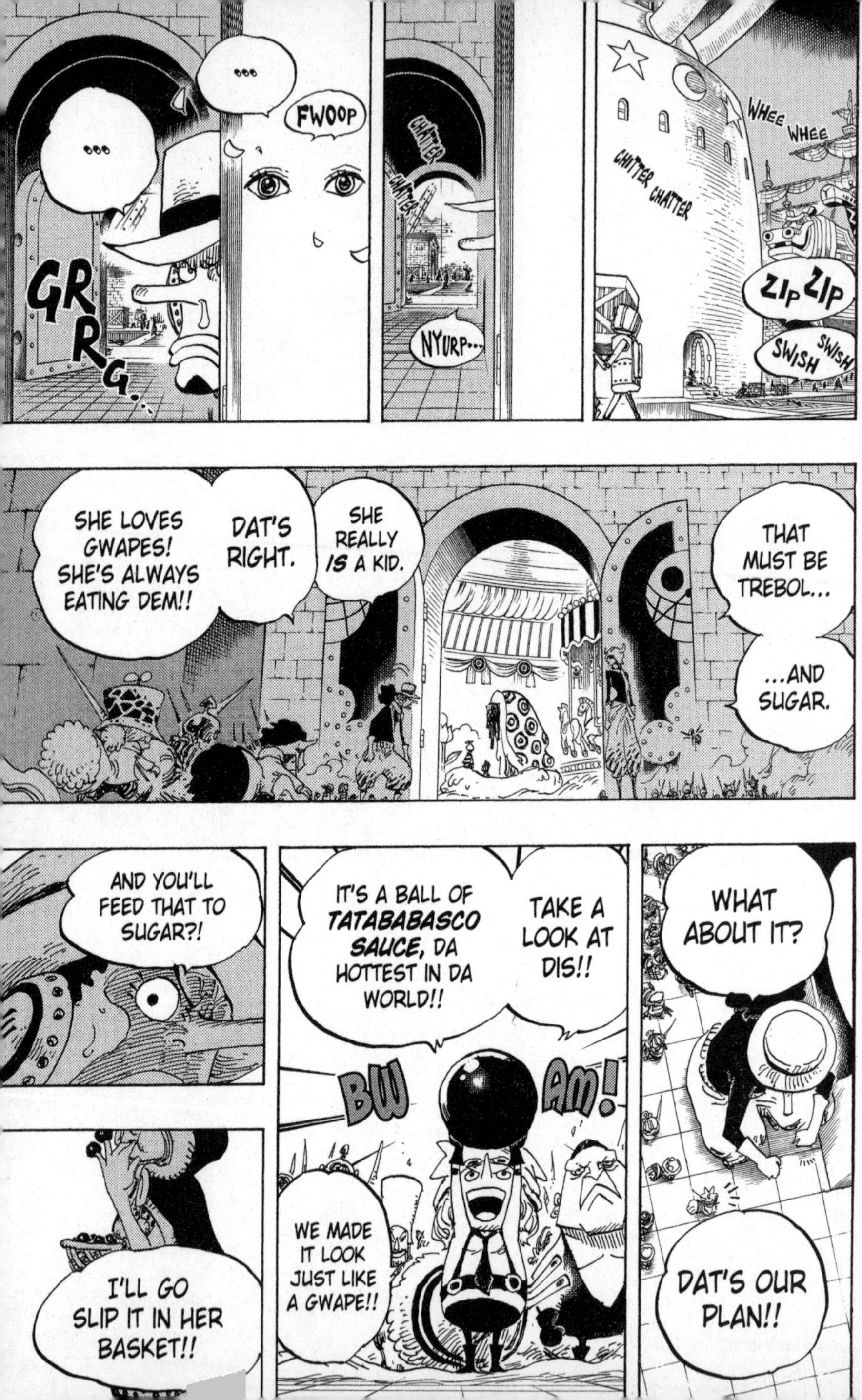
WHEE WHEE
CHATTER CHATTER
ZIP ZIP
SWISH SWISH
CHATTER CHATTER
NYURP...
FWOOP
...
...
GRRRG...
THAT MUST BE TREBOL...
...AND SUGAR.
SHE REALLY *IS* A KID.
DAT'S RIGHT.
SHE LOVES GWAPES! SHE'S ALWAYS EATING DEM!!
WHAT ABOUT IT?
DAT'S OUR PLAN!!
TAKE A LOOK AT DIS!!
IT'S A BALL OF ***TATABABASCO SAUCE,*** DA HOTTEST IN DA WORLD!!
BWAM!
WE MADE IT LOOK JUST LIKE A GWAPE!!
AND YOU'LL FEED THAT TO SUGAR?!
I'LL GO SLIP IT IN HER BASKET!!

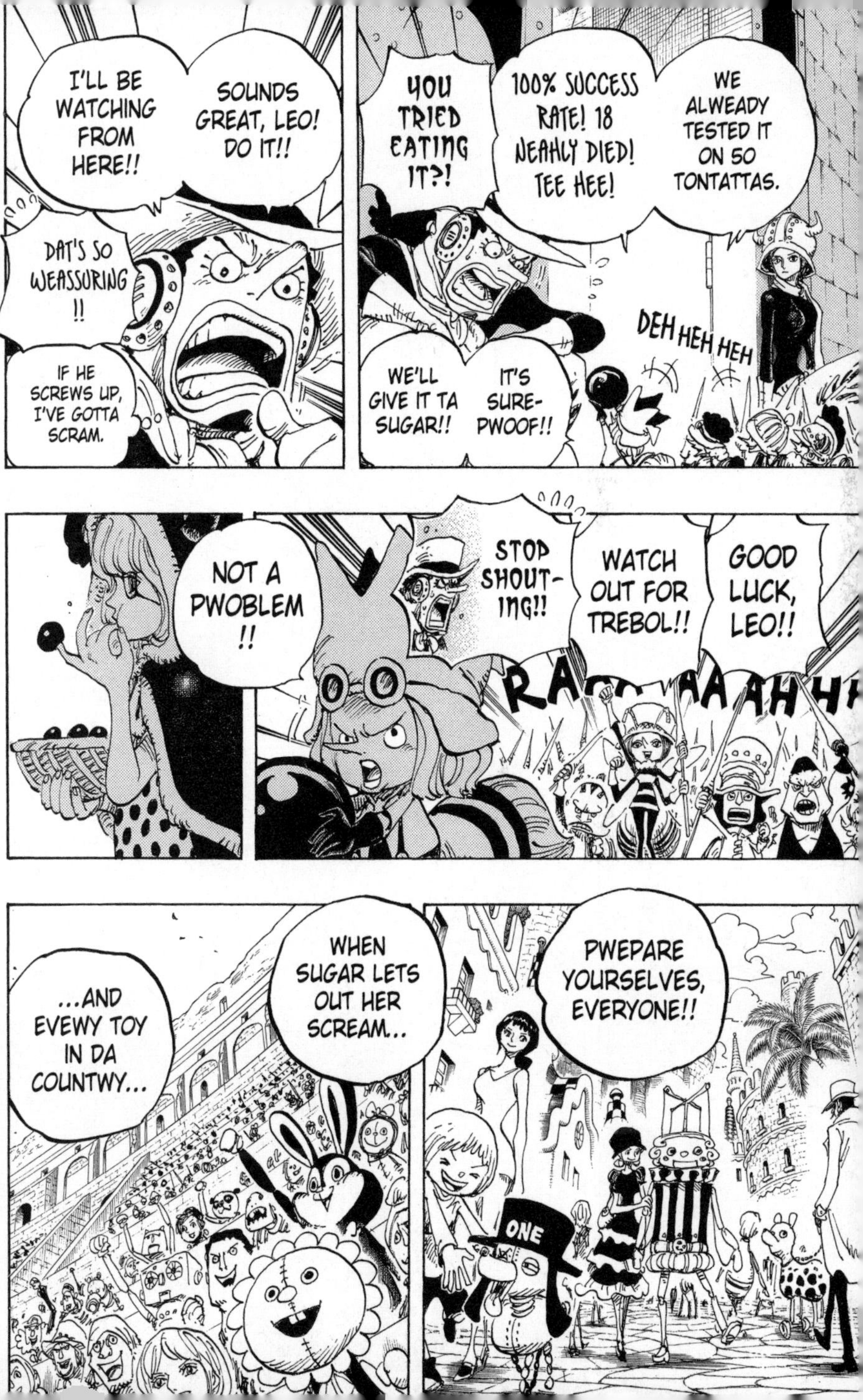
WE ALWEADY TESTED IT ON 50 TONTATTAS.
100% SUCCESS RATE! 18 NEAHLY DIED! TEE HEE!
YOU TRIED EATING IT?!
DEH HEH HEH
IT'S SURE-PWOOF!!
WE'LL GIVE IT TA SUGAR!!
SOUNDS GREAT, LEO! DO IT!!
I'LL BE WATCHING FROM HERE!!
DAT'S SO WEASSURING!!
IF HE SCREWS UP, I'VE GOTTA SCRAM.
GOOD LUCK, LEO!!
WATCH OUT FOR TREBOL!!
STOP SHOUTING!!
NOT A PWOBLEM!!
PWEPARE YOURSELVES, EVERYONE!!
ONE
WHEN SUGAR LETS OUT HER SCREAM...
...AND EVEWY TOY IN DA COUNTWY...

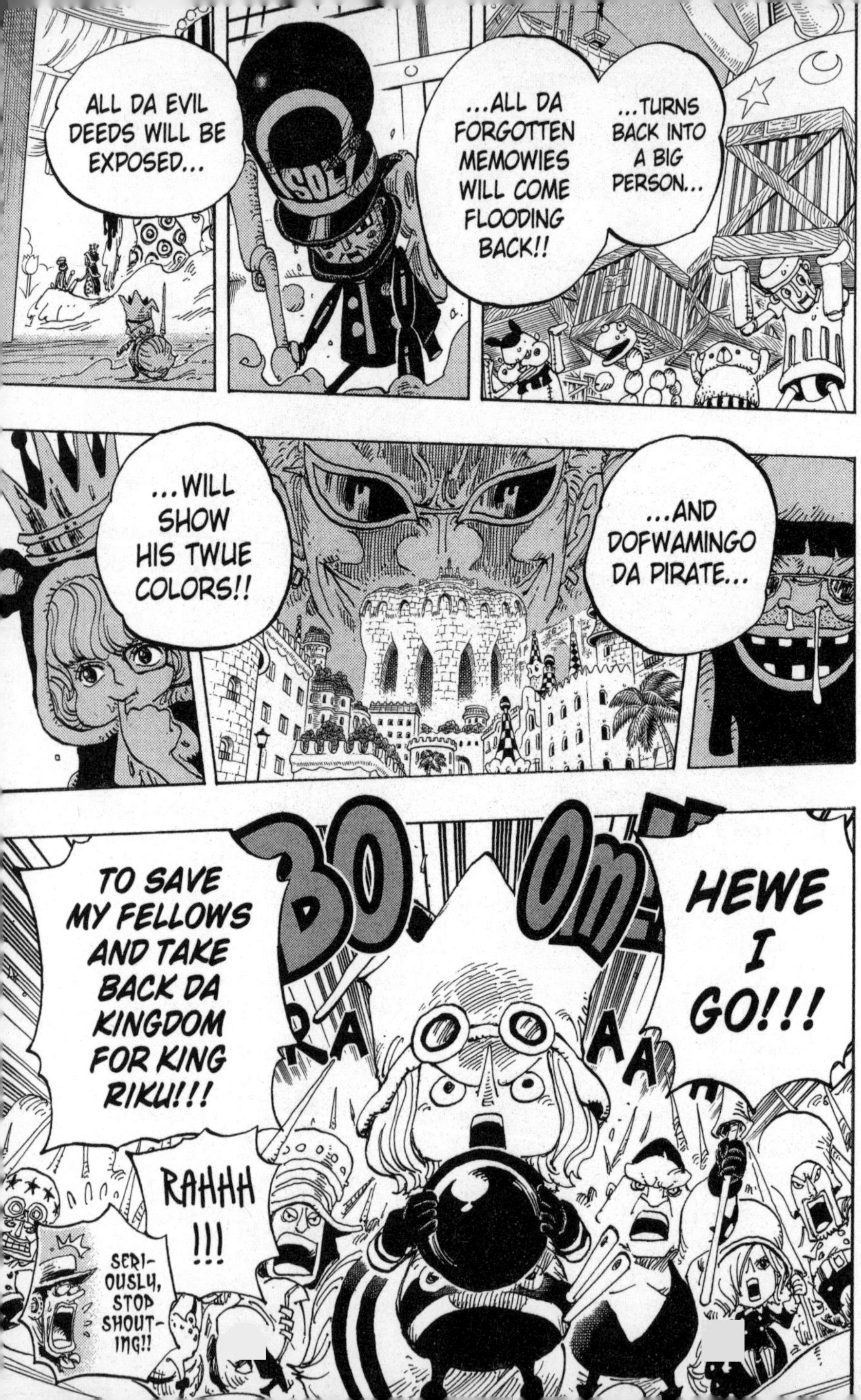
...TURNS BACK INTO A BIG PERSON...
...ALL DA FORGOTTEN MEMOWIES WILL COME FLOODING BACK!!
ALL DA EVIL DEEDS WILL BE EXPOSED...
...AND DOFWAMINGO DA PIRATE...
...WILL SHOW HIS TWUE COLORS!!
HEWE I GO!!!
BOOM
TO SAVE MY FELLOWS AND TAKE BACK DA KINGDOM FOR KING RIKU!!!
RAHHH !!!
SERI-OUSLY, STOP SHOUT-ING!!

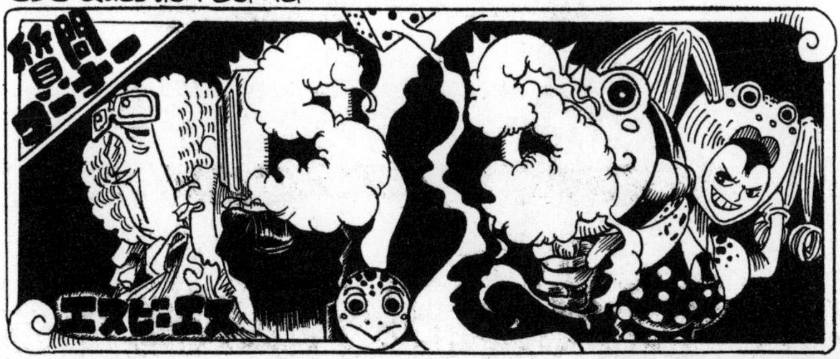
質問コーナー
エスビーエス
(Michi Nakahara, Tottori)

Q: They say that Luffy's Supreme King Haki can knock out fifty thousand, but what about Nami's Happiness Punch?

--Captain Nobuo

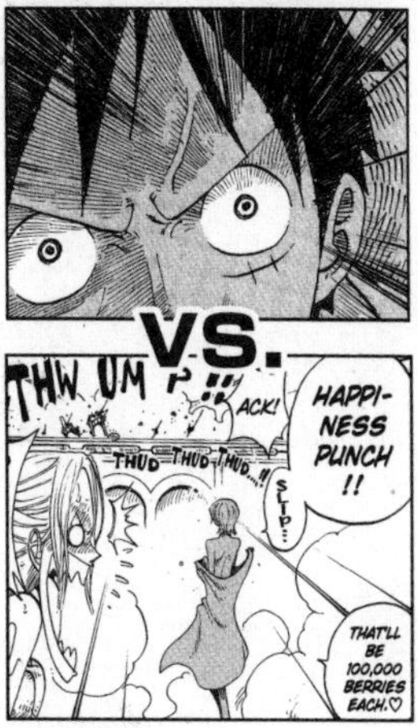
VS.
HAPPINESS PUNCH!!
ACK!
THW UMP!!
THUD THUD THUD...!!
SLIP...
THAT'LL BE 100,000 BERRIES EACH.♡

A: Ooh, good question. That's a tough matchup. Of course, in person, the Happiness Punch only affects those who can see it, so it's no match for Luffy. However, if you can use visual transponder snails, Luffy's Haki won't travel over the airwaves, but Nami can lay waste to the entire world, so I think she would win. Even worse, Nami's Happiness Punch costs 100,000 berries per person, which is deadly to anyone's pocketbook. In a way, it's much crueler than Haki.

Q: I want to know when the Straw Hats go to sleep and wake up!

--Fujiyama

A: That's a very interesting question. They don't seem to get into a rhythm very often, but here's the general idea. (S) stands for sleep, and (W) stands for wake.

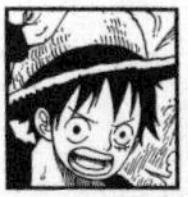
(S) When he's tired
(W) When his eyes open
(About five hours of sleep)

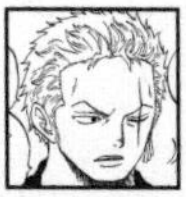
(S) 4:00 AM
(W) 7:00 AM
(Plus naps)

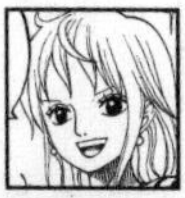
(S) 11:00 PM
(W) 7:00 AM

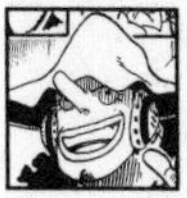
(S) 1:00 AM
(W) 8:00 AM

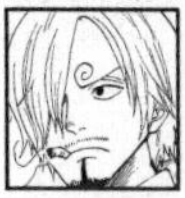
(S) 12:00 AM
(W) 5:00 AM

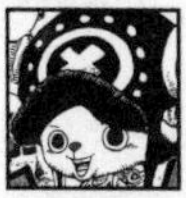
(S) 9:00 PM
(W) 7:00 AM
(Plus naps)

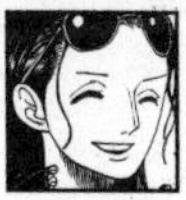
(S) 11:00 PM
(W) 6:00 AM

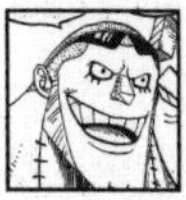
(S) 1:00 AM
(W) 9:00 AM

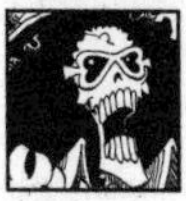
(S) 12:00 AM
(W) 5:00 AM

A: When they sail at night, the ship needs guards at the fore and aft, so there are always two awake at any moment. Everyone switches out in two-hour shifts. It's very rare that they're all asleep at once.

Chapter 738:
TREBOL ARMY, SPECIAL OFFICER SUGAR

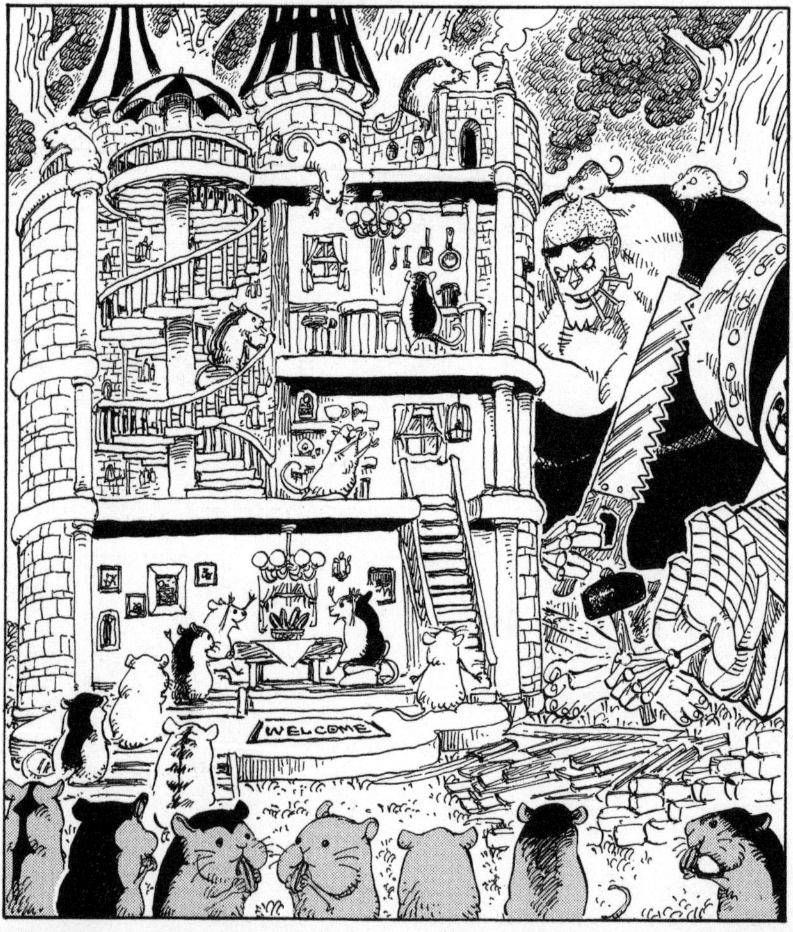
WELCOME

REQUEST: "FRANKY BUILDS A MINIATURE HOUSE FOR SOME HAMSTERS" BY NODA SKYWALKER FROM OSAKA

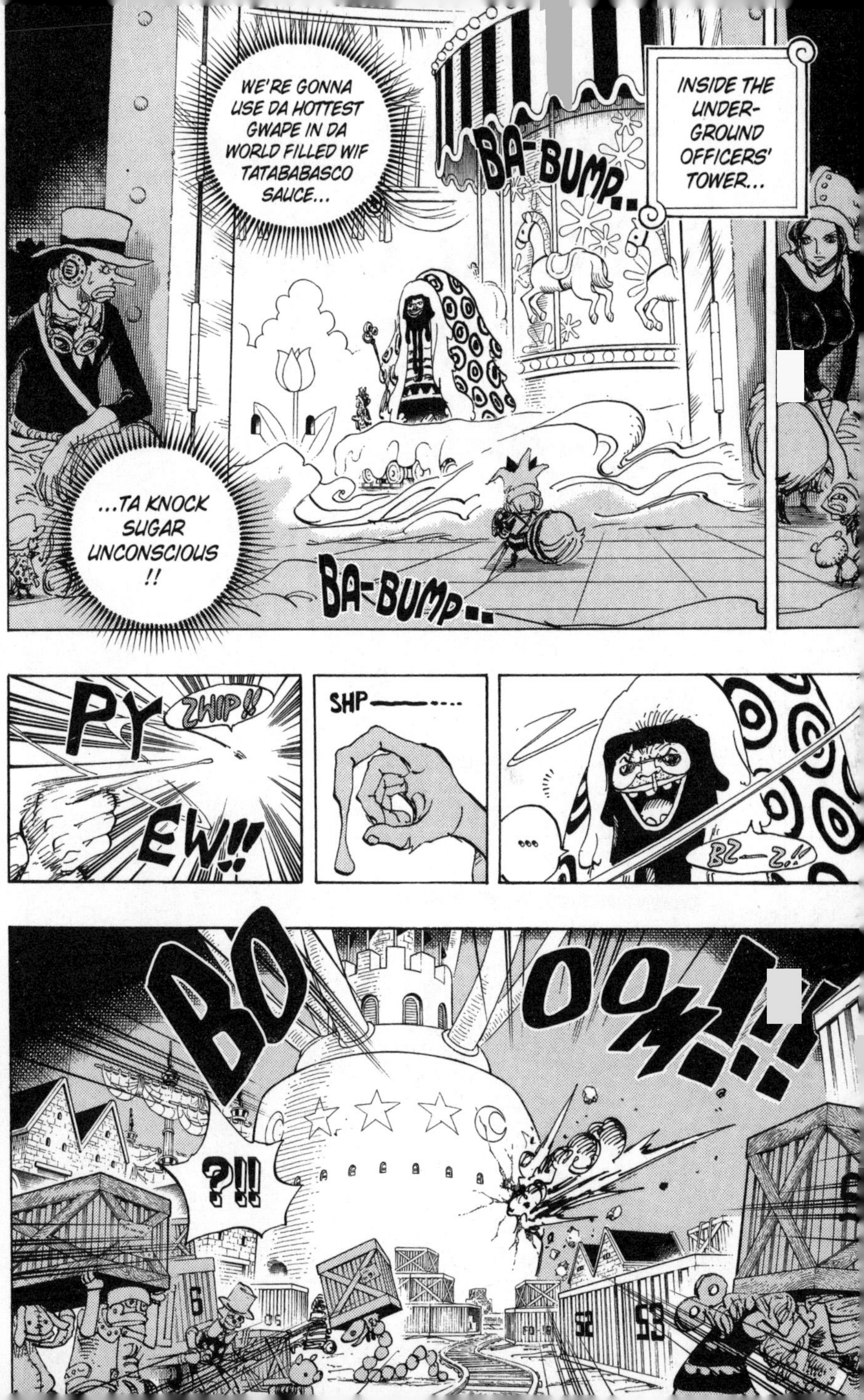
INSIDE THE UNDERGROUND OFFICERS' TOWER...
BA-BUMP..
WE'RE GONNA USE DA HOTTEST GWAPE IN DA WORLD FILLED WIF TATABABASCO SAUCE...
...TA KNOCK SUGAR UNCONSCIOUS !!
BA-BUMP..
BZ—Z!!
...
SHP———....
PYEW!!
ZHIP!!
BOOOM!!!
?!!

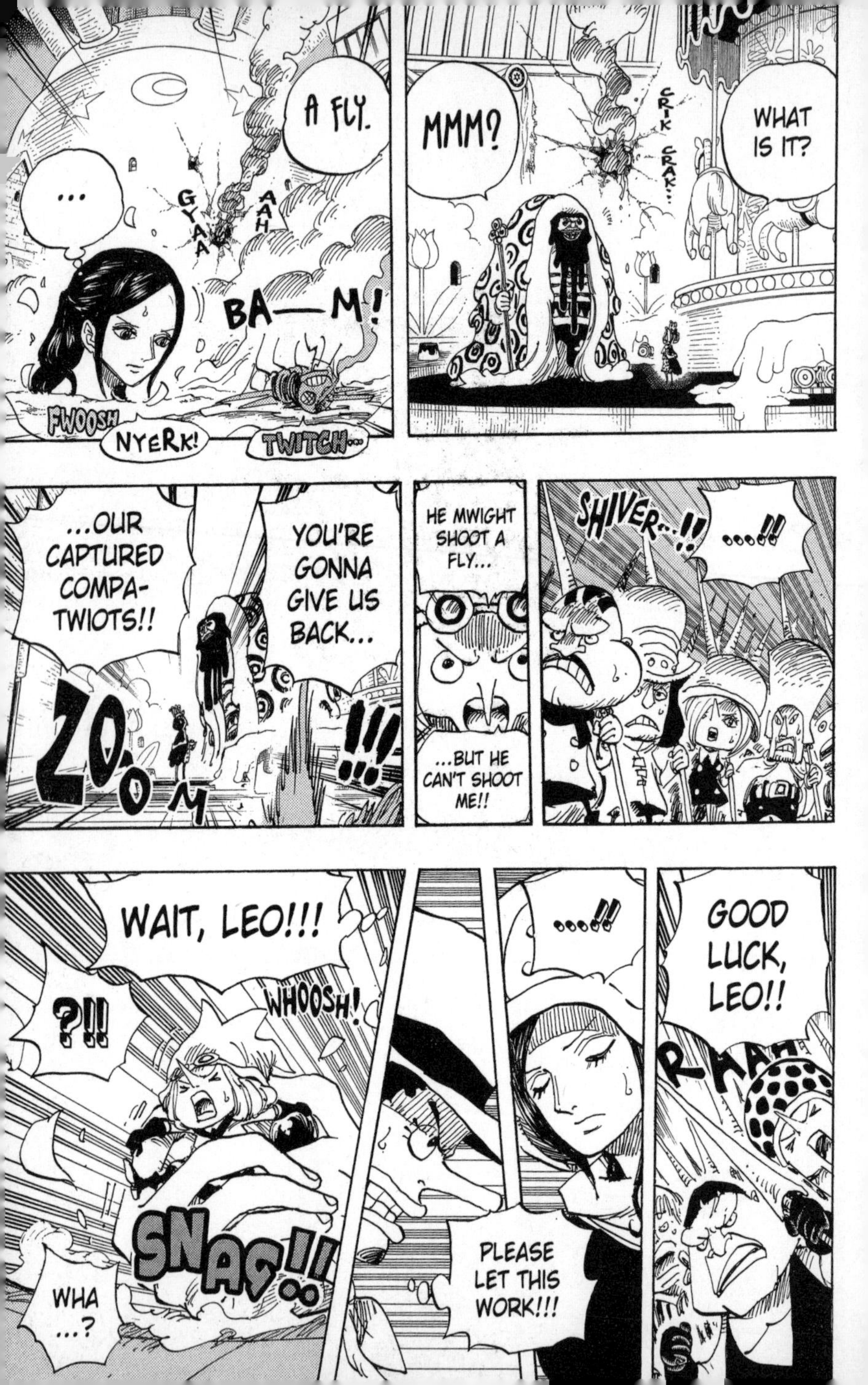
WHAT IS IT?
CRIK CRAK...
MMM?
A FLY.
AAH
GYAA
...
BA—M!
TWITCH...
NYERK!
FWOOSH
...!!
SHIVER...!!
HE MWIGHT SHOOT A FLY...
...BUT HE CAN'T SHOOT ME!!
YOU'RE GONNA GIVE US BACK...
...OUR CAPTURED COMPA-TWIOTS!!
!!!
ZOOM
GOOD LUCK, LEO!!
RAAH
...!!
PLEASE LET THIS WORK!!!
WAIT, LEO!!!
WHOOSH!
?!!
SNAG!!!
WHA ...?

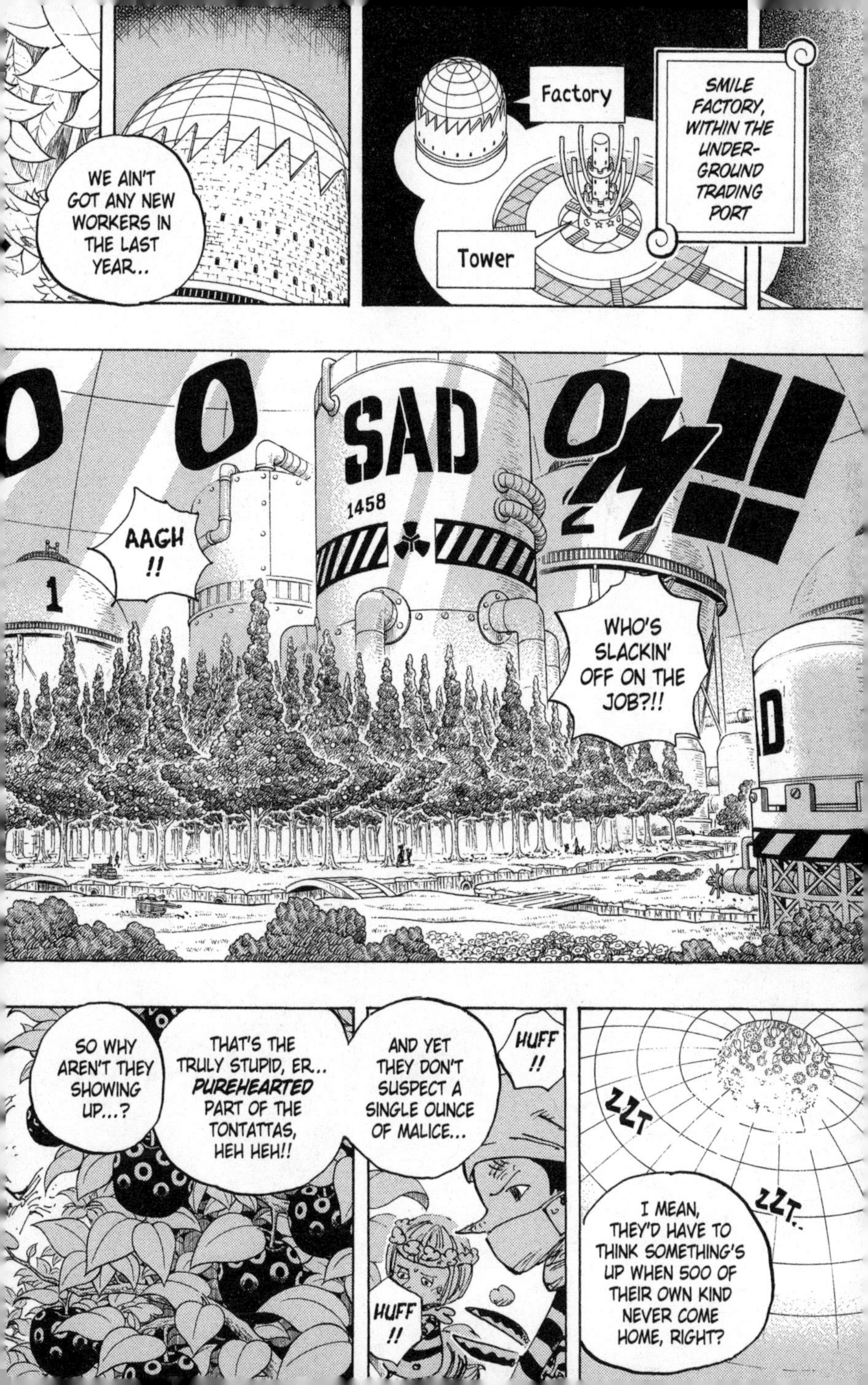
SMILE FACTORY, WITHIN THE UNDERGROUND TRADING PORT
Factory
Tower
WE AIN'T GOT ANY NEW WORKERS IN THE LAST YEAR...
DOSADON!!
WHO'S SLACKIN' OFF ON THE JOB?!!
AAGH!!
ZZT
ZZT..
I MEAN, THEY'D HAVE TO THINK SOMETHING'S UP WHEN 500 OF THEIR OWN KIND NEVER COME HOME, RIGHT?
HUFF!!
AND YET THEY DON'T SUSPECT A SINGLE OUNCE OF MALICE...
HUFF!!
THAT'S THE TRULY STUPID, ER... *PUREHEARTED* PART OF THE TONTATTAS, HEH HEH!!
SO WHY AREN'T THEY SHOWING UP...?

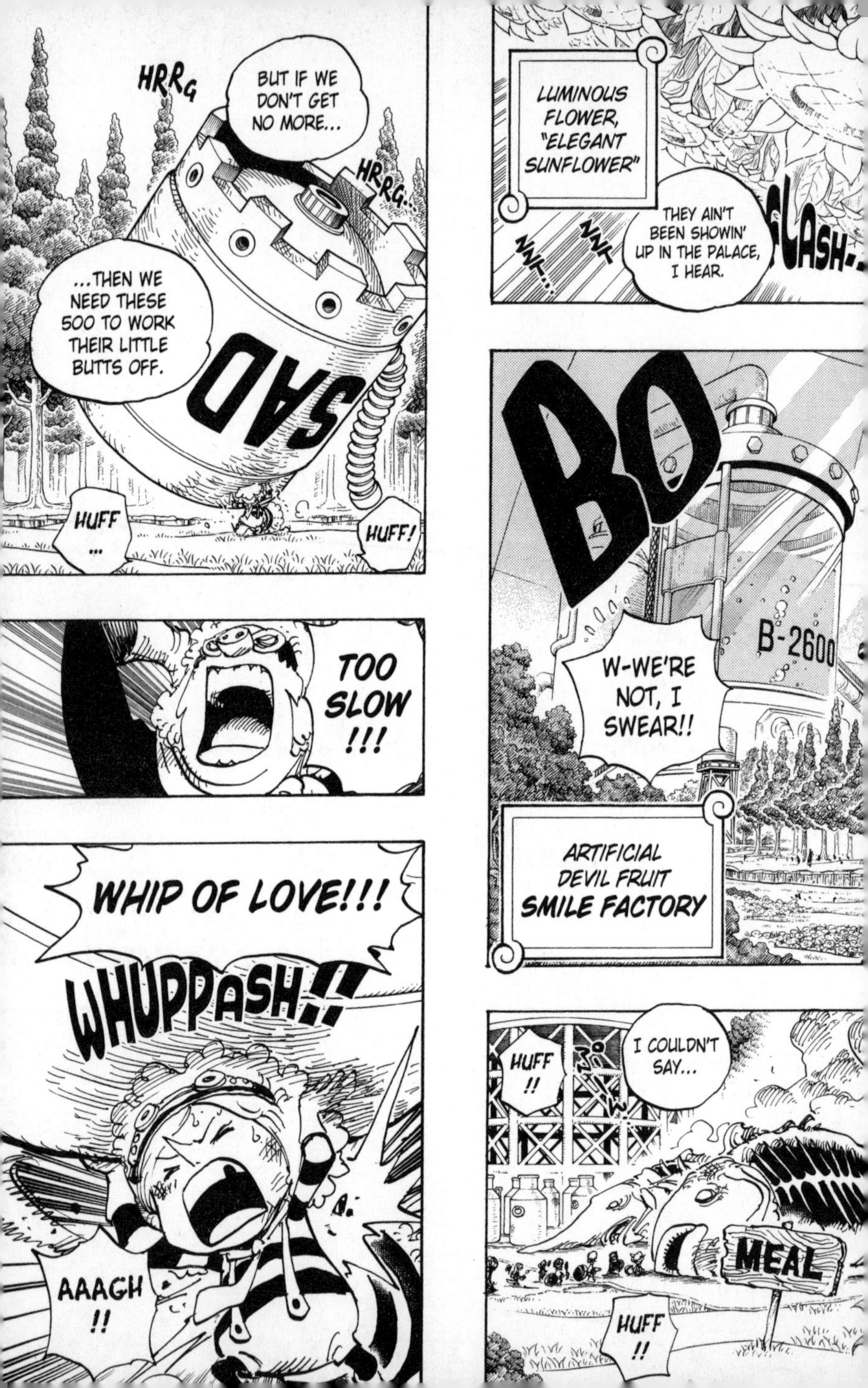
LUMINOUS FLOWER, "ELEGANT SUNFLOWER"
ZZNT ZZNT...
THEY AIN'T BEEN SHOWIN' UP IN THE PALACE, I HEAR.
FLASH...
BO
B-2600
W-WE'RE NOT, I SWEAR!!
ARTIFICIAL DEVIL FRUIT SMILE FACTORY
I COULDN'T SAY...
HUFF !!
MEAL
HUFF !!
HRRG
BUT IF WE DON'T GET NO MORE...
HRRG...
...THEN WE NEED THESE 500 TO WORK THEIR LITTLE BUTTS OFF.
SAD
HUFF!
HUFF ...
TOO SLOW !!!
WHIP OF LOVE!!!
WHUPPASH!!
AAAGH !!

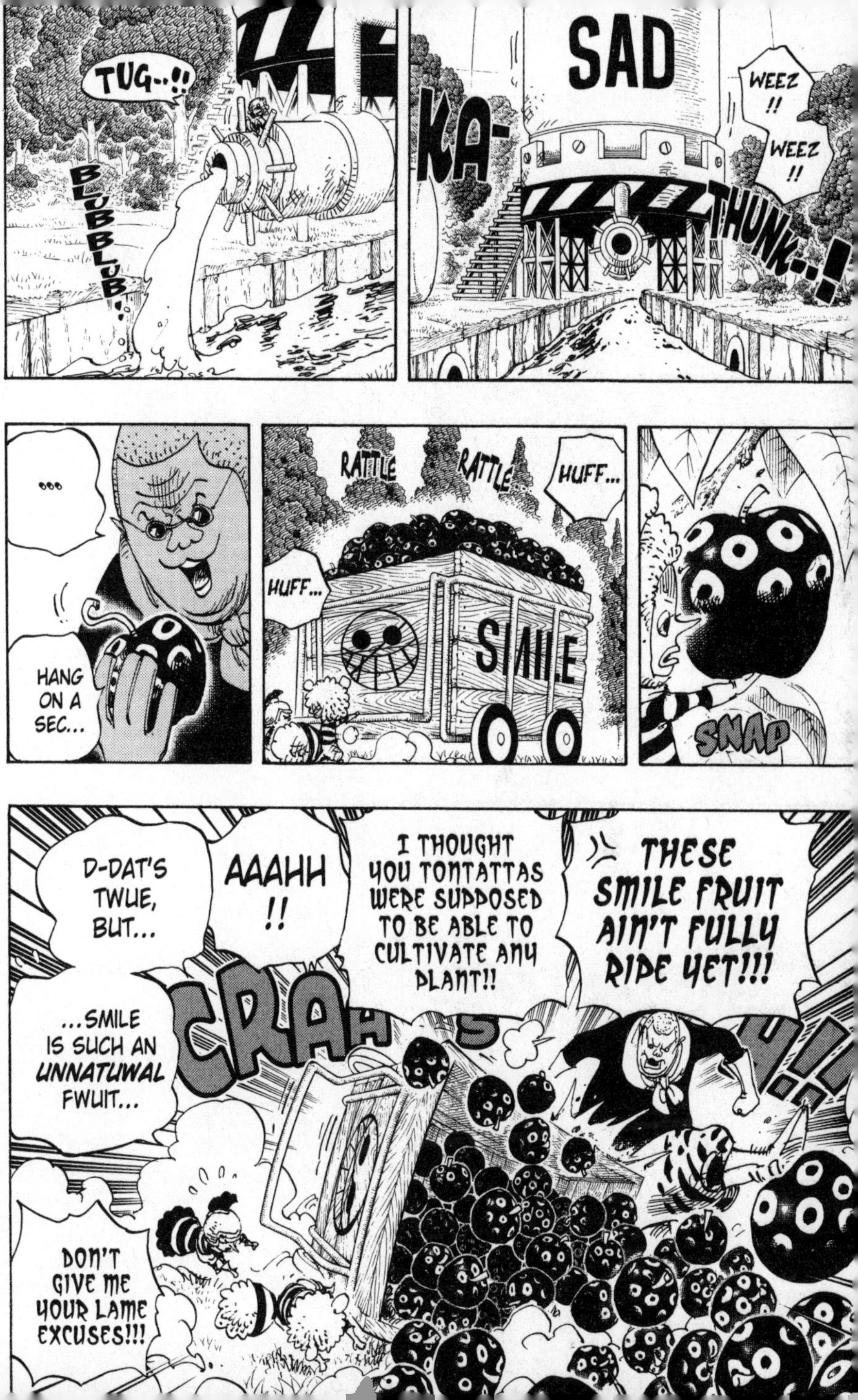
WEEZ !!
WEEZ !!
SAD
KA-
THUNK..!!
TUG..!!
BLUBBLUB
SNAP
HUFF...
RATTLE
RATTLE
HUFF...
SMILE
...
HANG ON A SEC...
THESE SMILE FRUIT AIN'T FULLY RIPE YET!!!
I THOUGHT YOU TONTATTAS WERE SUPPOSED TO BE ABLE TO CULTIVATE ANY PLANT!!
AAAHH !!
D-DAT'S TWUE, BUT...
...SMILE IS SUCH AN UNNATUWAL FWUIT...
DON'T GIVE ME YOUR LAME EXCUSES!!!

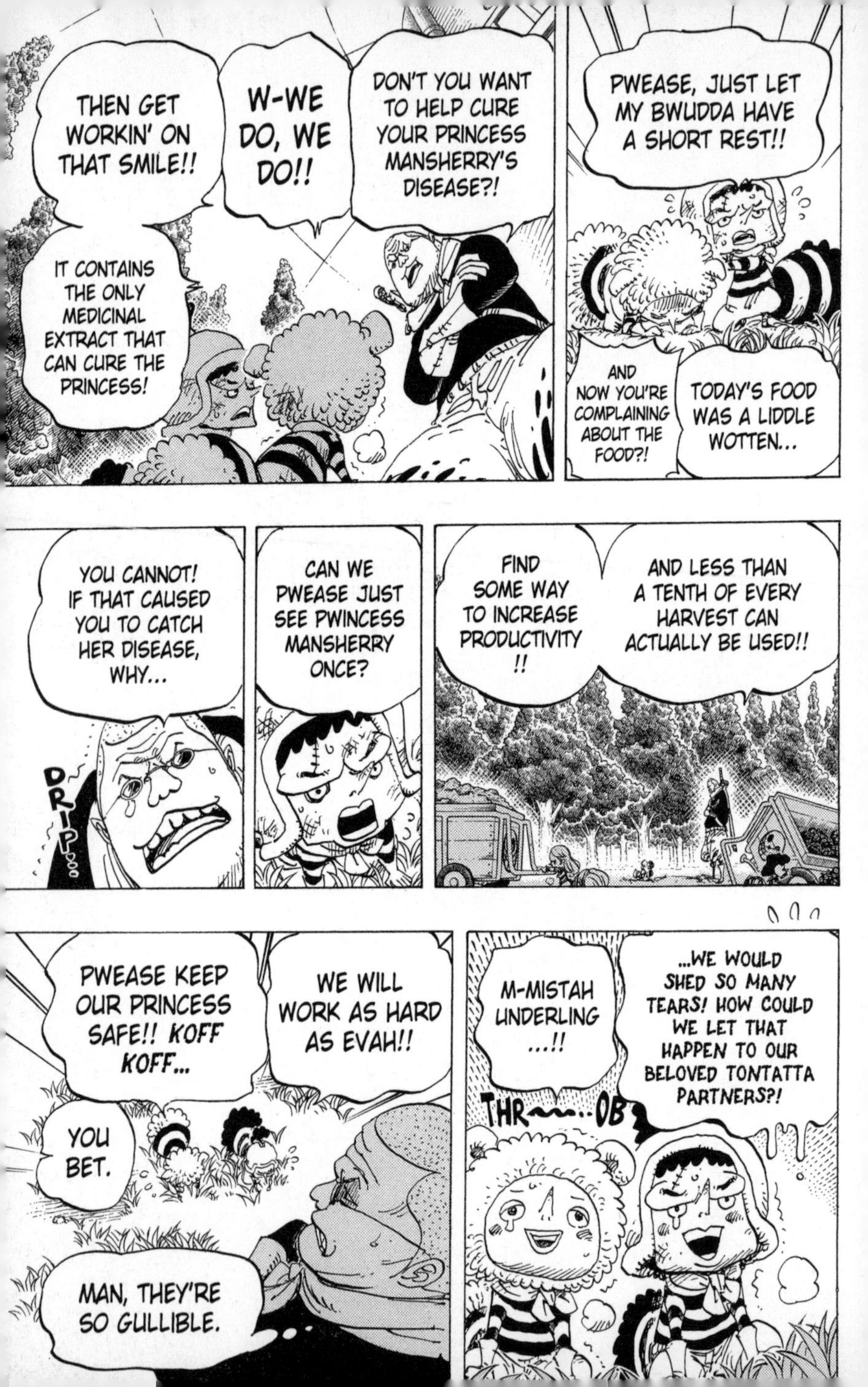
PWEASE, JUST LET MY BWUDDA HAVE A SHORT REST!!
TODAY'S FOOD WAS A LIDDLE WOTTEN...
AND NOW YOU'RE COMPLAINING ABOUT THE FOOD?!
DON'T YOU WANT TO HELP CURE YOUR PRINCESS MANSHERRY'S DISEASE?!
W-WE DO, WE DO!!
THEN GET WORKIN' ON THAT SMILE!!
IT CONTAINS THE ONLY MEDICINAL EXTRACT THAT CAN CURE THE PRINCESS!
AND LESS THAN A TENTH OF EVERY HARVEST CAN ACTUALLY BE USED!!
FIND SOME WAY TO INCREASE PRODUCTIVITY!!
CAN WE PWEASE JUST SEE PWINCESS MANSHERRY ONCE?
YOU CANNOT! IF THAT CAUSED YOU TO CATCH HER DISEASE, WHY...
DRIP
...WE WOULD SHED SO MANY TEARS! HOW COULD WE LET THAT HAPPEN TO OUR BELOVED TONTATTA PARTNERS?!
M-MISTAH UNDERLING...!!
THR~~~OB
WE WILL WORK AS HARD AS EVAH!!
PWEASE KEEP OUR PRINCESS SAFE!! KOFF KOFF...
YOU BET.
MAN, THEY'RE SO GULLIBLE.

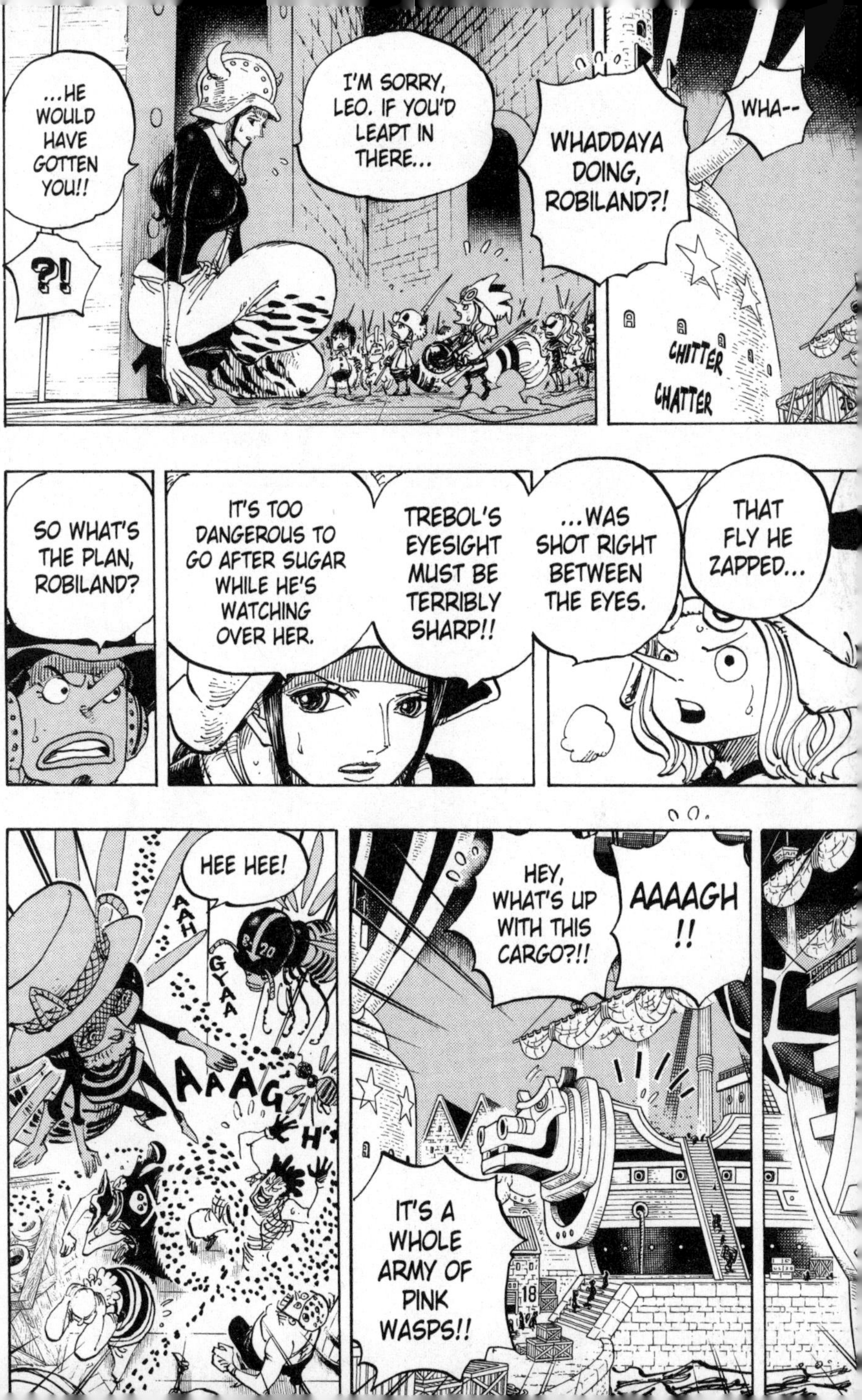
WHA--
WHADDAYA DOING, ROBILAND?!
CHITTER
CHATTER
I'M SORRY, LEO. IF YOU'D LEAPT IN THERE...
...HE WOULD HAVE GOTTEN YOU!!
?!
THAT FLY HE ZAPPED...
...WAS SHOT RIGHT BETWEEN THE EYES.
TREBOL'S EYESIGHT MUST BE TERRIBLY SHARP!!
IT'S TOO DANGEROUS TO GO AFTER SUGAR WHILE HE'S WATCHING OVER HER.
SO WHAT'S THE PLAN, ROBILAND?
AAAAGH !!
HEY, WHAT'S UP WITH THIS CARGO?!!
IT'S A WHOLE ARMY OF PINK WASPS!!
HEE HEE!
AAH
GYAA
AAAGH

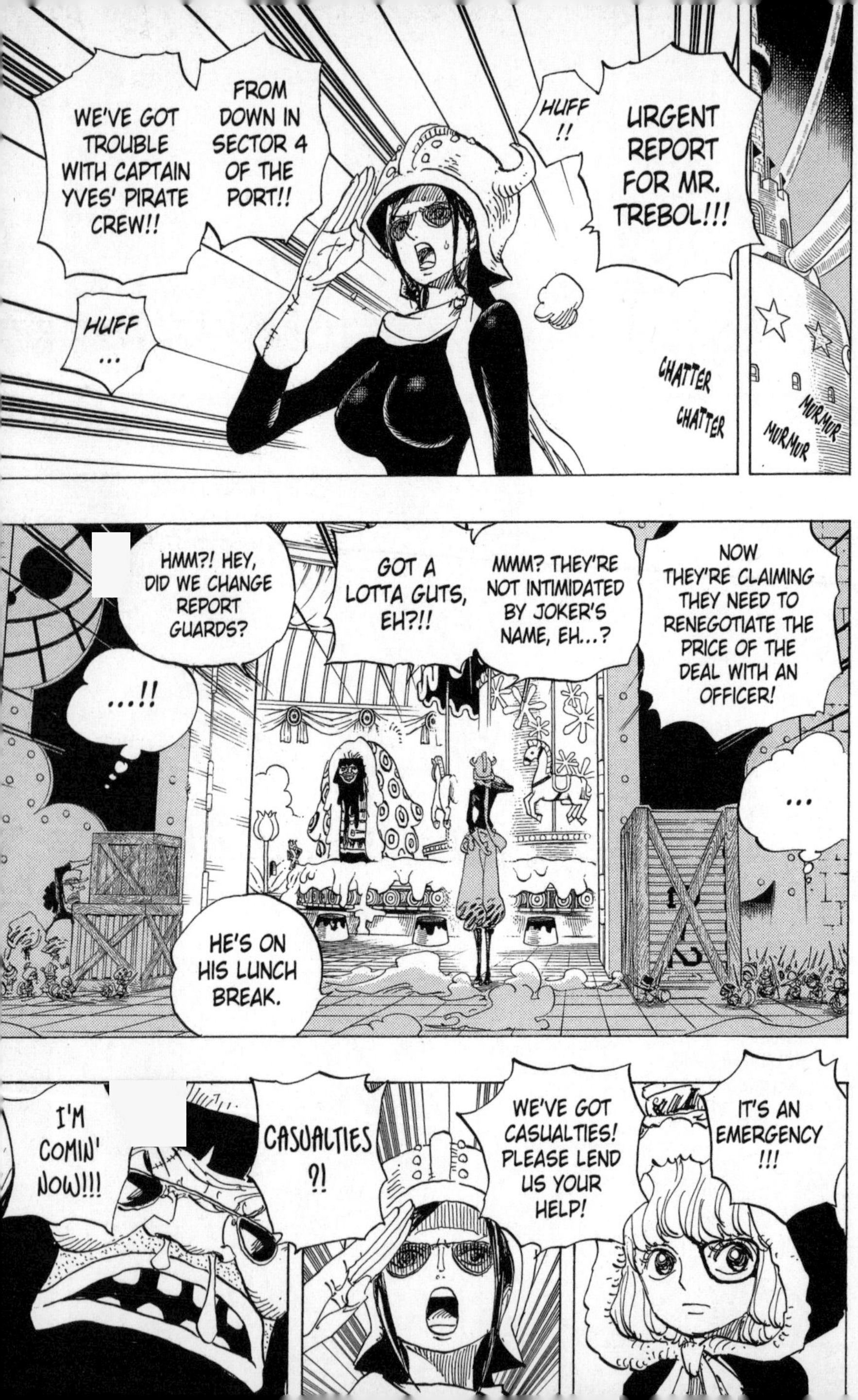
MURMUR
MURMUR
URGENT REPORT FOR MR. TREBOL!!!
HUFF !!
FROM DOWN IN SECTOR 4 OF THE PORT!!
WE'VE GOT TROUBLE WITH CAPTAIN YVES' PIRATE CREW!!
CHATTER
CHATTER
HUFF ...
NOW THEY'RE CLAIMING THEY NEED TO RENEGOTIATE THE PRICE OF THE DEAL WITH AN OFFICER!
MMM? THEY'RE NOT INTIMIDATED BY JOKER'S NAME, EH...?
GOT A LOTTA GUTS, EH?!!
...
HMM?! HEY, DID WE CHANGE REPORT GUARDS?
...!!
HE'S ON HIS LUNCH BREAK.
IT'S AN EMERGENCY !!!
WE'VE GOT CASUALTIES! PLEASE LEND US YOUR HELP!
CASUALTIES ?!
I'M COMIN' NOW!!!

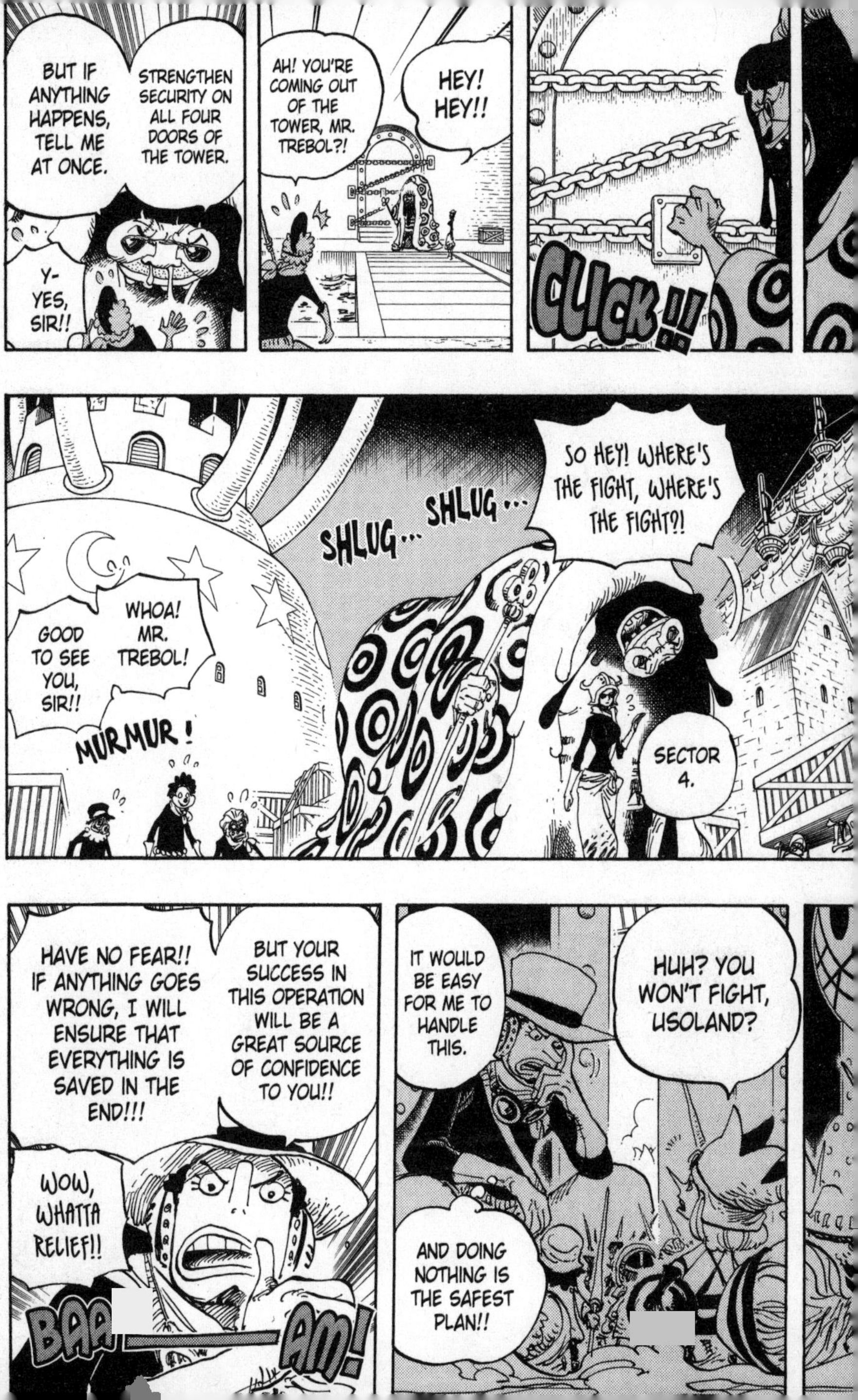

CLICK!!
HEY! HEY!!
AH! YOU'RE COMING OUT OF THE TOWER, MR. TREBOL?!
STRENGTHEN SECURITY ON ALL FOUR DOORS OF THE TOWER.
BUT IF ANYTHING HAPPENS, TELL ME AT ONCE.
Y- YES, SIR!!
SO HEY! WHERE'S THE FIGHT, WHERE'S THE FIGHT?!
SHLUG... SHLUG...
SECTOR 4.
WHOA! MR. TREBOL!
GOOD TO SEE YOU, SIR!!
MURMUR!
HUH? YOU WON'T FIGHT, USOLAND?
IT WOULD BE EASY FOR ME TO HANDLE THIS.
AND DOING NOTHING IS THE SAFEST PLAN!!
BUT YOUR SUCCESS IN THIS OPERATION WILL BE A GREAT SOURCE OF CONFIDENCE TO YOU!!
HAVE NO FEAR!! IF ANYTHING GOES WRONG, I WILL ENSURE THAT EVERYTHING IS SAVED IN THE END!!!
WOW, WHATTA RELIEF!!
BAAA—AM!

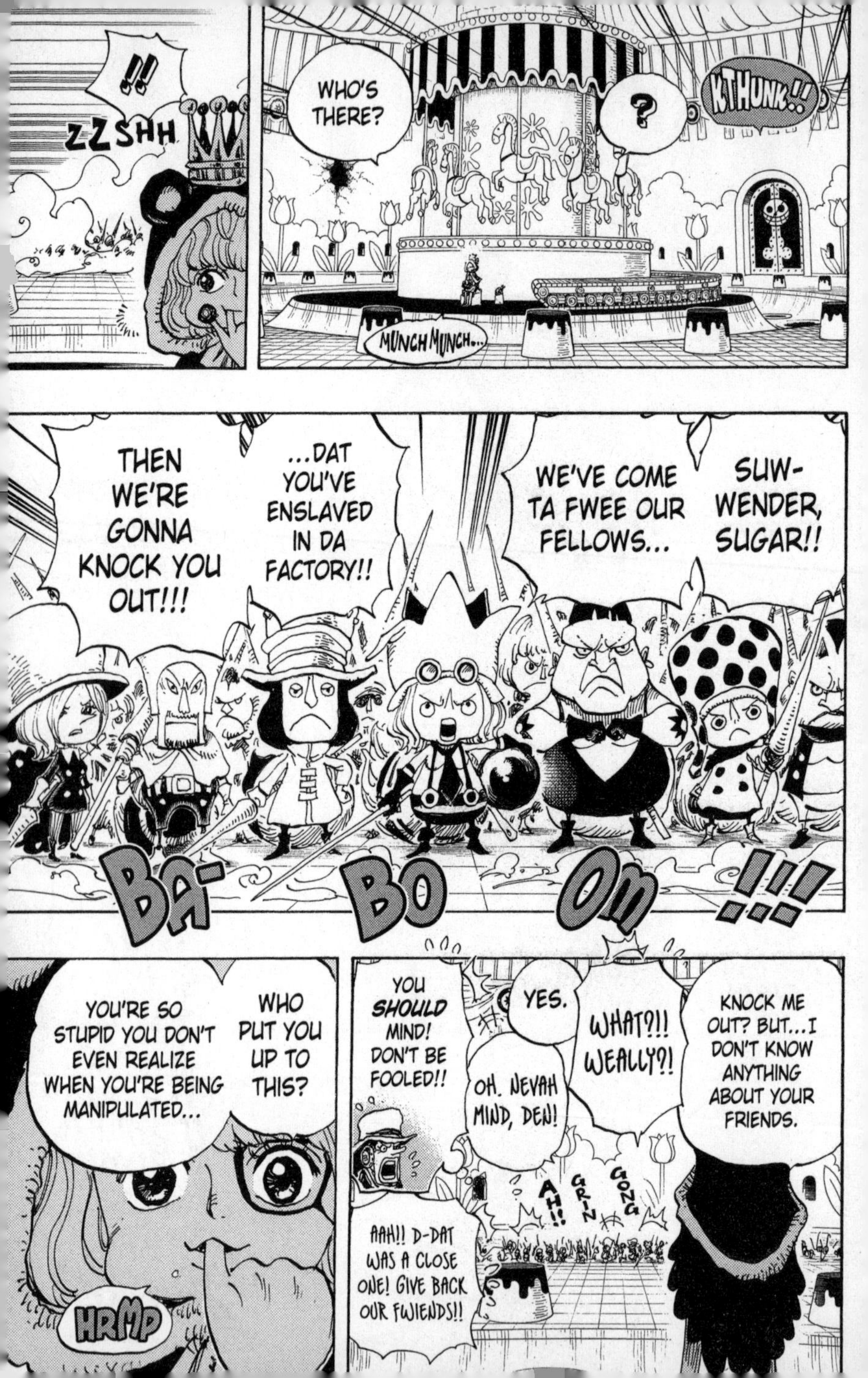
KTHUNK!!
?
WHO'S THERE?
MUNCH MUNCH...
!!
ZZSHH
SUW-WENDER, SUGAR!!
WE'VE COME TA FWEE OUR FELLOWS...
...DAT YOU'VE ENSLAVED IN DA FACTORY!!
THEN WE'RE GONNA KNOCK YOU OUT!!!
BA-BO-OM!!!
KNOCK ME OUT? BUT...I DON'T KNOW ANYTHING ABOUT YOUR FRIENDS.
WHAT?!! WEALLY?!
YES.
OH. NEVAH MIND, DEN!
YOU SHOULD MIND! DON'T BE FOOLED!!
GONG
GRIN
AH!!
AAH!! D-DAT WAS A CLOSE ONE! GIVE BACK OUR FWIENDS!!
WHO PUT YOU UP TO THIS?
YOU'RE SO STUPID YOU DON'T EVEN REALIZE WHEN YOU'RE BEING MANIPULATED...
HRMP

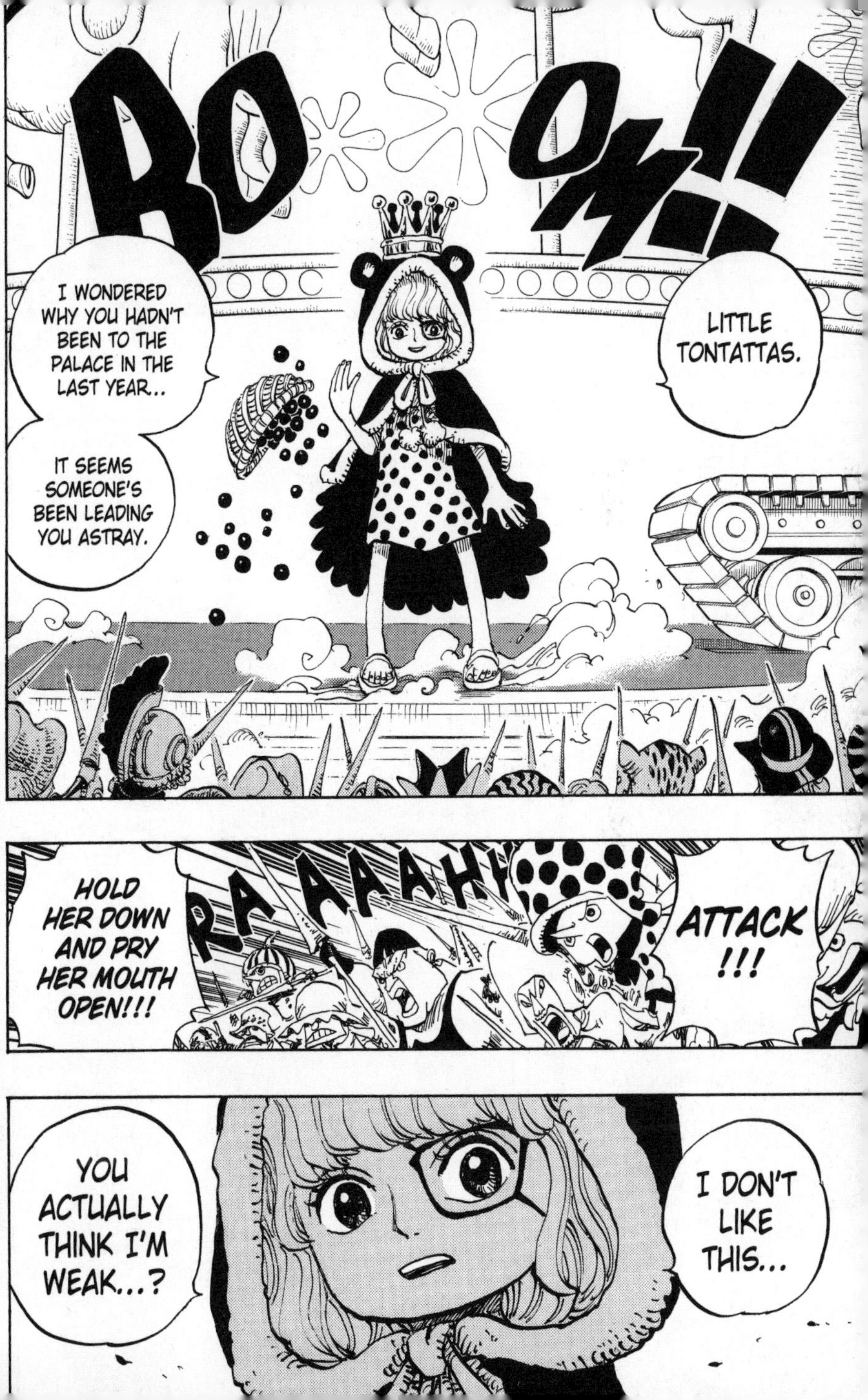
BOOM!!
LITTLE TONTATTAS.
I WONDERED WHY YOU HADN'T BEEN TO THE PALACE IN THE LAST YEAR...
IT SEEMS SOMEONE'S BEEN LEADING YOU ASTRAY.
ATTACK!!!
RAAAAH
HOLD HER DOWN AND PRY HER MOUTH OPEN!!!
I DON'T LIKE THIS...
YOU ACTUALLY THINK I'M WEAK...?

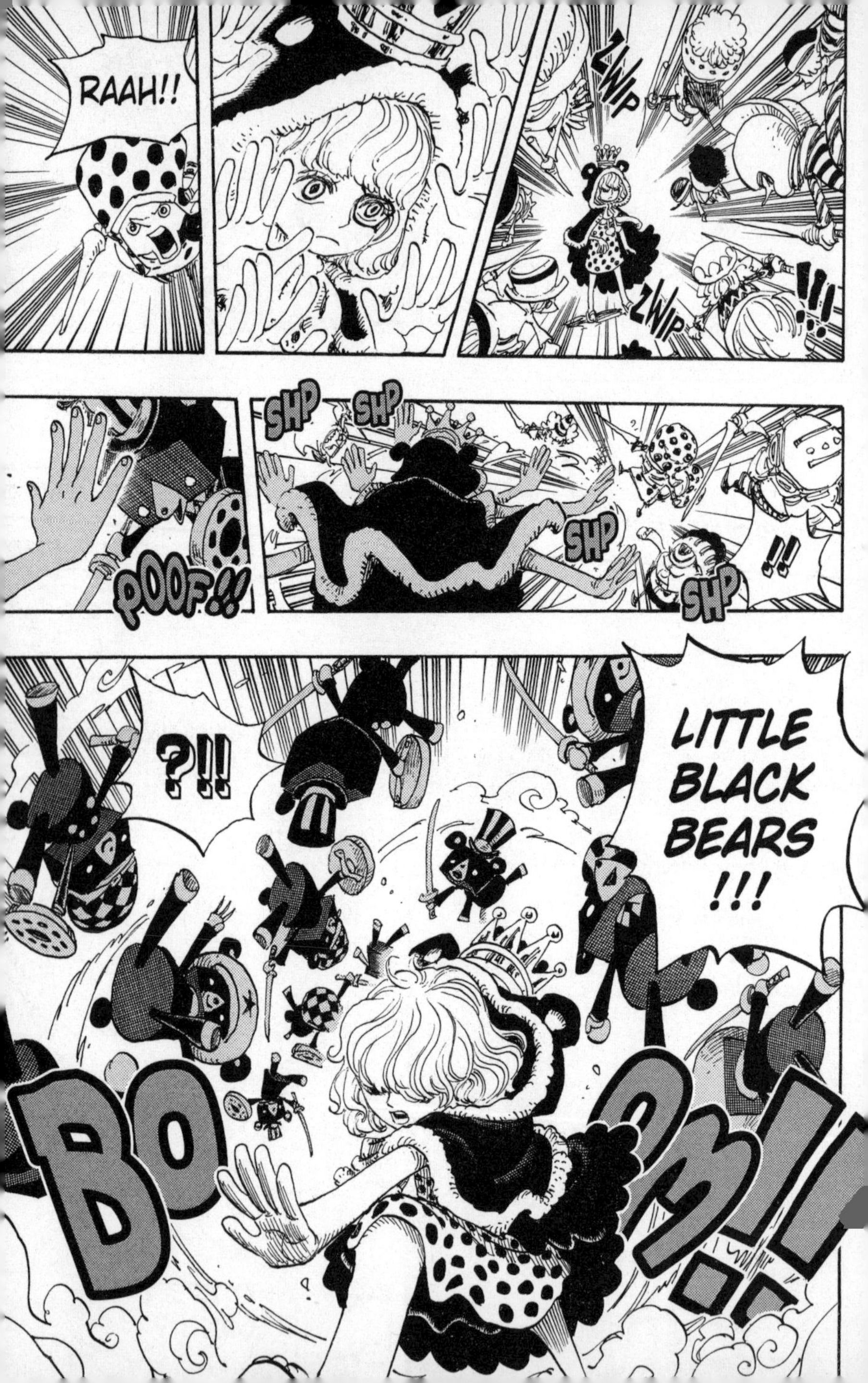

ZWIP
ZWIP
!!!
RAAH!!
SHP
SHP
SHP
SHP
!!
POOF!!
LITTLE BLACK BEARS!!!
?!!
BOOM!!

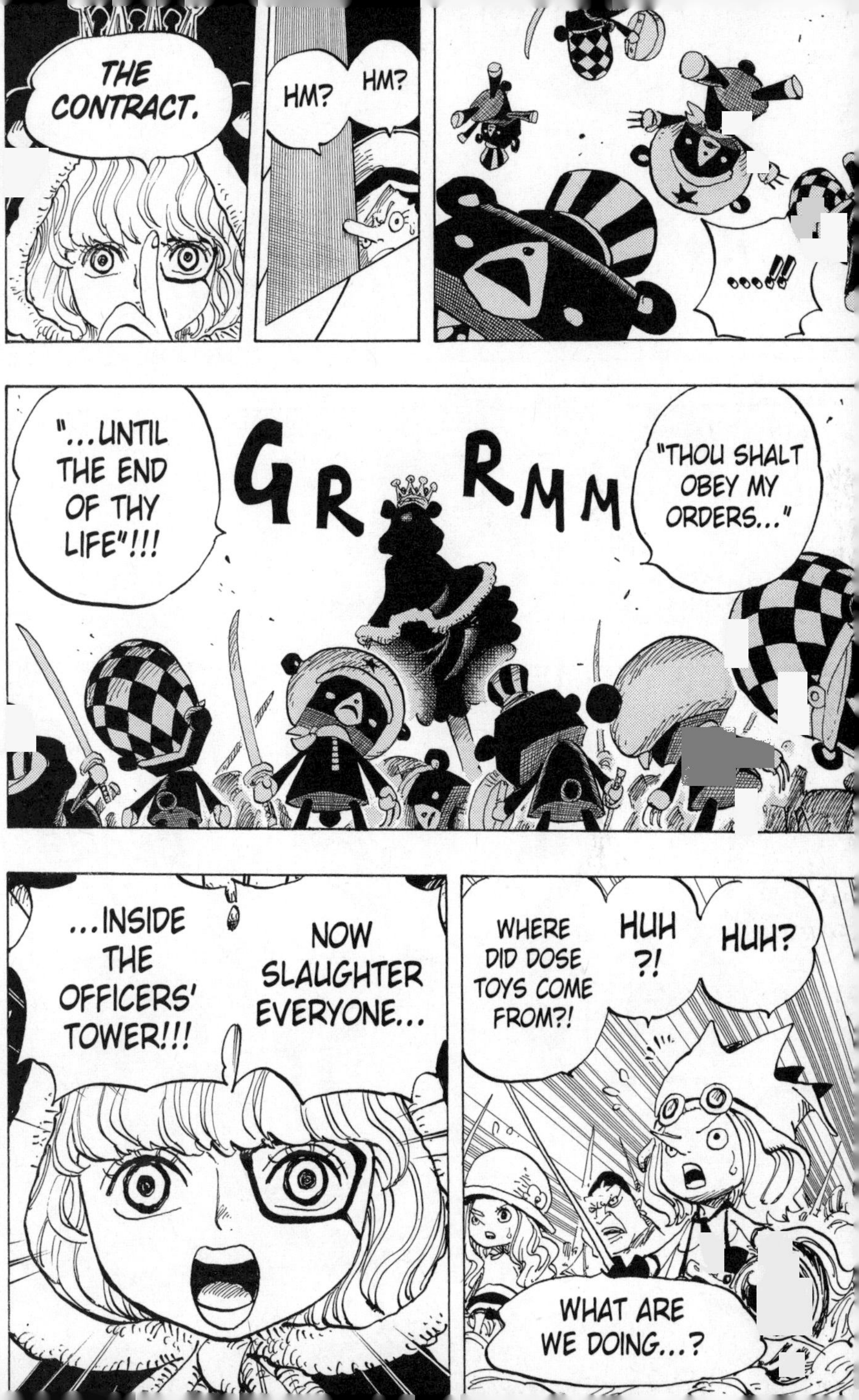
....!!
HM?
HM?
THE CONTRACT.
"THOU SHALT OBEY MY ORDERS..."
GRRMM
"...UNTIL THE END OF THY LIFE"!!!
HUH?
HUH ?!
WHERE DID DOSE TOYS COME FROM?!
WHAT ARE WE DOING...?
NOW SLAUGHTER EVERYONE...
...INSIDE THE OFFICERS' TOWER!!!

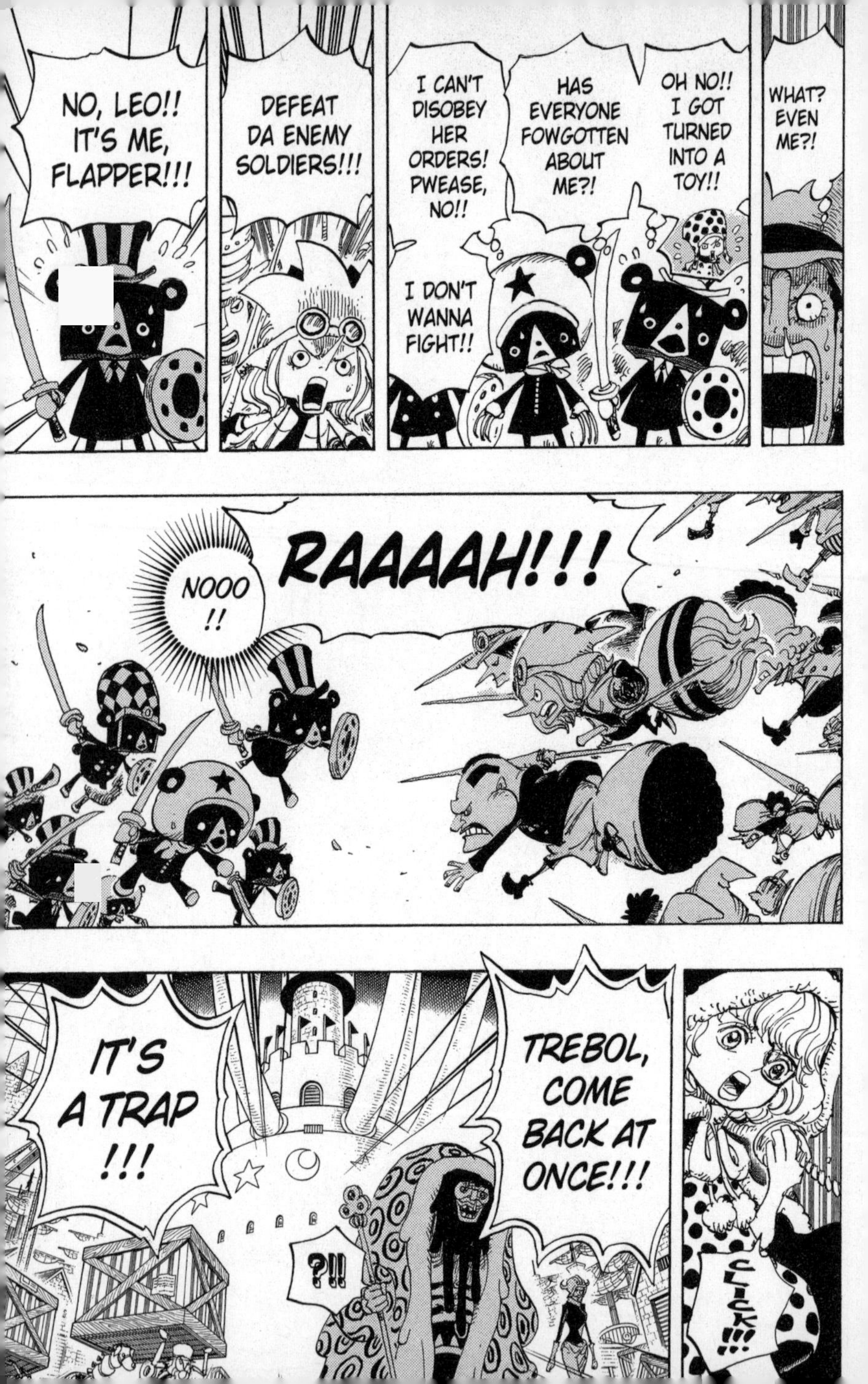
WHAT? EVEN ME?!
OH NO!! I GOT TURNED INTO A TOY!!
HAS EVERYONE FOWGOTTEN ABOUT ME?!
I CAN'T DISOBEY HER ORDERS! PWEASE, NO!!
I DON'T WANNA FIGHT!!
DEFEAT DA ENEMY SOLDIERS!!!
NO, LEO!! IT'S ME, FLAPPER!!!
RAAAAH!!!
NOOO !!
CLICK!!!
TREBOL, COME BACK AT ONCE!!!
?!!
IT'S A TRAP !!!

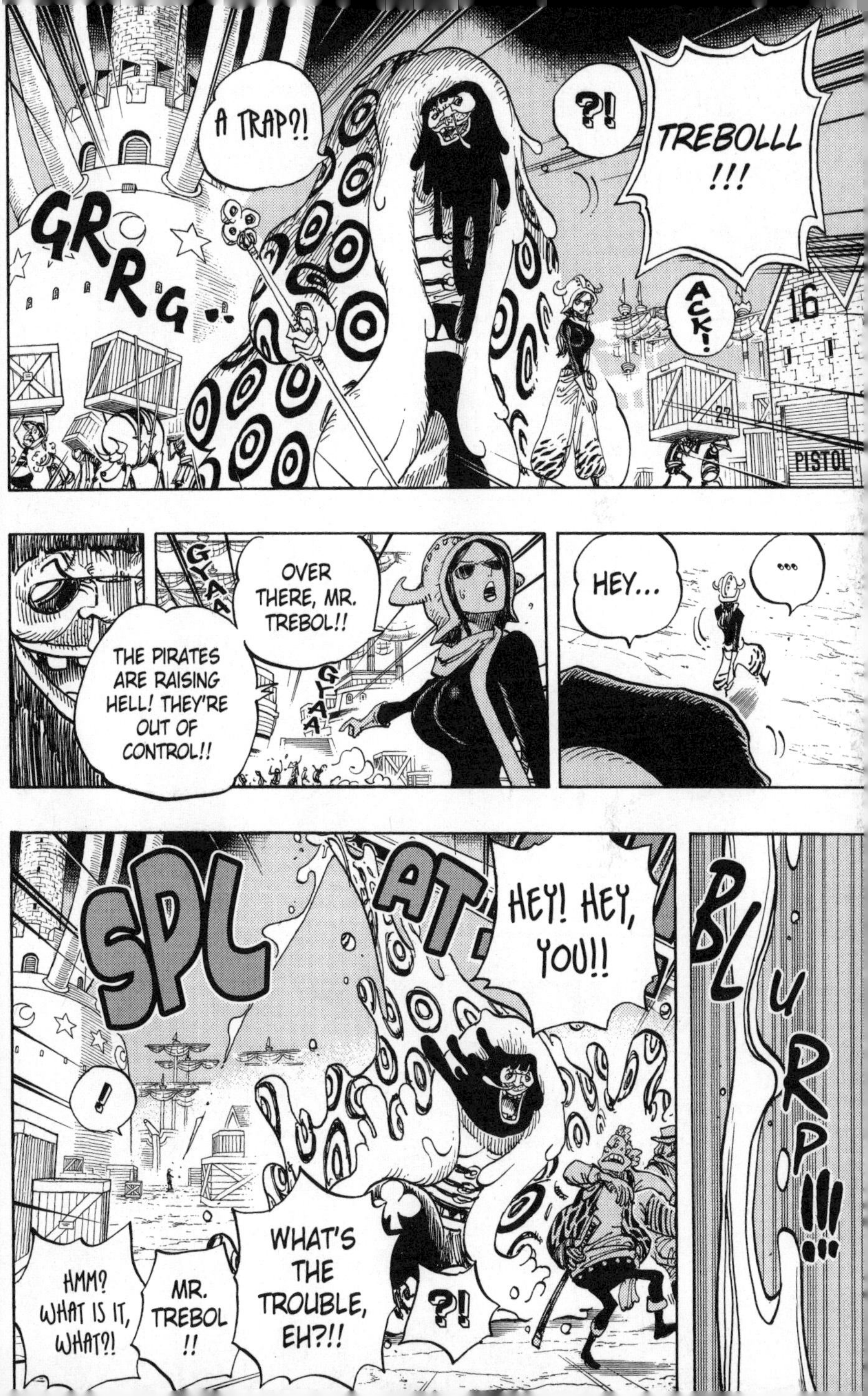
TREBOLLL !!!
?!
A TRAP?!
ACK!
GRRG
16
27
PISTOL
...
HEY...
OVER THERE, MR. TREBOL!!
GYAA
THE PIRATES ARE RAISING HELL! THEY'RE OUT OF CONTROL!!
GYAA
BLURP!!!
HEY! HEY, YOU!!
SPLAT
!
?!
WHAT'S THE TROUBLE, EH?!!
MR. TREBOL!!
HMM? WHAT IS IT, WHAT?!

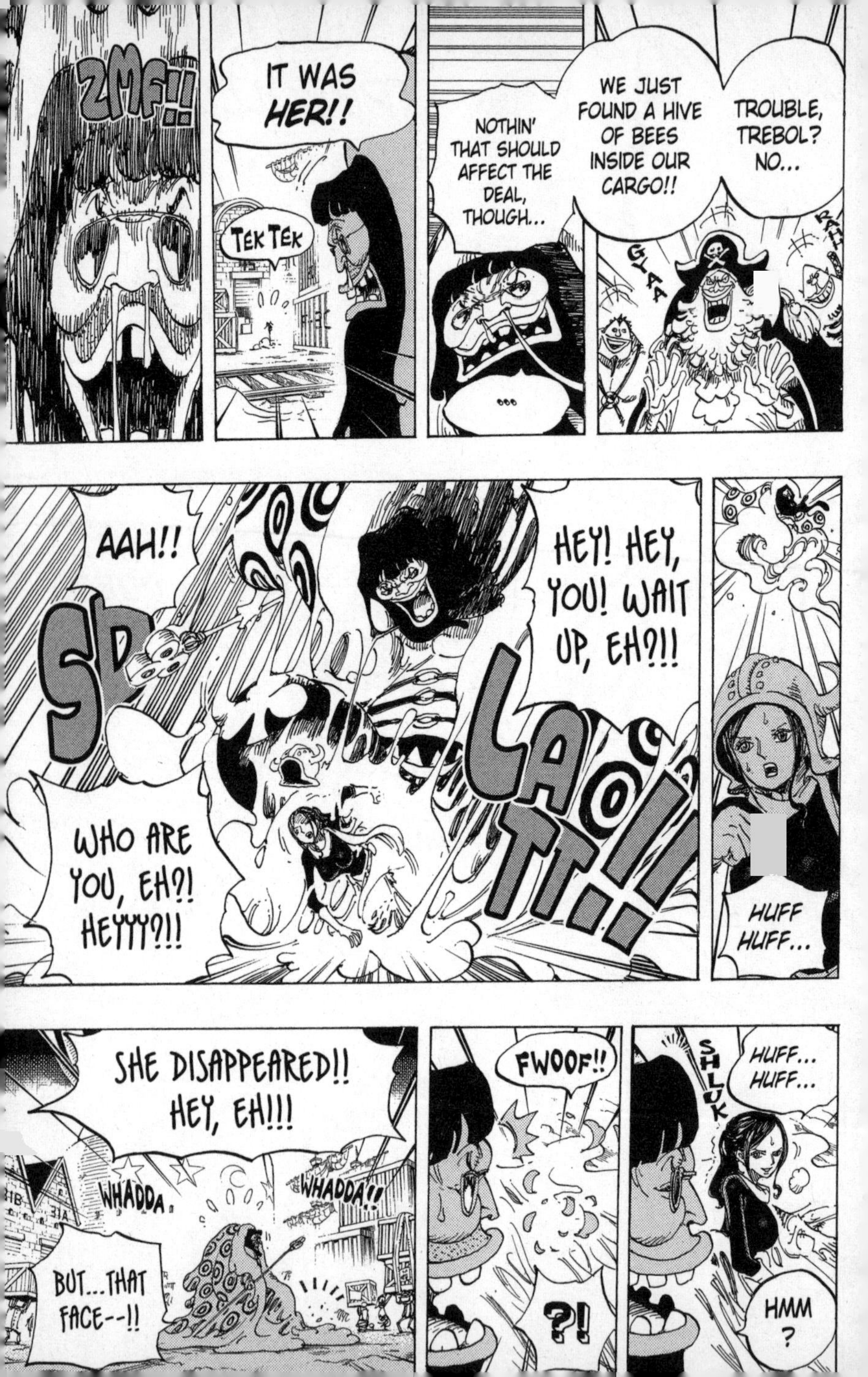

TROUBLE, TREBOL? NO...
WE JUST FOUND A HIVE OF BEES INSIDE OUR CARGO!!
GYAA
NOTHIN' THAT SHOULD AFFECT THE DEAL, THOUGH...
...
IT WAS HER!!
TEK TEK
ZMF!!
HUFF HUFF...
HEY! HEY, YOU! WAIT UP, EH?!!
LAOTT!!
AAH!!
WHO ARE YOU, EH?! HEYYY?!!
SHLUK
HUFF... HUFF...
HMM?
FWOOF!!
?!
SHE DISAPPEARED!! HEY, EH!!!
WHADDA!!
WHADDA
BUT...THAT FACE--!!

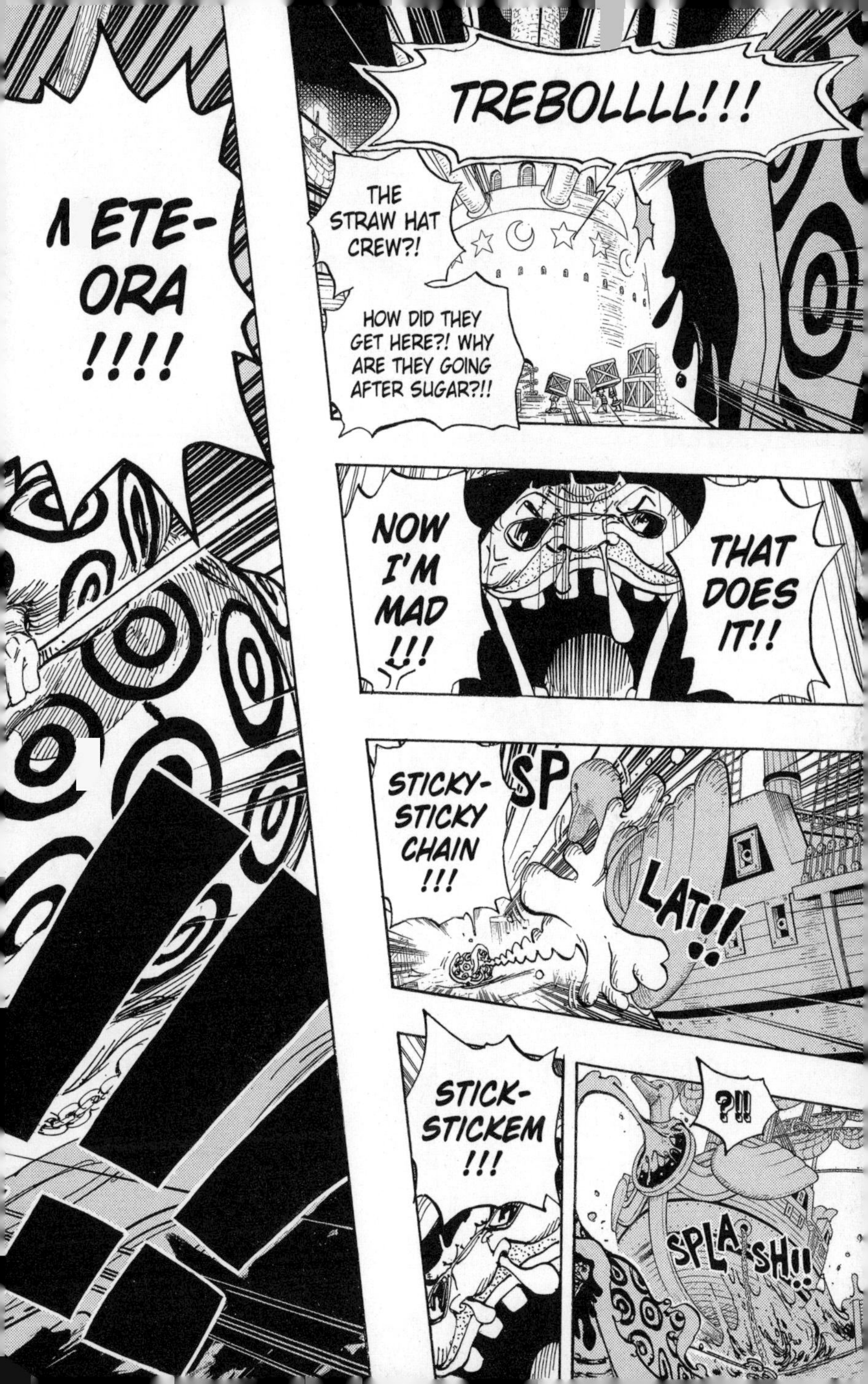
TREBOLLLL!!!
THE STRAW HAT CREW?!
HOW DID THEY GET HERE?! WHY ARE THEY GOING AFTER SUGAR?!!
THAT DOES IT!!
NOW I'M MAD!!!
SP
STICKY-STICKY CHAIN!!!
LAT!!
?!!
SPLASH!!
STICK-STICKEM!!!
ETE-ORA!!!!

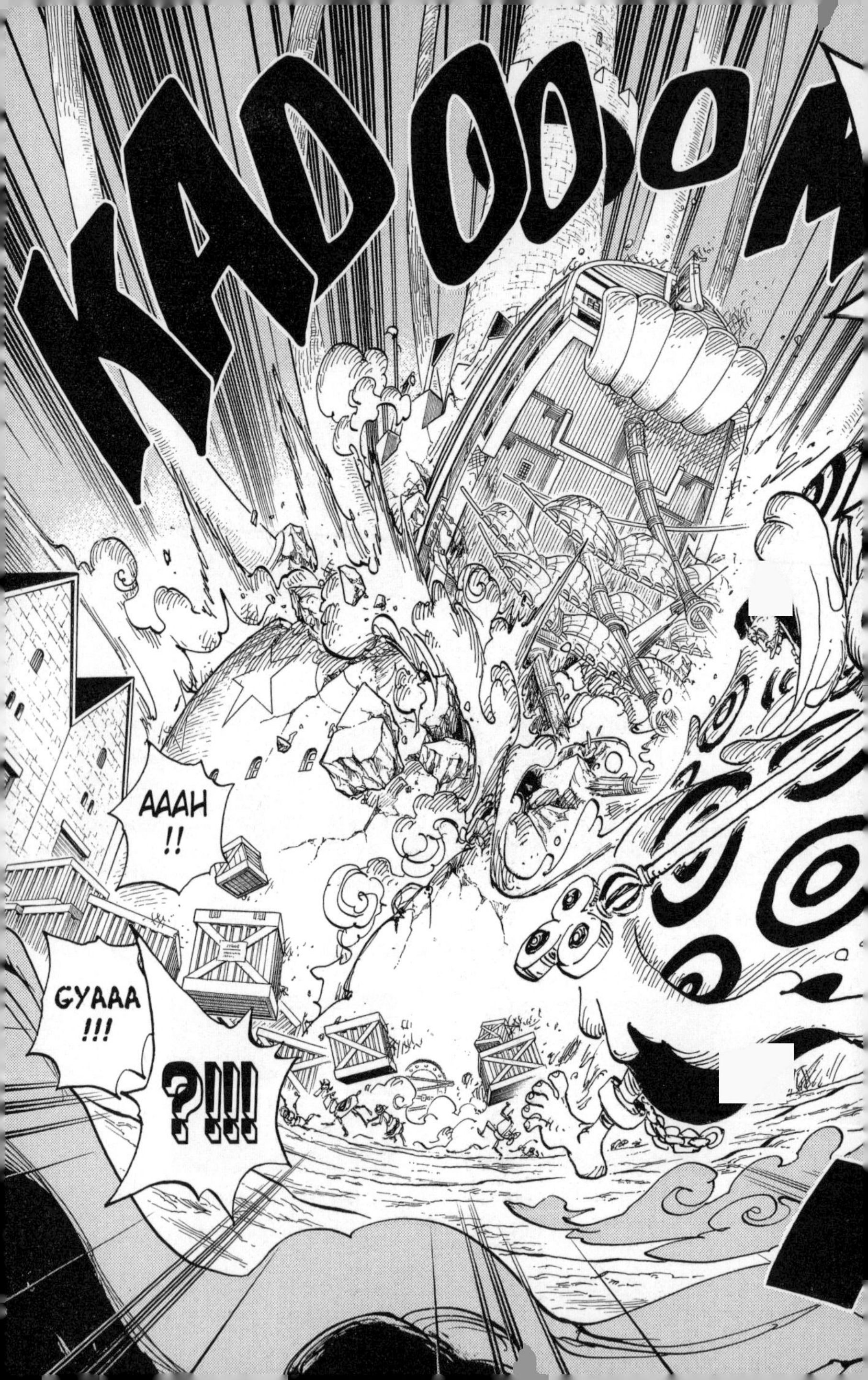
KADOOOM
AAAH !!
GYAAA !!!
?!!!

SBS Question Corner

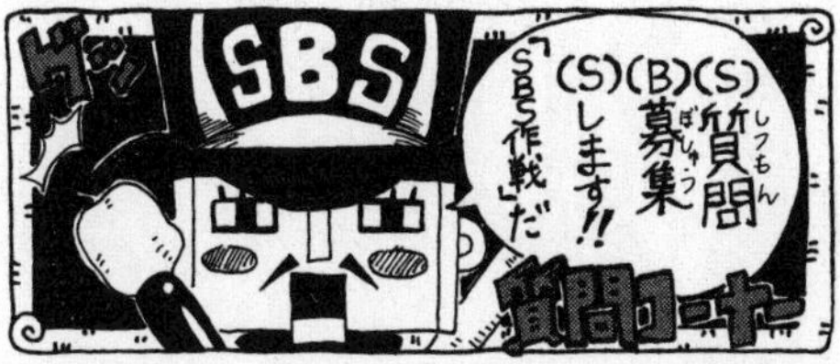
SBS
(S)(B)(S)質問募集します!!
「SBS作戦」だ
質問コーナー

(Haru, Nagano)

A: Well, I'm sad to announce that I've lost the postcard that was sent with this request. (sweat drop) Basically, someone wrote in to ask me to draw the Jolly Rogers of all the Worst Generation members...and I lost it as I was drawing them. I'm so sorry...but I will grant your request! Thanks for writing in! I won't bother with the flags I've already drawn.

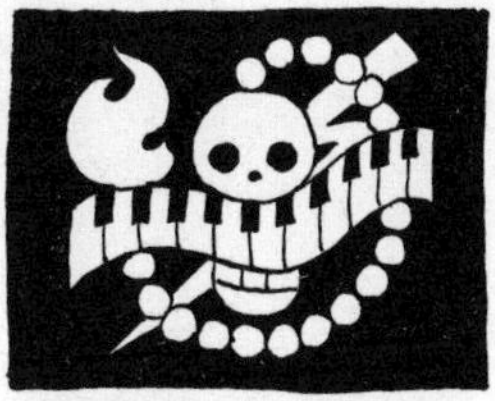

On-Air Pirates
(Scratchmen Apoo)

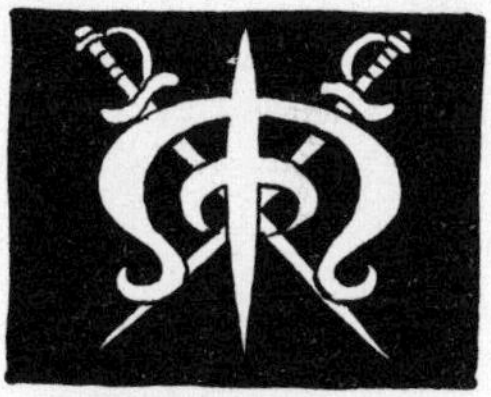

Drake Pirates
(X. Drake)

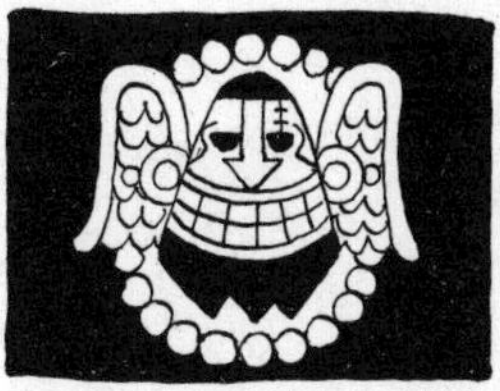

Fallen Monk Pirates
(Urouge)

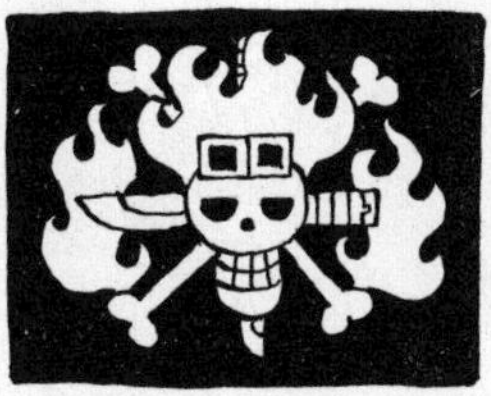

Kid Pirates
(Eustass "Captain" Kid)

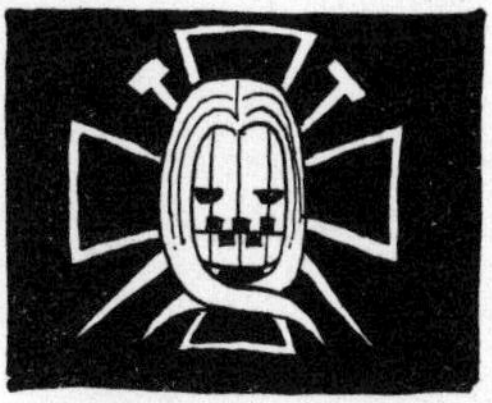

Hawkins Pirates
(Basil Hawkins)

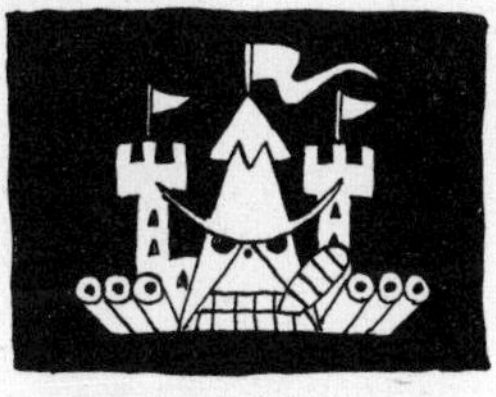

Firetank Pirates
(Capone "Gang" Bege)

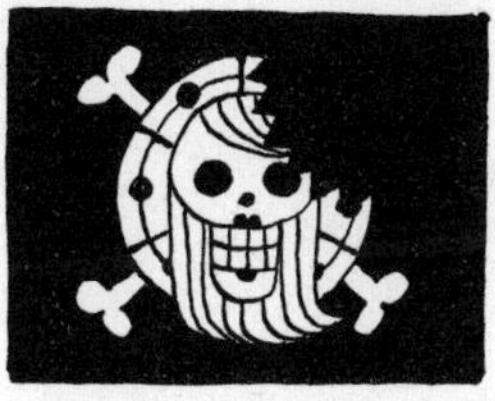

Bonney Pirates
(Jewelry Bonney)

A: Well, that's all for now. The SBS is over!! See you next volume!!

Chapter 739:
CAPTAIN

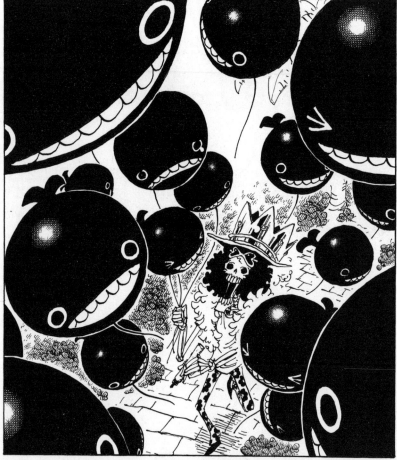

REQUEST: "BROOK SKIPPING ALONG DRAWING
LABOON BALLOONS" BY DOKURO FROM KYOTO

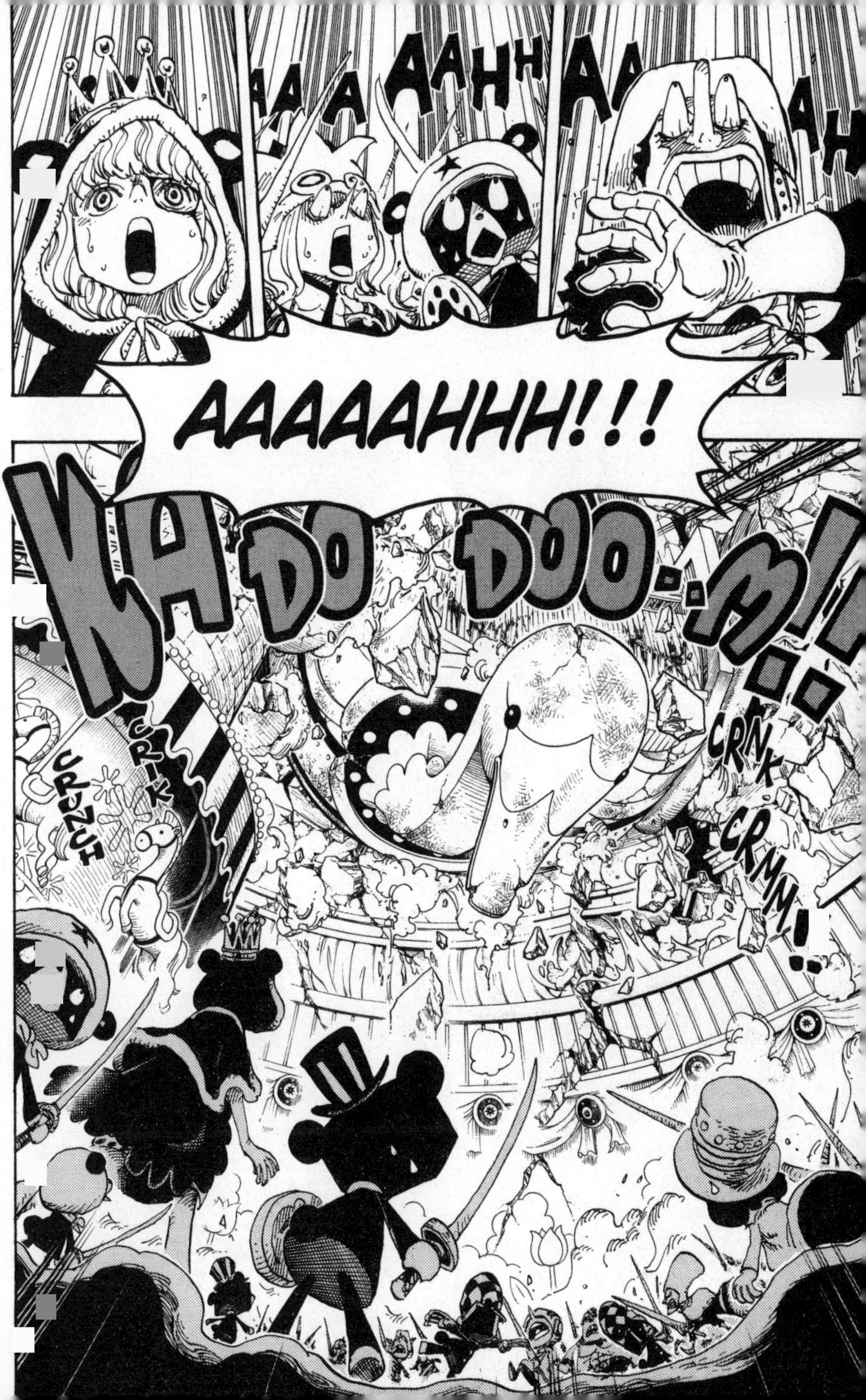
AAAAHHAAAAH
AAAAAHHH!!!
KA DO DOO--M!!
CRNK
CRMM!!
CRIK
CRUNCH

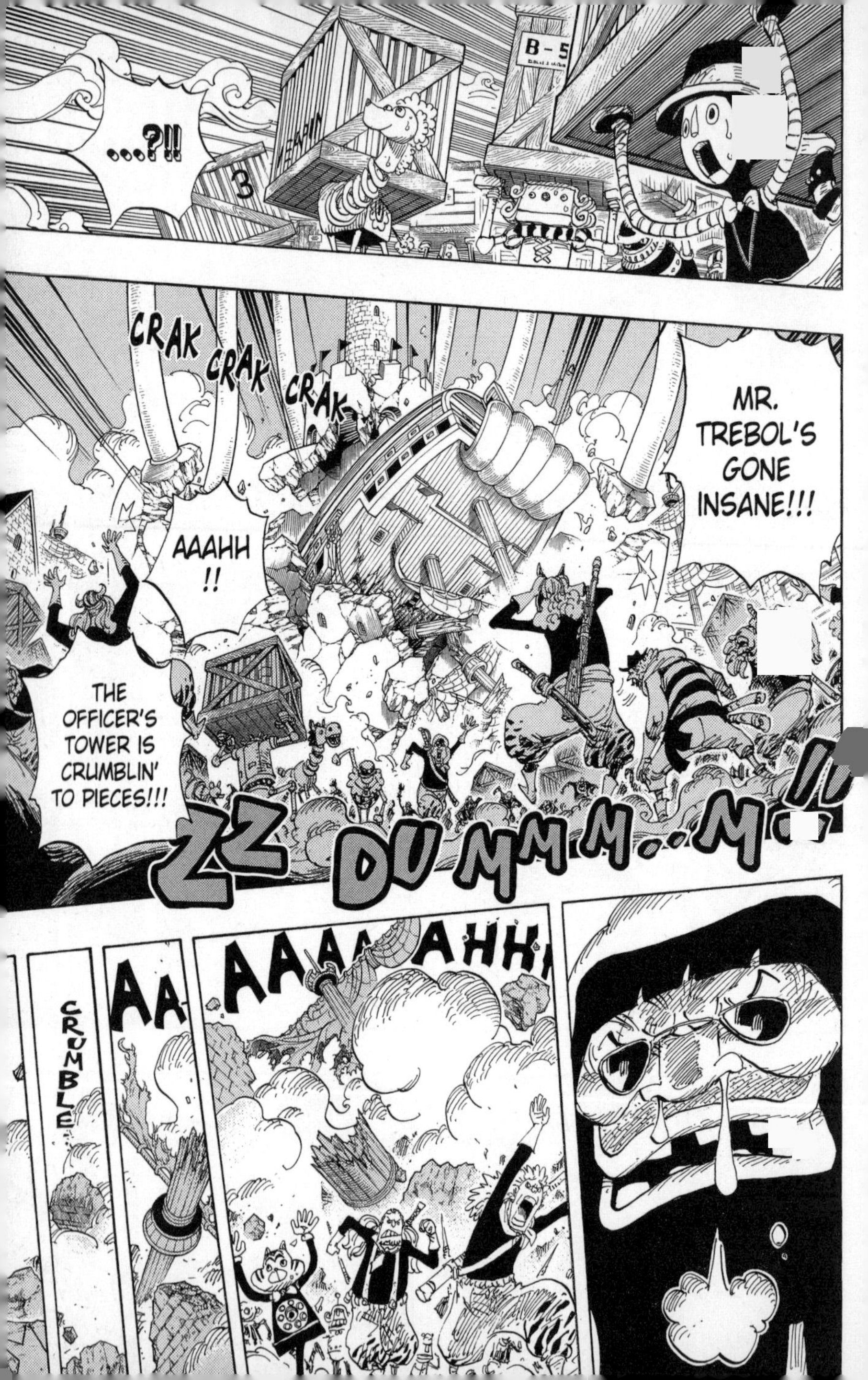
...?!!
CRAK
CRAK
CRAK
MR. TREBOL'S GONE INSANE!!!
AAAHH !!
THE OFFICER'S TOWER IS CRUMBLIN' TO PIECES!!!
ZZ DU MMM...M...!!
AAAAAHH
AA
CRUMBLE...

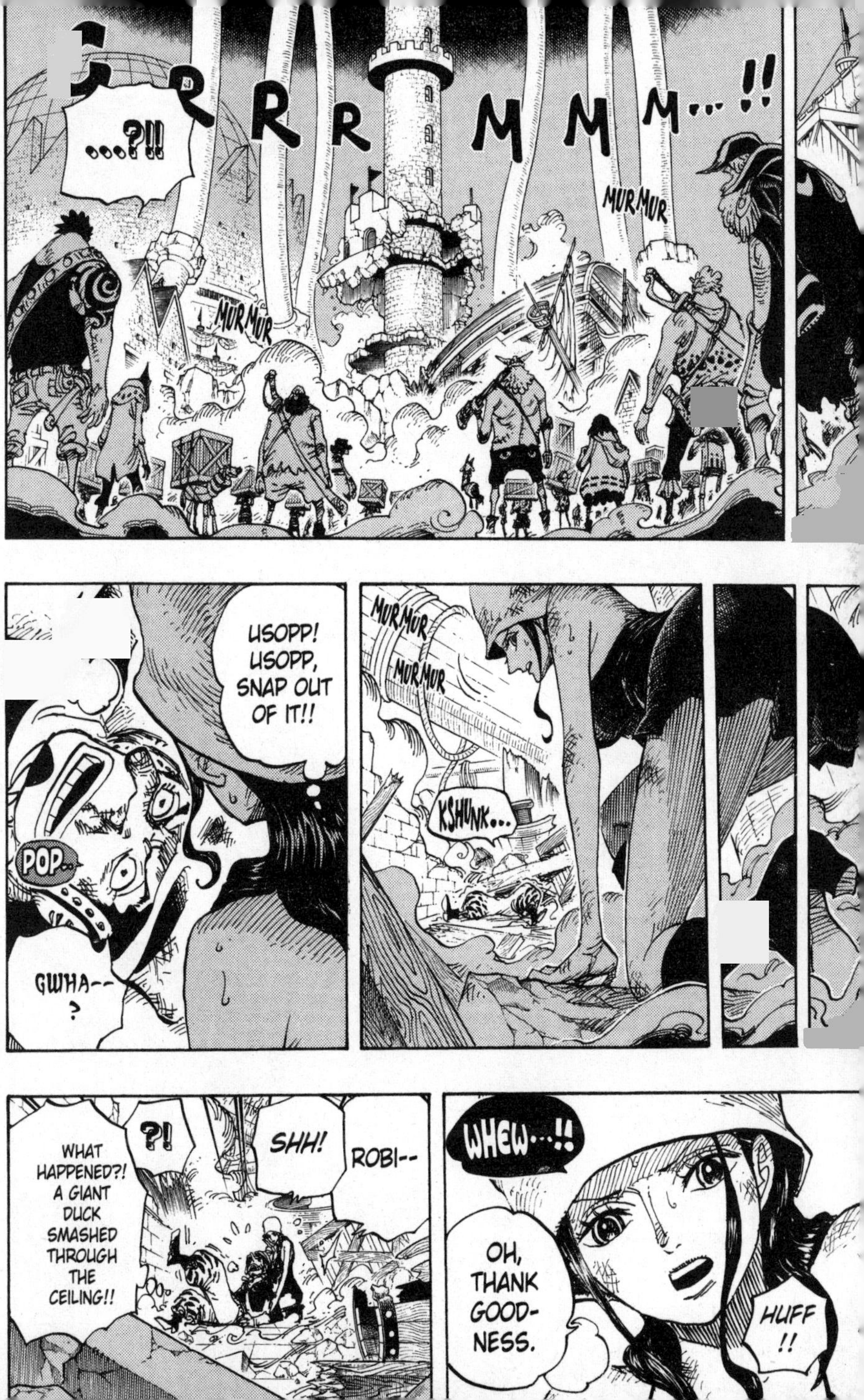
GRRRMMM...!!
...?!!
MUR MUR
MUR MUR
MUR MUR
MUR MUR
KSHUNK...
USOPP! USOPP, SNAP OUT OF IT!!
POP..
GWHA-- ?
WHEW...!!
OH, THANK GOOD-NESS.
HUFF!!
ROBI--
SHH!
?!
WHAT HAPPENED?! A GIANT DUCK SMASHED THROUGH THE CEILING!!

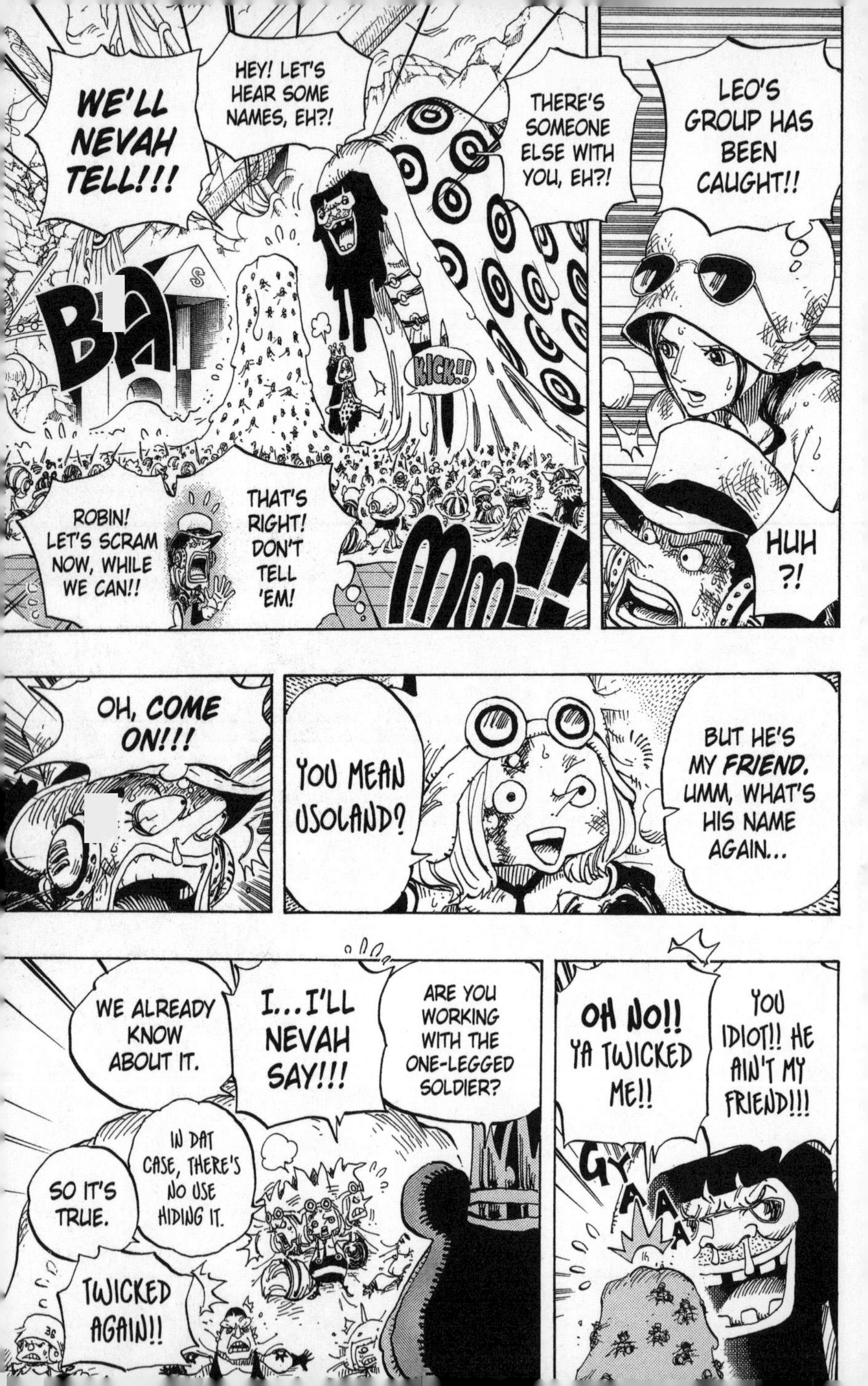
LEO'S GROUP HAS BEEN CAUGHT!!
HUH ?!
THERE'S SOMEONE ELSE WITH YOU, EH?!
HEY! LET'S HEAR SOME NAMES, EH?!
WE'LL NEVAH TELL!!!
KICK!!
BA
THAT'S RIGHT! DON'T TELL 'EM!
ROBIN! LET'S SCRAM NOW, WHILE WE CAN!!
BUT HE'S MY FRIEND. UMM, WHAT'S HIS NAME AGAIN...
YOU MEAN USOLAND?
OH, COME ON!!!
YOU IDIOT!! HE AIN'T MY FRIEND!!!
OH NO!! YA TWICKED ME!!
GYAAAA
ARE YOU WORKING WITH THE ONE-LEGGED SOLDIER?
I...I'LL NEVAH SAY!!!
WE ALREADY KNOW ABOUT IT.
IN DAT CASE, THERE'S NO USE HIDING IT.
SO IT'S TRUE.
TWICKED AGAIN!!

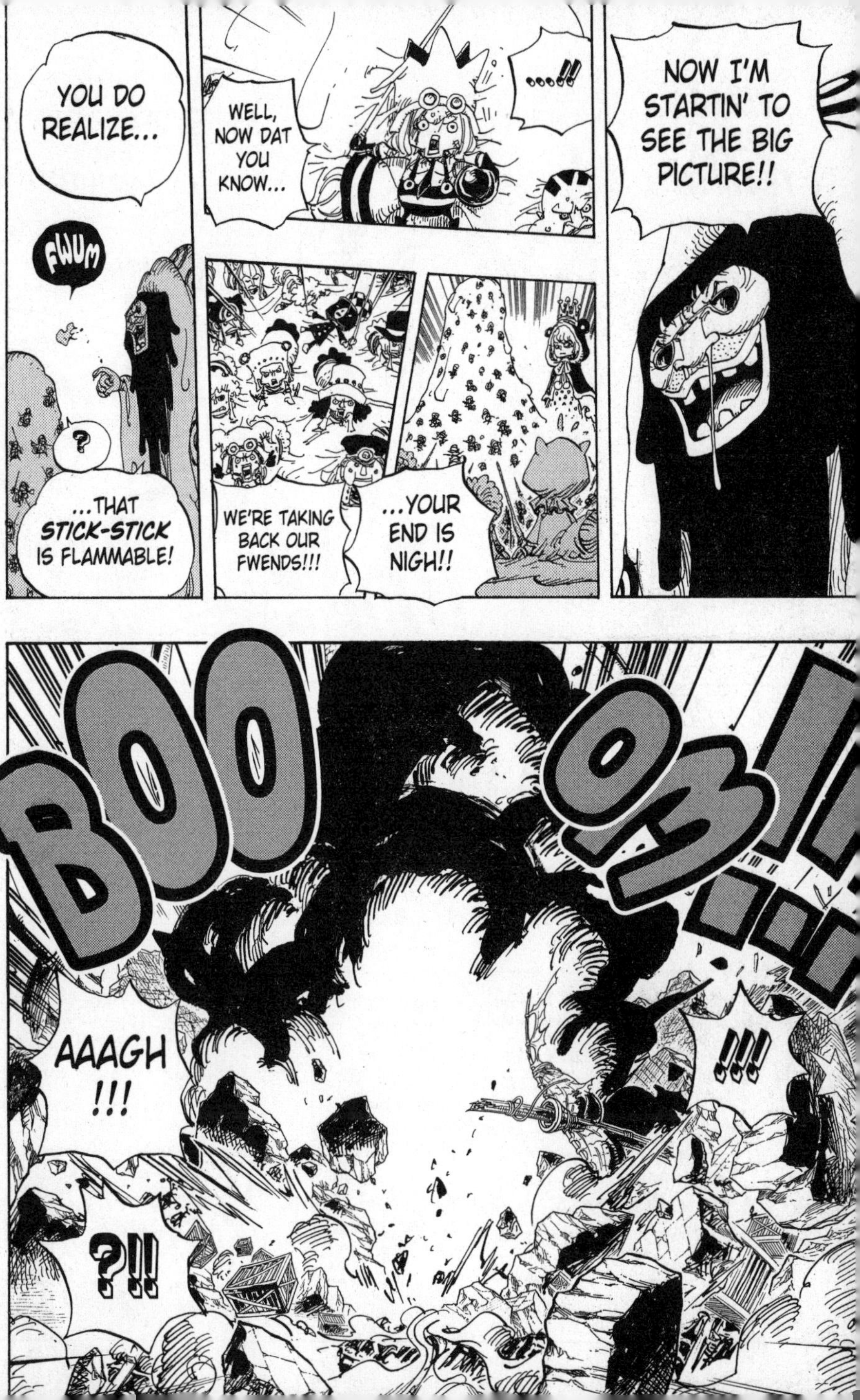
NOW I'M STARTIN' TO SEE THE BIG PICTURE!!
....!!
WELL, NOW DAT YOU KNOW...
...YOUR END IS NIGH!!
WE'RE TAKING BACK OUR FWENDS!!!
YOU DO REALIZE...
FWUM
?
...THAT STICK-STICK IS FLAMMABLE!
BOOOOM!!
!!!
AAAGH!!!
?!!

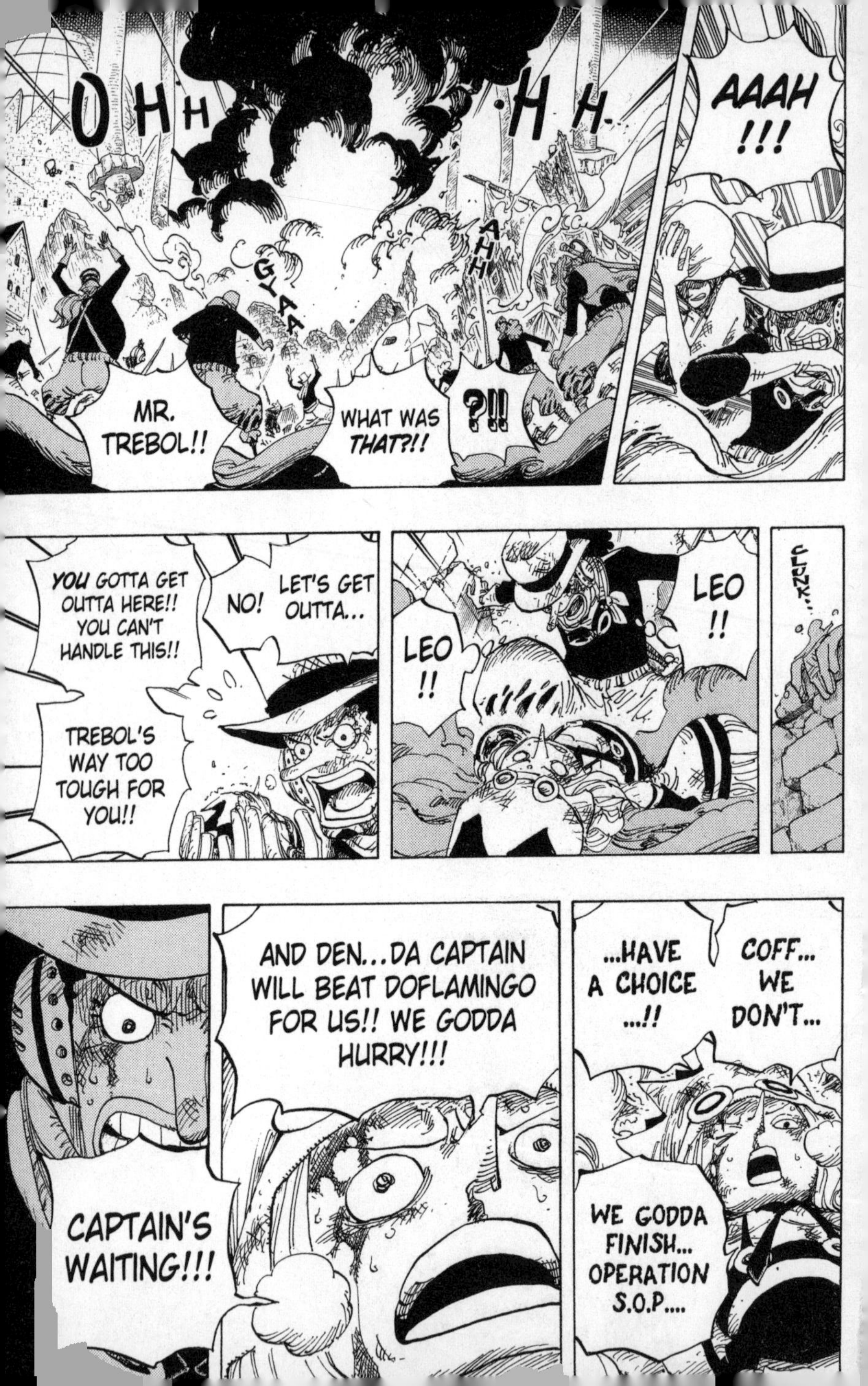
AAAH!!!
OHH H H H
AHH
GYAAA
?!!
WHAT WAS THAT?!!
MR. TREBOL!!
CLUNK...
LEO!!
LEO!!
NO! LET'S GET OUTTA...
YOU GOTTA GET OUTTA HERE!! YOU CAN'T HANDLE THIS!!
TREBOL'S WAY TOO TOUGH FOR YOU!!
COFF... WE DON'T...
...HAVE A CHOICE ...!!
WE GODDA FINISH... OPERATION S.O.P....
AND DEN...DA CAPTAIN WILL BEAT DOFLAMINGO FOR US!! WE GODDA HURRY!!!
CAPTAIN'S WAITING!!!

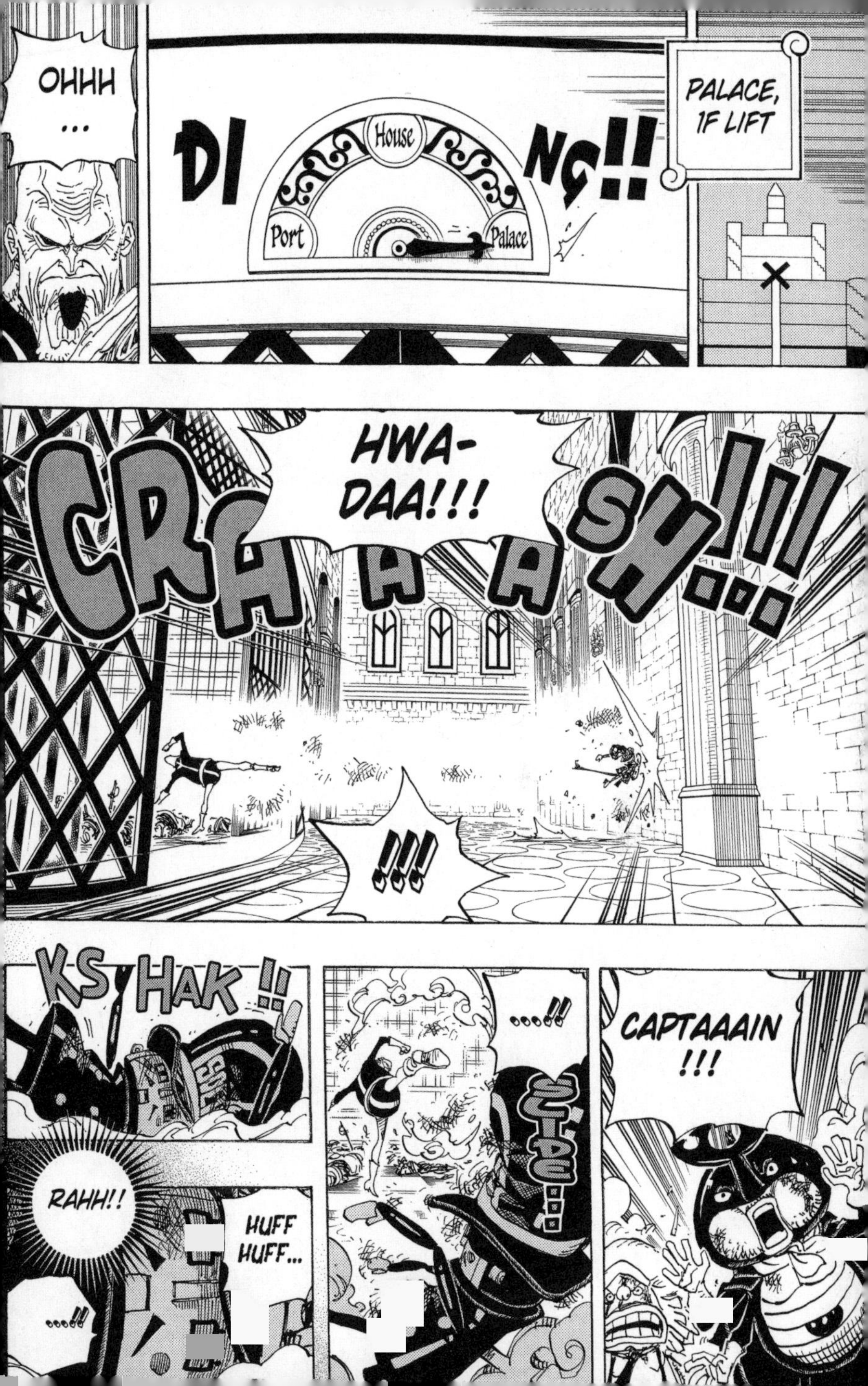
PALACE, 1F LIFT
DING!!
House
Port
Palace
OHHH ...
CRAAASH!!!
HWA-DAA!!!
!!!
CAPTAAAIN !!!
...!!
SLIDE...
KSHAK!!
RAHH!!
HUFF HUFF...
...!!

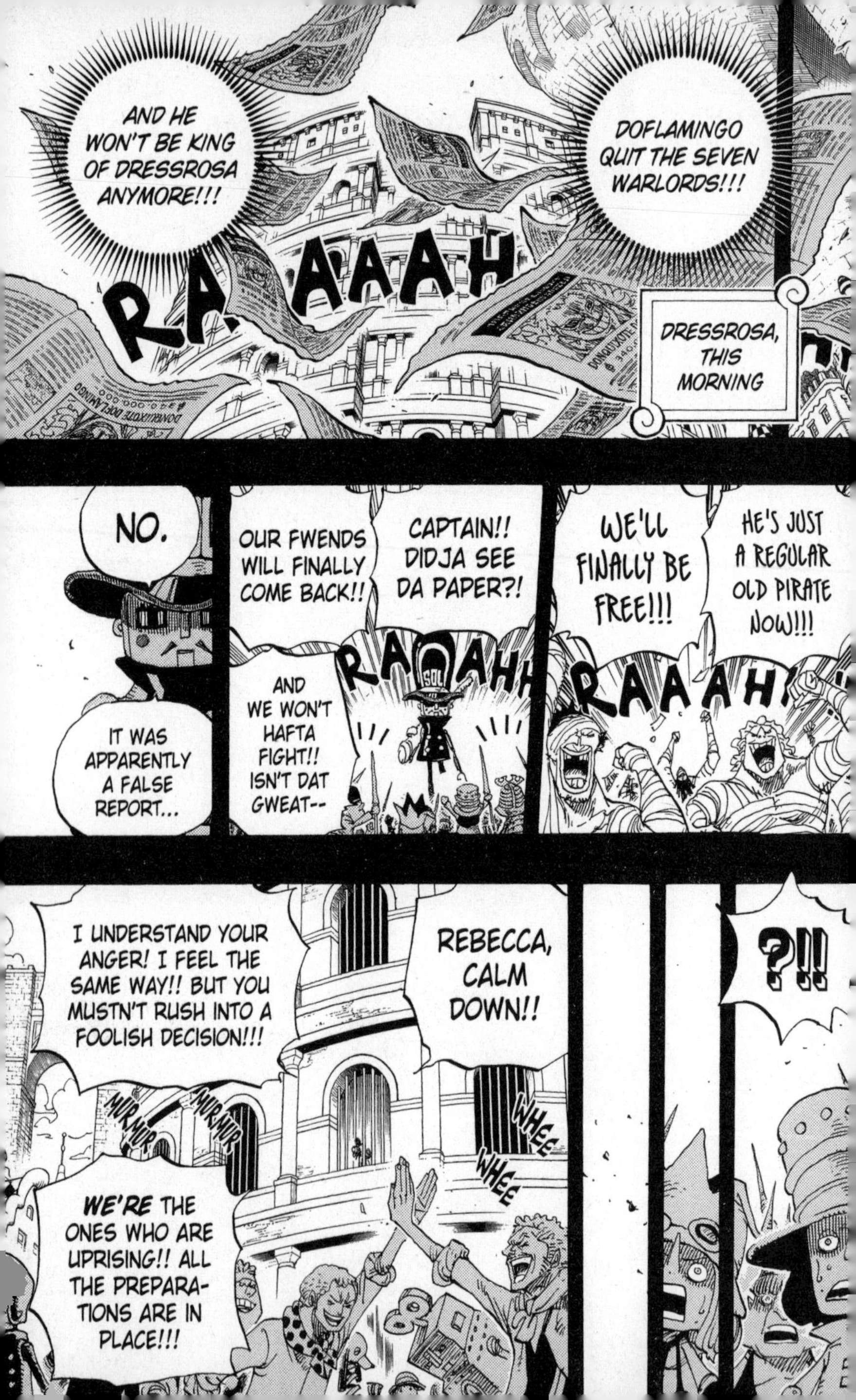
DRESSROSA, THIS MORNING
DOFLAMINGO QUIT THE SEVEN WARLORDS!!!
AND HE WON'T BE KING OF DRESSROSA ANYMORE!!!
RAAAAH
HE'S JUST A REGULAR OLD PIRATE NOW!!!
WE'LL FINALLY BE FREE!!!
RAAAH!
CAPTAIN!! DIDJA SEE DA PAPER?!
OUR FWENDS WILL FINALLY COME BACK!!
RAAAHH
AND WE WON'T HAFTA FIGHT!! ISN'T DAT GWEAT--
NO.
IT WAS APPARENTLY A FALSE REPORT...
?!!
REBECCA, CALM DOWN!!
I UNDERSTAND YOUR ANGER! I FEEL THE SAME WAY!! BUT YOU MUSTN'T RUSH INTO A FOOLISH DECISION!!!
WHEE WHEE
MURMUR MURMUR
WE'RE THE ONES WHO ARE UPRISING!! ALL THE PREPARATIONS ARE IN PLACE!!!

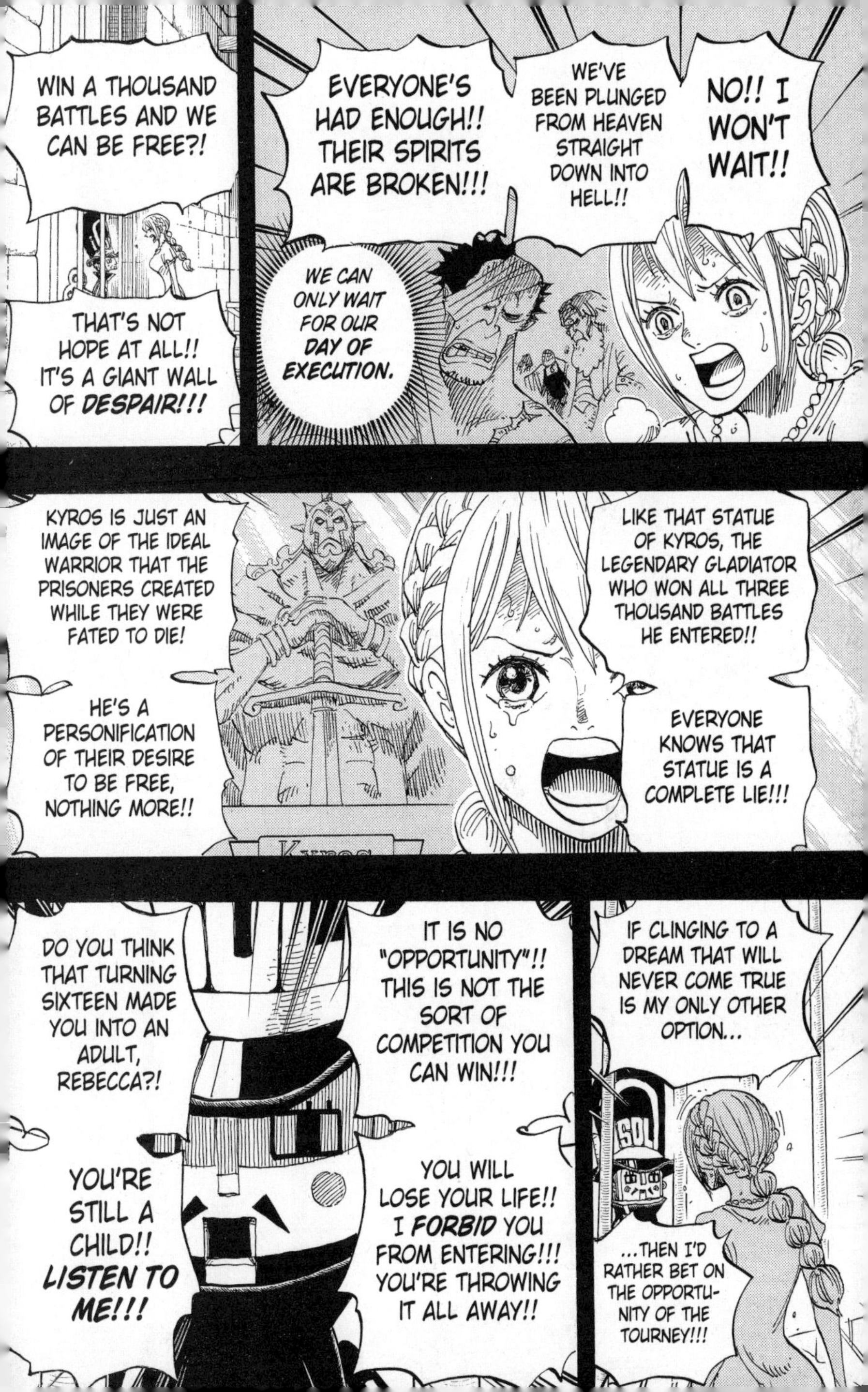
NO!! I WON'T WAIT!!
WE'VE BEEN PLUNGED FROM HEAVEN STRAIGHT DOWN INTO HELL!!
EVERYONE'S HAD ENOUGH!! THEIR SPIRITS ARE BROKEN!!!
WE CAN ONLY WAIT FOR OUR *DAY OF EXECUTION.*
WIN A THOUSAND BATTLES AND WE CAN BE FREE?!
THAT'S NOT HOPE AT ALL!! IT'S A GIANT WALL OF ***DESPAIR!!!***
LIKE THAT STATUE OF KYROS, THE LEGENDARY GLADIATOR WHO WON ALL THREE THOUSAND BATTLES HE ENTERED!!
EVERYONE KNOWS THAT STATUE IS A COMPLETE LIE!!!
KYROS IS JUST AN IMAGE OF THE IDEAL WARRIOR THAT THE PRISONERS CREATED WHILE THEY WERE FATED TO DIE!
HE'S A PERSONIFICATION OF THEIR DESIRE TO BE FREE, NOTHING MORE!!
IF CLINGING TO A DREAM THAT WILL NEVER COME TRUE IS MY ONLY OTHER OPTION...
...THEN I'D RATHER BET ON THE OPPORTUNITY OF THE TOURNEY!!!
IT IS NO "OPPORTUNITY"!! THIS IS NOT THE SORT OF COMPETITION YOU CAN WIN!!!
DO YOU THINK THAT TURNING SIXTEEN MADE YOU INTO AN ADULT, REBECCA?!
YOU WILL LOSE YOUR LIFE!! I ***FORBID*** YOU FROM ENTERING!!! YOU'RE THROWING IT ALL AWAY!!
YOU'RE STILL A CHILD!! ***LISTEN TO ME!!!***

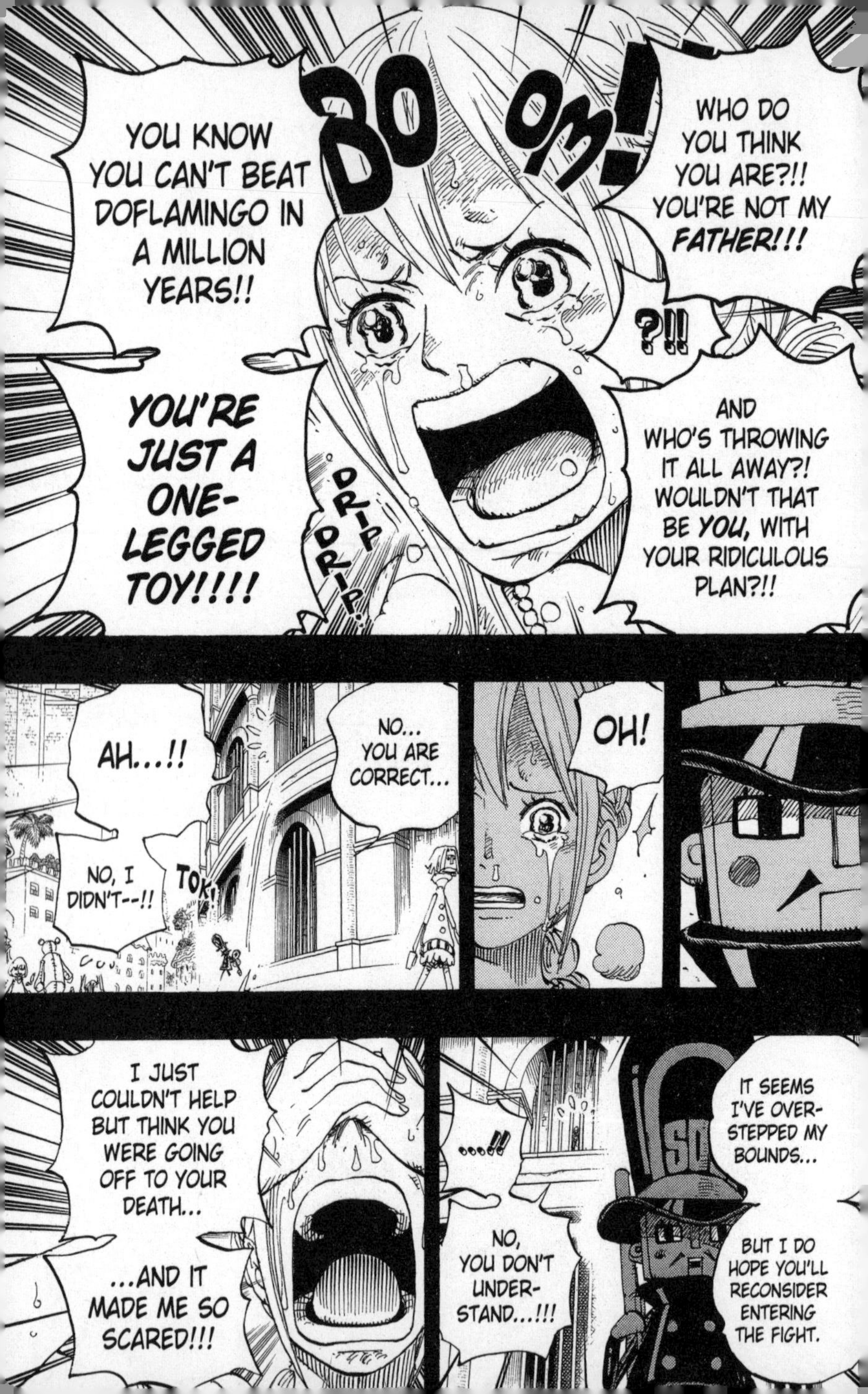
WHO DO YOU THINK YOU ARE?!! YOU'RE NOT MY *FATHER!!!*
BOOM!
YOU KNOW YOU CAN'T BEAT DOFLAMINGO IN A MILLION YEARS!!
?!!
AND WHO'S THROWING IT ALL AWAY?! WOULDN'T THAT BE *YOU,* WITH YOUR RIDICULOUS PLAN?!!
DRIP DRIP
YOU'RE JUST A ONE-LEGGED TOY!!!!
OH!
NO... YOU ARE CORRECT...
AH...!!
TOK!
NO, I DIDN'T--!!
IT SEEMS I'VE OVER-STEPPED MY BOUNDS...
...!!
BUT I DO HOPE YOU'LL RECONSIDER ENTERING THE FIGHT.
NO, YOU DON'T UNDER-STAND...!!!
I JUST COULDN'T HELP BUT THINK YOU WERE GOING OFF TO YOUR DEATH...
...AND IT MADE ME SO SCARED!!!

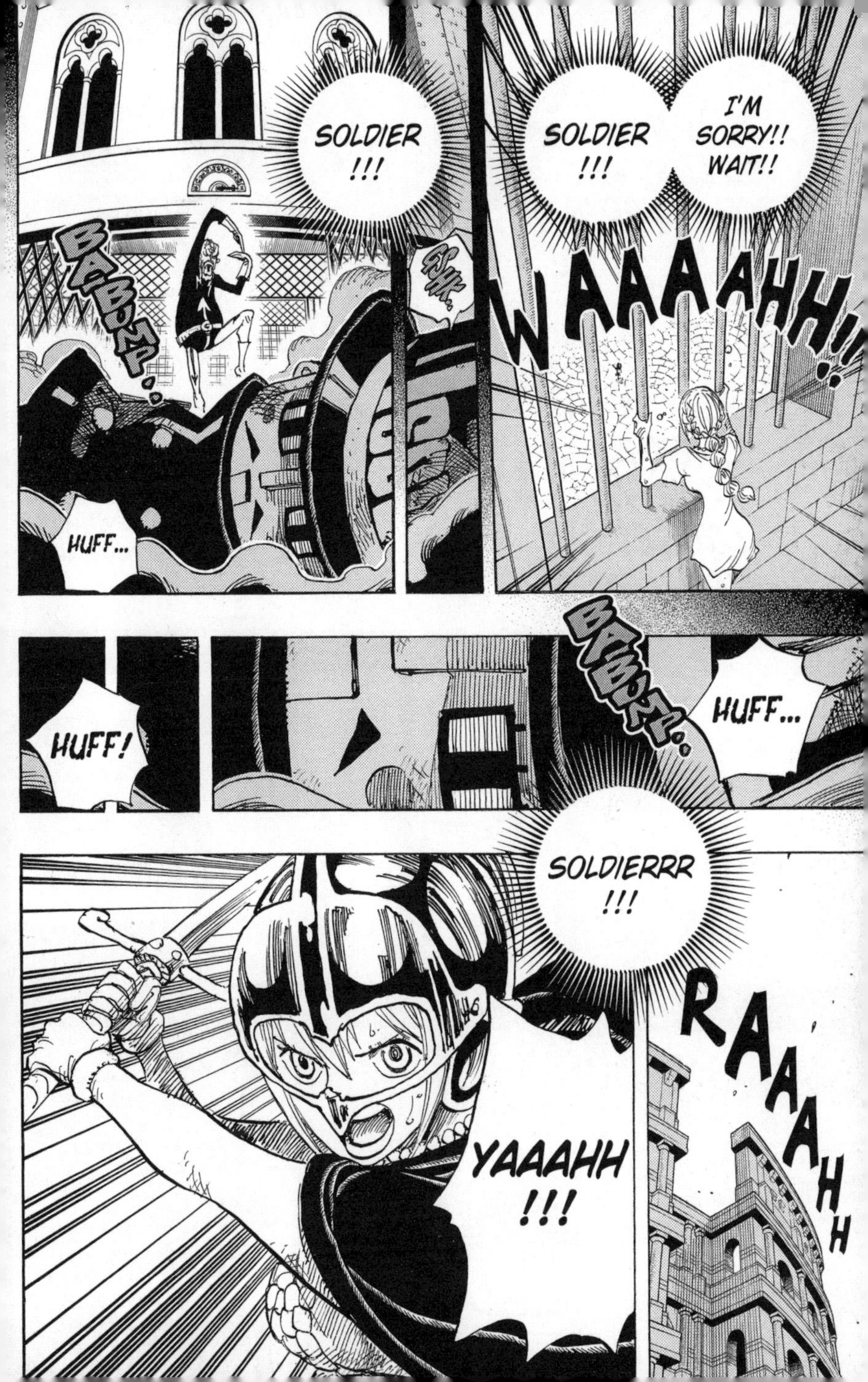
I'M SORRY!! WAIT!!
SOLDIER !!!
WAAAAHH!!
SOLDIER !!!
GSHK
BABUMP..
HUFF...
HUFF...
BABUMP..
HUFF!
SOLDIERRR !!!
RAAAAHH
YAAAHH !!!

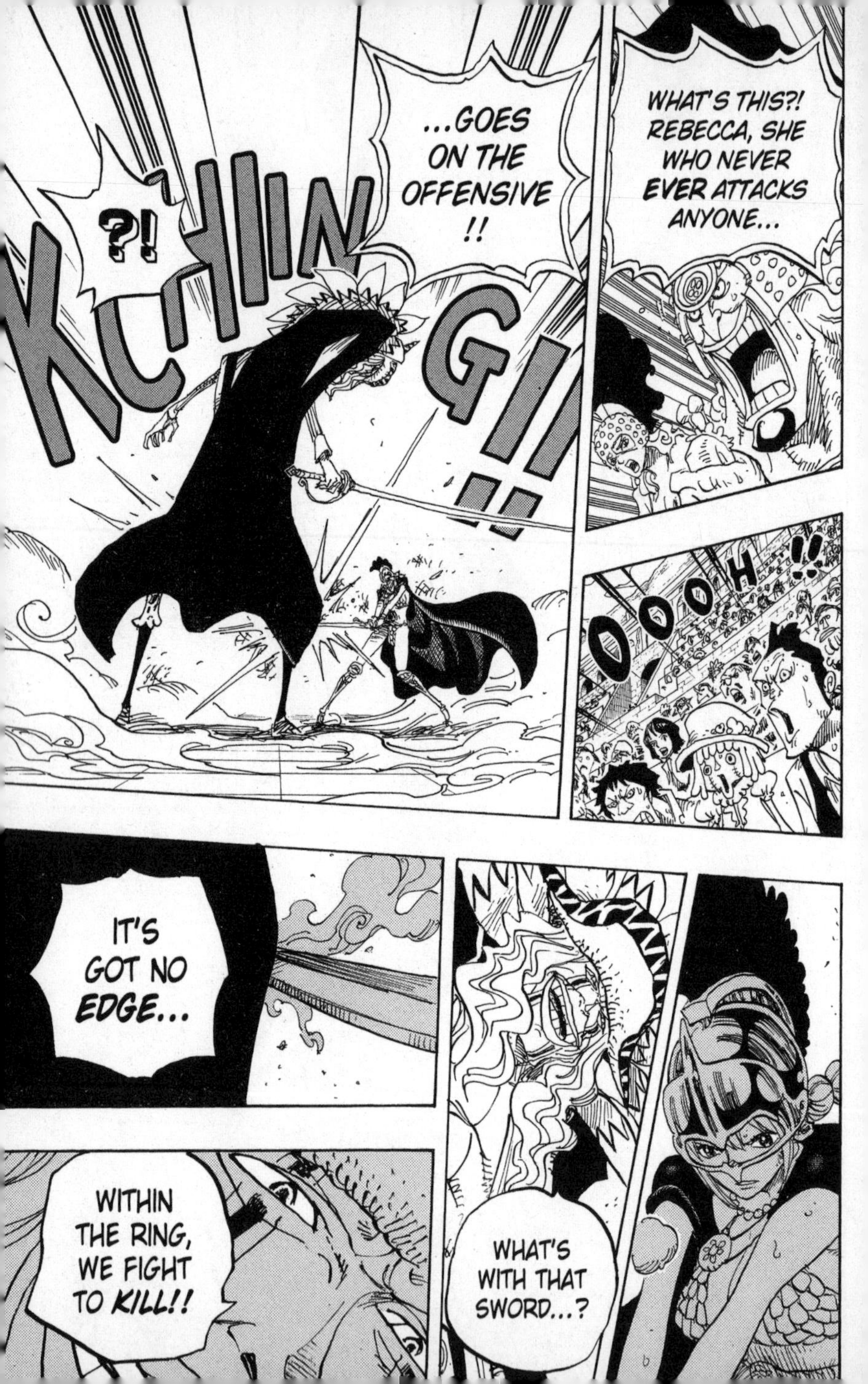
WHAT'S THIS?! REBECCA, SHE WHO NEVER EVER ATTACKS ANYONE...
OOOOH!!
...GOES ON THE OFFENSIVE !!
?!
KCHIIN
GI!!
WHAT'S WITH THAT SWORD...?
IT'S GOT NO EDGE...
WITHIN THE RING, WE FIGHT TO KILL!!

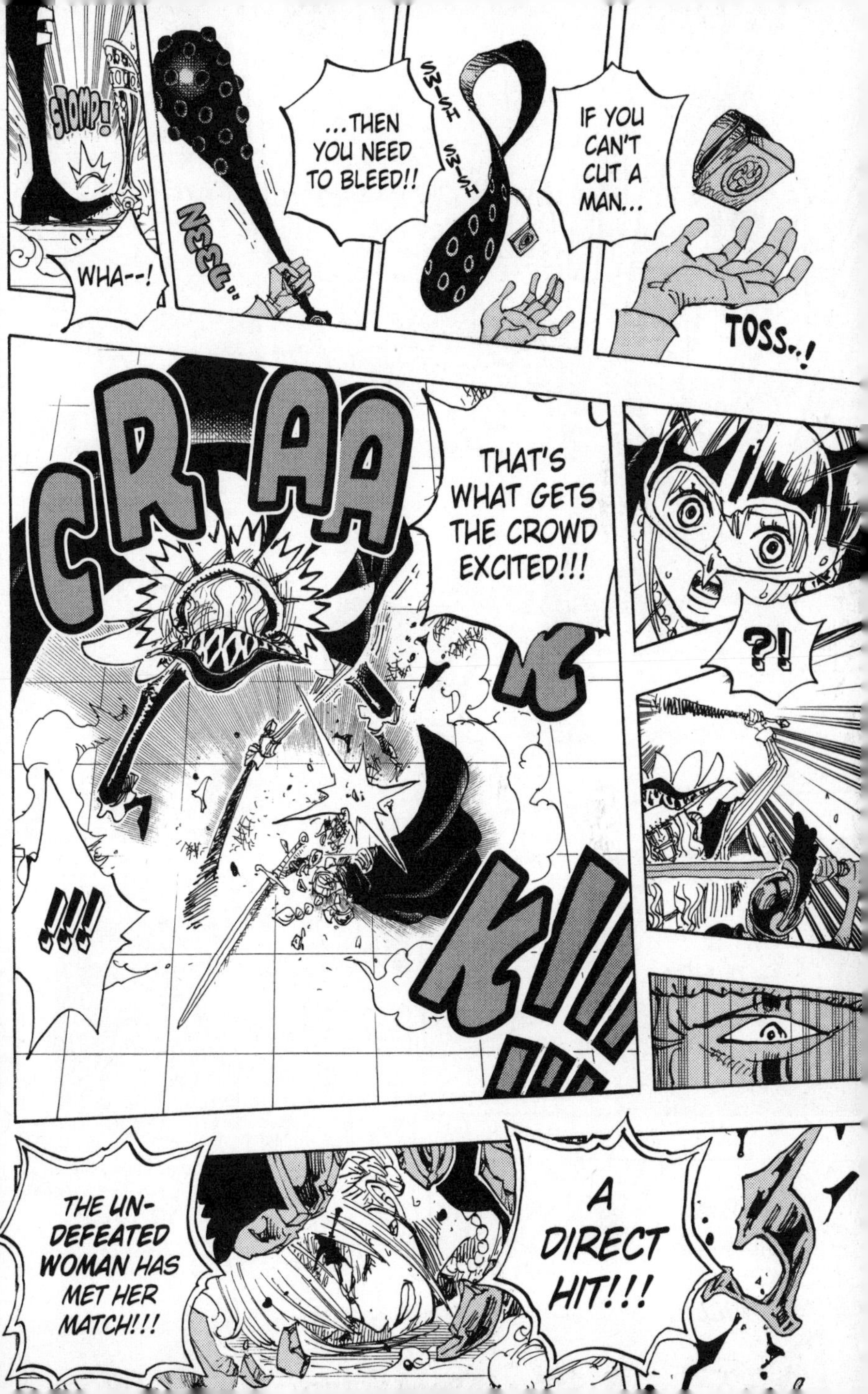

TOSS..!
IF YOU CAN'T CUT A MAN...
SWISH SWISH
...THEN YOU NEED TO BLEED!!
WHA--!
STOMP!
?!
THAT'S WHAT GETS THE CROWD EXCITED!!!
CRAACK!!!
!!!
A DIRECT HIT!!!
THE UN-DEFEATED WOMAN HAS MET HER MATCH!!!

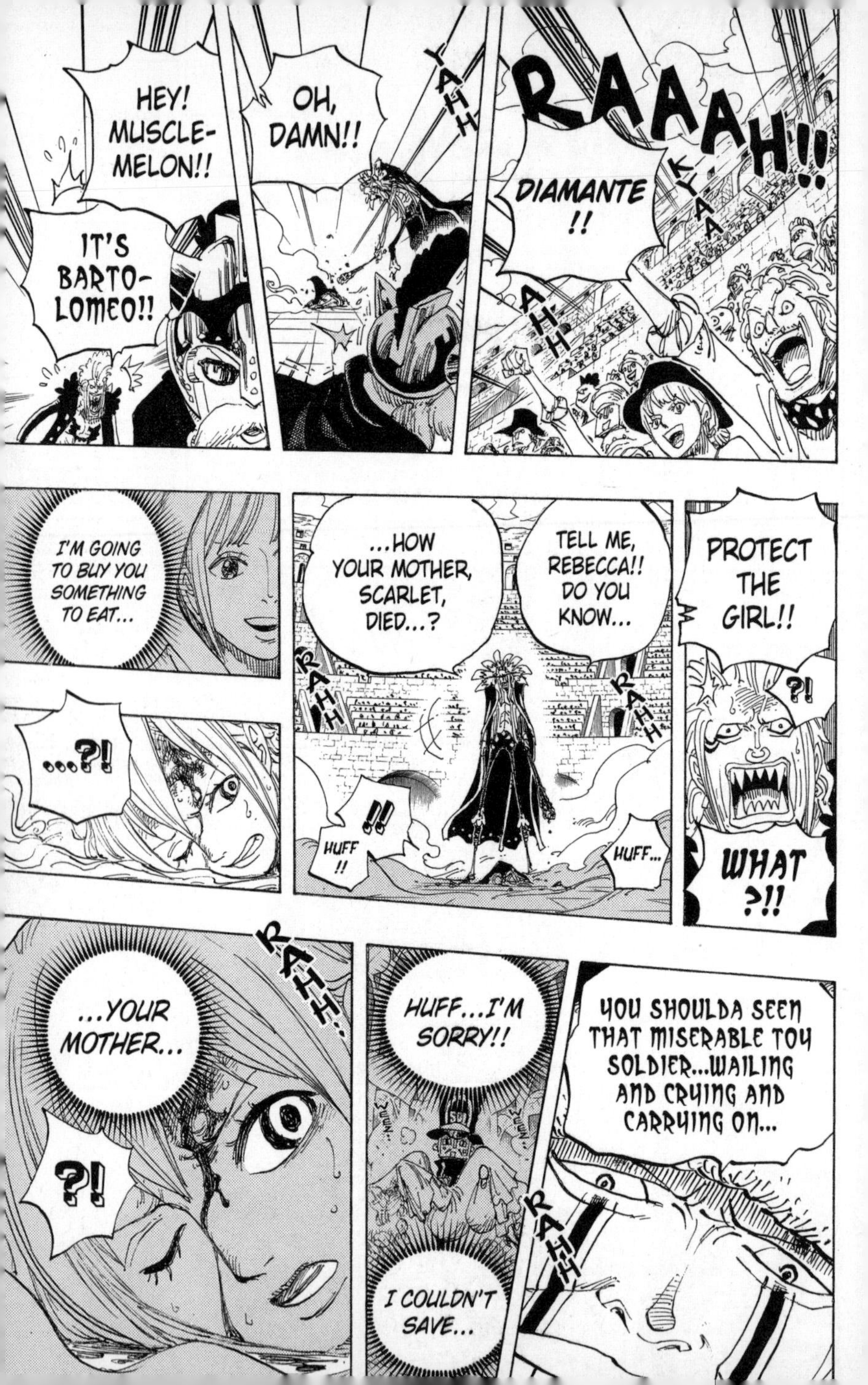
RAAAAH!!
DIAMANTE!!
KYAA
AHH
YAHH
OH, DAMN!!
HEY! MUSCLE-MELON!!
IT'S BARTO-LOMEO!!
PROTECT THE GIRL!!
?!
WHAT?!!
TELL ME, REBECCA!! DO YOU KNOW...
...HOW YOUR MOTHER, SCARLET, DIED...?
RAHH
RAHH
HUFF...
!!
HUFF!!
I'M GOING TO BUY YOU SOMETHING TO EAT...
...?!
YOU SHOULDA SEEN THAT MISERABLE TOY SOLDIER...WAILING AND CRYING AND CARRYING ON...
RAHH
HUFF...I'M SORRY!!
I COULDN'T SAVE...
RAHH...
...YOUR MOTHER...
?!

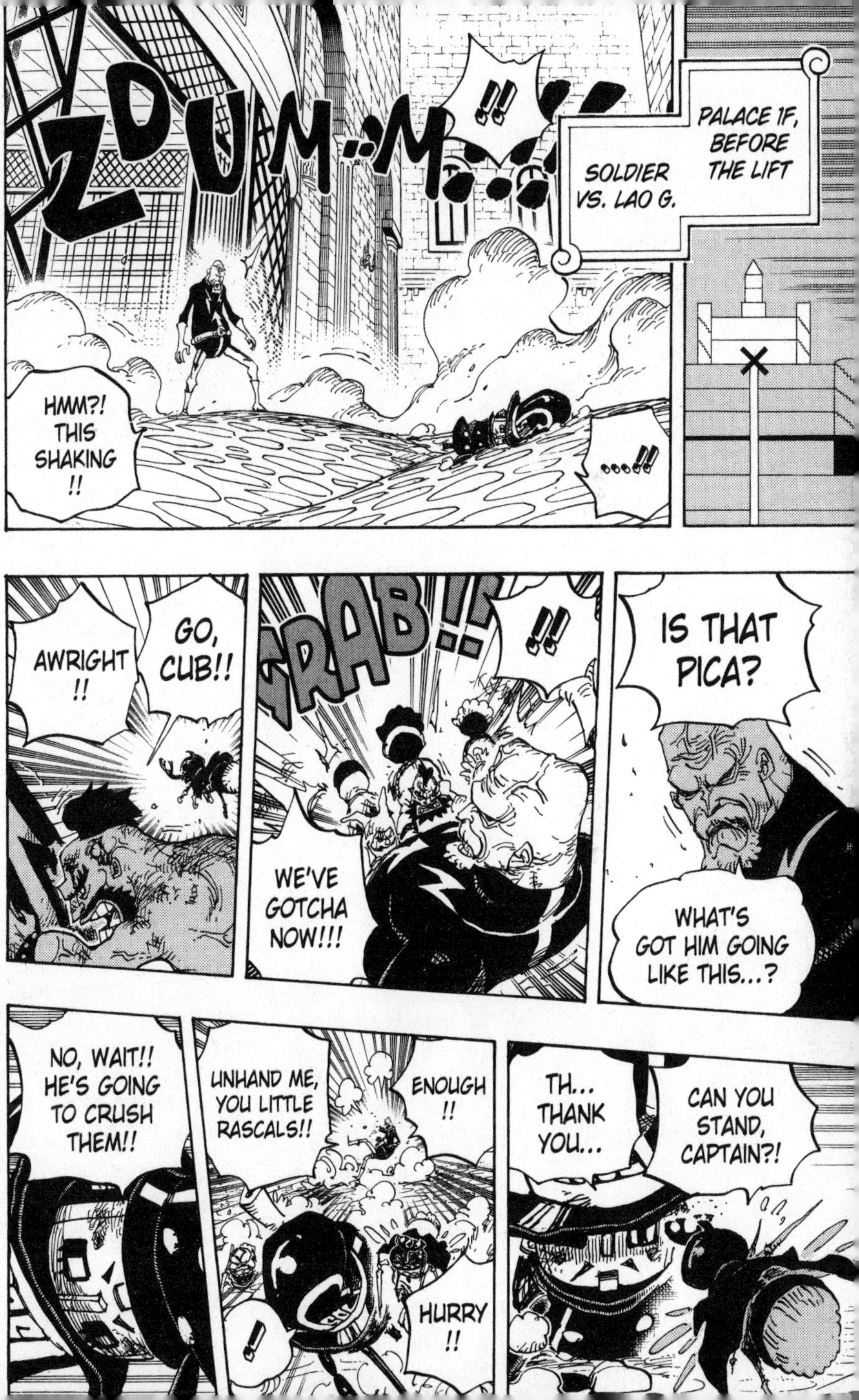
PALACE 1F, BEFORE THE LIFT
SOLDIER VS. LAO G.
ZDUM...M!!
...!!
HMM?! THIS SHAKING!!
IS THAT PICA?
WHAT'S GOT HIM GOING LIKE THIS...?
!!
GRAB!!
WE'VE GOTCHA NOW!!!
GO, CUB!!
AWRIGHT!!
CAN YOU STAND, CAPTAIN?!
TH... THANK YOU...
ENOUGH!!
UNHAND ME, YOU LITTLE RASCALS!!
HURRY!!
!
NO, WAIT!! HE'S GOING TO CRUSH THEM!!

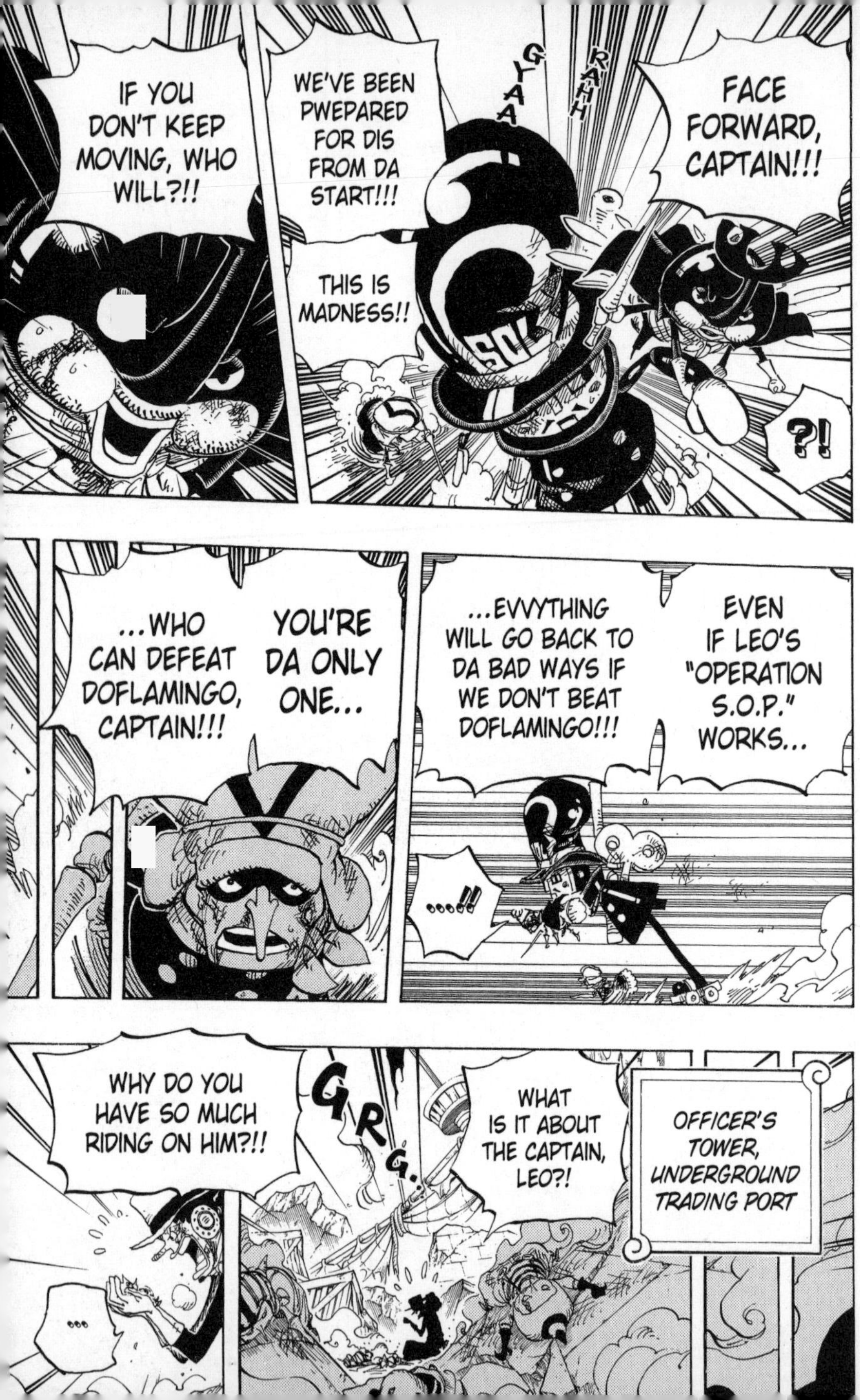
FACE FORWARD, CAPTAIN!!!
?!
RAHH
GYAAA
WE'VE BEEN PWEPARED FOR DIS FROM DA START!!!
THIS IS MADNESS!!
IF YOU DON'T KEEP MOVING, WHO WILL?!!
EVEN IF LEO'S "OPERATION S.O.P." WORKS...
...EVVYTHING WILL GO BACK TO DA BAD WAYS IF WE DON'T BEAT DOFLAMINGO!!!
....!!
YOU'RE DA ONLY ONE...
...WHO CAN DEFEAT DOFLAMINGO, CAPTAIN!!!
OFFICER'S TOWER, UNDERGROUND TRADING PORT
WHAT IS IT ABOUT THE CAPTAIN, LEO?!
GRG..
WHY DO YOU HAVE SO MUCH RIDING ON HIM?!!
...

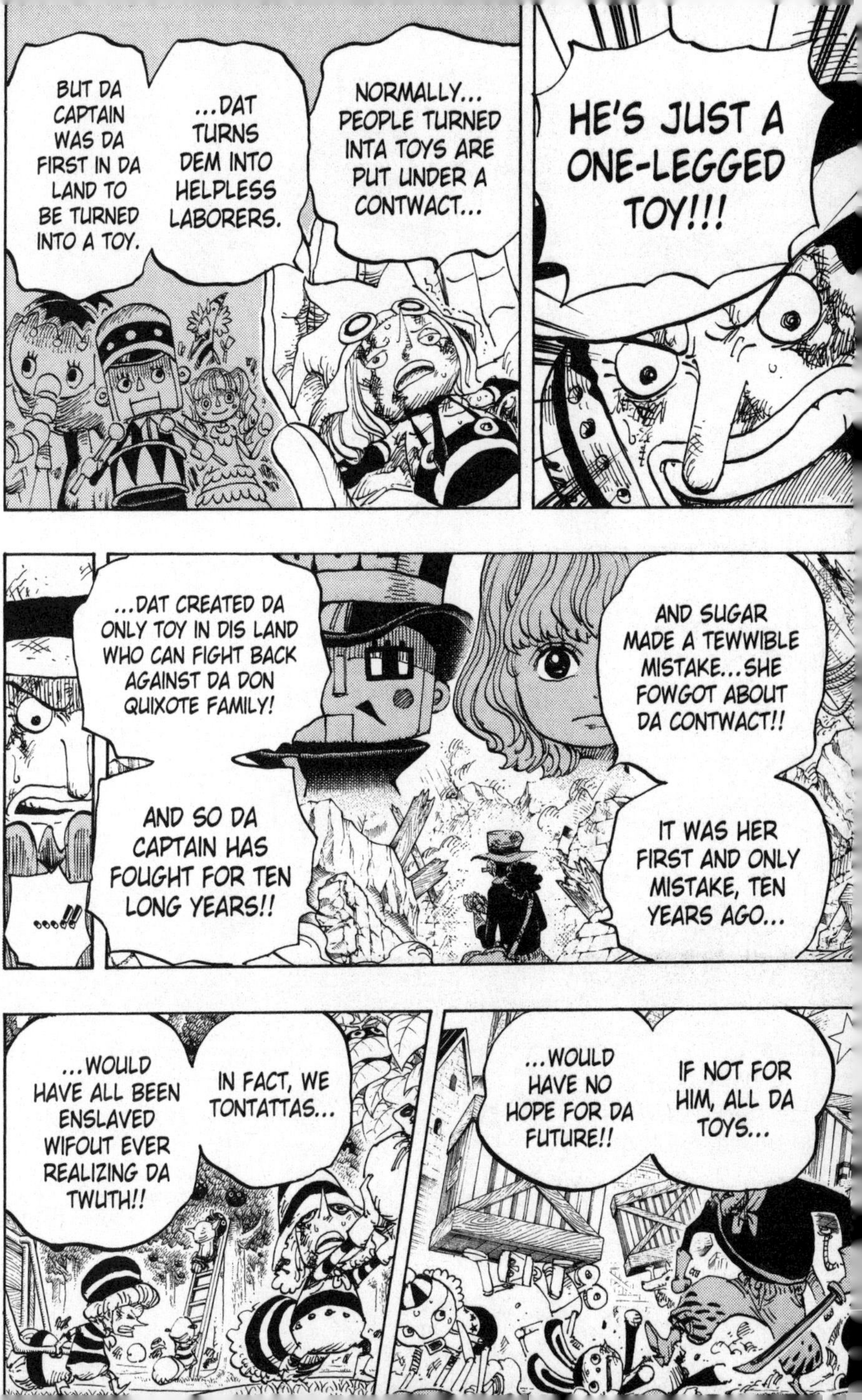
HE'S JUST A ONE-LEGGED TOY!!!
NORMALLY... PEOPLE TURNED INTA TOYS ARE PUT UNDER A CONTWACT...
...DAT TURNS DEM INTO HELPLESS LABORERS.
BUT DA CAPTAIN WAS DA FIRST IN DA LAND TO BE TURNED INTO A TOY.
AND SUGAR MADE A TEWWIBLE MISTAKE...SHE FOWGOT ABOUT DA CONTWACT!!
IT WAS HER FIRST AND ONLY MISTAKE, TEN YEARS AGO...
...DAT CREATED DA ONLY TOY IN DIS LAND WHO CAN FIGHT BACK AGAINST DA DON QUIXOTE FAMILY!
AND SO DA CAPTAIN HAS FOUGHT FOR TEN LONG YEARS!!
....!!
IF NOT FOR HIM, ALL DA TOYS...
...WOULD HAVE NO HOPE FOR DA FUTURE!!
IN FACT, WE TONTATTAS...
...WOULD HAVE ALL BEEN ENSLAVED WIFOUT EVER REALIZING DA TWUTH!!

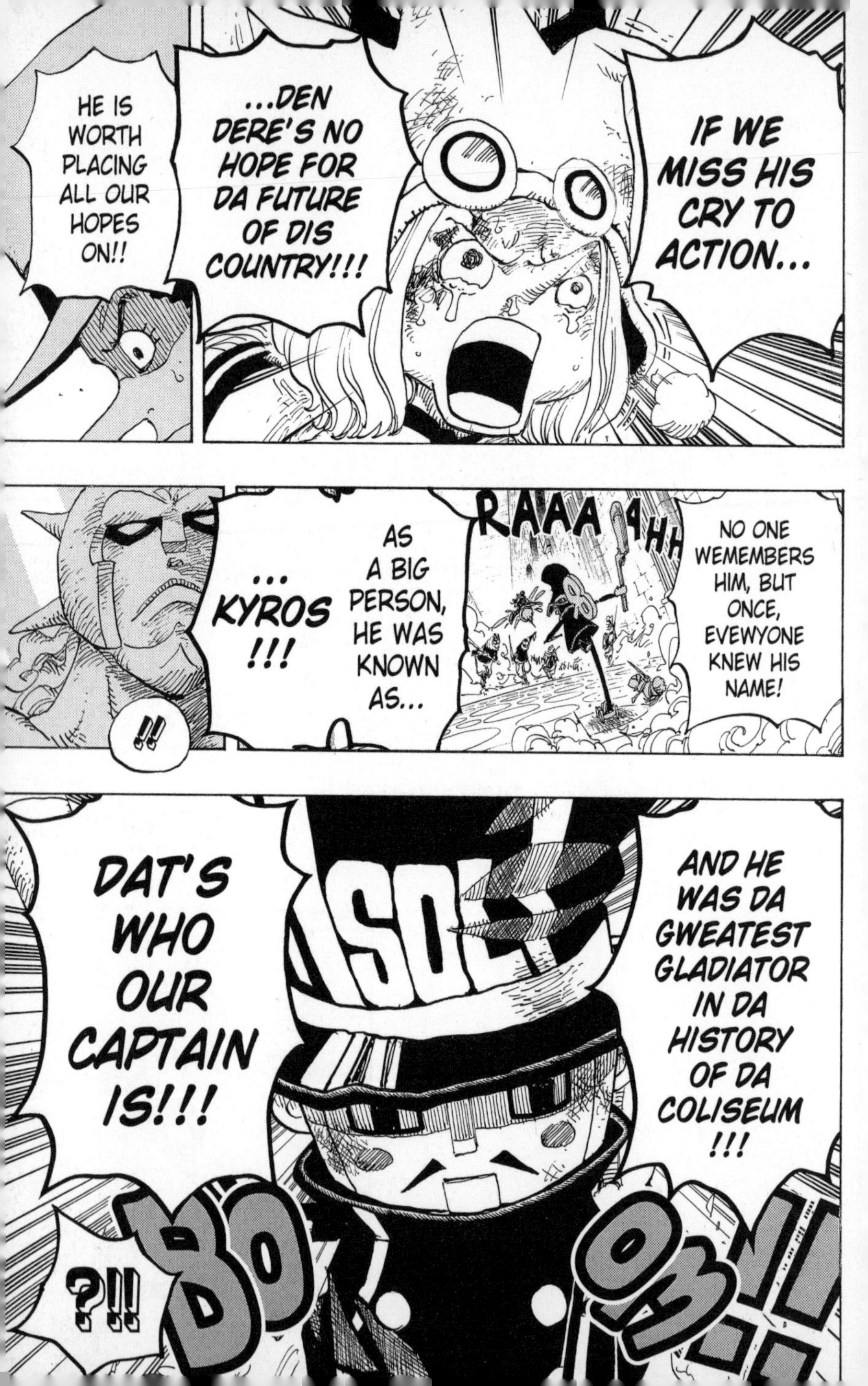
IF WE MISS HIS CRY TO ACTION...
...DEN DERE'S NO HOPE FOR DA FUTURE OF DIS COUNTRY!!!
HE IS WORTH PLACING ALL OUR HOPES ON!!
NO ONE WEMEMBERS HIM, BUT ONCE, EVEWYONE KNEW HIS NAME!
AS A BIG PERSON, HE WAS KNOWN AS...
...KYROS!!!
!!
AND HE WAS DA GWEATEST GLADIATOR IN DA HISTORY OF DA COLISEUM!!!
DAT'S WHO OUR CAPTAIN IS!!!
?!!

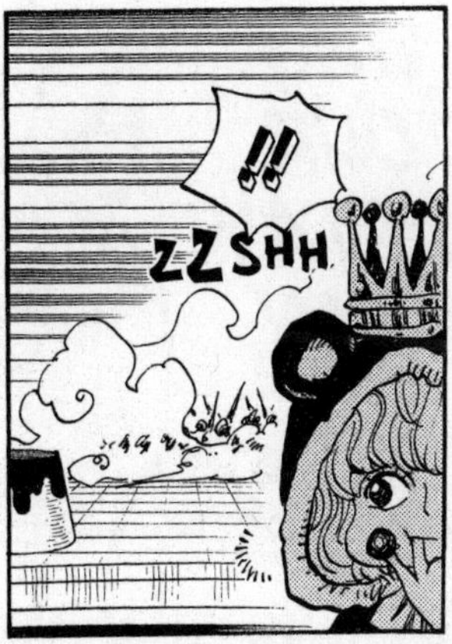
!!
ZZSHH

Chapter 740:

ITS IN YOUR HANDS!!!

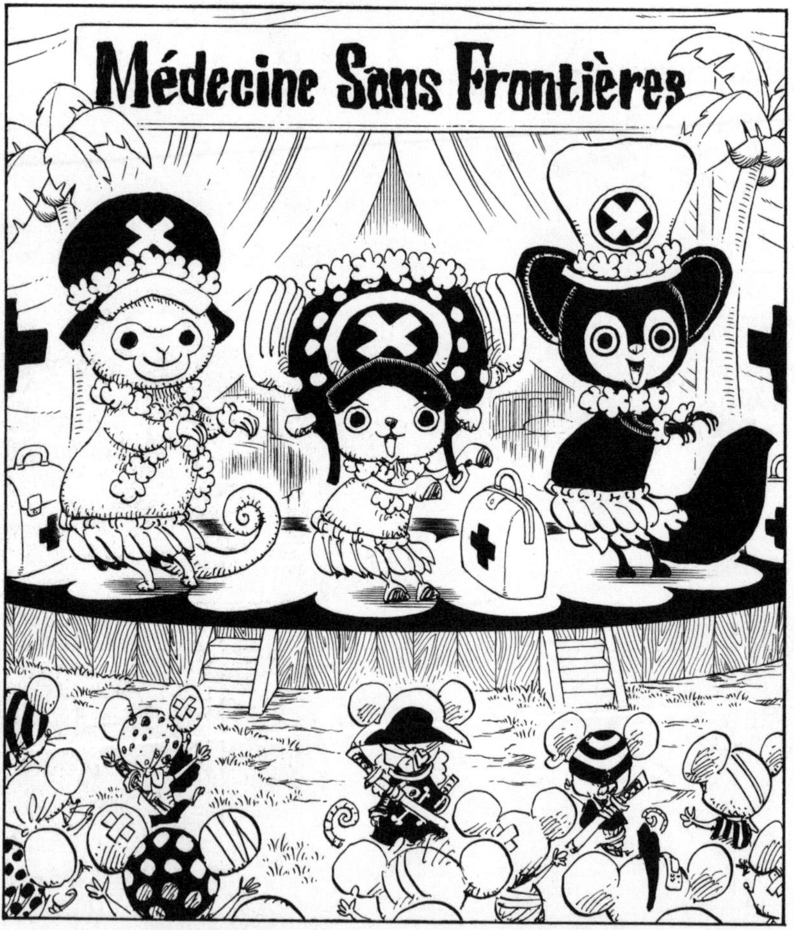
Médecine Sans Frontières

REQUEST: "CHOPPER DOING A HAWAIIAN HULA DANCE WITH A CUSCUS AND AN AYE-AYE" BY OSAMU FUJITA

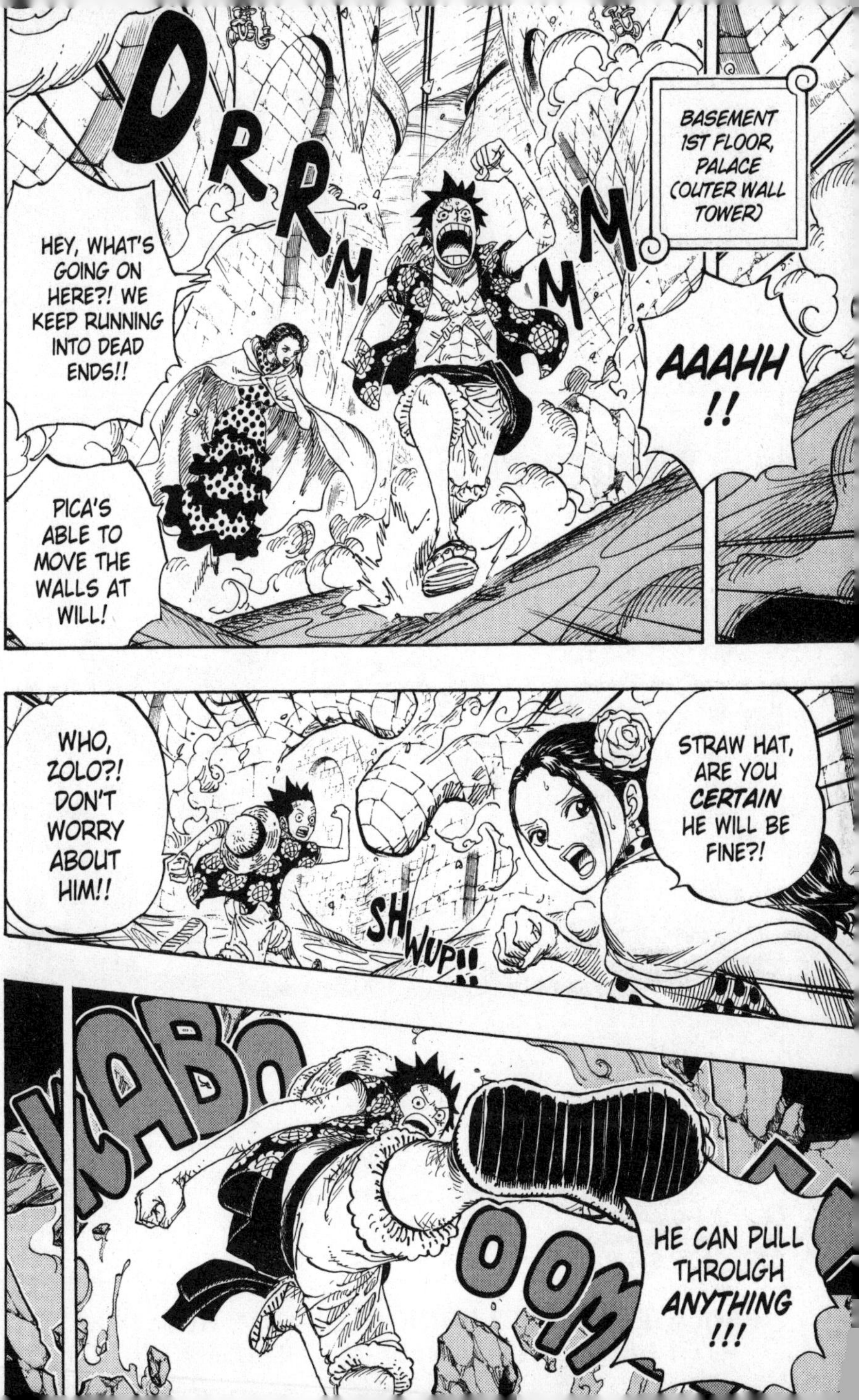
BASEMENT 1ST FLOOR, PALACE (OUTER WALL TOWER)
DRRRMMM
AAAHH!!
HEY, WHAT'S GOING ON HERE?! WE KEEP RUNNING INTO DEAD ENDS!!
PICA'S ABLE TO MOVE THE WALLS AT WILL!
STRAW HAT, ARE YOU CERTAIN HE WILL BE FINE?!
WHO, ZOLO?! DON'T WORRY ABOUT HIM!!
SHWUP!!
KABOOOM
HE CAN PULL THROUGH ANYTHING!!!

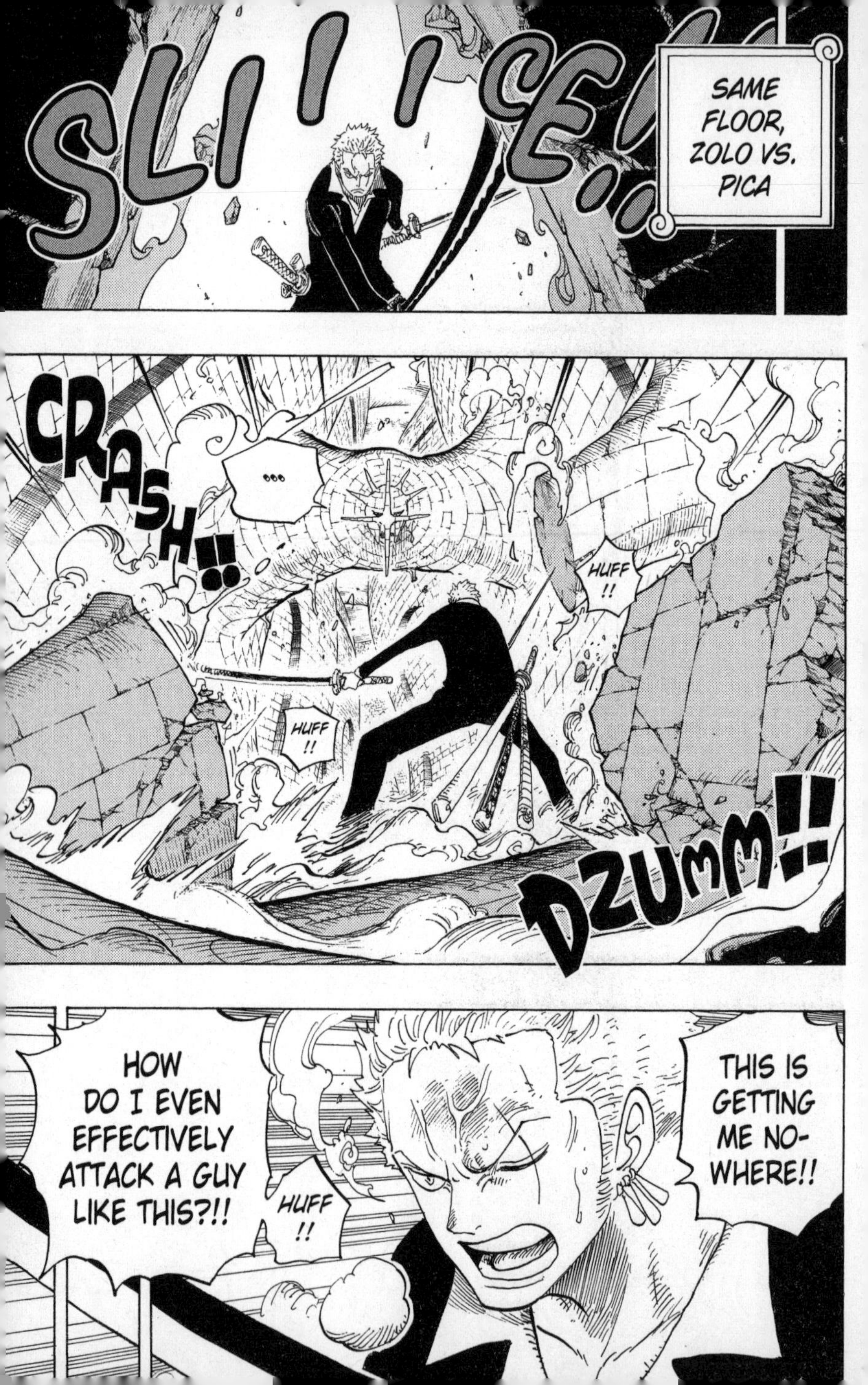
SAME FLOOR, ZOLO VS. PICA
SLIIICE!!
CRASH!!
...
HUFF !!
HUFF !!
DZUMM!!
THIS IS GETTING ME NO-WHERE!!
HUFF !!
HOW DO I EVEN EFFECTIVELY ATTACK A GUY LIKE THIS?!!

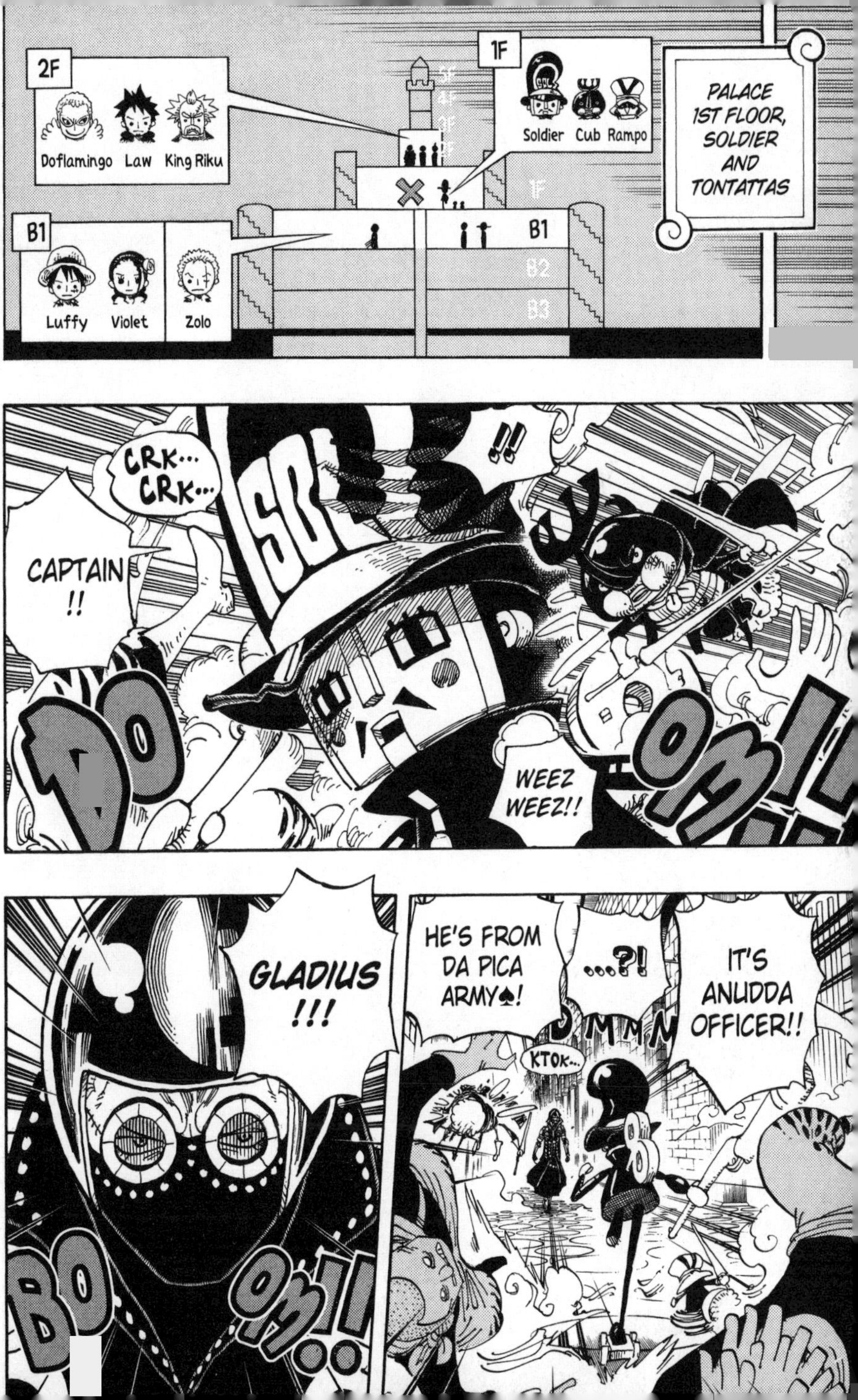
PALACE 1ST FLOOR, SOLDIER AND TONTATTAS
1F
Soldier
Cub
Rampo
2F
Doflamingo
Law
King Riku
B1
B1
Zolo
Luffy
Violet
!!
WEEZ WEEZ!!
CRK... CRK...
CAPTAIN!!
IT'S ANUDDA OFFICER!!
...?!
HE'S FROM DA PICA ARMY♠!
KTOK...
GLADIUS!!!

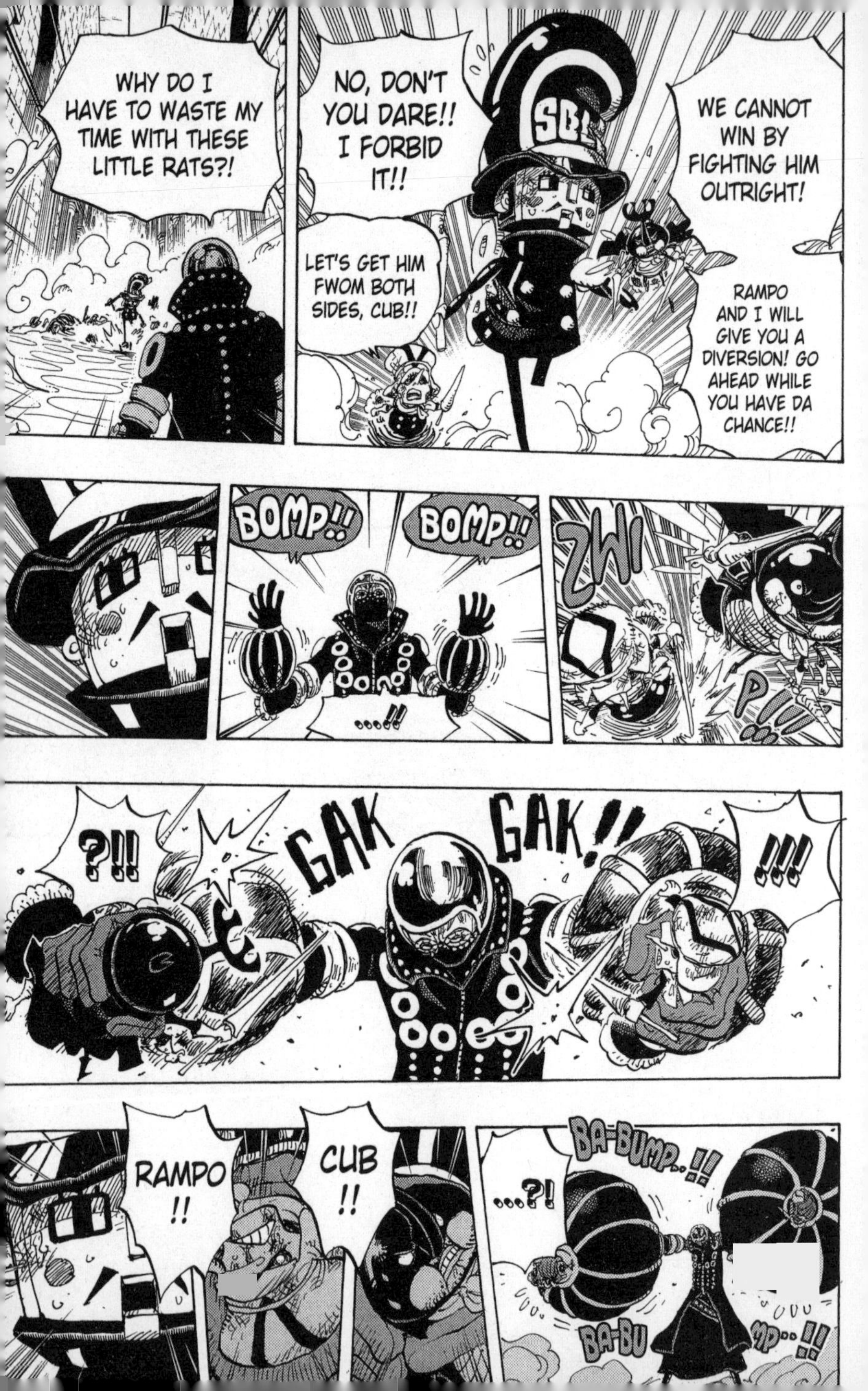
WE CANNOT WIN BY FIGHTING HIM OUTRIGHT!
RAMPO AND I WILL GIVE YOU A DIVERSION! GO AHEAD WHILE YOU HAVE DA CHANCE!!
NO, DON'T YOU DARE!! I FORBID IT!!
LET'S GET HIM FWOM BOTH SIDES, CUB!!
WHY DO I HAVE TO WASTE MY TIME WITH THESE LITTLE RATS?!
ZWI
P!!!
BOMP!!
BOMP!!
....!!
!!!
GAK GAK!!
?!!
BA-BUMP..!!
...?!
BA-BU
MP..!!
CUB!!
RAMPO!!

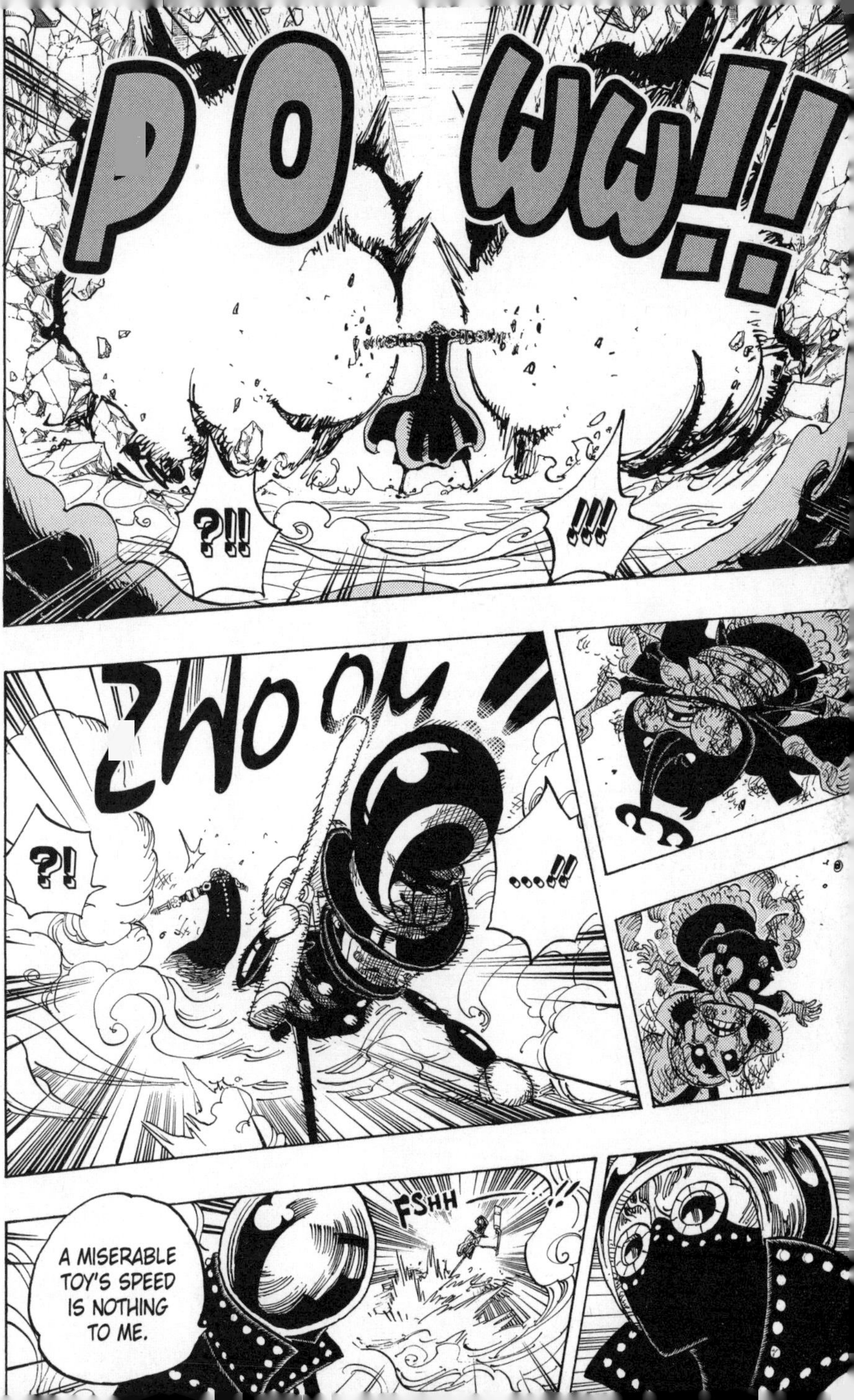
POWW!!
!!!
?!!
ZHOOM!!
....!!
?!
FSHH
A MISERABLE TOY'S SPEED IS NOTHING TO ME.

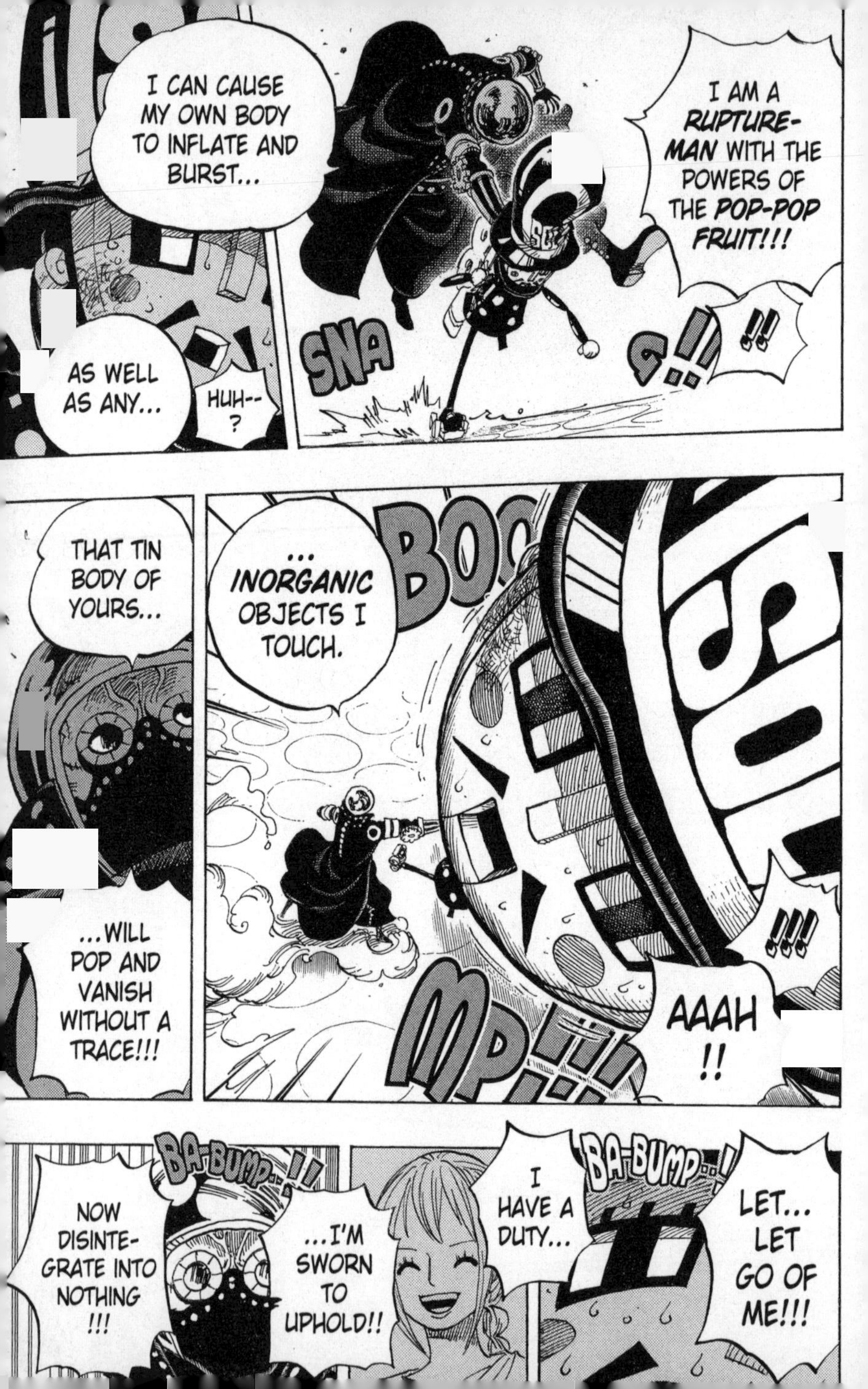
I AM A RUPTURE-MAN WITH THE POWERS OF THE POP-POP FRUIT!!!
SNA
G!!
!!
I CAN CAUSE MY OWN BODY TO INFLATE AND BURST...
AS WELL AS ANY...
HUH-- ?
... INORGANIC OBJECTS I TOUCH.
BOO
MP!!
!!!
AAAH !!
THAT TIN BODY OF YOURS...
...WILL POP AND VANISH WITHOUT A TRACE!!!
BA-BUMP..!
LET... LET GO OF ME!!!
I HAVE A DUTY...
...I'M SWORN TO UPHOLD!!
BA-BUMP..!!
NOW DISINTE-GRATE INTO NOTHING !!!

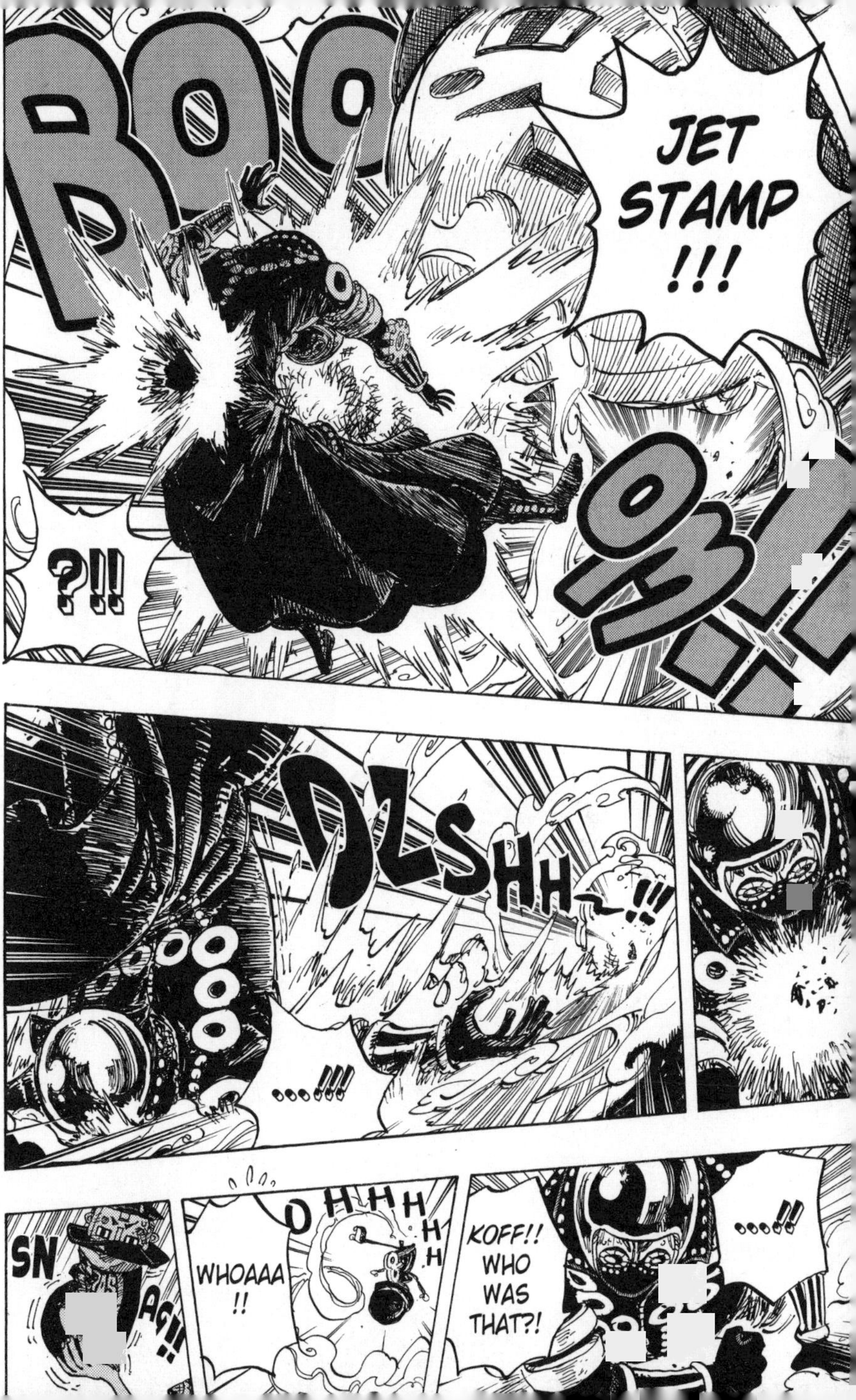
JET STAMP !!!
BOO
OM!!
?!!
DZSHH~!!!
...!!!
...!!
KOFF!! WHO WAS THAT?!
OHHHHHH
WHOAAA !!
SN
AG!!

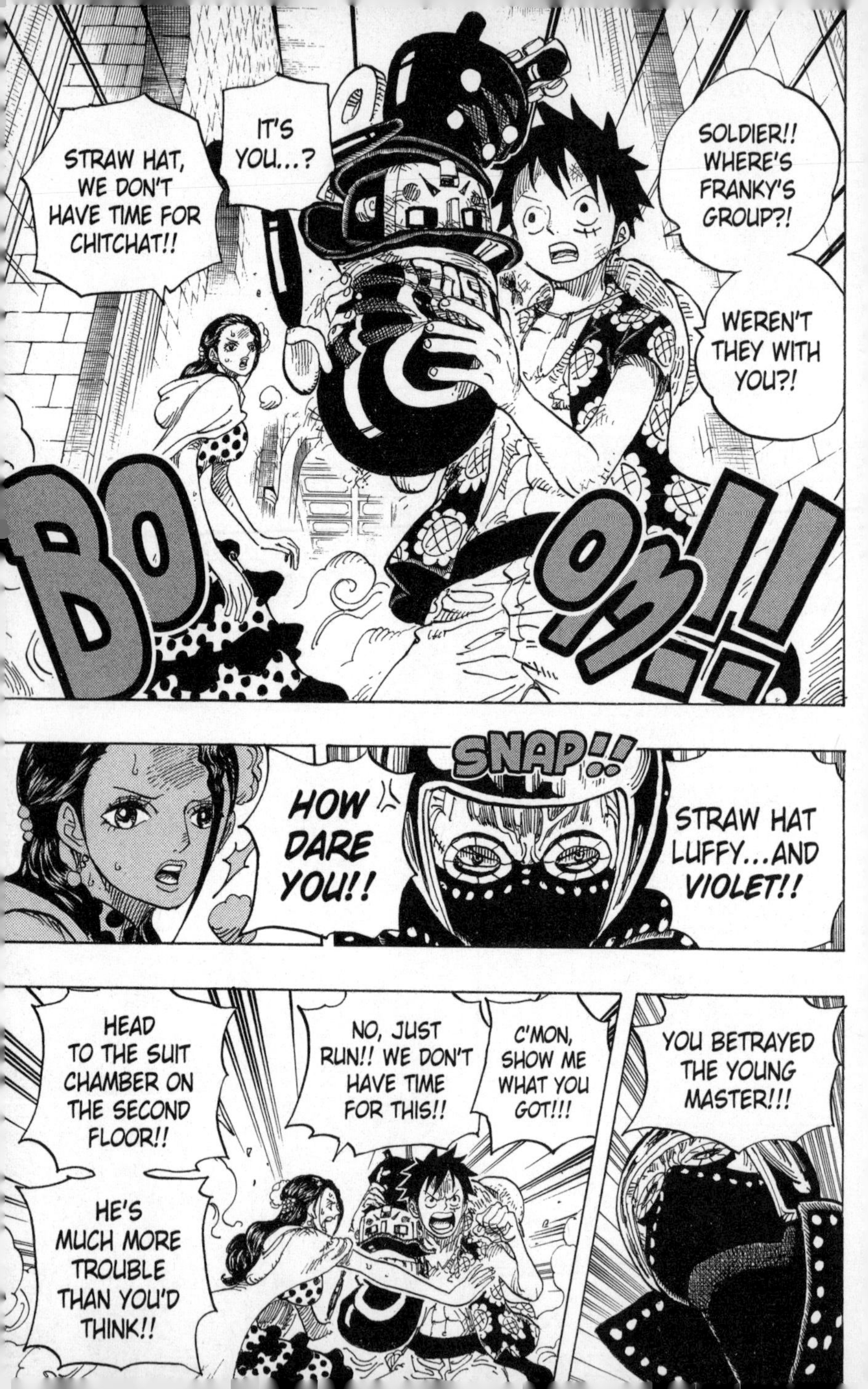
SOLDIER!! WHERE'S FRANKY'S GROUP?!
WEREN'T THEY WITH YOU?!
IT'S YOU...?
STRAW HAT, WE DON'T HAVE TIME FOR CHITCHAT!!
BOOM!!
SNAP!!
STRAW HAT LUFFY...AND VIOLET!!
HOW DARE YOU!!
YOU BETRAYED THE YOUNG MASTER!!!
C'MON, SHOW ME WHAT YOU GOT!!!
NO, JUST RUN!! WE DON'T HAVE TIME FOR THIS!!
HEAD TO THE SUIT CHAMBER ON THE SECOND FLOOR!!
HE'S MUCH MORE TROUBLE THAN YOU'D THINK!!

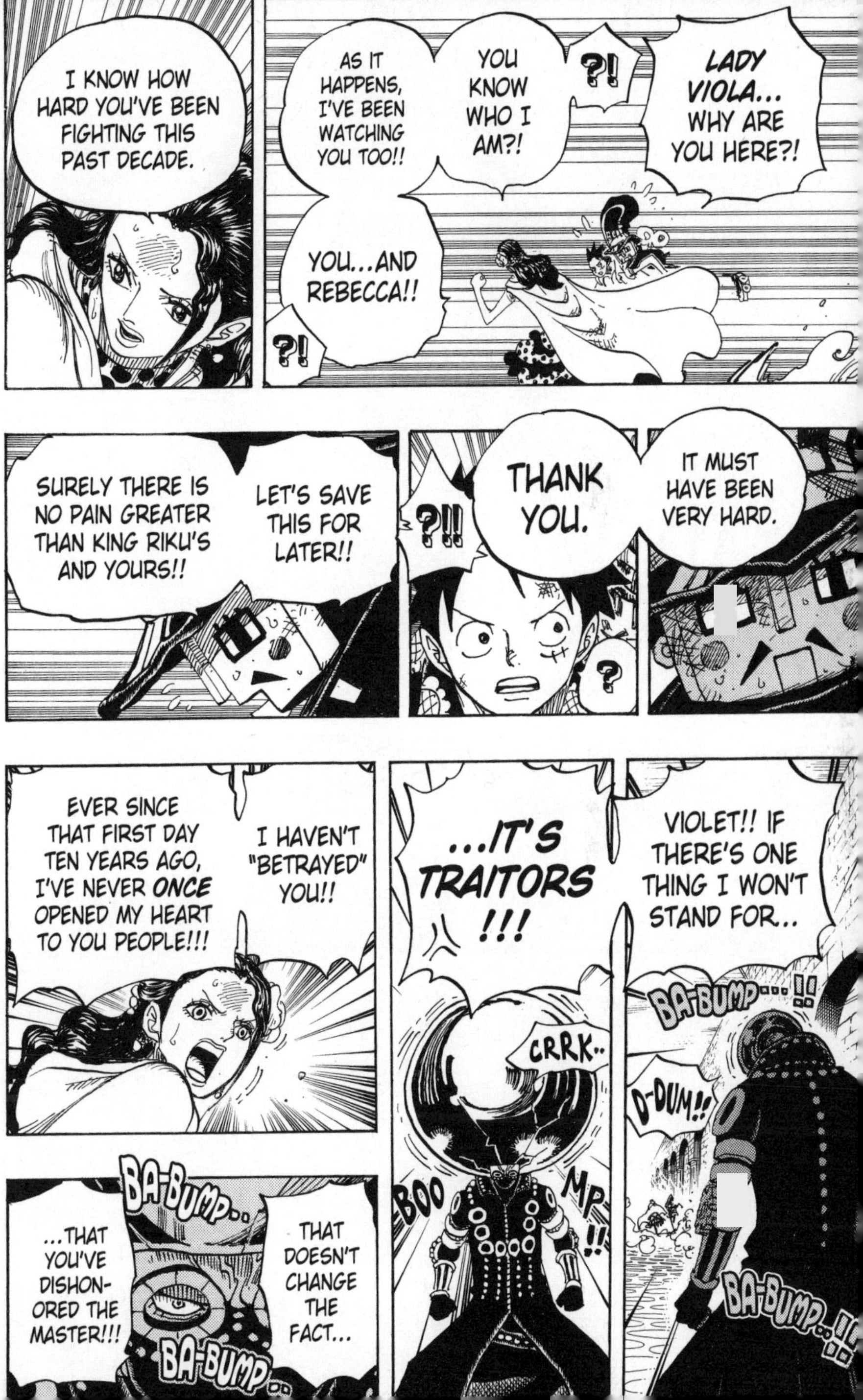
LADY VIOLA... WHY ARE YOU HERE?!
?!
YOU KNOW WHO I AM?!
AS IT HAPPENS, I'VE BEEN WATCHING YOU TOO!!
YOU...AND REBECCA!!
?!
I KNOW HOW HARD YOU'VE BEEN FIGHTING THIS PAST DECADE.
IT MUST HAVE BEEN VERY HARD.
THANK YOU.
?!!
?
LET'S SAVE THIS FOR LATER!!
SURELY THERE IS NO PAIN GREATER THAN KING RIKU'S AND YOURS!!
VIOLET!! IF THERE'S ONE THING I WON'T STAND FOR...
BA-BUMP...!!
D-DUM!!
BA-BUMP..!!
...IT'S TRAITORS!!!
CRRK..
BOOMP!!
I HAVEN'T "BETRAYED" YOU!!
EVER SINCE THAT FIRST DAY TEN YEARS AGO, I'VE NEVER ONCE OPENED MY HEART TO YOU PEOPLE!!!
THAT DOESN'T CHANGE THE FACT...
...THAT YOU'VE DISHONORED THE MASTER!!!
BA-BUMP..
BA-BUMP..

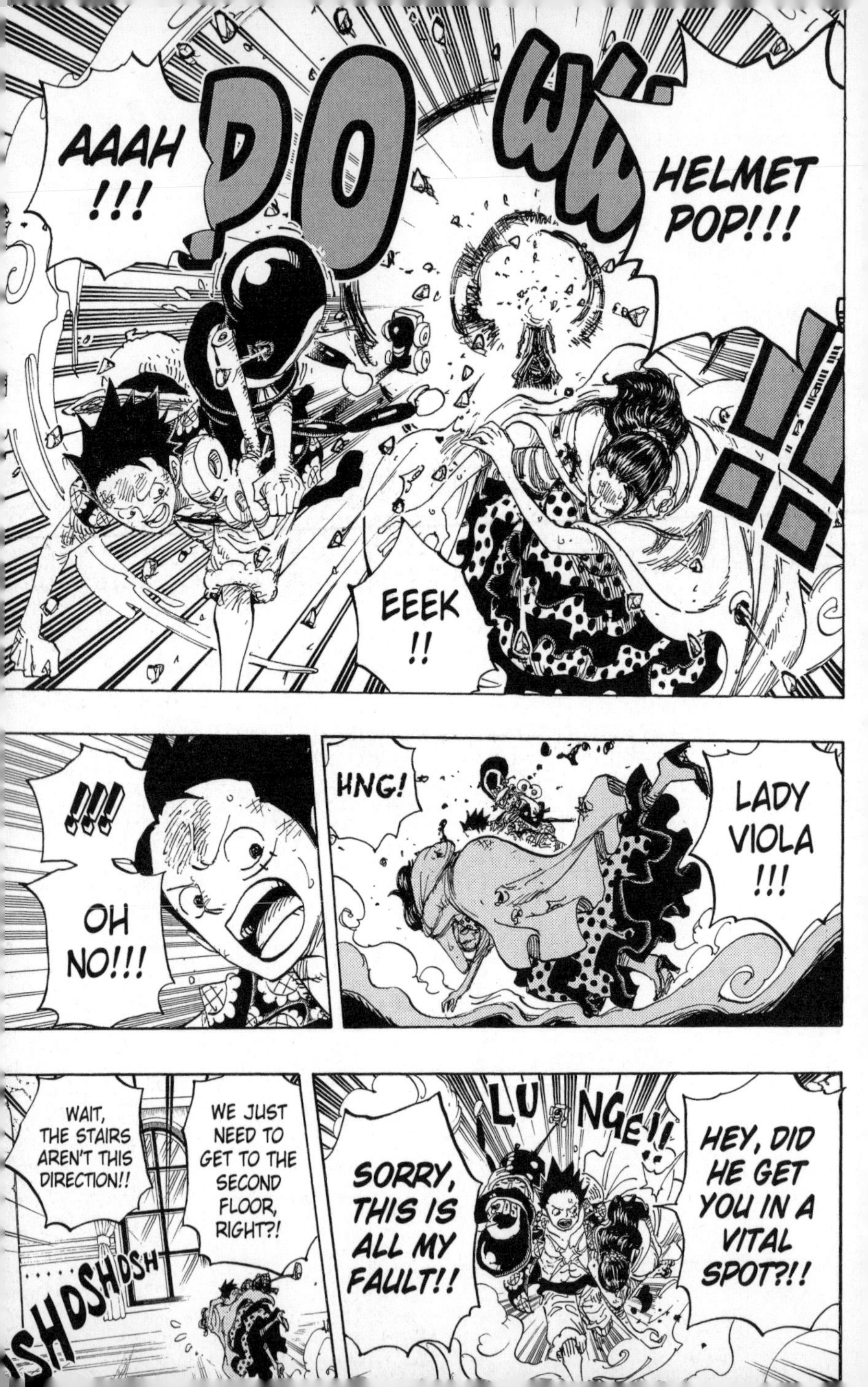
HELMET POP!!!
AAAH !!!
EEEK !!
LADY VIOLA !!!
HNG!
!!!
OH NO!!!
HEY, DID HE GET YOU IN A VITAL SPOT?!!
LUNGE!!
SORRY, THIS IS ALL MY FAULT!!
WE JUST NEED TO GET TO THE SECOND FLOOR, RIGHT?!
WAIT, THE STAIRS AREN'T THIS DIRECTION!!
SHDSHDSH

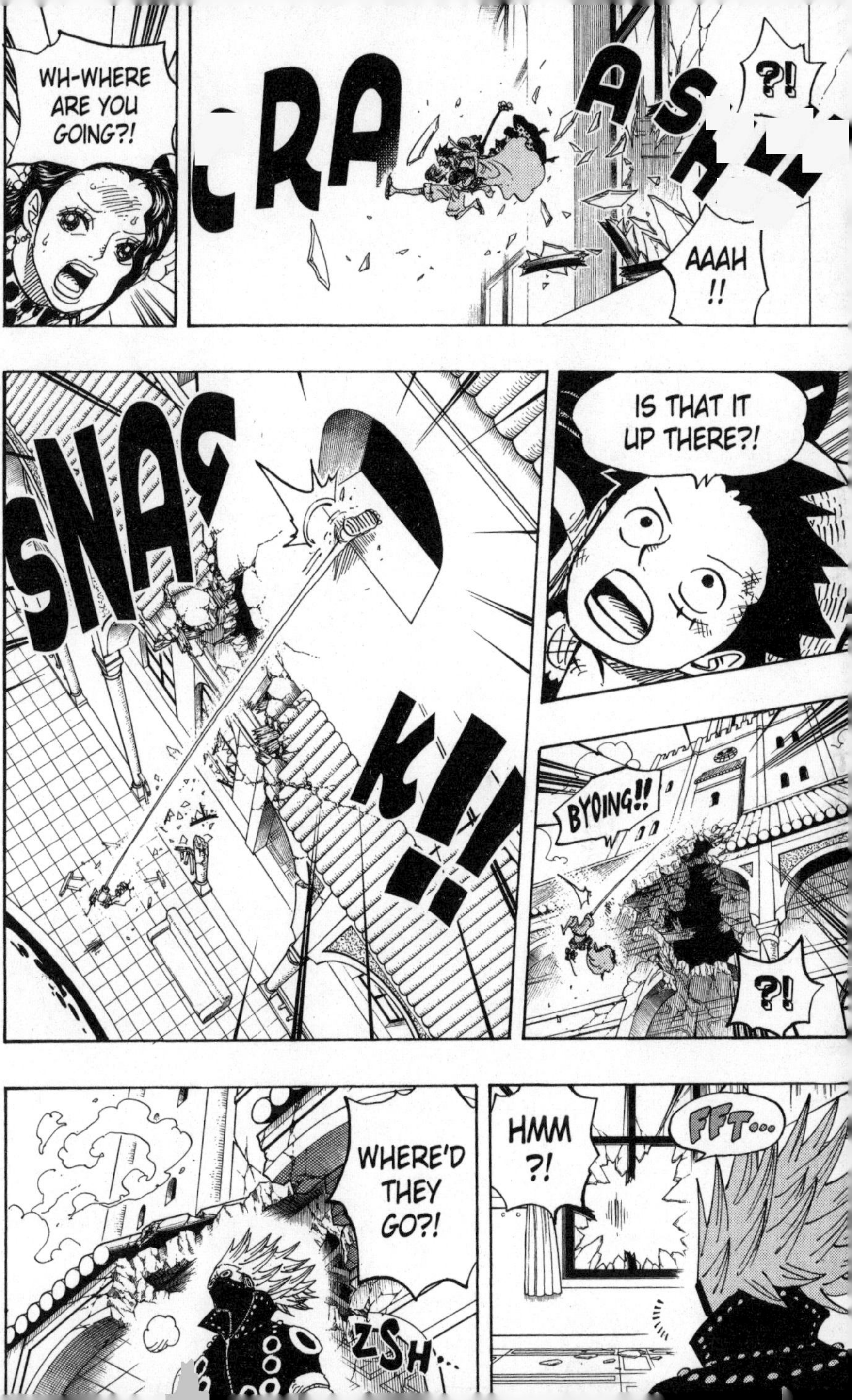
?!
CRAASH
AAAH !!
WH-WHERE ARE YOU GOING?!
IS THAT IT UP THERE?!
BYOING!!
?!
SNACK!!
FFT...
HMM ?!
WHERE'D THEY GO?!
ZSH...

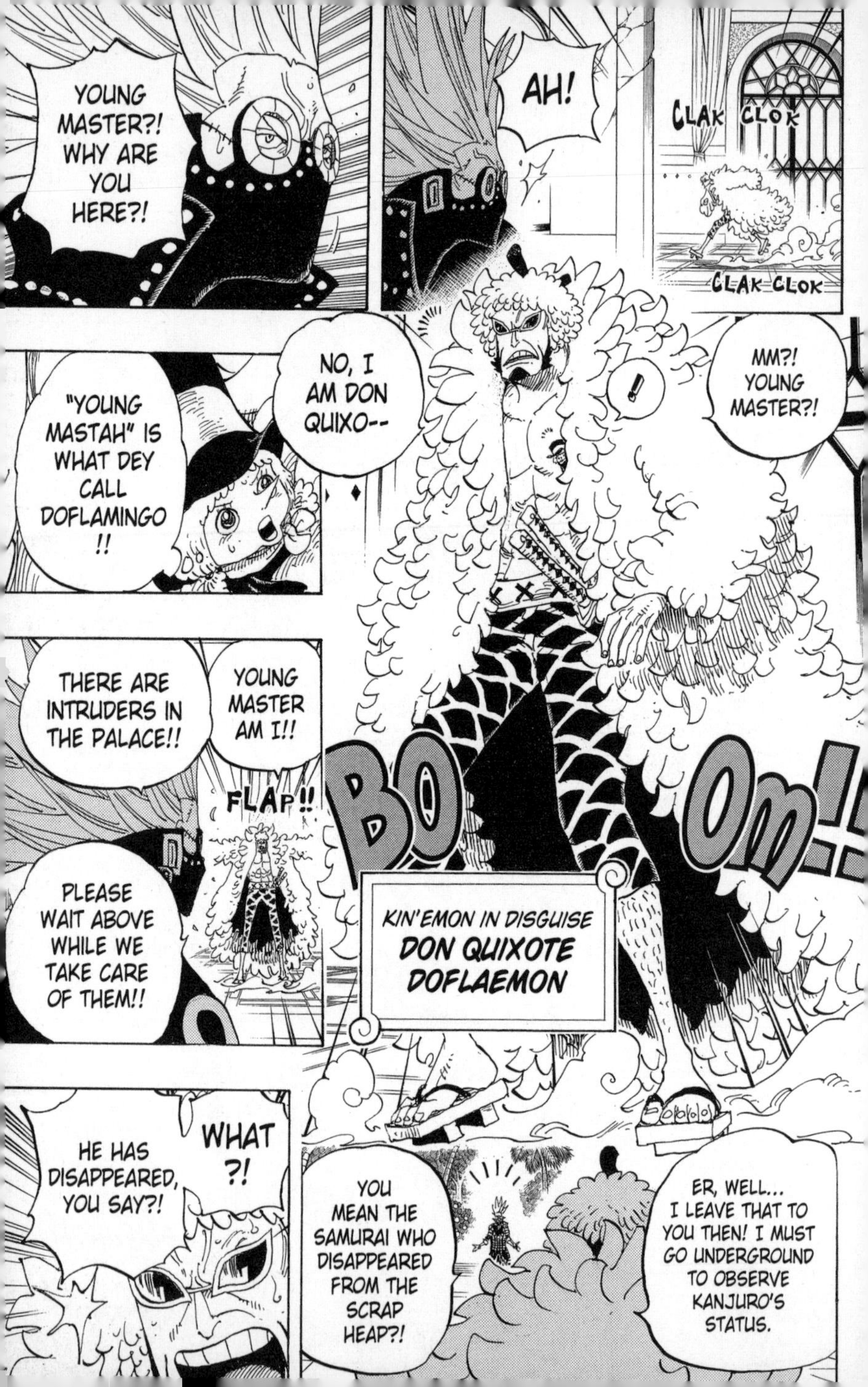
CLAK CLOK
CLAK CLOK
AH!
YOUNG MASTER?! WHY ARE YOU HERE?!
MM?! YOUNG MASTER?!
!
NO, I AM DON QUIXO--
BOOM!!
KIN'EMON IN DISGUISE
DON QUIXOTE DOFLAEMON
"YOUNG MASTAH" IS WHAT DEY CALL DOFLAMINGO!!
YOUNG MASTER AM I!!
THERE ARE INTRUDERS IN THE PALACE!!
FLAP!!
PLEASE WAIT ABOVE WHILE WE TAKE CARE OF THEM!!
ER, WELL... I LEAVE THAT TO YOU THEN! I MUST GO UNDERGROUND TO OBSERVE KANJURO'S STATUS.
YOU MEAN THE SAMURAI WHO DISAPPEARED FROM THE SCRAP HEAP?!
WHAT?!
HE HAS DISAPPEARED, YOU SAY?!

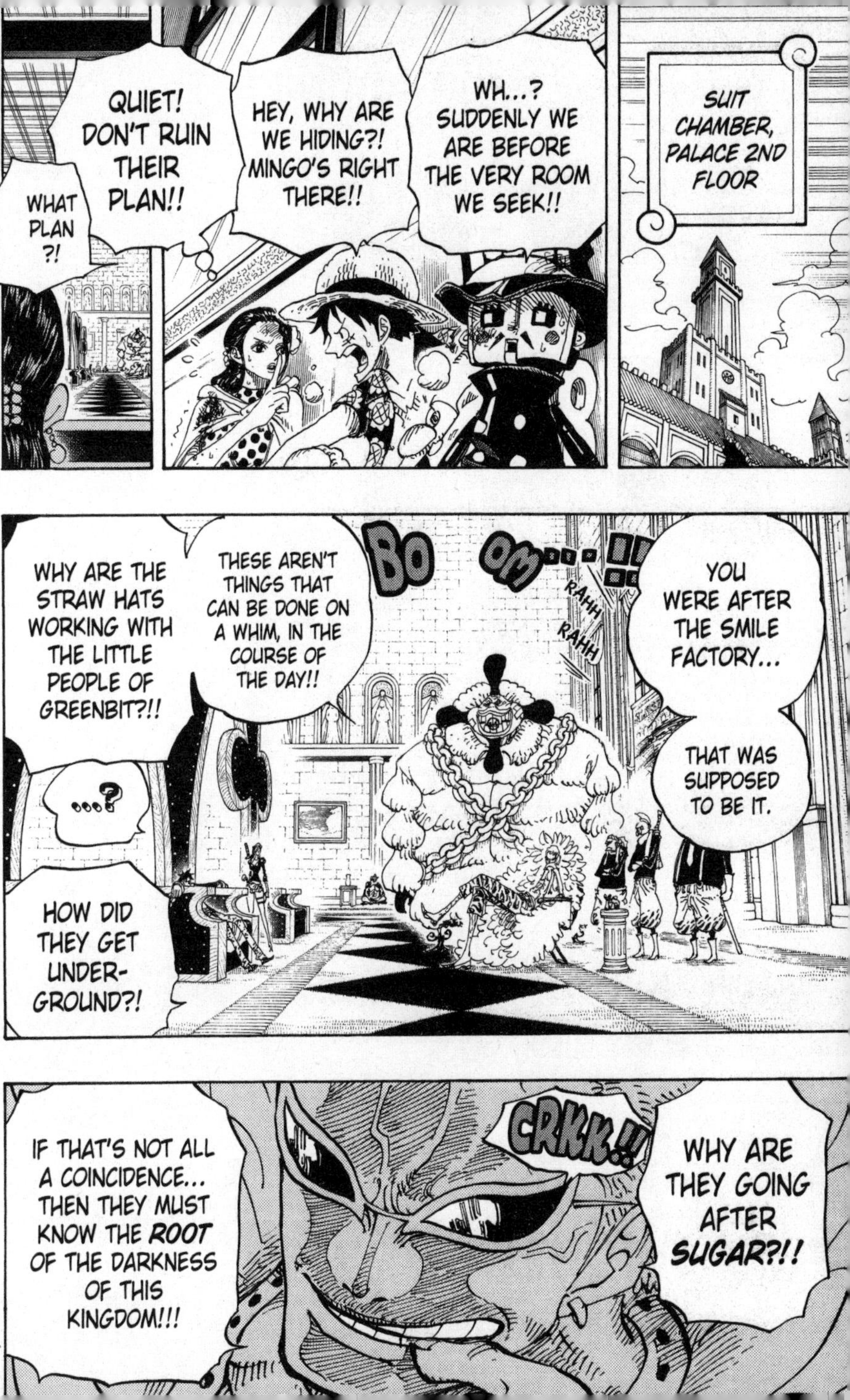
SUIT CHAMBER, PALACE 2ND FLOOR
WH...? SUDDENLY WE ARE BEFORE THE VERY ROOM WE SEEK!!
HEY, WHY ARE WE HIDING?! MINGO'S RIGHT THERE!!
QUIET! DON'T RUIN THEIR PLAN!!
WHAT PLAN ?!
YOU WERE AFTER THE SMILE FACTORY...
THAT WAS SUPPOSED TO BE IT.
BOOM...!!
RAHH
RAHH
THESE AREN'T THINGS THAT CAN BE DONE ON A WHIM, IN THE COURSE OF THE DAY!!
WHY ARE THE STRAW HATS WORKING WITH THE LITTLE PEOPLE OF GREENBIT?!!
...?
HOW DID THEY GET UNDER-GROUND?!
CRKK!!
WHY ARE THEY GOING AFTER *SUGAR*?!!
IF THAT'S NOT ALL A COINCIDENCE... THEN THEY MUST KNOW THE *ROOT* OF THE DARKNESS OF THIS KINGDOM!!!

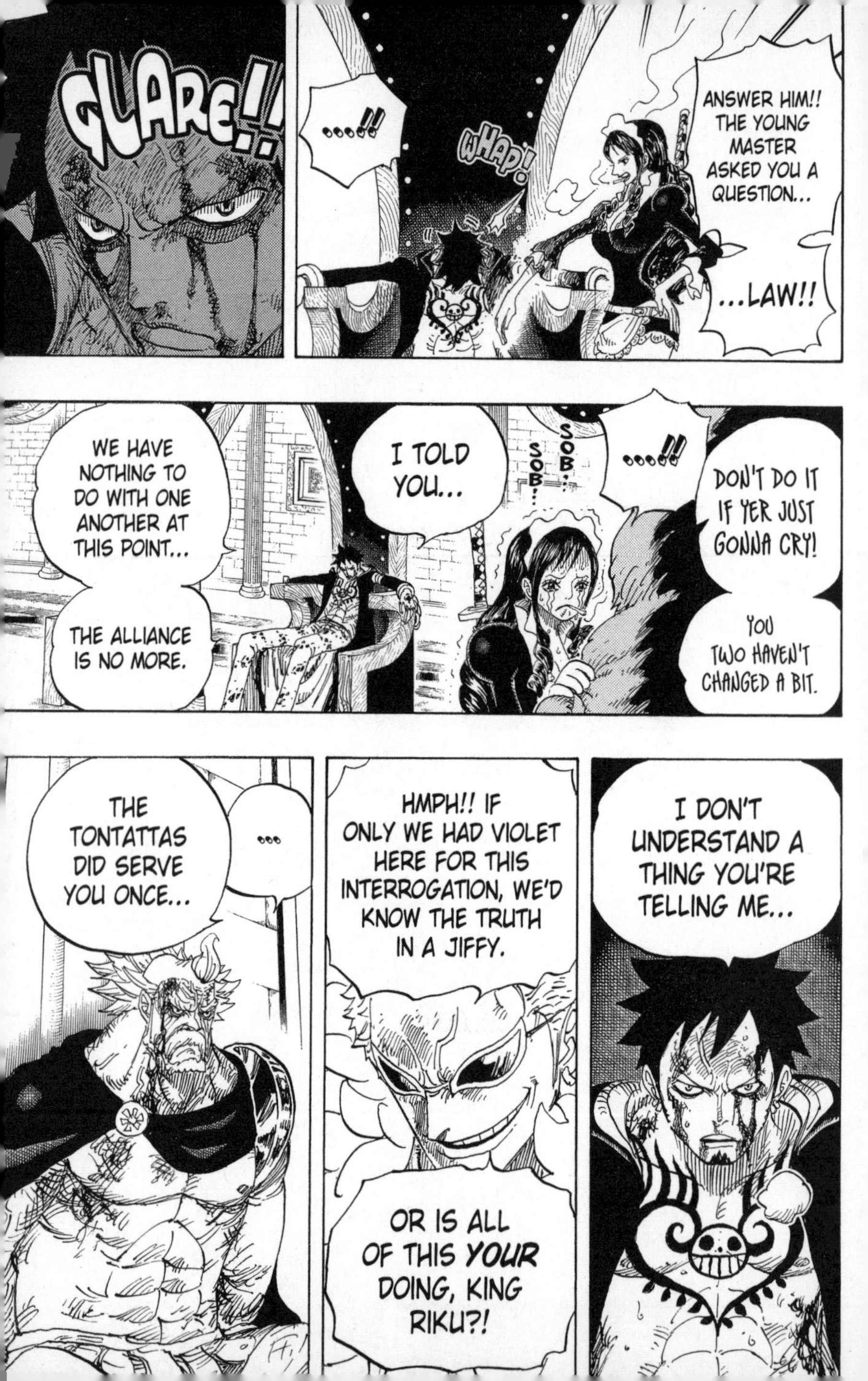
ANSWER HIM!! THE YOUNG MASTER ASKED YOU A QUESTION...
...LAW!!
WHAP!
...!!
GLARE!!
...!!
DON'T DO IT IF YER JUST GONNA CRY!
YOU TWO HAVEN'T CHANGED A BIT.
SOB SOB
I TOLD YOU...
WE HAVE NOTHING TO DO WITH ONE ANOTHER AT THIS POINT...
THE ALLIANCE IS NO MORE.
I DON'T UNDERSTAND A THING YOU'RE TELLING ME...
HMPH!! IF ONLY WE HAD VIOLET HERE FOR THIS INTERROGATION, WE'D KNOW THE TRUTH IN A JIFFY.
OR IS ALL OF THIS *YOUR* DOING, KING RIKU?!
THE TONTATTAS DID SERVE YOU ONCE...
...

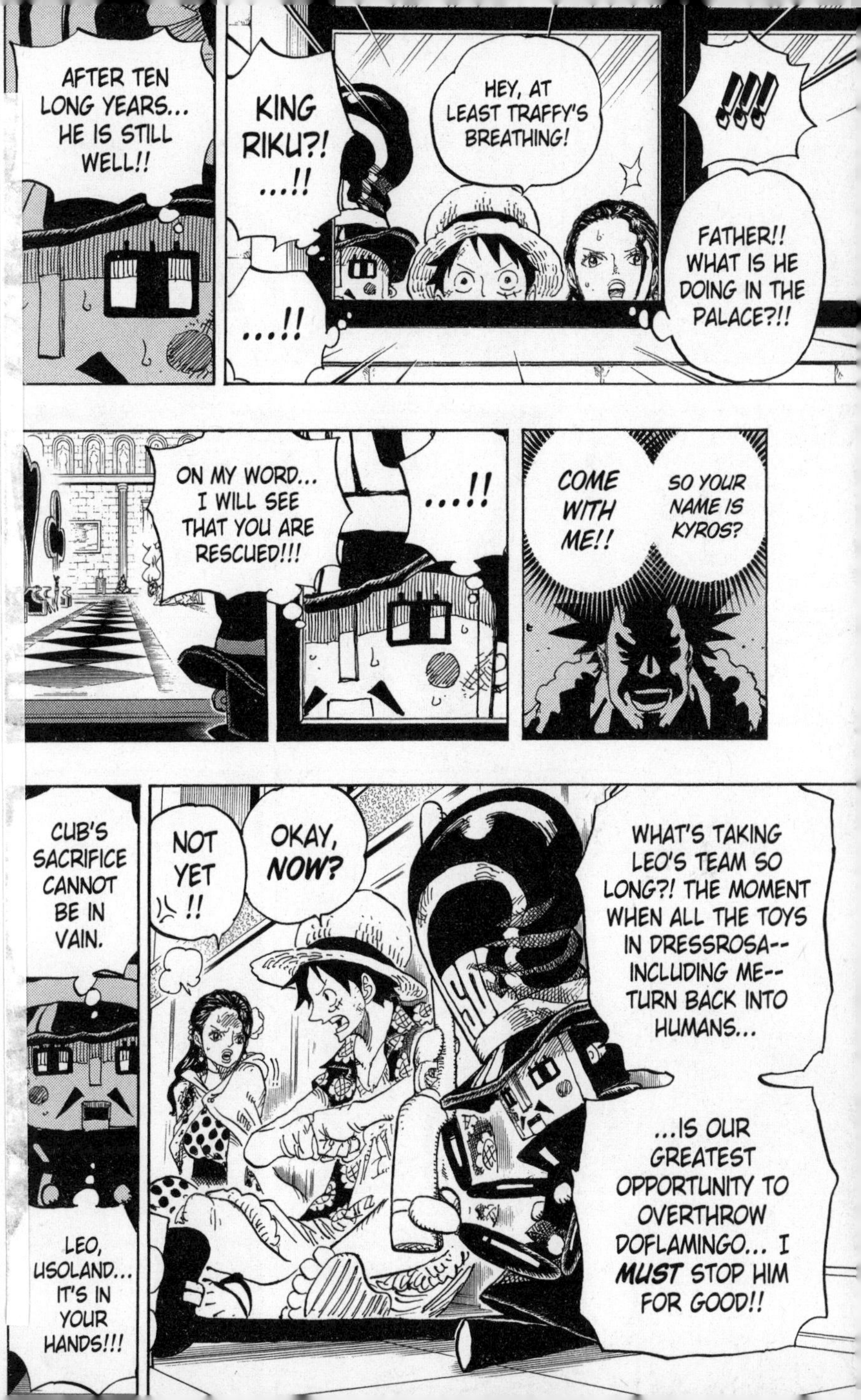
!!!
FATHER!! WHAT IS HE DOING IN THE PALACE?!!
HEY, AT LEAST TRAFFY'S BREATHING!
KING RIKU?! ...!!
...!!
AFTER TEN LONG YEARS... HE IS STILL WELL!!
SO YOUR NAME IS KYROS?
COME WITH ME!!
...!!
ON MY WORD... I WILL SEE THAT YOU ARE RESCUED!!!
WHAT'S TAKING LEO'S TEAM SO LONG?! THE MOMENT WHEN ALL THE TOYS IN DRESSROSA-- INCLUDING ME-- TURN BACK INTO HUMANS...
...IS OUR GREATEST OPPORTUNITY TO OVERTHROW DOFLAMINGO... I MUST STOP HIM FOR GOOD!!
OKAY, NOW?
NOT YET!!
CUB'S SACRIFICE CANNOT BE IN VAIN.
LEO, USOLAND... IT'S IN YOUR HANDS!!!

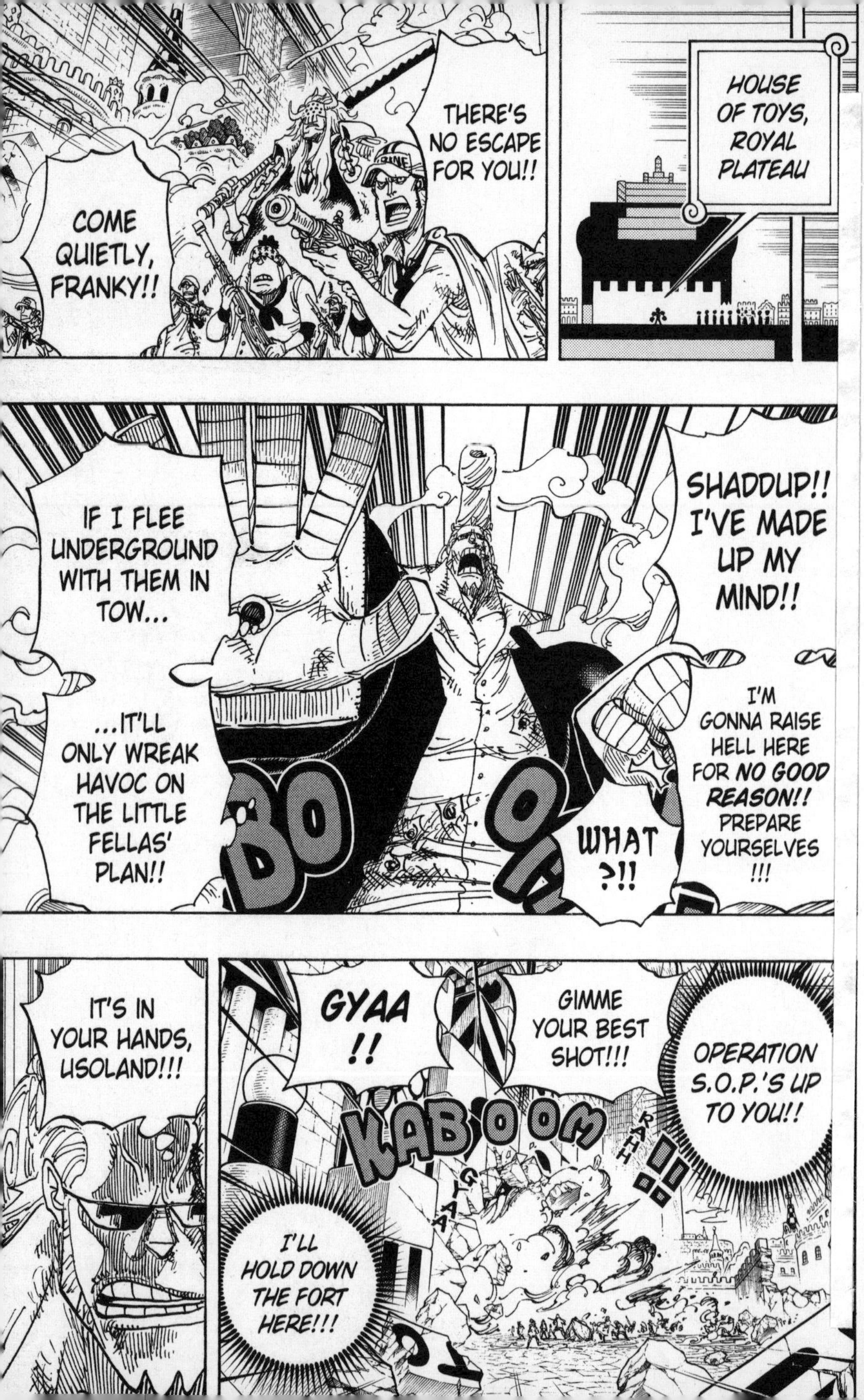
HOUSE OF TOYS, ROYAL PLATEAU
THERE'S NO ESCAPE FOR YOU!!
COME QUIETLY, FRANKY!!
SHADDUP!! I'VE MADE UP MY MIND!!
I'M GONNA RAISE HELL HERE FOR NO GOOD REASON!! PREPARE YOURSELVES!!!
IF I FLEE UNDERGROUND WITH THEM IN TOW...
...IT'LL ONLY WREAK HAVOC ON THE LITTLE FELLAS' PLAN!!
WHAT?!!
OPERATION S.O.P.'S UP TO YOU!!
GIMME YOUR BEST SHOT!!!
GYAA!!
KABOOOM!!
RAHH
GYAA
I'LL HOLD DOWN THE FORT HERE!!!
IT'S IN YOUR HANDS, USOLAND!!!

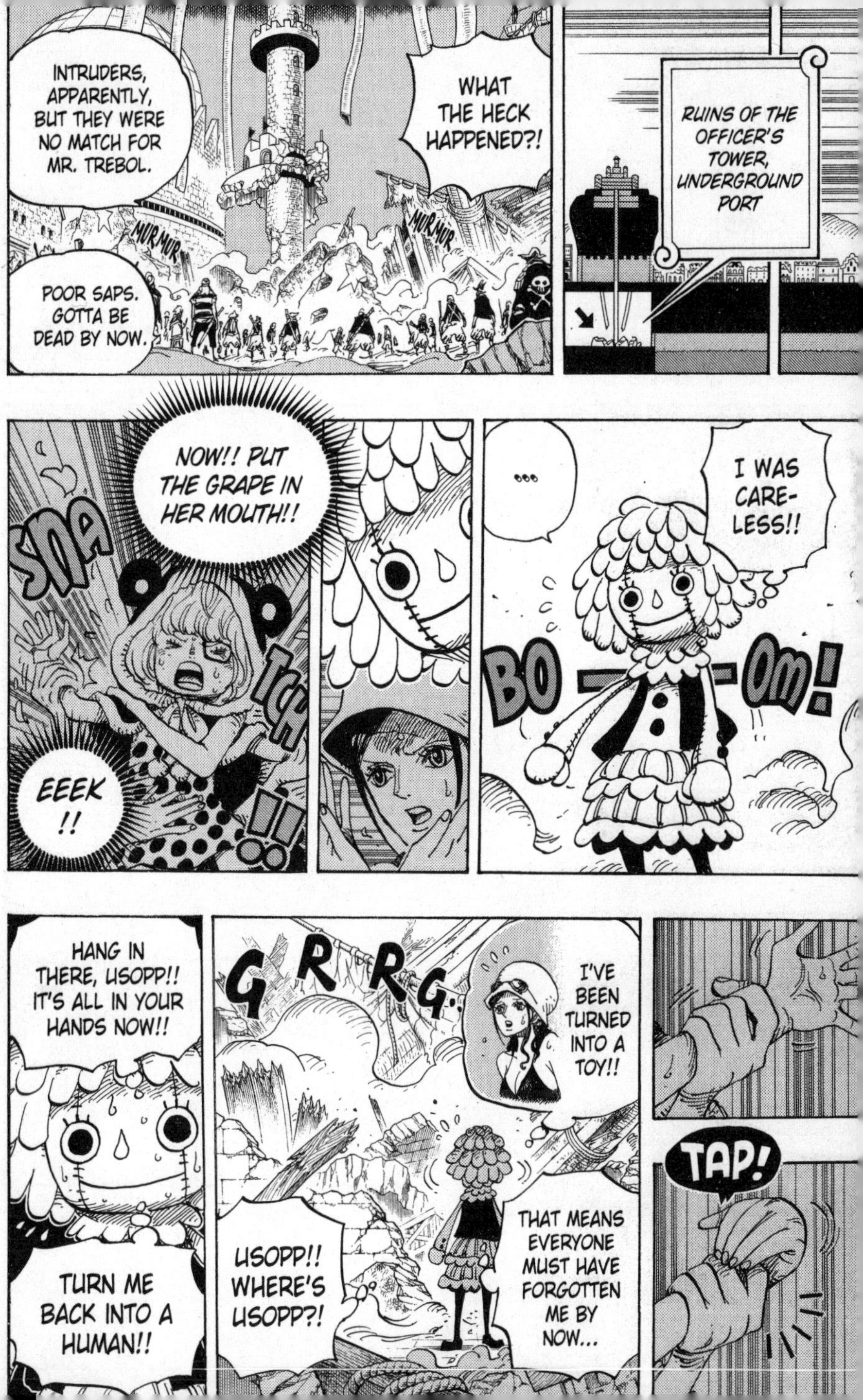
RUINS OF THE OFFICER'S TOWER, UNDERGROUND PORT
WHAT THE HECK HAPPENED?!
INTRUDERS, APPARENTLY, BUT THEY WERE NO MATCH FOR MR. TREBOL.
MURMUR
MURMUR
POOR SAPS. GOTTA BE DEAD BY NOW.
I WAS CARE-LESS!!
...
BO—OM!
NOW!! PUT THE GRAPE IN HER MOUTH!!
SNA
TCH!!
EEEK!!
TAP!
GRRRG
I'VE BEEN TURNED INTO A TOY!!
THAT MEANS EVERYONE MUST HAVE FORGOTTEN ME BY NOW...
USOPP!! WHERE'S USOPP?!
HANG IN THERE, USOPP!! IT'S ALL IN YOUR HANDS NOW!!
TURN ME BACK INTO A HUMAN!!

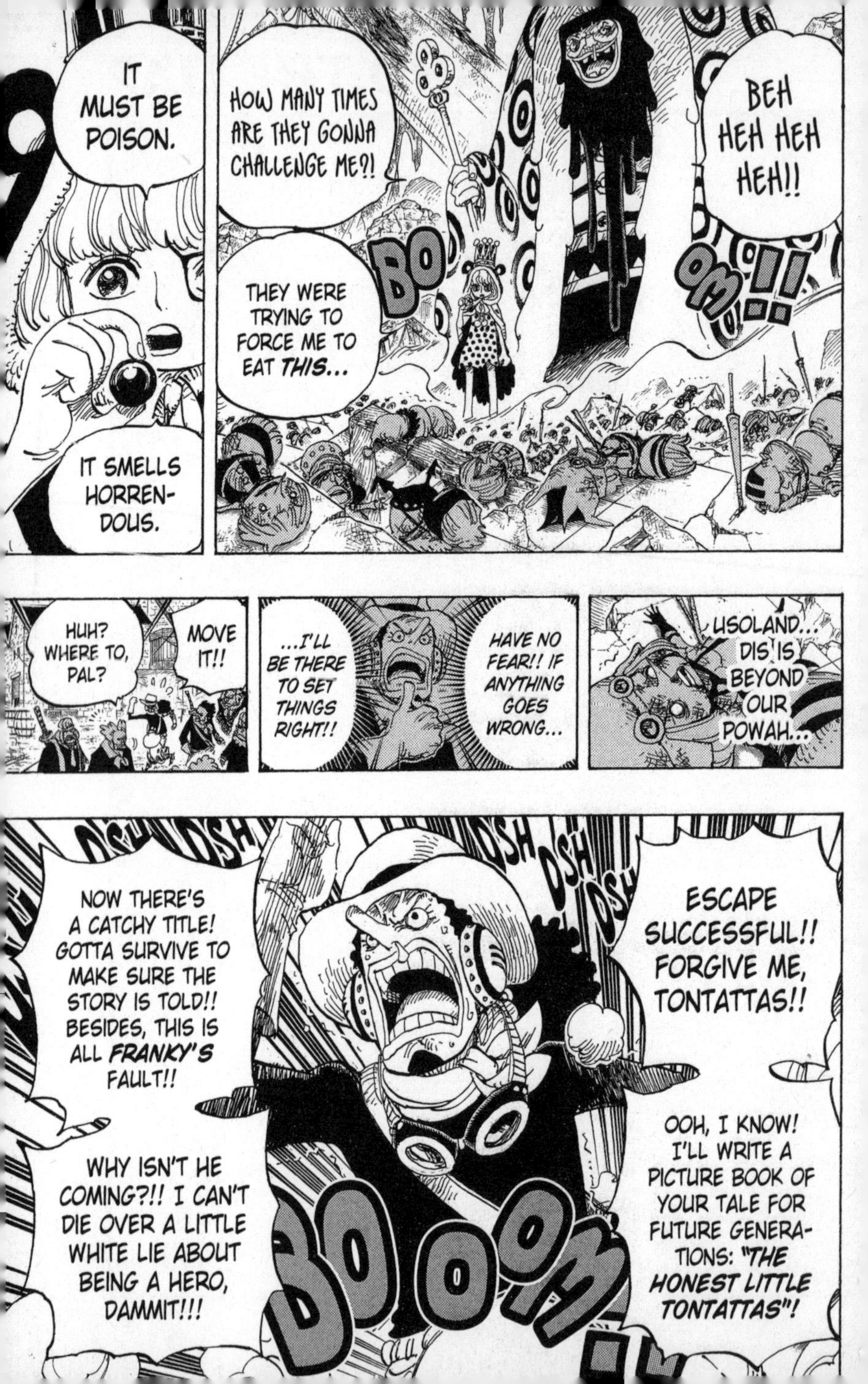
BEH HEH HEH HEH!!
BOOM!!
HOW MANY TIMES ARE THEY GONNA CHALLENGE ME?!
THEY WERE TRYING TO FORCE ME TO EAT *THIS*...
IT MUST BE POISON.
IT SMELLS HORREN-DOUS.
USOLAND... DIS IS BEYOND OUR POWAH...
HAVE NO FEAR!! IF ANYTHING GOES WRONG...
...I'LL BE THERE TO SET THINGS RIGHT!!
MOVE IT!!
HUH? WHERE TO, PAL?
DSH DSH DSH DSH
ESCAPE SUCCESSFUL!! FORGIVE ME, TONTATTAS!!
OOH, I KNOW! I'LL WRITE A PICTURE BOOK OF YOUR TALE FOR FUTURE GENERA-TIONS: *"THE HONEST LITTLE TONTATTAS"*!
NOW THERE'S A CATCHY TITLE! GOTTA SURVIVE TO MAKE SURE THE STORY IS TOLD!! BESIDES, THIS IS ALL *FRANKY'S* FAULT!!
WHY ISN'T HE COMING?!! I CAN'T DIE OVER A LITTLE WHITE LIE ABOUT BEING A HERO, DAMMIT!!!
BOOOM!!

USOLAND THE LIAR

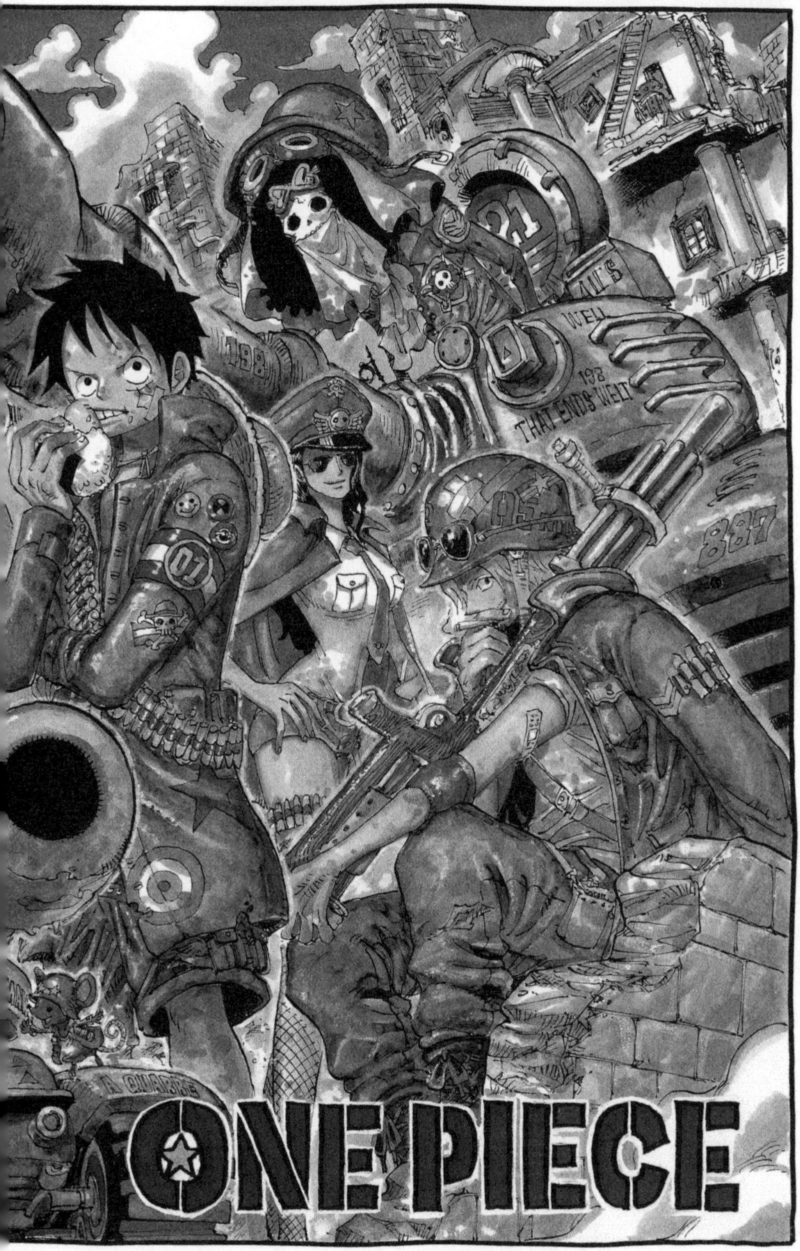
ONE PIECE

Chapter 741:

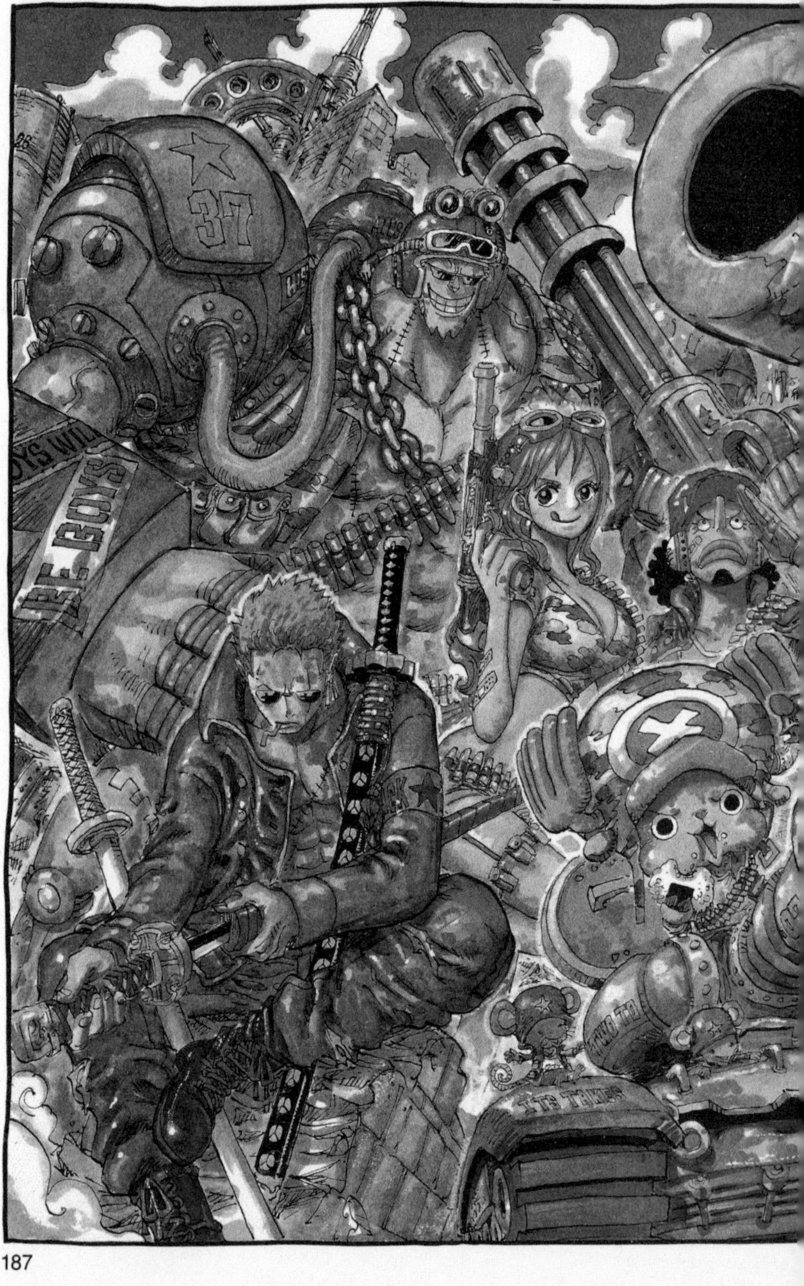

vol. 74
ONE PIECE

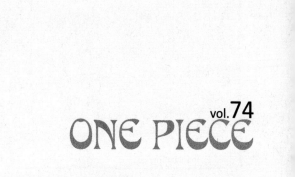

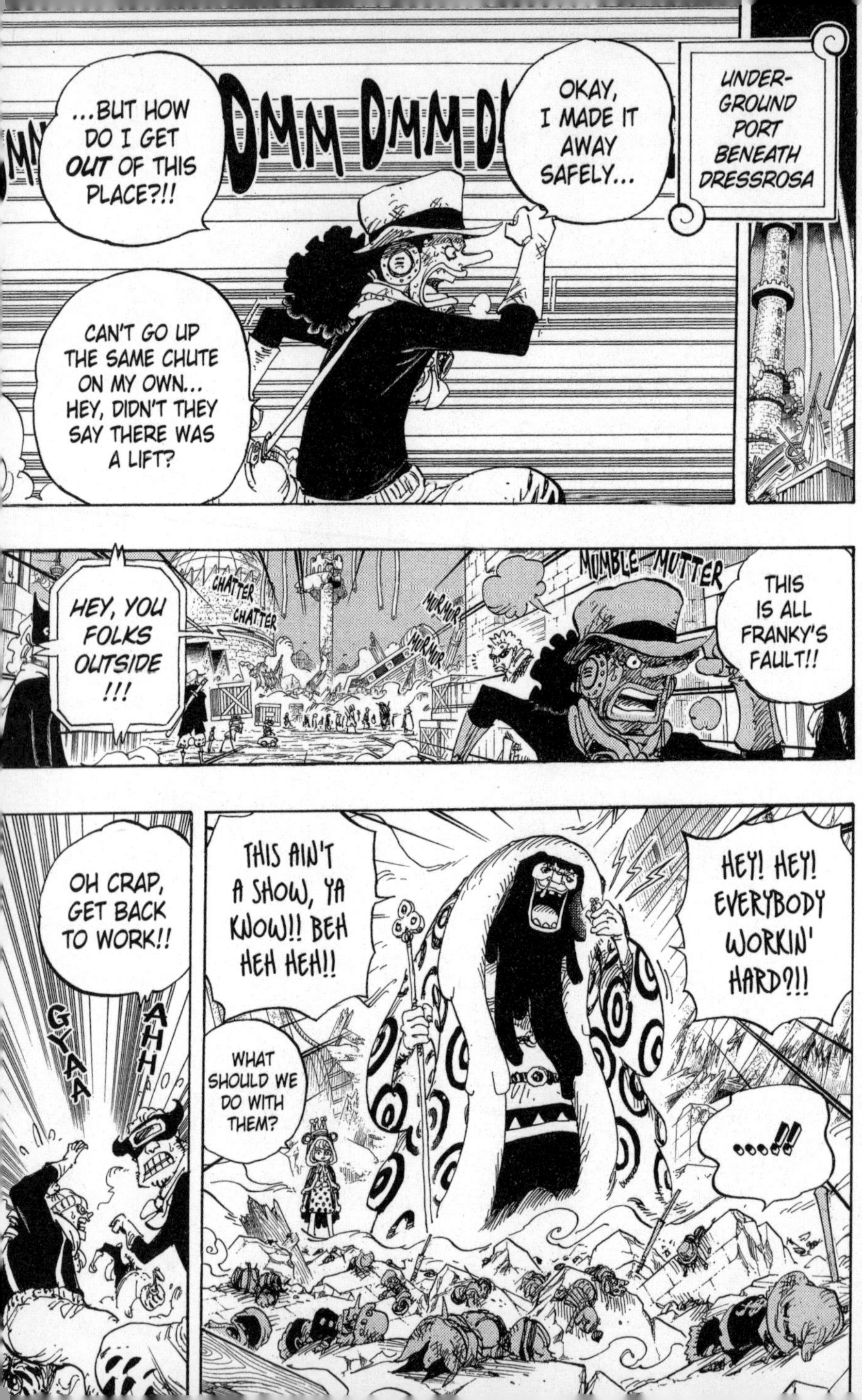
UNDERGROUND PORT BENEATH DRESSROSA
OKAY, I MADE IT AWAY SAFELY...
DMM DMM
...BUT HOW DO I GET OUT OF THIS PLACE?!!
CAN'T GO UP THE SAME CHUTE ON MY OWN... HEY, DIDN'T THEY SAY THERE WAS A LIFT?
THIS IS ALL FRANKY'S FAULT!!
MUMBLE MUTTER
MURMUR
MURMUR
CHATTER
CHATTER
HEY, YOU FOLKS OUTSIDE !!!
HEY! HEY! EVERYBODY WORKIN' HARD?!!
THIS AIN'T A SHOW, YA KNOW!! BEH HEH HEH!!
...!!
WHAT SHOULD WE DO WITH THEM?
OH CRAP, GET BACK TO WORK!!
AHH
GYAA

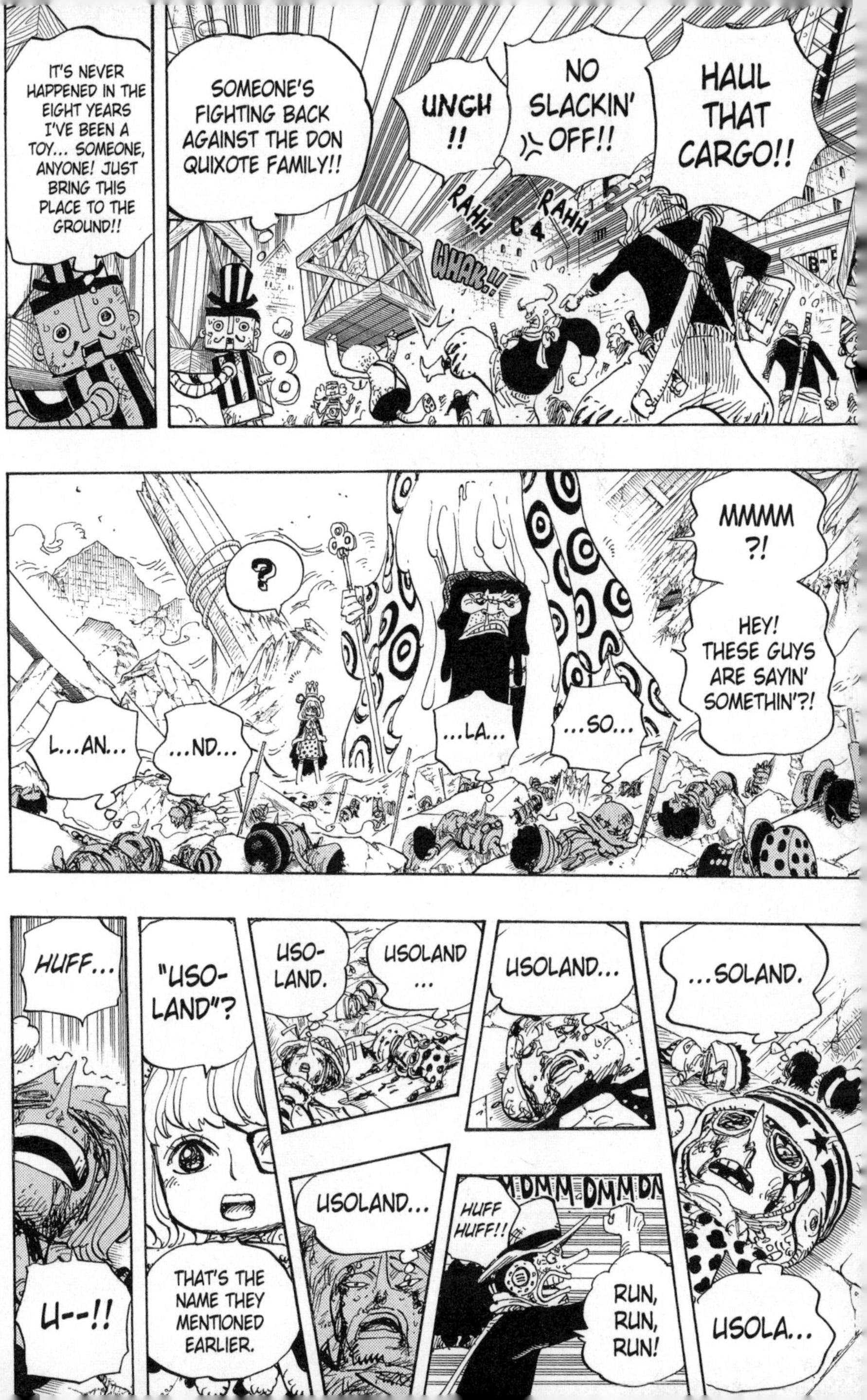
HAUL THAT CARGO!!
NO SLACKIN' OFF!!
UNGH !!
RAHH
RAHH
WHAK!!
SOMEONE'S FIGHTING BACK AGAINST THE DON QUIXOTE FAMILY!!
IT'S NEVER HAPPENED IN THE EIGHT YEARS I'VE BEEN A TOY... SOMEONE, ANYONE! JUST BRING THIS PLACE TO THE GROUND!!
MMMM ?!
HEY! THESE GUYS ARE SAYIN' SOMETHIN'?!
?
...SO...
...LA...
...ND...
L...AN...
...SOLAND.
USOLA...
USOLAND...
USOLAND ...
USO- LAND.
DMMM DMMM
HUFF HUFF!!
RUN, RUN, RUN!
USOLAND...
"USO- LAND"?
THAT'S THE NAME THEY MENTIONED EARLIER.
HUFF...
U--!!

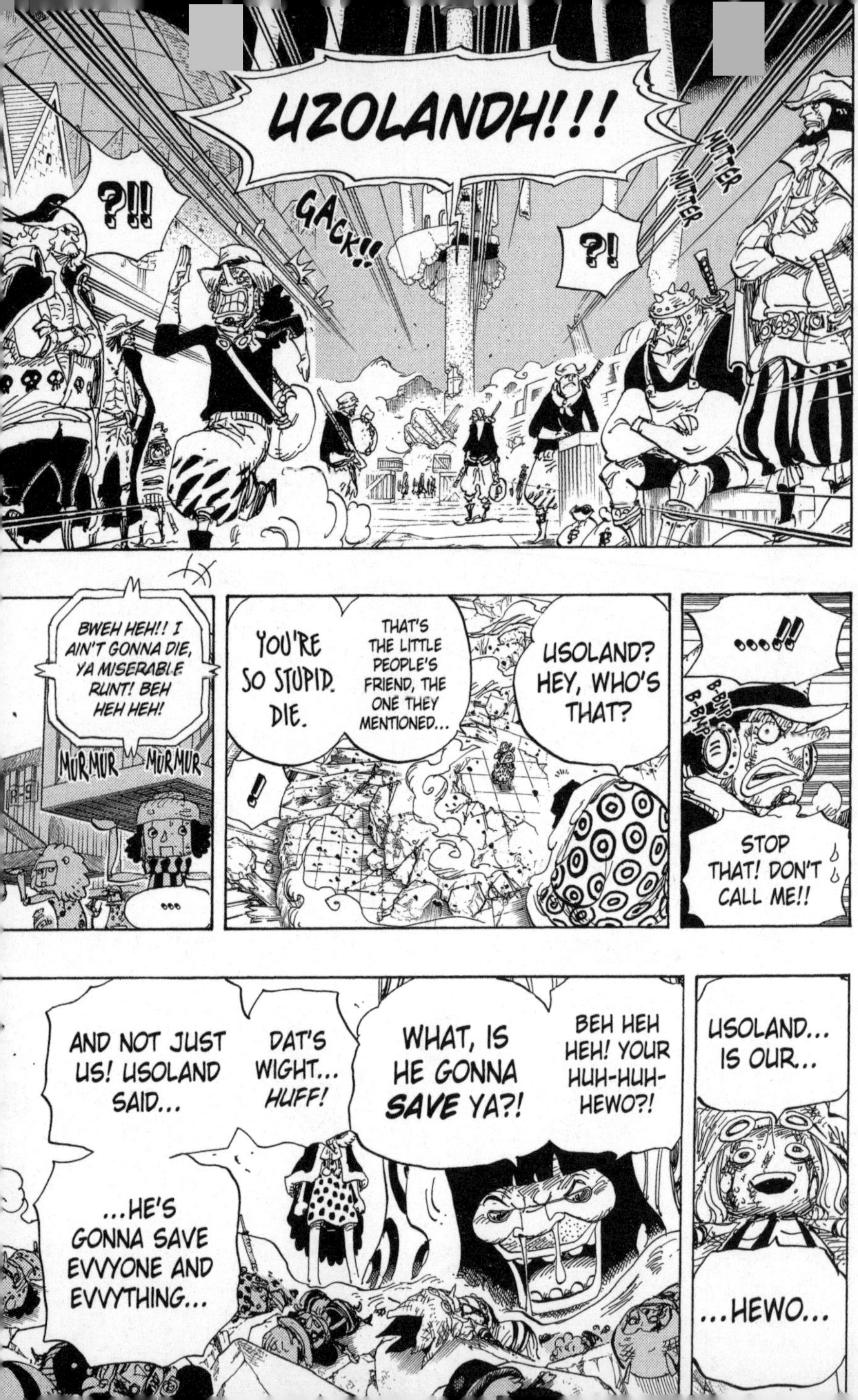
UZOLANDH!!!
MUTTER MUTTER
?!
GACK!!
?!!
...!!
B-BMP B-BMP
STOP THAT! DON'T CALL ME!!
USOLAND? HEY, WHO'S THAT?
THAT'S THE LITTLE PEOPLE'S FRIEND, THE ONE THEY MENTIONED...
YOU'RE SO STUPID. DIE.
!
BWEH HEH!! I AIN'T GONNA DIE, YA MISERABLE RUNT! BEH HEH HEH!
MURMUR MURMUR
...
USOLAND... IS OUR...
...HEWO...
BEH HEH HEH! YOUR HUH-HUH-HEWO?!
WHAT, IS HE GONNA SAVE YA?!
DAT'S WIGHT... HUFF!
AND NOT JUST US! USOLAND SAID...
...HE'S GONNA SAVE EVVYONE AND EVVYTHING...

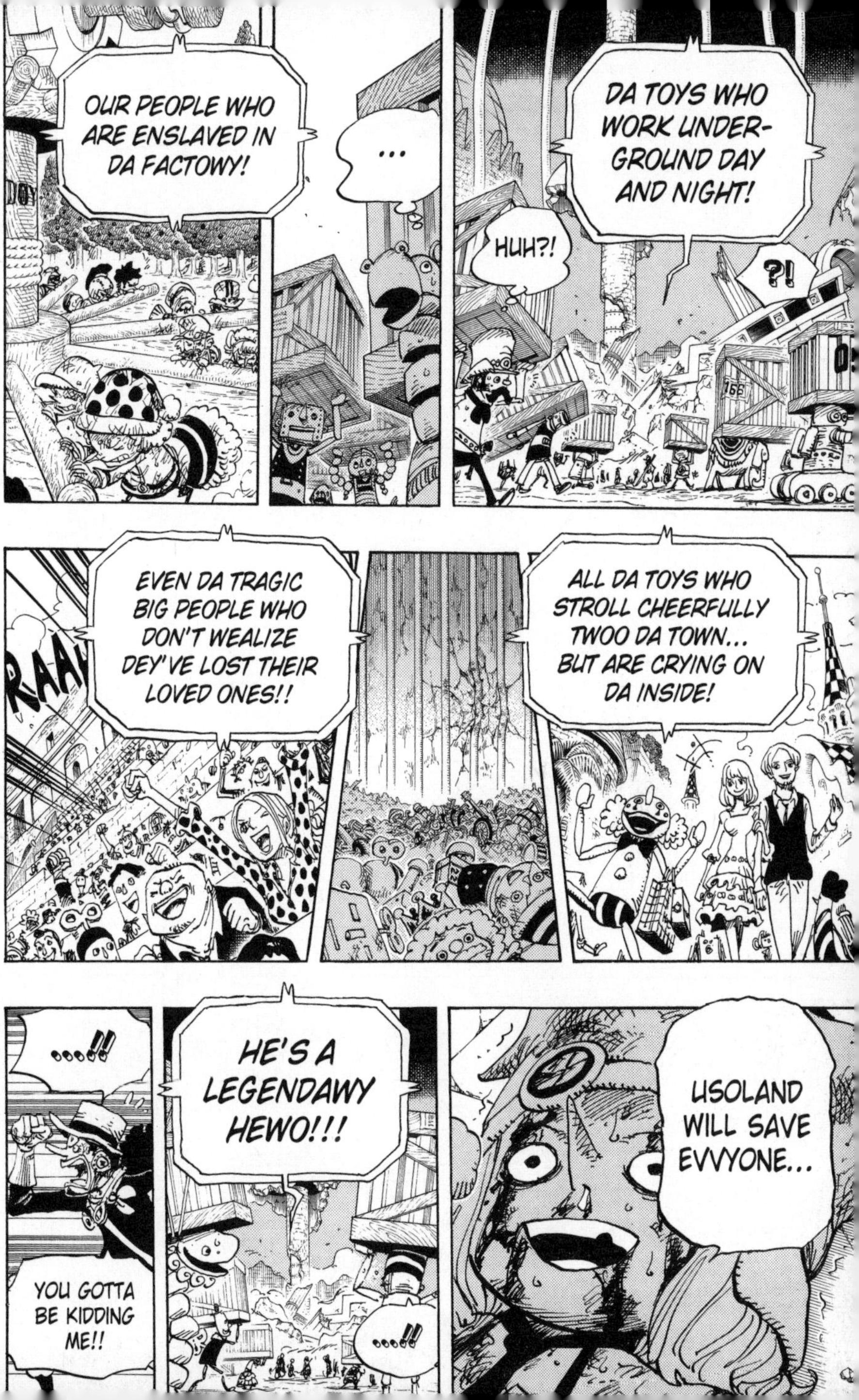
DA TOYS WHO WORK UNDER-GROUND DAY AND NIGHT!
?!
HUH?!
...
OUR PEOPLE WHO ARE ENSLAVED IN DA FACTOWY!
ALL DA TOYS WHO STROLL CHEERFULLY TWOO DA TOWN... BUT ARE CRYING ON DA INSIDE!
EVEN DA TRAGIC BIG PEOPLE WHO DON'T WEALIZE DEY'VE LOST THEIR LOVED ONES!!
RAAH
USOLAND WILL SAVE EVVYONE...
HE'S A LEGENDAWY HEWO!!!
....!!
....!!
YOU GOTTA BE KIDDING ME!!

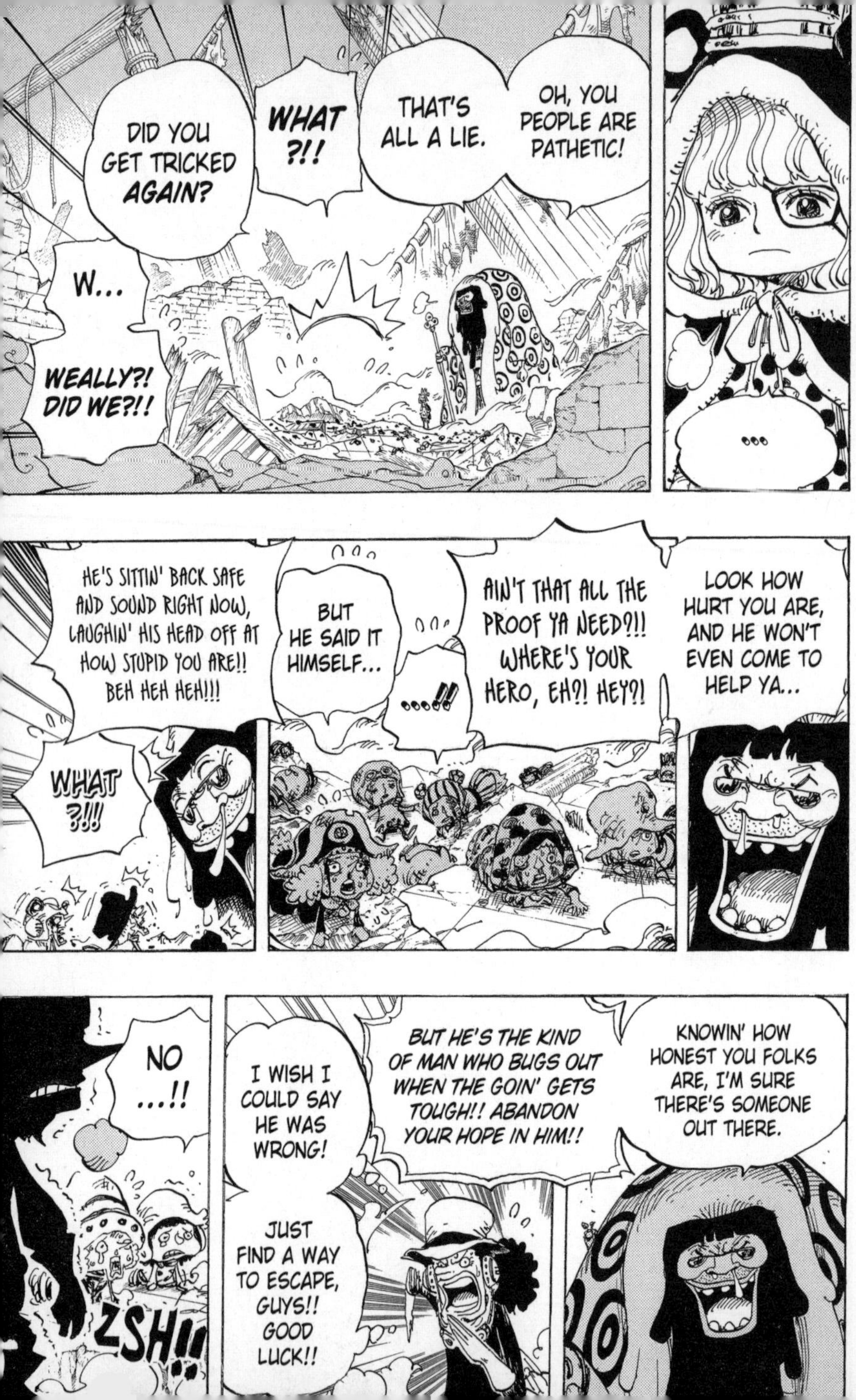
...
OH, YOU PEOPLE ARE PATHETIC!
THAT'S ALL A LIE.
WHAT ?!!
DID YOU GET TRICKED AGAIN?
W...
WEALLY?! DID WE?!!
LOOK HOW HURT YOU ARE, AND HE WON'T EVEN COME TO HELP YA...
AIN'T THAT ALL THE PROOF YA NEED?!!! WHERE'S YOUR HERO, EH?! HEY?!
BUT HE SAID IT HIMSELF...
....!!
HE'S SITTIN' BACK SAFE AND SOUND RIGHT NOW, LAUGHIN' HIS HEAD OFF AT HOW STUPID YOU ARE!! BEH HEH HEH!!!
WHAT ?!!!
KNOWIN' HOW HONEST YOU FOLKS ARE, I'M SURE THERE'S SOMEONE OUT THERE.
BUT HE'S THE KIND OF MAN WHO BUGS OUT WHEN THE GOIN' GETS TOUGH!! ABANDON YOUR HOPE IN HIM!!
I WISH I COULD SAY HE WAS WRONG!
JUST FIND A WAY TO ESCAPE, GUYS!! GOOD LUCK!!
NO ...!!
ZSH!!

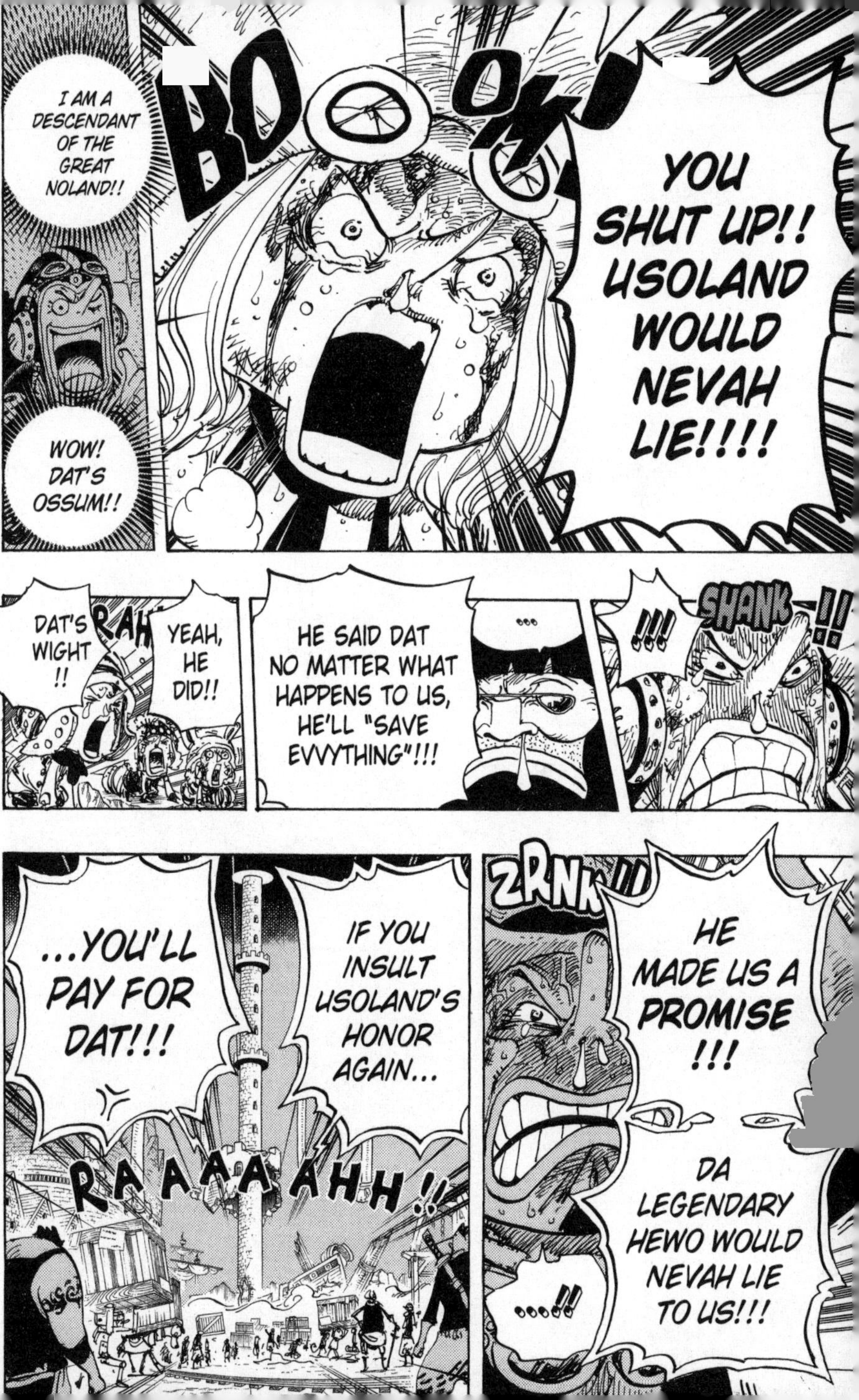
BOOOM!
YOU SHUT UP!! USOLAND WOULD NEVAH LIE!!!!
I AM A DESCENDANT OF THE GREAT NOLAND!!
WOW! DAT'S OSSUM!!
SHANK!!
!!!
...
HE SAID DAT NO MATTER WHAT HAPPENS TO US, HE'LL "SAVE EVVYTHING"!!!
YEAH, HE DID!!
RAH
DAT'S WIGHT!!
ZRNK!!
HE MADE US A PROMISE!!!
DA LEGENDARY HEWO WOULD NEVAH LIE TO US!!!
...!!
IF YOU INSULT USOLAND'S HONOR AGAIN...
...YOU'LL PAY FOR DAT!!!
RAAAAAHH!!

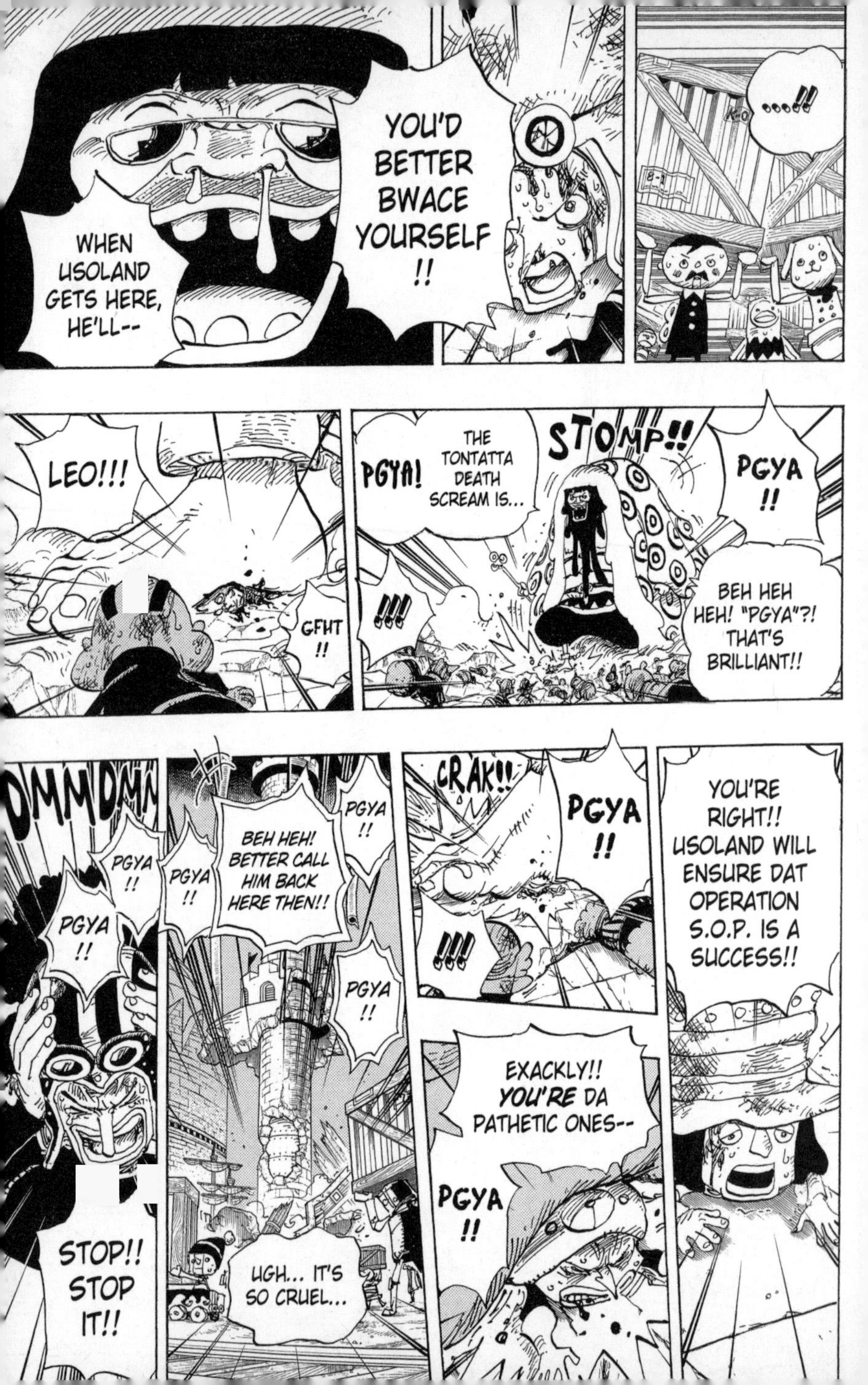
....!!
YOU'D BETTER BWACE YOURSELF!!
WHEN USOLAND GETS HERE, HE'LL--
STOMP!!
PGYA!!
BEH HEH HEH! "PGYA"?! THAT'S BRILLIANT!!
THE TONTATTA DEATH SCREAM IS...
PGYA!
!!!
LEO!!!
GFHT!!
YOU'RE RIGHT!! USOLAND WILL ENSURE DAT OPERATION S.O.P. IS A SUCCESS!!
PGYA!!
CRAK!!
!!!
EXACKLY!! YOU'RE DA PATHETIC ONES--
PGYA!!
PGYA!!
BEH HEH! BETTER CALL HIM BACK HERE THEN!!
PGYA!!
PGYA!!
UGH... IT'S SO CRUEL...
DMMDM
PGYA!!
PGYA!!
STOP!! STOP IT!!

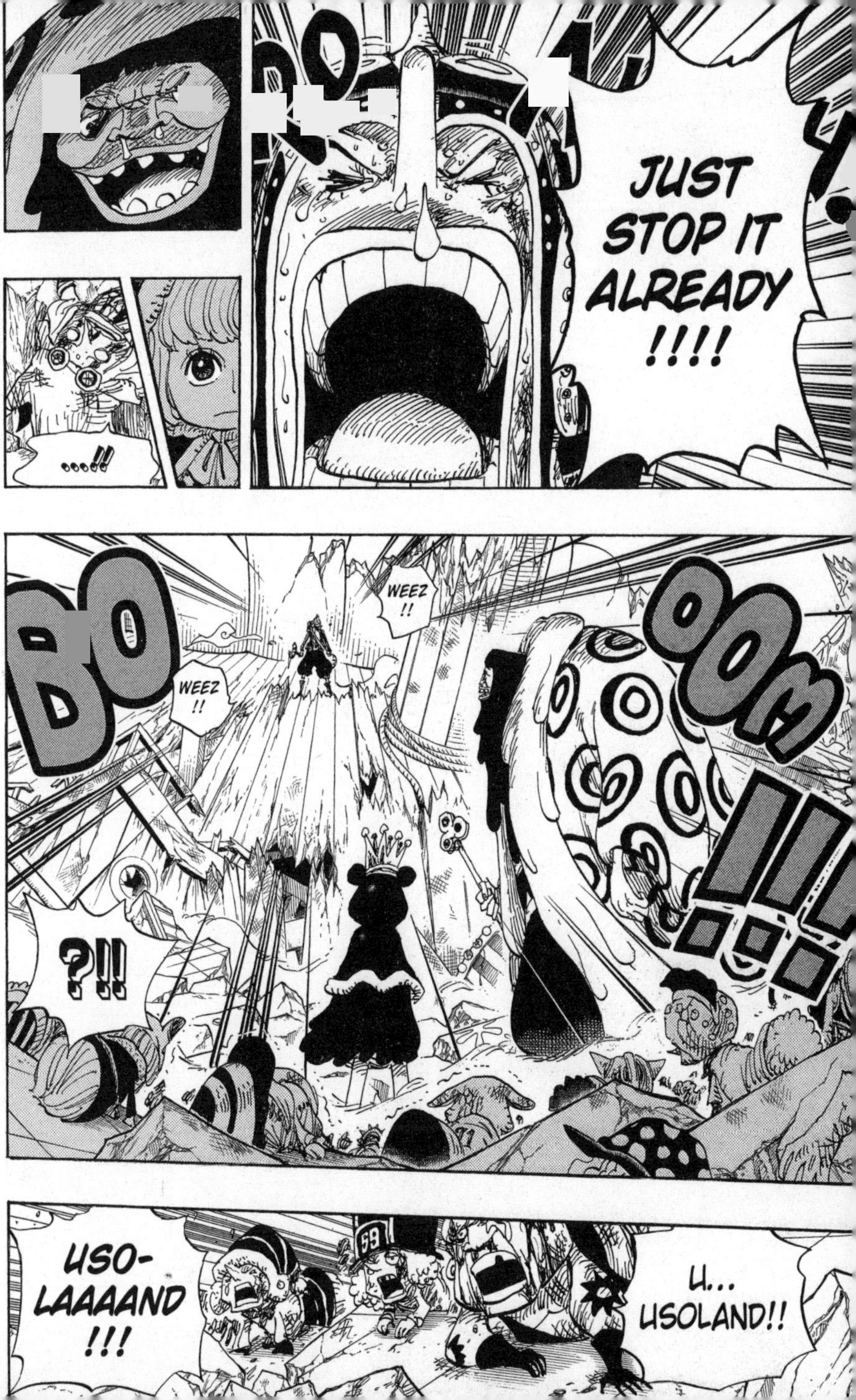
JUST STOP IT ALREADY !!!!
....!!
BO
OOM!!
WEEZ !!
WEEZ !!
?!!
U... USOLAND!!
USO- LAAAAND !!!

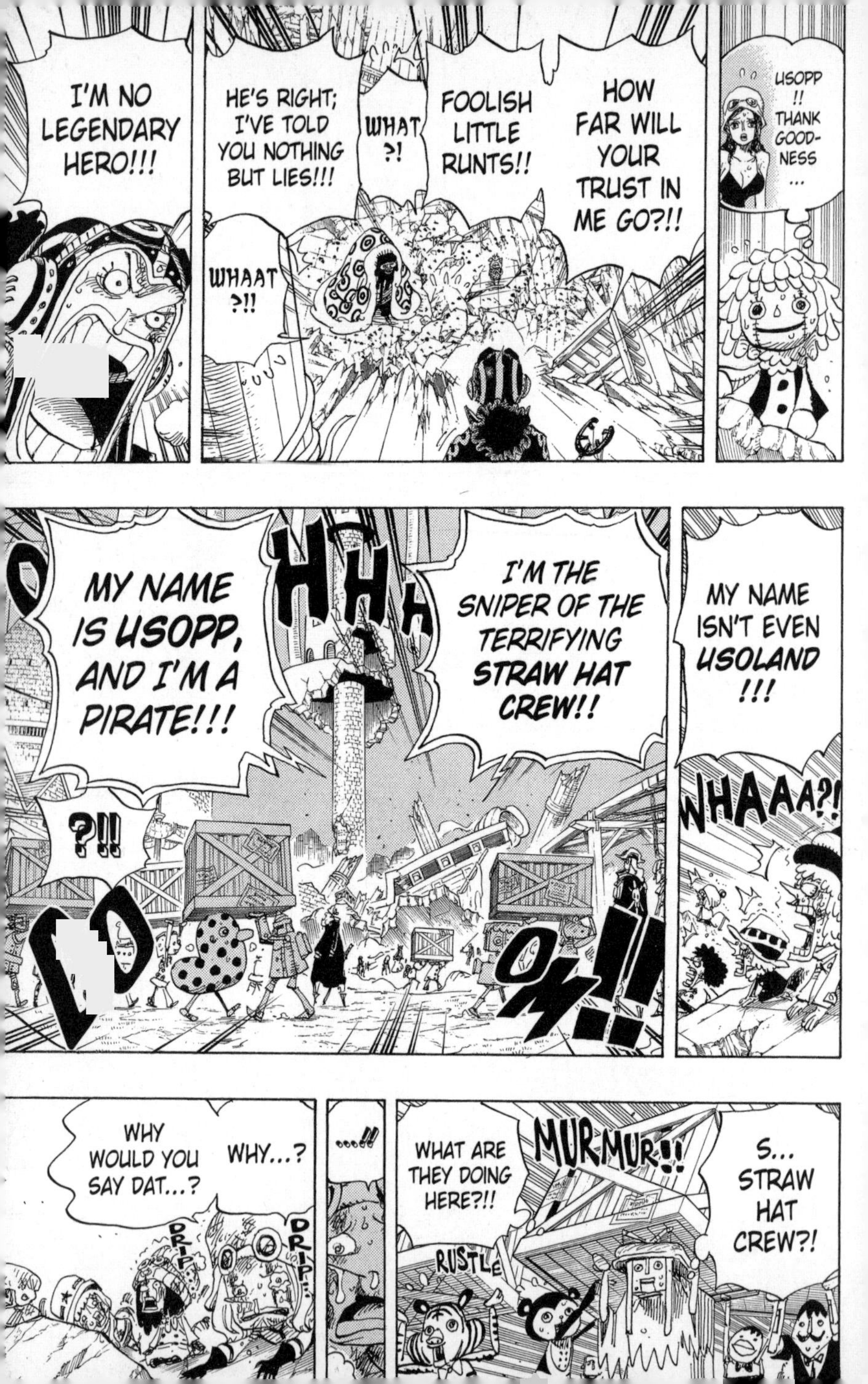
USOPP !! THANK GOODNESS ...
HOW FAR WILL YOUR TRUST IN ME GO?!!
FOOLISH LITTLE RUNTS!!
WHAT ?!
HE'S RIGHT; I'VE TOLD YOU NOTHING BUT LIES!!!
WHAAT ?!!
I'M NO LEGENDARY HERO!!!
MY NAME ISN'T EVEN USOLAND !!!
WHAAA?!
I'M THE SNIPER OF THE TERRIFYING STRAW HAT CREW!!
MY NAME IS USOPP, AND I'M A PIRATE!!!
?!!
HHH
OH!!
S... STRAW HAT CREW?!
MURMUR!!
WHAT ARE THEY DOING HERE?!!
RUSTLE
...!!
WHY...?
WHY WOULD YOU SAY DAT...?
DRIP
DRIP

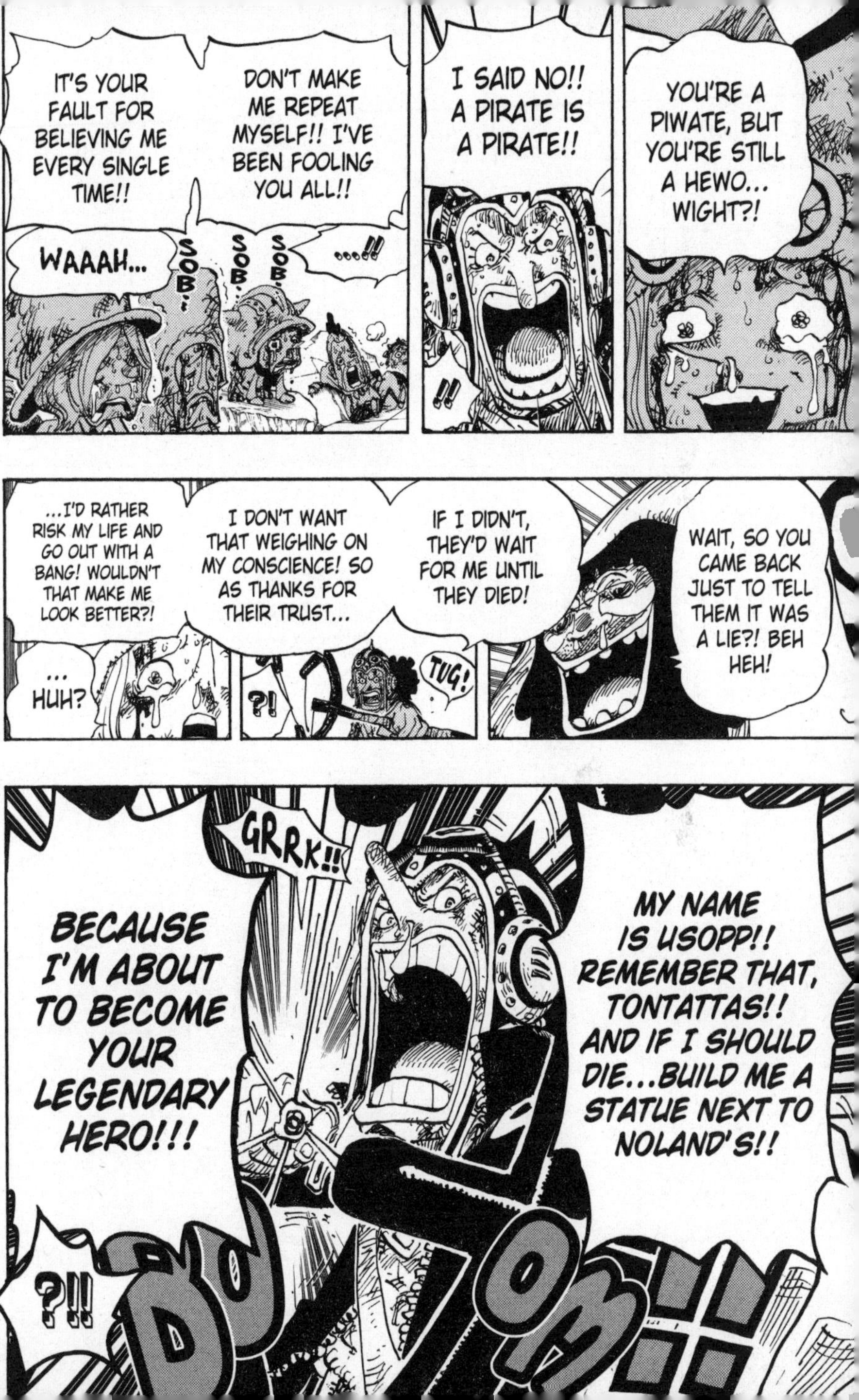
YOU'RE A PIWATE, BUT YOU'RE STILL A HEWO... WIGHT?!
I SAID NO!! A PIRATE IS A PIRATE!!
!!
DON'T MAKE ME REPEAT MYSELF!! I'VE BEEN FOOLING YOU ALL!!
IT'S YOUR FAULT FOR BELIEVING ME EVERY SINGLE TIME!!
....!!
SOB...
SOB...
SOB...
WAAAH...
WAIT, SO YOU CAME BACK JUST TO TELL THEM IT WAS A LIE?! BEH HEH!
IF I DIDN'T, THEY'D WAIT FOR ME UNTIL THEY DIED!
I DON'T WANT THAT WEIGHING ON MY CONSCIENCE! SO AS THANKS FOR THEIR TRUST...
TUG!
?!
...I'D RATHER RISK MY LIFE AND GO OUT WITH A BANG! WOULDN'T THAT MAKE ME LOOK BETTER?!
... HUH?
MY NAME IS USOPP!! REMEMBER THAT, TONTATTAS!! AND IF I SHOULD DIE...BUILD ME A STATUE NEXT TO NOLAND'S!!
GRRRK!!
BECAUSE I'M ABOUT TO BECOME YOUR LEGENDARY HERO!!!
?!!
DOOOM!!

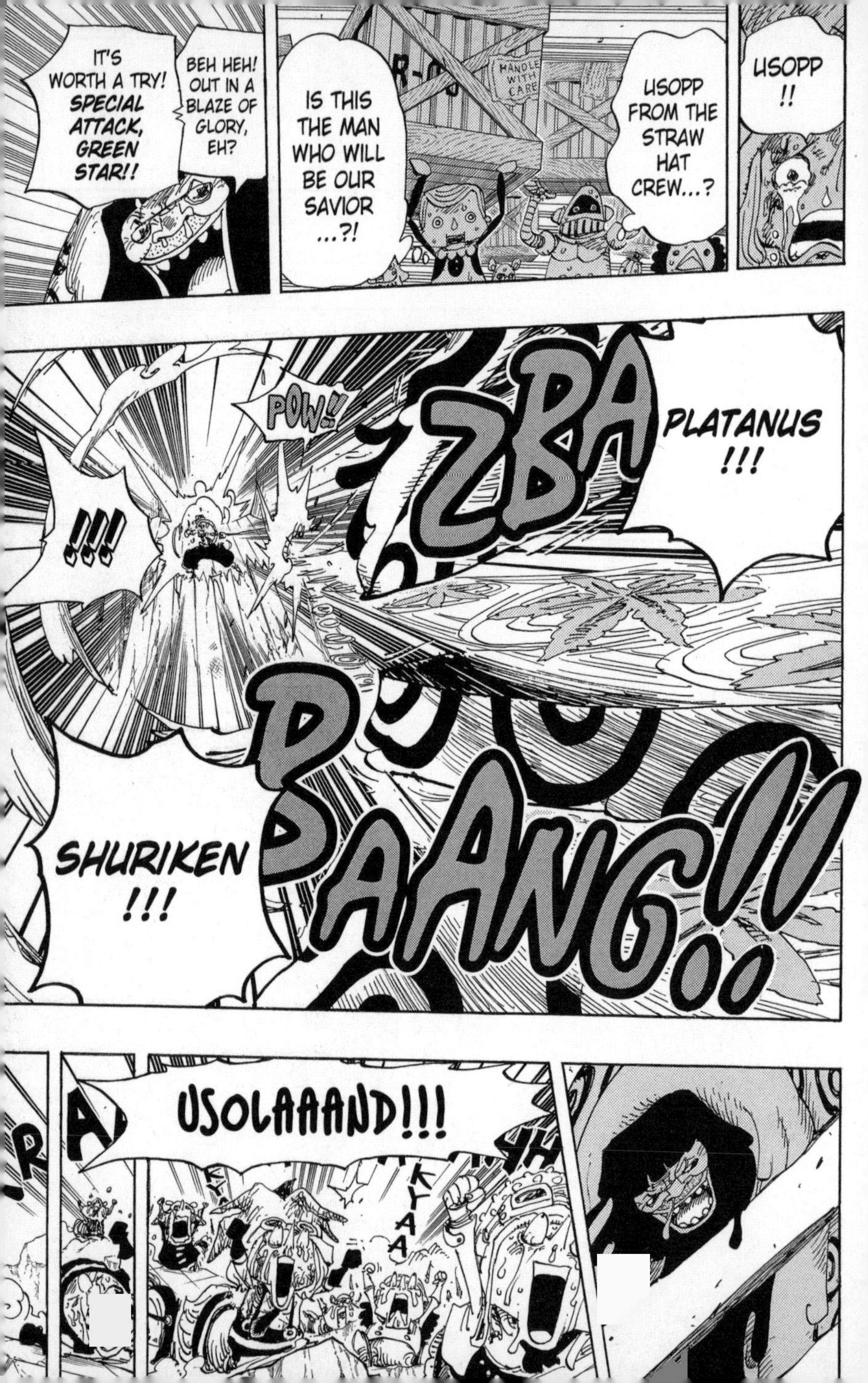
USOPP !!
USOPP FROM THE STRAW HAT CREW...?
IS THIS THE MAN WHO WILL BE OUR SAVIOR ...?!
HANDLE WITH CARE
BEH HEH! OUT IN A BLAZE OF GLORY, EH?
IT'S WORTH A TRY! SPECIAL ATTACK, GREEN STAR!!
PLATANUS !!!
ZBA
POW!!
!!!
SHURIKEN !!!
BAANG!!
USOLAAAND!!!
KYAA
KYAA

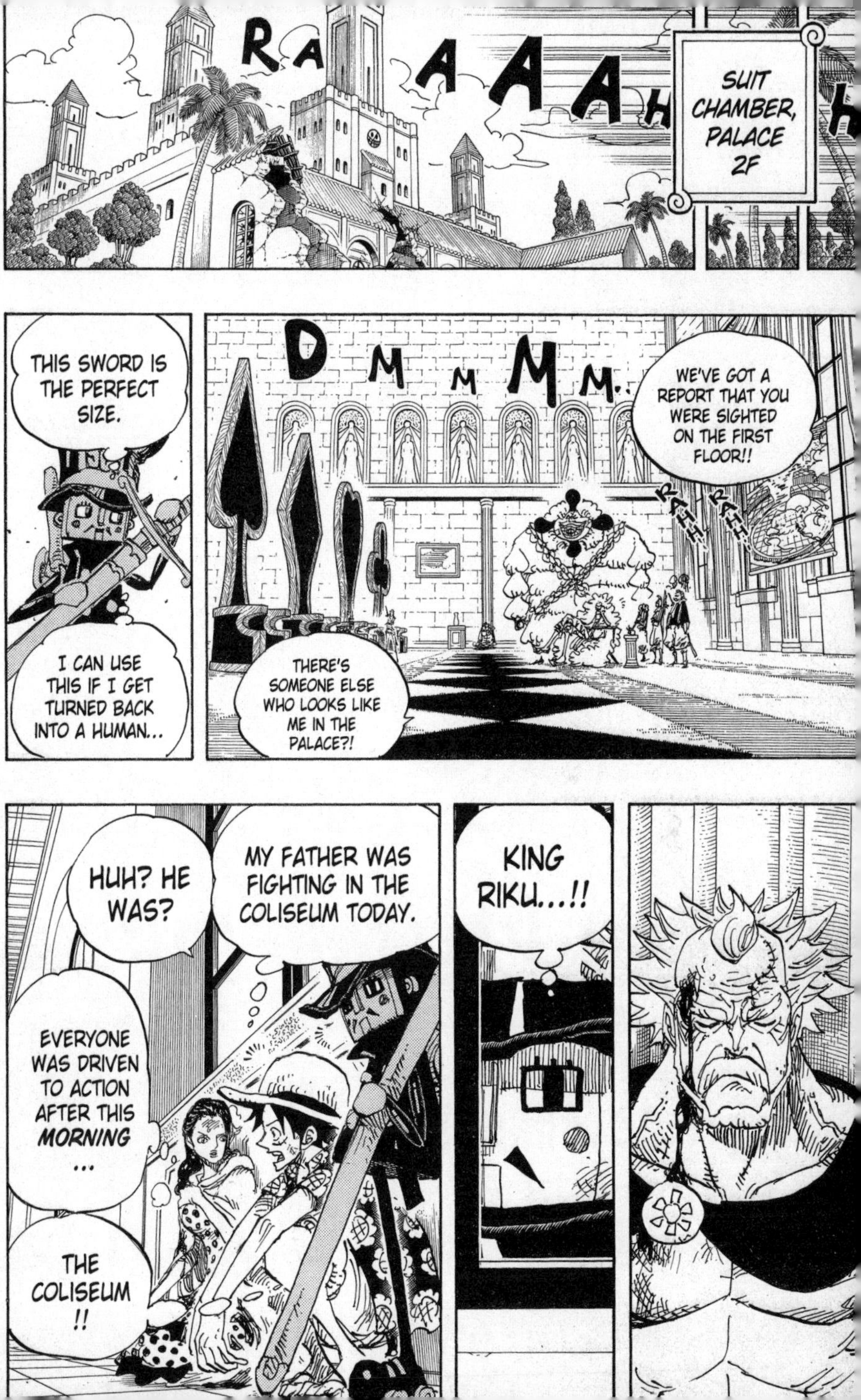
SUIT CHAMBER, PALACE 2F
RAAAAHh
DMMM..
WE'VE GOT A REPORT THAT YOU WERE SIGHTED ON THE FIRST FLOOR!!
RAHH RAHH
THERE'S SOMEONE ELSE WHO LOOKS LIKE ME IN THE PALACE?!
THIS SWORD IS THE PERFECT SIZE.
I CAN USE THIS IF I GET TURNED BACK INTO A HUMAN...
KING RIKU...!!
MY FATHER WAS FIGHTING IN THE COLISEUM TODAY.
HUH? HE WAS?
EVERYONE WAS DRIVEN TO ACTION AFTER THIS *MORNING* ...
THE COLISEUM !!

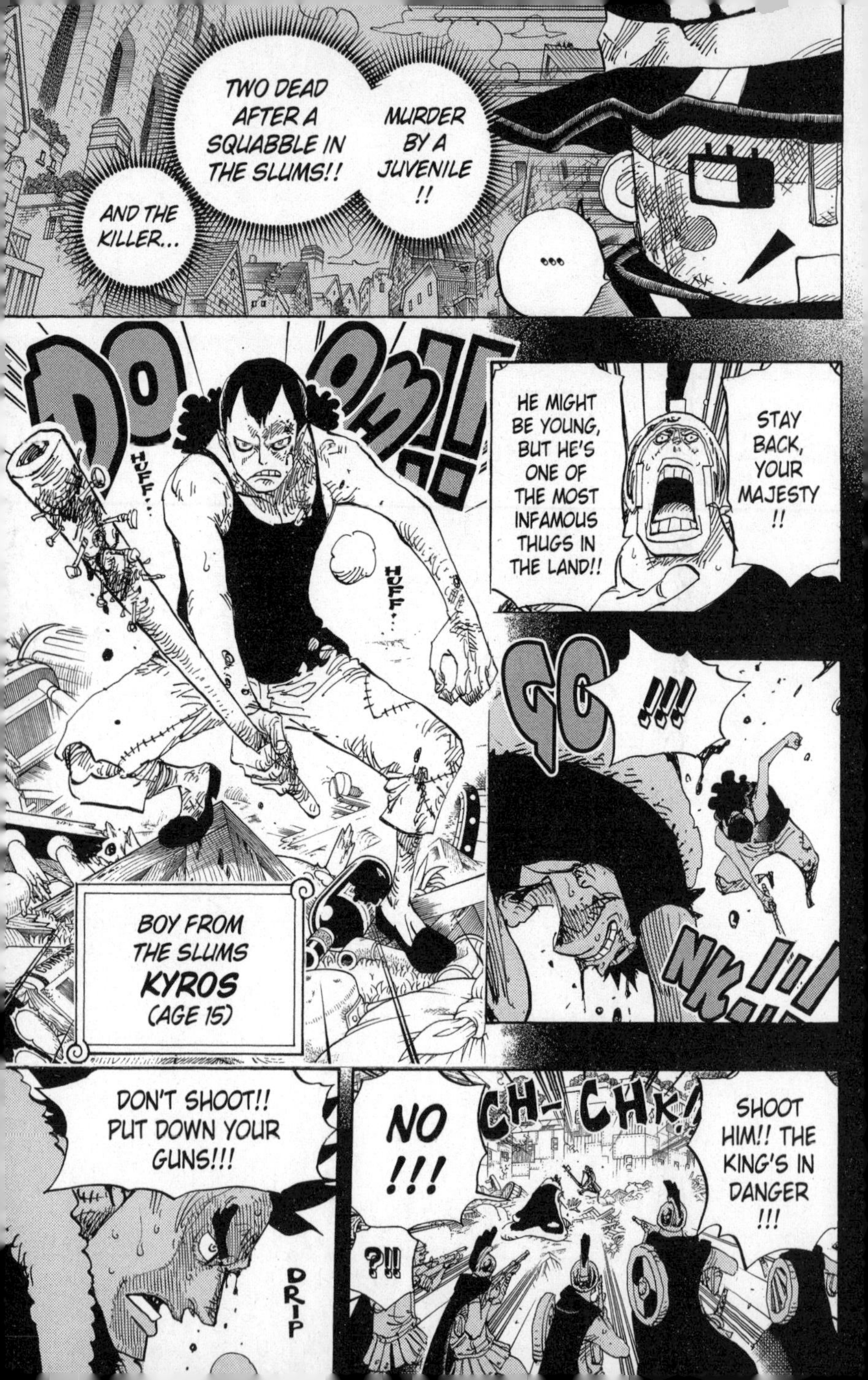
...
MURDER BY A JUVENILE!!
TWO DEAD AFTER A SQUABBLE IN THE SLUMS!!
AND THE KILLER...
STAY BACK, YOUR MAJESTY!!
HE MIGHT BE YOUNG, BUT HE'S ONE OF THE MOST INFAMOUS THUGS IN THE LAND!!
GO!!!
NK...!!
DOOM!!
HUFF...
HUFF...
BOY FROM THE SLUMS
KYROS
(AGE 15)
SHOOT HIM!! THE KING'S IN DANGER!!!
CH-CHK!
NO!!!
?!!
DON'T SHOOT!! PUT DOWN YOUR GUNS!!!
DRIP

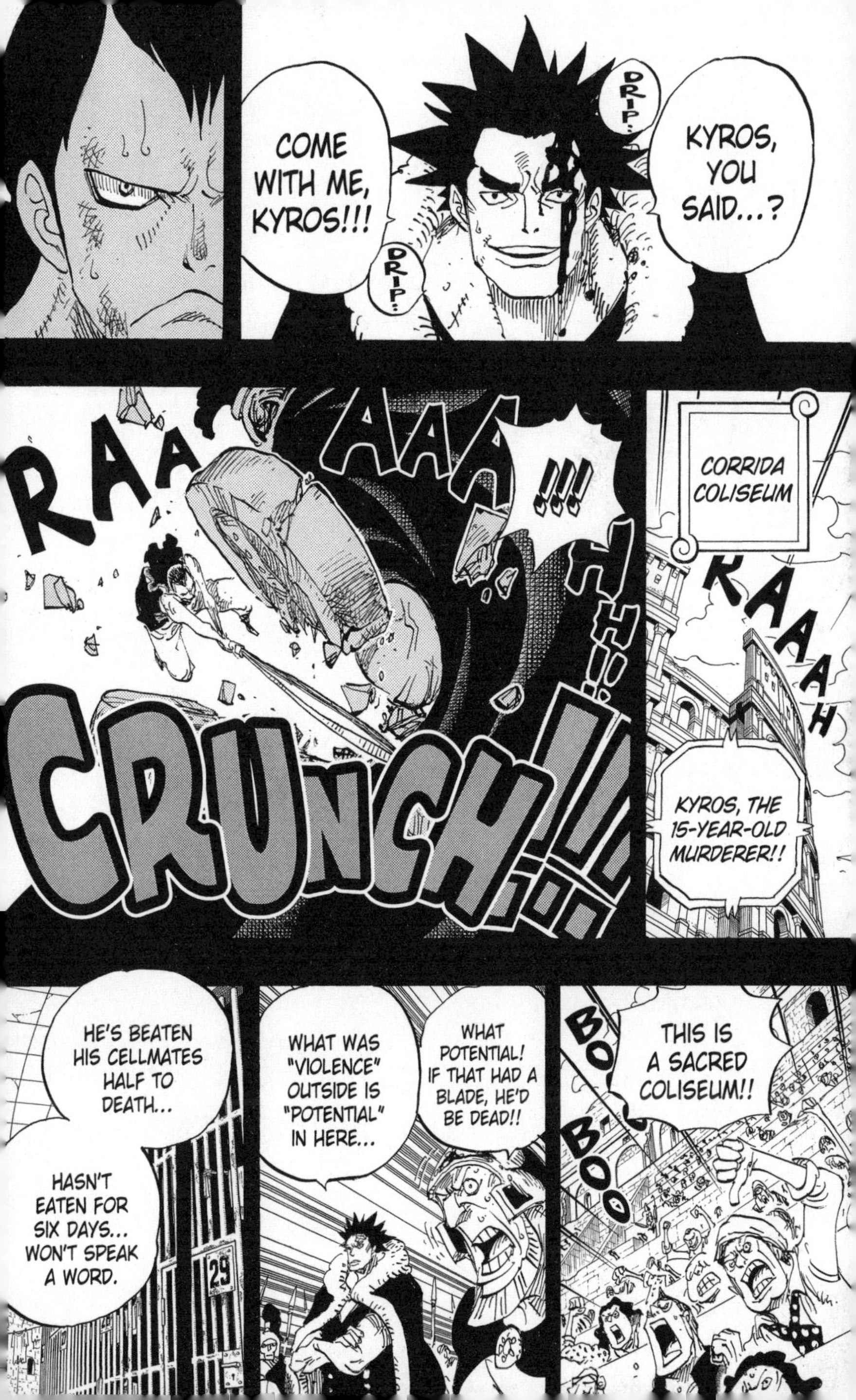
KYROS, YOU SAID...?
DRIP...
COME WITH ME, KYROS!!!
DRIP...
CORRIDA COLISEUM
RAAAAH
KYROS, THE 15-YEAR-OLD MURDERER!!
RAAAAHH!!!
CRUNCH!!!!
BOO BOO
THIS IS A SACRED COLISEUM!!
WHAT POTENTIAL! IF THAT HAD A BLADE, HE'D BE DEAD!!
WHAT WAS "VIOLENCE" OUTSIDE IS "POTENTIAL" IN HERE...
HE'S BEATEN HIS CELLMATES HALF TO DEATH...
HASN'T EATEN FOR SIX DAYS... WON'T SPEAK A WORD.
29

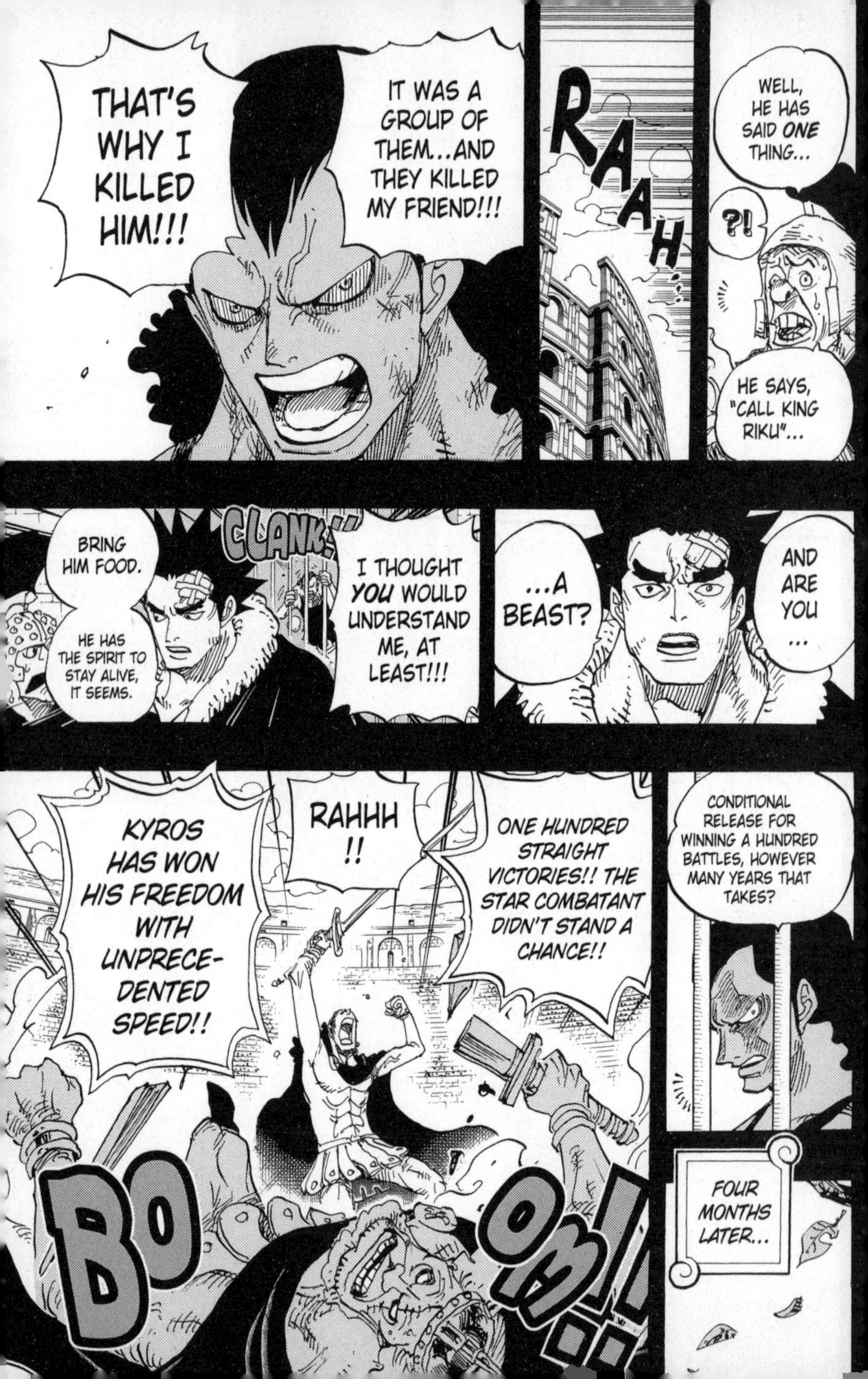
WELL, HE HAS SAID ONE THING...
?!
HE SAYS, "CALL KING RIKU"...
RAAAH...
IT WAS A GROUP OF THEM...AND THEY KILLED MY FRIEND!!!
THAT'S WHY I KILLED HIM!!!
AND ARE YOU...
...A BEAST?
I THOUGHT YOU WOULD UNDERSTAND ME, AT LEAST!!!
CLANK
BRING HIM FOOD.
HE HAS THE SPIRIT TO STAY ALIVE, IT SEEMS.
CONDITIONAL RELEASE FOR WINNING A HUNDRED BATTLES, HOWEVER MANY YEARS THAT TAKES?
FOUR MONTHS LATER...
ONE HUNDRED STRAIGHT VICTORIES!! THE STAR COMBATANT DIDN'T STAND A CHANCE!!
RAHHH!!
KYROS HAS WON HIS FREEDOM WITH UNPRECE-DENTED SPEED!!
BOOM!!

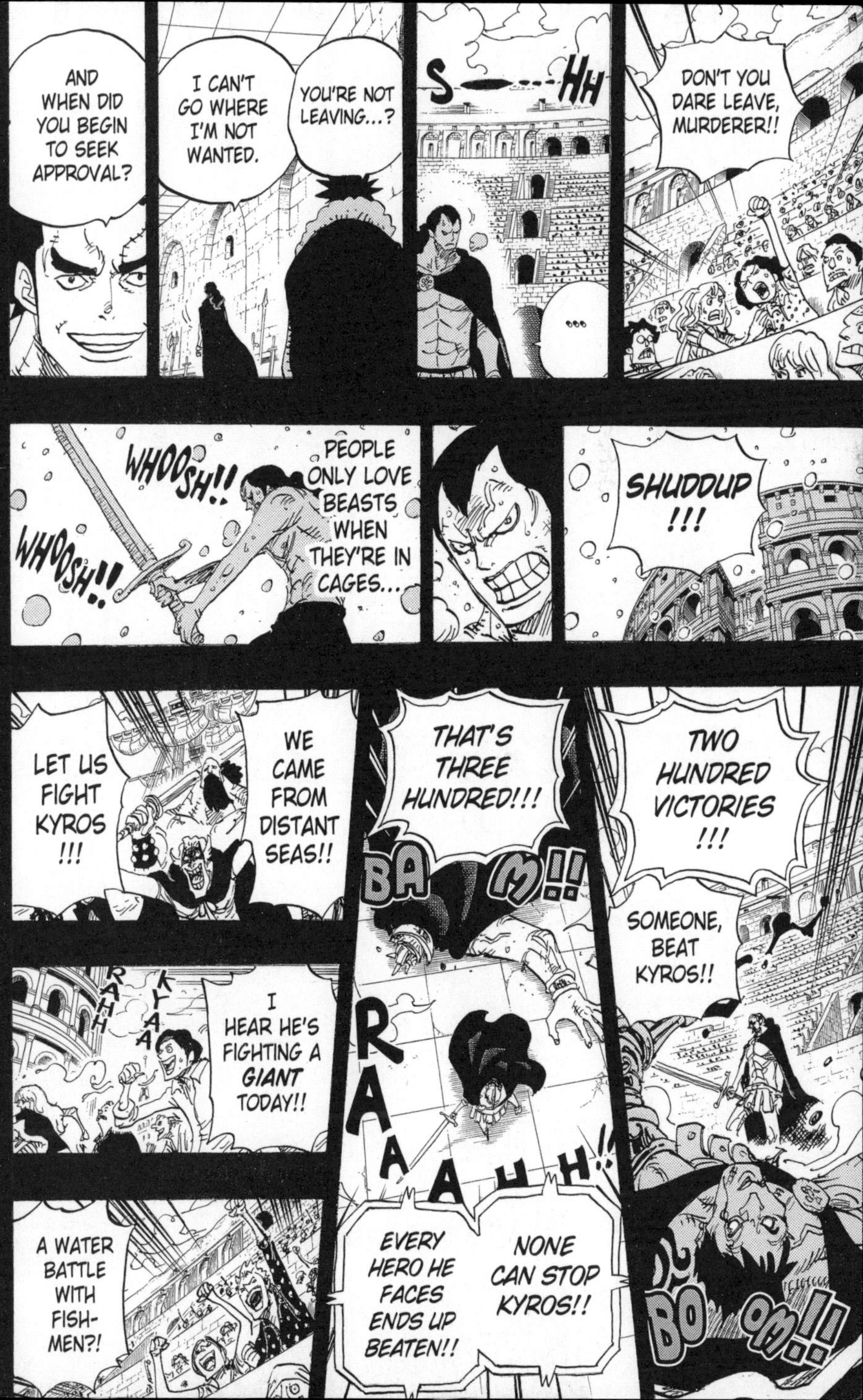
DON'T YOU DARE LEAVE, MURDERER!!
S—HH
...
YOU'RE NOT LEAVING...?
I CAN'T GO WHERE I'M NOT WANTED.
AND WHEN DID YOU BEGIN TO SEEK APPROVAL?
SHUDDUP!!!
PEOPLE ONLY LOVE BEASTS WHEN THEY'RE IN CAGES...
WHOOSH!!
WHOOSH!!
TWO HUNDRED VICTORIES!!!
SOMEONE, BEAT KYROS!!
BOOM!!
THAT'S THREE HUNDRED!!!
BAM!!
RAAAAH!!
NONE CAN STOP KYROS!!
EVERY HERO HE FACES ENDS UP BEATEN!!
WE CAME FROM DISTANT SEAS!!
LET US FIGHT KYROS!!!
I HEAR HE'S FIGHTING A GIANT TODAY!!
KYAA
RAHH
A WATER BATTLE WITH FISH-MEN?!

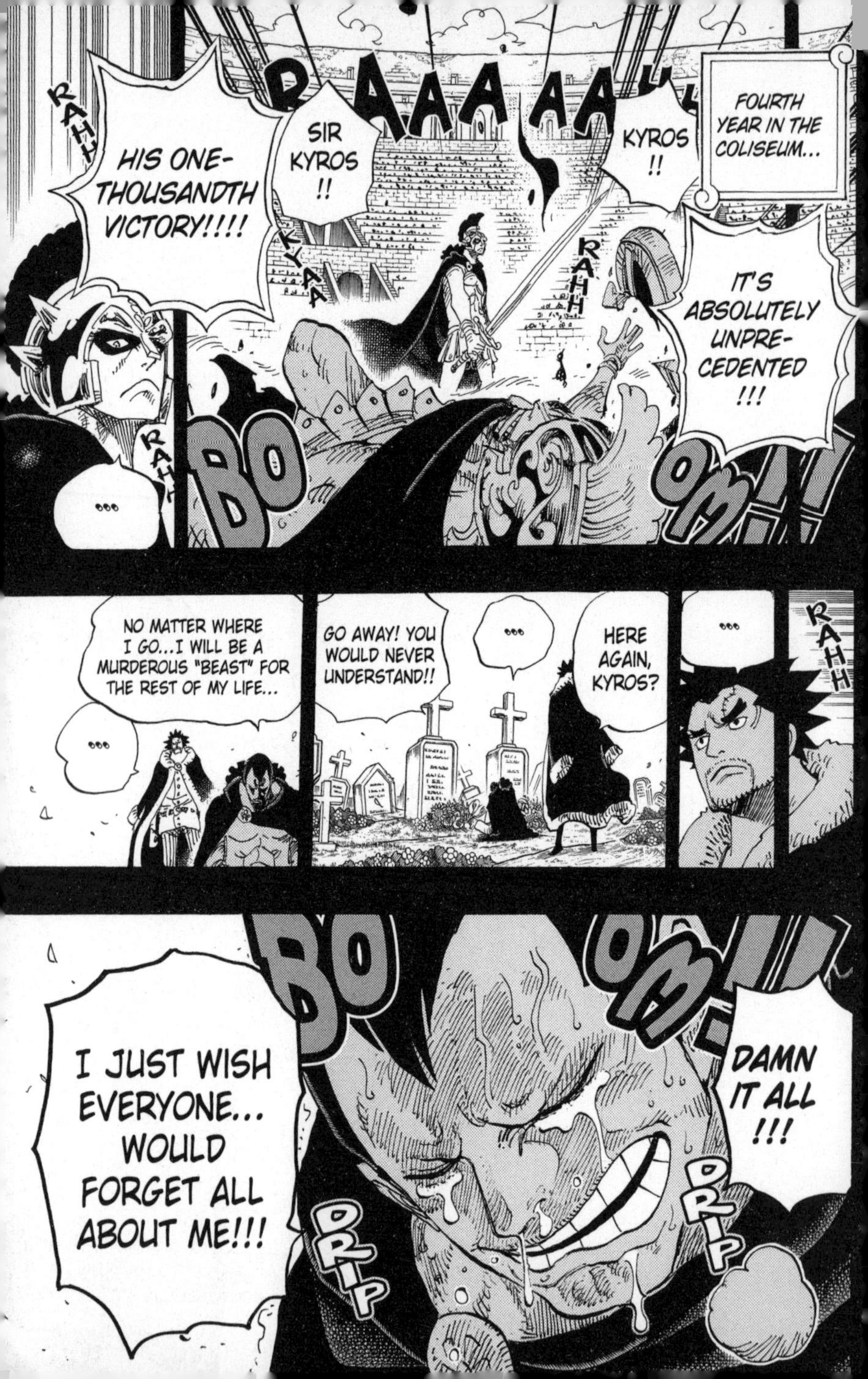
FOURTH YEAR IN THE COLISEUM...
KYROS !!
SIR KYROS !!
RAHH
HIS ONE-THOUSANDTH VICTORY!!!!
IT'S ABSOLUTELY UNPRECEDENTED !!!
RAHH
KYAA
RAHH
BOOM!!
...
RAHH
...
HERE AGAIN, KYROS?
...
GO AWAY! YOU WOULD NEVER UNDERSTAND!!
NO MATTER WHERE I GO...I WILL BE A MURDEROUS "BEAST" FOR THE REST OF MY LIFE...
...
BOOM!!
DAMN IT ALL !!!
I JUST WISH EVERYONE... WOULD FORGET ALL ABOUT ME!!!
DRIP
DRIP

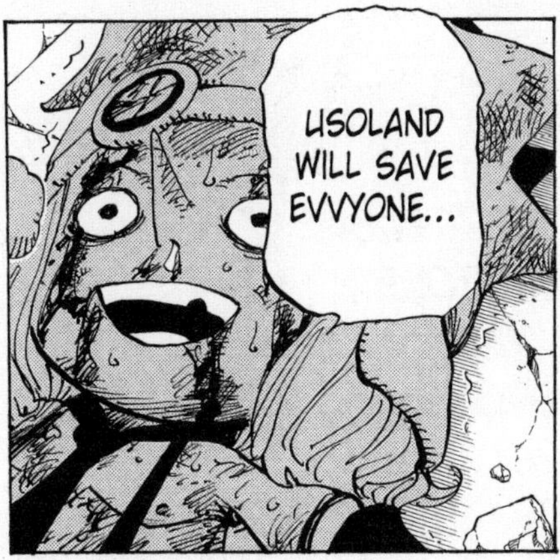
USOLAND WILL SAVE EVVYONE...

Chapter 742:

EVER AT YOUR SIDE

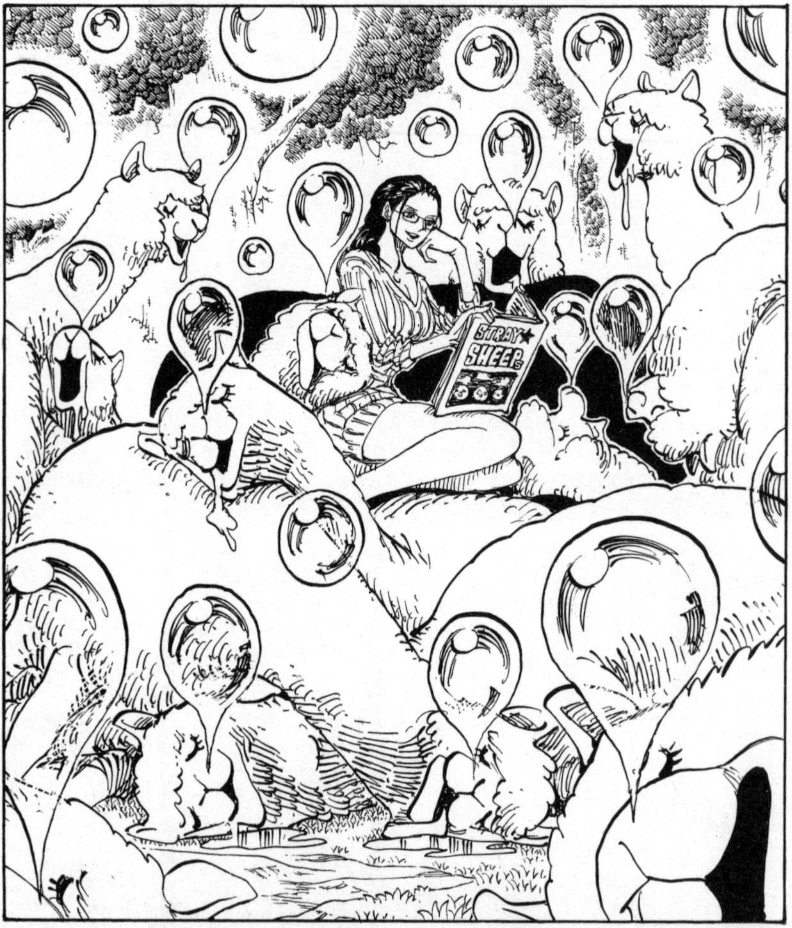
STRAY
SHEEP

REQUEST: "ROBIN READS A STORY TO NAPPING ALPACAS" BY MARU-CHAN FROM TOCHIGI

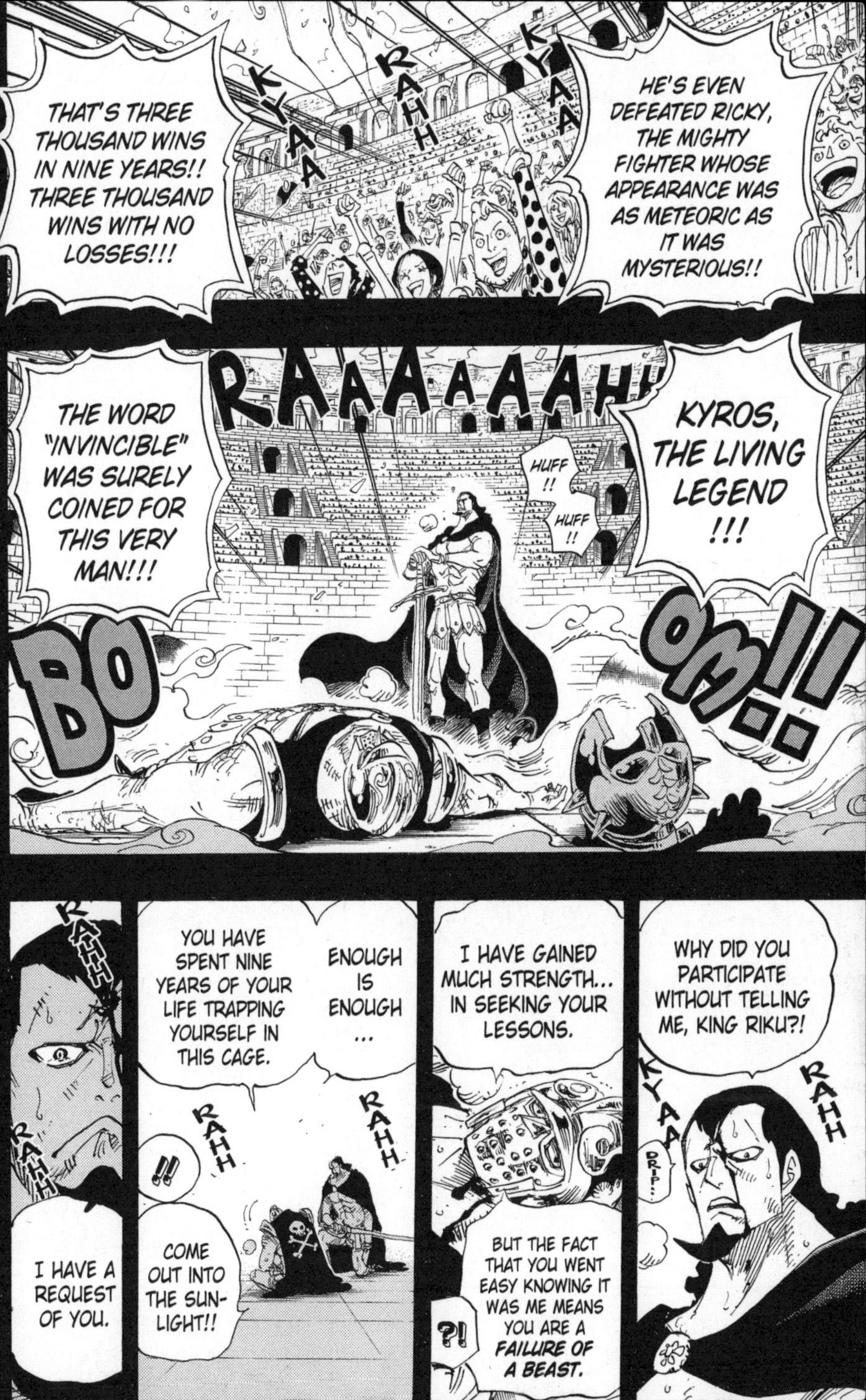
HE'S EVEN DEFEATED RICKY, THE MIGHTY FIGHTER WHOSE APPEARANCE WAS AS METEORIC AS IT WAS MYSTERIOUS!!
KYAA
RAHH
KYAA
THAT'S THREE THOUSAND WINS IN NINE YEARS!! THREE THOUSAND WINS WITH NO LOSSES!!!
RAAAAAAH!
KYROS, THE LIVING LEGEND!!!
HUFF!!
HUFF!!
THE WORD "INVINCIBLE" WAS SURELY COINED FOR THIS VERY MAN!!!
BOOM!!
WHY DID YOU PARTICIPATE WITHOUT TELLING ME, KING RIKU?!
RAHH
KYAA
DRIP...
I HAVE GAINED MUCH STRENGTH... IN SEEKING YOUR LESSONS.
BUT THE FACT THAT YOU WENT EASY KNOWING IT WAS ME MEANS YOU ARE A ***FAILURE OF A BEAST.***
?!
ENOUGH IS ENOUGH...
YOU HAVE SPENT NINE YEARS OF YOUR LIFE TRAPPING YOURSELF IN THIS CAGE.
RAHH
RAHH
!!
COME OUT INTO THE SUN-LIGHT!!
RAHH
RAHH
I HAVE A REQUEST OF YOU.

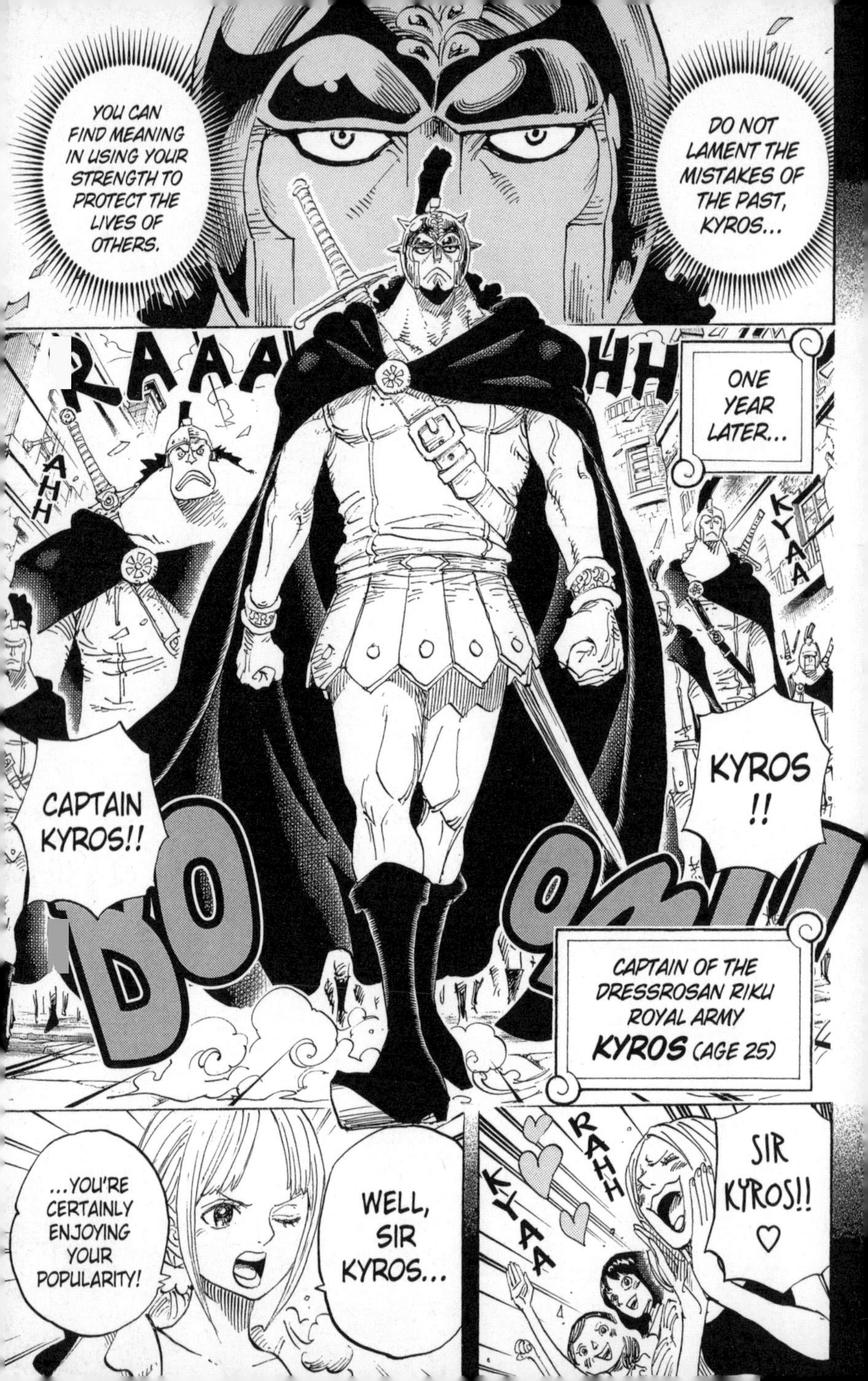
DO NOT LAMENT THE MISTAKES OF THE PAST, KYROS...
YOU CAN FIND MEANING IN USING YOUR STRENGTH TO PROTECT THE LIVES OF OTHERS.
ONE YEAR LATER...
KYAA
KYROS !!
AHH
CAPTAIN KYROS!!
CAPTAIN OF THE DRESSROSAN RIKU ROYAL ARMY KYROS (AGE 25)
SIR KYROS!! ♡
RAHH
KYAA
WELL, SIR KYROS...
...YOU'RE CERTAINLY ENJOYING YOUR POPULARITY!

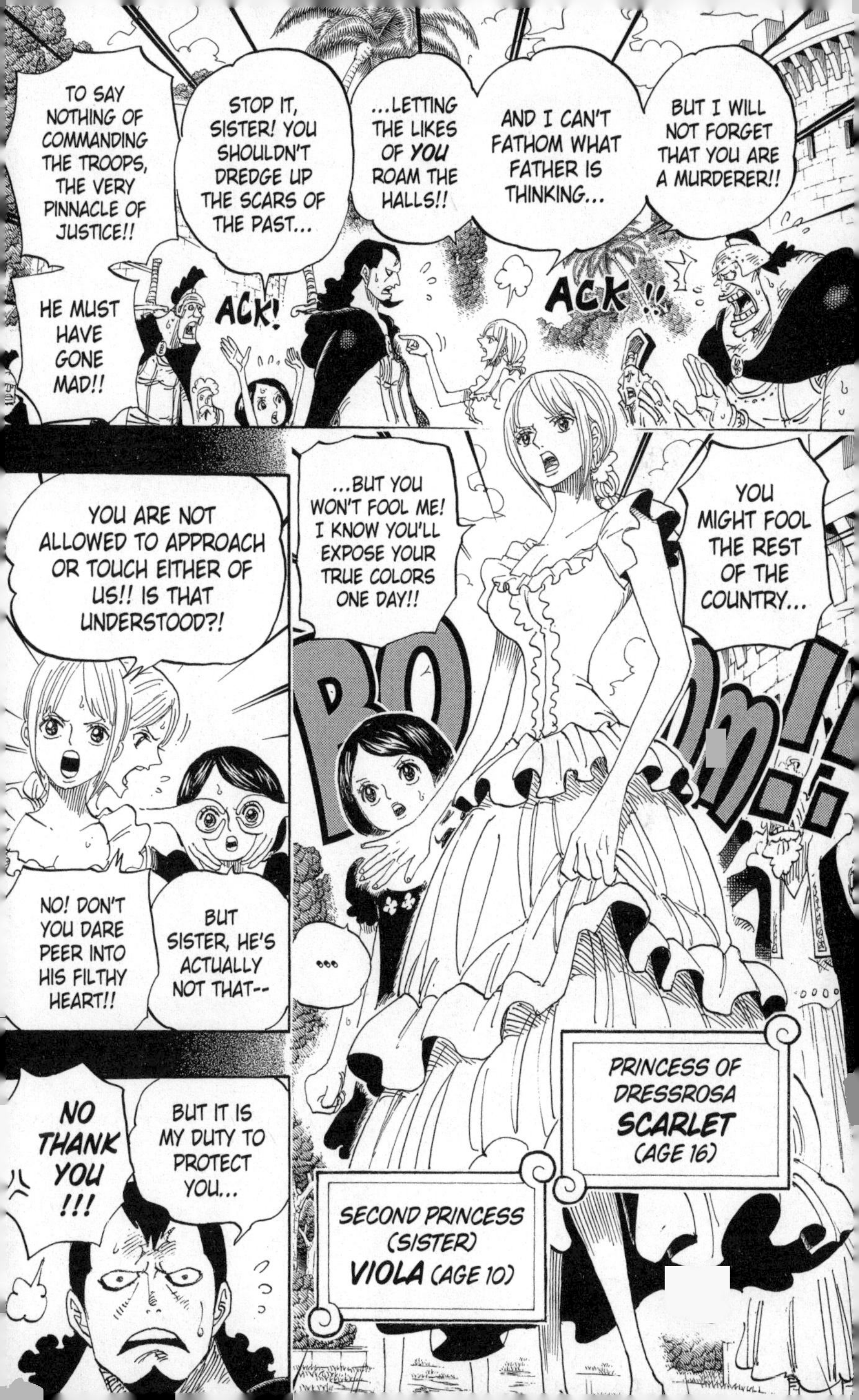
BUT I WILL NOT FORGET THAT YOU ARE A MURDERER!!
AND I CAN'T FATHOM WHAT FATHER IS THINKING...
...LETTING THE LIKES OF YOU ROAM THE HALLS!!
STOP IT, SISTER! YOU SHOULDN'T DREDGE UP THE SCARS OF THE PAST...
TO SAY NOTHING OF COMMANDING THE TROOPS, THE VERY PINNACLE OF JUSTICE!!
ACK!!
ACK!
HE MUST HAVE GONE MAD!!
YOU MIGHT FOOL THE REST OF THE COUNTRY...
...BUT YOU WON'T FOOL ME! I KNOW YOU'LL EXPOSE YOUR TRUE COLORS ONE DAY!!
...
PRINCESS OF DRESSROSA SCARLET (AGE 16)
SECOND PRINCESS (SISTER) VIOLA (AGE 10)
YOU ARE NOT ALLOWED TO APPROACH OR TOUCH EITHER OF US!! IS THAT UNDERSTOOD?!
BUT SISTER, HE'S ACTUALLY NOT THAT--
NO! DON'T YOU DARE PEER INTO HIS FILTHY HEART!!
BUT IT IS MY DUTY TO PROTECT YOU...
NO THANK YOU!!!

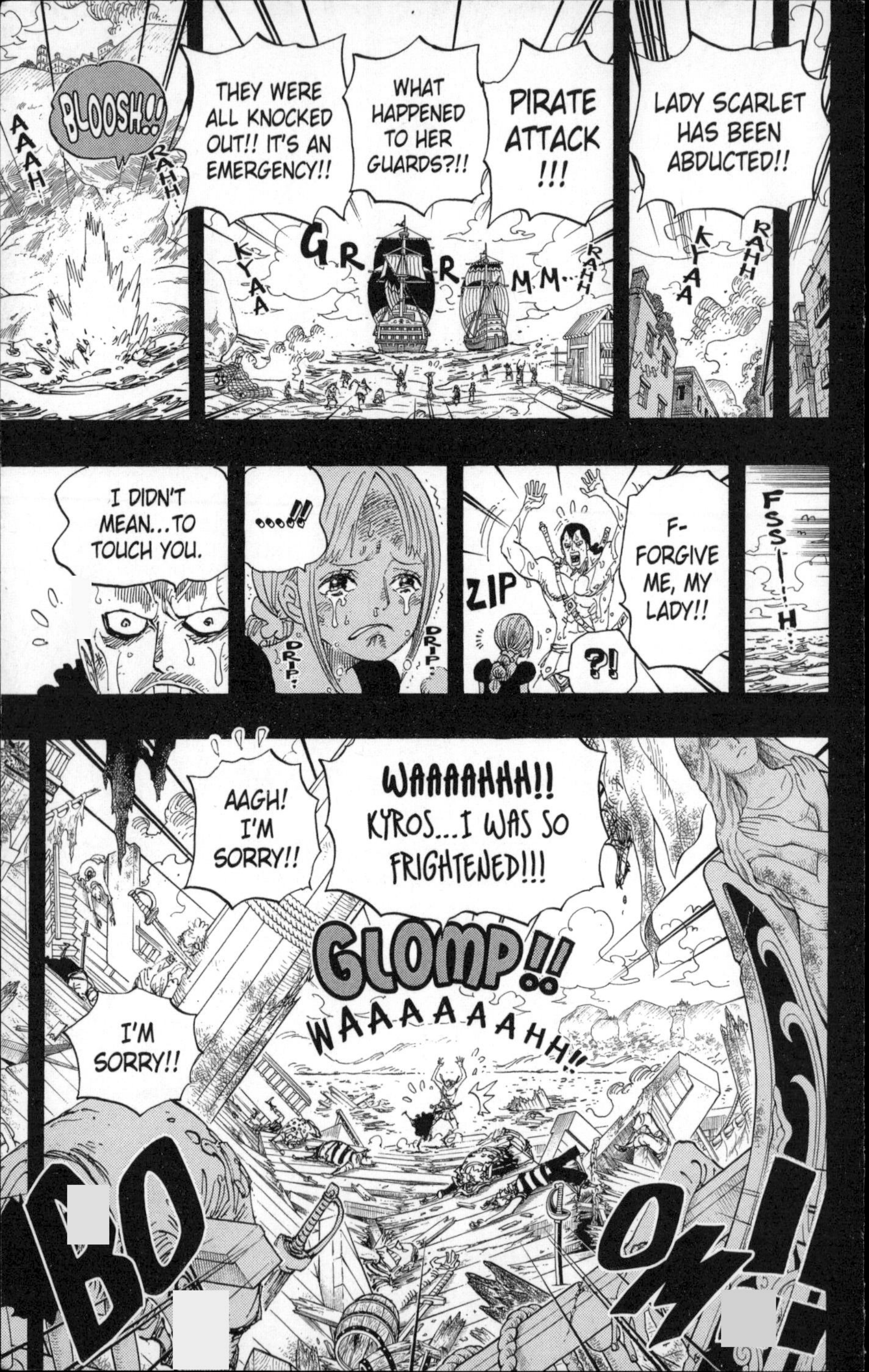
LADY SCARLET HAS BEEN ABDUCTED!!
KYAA
RAHH
PIRATE ATTACK!!!
WHAT HAPPENED TO HER GUARDS?!!
THEY WERE ALL KNOCKED OUT!! IT'S AN EMERGENCY!!
GRRRMM...
KYAA
RAHH
BLOOSH!!
AAAAH
RAHH...
FSSS...H
F- FORGIVE ME, MY LADY!!
ZIP
?!
....!!
DRIP
DRIP
I DIDN'T MEAN...TO TOUCH YOU.
WAAAAAHH!! KYROS...I WAS SO FRIGHTENED!!!
AAGH! I'M SORRY!!
GLOMP!!
WAAAAAAAHH!!
I'M SORRY!!
BOOM!

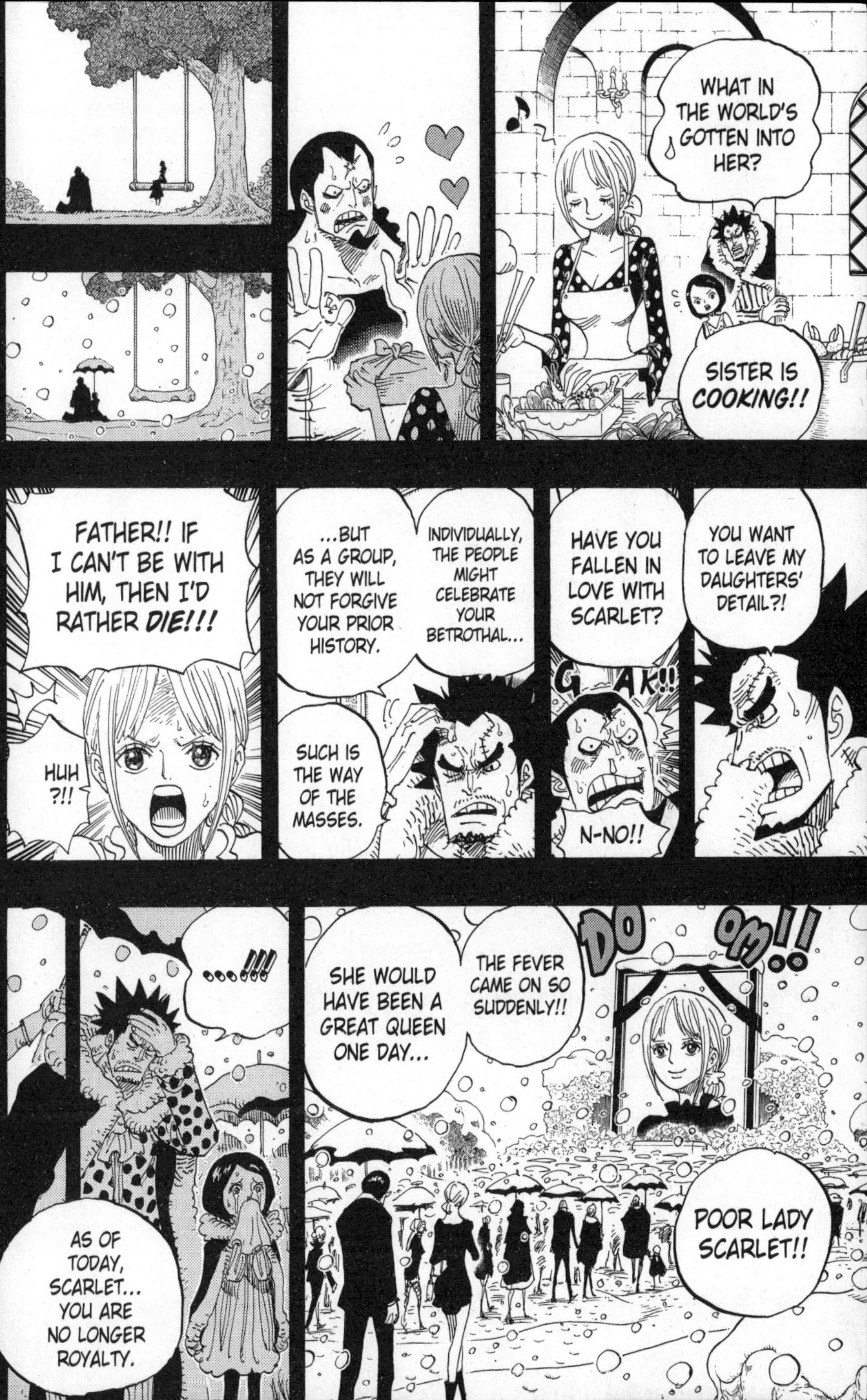
WHAT IN THE WORLD'S GOTTEN INTO HER?
SISTER IS COOKING!!
YOU WANT TO LEAVE MY DAUGHTERS' DETAIL?!
HAVE YOU FALLEN IN LOVE WITH SCARLET?
GAK!!
N-NO!!
INDIVIDUALLY, THE PEOPLE MIGHT CELEBRATE YOUR BETROTHAL...
...BUT AS A GROUP, THEY WILL NOT FORGIVE YOUR PRIOR HISTORY.
SUCH IS THE WAY OF THE MASSES.
FATHER!! IF I CAN'T BE WITH HIM, THEN I'D RATHER DIE!!!
HUH?!!
DOOM!!
THE FEVER CAME ON SO SUDDENLY!!
SHE WOULD HAVE BEEN A GREAT QUEEN ONE DAY...
POOR LADY SCARLET!!
......!!!
AS OF TODAY, SCARLET... YOU ARE NO LONGER ROYALTY.

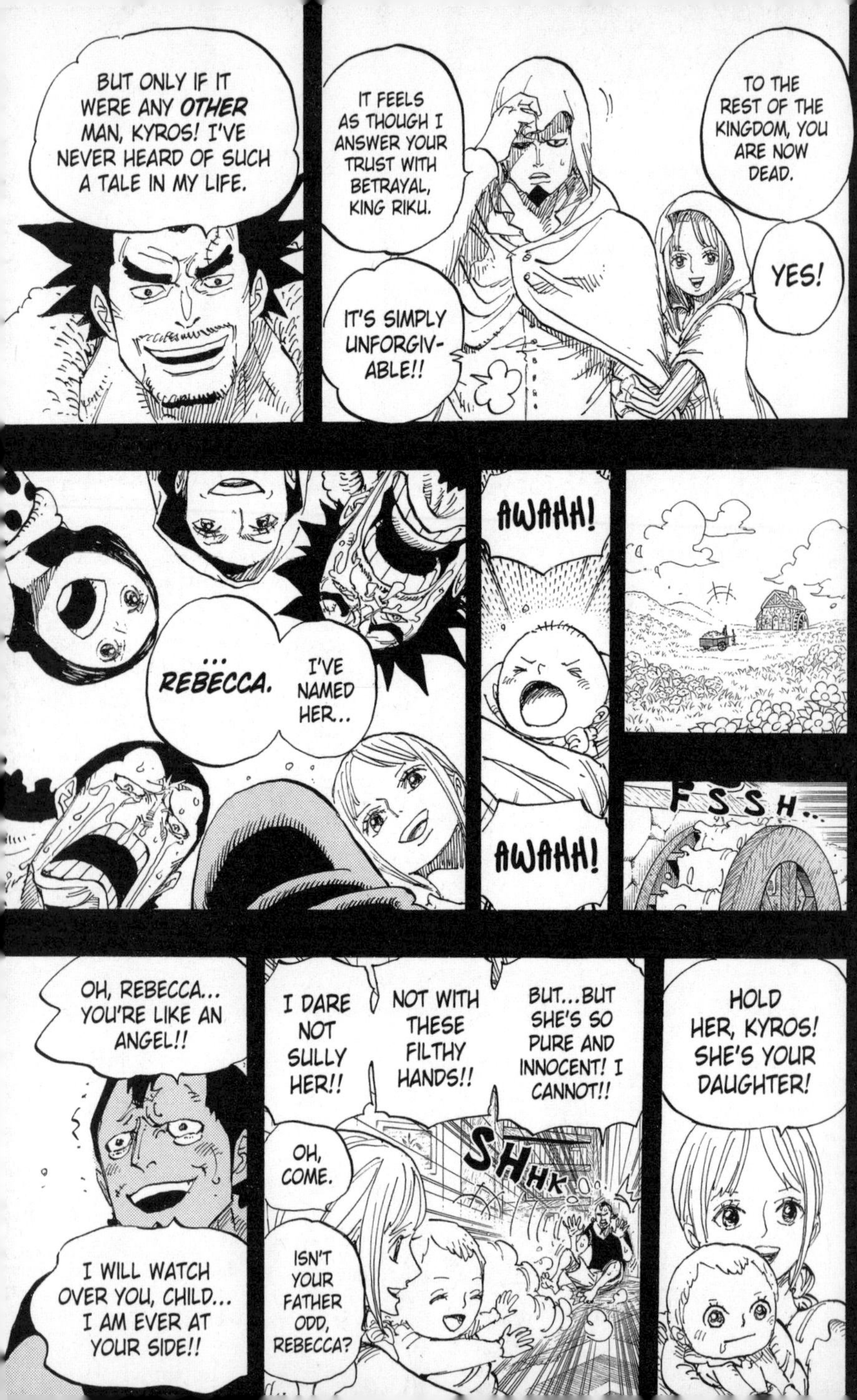
TO THE REST OF THE KINGDOM, YOU ARE NOW DEAD.
YES!
IT FEELS AS THOUGH I ANSWER YOUR TRUST WITH BETRAYAL, KING RIKU.
IT'S SIMPLY UNFORGIV-ABLE!!
BUT ONLY IF IT WERE ANY *OTHER* MAN, KYROS! I'VE NEVER HEARD OF SUCH A TALE IN MY LIFE.
FSSH...
AWAHH!
AWAHH!
I'VE NAMED HER...
... *REBECCA.*
HOLD HER, KYROS! SHE'S YOUR DAUGHTER!
BUT...BUT SHE'S SO PURE AND INNOCENT! I CANNOT!!
NOT WITH THESE FILTHY HANDS!!
I DARE NOT SULLY HER!!
SHHK
OH, COME.
ISN'T YOUR FATHER ODD, REBECCA?
OH, REBECCA... YOU'RE LIKE AN ANGEL!!
I WILL WATCH OVER YOU, CHILD... I AM EVER AT YOUR SIDE!!

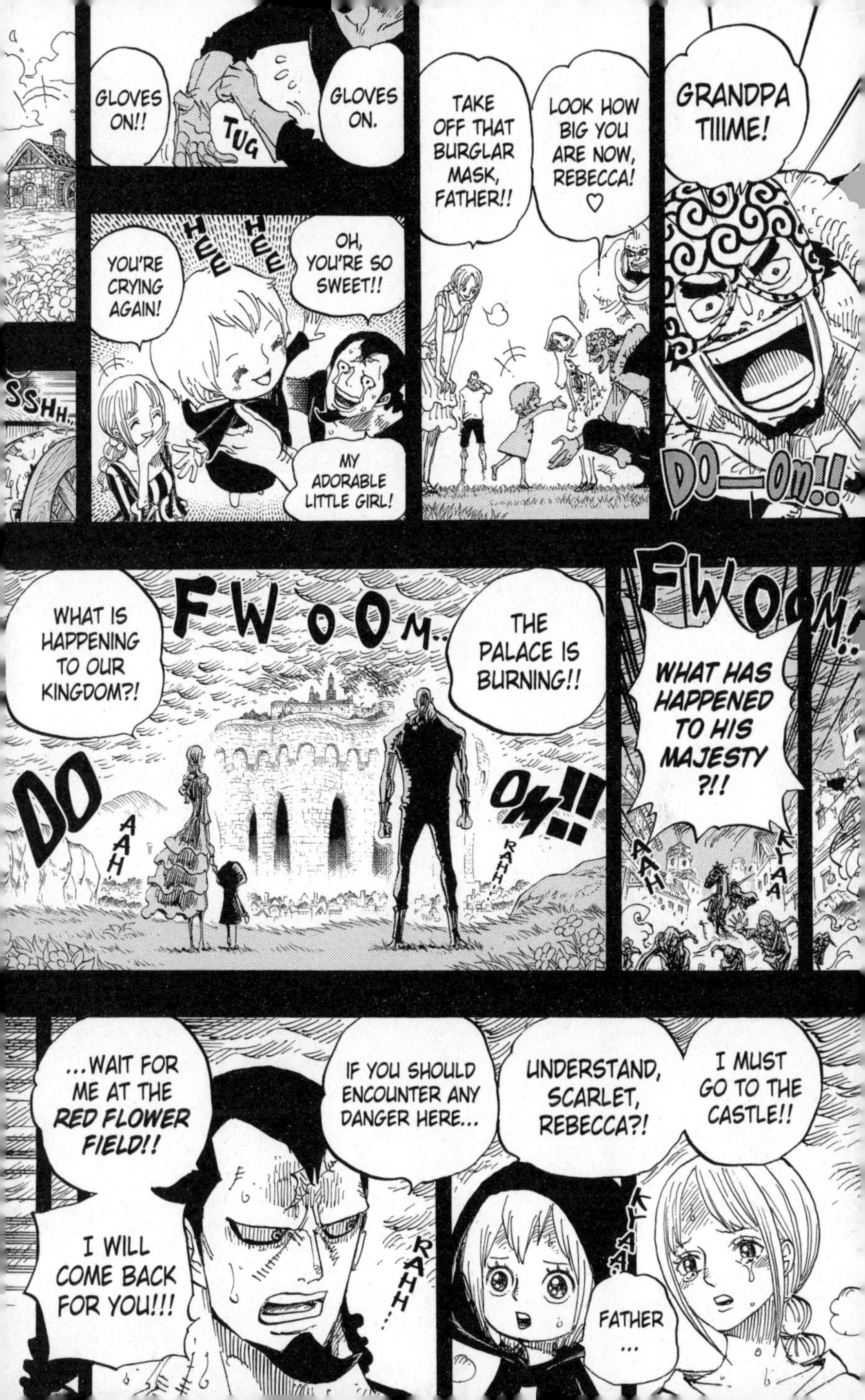
GRANDPA TIIIME!
DO—OM!!
LOOK HOW BIG YOU ARE NOW, REBECCA! ♡
TAKE OFF THAT BURGLAR MASK, FATHER!!
GLOVES ON.
TUG
GLOVES ON!!
OH, YOU'RE SO SWEET!!
HEE HEE
YOU'RE CRYING AGAIN!
MY ADORABLE LITTLE GIRL!
SSHH..
FWOOOM..
WHAT HAS HAPPENED TO HIS MAJESTY ?!!
KYAA
AAH
THE PALACE IS BURNING!!
FWOOOM..
WHAT IS HAPPENING TO OUR KINGDOM?!
RAHH!!
DOOM!!
AAAH
I MUST GO TO THE CASTLE!!
UNDERSTAND, SCARLET, REBECCA?!
KYAA
FATHER ...
IF YOU SHOULD ENCOUNTER ANY DANGER HERE...
...WAIT FOR ME AT THE RED FLOWER FIELD!!
RAHH...
I WILL COME BACK FOR YOU!!!

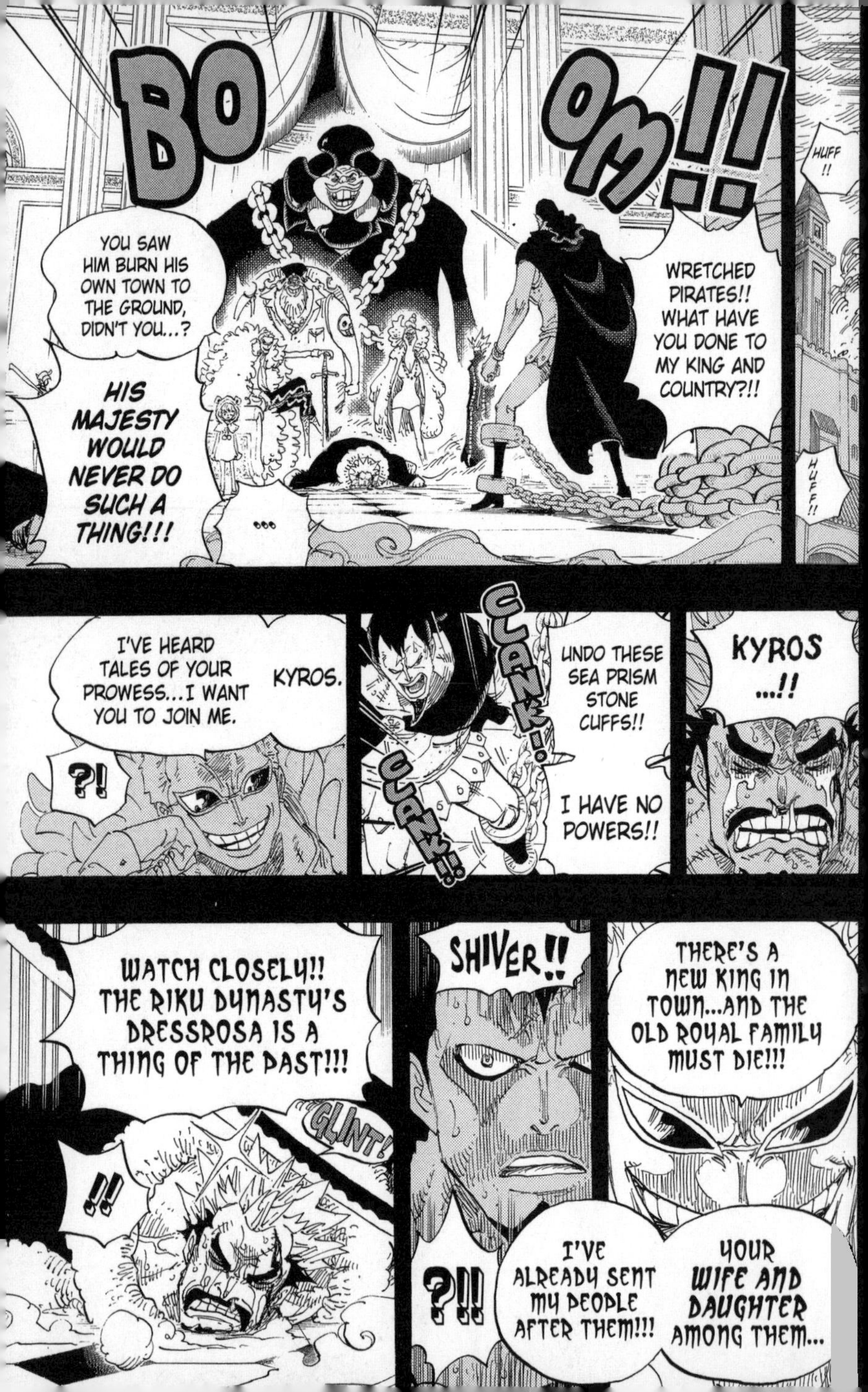
BOOM!!
HUFF!!
WRETCHED PIRATES!! WHAT HAVE YOU DONE TO MY KING AND COUNTRY?!!
HUFF!!
YOU SAW HIM BURN HIS OWN TOWN TO THE GROUND, DIDN'T YOU...?
HIS MAJESTY WOULD NEVER DO SUCH A THING!!!
...
KYROS ...!!
CLANK!
CLANK!!
UNDO THESE SEA PRISM STONE CUFFS!!
I HAVE NO POWERS!!
KYROS.
I'VE HEARD TALES OF YOUR PROWESS...I WANT YOU TO JOIN ME.
?!
THERE'S A NEW KING IN TOWN...AND THE OLD ROYAL FAMILY MUST DIE!!!
I'VE ALREADY SENT MY PEOPLE AFTER THEM!!!
YOUR WIFE AND DAUGHTER AMONG THEM...
SHIVER!!
?!!
WATCH CLOSELY!! THE RIKU DYNASTY'S DRESSROSA IS A THING OF THE PAST!!!
GLINT!
!!

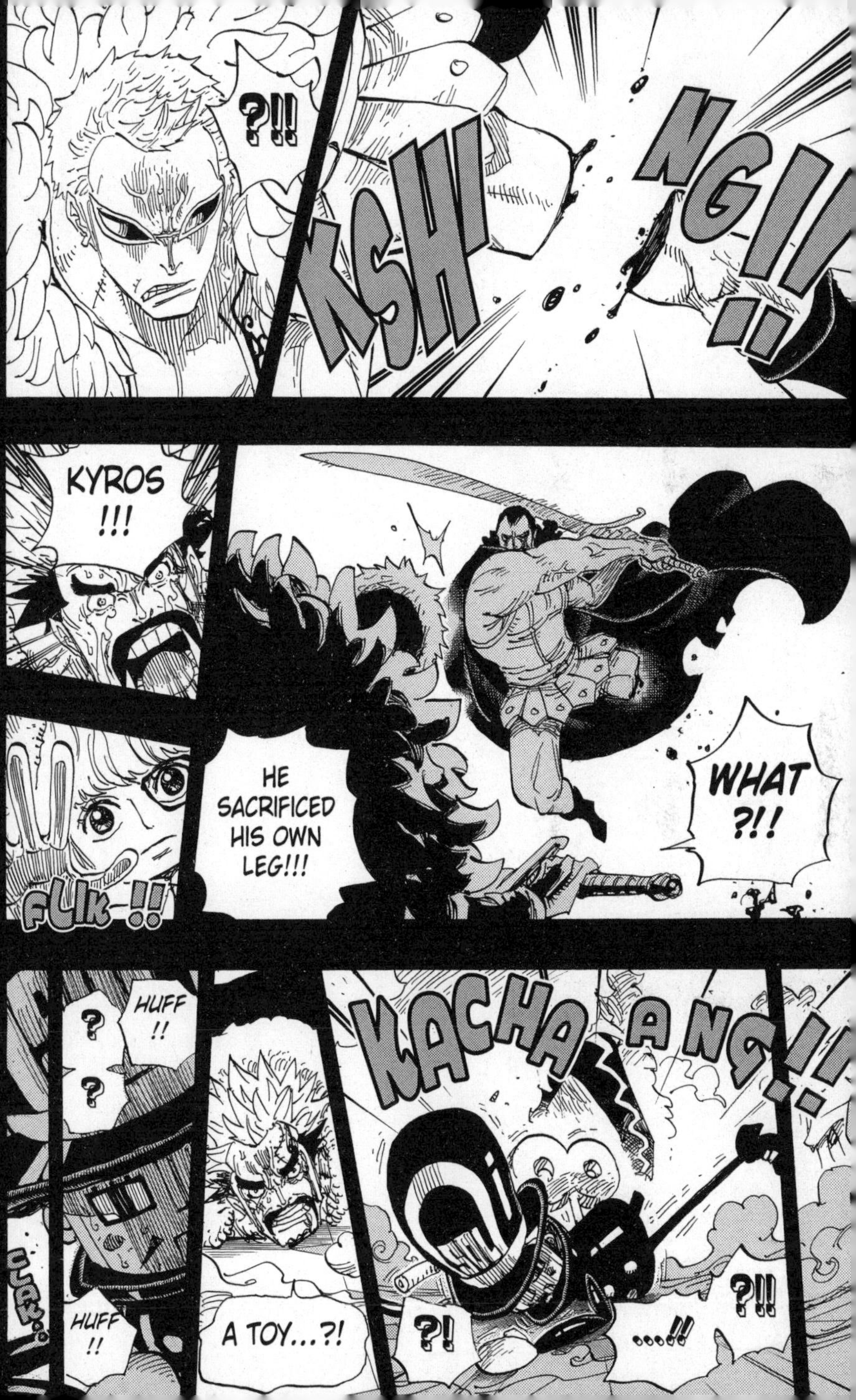
KSHING!!
?!!
WHAT ?!!
HE SACRIFICED HIS OWN LEG!!!
KYROS !!!
FLIK!!
KACHA ANG!!
?!!
...!!
?!
A TOY...?!
HUFF !!
?
?
HUFF !!
CLAK..

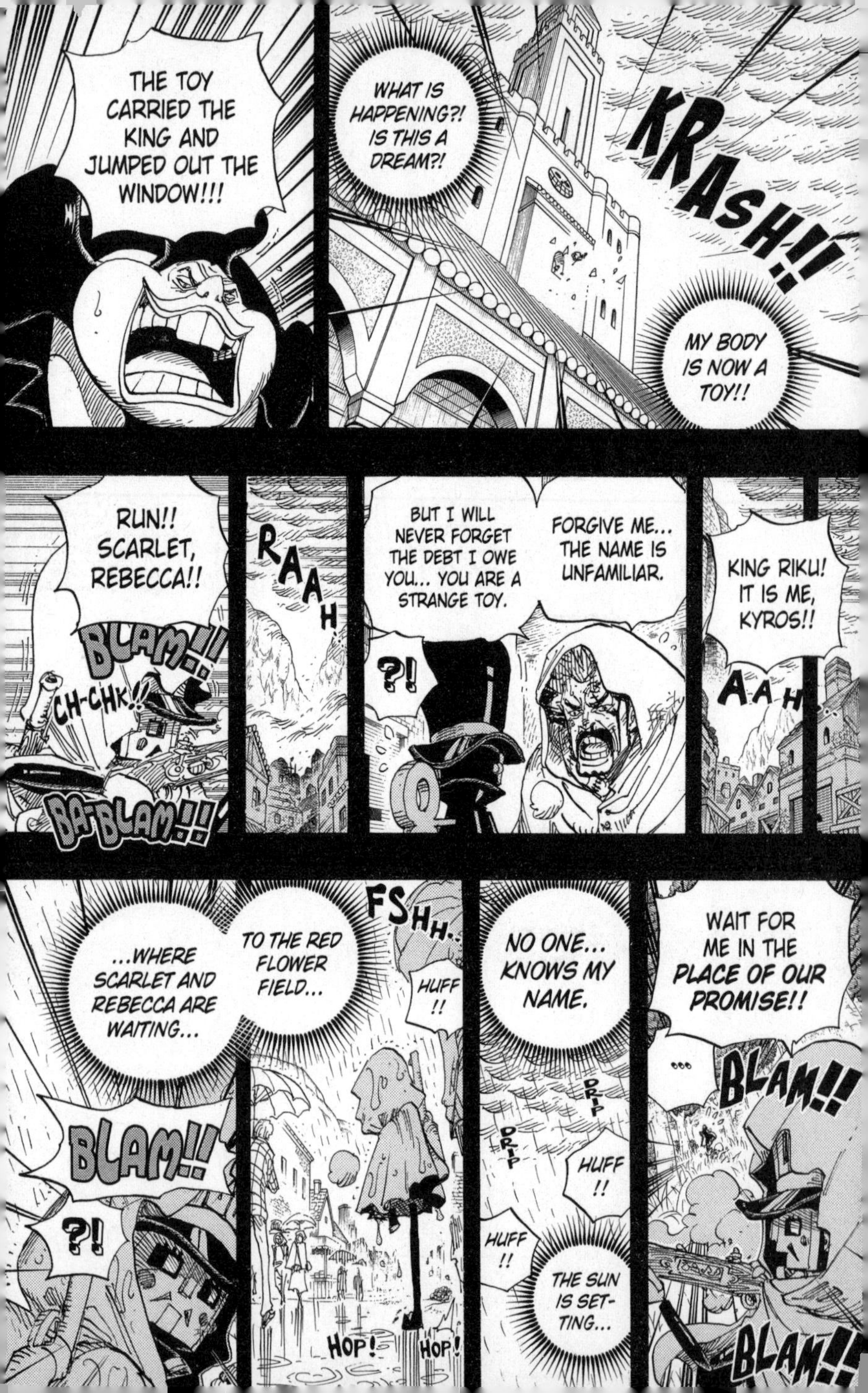
KRASH!!
WHAT IS HAPPENING?! IS THIS A DREAM?!
MY BODY IS NOW A TOY!!
THE TOY CARRIED THE KING AND JUMPED OUT THE WINDOW!!!
KING RIKU! IT IS ME, KYROS!!
AAH
FORGIVE ME... THE NAME IS UNFAMILIAR.
BUT I WILL NEVER FORGET THE DEBT I OWE YOU... YOU ARE A STRANGE TOY.
?!
RAAAH
RUN!! SCARLET, REBECCA!!
BLAM!!!
CH-CHK!!
BA-BLAM!!!
WAIT FOR ME IN THE PLACE OF OUR PROMISE!!
...
BLAM!!
BLAM!!
NO ONE... KNOWS MY NAME.
DRIP
DRIP
HUFF!!
HUFF!!
THE SUN IS SET-TING...
FSHH..
TO THE RED FLOWER FIELD...
HUFF!!
HOP!
HOP!
...WHERE SCARLET AND REBECCA ARE WAITING...
BLAM!!
?!

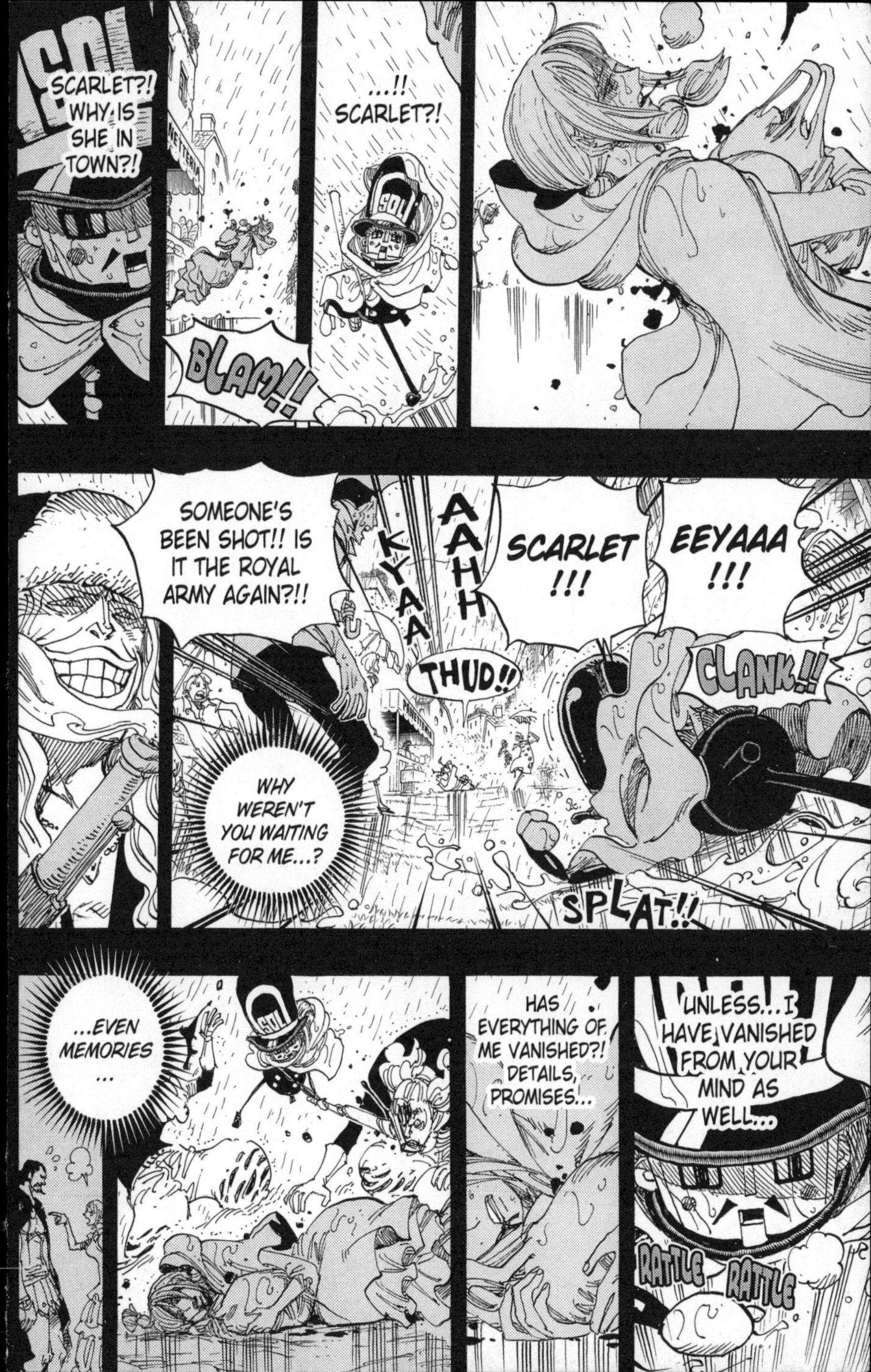
...!!
SCARLET?!
BLAM!!
SCARLET?! WHY IS SHE IN TOWN?!
EEYAAA!!!
CLANK!!
SCARLET!!!
AAAHH
KYAAA
THUD!!
SOMEONE'S BEEN SHOT!! IS IT THE ROYAL ARMY AGAIN?!!
WHY WEREN'T YOU WAITING FOR ME...?
SPLAT!!
UNLESS... I HAVE VANISHED FROM YOUR MIND AS WELL...
RATTLE RATTLE
HAS EVERYTHING OF ME VANISHED?! DETAILS, PROMISES...
...EVEN MEMORIES...

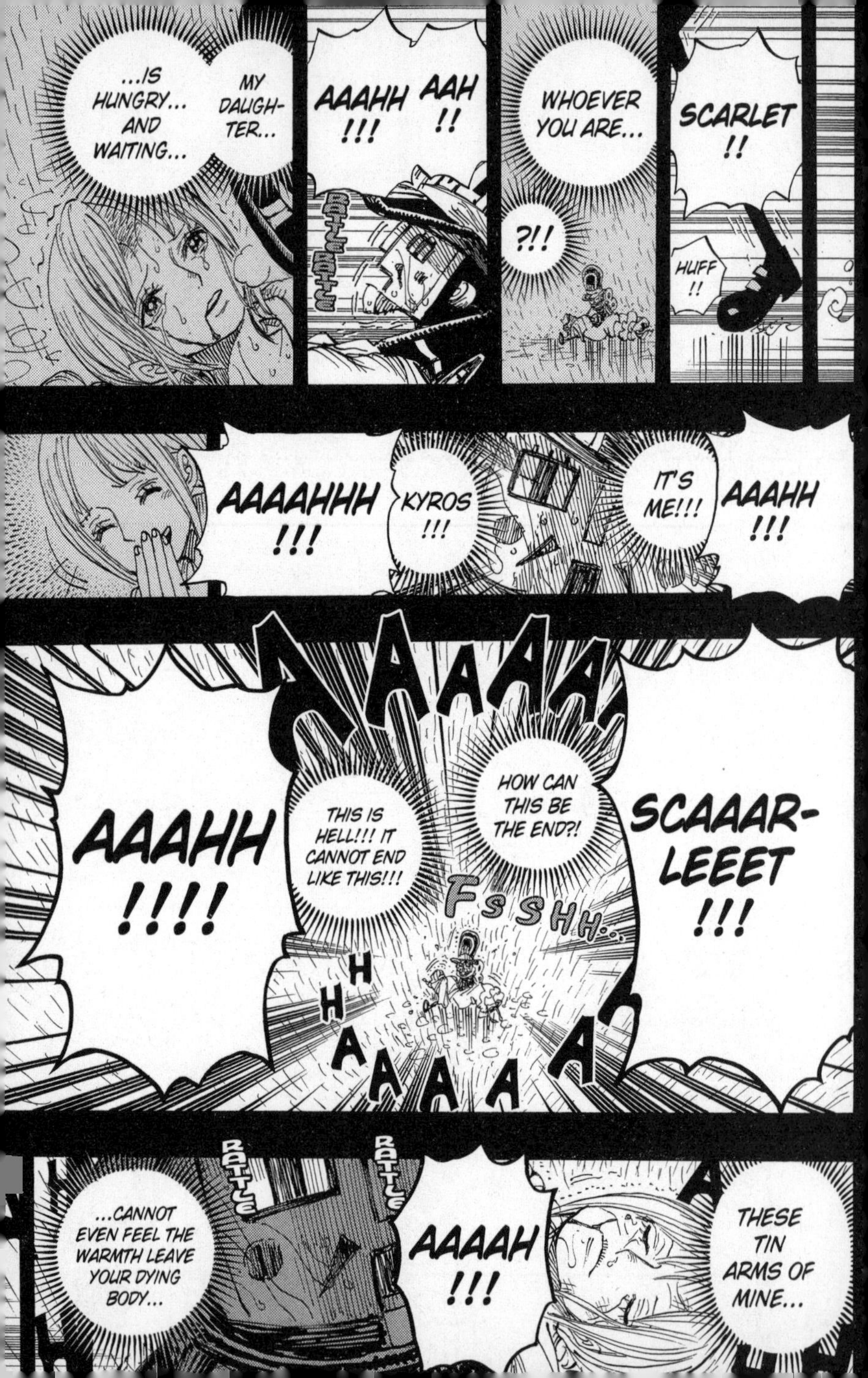
SCARLET !!
HUFF !!
WHOEVER YOU ARE...
?!!
AAH !!
AAAHH !!!
RATTLE RATTLE
MY DAUGHTER...
...IS HUNGRY... AND WAITING...
AAAHH !!!
IT'S ME!!!
KYROS !!!
AAAAHHH !!!
AAAAAHHAAAAA
SCAAAR-LEEET !!!
HOW CAN THIS BE THE END?!
THIS IS HELL!!! IT CANNOT END LIKE THIS!!!
FSSHH...
AAAHH !!!!
THESE TIN ARMS OF MINE...
AAAAH !!!
RATTLE
RATTLE
...CANNOT EVEN FEEL THE WARMTH LEAVE YOUR DYING BODY...

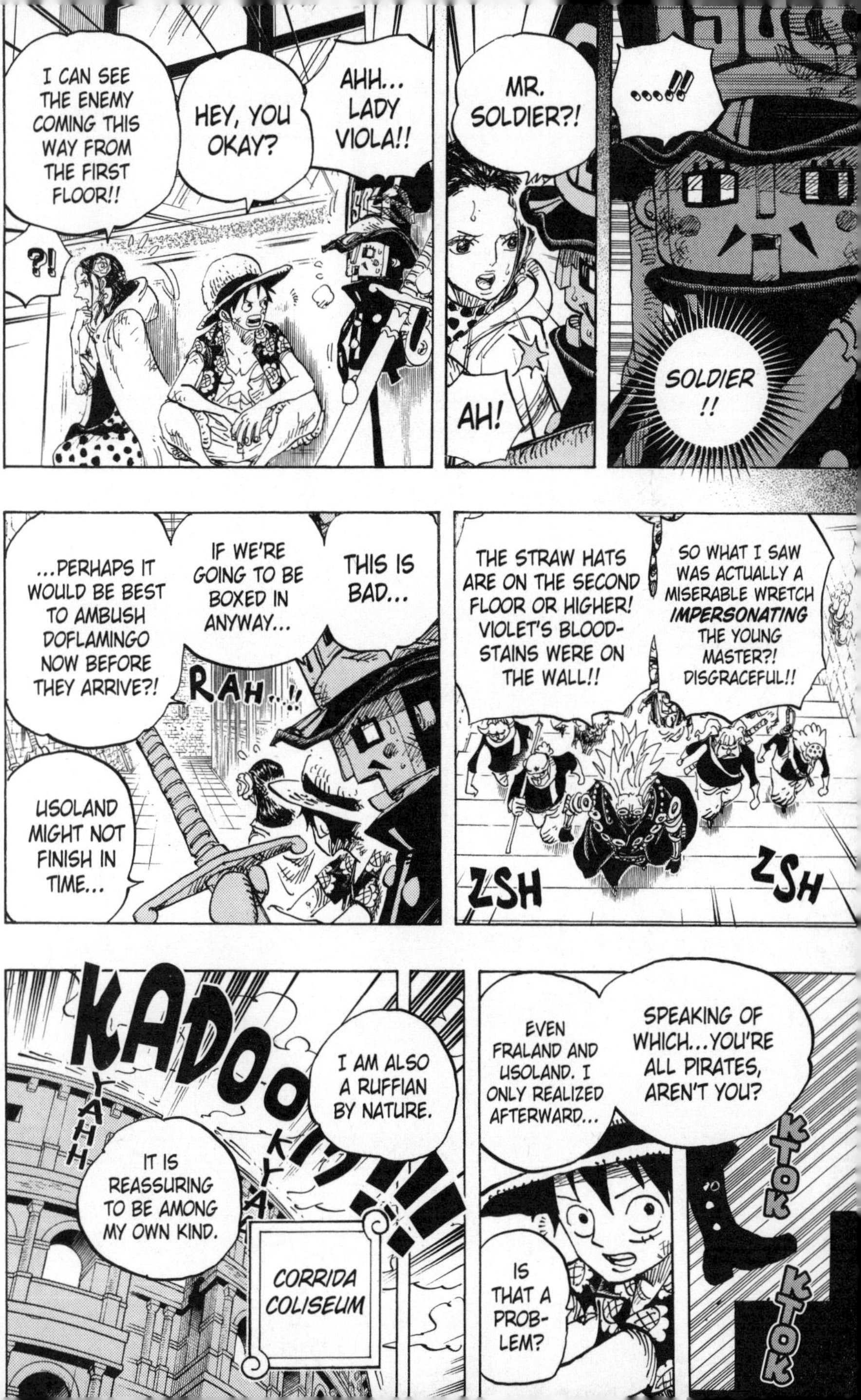
...!!
SOLDIER!!
MR. SOLDIER?!
AH!
AHH... LADY VIOLA!!
HEY, YOU OKAY?
I CAN SEE THE ENEMY COMING THIS WAY FROM THE FIRST FLOOR!!
?!
SO WHAT I SAW WAS ACTUALLY A MISERABLE WRETCH *IMPERSONATING* THE YOUNG MASTER?! DISGRACEFUL!!
THE STRAW HATS ARE ON THE SECOND FLOOR OR HIGHER! VIOLET'S BLOOD-STAINS WERE ON THE WALL!!
ZSH
ZSH
THIS IS BAD...
IF WE'RE GOING TO BE BOXED IN ANYWAY...
...PERHAPS IT WOULD BE BEST TO AMBUSH DOFLAMINGO NOW BEFORE THEY ARRIVE?!
RAH...!!
USOLAND MIGHT NOT FINISH IN TIME...
SPEAKING OF WHICH...YOU'RE ALL PIRATES, AREN'T YOU?
EVEN FRALAND AND USOLAND. I ONLY REALIZED AFTERWARD...
KTOK
KTOK
IS THAT A PROB-LEM?
I AM ALSO A RUFFIAN BY NATURE.
KADOO
YAHH
KYAA
IT IS REASSURING TO BE AMONG MY OWN KIND.
CORRIDA COLISEUM

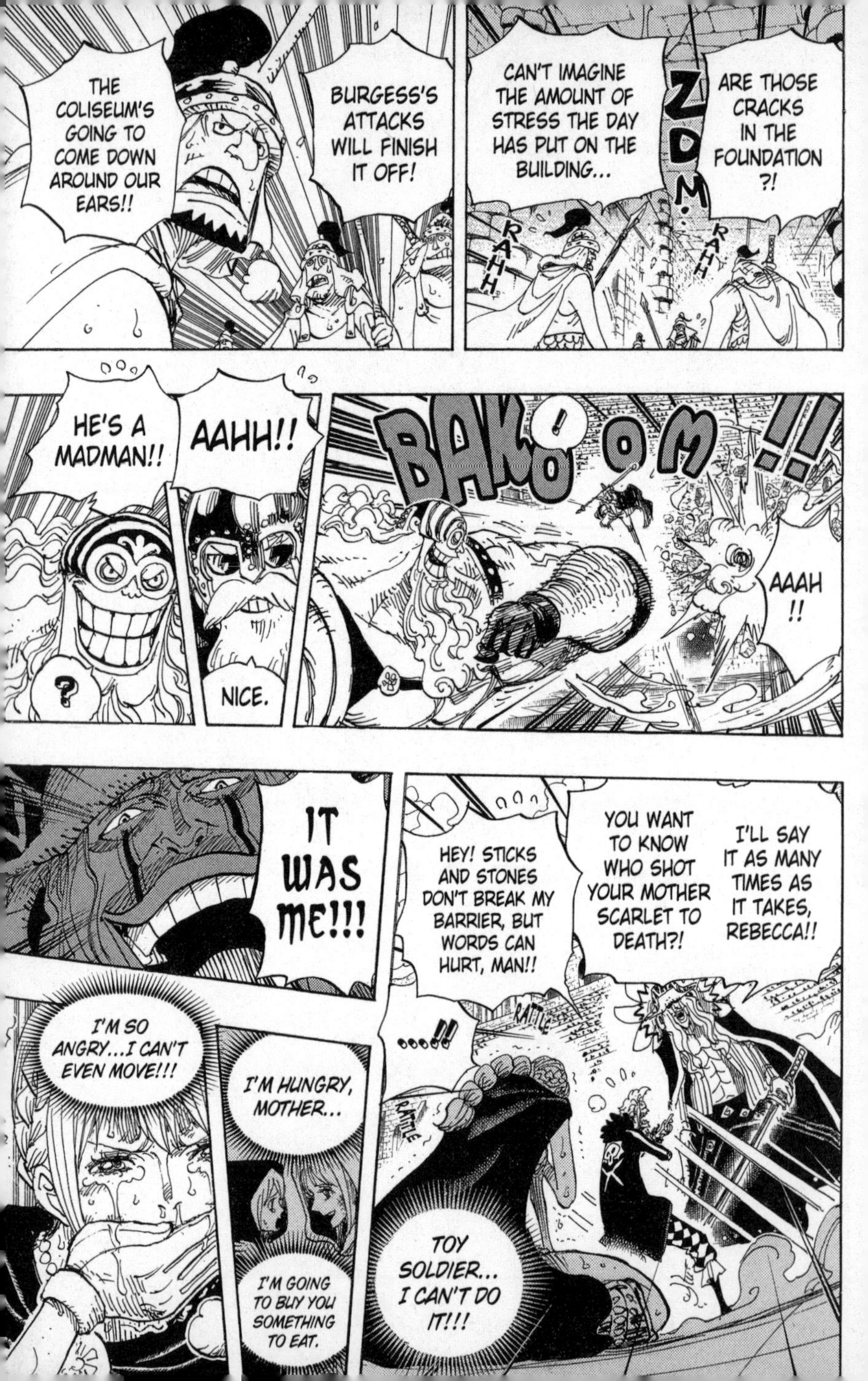
ARE THOSE CRACKS IN THE FOUNDATION ?!
ZDM
CAN'T IMAGINE THE AMOUNT OF STRESS THE DAY HAS PUT ON THE BUILDING...
RAHH
RAHH
BURGESS'S ATTACKS WILL FINISH IT OFF!
THE COLISEUM'S GOING TO COME DOWN AROUND OUR EARS!!
BAKOOM!!
AAAH !!
AAHH!!
NICE.
HE'S A MADMAN!!
?
I'LL SAY IT AS MANY TIMES AS IT TAKES, REBECCA!!
YOU WANT TO KNOW WHO SHOT YOUR MOTHER SCARLET TO DEATH?!
HEY! STICKS AND STONES DON'T BREAK MY BARRIER, BUT WORDS CAN HURT, MAN!!
IT WAS ME!!!
RATTLE
...!!
RATTLE
TOY SOLDIER... I CAN'T DO IT!!!
I'M HUNGRY, MOTHER...
I'M GOING TO BUY YOU SOMETHING TO EAT.
I'M SO ANGRY...I CAN'T EVEN MOVE!!!

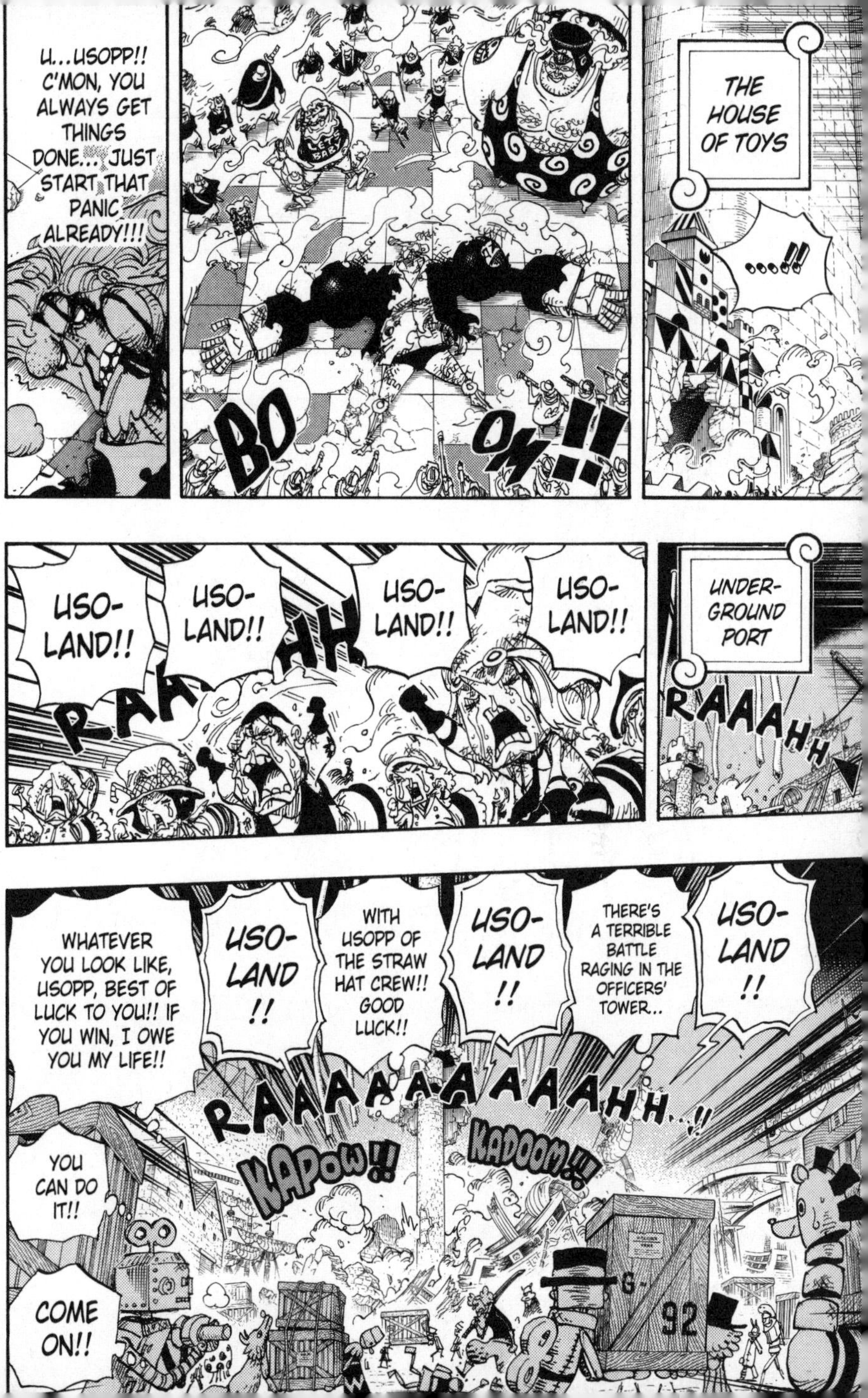
THE HOUSE OF TOYS
....!!
BOOM!!
U...USOPP!! C'MON, YOU ALWAYS GET THINGS DONE... JUST START THAT PANIC ALREADY!!!
UNDER-GROUND PORT
RAAAHH
USO-LAND!!
USO-LAND!!
USO-LAND!!
USO-LAND!!
RAAAHH
USO-LAND !!
THERE'S A TERRIBLE BATTLE RAGING IN THE OFFICERS' TOWER...
USO-LAND !!
WITH USOPP OF THE STRAW HAT CREW!! GOOD LUCK!!
USO-LAND !!
WHATEVER YOU LOOK LIKE, USOPP, BEST OF LUCK TO YOU!! IF YOU WIN, I OWE YOU MY LIFE!!
RAAAAAAAAAAHH...!!
KADOOM!!
KAPOW!!
YOU CAN DO IT!!
COME ON!!

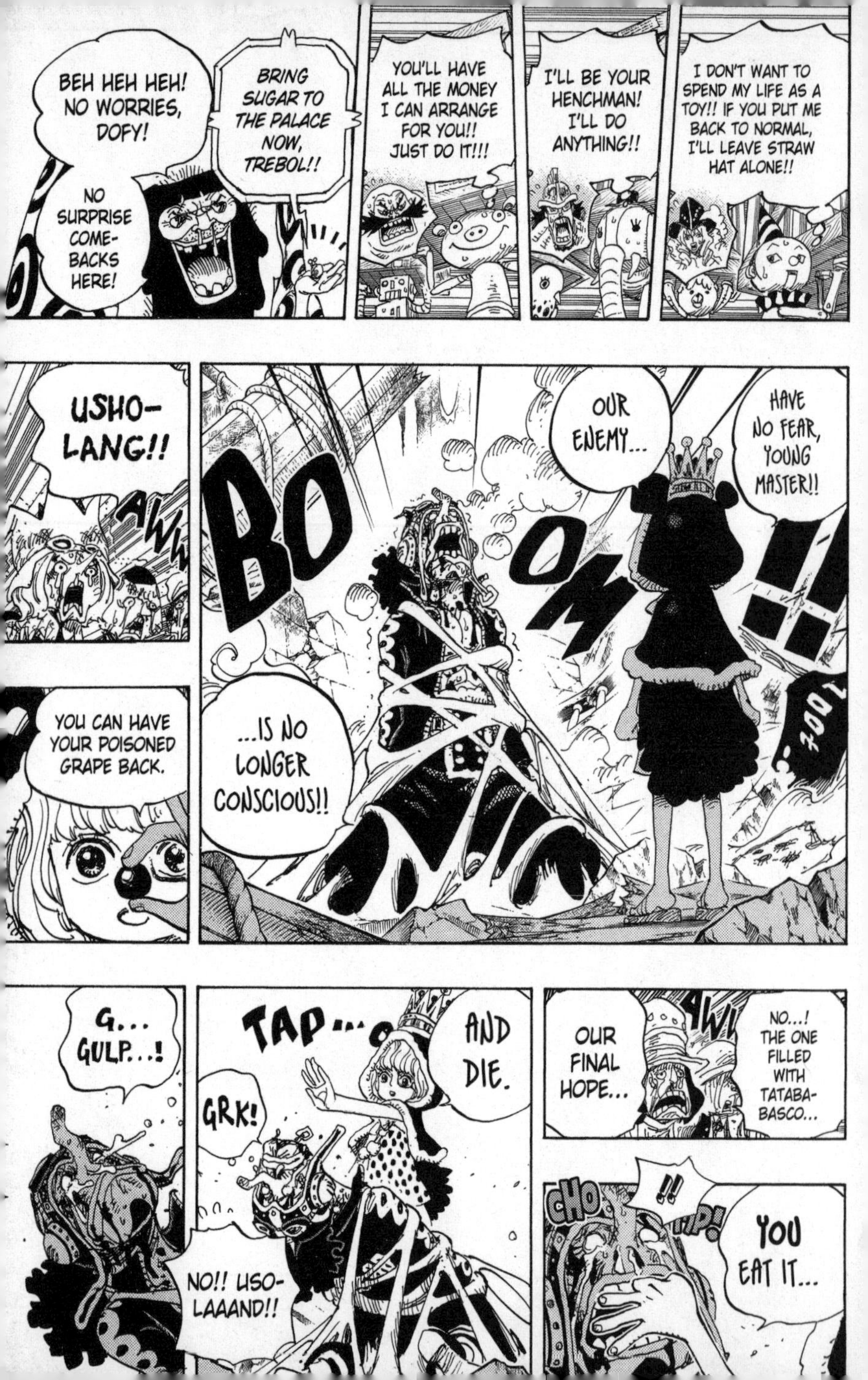
I DON'T WANT TO SPEND MY LIFE AS A TOY!! IF YOU PUT ME BACK TO NORMAL, I'LL LEAVE STRAW HAT ALONE!!
I'LL BE YOUR HENCHMAN! I'LL DO ANYTHING!!
YOU'LL HAVE ALL THE MONEY I CAN ARRANGE FOR YOU!! JUST DO IT!!!
BRING SUGAR TO THE PALACE NOW, TREBOL!!
BEH HEH HEH! NO WORRIES, DOFY!
NO SURPRISE COME-BACKS HERE!
HAVE NO FEAR, YOUNG MASTER!!
OUR ENEMY...
BOOM!!
TOOT
...IS NO LONGER CONSCIOUS!!
USHO-LANG!!
AWW
YOU CAN HAVE YOUR POISONED GRAPE BACK.
NO...! THE ONE FILLED WITH TATABA-BASCO...
AWW
OUR FINAL HOPE...
YOU EAT IT...
!!
CHOMP!
AND DIE.
TAP...
GRK!
NO!! USO-LAAAND!!
G... GULP...!

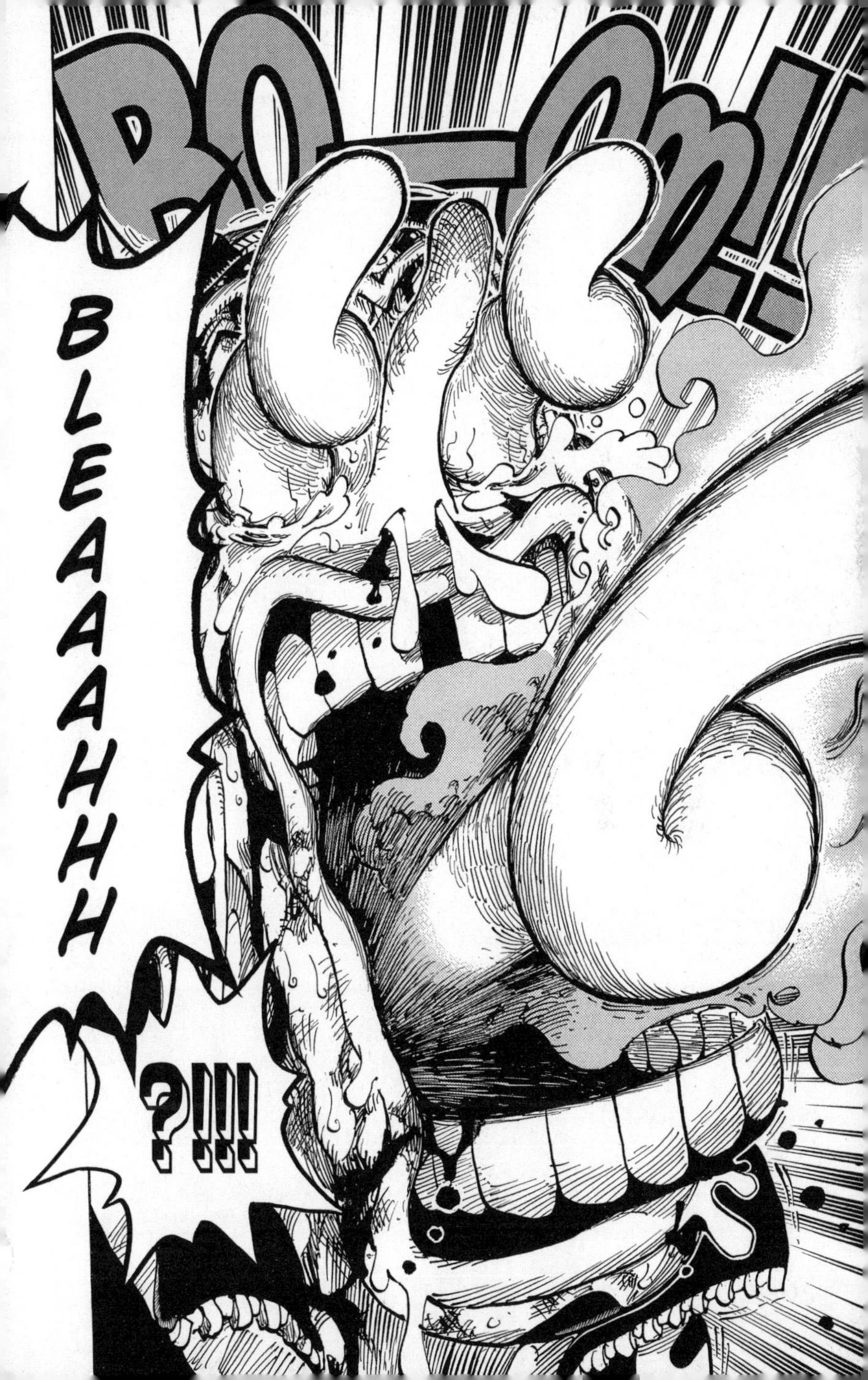
BLEAAAAHHH
?!!!

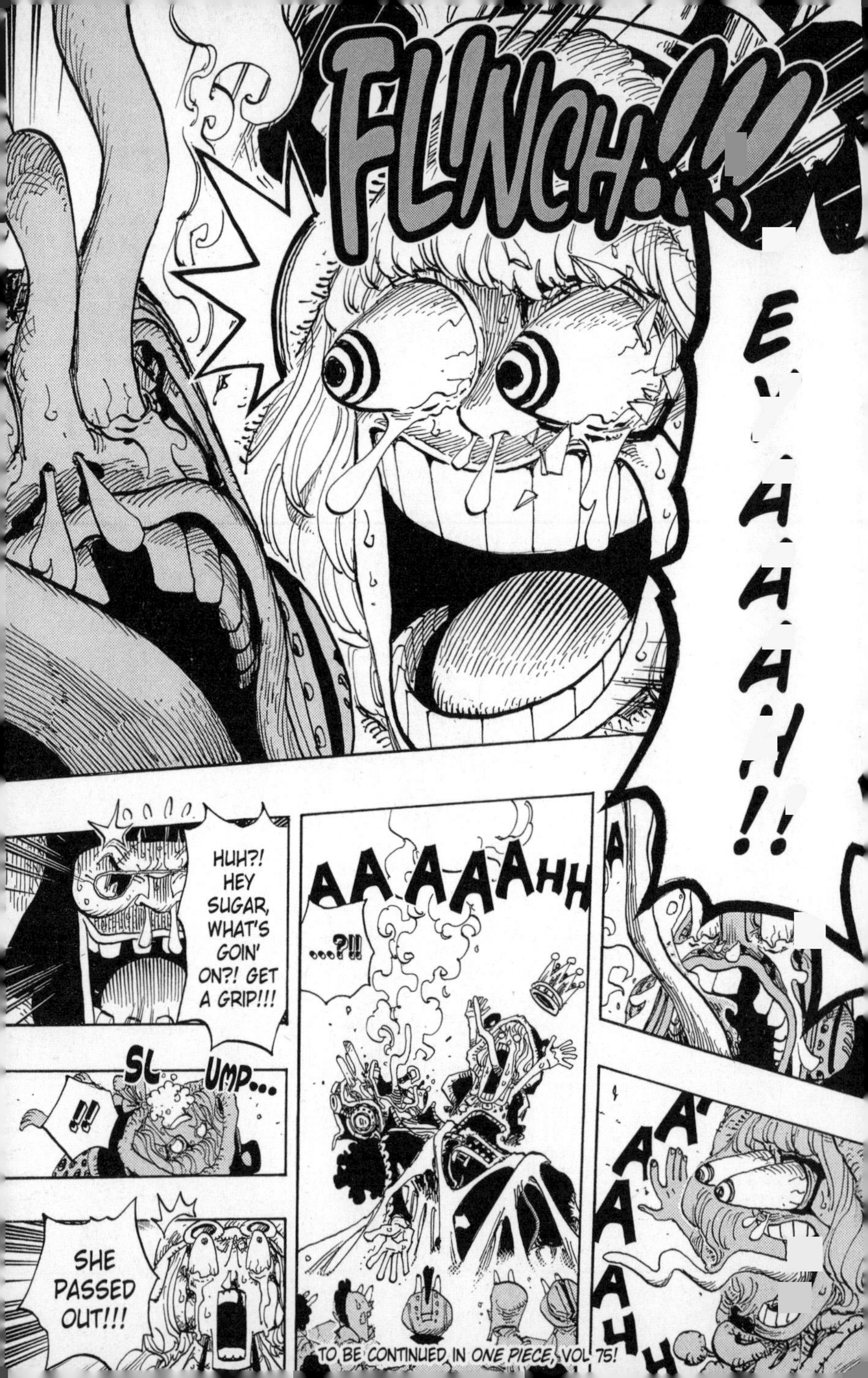
FLINCH!!!!
EYAAAAH!!
A
AAAAAH
AAAAAHH
...?!!
HUH?! HEY SUGAR, WHAT'S GOIN' ON?! GET A GRIP!!!
SLUMP...
!!
SHE PASSED OUT!!!

TO BE CONTINUED IN ONE PIECE, VOL 75!

COMING NEXT VOLUME:

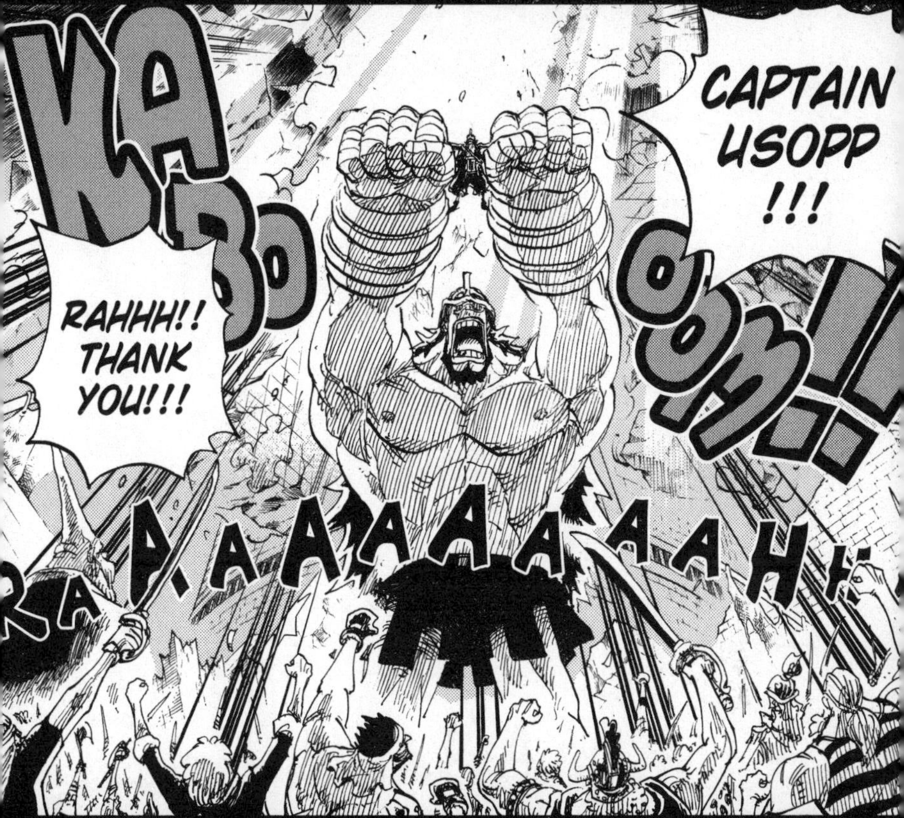
CAPTAIN USOPP!!!
RAHHH!! THANK YOU!!!

Usopp has done it! With Sugar knocked out, Dressrosa will finally awaken from the nightmare it was put under by Doflamingo. But the Warlord won't take this turn of events lying down. And when Doflamingo launches a dastardly counterattack, how will the Straw Hats respond?!

ON SALE AUGUST 2015!

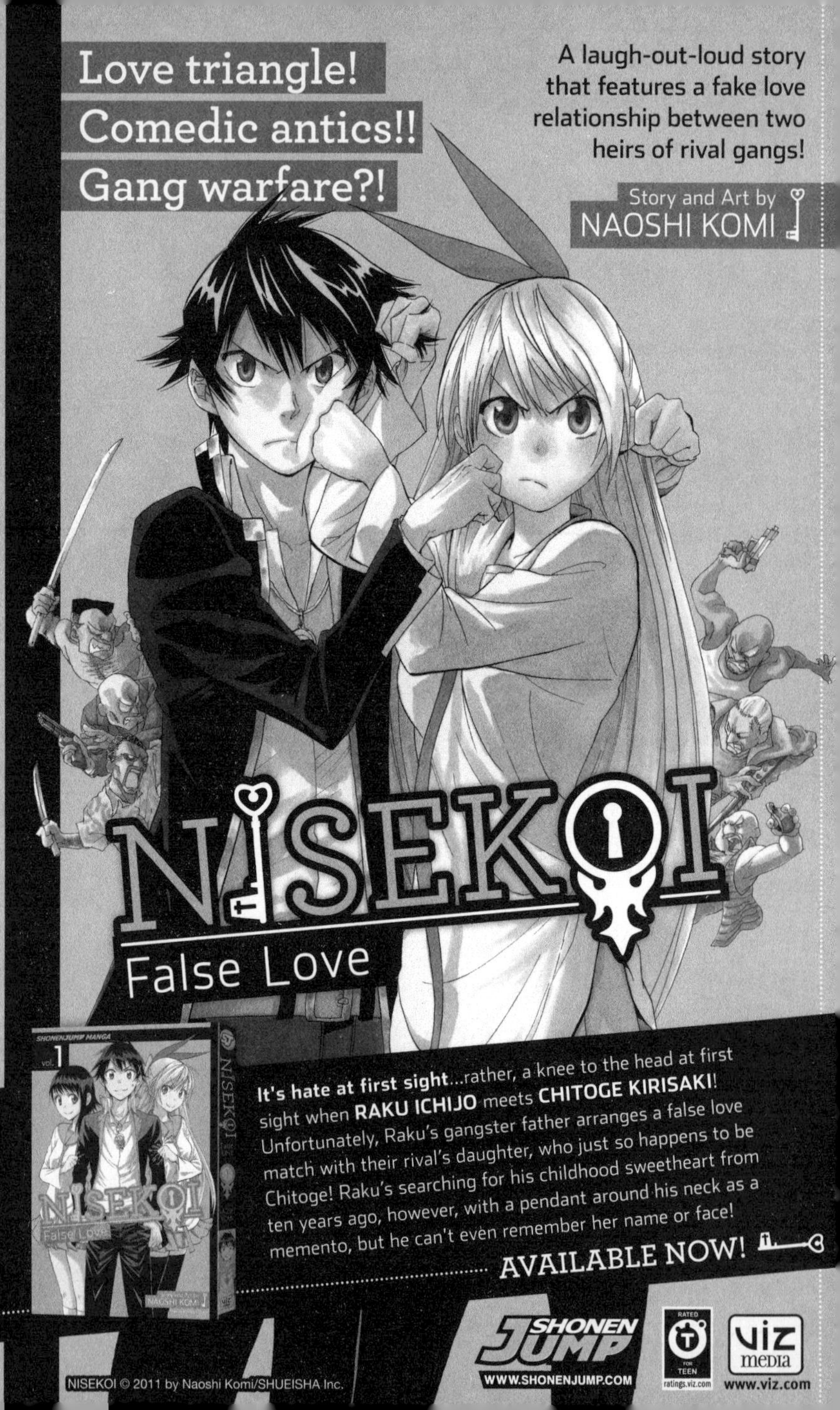
Love triangle!
Comedic antics!!
Gang warfare?!
A laugh-out-loud story that features a fake love relationship between two heirs of rival gangs!
Story and Art by
NAOSHI KOMI
NISEKOI
False Love
SHONENJUMP MANGA
vol. 1
It's hate at first sight...rather, a knee to the head at first sight when RAKU ICHIJO meets CHITOGE KIRISAKI! Unfortunately, Raku's gangster father arranges a false love match with their rival's daughter, who just so happens to be Chitoge! Raku's searching for his childhood sweetheart from ten years ago, however, with a pendant around his neck as a memento, but he can't even remember her name or face!
AVAILABLE NOW!
SHONEN JUMP
WWW.SHONENJUMP.COM
RATED T FOR TEEN
ratings.viz.com
viz media
www.viz.com
NISEKOI © 2011 by Naoshi Komi/SHUEISHA Inc.

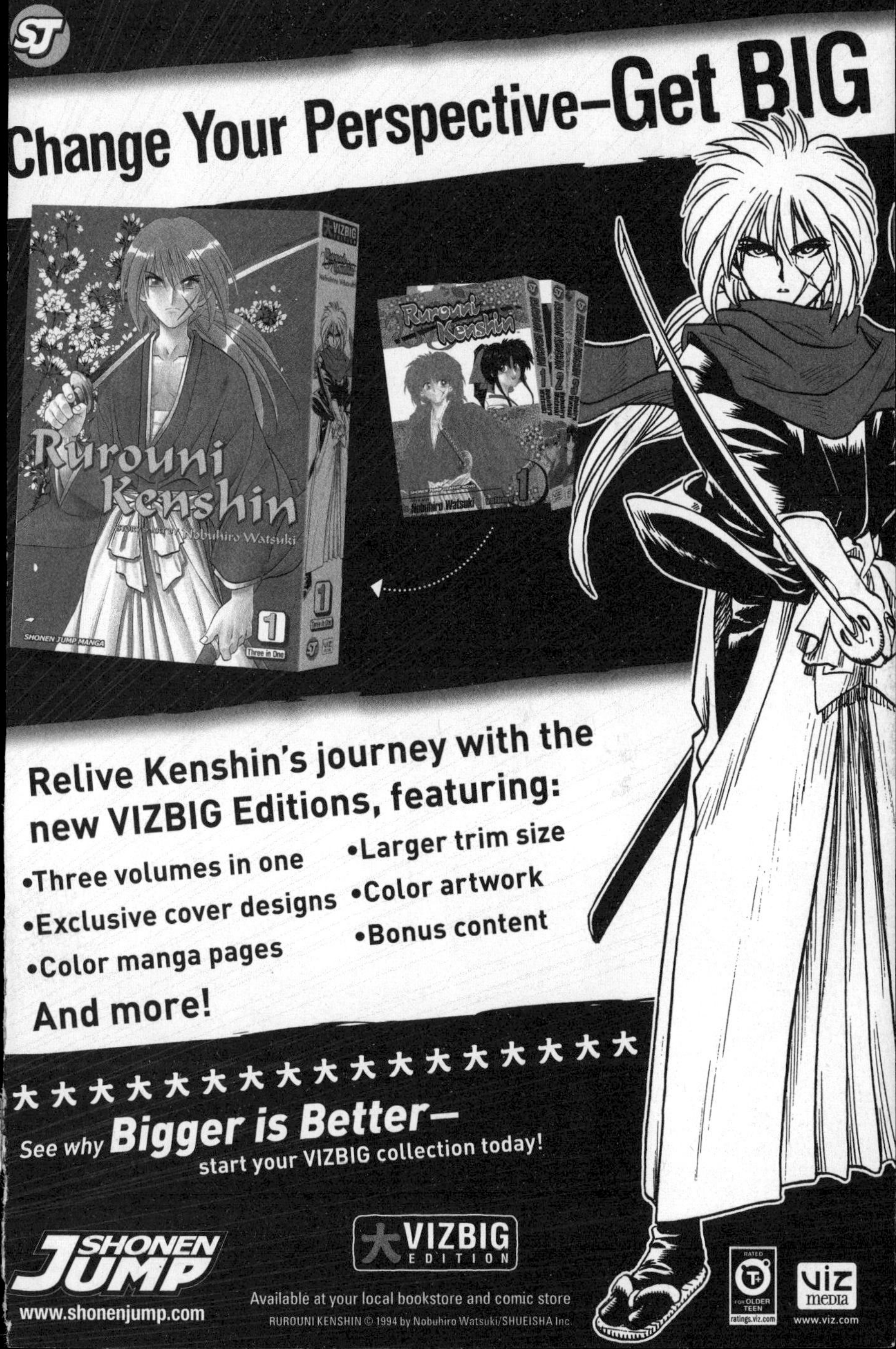
SJ
Change Your Perspective–Get BIG
Rurouni Kenshin
Nobuhiro Watsuki
SHONEN JUMP MANGA
1
Three in One
Relive Kenshin's journey with the new VIZBIG Editions, featuring:
•Three volumes in one
•Exclusive cover designs
•Color manga pages
•Larger trim size
•Color artwork
•Bonus content
And more!
See why Bigger is Better—
start your VIZBIG collection today!
SHONEN JUMP
www.shonenjump.com
VIZBIG EDITION
Available at your local bookstore and comic store
RUROUNI KENSHIN © 1994 by Nobuhiro Watsuki/SHUEISHA Inc.
RATED T+ FOR OLDER TEEN
ratings.viz.com
viz media
www.viz.com

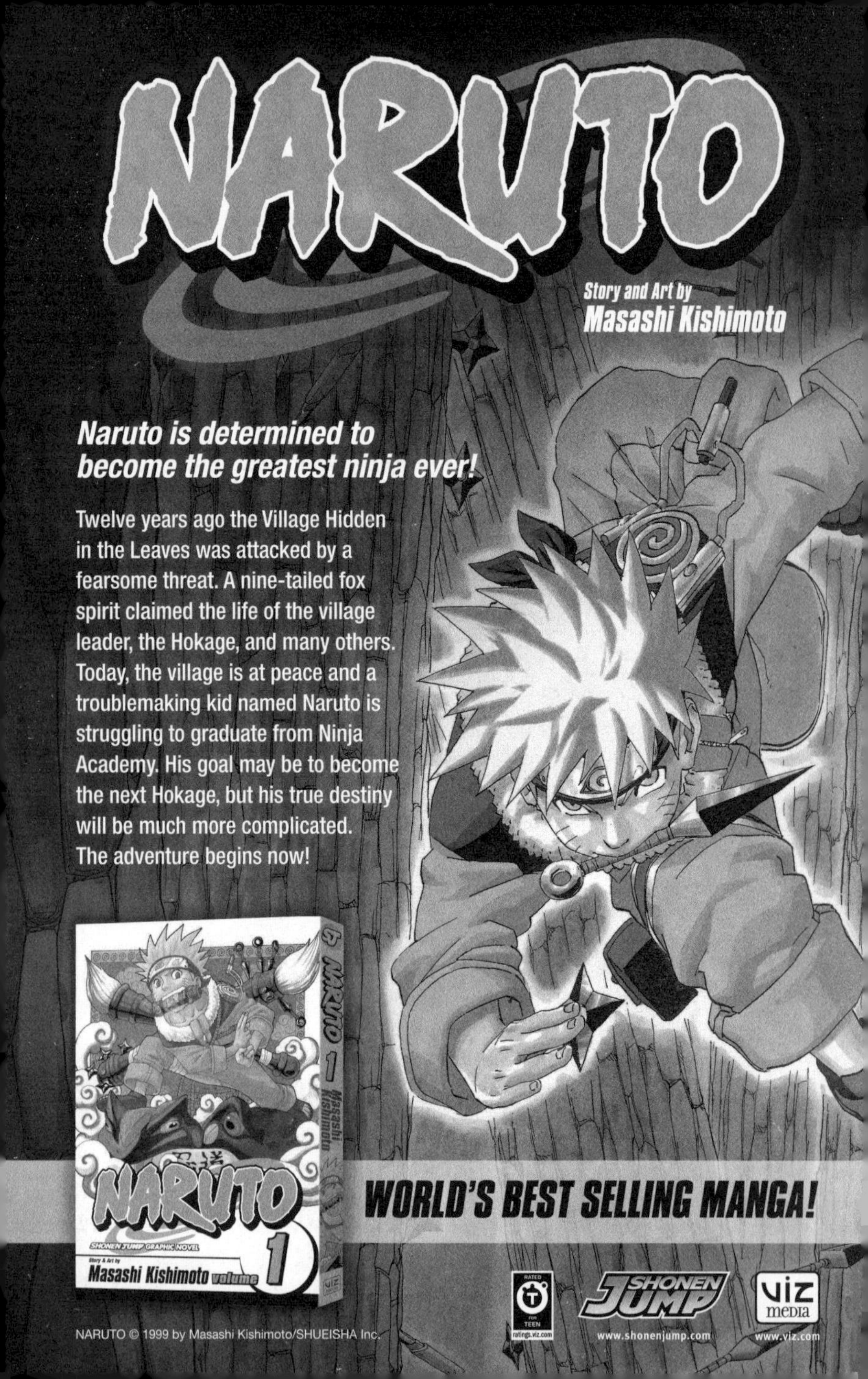
NARUTO
Story and Art by
Masashi Kishimoto
Naruto is determined to become the greatest ninja ever!
Twelve years ago the Village Hidden in the Leaves was attacked by a fearsome threat. A nine-tailed fox spirit claimed the life of the village leader, the Hokage, and many others. Today, the village is at peace and a troublemaking kid named Naruto is struggling to graduate from Ninja Academy. His goal may be to become the next Hokage, but his true destiny will be much more complicated. The adventure begins now!
NARUTO
1
Masashi Kishimoto
SHONEN JUMP GRAPHIC NOVEL
Story & Art by
Masashi Kishimoto volume 1
WORLD'S BEST SELLING MANGA!
RATED
T
FOR TEEN
ratings.viz.com
SHONEN JUMP
www.shonenjump.com
VIZ media
www.viz.com
NARUTO © 1999 by Masashi Kishimoto/SHUEISHA Inc.

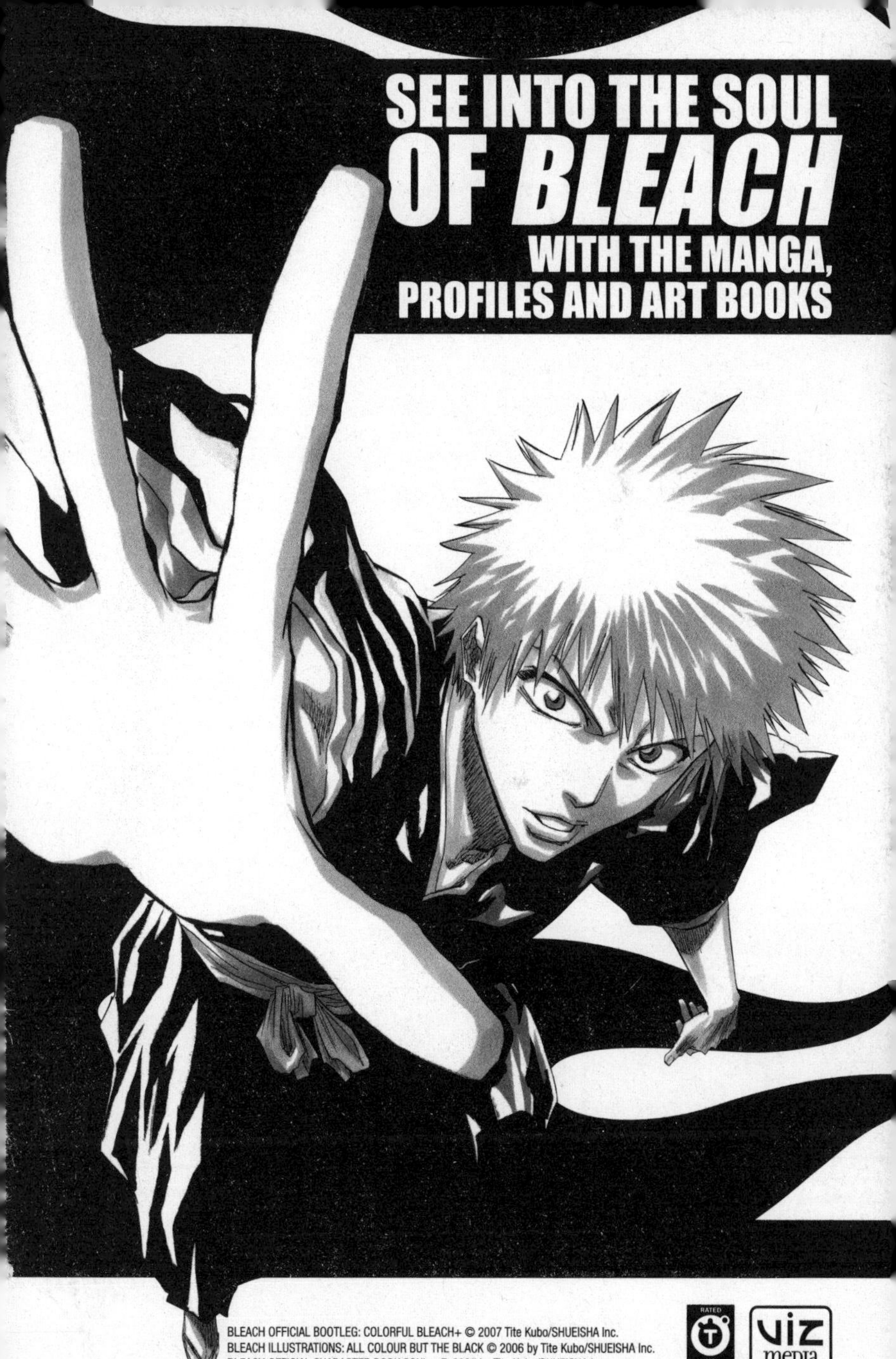
SEE INTO THE SOUL
OF BLEACH
WITH THE MANGA,
PROFILES AND ART BOOKS

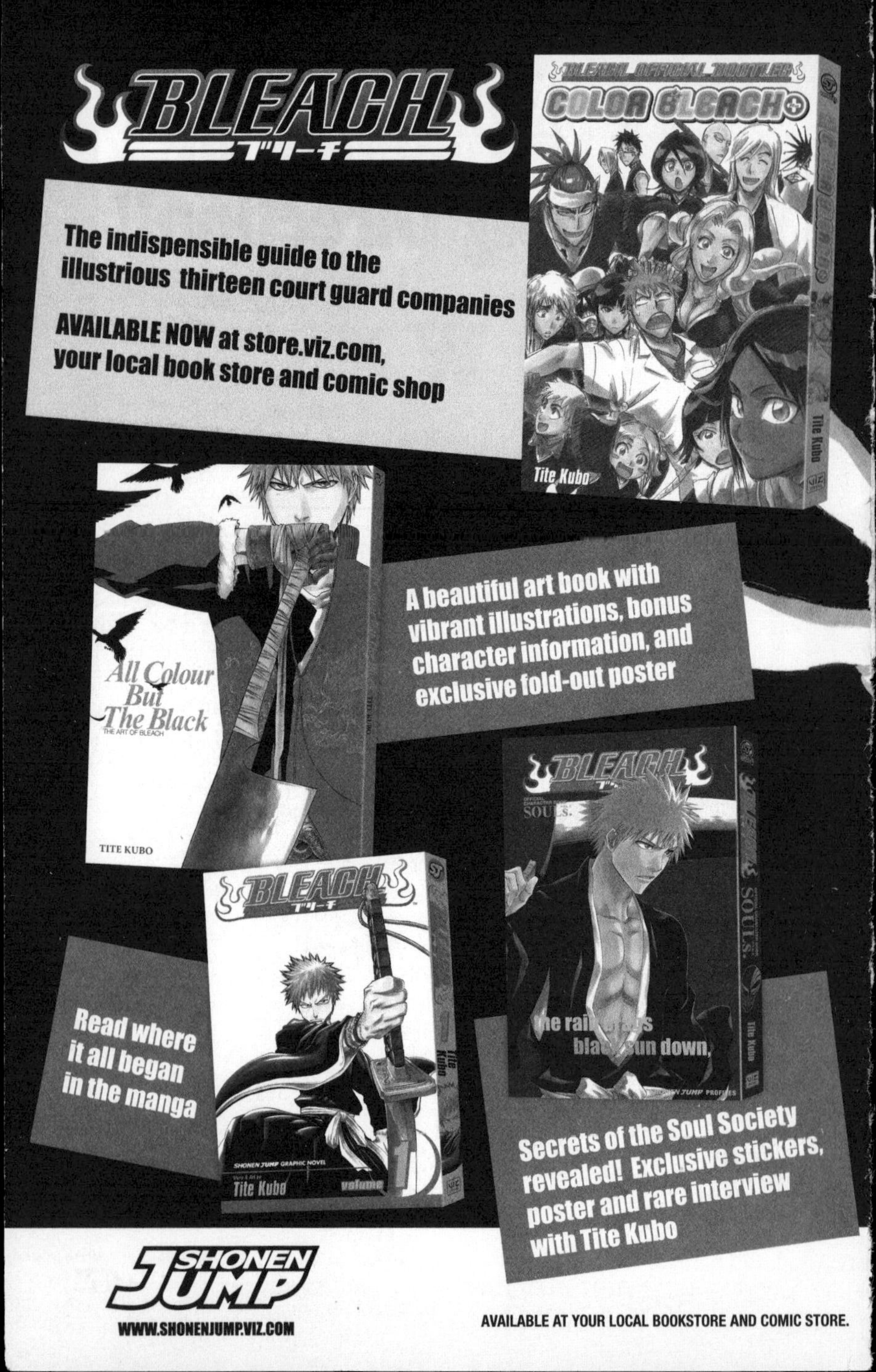
BLEACH
ブリーチ
The indispensible guide to the illustrious thirteen court guard companies
AVAILABLE NOW at store.viz.com, your local book store and comic shop
COLOR BLEACH+
Tite Kubo
All Colour But The Black
THE ART OF BLEACH
TITE KUBO
A beautiful art book with vibrant illustrations, bonus character information, and exclusive fold-out poster
BLEACH
SOULS.
Read where it all began in the manga
BLEACH
ブリーチ
SHONEN JUMP GRAPHIC NOVEL
Tite Kubo
volume 1
Secrets of the Soul Society revealed! Exclusive stickers, poster and rare interview with Tite Kubo
SHONEN JUMP
WWW.SHONENJUMP.VIZ.COM
AVAILABLE AT YOUR LOCAL BOOKSTORE AND COMIC STORE.

You're Re[ading]
the Wrong [Way]

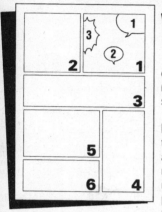

W hoops! Guess what? You're starting at the wrong end of the comic!

...It's true! In keeping with the original Japanese format, **One Piece** is meant to be read from right to left, starting in the upper-right corner.

Unlike English, which is read from left to right, Japanese is read from right to left, meaning that action, sound effects and word-balloon order are completely reversed...something which can make readers unfamiliar with Japanese feel pretty backwards themselves. For this reason, manga or Japanese comics published in the U.S. in English have sometimes been published "flopped"—that is, printed in exact reverse order, as though seen from the other side of a mirror.

By flopping pages, U.S. publishers can avoid confusing readers, but the compromise is not without its downside. For one thing, a character in a flopped manga series who once wore in the original Japanese version a T-shirt emblazoned with "M A Y" (as in "the merry month of") now wears one which reads "Y A M"! Additionally, many manga creators in Japan are themselves unhappy with the process, as some feel the mirror-imaging of their art skews their original intentions.

We are proud to bring you Eiichiro Oda's **One Piece** in the original unflopped format. For now, though, turn to the other side of the book and let the journey begin...!

—Editor ◀ • • •